China Under Mao:
Politics Takes Command

China Under Mao:
Politics Takes Command

A Selection of Articles from *The China Quarterly*

Edited by

Roderick MacFarquhar

THE M.I.T. PRESS

Massachusetts Institute of Technology
Cambridge, Massachusetts and London, England

Library of Congress Catalog Card Number: 66-25630
Printed in the United States of America

Introduction

by RODERICK MacFARQUHAR

The China Quarterly first appeared in January 1960 during what in retrospect seems like a transition period in the internal history of China. The years immediately prior to the appearance of our first number were turbulent, with radical changes of direction and policy. In the summer of 1955, after years of intermittent pressure, Mao Tse-tung personally called for a big push towards cooperative farming. The results exceeded even his expectations, and by the spring of 1956 most of China's peasants were organised in Soviet-style collectives.[1] Despite the rapidity of the change, China experienced far less disruption from collectivisation than the Soviet Union had done 25 years earlier, perhaps because of superior organisation and better preparation. This "high tide of socialism" also embraced the effective nationalisation or collectivisation of the country's industry and commerce.

Satisfied with the achievement of these ideological goals, an achievement that secured them even greater control over the country, China's leaders turned their primary attention to economic development. They realised that this task required the cooperation of all Chinese but particularly those with education, skills, experience, and initiative, even though many of these would be Western-trained intellectuals or the richer peasants, whom the party viewed with suspicion. Even before de-Stalinisation commenced in the Soviet Union and Eastern Europe, the Chinese set about relaxing the party's grip on these elements in Chinese society. In January 1956, Chou En-lai promised better working and living conditions to the intellectuals; in May of the same year, Mao himself confirmed the new policy, calling for a hundred flowers to bloom and a hundred schools to contend.

The unforeseen effects of de-Stalinisation in Eastern Europe, notably the Hungarian revolt, did not deter Mao; if anything they spurred him on, and in February 1957 he proclaimed the need to resolve peacefully "contradictions among the people" and in particular between leaders and led. At the end of April, the Communist party launched a campaign to rectify its methods of work and called upon the educated sections of society to voice criticisms. When the invitation was accepted, how-

[1] See Roy Hofheinz, "Rural Administration in Communist China," p. 99 below, and Kenneth Walker, "Collectivisation in Retrospect: The 'Socialist High Tide' of Autumn 1955–Spring 1956," *The China Quarterly*, No. 26.

ever, Mao came to realise the extent of disenchantment among wide sections of the Chinese intelligentsia. With his memories of the political impact of student riots during his own youth, Mao must have been particularly alarmed that unrest should have developed in the universities, especially since the students had been brought up under communism.[2] Mao and his colleagues quickly decided that the torrent of criticism had to be dammed, and on June 8, 1957, they launched a counterattack on the "bourgeois rightists" who had been so unwary as to express their hopes and fears. In the aftermath of the shock it had received, the party called for increased militancy, and at the second session of its Eighth Congress in April 1958, Liu Shao-ch'i (now head of state and Mao's heir apparent) linked the renewed emphasis on political correctness with militancy on the economic front. The year 1958 became the one of the "great leap forward".

Though China had completed her First Five-Year Plan in 1957 with considerable success, the overall increases in production evidently did not satisfy the Chinese leaders, who were faced with an annual increase in population of about 12 million on a base pushing 600 million in 1953.[3] Besides, conventional Soviet methods of economic development entailed dependence on the educated élite, with whom Mao must have been disillusioned. Manual labour now had to make up for technical expertise.[4] The "great leap forward" represented an attempt to achieve rapid economic progress by the massive mobilisation of dedicated manpower,[5] an attempt symbolised by the backyard steel campaign. In this campaign all Chinese, almost without distinction of age, sex, or occupation, were instructed to set up small furnaces in which they attempted to make steel. The campaign was highly wasteful of manpower and materials and was soon abandoned.

The "leap" was accompanied by the amalgamation of the recently founded collectives into "people's communes", which some enthusiastic party officials thought would be the means of realising communism in China almost overnight. Mao himself apparently saw the communes as the new basic units of society, designed to bridge the gulf between town and country, between intellectuals, workers, and peasants.

The pace proved too hot and the economic dislocation too widespread for the leap forward to be maintained at its original tempo, especially as the economic situation became graver under the impact of "three

---

[2] René Goldman, "The Rectification Campaign at Peking University," p. 255 below; Immanuel C. Y. Hsu, "The Reorganisation of Higher Education in Communist China, 1949–61," p. 271 below.

[3] Choh-ming Li, "Economic Development," p. 147 below.

[4] Robert D. Barendsen, "The Agricultural Middle School in Communist China," p. 303 below.

[5] S. H. Chen, "Multiplicity in Uniformity: Poetry and the Great Leap Forward," p. 392 below.

bitter years" (1959–61) of natural calamities.[6] As early as August 1959, the regime admitted that the production figures for 1958 had been greatly overestimated, and the retreat to realism continued even though some of those who had advocated it all along fell by the wayside.[7] Centralised direction of the economy was strengthened under the slogan of "taking the whole country as a coordinated chess game", while the powers of the communes were considerably reduced.[8] A fresh attempt was even made to recapture the enthusiasm of the intellectuals with the launching in 1961 of a controlled "hundred flowers" campaign.[9] Chinese secret military magazines now available in the West reveal the existence of widespread unrest and even rebellion in some parts of the country which helped spur such moves.[10] In the early summer of 1962, the sudden surge of some 100,000 refugees across the border into Hong Kong gave the outside world some idea of the critical situation within China.[11]

China spent the first half of the sixties recovering from the dislocation of the leap forward, the natural disasters of 1959–61, and the withdrawal of Soviet technologists in 1960.[12] Not until 1966 did this transitional recovery period seem to be ending when Peking announced the launching of the Third Five-Year Plan, three years after the conclusion of the second one. No figures of recent achievements or current targets were released, contrary to pre-leap practice, but Premier Chou En-lai indicated that production in important items did exceed 1957 levels but not those of 1958.[13]

In the past two years, with the reestablishment of equilibrium and self-confidence, the party has seemed to be girding itself once more for a new surge forward. The leaders see their prime task as ensuring the preservation of Maoist revolutionary zeal among their heirs and successors.[14] This renewed ideological militancy with its emphasis on the supremacy of politics in all things, of "redness" over "expertness", is hard to square with the apparently still continuing commonsense approach to economics. Presumably China's leaders are keen to avert

[6] W. K., "Communist China's Agricultural Calamities," p. 163 below.

[7] David A. Charles, "The Dismissal of Marshal P'eng Teh-huai," p. 20 below; Ellis Joffe, "The Conflict between Old and New in the Chinese Army," p. 34 below.

[8] Gargi Dutt, "Some Problems of China's Rural Communes," p. 119 below.

[9] See Dennis Doolin, "The Revival of the Hundred Flowers Campaign: 1961," *The China Quarterly*, No. 8.

[10] John Wilson Lewis, "China's Secret Military Papers," p. 58 below.

[11] See Frank Robertson, "Refugees and Troop Moves—A Report from Hong Kong," *The China Quarterly*, No. 11.

[12] Choh-ming Li, "China's Industrial Development, 1958–63," p. 175 below; Franz Schurmann, "China's New Economic Policy," p. 211 below.

[13] See W. K., "China's Third Five-Year Plan," *The China Quarterly*, No. 25.

[14] Benjamin Schwartz, "Modernisation and the Maoist Vision," p. 3 below; Donald W. Klein, "The Next Generation of Chinese Communist Leaders," p. 69 below.

further disruption of the economy but at the same time are convinced that the maintenance of national morale by education and propaganda is vital. The result has been a "great cultural revolution" in the shape of a growing cult of the "thought of Mao Tse-tung", with the works of the leader being cited as indispensable inspiration at every turn in a true revolutionary's daily life. And as politics takes command again, once more senior members of the party are being purged as at the time of the leap.

If 1960 was part of a transitional period in domestic politics, in foreign policy it was more like a watershed. It was in this year that China's increasingly vociferous demands for Communist militancy against the West finally erupted in open polemics with the Soviet Union.[15] Undeterred by Soviet economic and political pressure and their own internal difficulties, the Chinese have continually reiterated their demands for the Soviet Communist party to give in and adopt Chinese policies. Failing to obtain this, Peking has denounced Khrushchev and his successors as traitors to the revolutionary cause. In the belief that the Soviet revolution is degenerating (and the fear of a similar development spurs on the current "cultural revolution" within China) Mao has attempted during the sixties to shape a new alliance among the underdeveloped countries.[16] This was not to be based on the "Bandung spirit" of the second half of the fifties—that lay shattered in the Himalayas in the aftermath of the Tibetan revolt and the first border clashes with India in 1959. The Chinese now denounced men like Nehru and sought their allies either among friendly Communist leaders like Kim Il Sung of North Korea, Castro in Cuba, and Aidit in Indonesia, or among sympathetic though non-Communist Afro-Asians like Sukarno, Nkrumah, Sekou Touré, and Ben Bella. Even a princely ruler like Sihanouk of Cambodia or a basically anti-Communist military leader like President Ayub Khan of Pakistan were acceptable allies if their policies became sufficiently anti-American and pro-Chinese.

But even in Africa, which the Chinese considered to be the "storm centre" of the world revolution, Premier Chou found that Peking's denunciation of the UN and the partial test ban treaty fell on unreceptive ears.[17] The Chinese had to accept the abandonment of the projected second Bandung conference when they realised that it would not adopt the kind of anti-American and anti-Soviet positions they desired. Suddenly, too, China's friends were being overthrown or undermined—Ben Bella, Sukarno, Subandrio and Aidit, Pakistani Foreign Minister Bhutto, and Nkrumah while he was actually in Peking—or were beginning to

---

[15] Richard Lowenthal, "Diplomacy and Revolution," p. 425 below.
[16] A. M. Halpern, "China in the Postwar World," p. 483 below.
[17] W. A. C. Adie, "Chou En-lai on Safari," p. 462 below.

cool off like Castro and Kim Il Sung. In the early sixties the Chinese proclaimed themselves the leaders of the world revolution, but by the middle of the decade it was clear that the response had not lived up to their expectations. The image of China's power had been strengthened by the testing of three nuclear devices, but these explosions hardly compensated for the decline of her diplomatic position.[18] As of this writing, it is not yet clear what Peking's long-range reaction to these latest developments will be.

In making this selection from the first five years of *The China Quarterly,* I have had more than the usual editorial difficulty of deciding what to exclude, for the early sixties witnessed a tremendous growth in contemporary Chinese studies, particularly in the United States. I have in general chosen pieces because they contribute to our understanding of recent Chinese history with the intention of giving this volume an appeal beyond the immediate circle of specialists. I have also selected a few articles that have dealt with abiding principles of Chinese Communist theory and practice.[19] I have tried to cast the net wide to cover diverse spheres of Chinese life, partly to illustrate how Mao has attempted to implement his slogan of "politics takes command" in all things. The final collection can make no claim to be a comprehensive survey of the last few years, but I hope it will illuminate the major events of the period.

[18] Morton H. Halperin, "Chinese Nuclear Strategy," p. 449 below.
[19] H. F. Schurmann, "Organisational Principles of the Chinese Communists," p. 87 below; C. T. Hu, "Communist Education: Theory and Practice," p. 241 below; John M. H. Lindbeck, "The Organisation and Development of Science," p. 333 below; Howard Boorman, "The Literary World of Mao Tse-tung," p. 368 below; Ezra F. Vogel, "From Friendship to Comradeship: The Change in Personal Relations in Communist China," p. 407 below.

Contents

Politics and Organisation

Economic Development

China Under Mao:
Politics Takes Command

Politics and Organisation

Modernisation and the Maoist Vision—Some Reflections on Chinese Communist Goals

WHAT can be said at this point about the broad goals and motivations of the present Chinese Communist leadership? The question is, of course, distressingly imprecise and begs further definition. Is the leadership a monolithic group? Have its goals remained constant and unchanging? Is there a rigid Chinese Communist " goal structure," etc.?

On the question of leadership I shall simply adhere to the conventional hypothesis that Mao Tse-tung and those closest to him have played a leading role in determining basic policy shifts during the last fifteen years. There may have been moments when his presence has receded from the centre of the stage. In the early years after 1950, his role may have been somewhat inhibited by the awesome presence of Stalin. His influence may have flagged at the Wuhan meeting at the end of 1958 and after the retreat from the great leap forward. On the whole, however, one perceives the imprint of his outlook (probably developed in close collaboration with Liu Shao-ch'i) at almost every crucial turning point from the land reform campaign of 1950 to the present frenzied drive for " socialist education."

On the matter of goals, while there is certainly no rigid static " goal structure," while the relationship among goals has undoubtedly been enormously complex, problematic and shifting over time, it may nevertheless be possible to speak of a certain range of broad goals which has remained fairly constant and which may have set certain outer limits to the possibilities of policy choice. This does not mean, one should hasten to add, that the whole history of Communist China during the last fifteen years can be understood in terms of an unproblematic implementation of the leadership's goals. Unyielding objective conditions, unforeseen events and contingencies, and the recalcitrances of human nature have certainly been just as decisive as the goals of the leadership in shaping the history of China since 1949. Interpretations of events in Communist China have often swung wildly from the view that China is in an inert clay in the hands of the leaders who shape it as they will to the view that everything that has happened is a result of an iron

" objective necessity " which shapes all the leadership's decisions. All that will be urged in this article is that the goals of the leadership have been one of the factors shaping the course of events.

There has been much discussion of Chinese Communist goals during the last decade and a half and there is a certain range of broad assumptions which can be discerned in most analyses of the Chinese scene whether written by academic experts poring over Chinese Communist media or visitors who have been there. One such widely shared assumption is that the overriding, indeed, all-embracing goal of the Chinese Communist leadership is to achieve the modernisation of China or—put somewhat differently—everything that is happening in Communist China is an aspect of the process of modernisation. There is also the assumption that the basic goal of the leadership is the achievement of a certain vision of society spelled out in the scriptures of Marxism-Leninism-Maoism. This vision may involve aspects of what is called " modernisation " in the West, but modernisation is conceived of as a part of a much larger whole defined by the ideology. This view of the goals of the leadership is, of course, the avowed view of the leadership itself but is also shared by many others who may be ardently attracted to the vision or violently repelled by it. Another view places central stress on nationalism—on the goal of national power and prestige and on the achievement of world power status as quickly as possible. It is of course true that to the protagonists of the modernisation school nationalism is simply an " aspect " or " function " of some 'all-inclusive modernisation process and hence not to be considered under a separate rubric. To others it must be considered as a force in its own right. There is another view which may be said to concern motivation more than goals—namely, that the Chinese Communist leadership is essentially engrossed in the limitless " totalitarian " aggrandisement of its own power, both within China and in the world at large. There are undoubtedly other assumptions which can and have been made concerning the goals and motives of the leaders, but I shall confine my attention to these.

POWER

Turning first of all to the view that all the policies and decisions of the leadership are designed to maximise its power, we find that in recent years, particularly since the death of Stalin, there has been a distinct decline in the popularity of the " theory of totalitarianism " or all theories which stress the power drives of the leadership. There has, in fact, been a tendency on the part of some to brush aside the relevance of power considerations entirely on grounds which are a shade too facile. Power, we are told, is not an end in itself. It is functional to goals which lie beyond it or it plays a certain function in the larger social system, etc. It must always be explained in terms of " larger " social, historic and economic forces of which it is the mere instrument. One might say that for the whole course of human history power has always been " functional." It has always led to objective results, bad or good, which have survived its pursuit. This is just as true of Rameses and Ch'in Shih Huang-ti as it is of Mao Tse-tung. This by no means precludes the fact that it has also been pursued as an end in itself and that this pursuit has played its own role in human history. " Objectively " Macbeth may have been a most successful Scottish " state-builder " but this by no means proves that the side of him which Shakespeare chooses to depict is irrelevant to a discussion of his day-to-day political behaviour. Power has always been functional and always been demonic and the end is not yet in sight. What vitiates the narrow " power approach " is the assumption that a concern with the maintenance or expansion of power is necessarily incompatible with the pursuit of more general goals. If the Chinese Communist Party is conceived of as the sole effective instrument for achieving a certain vision of the good society or for making China a great world power or for consummating the process of modernisation, then the general goals and power considerations may actually reinforce and enhance each other.

Those who deny the relevance of power considerations might at this point maintain, however, that if power considerations and objective goals often move in the same direction why assign any particular causal weight to power considerations? In fact, however, at given points in time they may by no means move in the same direction. If one assumes that one of the basic domestic aims of the " hundred flowers " campaign was to provide the intelligentsia (a term which, of course, includes both professionals and academic and literary intellectuals) with an opportunity to participate more fully and freely in the economic and scientific development of China; if a reasoned judgment had been made that further economic and scientific development required the more positive participation of the intelligentsia, one can hardly say that the experiment was given time to prove itself. The fact that Mao Tse-tung was still vigorously supporting the programme in February 1957 only to allow himself to be won over to the opposition (which had undoubtedly been strong in the Party from the outset) within the next few months can hardly be due to its failure to produce spectacular economic results in the early months of 1957. The drive was speedily terminated when it seemed to involve a threat to the unlimited political power of the leadership. Similarly, while the purges of Kao Kang and Jao Shu-shih in 1954 and of P'eng Teh-huai in 1959 undoubtedly involved policy differences from the outset, it is quite clear that in the end these " anti-party elements " were associated with a threat to power. The vehemence with which the ideological remoulding of the army was carried on in the 1960–62 period can hardly be disassociated from this threat to power.

All of these instances, of course, involve not so much a concern for the expansion of power as for the preservation of power in being and it may well be one of the defects of the theory of totalitarianism that it dogmatically assumes that the concern for power must always be a concern for its maximisation. It makes no allowance for the possibility that a concern for the maintenance of power in being may, at times, outweigh the concern for its maximisation in the future. Nevertheless, the power approach reminds us that we are dealing with a group of men who know and savour power and its uses as much as any ruling group that has ever existed. They are not merely the embodiment of a social vision, or the destiny of China, or the process of modernisation. Mao's spectacular projection of his own authority in the Communist bloc and the world at large and the present hysterical cult of Mao in China may serve a certain vision of the world or be in line with certain policies but also admirably feed his limitless *hybris*. The factor of power is relevant to a discussion of all these policies and shifts in policy. Indeed, at points where the implementation of policy may seem to endanger power interests, it may be the most relevant factor of all.

MODERNISATION

If the ever-present concern with power by no means precludes the pursuit of broader goals—what are these broader goals? One widely accepted response is that the goal is the modernisation of China. One could, of course, devote volumes to a discussion of the meaning of this term and yet there does seem to be a kind of common core of shared meaning which is implicit at least in most American discussions. In general, it tends to mean something approximating Max Weber's conception of the process of rationalisation in all those spheres of social action—economic, political, military, legal, educational—which lend themselves to the application of " *Zwecksrationalität*." It involves the sustained attention to the most appropriate, " rational " and efficient methods for increasing man's ability to control nature and society for a variety of ends. Economists often treat it as being co-extensive with industrialisation and it is indeed in this area that the meaning of the term " rationalisation " can be most concretely elucidated. Weber himself in spite of his tendency to use the cover term " capitalism " (presumably an economic category) was just as much concerned with political bureaucracy, military development and legal " rationalisation." It tends to involve the notion of a highly developed division of labour of " functional specificity " with the corollary that men should have a degree of autonomy and authority within their various areas of competence. It also involves a stress on norms of universality rather than ascription and thus, should involve social mobility—the opening up of careers to talents. Looking at the whole concept from the point of view of China, one is inclined to stress that it also may involve a sober respect for objective conditions. The technician and, for that matter, the professional bureaucrat will be very conscious of the limits imposed by his materials and by the imperatives of the situation within which he operates.

Actually one can distinguish two versions of the concept of modernisation which may have quite different implications. One version treats the "process of modernisation" as a vast, indeed, an all-embracing impersonal historic force. Revolutions, ideologies, nationalism and the policies of governments are all surface eruptions of this underlying process which is independent of the wills of men and operates behind their backs very much like Hegel's "*Weltgeist*" or Marx's "mode of production." In the other version, modernisation becomes a conscious project or consciously entertained goal of large or small groups of men. The two versions may have quite different consequences for an analysis of the behaviour of the Chinese leadership. If modernisation is an all-enveloping force which controls all the acts both conscious and unconscious of the leadership, all their acts must be explained as a "function" of the modernisation process. The leadership may explicitly profess concern with other matters; it may even sincerely be concerned "subjectively" with other matters. In fact, all its behaviour is determined by the imperatives of the modernisation process. If, on the other hand, modernisation is a goal consciously pursued, it is not impossible that it may compete in the minds of the leadership with other goals. In fact, the decisions of the leadership may have something to do with shaping the order of priorities and strategies of the modernisation process itself.

The adherents of the monistic modernisation theory seldom if ever raise questions about the goals of modernisation itself. It is assumed that the goals are immanent in the process and that we know what they are. Among many Americans there is in fact the latent assumption that a fully modernised society will look exactly like the United States with all its social and cultural specificities. Even if we assume that modernisation is leading in the end of days to some universal homogenised human condition, *in processu* it is quite compatible with quite different conceptions of the priority of ends to be served. A highly advanced industrial society may be able to lavish equal resources on state power and prestige and welfare. A less developed society will have to make choices in this area and these choices may have a most profound effect on the strategy of modernisation.

NATIONALISM

Viewed in this light nationalism may be much more than a " function " of the modernisation process.   Where it occupies a central place, it may actually determine the strategy of modernisation.   To assume that Stalin's lop-sided emphasis on heavy industrial development was a function of Soviet nationalism seems to make much more sense than to assume that it was the only rational strategy of industrialisation in an underdeveloped area. Similarly one must assume that the apparent priority granted to nuclear development in China through all the recent shifts in economic strategy is related fundamentally to its nationalist goals rather than to any obvious imperative of the modernisation process.

The Chinese leadership's unquestioning adoption of this model after 1950 was due not simply to the fact that it was the orthodox Marxist-Leninist model of economic development but also to the fact that Stalin had in this model already bent Marxism-Leninism to national power purposes. As perfervid Chinese nationalists the Chinese leadership shared the preoccupations which lay behind Stalin's own choice of model. They were genuine Stalinists in their whole-hearted acceptance of Stalin's accommodation of Marxism-Leninism to the interests of a nation-state. It is thus entirely meaningful to stress that the speedy achievement of nationalist goals has been one of the unchanging central goals of the leadership which has shaped the priorities and strategy of the modernisation process itself. This does not mean that the leadership is not committed to the welfare goals which we associate with modernisation— with living standards, public health, literacy, etc.—but the relative priorities seem quite clear.

During the years from 1949–56 there can be little doubt that the goal of modernisation *on the Soviet model* was assiduously pursued by the Chinese Communist leadership in many sectors. After the Korean War we have a gradual implementation of the Soviet model of economic development. There is a movement towards the creation of a state structure with a modern bureaucratic apparatus and the professionalisation of the army on a Soviet model is vigorously pursued. It has indeed become the tendency among some to regard this eminently Soviet phase of Chinese development as the " modernising " phase *par excellence* as opposed to the irrationalities of subsequent phases. Yet as we know, the relationship of the whole Soviet development to the supposed prerequisites of modernisation has itself been the subject of endless, unresolved debates. Ideology is also deeply implicated in the whole Soviet development. What is mainly implied is that the Soviet model involves a stress on professionalisation, on a degree of autonomy for professional hierarchies, particularly in the industrial, state administrative and military spheres. Franz Schurmann has, for instance, stressed the emphasis during this period on the Soviet conception of managerial responsibility in industry (without necessarily regarding it as pre-eminently rational).

One of the most striking facts of recent Chinese Communist history (particularly since 1956) has been the gradual departure from the Soviet model of modernisation. Some have leaped to the conclusion that this marks the departure from a " rational " approach to modernisation. Yet it might well be argued that, in part, the departure from the Soviet model of modernisation was due to the realisation that this model was not applicable to China's real situation. The Chinese could not reduce the peasantry to a subsistence level and then ignore the agricultural sector. To keep their vast population alive at the barest subsistence level it became obvious that a maximum attention to agriculture was imperative. In the strictly economic sphere one might argue that the economic policy pursued after 1960 with its emphasis on " agriculture as the base " has been much more rational in terms of China's conditions than the model of the 1953–56 period. In fact, one might argue that during the whole period from the " Hundred Flowers " campaign to the present campaign for " socialist education " all policies have borne some relationship to the problems of modernisation.

THE MAOIST VISION OF THE GOOD SOCIETY

It nevertheless seems to me that if we are to understand some of the modes of response to these problems which have emerged since 1956, we must introduce another broad goal area which might be called ideological but which I shall refer to as the Maoist vision of the good society.

The vision involves not only a conception of the good society of the future but also a sanctified image of the methods by which this vision is to be achieved. Certainly Marxist-Leninist-Stalinist ideology is one of the main sources of this vision, but this does not preclude the possibility that in some of its aspects it coincides with certain traditional Chinese habits of thought and behaviour. It draws above all on the actual experience of the Communist movement during the thirties and forties, and the interpretation of this experience enshrined in the Yenan writings of Mao Tse-tung and Liu Shao-ch'i. As has often been pointed out, the " Yenan syndrome " seems to occupy a central, hallowed place in the vision of Mao Tse-tung and most of the elements which form part of the Maoist vision first appear, at least in their embryonic form, during this period.

The phrase "Maoist vision" seems to describe a static frame of reference and almost suggests something like an "operational code" which may provide a key to all the shifts and twists of Party policy since 1949. On the contrary, there is absolutely no reason to assume that it provided Mao with any prevision of the circumstances which were to give rise to the "Hundred Flowers" campaign or the "great leap forward" campaign, or to the circumstances which were to lead to their abrupt demise. Not all elements of the vision have been equally prominent at all times and some of them have only been made fully explicit in the course of time. Many elements of the vision are highly ambivalent ("dialectic") lending themselves to the support of quite opposing policies. And yet when viewed in the abstract, there is a kind of rough coherence among them.

Not only has the pursuit of this vision often cut across other goals of the leadership but has with varying degrees of intensity conditioned the manner in which these other goals have been pursued. Some elements of the vision have had an obvious and almost unremitting impact on reality. The enormous energies invested since 1949 in the effort to achieve the spiritual transformation of the entire Chinese people whether in the form of "study" (hsüeh-hsi), "thought reform," "remoulding," "education through labour" or "socialist education" is one of the most obvious instances. At another level, some elements of the vision have been invoked and made most explicit in connection with certain specific campaigns—such as the notion of "contradictions among the people" at the time of the "Hundred Flowers" campaign or the emphasis on "subjective forces," "revolutionary romanticism" and "man as the decisive factor" at the time of the "great leap forward." One is tempted to say that, when invoked in this way, these ideological themes simply serve to confirm the infallibility of the "thought of Mao Tse-tung" in the face of all shifts and twists in line, and—particularly since 1956—to confirm ever more emphatically the autonomy and originality of the "Chinese path." Undoubtedly they do serve this purpose. Yet while these themes are hardly the "sufficient causes" of the campaigns of 1956, 1958 or other new departures, the genuine belief in the assumptions implicit in them may well explain the high confidence and élan with which these campaigns are pressed. One simply has to peruse Mao's comments in such works as *The Socialist Upsurge in China's Countryside* (1955) to appreciate the fervour of his belief in those "facts" which seem to support his vision. At another level, however, elements of the vision are obviously manipulated simply as ideology in the narrowest sense. Thus the fact that the slogans of the

"Hundred Flowers" movement and of the great leap continue to live on into periods when they no longer apply is obviously a device designed to prove that Mao's contributions to the storehouse of Marxism-Leninism are irrevocable and cumulative.

CONSENSUS AND COLLECTIVISM

What are some of the essential elements of the Maoist vision? There is first of all the overriding commitment to a society united by something approaching a total consensus and a society marked by radical collectivism. It may seem superfluous to speak of the collectivist goal of a Communist society, and yet the image of collectivity which has emerged in China, particularly since 1958, seems somewhat different in kind from that projected in the Soviet Union. The emphasis on the individual's total self-abnegation and total immersion in the collectivity as ultimate goods; the frequent reference to the model of military life with its nostalgic allusions to the heroic and idyllic guerrilla bands of the past are particular characteristics of the Maoist projection of the future. Lenin's own projection of Utopia in *State and Revolution* still draws heavily on Marx's own meagre and vague descriptions which, as we know, speak in terms of the total liberation and self-fulfilment of the individual. Whether this language makes Marx a sort of ultimate liberal as some of his interpreters would have us believe, may be open to serious doubt, yet there is the fact that the individual and his situation does play a central role in Marx's Utopia. While the Soviet official ideology has been as deeply suspicious of the whole notion of alienation in the young Marx as the Chinese, a somewhat crasser form of the concern with the interests of the individual can nevertheless be discerned in its projection of Communism. The Maoist version on the other hand projects a kind of collectivist mysticism. Commenting on the European and Soviet discussions of Marxism, Chou Yang states " that in advocating the return of Man to himself they are actually advocating absolute individual freedom and asking the people who live under Socialism to return to the human nature of bourgeois individualism and to restore the capitalism by which it is fostered." [1]

Even more characteristic has been the enormous emphasis on the power of spiritual transformation (indoctrination seems to be far too weak a term) to bring about this society of collective man. The hope is that of a kind of internalised total consensus achieved mainly by spiritual methods. The ultimate roots of this emphasis may be sought in Lenin's own emphasis on the conscious factor (further extended by

[1] *Peking Review*, "Fighting Task of Workers in Philosophy and Social Science," January 3, 1964.

Stalin) perhaps fed to some extent by the Confucian faith in the power of moral influence. Its more immediate background is to be sought in the circumstances of the Yenan period when the methods of " remoulding " were first applied to members and prospective members of the Communist Party. The notion was later vastly extended to include the whole " people " including the " national bourgeoisie " however defined. The doctrine that all can be saved—even some " counter-revolutionary elements "—has, of course, always been heavily qualified by the retention of the class notion. People of the wrong classes are not easily transformed, and continue to generate poisons of wrong thought. Yet they *can* be transformed while those of good class background *can* be led astray. In the end the main criterion for assigning persons to the " people " or " non-people " is to be sought in their spiritual attitudes rather than in the facts of their class origin. The doctrine of salvation stresses simultaneously that almost all men may be saved; that salvation is enormously difficult for all men, and that backsliding is an ever present possibility. Paradoxically the emphasis on spiritual transformation may lend itself to quite disparate policies. The " Hundred Flowers " campaign may have been predicated on the genuine belief that the intelligentsia had been basically transformed during the 1949–55 period, while the " anti-rightist " campaign of 1957 was based on precisely the opposite assumption. The " great leap forward " may have been based on the assumption that the " masses " (unlike the intelligentsia) had been basically transformed and that their " subjective forces " were at the disposal of the leadership while the present campaign of " Socialist education " seems to be predicated on the assumption that there is still much work to be done.

" POPULISM "

The emphasis on spiritual transformation is closely linked to the " populist " theme—because the whole people (defined as a union of four classes) can be transformed, the whole Chinese people can participate in the building of Socialism and Communism. This doctrine finds its formal institutional expression in the coalition structure of government, and can, of course, be harnessed to the nationalist goals of the régime as well as to project the Chinese model to the " emerging world " where there is such an obvious political need to " unite with whom one can unite." The obverse side of the formula—the notion that the " people " is not homogeneous but composed of different classes which still engender " non-antagonistic " (and even antagonistic) contradictions, has, however, been of equal importance. It has justified the need for constant vigilance and unremitting indoctrination, but was also used to justify the vaguely defined legitimate area of "blooming and contending" of the "Hundred Flowers" period. On this side, it is particularly closely linked to another element of the Maoist vision, namely, the enormous stress on struggle, conflict and high tension as positive values. Mao Tse-tung's commitment to these values probably preceded his conversion to Marxism-Leninism and has, as we know, even coloured his vision of the utopian future which he seems reluctant to think of in terms of stasis and total harmony. When directed against those defined as the outer enemy, struggle makes for solidarity "within the people." On another level, however, the enemy must be conceived of as ever present in the minds of the people itself in the form of "bourgeois thought." The struggle against this bourgeois thought is not only a negative factor. "Fighting against wrong ideas is like being vaccinated— a man develops greater immunity from disease after the vaccine takes effect. Plants raised in hot-houses are not likely to be robust." [2] At the time when it was uttered, this doctrine was linked to the lenient policies of the "Hundred Flowers" period. One can easily see how the same doctrine can be given a much more draconic interpretation.

Another element of the vision which is closely linked to the emphasis on spiritual transformation and collectivity is the stress on man rather than weapons or tools as the "decisive force in history." By transforming men's minds and consolidating their collective energies one can achieve enormous results in spheres where others have relied on material power. Here again the Yenan experience provides the shining example. Where one has mobilised the collective energies of men, motivated by the Maoist vision, economic advancement, national power and social transformation are no longer purely dependent on "material prerequisites."

Another theme which has been stressed, with varying degrees of intensity, is the necessity of contact with the masses, and "participation in physical labour" on the part of intellectuals, students, professionals and lower bureaucrats. This may reflect the genuine belief that "participation in labour" is a form of thought reform which will induce respect for physical labour and keep these elements from over-weening pretensions. At the same time it is made crystal clear that one is not free to find among the masses any view of reality which contradicts the Maoist vision.

THE ROLE OF THE COMMUNIST PARTY

Finally there is the enormous pivotal role of the Communist Party as the "proletarian" vanguard of society. Again, we seem to be dealing here with standard Marxist-Leninist doctrine, but as has been pointed

---

[2] "Correct Handling of Contradictions among the People," Bowie and Fairbank, *Communist China 1955–59* (Cambridge, Mass.: Harvard University Press, 1962), p. 289.

out by many, the Party has probably played a more crucial and concrete role in China than in the Soviet Union at least during the lifetime of Stalin. The transformation of the Chinese people must be carried out by the Party. Ideally speaking, the Party maintains its supremacy not simply by dint of its organisational machinery but by its ability to internalise its " proletarian nature " into every party member. The " proletarian nature " of the Party no longer resides, of course, primarily in the industrial workers but has become a kind of spiritual essence embodied in the Party and yet still endowed with all those transcendental and universal qualities which Marx attributes to the working class. It is this idea of the " proletarian nature " of the Party which sets strict limits to the whole populist drift of the Chinese vision. In fact since the beginning of the Sino-Soviet conflict, the Party has stressed its proletarian nature more than ever. The Party does not derive its transcendent moral status and historic role in China or in the world at large from the fact that it merely represents the Chinese people, but from a higher source. The Party may serve the interests of Chinese nationalism but it does so from a supra-national stance.

Within China itself the Party ought to be the nervous system of society and should play a commanding role in every sphere of social and cultural endeavour. The ideal Communist cadre is not only a paragon of selflessness but potentially omnicompetent. Ideally it is also the Party which is in direct communication with the " worker-peasant-soldier " masses and which reflects what the masses want and need or rather what they ought to want and need in a Maoist universe. Thus whenever there is a stress on the " mass line," one may assume that the decision-making function of the local party fraction is being stressed. Yet all of this still leaves open the possibilities that the Party ranks, as opposed to the Supreme leader, are vulnerable to error and backsliding.

MAO'S VISION AND MODERNISATION

These it seems to me are some of the more salient elements of the Maoist vision. What have been the relations of this vision to the goal of modernisation?

The official view of the present leadership is that the vision—no matter how its interpretation may fluctuate—not only provides the most effective means for achieving modernisation, but is also an end in itself. The only desirable modernisation is a modernisation which can be incorporated into the Maoist vision. At the other extreme, we have the view that the vision runs completely athwart the prerequisites of modernisation or that it is a sort of rationalisation of the failures and difficulties of modernisation in China. One makes a virtue of necessity according to this view because the necessity is intractable. Where weapons and capital are scarce what is to be lost in stressing the organisation of human energies? Where material incentives are not available, why not stress the "Communist ethic"? Oddly enough, the official ideology also seems to stress the relation of necessity to virtue. It was, after all, the peculiarities of Chinese conditions which made possible the stress on guerrilla warfare. It is the "poverty and blankness" of China, Mao insists in 1958, which makes possible the achievement of Communism long before the insidious corruptions of capitalism and revisionism have set in. The fact that "virtue" is associated with necessity by no means implies that the belief in virtue may not be genuine and fervent particularly since the belief is also linked to the power interests of the leadership.

Surveying the history of the People's Republic since 1949, we find that various elements of the vision play an enormous role in the enormous effort of the first few years to bring about political and ideological consolidation. "Study," "thought reform," "confession," etc., were applied on various levels not only to prospective party members but to the "people" as a whole. The "small group" technique and the technique of mass organisation were universally applied. The Party seemed to be proving that totalitarian consolidation of a people could be carried out effectively by relying on "man" rather than technology. Except for those defined as counter-revolutionaries and reactionaries, there was considerable reason for belief that the spiritual transformation was succeeding. Some parts of the vision seemed, and seem, to be quite compatible with certain aspects of modernisation. Many tasks of public health, police work, social control and even economic undertakings, which depend primarily on labour intensivity, lend themselves to Maoist methods.

THE RELEVANCE OF THE SOVIET MODEL

However, while the vision did permeate large sectors of political and social activity, in the areas most crucial to the modernisation effort— particularly as related to state power goals—it was the Soviet model which was followed. This involved some retreat in the concept of Party omnicompetence, considerable emphasis on a "rational" division of labour and professionalisation and some emphasis on the need for a professional state bureaucracy. This does not mean that one should see an absolute antagonism between the Soviet model of modernisation and the Maoist vision. Obviously the gravitation toward the total nationalisation of industry and the collectivisation of agriculture was entirely in line with both. In fact, it may well have been high confidence and exuberance (as well as a desperate sense of haste) induced by the success of his vision in the political and social spheres which led Mao and those closest to him in 1955 to feel that collectivisation could be speedily consummated in China without the dire effects it had produced in the Soviet Union. The fact remains, however, that on the whole Mao modestly deferred to the " superior experience " of the Soviet Union in these areas.

With the beginning of the " Hundred Flowers " experiment, the picture becomes more complex. On the one hand the experiment seems to mark a further concession to the requirements of modernisation. This can be discerned in the effort to give professionals and specialists a greater sense of security and freedom, in the rectification campaign directed against the Party with the implied admission that in some areas the specialists knew more than the Party and even in the new concern with legal codification. The campaign also seems to have coincided, however, with some dawning doubts about the complete applicability of the Soviet model of modernisation to Chinese conditions. These doubts were certainly encouraged by the death of Stalin and the new winds blowing in the Communist bloc itself. This new emphasis on the requirements of modernisation as well as the doubts about the Soviet model did not, however, necessarily diminish the role of the Maoist vision. On the contrary, the " Hundred Flowers " formula was presented as a precious new contribution of Mao Tse-tung (the first since 1949) to the storehouse of Marxism-Leninism and it is, of course, quite easy to see how many ambivalent elements of the vision lent themselves to the " soft " interpretation of this period. In fact, Mao may have genuinely believed that in the course of thought reform " the political outlook of the Chinese intellectuals has undergone a fundamental change." [3] The growing doubts about the complete applicability of the Soviet model of modernisation may have even encouraged the view that the Maoist vision was applicable in areas where " Soviet experience " had hitherto reigned supreme.

In fact the " great leap forward " and commune movement of 1957–1959 mark the high tide of the application of the Maoist vision to the very tasks of modernisation. If the intelligentsia had shown its fundamental untrustworthiness, the subjective forces of the masses [4] were still available for heaven-storming feats. The emphasis on man as the decisive factor, on the negligible role of " material prerequisites," on the superior efficacy of collective subjective forces and on the

---

[3] Lu Ting-yi, " Let Hundred Flowers Blossom; Let a Hundred Schools Contend," Bowie and Fairbank, *op. cit.*, p. 154.
[4] Whatever may have been the discontents revealed in 1956–57, the peasants had, after all, been collectivised without producing anything resembling the effects of collectivisation in the Soviet Union.

omnicompetence of the Party all enter into this experiment, and give it its utopian, apocalyptic flavour.

CONTRACTION AND REVIVAL

The retreat from the Great Leap in 1960–62 again seems to mark a return to a sober estimate of the requirements of modernisation but no longer on an exclusively Soviet model. It also seems to mark a contraction in the influence of the Maoist vision even though the new economic model with its emphasis on "agriculture as the base" was quite distinctly Chinese. One may, in fact, argue as has been suggested that the modernisation policies of this period are much more "rational" in terms of Chinese realities than the policies of the Soviet period. They have led, it would appear, to a substantial economic recovery. Yet, as we know, ever since the end of 1962 there has again been a rising crescendo of emphasis on "socialist education." At this very moment the Maoist vision, in one of its most extreme formulations, again occupies the centre of the stage. The beginnings of this new revival are perhaps to be discerned in the crisis surrounding the army in the 1959–62 period. As we know, P'eng Teh-huai, who seems to have become the spokesman of military professionalism and perhaps of professionalism in general, had also become an "anti-party" element, that is a menace in the realm of power, while the crisis of morale in the army revealed in the *Bulletin of Activities* (*Kung-tso T'ung-hsun*) documents suggested that the threat to the vision, at least in this sphere, was also regarded as a threat to power. Thus the campaign of "Socialist education" was begun very early in the army, and having been judged a success, we find the army projected as a model for society as a whole. Here again we note what Stuart Schram has called Mao's "military deviation"—his tendency to think of a well-indoctrinated army as providing a paradigm of Communist life.

The return of large numbers of students to the countryside involving as it did the frustration of hopes for advancement in urban society, also created a serious problem of morale which seemed to call for drastic therapy in terms of spiritual transformation. Beyond this, the growing intensity of the Sino-Soviet conflict has strongly impelled the leadership to project the Maoist vision onto the world at large as the very embodiment of "true Marxism-Leninism."

Above all, however, there is the fact that the ageing Mao and those closest to him are genuinely concerned with the survival of the vision. The whole current fervid campaign of "Socialist education" is permeated more by a kind of pervasive anxiety than by a mood of high confidence. The leadership may be quite optimistic about China's present economic situation and posture in the world at large, but it is precisely in the ideological sphere that one detects a mood of concern. The intelligentsia had shown its unreliability at the time of the " Hundred Flowers " campaign. Even the masses had shown their inability to live up to Mao's expectations at the time of the " great leap forward." Indeed, it is now implied that the spontaneous inertial movement of things runs counter to the vision. " The restoration of capitalism," states Chou En-lai (and here he is undoubtedly the spokesman of Mao Tse-tung), " is not inevitable. In China we have a firm and fighting Marxist-Leninist Party, a proletarian Power which is increasingly consolidating itself, a powerful and revolutionary People's Liberation Army, an enormous number of cadres, a people of high political consciousness and a glorious revolutionary tradition. Of especial importance is the fact that our Party and State can count on a leading nucleus guided by the thought of Mao Tse-tung. All of this makes the restoration of capitalism very difficult in our country." [5]

There is here, of course, an oblique implication that the Soviet Union lacks these reassuring features. The whole thrust of the passage suggests, however, that what mainly stands between China and the " restoration of capitalism " is the Maoist vision. It is noteworthy that there is no reference to the " Socialist structure " of Chinese society as one of the factors preventing such a restoration.

While the " Socialist education " campaign has, however, fallen with an enormous weight on the literary, artistic and cultural spheres and perhaps on all non-vocational areas of social life, while the cult of Mao has been raised to unprecedented heights, it is still not clear whether it has again been allowed to affect the strategy of modernisation, particularly in the economic sphere. In fact, one may speculate that in the areas of highest priority—such as nuclear development—the Maoist vision has never been allowed to interfere with the requirements of technology. As far as one can judge at the present, experts are now expected to be diffused with redness even while devoting a maximum of attention to expertise and the system of higher education is more oriented than ever to the production of experts. Yet all this may change. It would certainly be the gravest of errors to assume that because the 1960 economic strategy has proven fairly successful, economic considerations will necessarily override the concern with the " succession to the revolutionary heritage."

The leadership's concern is probably justified. It is difficult to believe that the vision will survive at least in its present extreme form. It is difficult to believe not only, or even primarily, because in some of

5 " Report on the Work of the Government," *Peking Review*, Jan. 1, 1965.

its aspects it runs counter to the requirements of modernisation. Even more immediately, it involves such a constricted and terribly simplified view of human life that one is inclined to doubt whether it is humanly viable. In terms of modernisation, however, it is difficult to believe that the vision will be allowed in the long run to interfere particularly with those aspects of modernisation most relevant to the achievement of national power. While the vision may retreat, however, we are in no position to foresee the extent of the retreat or to predict what will remain. Modernisation may not be fully compatible with the Maoist vision but neither has it been fully compatible with Jeffersonian democracy. China may depart from the Maoist vision yet still move into a future uniquely its own. As long as Mao and those close to him remain at the helm, we may expect them to be as much concerned with the vision as with any of the other goals of the régime.

The Dismissal of Marshal P'eng Teh-huai

By DAVID A. CHARLES

THERE is little reason for thinking that the anti-rightist campaign of 1957–58, which closed the Hundred Flowers interlude, was undertaken in order to overcome an organised opposition in the central leadership of the Chinese Communist Party rather than to deal with a political situation that was clearly getting out of hand. The victims were either bourgeois intellectuals and members of the so-called "democratic parties" or communist officials of the second rank, for the most part provincial administrators. Their fate presumably strengthened the hand of the doctrinaires in the Party and weakened the will of the moderates to oppose the extravagances of the subsequent "great leap forward"; and there are doubtless many in China as well as the West who believe that Mao's personal involvement in the fiasco of liberalisation may have constituted the first stage in a process which would lead eighteen months later to his withdrawal from the chairmanship of the republic. The political repercussions were, however, long-term; the immediate effect of the change of line may have been to cement rather than undermine the solidarity of the leaders.

The campaign against the "right-wing opportunists" launched after the eighth plenum of the Central Committee, held at Lushan in August 1959, was a very different affair. Its denunciation of "rightism" had an air of paradox, since the régime, as was shown by the announcement in the same communiqué of the transfer of ownership from the communes to the production brigade, was itself swinging slowly but inexorably to the right.[1] And the impression that on this occasion personalities rather than policies were involved was strengthened by the extraordinary virulence of the press campaign, accompanied as it was by the passionate reaffirmation of policies, which could be seen to have failed, at least as originally conceived, and by an emotional rallying round the person of Mao and exaggerated adulation of his leadership.

---

[1] The transfer, although announced at Lushan, had perhaps been discussed at the Wuhan plenum in December 1958 and may have been decided in principle at the enlarged meeting of the Politburo held without publicity at Chengchow in the following February. In any case, the turning point had come at Wuhan with the abandonment of the more ambitious claims made for the communes. Lushan neither halted the retreat from the communes nor reversed the trend towards the more rational planning: at the most it may have slowed down the implementation of policies which were already being put into effect.

At the end of September came the announcement of the replacement of Marshal P'eng Teh-huai, the Minister of Defence, by Marshal Lin Piao, the hero of the revolutionary war, and of General Huang K'o-ch'eng, the Chief of Staff of the Army and P'eng's senior vice-minister, by General Lo Jui-ch'ing, the Minister of Public Security and a man whose record was more that of a policeman than a soldier. At the same time, in an unprecedentedly long list of appointments and removals, two Vice-Ministers of Foreign Affairs, Chang Wen-t'ien and Wang Chia-hsiang, failed to secure re-nomination. And a few days later, the absence of Ch'en Yun from the October celebrations in Peking provided the first proof of his fall from grace.[2] With the exception of Wang Chia-hsiang, who quickly rehabilitated himself, they were all consigned to an obscurity from which they have barely, if at all, emerged.

All of this fitted into the pattern of what, to borrow the jargon of the Kremlinologists, could be described as a " power-struggle " in the top leadership. The failure to name the rightist leaders could be explained as due to a desire to maintain the semblance of unity by which the Chinese Party has always set such store. Nor was there any evidence, for all the talk of deviationists at every level, that the purge was in fact being extended to the lower ranks of the Party on anything like the scale of earlier campaigns; indeed, as if to emphasise the difference, the authorities took the occasion of the dismissal of P'eng Teh-huai to rehabilitate a number of rightists of 1957 and earlier vintages.

This interpretation of the anti-rightist campaign of 1959—that the Party had to deal with a palace intrigue rather than a popular movement —was that of most Western observers at the time. It is confirmed by reports which have come out of China during the subsequent two years. We can now assert with confidence that P'eng was the leader of an " anti-party " group in the Politburo which made its challenge at the Lushan plenum, where P'eng read a memorandum attacking the whole policy of the Party; that P'eng's attack had been made with the knowledge of the Russians, for he, without the knowledge of the Politburo, had written a letter to the Soviet party criticising the great leap forward and the communes for which Moscow had already revealed its distaste; that his principal associate was Chang Wen-t'ien and that at Lushan or earlier he had enlisted the support of the veteran and highly respected Lin Po-chü; that Khrushchev's refusal to apologise for this intervention in Chinese domestic affairs perhaps precipitated the acute phase of the Sino-Soviet dispute; and that at the Bucharest and Moscow Conferences in the following year Khrushchev continued to defend his actions and

---

[2] As pointed out below, Ch'en Yun's elimination from power may in fact have preceded the Lushan plenum.

the right of the Soviet party to hold private discussions with leading members of other parties, whether Chinese or Albanian.[3]

The reports confirm that, as most Western observers had conjectured, the background to the case of P'eng Teh-huai was a dispute on nuclear strategy. Whether or not, as Lin Piao was subsequently to allege, P'eng had actively resisted Party control of the Army his original offence was that he had questioned the continuing validity of Mao's theories on partisan warfare; had come out in favour of a professional army employed as soldiers rather than auxiliary agricultural workers; and had opposed the concept of a nation in arms and its expression in the creation of an enormous untrained militia.[4]

P'eng's " rightism " may well have been conditioned by such military considerations. Thus his dislike of the communes perhaps sprang from their integration with the militia and the effect on the morale of a peasant army of the upheaval they caused in agrarian life; and it is likely enough that the plans of the Ministry of Defence for modernisation were disrupted by the diversion of effort into the extravagances of the great leap forward. In the same way, his disapproval of the breach with Moscow could plausibly be explained by a reluctance to quarrel with China's only supplier of modern weapons. It is clear, however, that, whether or not for tactical reasons, P'eng preferred to concentrate his attack on the political and economic policies of the Party rather than air his professional grievances. Throughout P'eng acted as a senior member of the Politburo rather than as a dissatisfied Minister of Defence. He was

---

[3] The number of these reports and their general concordance on the main points at issue show how difficult it is for the Chinese Communists, at a time when they are actively encouraging contacts with the West, to keep the outside world permanently in ignorance of major political developments in the country. Some of the reports reflect the briefing which all Party members received at the time of the events. Others derive from a revival of Party interest in the 1959 affair which coincided with the exacerbation of Sino-Soviet relations in the summer of 1960. On this occasion selected cadres were told about P'eng Teh-huai's contacts with the Soviet leadership— an aspect of the case which had been concealed in the earlier general briefing. While it would be hazardous to suggest on the evidence available that the Chinese have actually wished the information to reach the West, they must have been aware that secrecy was unlikely to be maintained indefinitely in view of the wide circulation given to the information in a party of some 17 millions.

[4] Alice Hsieh, in her article " Communist China and Nuclear Warfare " (*The China Quarterly*, No. 2, 1960), having identified P'eng on the strength of a speech in 1955 as a supporter and not an opponent of Mao's " partisan " theories of war, suggested that his dismissal was intended to solve a dispute between the " Maoist " Ministry of Defence and the more professionally minded General Staff, with Lin Piao as the reconciler of the two views. Reference to Lin Piao's Tenth Anniversary speech does not however bear out Mrs. Hsieh's contention that Lin placed equal emphasis on the importance of political control and modernisation. Indeed he stressed that politics is the " predominant " side and proclaimed the Party's belief that " although equipment, and technique are important the human factor is even more important." While P'eng may have been a comparatively late convert to the " professional " viewpoint it would have been paradoxical if he had not only been got rid of but disgraced for upholding the orthodox Maoist strategical theories which would soon be reiterated in the Lenin Anniversary, and many other articles.

disgraced as the leader of an " anti-party group " and not as the proponent of unacceptable military theories.

There is little evidence on which to speculate about the origins of P'eng Teh-huai's movement and its ramifications. Ch'en Yun, although his elimination from power was not noted in the West till his failure to appear in Peking for the October 1 celebrations, was in fact little in evidence throughout 1959 and relapsed into obscurity after his March article in the *People's Daily*. He may not even have been present at the Lushan plenum [5] and, although sharing P'eng's dislike of the Party's economic policies, does not seem to have played any significant part in the intrigue. Chang Wen-t'ien on the other hand was deeply involved. Indeed, while keeping himself in the background he may well have been the moving spirit. P'eng himself has had little experience of political activity; and, even if Chang did not actually write P'eng's letter to the Soviet Party and his subsequent Lushan memorandum, we may suspect that the former Chinese representative on the Comintern and Ambassador to Moscow was the dissidents' link with the Russians.

On April 24, while the National People's Congress (April 18–28) was still in session, P'eng started on a " military good-will " mission to the capitals of the Warsaw Pact Powers, which was to keep him out of the country for some seven weeks. On the same day, and probably by the same aeroplane, Chang Wen-t'ien left for Warsaw as Chinese observer at a meeting of the foreign ministers of the Warsaw Pact Powers. This simultaneous departure was almost certainly a coincidence. Chang Wen-t'ien, as senior Vice-Minister of Foreign Affairs, would naturally represent his Minister in view of the latter's commitments at the National People's Congress; nor, in the case of P'eng, should too much stress perhaps be laid on the obvious analogy with the experience of Marshal Zhukov, who in 1957 was sent to Yugoslavia and Albania on an unexpectedly protracted tour which was clearly a put-up job to keep him out of the country while action was taken against him. So far from being eliminated during their absence, P'eng and Chang were, on April 28, confirmed in their offices and were still strong enough three months later to challenge the leadership. Whatever lobbying there may have been behind the scenes at the National People's Congress, it is unlikely that in April either the dominant faction or their critics regarded the time as ripe for a show-down.

On arrival in Moscow, and again on June 2, P'eng Teh-huai met the Moscow Commander, Marshal Moskalenko, who was surprisingly unsympathetic. On May 25, P'eng had a cordial meeting with

---

[5] He does not seem to figure in the photograph published by the *People's Daily* on August 27. Identification is however difficult and his absence from the photograph might in any case have been due to his having come out in support of P'eng.

Khrushchev in Tirana; and it may have been on this occasion that he delivered the letter to the Soviet Party which was to cause so much bad blood between the two countries. He finally got back to Peking, via Outer Mongolia, on June 13, having travelled from Moscow to Ulan Bator in the company of Marshal Koniev.

After his return P'eng seems to have held his hand while the Party was preparing to scale down the fantastic claims for the 1958 harvest and publicly shift policy on the communes. He was, however, busy—or so the Party afterwards alleged—collecting statistics and other evidence to prove the inadequacies of the great leap forward. What happened when he finally came out into the open at the eighth plenum of the Central Committee, held at Lushan from August 2 to August 16, can only be deduced from the tendentious accounts which Party members subsequently received. It is known, however, that P'eng proposed a resolution which attacked the Party's political and economic policies and that he set out his views in an extremely lengthy memorandum which he read to the meeting; that Lin Po-ch'ü, who had long stood for moderation, commented favourably on P'eng's initiative, which received the full support of Chang Wen-t'ien, General Huang K'o-cheng and a number of lesser personalities, while a good many other speakers at first wavered. P'eng's colleagues in the Politburo were surprised, or affected to be surprised, at his action and finally carried a counter-resolution which uncompromisingly rejected P'eng's criticisms, reaffirmed the entire correctness of the Party's line and, while admitting the right of P'eng to express his views in the Politburo, condemned him for factional activity in lobbying members of the Central Committee. There is unfortunately little evidence on which to assess the chances which P'eng and his friends had of success. Defeat, as is usually the case when the leadership of a Communist Party is unsuccessfully attacked, was overwhelming and perhaps appeared to be more easily achieved owing to the speed with which the waverers abandoned their rebellious colleagues as soon as the issue seemed to be decided.

A good deal is known about the content of P'eng's memorandum. After dealing fairly briefly with the shortcomings of the communes, which he attributed to their having been set up without adequate preparation, P'eng went on to criticise the conduct of the mass campaigns in industry and agriculture, without however disputing the correctness of Mao's "general line." He soon came to his main theme—the shortcomings of the great leap forward. The blunders and the waste of the small blast furnaces were dealt with at length. They had, he alleged, even been set up in places where coal was unobtainable, so that the peasants had had to cut the trees down and feed the furnaces with ordinary firewood. Yet so great had been the enthusiasm for the new idea that the undisclosed target had been to overtake British steel production not in fifteen years as announced but in ten years and United States production in 15–20 years.

Many of P'eng's shafts such as his ascription of the great leap forward to " petty bourgeois fanaticism " and his reminder that the Communists used to condemn the Kuomintang for ruling the nation through the Party, stuck sufficiently to be quoted as the views of the anonymous rightists in the subsequent press campaign. The Party did not, however, venture to comment publicly on P'eng's bitter denunciation of their claims to have raised the standard of living of the masses. According to his statistics, in 1933–53 adults were getting one catty (half a kilogram) of rice a day and children three-quarters of a catty. In 1956 they got three-quarters of a catty and two-thirds of a catty respectively. In 1958 this had been reduced to half a catty and one-quarter of a catty in many areas. The masses could not survive on such a diet and had been reduced to eating algae, cotton-leaves and leaves of the mustard plant. If their rations were not improved, there would be a repetition of the riots which had taken place in 1957.[6]

Whether because they had been genuinely taken aback by the boldness of P'eng's onslaught or because they wished to allow his associates every opportunity for declaring themselves, the Party leaders allowed a protracted debate which was by no means one-sided. Indeed, at one stage there was an emotional scene when Mao, in reply to a suggestion that the disgrace of P'eng might be the signal for a revolt by the armed forces due to his popularity with them and in the country, declared with tears in his eyes that, if this happened, he would go back to the villages and recruit another army. The generals present then got up in turn and pledged their loyalty to Mao and to the Central Committee.

Of P'eng's supporters, Lin Po-ch'ü at least seems to have held out to the end. While not subjected to indignities, Lin had subsequently to make a self-criticism and was still under a cloud when he died in May 1960 and was accorded a national funeral. This was the occasion for P'eng's only publicly recorded appearance since his fall.

P'eng himself was treated more harshly. After his arrest and a period of intensive re-indoctrination, he made a formal confession in the shape of a short letter to Mao in which he alluded to his errors, regretted that he had failed to follow Mao's guidance and asked to be allowed to

---

[6] These incidents, which were referred to in the Chinese press at the time, included a demonstration in early June by some 2,000 peasants from Kungan and Shih Shou in Hupeh and An Hsiang and Hua Jung in Hunan who joined hands and staged a demonstration at a village called Huang Shan Tou on the border between the two provinces. This was firmly suppressed with some loss of life. Subsequently there was serious student unrest in the Wuhan area, which was widely publicised. Mass trials for counter-revolutionary activity were also reported in the press.

rehabilitate himself by working as a peasant. Although P'eng's letter could not be regarded by Communist standards as an adequate exercise in self-criticism, Mao, in an equally brief reply, after paying tribute to P'eng's services in the revolution, advised against manual labour in view of P'eng's age but suggested that he should visit factories in order to obtain first-hand experience of the masses at work.[7] After completing his tour of Chinese industry, P'eng was sent as superintendent (or, according to some other accounts, deputy superintendent) of the much publicised and appropriately named " Sino-Soviet Friendship " State Farm in Heilungkiang. Nominally, he retains his membership of the Politburo.

Only P'eng's confession was divulged to the Party. Apart from Huang K'o-ch'eng and Chang Wen-t'ien, Chou Hsiao-chou, the provincial secretary of Hunan, seems to have been the only associate of P'eng's who was denounced by name to the cadres. His defection must have been a particularly bitter blow to Mao, since it emphasised the connection of his own province with the movement of his fellow Hunanese, P'eng Teh-huai and Huang K'o-ch'eng. Chou had served under Huang K'o-ch'eng when the latter was provincial secretary of Hunan (1949–52) and since 1953 had held that post. He has not been heard of since his removal, which was announced on September 27. Huang K'o-ch'eng has also faded into complete obscurity; nor has Chang Wen-t'ien made any public appearances, except at the commemoration of Lenin's birthday in April 1960 and at this year's October 1 celebration in Peking.

In the meantime the press campaign against the group had got under way. It opened quietly with two *People's Daily* editorials on August 6 and 7, four days after the plenum opened. Both articles were careful to limit their criticism to the spread of rightist " ideas " and avoid giving the impression that important personalities were involved. Nothing more was heard of " rightism " till August 16, the day the plenum ended, when a *Red Flag* article took up the theme. Again the tone was moderate: indeed *Red Flag*, while admitting that " dangerous " rightist-inclined tendencies actually existed now implied that they could be easily cured by urging that " help " should be extended to comrades, who had fallen a victim to them, in accordance with the principle of " treat the sickness to save the patient."

The main offensive was launched only ten days later on August 26, when the resolution of the Lushan plenum was published simultaneously with a speech by Chou En-lai to the Standing Committee of the National People's Congress. Both documents were significant for the fact that

---

[7] Reports that P'eng Teh-huai at one stage worked on the Shum Chun reservoir in Kwangtung may therefore be discounted.

what had previously been called rightist sentiments were for the first time classified as right-opportunist sentiments, *i.e.*, those who held them were not only misguided but heretical. Reference in the plenum resolution to " hostile enemy elements within the country " and " unfirm " cadres tainted from right-opportunist sentiments was matched by Chou's description of " reactionaries at home and abroad " and " bourgeois rightists " with possible sympathisers in the Party. The foreign theme, which in view of subsequent developments must always be regarded as containing a possible allusion to the Soviet Union rather than Yugoslavia, was taken up in a *People's Daily* editorial of the following day which claimed that the right opportunists had " joined the hostile elements at home and abroad in a campaign of slander and have attempted to create ideological and political confusion by killing the initiative of the masses." The article was also notable for calling the right opportunists " incorrigible " and admitting that " bourgeois anti-Socialism " existed within the Party and constituted a major danger. On August 30, *Red Flag*, in sharp contrast with its more lenient attitude of August 16, denounced the pessimism of the right opportunists as " criminal activity against the cause of building Socialism."

In September, references started to appear to the great heretics of the past. On September 1 the *People's Daily* recalled the cases of Kautsky, Plekhanov and Ch'en Tu-hsiu in China, to show that proletarian revolutionaries could " degenerate " into bourgeois revolutionaries. On September 4 the same paper described a " small number of right opportunists " as " enemy supporters and agents of the revolutionary ranks." On September 7 *The Chinese Youth Newspaper* referred to the possibility that rightists might hold " responsible positions " as " unit leaders " in the Party; and two days later the *People's Daily* warned comrades with rightist tendencies that they might " not be able to weather the storm." During the same month some articles in the provincial press for the first time linked the rightists with the Soviet Union by accusing them of advocating blind adherence to the Soviet model.

On September 16 came the announcement of the dismissals, and the public campaign reached its climax with the extraordinary Tenth Anniversary article of Liu Lan-t'ao, published on September 28. The violence of its language was in strong contrast with the moderation shown by other contributions to the series when discussing right opportunism : indeed the *Peoples' Daily* in its editorial on National Day did not refer to the subject at all. The appearance of the article to coincide with Khrushchev's arrival in Peking may well have been deliberate.

Apart from the proof which it provided of the seriousness with which the party regarded the affair, Liu's article was noteworthy for the light which it threw on the position of the dissidents. Particularly interesting was the charge that the right opportunists had denounced the practice of placing the first secretary in command as "dictatorship" and "undemocratic." (This like so much else in the programme of the rightists of 1959 is now virtually the official line.) And Liu's eulogy of Mao's leadership as "indispensable to the success of the revolution" indicated that the deviationists had challenged this leadership.

The campaign continued through October and November with major articles by K'o Ch'ing-shih in *Red Flag* of November 1 and by Ch'en Po-ta in the issue of November 16. Neither added much to what had already been said, except for the accusation that the rightists were also revisionists. Their Socialism according to K'o Ch'ing-shih, "is the so-called socialism in the minds of the modern revisionists, who are traitors to Marxism-Leninism." Ch'en Po-ta linked them with the "bourgeois rightists" of 1957, claiming that both agreed with the "modern revisionists in various nations" in that they all identified the dictatorship of the proletariat with the non-party system. Both articles however provided useful summaries of the programme of the dissidents through the eyes of their opponents. According to K'o Ch'ing-shih it was "to oppose the general line of the party on socialist construction, to oppose the tremendous leap forward and to oppose the peoples communes." Ch'en Po-ta summarised rightist opposition to the general line as consisting of two articles: "article number one is opposition to the party leadership, and article number two is opposition to the mass campaign."

Space does not permit a more detailed analysis of the voluminous press and radio campaign. It is of interest not only as source material for reconstructing the arguments used by the dissidents but also for the evidence which it provides of the extent to which the party was shaken by the affair. The muted opening of the press campaign while the Lushan plenum was in session and the ten days delay in issuing the communiqué and launching the main offensive could be regarded as evidence of careful orchestration by the Communist authorities. An alternative, and perhaps more plausible, interpretation of the weak initial reaction to P'eng's onslaught is that the Party was playing for time. Certainly the *People's Daily* editorials of August 6 and 7 and the *Red Flag* article of August 16 were singularly ineffective as a reply to the Marshal's memorandum. Whether or not the issue had in fact already been decided, they do not give the impression that the Party had made up its mind how to deal with the revolt.

Indoctrination of party members was carried on at the same time as the press campaign. Several thousand cadres of the Ministry of Defence and National Defence establishments met to denounce the activities of P'eng Teh-huai and Huang K'o-ch'eng; and similar meetings were held at the Ministry of Foreign Affairs to criticise Chang Wen-t'ien. In due course Party members throughout the country were briefed down to the lowest level.

The principal item on the agenda at these nation-wide meetings was the reading and discussion of a long document which outlined the activities of the dissidents stigmatising them as an " anti-Party " group which had operated under P'eng to destroy the unity of the Party. The main attack was on P'eng, and the statement included a list of sixteen specific charges against him. Most of these dealt with incidents in his past career with the object of proving that he had " failed to pass the bourgeois-democratic stage of the revolution," *i.e.*, had never been a true Communist at all. As a former bourgeois (*i.e.*, Kuomingtang) officer, he was accused of having joined the Communists merely out of opportunism and compared to a capitalist who invests his money wherever it will show him a profit. P'eng's subsequent military career was the subject of further charges. He was said, while winning a tactical victory over the Japanese in the Battle of the Hundred Regiments, to have committed a gross strategical blunder by prematurely exposing the strength of the Communists, which Mao had always been careful to conceal.[8] The result was that Chiang Kai-shek decided to concentrate on eliminating the internal rather than the external enemy, while the Japanese and their Chinese puppets delivered a co-ordinated attack on the Communists and their supply lines. Many of the nuclei which had been operating behind the Japanese lines and would otherwise have expanded into military bases, were wiped out or had to join the main Communist forces. The economic situation became so bad that half the army had to be demobilised and the remainder ordered to become self-supporting. Even padded winter clothing could not be obtained. All these disasters were to be attributed to P'eng's folly in abandoning Mao's tactic of partisan and guerilla warfare. P'eng was also accused of having repeatedly ignored the directives of the Central Committee. Thus he was said to have fought the fifth and last battle of the Korean War on his own initiative, thereby becoming guilty of gross insubordination.[9]

Owing to the absence of publicity even within the Party it is difficult to determine the extent of the purge which followed the fall of the leaders.

---

[8] The so-called Battle of the Hundred (or Hundred and Fifteen) Regiments was fought from August 20 to December 5, 1940.

[9] According to Western reckoning, the fifth battle of the Korean War was the unsuccessful Chinese attack of April 1951, in which the Gloucesters were involved. The reference may however be to the final Chinese offensive against the South Korean troops, which was launched just before the armistice, apparently in order to secure last-minute gains of territory and overcome South Korean objections to an armistice. If this is the reference, it is strange that the Central Committee should disclaim responsibility for so political an operation.

At the Ministry of Defence, two of Huang K'o-ch'eng's fellow Vice-Ministers, General Li Ta,[10] P'eng's Chief of Staff in Korea, and General Hsiao K'o, were removed at the same time as Huang but given other minor appointments, Li Ta becoming Vice-Chairman of the Physical Culture and Sports Commission and Hsiao K'o Vice-Minister of State Farms and Land Reclamation. General Hung Hsueh-ch'ih, the Head of Rear Services of the P.L.A., was removed on October 14 and has not since been heard of. He was Head of the Rear Services of the C.P.V. in Korea under P'eng and then served as Deputy Head of Rear Services under Huang K'o-ch'eng, moving up to Head of Rear Services when Huang became Chief of Staff. At about the same time the Commander of the Peking Garrison, General Yang Ch'eng-wu, was transferred to the Ministry of Defence, where he would not have command of troops. These seem to be the only publicly announced moves in the Army which could be regarded as directly concerned with the P'eng affair.

The civilian changes announced in the September 16 list of appointments and removals are difficult to analyse since, no doubt deliberately, they included a large proportion of routine changes, a good many of which probably dated from some time previously. Certainly there is reason for thinking that the opportunity was taken to remove, or announce the removal, of a good many administrators, particularly in the economic field, who had supported the more moderate policies of Ch'en Yun; and a long list can be compiled of officials who were not given other appointments or removed into positions where they could exercise little influence.[11] On the other hand, Ch'en Yun's direct involvement in P'eng's intrigues certainly cannot be regarded as proven. While it is possible that, in view of Ch'en's seniority, the Party deliberately concealed from the cadres the fact of his complicity, it is perhaps more likely that P'eng and Chang decided to mobilise support in the Central Committee and appeal to the Soviet Party only after Ch'en Yun and what may be called the legal opposition had withdrawn into sulky silence.

---

10 Li Ta is presumably now in reasonably good odour since he served as Field-Marshal Montgomery's conducting officer in China.

11 They include: Lo Shih-yü, Deputy Director of the State Council's Central Administrative Bureau of Industry and Commerce; the directorate of the Fourth General Office of the State Council on its incorporation into the newly constituted General Office for Industry and Communications, *viz.*, the Director, Chia T'o-fu (who in 1949 had served under P'eng in the North West and subsequently under Kao Kang), and the two Deputy-Directors, Chou Kuang-ch'un and Sung Shao-wen (who however retained his appointment as Vice-Chairman of the National Construction Committee till its abolition in January 1961); a Vice-Minister of Food, Kao Chin-ch'un, who at the end of the war had been P'eng's principal civilian collaborator in Sinkiang; a Vice-Minister of Education, Ch'en Tseng-ku; a Deputy-Director of the People's Bank of China, Ts'ui Kuang: at least one Vice-Chairman of the State Planning Commission, Ni Wei; the Director of the Counsellors Office of the State Council and Deputy Secretary-General of the State Council, T'ao Hsi-chin; and two Vice-Ministers of Health, Fu Lien-chang and Wu Yun-fu.

The failure of P'eng's attempt at direct action would naturally affect the position of all those who sympathised with his views, whether or not they had actively participated in his movement.

But P'eng's challenge to the leadership was not only a manifestation of discontent with the internal policies of the dominant faction. It also had a profound effect on Sino-Soviet relations. At what stage the Politburo learnt of P'eng's letter to the Soviet Party remains obscure. Even if P'eng took the natural precaution of writing his letter when safe on Soviet territory, he may have been betrayed by a member of his entourage. Nor is a leak on the Soviet side inconceivable. To mention only one possibility, we now know from the revelations of the 22nd Soviet Party Congress that Molotov, when Ambassador in Outer Mongolia, was opposing the official Soviet line on the possibility of co-existence and that in April 1960 he set out his views in an article for the Lenin Anniversary which was rejected by *Kommunist* at the same time as the Chinese were publishing their notorious series of polemics on the same topic. Certainly if P'eng was indiscreet enough, when passing through Ulan Bator on his way back from his European trip, to reveal anything of his conversations with Khrushchev to Molotov or his contacts, there would have been every possibility of his confidences reaching the Chinese.

The alternative theory is that the Politburo learnt of P'eng's contacts with the Russians only after his arrest and interrogation. Such a hypothesis perhaps fits in better with what is known of the course of Sino-Soviet relations. Khrushchev's announcement of his intention to visit the United States almost coincided with the opening of the Lushan plenum. Western observers at the time stressed the reservations expressed in Chinese official statements welcoming the Soviet move. More striking perhaps, in retrospect, is their comparative warmth. For all its doubt about the seriousness of American intentions, the *People's Daily*, with its references to the " melting of ice-bergs " and the " real possibility of a détente," set out a theory of summitry which would soon become rank heresy; and on August 16, *Red Flag* published an extraordinary article by the authoritative " Yü Chao-li " entitled " Peaceful Competition is an Inevitable Trend " in which, after quoting Marx, traditional Chinese sayings and even the Bible—" They who take the sword shall perish by the sword "—the writer concluded that anyone who denied his thesis " would stand convicted and condemned before the bar of history." [12] The Chinese are often slow to react officially; but it is hard to believe that they could have authorised so wholehearted an endorsement of the

---

[12] This article may be compared with the bitter and uncompromising attack on American Imperialism which appeared in *Red Flag* under the same pseudonym on September 16, the day Khrushchev arrived in the United States.

Soviet line after they had got to know that a member of the Politburo was in secret, and from their point of view treasonable, correspondence with the Russians. On September 9, Tass fired the first broadside in the current Sino-Soviet dispute by publishing a communique virtually disavowing China in her dispute with India. A sharp reaction by the Chinese to the discovery that the Soviet Union had prior knowledge of P'eng's views and rejection by the Russians of their protests would explain a deliberate provocation of China—which was not required by the interest of the Soviet Union in improving her relations with India and the West or by the failure of China to fall into line, however reluctantly, with the rest of the Communist *bloc* when Khrushchev dramatically announced his plans for a détente with " the main enemy."

In any event, the incident continued to poison Sino-Soviet relations. Khrushchev refused to apologise for his interference in the internal politics of China; and the issue remained unsettled after his unsatisfactory visit to Peking on his way back from the United States. In March 1960 the Chinese resurrected Chang Wen-t'ien from the obscurity in which he had lived since his dismissal after Lushan had him denounced at special Party meetings as a right opportunist who had propagated the erroneous view that China should concentrate on obtaining diplomatic recognition from as many countries as possible, including the United States, and that peaceful co-existence in accordance with Five Principles and Bandung should be the basis of China's foreign policy. Chang was said to have opposed the Party's line which was that peaceful co-existence was a means to an end and not an end in itself, and that China should broaden the front in the fight against the main enemy, United States imperialism, by actively mobilising the forces in neutral countries which were hostile to the imperialists. It seems to have been at these meetings that some at least of the cadres learnt of P'eng's letter to the Soviet Party, the existence of which had not been referred to at the earlier briefings.

At the Bucharest Conference in the following June Khrushchev carried the war into the Chinese camp by openly accusing the Chinese of persecuting any comrade who had contacts with the Soviet Party. After referring to the case of P'eng Teh-huai and his dismissal for communicating his views to the Soviet Party, Khrushchev went on to defend the memory of Kao Kang, whose only offence, he suggested, had been that he opposed the incorrect policies of the Chinese Party towards the Soviet Union.

We may expect that, if and when China and Russia start open recriminations against each other, Soviet propaganda will provide fresh material for appreciating the place of the P'eng Teh-huai episode in the recent history of the Chinese Communist Party and in the Sino-Soviet dispute. In the meantime two points may be made. First, the mistake of P'eng and his associates was that they struck too soon. If they had held their hand, China at a time of acute food shortages, economic recession and mounting discontent, would now find herself with a Minister of Defence, a Chief of Staff and other leading personalities who were prepared to treat privately with the Russians in order to establish sanity in the leadership.

Secondly, the extraordinary bitterness of the current controversy between China and the Soviet Union becomes easier to understand when we realise that it was set off by the same kind of outrage to national sentiment as produced the breach between the Soviet Union and Albania. The disgraced members of the Albanian Politburo were, in the view of their colleagues, caught intriguing with the Russians or, as Khrushchev preferred to put it at the 22nd Congress, " had the courage honourably and openly to express their disagreement and come out for the solidarity of Albania with the Soviet Union." P'eng Teh-huai did no less. In both cases Khrushchev refused to disown his friends; in both cases economic sanctions were applied by the withdrawal of technicians and the denial of effective assistance at a time of agricultural crisis; nor were any but the obscurest hints of friction allowed to appear for many months in the Party press. The strange friendship of the Chinese and Albanian Parties is based not only on ideological sympathies but on the memory of a similar experience at the hands of the Soviet Union.

The Conflict between Old and New in the Chinese Army*

By ELLIS JOFFE

ONE of the most pressing needs of the Chinese Communists when they
established their régime, was to convert the sprawling semi-guerrilla force
which had brought them to power into a modern army capable of maintaining that power. China's leaders were acutely aware of this need
and they lost little time in launching the armed forces on the long
march to modernisation. No modernisation, however, could have
succeeded without large numbers of officers skilled in running a
complex military establishment. The Red Army commanders, though
resourceful and battle-tested, were by and large not equipped for
this task. It was necessary, therefore, to develop a professional officer
corps.

The leadership made a conscious and concerted effort to meet this
need, and this effort has been reinforced by the very process of military
modernisation which has been conducive to the growth of professionalism. But if this solved one problem, it created another. The professional
officers [1] developed views and values which have brought the army
into conflict with the Party on a number of issues. Essentially this
is a conflict between generations differing in experience, outlook and
responsibilities. The protagonists are the veteran leaders of the
" guerrilla generation " on the one hand, and the younger officers of
an increasingly " professional generation " on the other. Although
both generations are Party members,[2] and although both desire a
modern army, they tend to see things in a different light; the viewpoint
of the officers is more " expert," that of the Party leadership more " red."

What were the circumstances which produced the " professional
generation "? What are their views and how do they differ from those

---

* The article is based on a study which I am preparing for the East Asian Research
Center, Harvard University.

1 For reasons of style, the phrases " the professional officers " and " some professional
officers " are used interchangeably throughout the article. This, however, does not
imply that I am referring to the entire professional officer corps. Although it is
impossible to determine what percentage of the officers may be termed " professionals," it is clear that only a part of the officer corps has been involved in
this conflict.

2 No figures are available on how many officers are Party members, but it may be
safely assumed that all the high-ranking officers and the overwhelming majority of
the junior officers belong to the Party.

34

of their superiors? How has the leadership met the challenge to its beliefs? This article is a preliminary attempt to shed some light on these questions.

MODERNISATION AND PROFESSIONALISM

The growth of a professional officer corps, and its consequent conflict of views with the Party, is inextricably connected with the modernisation of the armed forces. For it was this transformation that has nourished professionalism. Before this the revolutionary nature of the army militated against the development of professionalism.[3] The army's primitive equipment and rudimentary staff system obviated the need for, and indeed precluded, specialisation. Its irregular, and "democratic" character, and its intimate relationship with the population blurred the distinctions between ranks, and between soldiers and civilians. The close merging of political and military doctrine and tasks led to the fusing of political and military leadership.

It has sometimes been asserted that China's leaders, irrevocably committed to a "guerrilla mentality," have underestimated the importance of modernising the army. This is an oversimplification. Although the revolutionary concepts of the veteran leaders have been decisive in their conflict with the officers, there is no evidence that they denied the need for transforming the army into a modern force. On the contrary, there is ample evidence to show that they were fully aware of the need to usher the army into the modern era [4] realised that professional officers were required to do the ushering [5]; and initiated measures to meet these needs. What were these measures and what impact did they have upon the growth of professionalism? This question must be approached on several levels.

Technological modernisation

First of all weapons had to be modernised and standardised. In 1949, however, the Chinese Communists were in no position to carry out a swift and sweeping transformation of their weapons and probably they turned

---

[3] There is no space to sketch the salient features of the Chinese Red Army before 1949. Its "non-professional" nature in terms of weapons, training, organisation and political work is examined in some detail in Ellis Joffe's "The Chinese Red Army 1927–1949 and the 'Man-Over-Weapons' Doctrine," unpublished paper, Harvard University, January 1964.

[4] See, for example, New China News Agency (NCNA), July 31, 1951, in *Current Background* (CB) (Hong Kong: U.S. Consulate-General), No. 208; NCNA, July 31, 1952, *ibid.*; *Jen-min Jih-pao* (*People's Daily*) editorial, NCNA, July 24, 1954, *Survey of the China Mainland Press* (SCMP) (Hong Kong: U.S. Consulate-General), No. 856, pp. 54–55.

[5] See, for example, *People's Daily* editorial, NCNA, February 15, 1955, CB, No. 314, p. 18; *Eighth National Congress of the Communist Party of China* (Peking: 1956), II, Speeches, pp. 29–30.

immediately to the Soviet Union for help. There are indications that the Sino-Soviet Treaty of 1950 contained secret provisions for military assistance,[6] but it is unlikely that the suspicious Stalin was in a hurry to give weapons to the Chinese. There is no doubt, however, that the intervention of the Chinese in the Korean War to wage a costly fight not of their own making forced the Russians to come to their aid with large quantities of military hardware.[7] This aid served as a springboard for the Chinese Army's leap into the era of modern conventional warfare.

It is more difficult to evaluate the less tangible aspects of the Korean War's impact on the Chinese military leaders, but there can be little doubt that it was a traumatic experience for them. It hammered home the fact that their army had to undergo a thorough transformation before it could lock horns with a modern military force. It exposed them to the manifold problems of modern warfare for which their vast storehouse of experience provided no solutions. And it dramatically demonstrated the limitations of their hitherto successful strategy and tactics.

From the Korean War to 1960 the modernisation of the Chinese army proceeded at a steady pace. With the aid of advisers and modern, although not the latest, Soviet equipment, the Chinese transformed their infantry force into a complex, well balanced, conventional army with numerous specialised arms and support and service units, backed by a network of military industries.[8]

Training professional officers

To run this huge and increasingly complex military machine required vast numbers of officers with special skills. To meet this need the Communists set up military academies in the early months of their rule.[9] The graduates of these academies formed the backbone of the new officer corps. With the growing complexity and diversity of the armed forces the original handful of schools have mushroomed into a network of at least 67 military academies, covering a wide variety of specialised subjects.[10] The main training ground of the professional officer is, of course,

---

[6] See, for example, *Kung-jen Jih-pao (Daily Worker)*, July 31, 1955, SCMP, No. 1163, p. 261.

[7] *Cf.* Raymond L. Garthoff, "Sino-Soviet Military Relations," *The Annals* (of the American Academy of Political and Social Science), September 1963, pp. 84–85.

[8] For an estimate of China's armed forces, see *The Communist Bloc and the Western Alliances: The Military Balance 1962–1693* (London: The Institute for Strategic Studies, 1964), p. 8; *The Christian Science Monitor*, February 21, 1964.

[9] Derk Bodde, *Peking Diary: A Year of Revolution* (New York: 1950), pp. 117–118; NCNA, December 1, 1950, SCMP, No. 21, pp. 13–14; *People's Daily* editorial, NCNA, December 1, 1950, *ibid.* pp. 15–16; NCNA, December 9, 1950, SCMP, No. 27, pp. 17–18; NCNA, December 25, 1950, SCMP, No. 37, pp. 20–22.

[10] *Communist China: Ruthless Enemy or Paper Tiger?* (Department of the Army, Pam 20–61: 1962), Appendix G (Chinese Communist Military Organisation).

the military academy, but special efforts are also made to promote research in military science and to disseminate information to keep the officers in the units abreast of the latest developments.[11]

Formation of a professional officer corps

No single event probably contributed more to the growth of professionalism than the adoption of the " Regulations on the Service of Officers " in February 1955.[12]   The introduction of these regulations fundamentally altered the informal, egalitarian, " democratic " and non-professional nature of the Chinese Comunist officer corps as it had been moulded during more than two decades of revolutionary warfare.[13]

For the first time officers in the Chinese Red Army were classified according to their fields of specialisation, and ranks were established.[14] Regular channels were set up for entry into the officer corps and for advancement on the basis of professional competence.[15]   The regulations also required the officers to wear shoulder-boards and insignia in accordance with their rank.[16]   Shortly after the regulations were adopted, the old system of providing both officers and men with food and a small allowance in lieu of salaries was replaced by cash payments.   The present scale of pay—which ranges from U.S. $2.50 per month for a private to $192–236 for a full general [17]—is indicative of the new differentiations. With the conferment of military titles and honours on the army leaders in September 1955,[18] the Chinese officer corps acquired all the trappings typical of a regular army.

The introduction of conscription in July 1955 capped the process of putting the army on a regular footing.   Until then, the Communists had relied on " volunteers."   Under the Conscription Law,[19] all male citizens have the duty to serve in the armed forces upon reaching the age of eighteen, and it is estimated that some 700,000 are called up for military service each year.[20]   Conscription has thus brought into sharp focus the distinction between the amateur citizen-soldier and the professional officer.

Cumulatively, these developments spelled the end of the irregular,

---

[11] *Chung-kuo Ch'ing-nien Pao (The Chinese Youth Newspaper)*, November 3, 1956, SCMP, No. 1416, pp. 7–8; NCNA, March 16, 1958, SCMP, No. 1736, p. 2.

[12] NCNA, February 9, 1955, CB, No. 312.

[13] See Joffe, pp. 35–39.

[14] Regulations, Articles 4, 7, 8.

[15] Articles 11, 15, 17.

[16] Article 24.

[17] Edgar Snow, *The Other Side of the River: Red China Today* (New York: Random House, 1962), p. 289.

[18] CB, No. 368, pp. 1–2.

[19] CB, No. 344.

[20] *The Communist Bloc and the Western Alliances*, p. 8.

egalitarian and informal guerrilla officer, and cleared the ground for the emergence of a status-conscious, professional officer corps.

Soviet aid and advice

Despite the immense importance of the Soviet Union's role in creating a modern and professional Chinese army, it is difficult to detail, much less document, Soviet military aid and advice because this aspect of Sino-Soviet relations has been shrouded in a veil of official secrecy.

There is little doubt that most of the new Chinese military establishment has been built with Soviet equipment. To be sure, this was no handout; Peking paid for what it got, and these payments were financed by loans from the Soviet Union, which by mid-1957 reportedly amounted to about U.S.$2 billion.[21] Nevertheless, Soviet aid did lay the foundation and provide the vital push for the modernisation of China's armed forces.

With aid, came advice. Until the late fifties, Chinese leaders went all out to heap praise on the Soviet army and to underline the need for studying its "advanced experience." Concretely this meant that Soviet personnel played an important part in modernising the Chinese armed forces. Soviet advisers arrived in China in late 1950 and remained, probably in declining numbers, until 1960.[22] Many Chinese officers are believed to have been sent to study in the Soviet Union.[23] The importance of the Russian influence is reflected in the reorganisation of the Chinese military establishment along essentially Soviet lines.

No less important has been the impact of Soviet counsel and guidance on the Chinese officers, although of course this cannot be evaluated in tangible terms. Through their Soviet advisers and through Soviet military writings, the Chinese officers inevitably became acquainted with and assimilated doctrines and practices which in some basic respects differ markedly from those considered sacrosanct by their own leaders. This has led them to question the wisdom of their leaders on fundamental issues of military organisation and strategy. The Soviet organisation is more hierarchic and bureaucratic than the Chinese—particularly in its emphasis on unity of command compared with the Chinese stress on collective leadership—and, therefore, more acceptable to a professionally-

---

21 Allen S. Whiting, *Contradictions in the Moscow-Peking Axis* (Santa Monica: The RAND Corporation, RM-1992, September 24, 1957), pp. 5–6.

22 No details are available, but the establishment of a Russian language school among the first Chinese military academies was probably in response to the pressing need for interpreters and for Russian-speaking Chinese officers in anticipation of their dispatch to the Soviet Union.

23 Here too no details are available, but in 1954, for example, it was reported in Hong Kong that twenty regimental staff officers had been sent to the Kiev staff school. S. M. Chiu, "The Chinese Communist Army in Transition," *Far Eastern Survey*, Vol. XXVII, November 1958, p. 171.

oriented Chinese officer.[24] Soviet strategic influence assumed far-reaching implications in the mid-fifties, when it began to acknowledge that in a nuclear war military factors, rather than political ones, are decisive. Some Chinese officers apparently accepted this revision, which was tantamount to rejecting the revered military thought of Mao Tse-tung.[25] In sum, the precise nature of Soviet influence on the Chinese officers is a subject for speculation, but there is little doubt that it had an important impact on the growth of professionalism in the Chinese army.

A new division of labour

Of no less importance than the specific steps taken to build up a professional officer corps have been the changes stemming from the nature of the post-revolutionary environment. Throughout the revolutionary period and for several years after 1949 there was little to distinguish the political from the military leaders. The military and political élites were inextricably intertwined, and their tasks and experience were identical to a great extent. There was little ground, therefore, for the emergence of basic conflicts of views between the political and military leaders.

As the Party gradually came to grips with the manifold problems of state administration, tasks and responsibilities became increasingly specialised. Whereas in the insurrectionary milieu the same leader could be—and usually was—simultaneously qualified to handle several key jobs in different fields, today this is no longer possible. The efficient management of state affairs has necessitated a clear division of labour between the managers.

The new division of labour is illustrated in the shifts which have taken place in the functions of the élite since 1949.[26] Many top level leaders have drifted away from the daily direction of military affairs. On the other hand, those leaders who are concerned with the armed forces have become specialists. In other words, overall military policy at the highest levels is determined largely by men whose intimate relationship with military affairs has been limited in the main to the days of revolutionary warfare. While they are undoubtedly aware of the need for a modern military machine, they have only limited first-hand knowledge of modern warfare and the day-to-day problems of a complex army. In contrast to this, several of the important second-level leaders have, for a number

[24] See, for example, *Chieh-fang Chün Pao* (*Liberation Army News*), June 16, 1959, *Joint Publications Research Service* (JPRS), No. 10343/59, p. 4; *Liberation Army News* editorial, August 18, 1958, JPRS 10240/59, p. 40; *Liberation Army News*, August 29, 1958, JPRS 10239/59, pp. 31–33.

[25] Alice Langley Hsieh, *Communist China's Strategy in the Nuclear Era* (Englewood, New Jersey : Prentice-Hall, 1962), Chap. 2.

[26] Donald W. Klein, " The 'Next Generation' of Chinese Communist Leaders," *The China Quarterly*, No. 12, October–December 1962, pp. 65–66.

of years, tackled these matters from day to day, and it is reasonable to assume that, their " guerrilla " background notwithstanding, some of them have become fully aware of the problems of modern warfare and have adopted a " professional " viewpoint.

In sum, the professional officers may be grouped in two broad categories. First, young men who joined the army, or became officers, after 1949 and who were trained and became professionals as the army was being modernised; these officers presumably occupy the lower levels of the command structure. Secondly, veteran guerrilla officers who were assigned to specialised military duties in the early fifties and who have since been intimately involved in the complex problems of the modernised army; these officers hold positions on the General Staff and occupy important command posts.

The Elements of Conflict

It is difficult to pinpoint when tensions first appeared between the Party and the professional officers or to gauge their intensity at a particular time. The best barometer of these tensions is the Party's various campaigns to curb professionalism in the army. In broad outline, these campaigns appear to tie in with developments in the country at large, and especially with the rectification campaigns and the drives against intellectuals. In the army they seem to have started in 1956, gathered momentum in 1957, reached a climax in 1958 and continued through 1959. There is little doubt that friction between the Party and the officers over issues which we shall examine below was responsible for the dismissal of Marshal P'eng Teh-huai as Minister of Defence and General Huang K'o-ch'eng as Chief of the General Staff.[27] Under P'eng's successor, Marshal Lin Piao, a new attempt has been made to strengthen Party control over the armed forces. Lin's leadership, together with the scrapping of the great leap forward, the waning of the anti-professional euphoria which had accompanied it, and, perhaps, the drastic deterioration of Sino-Soviet relations, probably account for the muting of tension. There is no sign, however, that many of the sources of tension have been removed.

Before analysing these sources of tension, several caveats are in order. First, it cannot be overemphasised that this " conflict " over professionalism exists within a broader context of unity and harmony which is indeed striking. Secondly, it must be stressed again that the overwhelming majority of the officers are Party members, so that whatever conflict exists, it is strictly an intra-Party affair. Thirdly, we have chosen

---

[27] See below.

to deal with issues without associating them with personalities, primarily because given the fragmentary evidence, such an attempt must be relegated in large part to the realm of speculation and inference.[28]

Man or weapons?

Underlying all the points of conflict between the Party and the officers are two fundamentally different points of view on the relationship between man and weapons and, consequently, on the nature of the modernised army. The officers argue that in modern warfare material and technological factors are more important that the human element. They assert that, in contrast to the guerrilla period when primary reliance had to be placed on the human element, the outcome of a modern war depends primarily on the material resources of an army and the way in which they are used. For this reason, the development of weapons and their efficient operation should take priority over political considerations. In short, professionalism must take precedence over politics.[29]

Not so, insist the Party leaders. They do not deny the importance of weapons, but they believe in the inherent superiority of man over machines. To translate this superiority into reality, man has to be properly mobilised, indoctrinated and used—and only the Party is competent to do this. Hence politics must be placed above professionalism.[30]

It may be argued that this doctrine is merely the Party leaders' rationalisation for China's lack of atomic weapons, a smokescreen for the painful reality of military and technological inferiority. This is undoubtedly true. There is overwhelming evidence that China's leaders are acutely aware of the importance of nuclear weapons, that they are deeply distressed by the fact that China has none, that, whatever their bellicose statements, they have a healthy respect for an adversary who does, and that they are making every effort to join the nuclear club. But that is only one side of the coin. To stop short at this explanation and to consider this question solely in terms of the leadership's current needs is to disregard their whole historical experience, and there is every indication that this experience has left an indelible imprint on their thinking.[31]

What is that experience? Put simply, it is not the gun, but the man behind the gun that is decisive in determining the outcome of war, and the conditioning of man depends on political factors. The validity of this experience, assert the leaders, is not altered by the passage of time

[28] For an attempt to identify issues with personalities see Hsieh, *passim*.
[29] See, for example, *People's Daily*, July 28, 1961, SCMP, No. 2556, p. 2.
[30] See, for example, Lin Piao, *March Ahead Under the Red Flag of the Party's General Line and Mao Tse-tung's Military Thinking* (Peking, 1959), p. 17.
[31] Joffe, *passim*.

and the advance of technology. Although this view has been expressed in numerous statements, it can be argued that the leaders really do not believe what they say publicly, and such pronouncements are intended only for the population at large and for external consumption. Such an argument, however, is on shaky ground. The available issues of the army's secret *Kung-tso T'ung-hsun* (*Bulletin of Activities*) clearly show that there is a remarkable identity between published views and those voiced in inner Party circles.[32]

It is important to keep in mind that these differences between the leaders and the officers are basically a matter of degree. Both the officers and the leaders concede the necessity of being both " red " and " expert "; the gulf between them lies essentially in the emphasis which they place on the " red " and the "expert."

These divergent approaches underlie their conflicting viewpoints on the nature of the modernised army. The Party leaders agree, of course, that the army must be modernised, but they assert that modernisation must not basically alter its traditional doctrine, characteristics and practices. The " revolutionary " essence of the army must not change in the midst of change.[33]

The army must change with the changing times—this is the basic contention of the professional officers. In their view, modernisation is not something that can simply be tacked onto the " guerrilla " army; the substance of that army must change too.[34] In the following sections we shall see how these opposing viewpoints apply to concrete issues.

Relations between officers and men

The far-reaching changes which have taken place in the army since 1949 have brought about an estrangement between some officers and the rank and file. The main reason for this is that officers believe that the efficient operation of a modern, technically complex army requires discipline and " centralism," rather than " democracy " and individual initiative.[35] Other, less tangible, factors also undoubtedly contributed to the worsening of relations. The introduction of conscription and,

---

[32] See, for example, a document prepared by the Academy of Military Sciences, *Kung-tso T'ung-hsun* (*Bulletin of Activities*), No. 29, August 1, 1961. In an excellent analysis of these documents Professor Ralph L. Powell points out that " they provide convincing evidence that previously published statements of doctrine have generally represented official policy, even when they have been considered to be unrealistic in the atomic age. . . . The doctrine still claims that the two basic and unchanging factors in war are the dominance of men and of politics. . . ." Ralph L. Powell, *Politico-Military Relationships in Communist China* (Policy Research Study, External Research Staff, Bureau of Intelligence and Research, United States Department of State, October 1963), p. 19.

[33] *Liberation Army News* editorial, August 17, 1958, JPRS, No. 6471/59, p. 1.

[34] *Liberation Army News*, August 29, 1958, JPRS, No. 10239/59, p. 31.

[35] See, for example, *Eighth National Congress of the Communist Party of China*, p. 264.

consequently, the frequent rotation of enlisted men, has precluded the formation of ties which formerly grew out of long and intimate association. The whole range of measures adopted to make the officers professionals has tended to make them status-conscious and remote from the men. Finally, relations moulded during a revolutionary era of idealistic fervour and constant danger are bound to be very different from those formed in a period dominated by the dreary duties of a peacetime army.

These factors have combined to produce a situation which has caused grave concern to the Party leaders. They have blasted the officers for flagrantly flouting the cherished traditions of the revolutionary army. Some officers, it was said, looked upon discipline and " democracy " as diametrically opposed things, and stressed the former to the exclusion of the latter. They regarded the new status accorded them as a sign that the egalitarian traditions of the army had been abandoned, and felt free to lord it over the men. They set themselves on a pedestal, failed to mix with the men, showed no concern for their welfare, and abused their authority. They became armchair bureaucrats, neglected the " mass-line," and retaliated against critics. They exaggerated the importance of their professional training and hierarchical status, and scoffed at the practice of soliciting the opinions of the rank and file.[36]

Relations between officers and civilians

The estrangement between the ranks has been paralleled by a loosening of the close ties which had traditionally existed between the Chinese Communist forces and the peasant masses. Over-conscious of their new status and no longer dependent on the support of the population, some officers began to treat civilians in a high-handed and haughty manner. Such behaviour has drawn strong fire from the Party leaders. Some officers, it was said, blatantly disregarded the needs, well-being and feelings of the population. They requisitioned property from the peasants and destroyed crops during manoeuvres. They callously ignored safety rules on the road. They dabbled in black market operations. They and their dependants lived a life of luxury which alienated the masses. They used their position to pursue their romantic ambitions with village girls, even married ones. And they and their families showed contempt for physical labour.[37]

[36] See, for example, *People's Daily*, August 1, 1955, SCMP, No. 1106, pp. 4–9; *Liberation Army News* editorial, August 18, 1958, JPRS, No. 10240/59, p. 42; *Liberation Army News*, August 29, 1958, JPRS, 10239/59, p. 32.

[37] See, for example, *People's Daily*, August 1, 1955, SCMP, No. 1106, p. 7; NCNA, May 12, 1957, SCMP, No. 1547, p. 27; *Liberation Army News*, March 30, 1958, JPRS, No. 10239/59, p. 14.

Political controls in the army

Nowhere has the clash between politics and professionalism been more apparent and acute than in the friction generated by Party control in the army. This control is exercised through a hierarchy of Party committees, political commissars, political departments and Party members, a hierarchy which parallels the military chain of command from the highest to the lowest level. The Party committees are granted wide powers to formulate measures relating to the implementation of directives received from above and to supervise their enforcement. The decisions of the Party committee are handed over to the military commander and the political commissar for execution. Between these two there ostensibly exists a division of work to the effect that one is responsible for everything concerning military matters, the other for political affairs.[38]

Theory is one thing, practice another. Problems are bound to arise in the functional relationship between the military and political leaders, whatever the theoretical division of labour between them. These may stem from matters which are not clearly under the jurisdiction of either, or they may pertain to areas where the decision of one will affect the sphere of responsibility of the other. More important, when " politics take command," all other considerations are subordinate; this implies that the political functionary is entitled to meddle in everything that goes on within the unit.

In the event of a dispute between the officer and the commissar, the matter is presumably referred to the Party committee for resolution. It is extremely doubtful, however, whether the committee will judge a case on its merits. First, it must be remembered that the commissar is also the secretary of the committee,[39] *i.e.*, the top Party man on the spot, and from this position of power he wields great authority over the Party members. Second, it may be safely assumed that the committee is composed of the more " activist " elements among the Party members, and they can be expected to view everything through politically tinted lenses and to be receptive to the commissar's, rather than to the officer's opinions. In view of this, it is safe to say that in practice it is the commissar who manipulates the actions of the committee rather than the reverse. As a result, the officer may find himself in the frustrating position of being in effect subordinate to the man with whom nominally he shares command. If he and the commissar see eye to eye, things will work smoothly; however, in cases where they are at loggerheads, the

---

[38] See, for example, *Eighth National Congress of the Communist Party of China*, pp. 32–33; *Bulletin*, No. 3, January 7, 1961.
[39] *Liberation Army News* editorial, May 8, 1963, SCMP, No. 2984, p. 4.

existence of political controls may well hamper the ability of the military commander to exercise effective leadership and will generate friction.

Despite the potential incompatibility of political controls with professional leadership, there is little doubt that the system functioned well during the period of guerrilla warfare and in the early years of the Communist régime. Three reasons seem to account for this harmony. First, both the commanders and the commissars were veteran Party members with much the same experience and background in both political and military work. Second, the close interrelation of political and military tasks in the milieu of insurrection gave little basis for conflict. Third, in many cases the commander and the commissar were one and the same person.

With the modernisation of the army and the growth of professionalism, the latent elements of conflict have come to the surface. Some officers have assailed the system of political controls on the grounds that it is incompatible with a command structure that will function swiftly and smoothly, a requirement they deem vital in modern warfare.[40] Not only do they consider the Party committees and the commissars an obstacle to organisational efficiency, but they consider them incompetent to handle military affairs. In their view, it is the professional military men and not political functionaries who are best equipped to render judgment on military matters.[41] These officers did not stop short at criticising the political control system, but in some cases at least took direct action. Although only fragmentary evidence is available, it is clear that in certain instances the commanders pushed the commissars into the background or simply abolished this institution.[42] Perhaps more serious, from the Party's viewpoint, than the friction generated by the operations of the political control system was the startling fact, revealed in the *Bulletin of Activities*, that as late as 1960 many of the lower-level units simply had no such system.[43]

Such views and actions have been vehemently denounced by the Party leaders. They are deeply committed to the predominance of political considerations over all others, and assert that politics should always " take command." [44] They interpret the officers' contention that

[40] See, for example, *Liberation Army News* editorial, July 1, 1958, SCMP, No. 1881, p. 4; *Liberation Army News* editorial, August 1, 1958, SCMP, No. 1881, p. 2; NCNA-English, Peking, July 31, 1958, CB, No. 514, pp. 1–2; *Hsin Hunan Pao (New Hunan Daily)*, November 22, 1959, SCMP, No. 2155, p. 11.

[41] See, for example, *Liberation Army News* editorial, August 18, 1958, JPRS, 10240/59, p. 40.

[42] *Liberation Army News* editorial, July 1, 1958, SCMP, No. 1881, p. 4; *Liberation Army News*, May 23, 1958, SCMP, No. 1900, p. 9; *Liberation Army News*, June 16, 1958, JPRS, No. 10343/59, pp. 4–6; *Liberation Army News*, September 4, 1958, JPRS, No. 10240/59, pp. 18–19.

[43] *Bulletin*, No. 23, June 13, 1961, cited in Powell, p. 8; *Bulletin*, No. 3, January 7, 1961.

[44] See, for example, *Liberation Army News* editorial, July 1, 1958, SCMP, No. 1881, p. 4.

collective leadership is unsuitable for modern warfare as a camouflage for the officers' desire to loosen the Party's hold over the army, and they reject the argument that collective leadership is incompatible with efficiency on the grounds that even in a modern army collective decision-making by non-specialists is superior to individual decision-making by a specialist.[45]

Employment of the army for non-military purposes

The increasing tendency of the professional officers to view things through "expert" rather than "red" lenses has led them to assail another cherished policy of the Party leadership: the use of the army in the execution of economic and socio-political tasks.[46] Their objections to this policy were voiced on the grounds that the diversion of troops to non-military activities dissipates their energies and interferes with training. In a modern army, they maintain, training is a full-time job and the soldiers should devote all their time to this task, leaving the execution of non-military projects to civilians.[47]

Quite the contrary, assert the Party leaders. The employment of the army in construction, they maintain, has two important advantages: first, the socialist construction of the state will benefit from the use of troops on economic projects; second, participation in non-military activities is essential to the political and ideological conditioning of the troops, for it will heighten their appreciation of labour and will raise their Communist consciousness.[48]

The militia

The disfavour with which the officers have looked upon the turning of soldiers into peasant masses has been paralleled by their distaste for turning the peasants into soldiers through the militia. In the autumn of 1958, it will be recalled, the militia movement was revived with intense vigour and a frenetic campaign for a nation-at-arms swept the country.[49]

This campaign was anathema to the professional officers. In an era when combat is waged with complex and refined instruments of destruction manned by highly trained personnel, the spectre of hordes of peasants lugging rifles into battle can give little comfort to a professional officer. But the task of training the militia fell upon the army, and this

---

45 See, for example, *Liberation Army News*, August 29, 1958, JPRS, 10239/59, pp. 31–32.
46 For a brief discussion of the army's non-military activities see Ellis Joffe, " The Communist Party and the Army," *Contemporary China*, IV, 1961, pp. 55–59.
47 See, for example, *Hung Ch'i (Red Flag)*, No. 15, August 1, 1959, *Extracts from China Mainland Magazines* (ECMM) (Hong Kong: U.S. Consulate-General), No. 182, p. 7.
48 See, for example, NCNA, Peking, April 25, 1959, CB, No. 579, p. 2.
49 *Cf.* Ralph L. Powell, " Everyone a Soldier—The Communist Chinese Militia," *Foreign Affairs*, XXXIX, October 1960, pp. 101–111.

involved diverting men and precious equipment to the militiamen.[50]
To the officers this meant disrupting the regular programmes of the army
and allocating sparse resources to what many evidently considered a
worthless cause. They left no doubt that in their view the complex
business of war should be left to the troops trained for this task and
not to incompetent civilians.[51]

Nothing could be farther from the convictions of the Party leaders.
Their deeply rooted, almost mystical, belief in the power and potentiality
of mobilised masses was clearly brought out in their explanations of the
militia programme. Fighting between armies, they contend, is only one
form of warfare. In the war against Japan and the Nationalists it was
mobile and guerrilla warfare, based on the mobilisation of the masses,
that emerged victorious. The conclusion is clear to the Party leaders:
a " people's war " can defeat any enemy, whatever his weapons.[52]

Nuclear strategy and Sino-Soviet relations

A key element of disagreement involving the highest echelons of the
Party and the army has been the question of nuclear strategy. This
debate has been closely intertwined with the issue of economic versus
defence priorities and the nature of Sino-Soviet strategic relations.

It appears that, as we have already observed, by 1954–55 some
ranking Chinese officers had become fully aware of the implications of
nuclear weapons for modern warfare, partly as a result of the revision
in Soviet military thinking which was taking place at the time. They
stressed the threat of a surprise attack and the decisiveness of the first
blow in a nuclear conflict and, by implication, denied the feasibility of
Mao's doctrine of protracted war. They called for a rapid improvement
in China's defences and the maintenance of a large standing army. The
adoption of these proposals would have required the diversion of
resources from economic development—and it was primarily on this
score that their proposals were rejected by the leaders. They asserted
that economic construction must take precedence because a sound
industrial base is a prerequisite for strong defence. Like the officers, they
recognised that until China had a nuclear capability of her own, she
would be decisively dependent on the Soviet Union.

Recognition of this dependence coupled with an awareness of the
West's military superiority may account in part for the cautious course
which China pursued in foreign affairs after 1954.[53] But this shift was

---

50 NCNA, December 31, 1958, SCMP, No. 1934, p. 10.
51 See, for example, *Che-hsueh Yen-chiu*, No. 1, January 10, 1959, ECMM, No. 159,
p. 29.
52 See, for example, *Kiangsu Ch'ün-chung (Kiangsu Masses)*, No. 5, October 1, 1958,
ECMM, No. 150, p. 6.
53 The preceding section is drawn from Hsieh, Chap. 2.

short-lived. The successful testing of an ICBM and the orbiting of an earth satellite by the Russians in the autumn of 1957 had a profound effect on the Chinese. They now believed that the balance of power had shifted decisively in favour of the Communist bloc and thought that this superiority should be exploited through a more aggressive policy in support of " national liberation " wars. The Russians, however, thought otherwise. They did not share Peking's optimistic evaluation of the strategic balance, and were reluctant to foment local wars for fear of " escalation." [54] The cracks which had appeared in the alliance after Khrushchev's denunciation of Stalin in 1956 were growing wider.

Khrushchev was apparently unwilling to go too far in alienating the Chinese, at least at this time. The Soviet camp was still shaken by the dramatic developments of 1956—the Polish October and the Hungarian Uprising—and the Soviet leader had just emerged from a power struggle at home. He may have decided that at this juncture it was necessary to placate Peking. Perhaps for this reason Moscow made a momentous move: on October 15, 1957, the Chinese subsequently revealed, the two countries signed an agreement on " new technology and national defence," according to which the Soviet Union would give China a sample of an atomic bomb and technical data for its manufacture.[55] But far from placating Peking, the aftermath of this agreement was to have exactly the opposite effect.

Why this came about can only be speculated upon. It is conceivable that the Russians were far from eager to see Peking join the nuclear club and the pace of their assistance only frustrated the Chinese. Some time in 1958, perhaps on the eve of the Formosa Straits crisis, the Chinese may have outrightly asked the Russians for nuclear warheads; the Russians, it appears from later Chinese charges, refused—unless they maintained control over the weapons.[56] By this time the Chinese probably realised that they would have to go it alone. Perhaps partly due to this, their economic programme based on self-reliance, which was already under way, was pushed to the extreme, culminating in the " great leap forward " and the communes. Aggravated by the paucity of Moscow's aid and angered by Khrushchev's move toward a détente with the West, the Chinese began to challenge the Soviet leader's ideological primacy in the Communist movement and, possibly, to undermine his leadership by drumming up support against him in the bloc. By mid-1959 the Russians apparently had had enough; on June 20, the Chinese later claimed, they " unilaterally tore up " the agreement.[57] The conflict was moving inexorably towards a climax.

[54] Hsieh, pp. 76–96.   [55] *Peking Review*, No. 33, August 16, 1963, p. 14.
[56] Quoted in *The New York Times*, September 14, 1963.
[57] *Peking Review*, No. 33, August 16, 1963, p. 14.

It is possible that some Chinese military leaders had grave misgivings over a policy which led to rapidly mounting tension between Peking and Moscow. Moscow was not exactly generous with her nuclear arsenal to be sure, but she was obviously prepared to give something, and to military men, keenly aware of the importance of nuclear weapons and deeply apprehensive over China's vulnerability, that was better than nothing. For better or for worse, Russia was China's sole supplier of nuclear data and materials, and cutting off that source would retard China's chance of acquiring her own capability. No less important, the Russians still provided China with vital conventional equipment and supplies, and the officers may have feared that Moscow would be antagonised to the point of stopping this flow.

From their viewpoint, it may have seemed preferable to make political concessions to gain immediate military benefits, small as these might be, and they may have argued that efforts should be made to retain, and perhaps increase, Soviet assistance—at a price. That such a controversy was going on was indicated by the intensity of the campaign against the officers in mid-1958, a major theme of which was the need for self-reliance and opposition to dependence on the Soviet Union.[58] It is possible that Marshal P'eng Teh-huai, the then Minister of Defence, communicated his dissatisfaction to Khrushchev, perhaps in an attempt to head off the abrogation of the agreement; then, supported by some officers and other leading personalities, he blasted the leadership at the Lushan plenum of the Central Committee in August 1959.[59]

In September 1959 Marshal P'eng and the PLA's Chief of Staff, General Huang K'o-ch'eng, were removed from their posts. The circumstances surrounding this shake-up are veiled by official secrecy. In the *Bulletin of Activities*, P'eng and Huang are accused of many misdeeds relating to issues with which we have dealt in the previous pages.[60] They are not directly charged with colluding with the Soviet Union, though the documents speak of the need for eradicating their " erroneous

---

[58] See, for example, *Liberation Army News* editorial, August 1, 1958, SCMP, No. 1881, p. 2; *Liberation Army News* editorial, September 20, 1958, JPRS, No. 6471/59, pp. 21–24.

[59] David A. Charles, " The Dismissal of Marshal P'eng Teh-huai," *The China Quarterly*, No. 8, October–December 1961, pp. 63–76.

[60] In the *Bulletin of Activities*, P'eng and Huang were charged with representing the " military line of the propertied class," supporting an " erroneous or false line " not in accordance with Mao's ideology (*Bulletin*, No. 3, January 7, 1961; No. 1, January 1, 1961, cited in Powell, p. 2), promoting " dogmatism," " warlordism," " feudalism " and a " simple military point of view." They were blamed for disobeying the ideology and military thought of Mao while believing in and imitating foreign countries (*Bulletin*, No. 24, June 18, 1961; No. 29, August 1, 1961, cited in Powell, *ibid*.). Criticisms which probably include P'eng and Huang attacked " unreasonable military systems and formalities " (*Bulletin*, No. 11, March 2, 1961, cited in Powell, *ibid*.). In essence, as Powell observes, P'eng and Huang were accused of military professionalism (*ibid*. p. 3).

line " and " modern revisionism " in one breath.[61]   However, official
Chinese charges in 1963 and 1964 that Khrushchev supported anti-Party
elements in the CCP and praised them for opposing the Party's economic
policy [62] lend credence to the speculation that P'eng and Khrushchev
may have been up to something.   It was this economic policy and its
doctrinal implications that aroused Khrushchev's wrath, and it was
perhaps for this reason that, as it is believed, P'eng attacked the leadership on economic rather than military grounds.   The full story of this
episode, however, has yet to be told.

THE PARTY STRIKES BACK

The reaction of the Party leaders to the challenge posed by the professional officers, needless to say, has not been limited to criticism and verbal
rebuttals.   As the officers began to fire broadsides at Party leadership and
doctrine, the Party high command moved quickly to clamp down on them.

Tightening of political controls

First and foremost, the Party tightened its grip over the armed forces.
Essentially this has been done along two lines: the intensification of
indoctrination in the officer corps, and the consolidation of Party organisations in the military establishment, especially at the lower levels.   This,
of course, has always been the Party's preoccupation, but with the
growth of professionalism its efforts have been stepped up.

By 1956 a full-scale campaign to indoctrinate the officers was under
way.[63]   Simultaneously, Party organisations in the armed forces, and
especially the Party branches, were enlarged and overhauled in order
to augment their position of leadership *vis-à-vis* the officers.[64]   In the
first half of 1957, the tone for the rectification campaign in the army,
as elsewhere, was set by Mao's speech on contradictions.[65]   There is no
evidence that the torrent of devastating criticism which poured forth
from intellectual circles during the short-lived " hundred flowers " period
extended in any considerable degree to the army.[66]   Nevertheless, it
appears that during the subsequent anti-rightist campaign the Party took

---

61 *Bulletin*, No. 1, January 1, 1961; No. 7, February 1, 1961.
62 Quoted in *The New York Times*, September 14, 1963, and February 7, 1964.
63 NCNA, February 21, 1956, SCMP, No. 1241, p. 5; NCNA, December 22, 1956,
   SCMP, No. 1455, p. 7.
64 *Liberation Army News*, January 12, 1957, SCMP, No. 1616, pp. 14–15.
65 NCNA, May 12, 1957, SCMP, No. 1547, p. 27; NCNA, April 20, 1957, SCMP,
   No. 1524, p. 7.
66 This is also suggested by the fact that, as far as it is known, the anti-rightist campaign
   did not claim any important victims in the army—with one notable exception, Ch'en I,
   Director of the Cultural Department of the General Political Department, who was
   purged. See *People's Daily*, March 1, 1958.

the opportunity to strike out at the officers, branding them "right-wingers" and ominously linking their views with the ultimate crime of opposition to Communism in general.[67]

In 1958, and especially in the latter half of the year, the movement against professionalism soared to new heights of vehemence. The inculcation of Mao's military writings was pushed with unprecedented vigour [68] and special stress was put on the leadership role of the Party committees.[69] The military academies, where professional attitudes were most likely to originate and be nurtured, were a prime target of the drive. It is also likely that the influence of Soviet advisers was strongest in these schools, and perhaps this is one of the reasons why they bore the brunt of the campaign to instil Mao's teachings and to eradicate "dogmatism." The reports on what had to be eradicated in some of these academies indicate to what extent professionalism had taken root.[70]

After Lin Piao took over as Minister of Defence a new and extensive effort was made to reorganise and revitalise the political control system; this provides another indication that the system had deteriorated to a considerable degree. From July 1960 to February 1961 inspections, investigations and a purge were carried out in the army. Then the Party launched a campaign to recruit new members and to establish branch committees and Party groups in companies and platoons which had previously lacked Party organisations.[71]

Measures to improve relations with civilians

Hand in hand with the house-cleaning in the army, the Party moved to forestall what it considered a dangerous drift of the officers from the population at large. Here perhaps the most prickly problem was the glaring gap which had developed between the living standard of the officers and their dependants on the one hand and the populace on the other hand.

Since the adoption of the pay system thousands of officers' dependants had left their rural homes to stay at military posts. This, it was said, caused difficulties in providing supplies, services and employment, and adversely affected the work of the officers. More important, perhaps, was the awkward situation created by the fact that at a time when the

67 *Liberation Army News* editorial, NCNA, July 30, 1957, SCMP, No. 1588, p. 9.
68 *Liberation Army News*, January 16, 1958, SCMP, No. 1786, pp. 6–7, NCNA-English, July 31, 1958.
69 *Liberation Army News*, January 16, 1958, SCMP, No. 1786, p. 7.
70 NCNA, June 19, 1958, SCMP, No. 1802, p. 12; *Liberation Army News*, June 24, 1958, SCMP, No. 1817, pp. 16–17; *Liberation Army News*, May 5, 1958, JPRS, No. 10343/59, p. 39; *Liberation Army News*, June 20, 1958, JPRS, No. 10239/59, p. 34; *Liberation Army News*, August 8, 1958, JPRS, No. 10240/59, pp. 4–6.
71 *Bulletin*, No. 23, June 13, 1961, cited in Powell, p. 8.

peasants were under perennial pressure to increase production and cut down on consumption, the dependants were not only sideline spectators of their efforts but also led a much better life. Such a situation, it was said, dampened the enthusiasm of the peasants for work and alienated them from the armed forces. Taking all this into account, the Party ordered, in late 1957, that the dependants should go home and get down to work. Consequently, a mass migration of officers' families back to their villages was set in motion.[72]

Other measures aimed at levelling the living standards included a reduction in the quantity of provisions supplied to the armed forces and a lowering of the dependants' rations to the level for the population as a whole,[73] a reduction in the salaries of officers of divisional level and above,[74] and exhortations to the officers to be thrifty and to refrain from buying up commodities which were in short supply.[75] At the same time, steps were taken to put an end to the callous treatment of civilians by the military.[76]

" Officers to the ranks "

The whole campaign against professionalism was epitomised in the " officers to the ranks " movement, laid down by a General Political Department directive of September 20, 1958, which required every officer to spend a month as an ordinary soldier.[77] By February 1959 over 150,000 officers, including more than 160 generals, were reported to be cheerfully doing their stint as privates.[78] It was said that battle-hardened veterans of three decades of soldiering shed their gold-braided uniforms, donned a private's kit, and took orders from greenhorn corporals[79]; heads of logistics departments served as cooks[80]; divisional political commissars stood sentry duty[81]; colonels swept barrack floors and cleaned spittoons[82]; a major-general sang songs to entertain the troops accompanied by another general on the fiddle[83]; and so on. Few will argue that this phenomenon is probably unique in the annals of modern armies.

[72] NCNA, November 27, 1957, SCMP, No. 1668, pp. 18–19; also pp. 17, 19.
[73] Lanchow, *Kansu Jih-pao (Kansu Daily)*, September 18, 1957, SCMP, No. 1626, pp. 24–25.
[74] *Liberation Army News*, February 26, 1957, SCMP, No. 1625, p. 27.
[75] NCNA, January 12, 1957, SCMP, No. 1460, pp. 9–10.
[76] NCNA, June 14, 1957, SCMP, No. 1557, p. 6.
[77] NCNA-English, September 21, 1958.
[78] *People's Daily*, April 27, 1959, CB, No. 579, p. 5.
[79] *People's Daily*, June 24, 1958, SCMP, No. 1812, p. 1.
[80] *Ibid.*
[81] *Ibid.*
[82] See note 78, p. 6.
[83] NCNA, October 19, 1958, SCMP, No. 1891, p. 3.

Essentially this movement was intended as a panacea for the problems arising from the growing caste-consciousness of the officers. The Party sought to recreate the revolutionary climate of the past and to demonstrate forcefully to both officers and men that regardless of how the army has changed, its time-honoured traditions have not.[84] Assessing the programme, the Chinese have noted, to no great surprise, that it made the troops very happy.[85] The same could hardly be said for the officers. The strange metamorphosis forced upon them not only ran counter to what a professional officer would consider the requirements of status and discipline, but was probably also a source of considerable physical discomfort to them. That the officers were not exactly elated with the movement is evident in the fact that the Party felt compelled to defend it at length.[86] In any case, it appears that since the "great leap forward" was abandoned, this programme has been quietly dumped.

AFTER THE "LEAP"

In late 1960 the Party leaders scrapped the "great leap forward" and reluctantly returned to more sober and sensible policies. One reason for this has been the realisation that sheer muscle-power cannot perform miracles and that expertise cannot be dispensed with. Consequently, the stock of "experts" in relation to "reds" has risen markedly on the political exchange. There has been a renewed emphasis on expertise, and the scorn heaped on professional men in past years has given way to an admitted appreciation of the need for their talents.

This shift in attitude toward specialists has been reflected in the army. The deluge of denunciations which had descended on professional officers in previous years, especially in 1958, has almost stopped. In fact, since 1960 there does not appear to have been a campaign aimed specifically at the officers, though indoctrination drives intended for the army as a whole have, if anything, been stepped up.[87]

There are no indications, however, that the Party leaders have made any key concessions to the viewpoint of the professional officers. To be sure, it appears that in two important areas of disagreement the Party has modified its policy. First, the employment of troops in economic construction has been drastically curtailed. Whereas in 1958 the army devoted some 60 million work days to industrial and agricultural work,[88]

---

[84] See, for example, note 78, pp. 6–8.

[85] *Ibid.* pp. 7–8.

[86] *Hung Ch'i* (*Red Flag*), No. 4, February 16, 1959, JPRS, No. 9176/59.

[87] S. M. Chiu, "The PLA and the Party: Recent Developments," *Military Review*, XLIII, June 1963, pp. 58–66; *Bulletin*, No. 3, January 7, 1961.

[88] *Shih-shih Shou-ts'e* (*Current Handbook*), No. 3, February 6, 1959, ECMM, No. 167, p. 15.

in 1961 the number fell to 22 million.[89]   But this may have been due as much to the Party's reluctance to use troops in the countryside at a time of severe food shortages, and to the abandonment of many projects initiated during the "leap," as in deference to the officers' demands. Second, the militia movement appears to be on the wane, but this also is probably due to the abandonment of the "leap" and to the monumental mess into which the militia had deteriorated [90] rather than to the objections of the officers.   In short, while these may seem to be concessions, there is no evidence that they are the direct result of pressure by the officers, and there is no hint that any of the officers' arguments have been accepted.

Quite the contrary is true.   The Party has reaffirmed its basic views regarding the army and has taken steps to ensure their implementation. The " Regulations for PLA Management and Education on the Company Level " [91] and the " Four Sets of Regulations on Political Work in Company-Level Units of the PLA " [92] promulgated in 1961 were designed to strengthen the Party's political and organisational hold over the basic-level units of the armed forces.   But the most forceful and far-reaching reassertion of Party principles and practice was the publication in March 1963 of the "Regulations Governing PLA Political Work." [93]

The importance of these Regulations—the first such Regulations to be issued apart from a 1954 draft [94]—can hardly be exaggerated.   But their most striking feature is that they contain nothing new.   They bring together and formalise things which had been said many times before, but in no way do they diverge from previous patterns.   That it was necessary to do this is, as has been observed, a clear indication that much of what was supposed to be operational was in fact not so.   But at the same time the Party has left no doubt that it will bend every effort to remedy the defects and that it has no intention of modifying its stand, whatever the views of the professional officers.   Commenting on the Regulations, the army newspaper went through the whole gamut of issues which have been in dispute and restated emphatically and unequivocally that the Maoist doctrine remains the guiding light for all of them.[95]

89 NCNA-English, February 4, 1962.
90 For an illuminating report on the sorry state of the militia in Honan, see *Bulletin*, No. 4, January 11, 1961.
91 NCNA, July 5, 1961, SCMP, No. 2540, pp. 1–3.
92 NCNA, November 21, 1961, SCMP, No. 2630, pp. 1–3.
93 The text of these Regulations has apparently not been made public.   For a detailed description of their content, see *Liberation Army News* editorial, May 8, 1963 (reprinted in the *People's Daily*), SCMP, No. 2984, pp. 1–8.
94 The 1954 draft has been referred to several times, but apparently it has not been made public.
95 Note 92, p. 3.

The Party, in short, has conceded nothing in principle, but it is apparent that it has a long way to go before all its principles become practice.

How the drastic deterioration of Sino-Soviet relations has affected Party relations is an open question. It is likely that the removal of Marshal P'eng and his supporters has not removed the apprehension of some officers over the consequences of the rift. For one thing, the defensive value of the Soviet nuclear shield for China can now only be very limited. More important, outside aid, especially aircraft parts and aviation and vehicle fuel, is still indispensable for keeping China's military machine at maximum efficiency, to say nothing of modernising it. Such aid, however, has not been forthcoming. It is known that in mid-1960 the Soviet Union withdrew its military as well as non-military technicians, and drastically diminished its shipments of military equipment and supplies.[96] This has undoubtedly hit the army hard.[97]

Just how hard is suggested by China's apparent efforts to overcome the difficulties. One sign was the establishment in 1963 of three new Ministries of Machine Building, presumably to take charge of expanded military production. Another was the visit in September 1963 of a Chinese military delegation to Sweden, possibly to shop for supplies. A third is Peking's preoccupation with increasing petroleum production and importing oil.[98] However, in view of the country's sparse resources and economic priorities, it is unlikely that China's military industry can rapidly make up for the hardware which previously came from abroad. The efficiency of the armed forces will probably continue to decline in the near future, and it is possible that some officers are deeply distressed over this state of affairs.

There is no sign, however, of tension between the Party and the military. On the contrary, since 1960 there has been a notable absence of public criticism of the army, and recently the army has come in for unusual praise.[99] Could one reason for this harmony be that Moscow's disregard for Peking's view's, especially on the test ban treaty, has convinced the officers that China has only herself to depend upon? If so, then, ironically, the widening of the Sino-Soviet rift, which several years ago tended to drive the military and political leaders apart, has now drawn them closer together.

But if there is no sign of tension, there is also no sign that the sources of potential tension have been eliminated. " Redness " and

96 United States Department of State press release, August 20, 1963: *The Military Balance 1963–1964* (London : Institute for Strategic Studies, 1963), p. 9.
97 *The New York Times*, December 4, 1963, and March 1, 1964 ; *The Christian Science Monitor*, February 21, 1964.
98 *The Christian Science Monitor*, February 24, 1964 ; *The New York Times*, December 27, 1963.
99 See, for example, *Far Eastern Economic Review*, February 13, 1964.

" expertise " do not, in the final analysis, go together and some way out will eventually have to be found, perhaps by a new generation of more technically oriented leaders. However, given the Party's firm control over the army and its constant concern with maintaining that control, there is no reason to expect any major crisis in the relations between the Party and the army in the present circumstances.

China's Secret Military Papers

On August 5, 1963, the State Department released a set of secret Chinese military papers, which is the most illuminating first-hand material that scholars have had on the Chinese Communists since the Hoover Institution acquired the Yenan Documents in the mid-forties.

Twenty-nine issues of the secret military journal Kung-tso T'ung-hsun (Bulletin of Activities), *covering the period of January 1—August 26, 1961 are now available. Microfilm of the twenty-nine available issues of the Kung-tso T'ung-hsun can be had from the Photoduplication Service of the Library of Congress. Later in the year the Hoover Institution will be publishing an English translation of these papers, together with notes. It is thought that these copies of the* Bulletin *found their way out of China after Khambas over-ran a Chinese regimental post in Tibet in the late summer of 1961. They were most probably available within the State Department by early 1962.*

According to the General Political Department of the People's Liberation Army, the Bulletin *is an irregular secret publication produced by the Party for officers, at the regimental level or above, who belong to the Party. It was first published on January 1, 1961. The top secret issues of the* Bulletin *were distributed only to divisional officers. The missing issue in the available set, No. 9 may have been top secret and not acquired by the State Department.*

The Bulletin *contains extremely frank speeches by top military leaders, resolutions and reports of the Military Affairs Committee of the Central Committee as well as from other sections of the army. It was published by the General Political Department of the People's Liberation Army to expose political and technical weaknesses in the armed forces. In the last three years corrective measures have been pushed through. It is not certain, as yet, how effective these measures have been.*

China's Secret Military Papers: 'Continuities' and 'Revelations'

By JOHN WILSON LEWIS

CHINA'S rulers in 1961 surveyed their shattered dreams and then, with studied self-confidence, hailed the vitality of their revolutionary " mass-line " credo. This resolute re-affirmation of standard principles had a hollow ring, however, and doubts about the " real methods of control " employed during the years of retreat and readjustment coincided with angry charges that the language of the " mass-line " disguised terror and brutality on an appalling scale. In the confusion, fact has until recently seemed entwined irretrievably with propaganda and invective, but now a unique collection of the *Kung-tso T'ung-hsun* (*Bulletin of Activities*) makes it possible to disentangle the contradictory methods of control and leadership used in 1961 and to evaluate their widely varied effects in that crucial year.

REALITY AND DOGMA

The *Bulletin of Activities* confirms the genuine preoccupation of senior Party leaders with the mass line and with the galaxy of doctrinal slogans and techniques articulated in the years of revolution to support it. At the same time, a remarkably realistic mood permeates these military documents. It lends credence to the assertion that Party officials firmly believe in mass-line " investigation and research "; but it also reflects the shocking inability of those officials to imbue their subordinates with the spirit of the mass-line. In a period of acknowledged domestic chaos and even near anarchy, the *Bulletin* contains frank appraisals and reveals careful planning and responsive arrangements by the highest Communist cadres to meet the acute problems at hand.

A penetrating search for hard facts best characterises the tone of the *Bulletin*. For example, in the only report commented on by Mao Tse-tung in the journal, the following conversation is reported:

> Liu Sheng-hua, a deputy squad leader of the eighth squad, a poor farmer, stated during target practice last September: " When I am demobilised, I'll want only a gun." Others asked him: " What do you want a gun for?" He replied: " To fight the Party!" [1]

[1] *Kung-tso T'ung-hsun* (*Bulletin of Activities*), No. 11, March 2, 1961, p. 12.

58

With the same candour, other reports recount the details of popular disaffection, widespread starvation, cadre corruption and stupidity, loss of military morale and effectiveness, peasant uprisings, and economic disarray. Distraught by the food shortages in the rural areas, members of the Central Garrison Force ask bitterly " Does Chairman Mao, who lives in Peking, know the life of the peasants? " [2] Tied to the harsh realities of Chinese politics in 1961, Party officials did not dream of miracles,[3] rather they calculated painstakingly the progressive steps needed to salvage their revolution and regain the momentum lost in the " three hard years." Doctrine thus continued to be enforced because Peking's leaders held that rigid adherence to Maoism alone would insure the communication of accurate information to the Politburo and the implementation of effective policies at the production sites.

For this reason, the Party élite sought to weld the revolutionary ideal to the actual practice of the cadres and infused unusual vitality into its routine pronouncements on rectification, study, investigation and research, and physical labour. Real people dot the pages of the journal, and a careful reading of those pages should help dispel the myths that Communist exhortation has deprived Chinese of their souls or their wit, or has magically transformed grandiose schemes and silly hopes into reality. Peasants have become bored, they have resisted or cunningly misinterpreted official edicts, and they have " tuned out " the annoying propaganda barrage. The *Bulletin* conclusively demonstrates that hunger, disease and death have been more persuasive for the Chinese people than Radio Peking or the nearest cadre. Moreover, the *Bulletin* consistently ties thought reform policies to the tide of popular reaction that threatened to engulf the Party in 1961.

In this light the Chinese Communist Party refers to the political qualities derived from the revolutionary ideology as their " spiritual A-bomb "—a device infinitely superior to that in the hands of the Russians and Americans.[4] In the *Bulletin*, military leaders laud the efficacy of thought reform for the restoration of morale and rectitude within Party-led organisations, especially within the army itself. The unhealthy conditions in the People's Liberation Army in 1959–60 are emphatically blamed on the absence of political control and on the political errors of Marshal P'eng Teh-huai, Minister of Defence until September 1959. Throughout the *Bulletin*, the key Party figure directing the re-establishment of political dominion in the army is Marshal Lin

2 *Bulletin*, No. 1, January 1, 1961, p. 13.
3 *Bulletin*, No. 2, January 3, 1961, p. 3.
4 *Bulletin*, No. 29, August 1, 1961, p. 3. Among the political qualities enumerated are " political consciousness, bravery and sacrifice." By inference, these qualities are placed in opposition to the " erroneous feeling " that " modern war will destroy mankind "; *Bulletin*, No. 3, January 7, 1961, p. 14.

Piao, who is frequently flattered by the title "chief" (*tsung*) and by a
reference to his "leadership thought."[5] Lin, as the main actor, in
turn relies heavily on the writings and name of Mao Tse-tung to reinforce
his authority and bolster his claim to political orthodoxy. Organisationally, the Party directs military activities and policy under Lin Piao
through the Military Affairs Committee of the Central Committee,[6] and
all other military organs take their cue from the Military Affairs Committee or have been quietly abandoned in the general reorganisation since
1959. A resolution passed in December 1960 by the Military Affairs
Committee details the system of political control prescribed for the
Liberation Army,[7] while a separate directive governs the establishment of
Party committees by *hsien*-level armed forces departments of the government.[8] By late April 1961, the General Political Department of the
Liberation Army could report to the Central Committee and the Military
Affairs Committee that Party branches throughout the Army had been
re-organised, that new Party members had been recruited within it, and
that a systematic purge of "rotten" elements had been completed.[9]

The interplay of harsh reality and political dogma may be further
examined in a directive of the Military Affairs Committee and the
General Political Department which details the "key points in the
political work of the whole army in 1961." This directive of December 24,
1960, gave impetus to several ideological campaigns aimed at correcting
the manifestations of crisis and disorder in the army—anti-Party hostility,
poor training, lagging morale, illness and disinterest in political activities.
Three central movements which originate and culminate within the
pages of the *Bulletin* are those for strengthening political-ideological
work,[10] for "two recollections and three investigations" (*liang-i
san-ch'a*),[11] and for "management education" (*kuan-li chiao-yü*).[12]
In each of these three movements Party cadres underlined vital aspects

---

5 See, for example, *Bulletin*, No. 1, January 1, 1961, pp. 7–11, and *Bulletin*, No. 16,
April 10, 1961, p. 13.   The only other Chinese leader to receive flattery on the same
level as Mao is Liu Shao-ch'i.   See *People's Daily*, September 13, 1963.

6 For a careful treatment of the Military Affairs Committee in the light of the *Bulletin*,
see Ralph L. Powell, *Politico-Military Relationships in Communist China* (Washington: U.S. Department of State, unclassified, 1963), especially pp. 5–7.

7 *Bulletin*, No. 3, January 7, 1961, pp. 1–33.

8 *Bulletin*, No. 19, May 13, 1961, p. 12.

9 *Bulletin*, No. 23, June 13, 1961, pp. 1–6.

10 For the principal documents, see *Bulletin*, No. 1, January 1, 1961, pp. 1–21, No. 3,
January 7, 1961, pp. 1–33, and No. 6, January 27, 1961, pp. 12–14.

11 See, for example, *Bulletin*, No. 4, January 11, 1961, pp. 1–20, and No. 15, April 5,
1961, pp. 9–15.   The formal definition of *liang-i san-ch'a* is "recollection of class
suffering and national suffering and investigation of one's standpoint, will to fight
and work," *Bulletin*, No. 4, January 11, 1961, p. 11.

12 See *Bulletin*, No. 7, February 1, 1961, pp. 23–28; No. 13, March 20, 1961, pp. 1–15;
No. 14, March 29, 1961, pp. 1–2; No. 15, April 5, 1961, pp. 26–30; No. 16, April 19,
1961, p. 16; No. 18, April 30, 1961, pp. 12–23; No. 22, June 1, 1961, pp. 1–5; No. 23,
June 13, 1961, pp. 16–21; and No. 24, June 18, 1961, pp. 1–18.

of doctrine and extolled the line of integrating theory with practice. The "management education" movement in particular comprised a crucial but somewhat ponderous restatement of the complexities of the mass-line as applied to army life. With the other two movements it became closely integrated with the rectification movement announced at the Ninth Plenum of the Party's Eighth Central Committee (meeting between January 14–18, 1961), with the campaign for "investigation and research," [13] and with the "3–8" campaign begun in the spring of 1960.[14]

COMMON INTEREST IN SURVIVAL

The deft handling of the various movements and campaigns in 1961 supports the impression that the highest élite of the Chinese Communist Party and the Liberation Army is firmly united in upholding revolutionary ideology and suprisingly animated. Party leaders appear realistic enough to share a common interest in survival and effective Party operation, though a shared faith and personal commitment are also at work. The *Bulletin of Activities* offers no evidence that factions exist within the Party Central Committee, or any of its principal departments or committees, or between it and the organs of the state and army. Instead it shows that the highest leaders have drawn together in the face of mounting dissatisfaction and disinterest expressed by their subordinate cadres and the general population. No evidence ties P'eng Teh-huai to the sin of factionalism, although he is charged with damaging errors and deviations.[15] The *Bulletin* proves that many senior officials often

---

[13] See *Mao Tse-tung Lun Tiao-ch'a Yen-chiu* (*Mao Tse-tung on Investigation and Research*) (Hong Kong: San-lien shu-tien, 1961). One of the principal documents used in this campaign was Mao's *On Investigation Work*, written in 1930 but never published or referred to in official lists of his works. *Bulletin*, No. 15, April 5, 1961, pp. 1–8.

[14] The "3–8" campaign refers to three phrases and eight characters (or four words) which translate as follows: "steadfast and correct political direction, painstaking and frugal working style, flexible and mobile strategy and tactics; unity, earnestness, seriousness and activeness. For typical Chinese articles on the "3–8" campaign see *Survey of China Mainland Press* (Hong Kong: U.S. Consulate-General): Nos. 2270 (June 2, 1960), pp. 1–6; 2309 (August 3, 1960), pp. 2–4; and 2472 (April 10, 1961), pp. 1–6; and *Bulletin*, No. 3, January 7, 1961, pp. 13–14. The post-1960 "3–8" is only vaguely related to Mao's "3–8" military guidelines laid down from 1928 to 1947 and formalised in 1947 as the "Three Main Rules of Discipline and Eight Points for Attention." See Mao Tse-tung, *Selected Works* (Peking: Foreign Languages Press, 1961), IV, pp. 155–156. Other campaigns discussed in the *Bulletin* include: a campaign for frugality and economy; a movement to encourage the use of food substitutes; a movement against too many meetings, reports, documents, organisations and slogans; and a movement to foster high quality, technical skills.

[15] The *Bulletin* links P'eng, Huang K'o-ch'eng and Hung Hsueh-chih, but refers to them as "comrades." The military documents specifically accuse the trio of "representing the military line of the bourgeoisie" and "going counter to Chairman Mao's basic principles on building the military" while fostering "dogmatism, the purely military viewpoint and warlordism," *Bulletin*, No. 3, January 7, 1961, p. 3; and No. 24, June 18, 1961, p. 1.

drop " out of the news " because of extensive travel and pressure of
work, not declining political fortunes.

The tension which the *Bulletin* does reveal is between the different
generations within the Party and between levels of cadres. Obviously
this does not preclude similar tensions from occurring within the Central
Committee of the Party. But, the Central Committee's recognition of
conflict between generations and between the various levels of the
hierarchy would make it set a high premium on its own solidarity. An
operative consensus within its ranks would, in turn, need to result from
debate based on varied and controversial sources of information. This
is exactly what is shown in the *Bulletin*—active discussion and fairly
firm unity. The combination may not be perfect but the deficiencies
are a far cry from factions.

In the Maoist mind, a certain overlapping occurs between " inexperienced, post-1949 Party members " and " opportunist, corrupt
subordinates." Increasingly sensitive about their own ageing, Party
leaders muddle immaturity and irresponsibility and posit an identical
ideological solution for both. A speech by Marshal Yeh Chien-ying
highlights the intensity of the élite's concern in this regard when he
states " Man's death is a natural law. Man comes from nature and
returns to nature. This is a law." Thus, he continues, it is necessary
to leave some records " to be passed on to the younger generation." [16]
Then Yeh argues that the leadership should pay attention to those
at the meetings who do not applaud or who applaud in a forced
manner.[17] The minority who do not applaud are Party members and
comrades in the Liberation Army, but they entertain doubts and
different views and therefore must be carefully educated. Otherwise, he implies, the senior élite will be unable to prepare the
rules and ordinances for the guidance of the next generation.[18]
Similar comments in the *Bulletin* make the same points: the
differences between the " veterans " of the revolution and those
who joined after 1949; the necessity for the veterans to codify their
experiences before they " return to nature "; and the need for complete
political and ideological solidarity among the leading cadres (the
" veterans ") so that they might reach agreement on the codes as well
as lead the next generation properly. It is difficult to imagine an élite

---

16 *Bulletin*, No. 26, July 13, 1961, pp. 2–3.

17 *Ibid.*, pp. 3–4.

18 For the other major documents on the Military Affairs Committee meetings held to
prepare the ordinances and regulations, see *Bulletin*, No. 12, March 10, 1961, pp. 1–8;
and No. 29, August 1, 1961, pp. 1–11. For a Liberation Army notice on the writing
of battle histories which will relate both to reminiscences and the ordinance project,
see *Bulletin*, No. 14, March 29, 1961, p. 7.

acutely preoccupied with the applause and unity of its members—
and elsewhere with the proper hanging of the pictures of the members of
the Political Bureau's Standing Committee [19] and with other symbols of
solidarity—blithely tolerating factional quarrels so intense that they could
be exploited by the foreign press.

A comprehensive communications network further sustains unity
among the leaders.[20] Indeed, the *Bulletin* plays a key role in the extraordinary effort to keep senior military officers and cadres informed. From
January through August 1961, there were regular meetings with a fairly
systematic rotation of speakers and participants to insure lively discussions
and to make sure that senior officers and cadres knew of successive
problems and proposals. Some surprisingly large sessions " met " on the
telephone, while others broke up into small seminars of specialists from
the army and the Party. Most of the leading army marshals selectively
duplicated the investigations of lower levels in sample areas, and higher
echelons circulated reports, reference materials, and draft regulations
for study and comment down to the regimental level or even lower.

The conferences and symposia, including meetings to write ordinances
for use by the " next generation," invoked the words of Mao-Tse-tung
as final authority, and Party cadres ritually apotheosised the works of
" the Chairman " in all conceivable settings.[21] The fourth Chinese
volume of Mao's *Selected Works*, published in 1960, stands out as the
principal source for study and guidance. By adhering to the main theses
in the fourth volume, which covers Mao's writings from August 1945 to
September 1949, the major domestic and international deviations,
including the deviation of revisionism, could purportedly be corrected.
In addition, Party officials, while preparing directives and study guides,
intend to tap the data in two forthcoming volumes of the *Selected Works*,
supplements to the first four Chinese volumes, and in the substantial file
of unpublished papers by Mao, including his speeches in 1958 and 1959.[22]

REVELATIONS

The foregoing, in the main, outlines the principal " continuities " which
exist between the pages of the *Bulletin of Activities* and those of easily
acquired newspapers, journals and pamphlets. These continuities are

---

[19] *Bulletin*, No. 13, March 20, 1961, p. 24.
[20] High-level communications are related to general military communications and military
security in the *Bulletin*. On military communications work, see *Bulletin*, No. 20,
May 22, 1961, pp. 1–24. For major documents on security procedures, see *Bulletin*,
No. 8, February 6, 1961, pp. 20–31, which contains stories of men punished for
showing secret papers to their mistresses or for allegedly plotting to turn classified
data over to the U.S. Consulate-General in Hong Kong.
[21] For examples, see *Bulletin*, No. 6, January 27, 1961, pp. 1–11; and No. 16, April 19,
1961, pp. 13–16.
[22] *Bulletin*, No. 8, February 6, 1961, p. 14; and No. 26, July 13, 1961, p. 2.

found primarily in connection with doctrine. Furthermore, the exposition of Party doctrine in the military journal adds a wider dimension of reality and plausibility to Party principles and policies, and, in the context of the " revelations " described below, the " features " of Maoist doctrine appear somewhat less awe-inspiring that some people had once supposed. But the " revolutionary " leadership techniques also must be credited in large measure for salvaging the crumbling social order in 1961 and then for progressively restoring morale and discipline in the army and in the general populace. In skilled hands the mass-line still appears to have carried some of the old Yenan " magic."

That magic, however, had become a cruel hoax in the hands of ill trained or corrupt cadres, who showed the mass-line's potential for brute terror. From the Central Committee's published point of view at least, a foul trick had been played on the Chinese people by men who bear the Communist Party label but who acted the petty tyrant, and so fundamentally contributed to the disaster of the " three hard years." Even when the proper " adjustments " have been made for the usual negative tone in Party documents, with their penchant for blaming the " lower levels," the *Bulletin* makes a convincing case that dictatorial leaders in the rural areas took command of peasant groups and army units and grossly mishandled the mounting chaos set in motion by the great leap forward. Stories of the scope of this " betrayal " by Party and Liberation Army cadres and the popular reaction are sharply etched on the pages of the journal, and these constitute the " revelations " which in the future will give us pause as we venture beyond the safety of doctrine into the world of " objective realities."

Although no summary can possibly do justice to these stories, I shall attempt to suggest their content under these three rough headings: cadre leadership, military discipline and training, and social disorder and rural organisation.

Cadre leadership

Refugee reports and thinly disguised hints in the Communist Press have left little doubt that the Party has been seriously hampered in its operations by venal and ignorant cadres. Nevertheless, the journal reveals an unexpectedly large and harmful substratum of such cadres. Many cadres were charged with murder, rape and extreme forms of cruelty. In a report of the Nanking Military Region, for example, cadres were said to employ simple, inflexible and rough tactics.[23] They were accused of swearing, ridicule, name calling, and of torture and terror, including hanging people up by the hands and flogging them. Party

[23] *Bulletin*, No. 15, April 5, 1961, pp. 26–30.

officials found cadres who stripped men and women naked and maliciously shamed them before their fellow villagers as a punishment for petty thefts.[24] In general a large body of cadres spurned or misused mass-line techniques, and many wives of cadres behaved in a pompous and extravagant way.[25] One summary statement notes the effect of malpractices on the peasants in this way: " The glory of serving the people as cadres should be verified. To become cadres should not be considered as a shameful thing. It should be clearly explained that becoming cadres is quite different from doing bad deeds." [26]

Military discipline and training

The greatest value of the *Bulletin* perhaps lies in its treatment of Chinese Communist military affairs. Relations between the army and the Party, organisational problems, training programmes in the use of advanced weapons, basic defensive strategies to be followed in case of war, and difficulties in supply, security, staffing, repairing equipment, and accident prevention receive extensive and, for the Western student, unique treatment.[27] Although amazing improvement was displayed by the Liberation Army in October 1962 when it launched the offensive against India, many of the questions raised in the journal will have a lasting impact of the conduct and role of the Liberation Army. How does the army based on peasant conscripts maintain a high level of readiness and morale in time of peace? [28] How can discipline be sustained in the face of reports of starvation and maltreatment from the soldier's home village? [29] How can the " revolutionary spirit " be instilled when the number of veterans falls off annually? [30] And, when there is a food shortage within China, how can the Party ensure that the army is well enough fed so that its efficiency in not impaired and at the same time prevent the army from being a hub of special privilege? [31]

---

[24] *Bulletin*, No. 5, January 17, 1961, pp. 15–17.

[25] *Bulletin*, No. 7, February 1, 1961, pp. 1–12. For a sample article on cadre special privileges see No. 6, January 27, 1961, pp. 18–21.

[26] *Bulletin*, No. 6, January 27, 1961, pp. 15–17. Other important materials on the cadres are found in No. 11, March 2, 1961, pp. 24–33; and No. 28, July 29, 1961, pp. 9–18.

[27] Powell, *op. cit.*

[28] For the extensive documentation on training and readiness problems, see these articles in *Bulletin*, No. 2, January 3, 1961, pp. 22–32; No. 5, January 17, 1961, pp. 1–4; No. 8, February 6, 1961, pp. 1–10; No. 10, February 20, 1961, pp. 19–27; No. 11, March 2, 1961, pp. 1–18; No. 12, March 10, 1961, pp. 16–24; No. 14, March 29, 1961, pp. 23–26; No. 25, June 28, 1961, pp. 1–11; and No. 27, July 25, 1961, pp. 1–27.

[29] For a sample on the handling of letters and visits with family members in " disaster areas " see *Bulletin*, No. 1, January 1, 1961, pp. 16–21; No. 6, January 27, 1961, pp. 12–14; No. 7, February 1, 1961, pp. 29–32; No. 17, April 25, 1961, pp. 14–18; and No. 23, June 13, 1961, pp. 22–25.

[30] *Bulletin*, No. 14, March 29, 1961, pp. 27–29; No. 26, July 13, 1961, pp. 10–16.

[31] For a sample of the articles on health problems in the army and the use of food substitutes, see *Bulletin*, No. 6, January 27, 1961, pp. 22–27; No. 10, February 20,

In the *Bulletin*, the most striking examples of the collapse of military discipline are to be found in discussions of the militia. Reared in the Yenan image of invincible, dispersed armed units, the militia by 1960 were either an awesome liability or existed largely on paper.[32]   A January 1961 report, for example, stated that the Chinese people called the militia " rabid dogs, whippers, bandits and a group of tigers." [33] It continued that the conduct of the militiamen had seriously impaired the relationship between the Party and the peasant masses and had destroyed the reputation of the militiamen themselves. In Shangch'eng *hsien*, Honan, the militia leaders of thirteen communes led militiamen to search houses, rape women, and rob at gunpoint.[34]   According to another report, the Party had had to confiscate the weapons of the militia and put them in the hands of a few trusted peasants.[35]

Social disorder and rural organisation

Though largely inferred, a remarkable picture of new social breakdown in the " three hard years " is painted in the *Bulletin*. The near collapse of military discipline and the abandonment of mass-line procedures in some regions unquestionably aggravated the crisis in 1960 and threatened to upset the precarious balance of social order. Yet, it is hardly possible to witness the contest between " mass-line " and oppressive practices as a spectator might watch a football match. Though one might agree with the editors of the *Bulletin* that " antagonistic contradictions " had been revived throughout China,[36] doctrine itself—as well as the incredible blindness of Party leaders to the fact that in 1958–59 mass-line techniques existed largely in their minds rather than in what the cadres were doing—must bear the brunt of the blame. It was Party doctrine which removed all constraints from the cadres and then concentrated all mechanisms of power in their hands.

In any case, hunger and brutality precipitated widespread revolt and " armed banditry " in the aftermath of the commune failure. Challenged, the Party launched an all-out military and political effort to " suppress the counter-revolutionaries and pacify the countryside." [37]   Among other untidy events, terrible calamities are said to have occurred in Honan and

1961, pp. 28–32; No. 11, March 2, 1961, pp. 19–23; No. 13, March 20, 1961, pp. 16–20; No. 22, June 1, 1961, p. 17; No. 26, July 13, 1961, p. 17; and No. 29, August 1, 1961, pp. 12–15.

[32] The principal articles on the militia are in *Bulletin*, No. 4, January 11, 1961, pp. 21–27; No. 14, March 29, 1961, pp. 16–17; and No. 21, May 26, 1961, pp. 1–16.

[33] *Bulletin*, No. 5, January 17, 1961, p. 12.

[34] *Ibid*. p. 8.

[35] *Bulletin*, No. 4, January 11, 1961, pp. 21–27.

[36] *Bulletin*, No. 14, March 29, 1961, pp. 2–7.

[37] See especially *Bulletin*, No. 1, January 1, 1961, pp. 29–32; and No. 5, January 17, 1961, pp. 5–15.

Shantung, and those "calamities" appear to have constituted armed peasant revolt.[38] The Honan revolt, unreported in any known source until the *Bulletin* was released for publication by the State Department, apparently engulfed six of the seven special districts in the province and caused numerous casualties. In 1961, the memory of bloodshed in Honan and elsewhere greatly compounded the Party's tasks of "linking the leadership with the masses" and getting the population to support the régime's plans. It is in this light that the re-establishment of more traditional forms of leadership in China's rural areas in 1961–62 takes on special meaning.[39]

Bloody social disorder also shifted the Central Committee's attention from the ideological and mobilisation aspects of rural organisation to organisation for production and control. This shift was announced on April 4, 1961, in a speech by Liu Chih-chien and promulgated in the form of a "draft sixty-article charter" on the rural communes.[40] In the *Bulletin*, that charter, which was never published and was probably later superseded or revised, plays an important educational role. Party leaders did not simply work to elevate "political consciousness" within the Liberation Army for benefits in discipline and morale; they simultaneously expected the soldiers and officers to assist and even take the lead in stabilising the countryside once more. The rigorous quality of army life and the wide contacts of peasant conscripts made political training in the armed forces an extraordinarily effective instrument.

INTERNATIONAL AFFAIRS

In the Chinese scheme of things, revolutionary doctrine, if "properly" carried out, moulds the society and polity into an operative unit. When, in 1960, Party leaders became fully aware of the domestic upheaval that confronted them, they turned with missionary-like zeal to doctrinal positions which first had been given meaning in the years of revolutionary war. Indeed Party cadres who express themselves in the *Bulletin* recall other near-fatal periods—1927–29, 1934–35 and 1941–42—in which adherence to doctrine supposedly saved the day and out of which came a sharper understanding of the tools of revolution. The desire to duplicate the doctrinal revival of earlier years thus came to dominate the élite after 1960. In that crusading atmosphere principles of foreign

---

[38] In addition to the sources cited in note 37, see *Bulletin*, No. 4, January 11, 1961, pp. 21–27; and No. 21, May 26, 1961, pp. 9–16.

[39] See John W. Lewis, " The Leadership Doctrine of the Chinese Communist Party: The Lesson of the People's Commune," *Asian Survey*, III, No. 10 (October 1963), pp. 457–464.

[40] See *Bulletin*, No. 15, April 5, 1961, pp. 1–8; No. 17, April 25, 1961, pp. 1–7; No. 18, April 30, 1961, pp. 1–4; No. 19, May 13, 1961, pp. 1–14.

policy were caught up and transformed along with domestic policies and programmes.

Seven articles in the *Bulletin* deal with international affairs.[41] They cover general Chinese strategies and considerations as well as specific situations, issues and countries—including Laos, the Congo and Japan—which receive special attention. An article entitled " Several Principal Problems Concerning the Current International Situation " covers more general items [42] and, along with a discussion of the study of Mao's works,[43] sets forth those arguments about revisionism, peaceful co-existence, imperialism, struggle, Party supremacy, and the non-aligned which in 1963 became the keystones of the " proposal concerning the general line of the international Communist movement." [44] The article on " several principal problems " views the world situation in the form of a game in which each side plays for the " championship." Thus in the test of strength to come all outstanding issues with the United States " must be settled at the same time, if a settlement is expected." Moreover, in this all-or-nothing contest the Chinese consider the non-aligned Asians and Africans to be strategic pawns and seek to win more pawns through " wars of liberation " thereby turning the tide in China's favour. The article places Africa at the centre of the struggle and says: " When the revolution is ripe, the wave of revolution will roll up the Continent of Africa."

Parallels between China's domestic and foreign spheres and a recog-nition of her antagonistic stance on many international questions are, of course, not new. A reading of the military journal, however, changes the points of emphasis. As seen here, the Party leaders judge inter-national situations and derive external policies in the light of their domestic impact and their " doctrinal validity." Whereas doctrine at the domestic level may be bound to an obvious arena of " objective reality " through a conscious strategy of " investigation and research," no such arena or strategy exists for the Chinese in international affairs. Doctrine equips the Chinese to ascertain domestic but not international realities, and the more the sense of reality at home depends on doctrine the greater the psychological isolation in the world at large becomes. The " penetrating search for hard facts " noted above ends when one comes to the articles on international relations. Thus the process seems clear: domestic crisis, reasserted doctrine, international rigidity and isolation. The lesson is a melancholy one.

41 See *Bulletin*, No. 4, January 11, 1961, pp. 30–33; No. 6, January 27, 1961, pp. 30–32; No. 13, March 20, 1961, pp. 30–33; No. 14, March 29, 1961, pp. 30–32; No. 17, April 25, 1961, pp. 19–25; No. 22, June 1, 1961, pp. 13–16; and No. 29, August 1, 1961, pp. 16–17.   42 *Bulletin*, No. 17, April 25, 1961, pp. 19–25.
43 *Bulletin*, No. 8, February 6, 1961, pp. 11–19.
44 *People's Daily*, June 17, 1963.

The " Next Generation " of Chinese Communist Leaders [1]

By DONALD W. KLEIN

THE question of who will succeed Mao Tse-tung is a fascinating and important question.[2] The related question of the composite group of leaders which will emerge in about a decade is, if less fascinating, of at least equal importance, particularly given the increasing complexities of an industrialising society on the China mainland.

Are we actually nearing a period when the present hierarchy will begin to fade away? Seemingly we are, as a quick flashback to 1949 will illustrate. When the Chinese Communists came to power thirteen years ago, they were rightfully considered a young group of leaders. Their triumphant general in the field, Lin Piao, was just over forty, Chou En-lai just over fifty, and Mao himself in his mid-fifties. Among his international peers, Mao was fifteen years younger than Stalin, eleven younger than Attlee, and almost ten younger than Truman. To emphasise their youth in another way, only two men among the forty-four elected as full Central Committee (CC) members in 1945 died a natural death from that time until 1960.[3]

But with the passage of thirteen years, there is a complete reversal of this situation. We now find, to use comparatives, that the Chinese Politburo members average four years older than the Soviet Presidium members, and almost fourteen years older than those in the American cabinet, including Mr. Kennedy.[4]

---

1 This article is an expanded version of a paper presented at the annual meeting of the Association for Asian Studies, April 2–4, 1962, Boston. The writer would like to express his gratitude to Mr. John Ma of Cornell University, Mrs. Jane P. Shapiro and Mr. Ng Yong-sang, both of Columbia University, for valuable assistance on certain technical points.

2 For a thorough treatment of the succession issue, see Harold C. Hinton, " The Succession Problem in Communist China," *Current Scene* (Hong Kong), Vol. I, No. 7, July 19, 1961.

3 The two men were Kuan Hsiang-ying and Jen Pi-shih, who died in 1946 and 1950, respectively. Two others (Wang Jo-fei and Ch'in Pang-hsien) died in an air-crash in 1946. The case of Ch'en T'an-ch'iu remains a bit of a mystery; apparently he was killed (or executed) in Sinkiang *prior* to the Seventh Congress in 1945, a fact then unknown to the Party. Kao Kang was reported by the Communists to have committed suicide following his purge in 1954–55. The specific facts about Kao's accomplice, Jao Shu-shih, are unknown, but it seems safe to assume that he is either in prison or was executed. The person who died in 1960 was Politburo member Lin Po-ch'ü.

4 The nineteen full members of the Chinese Politburo average sixty-three years; the six alternates average fifty-nine. The combined figure, sixty-two years, is the one used here.

The Statistical Sample

In order to make comparisons between emerging Chinese leaders, the following breakdown serves as one means of probing the layers of leadership.

THE CCP CENTRAL COMMITTEE—FIVE LAYERS OF LEADERSHIP

Group	Number in Sample	Notes
I	36	The *full* members of the CC elected in 1945 at the Seventh Party Congress. Forty-four originally elected.
II	26	The *alternate* members of the CC elected in 1945 at the Seventh Party Congress. Thirty-three originally elected. With few exceptions, most of this group were promoted to full CC membership in 1956 at the Eighth Party Congress.
III	29	In addition to almost all of the surviving members of Groups I and II, thirty-three additional persons were made *full* CC members in 1956 at the Eighth Party Congress.
IV	58	The *alternate* CC members elected at the Eighth Party Congress in 1956. Seventy-three originally elected.
V	23	The *alternate* CC members elected at the Second Session of the Eighth Party Congress in 1958. Twenty-five originally elected.
Total sample :	172	

A few words beyond those in the "Notes" above should serve to give a better idea of these groups. Group I is made up of Mao Tse-tung's core group; as might be expected, the present Politburo comes mainly from this group. Second are those alternates of 1945—Group II. At the end of the Long March in 1935 Mao's forces took refuge in the Shensi Soviet—Mao's nod toward these men from the North is most clearly reflected in these 1945 alternates, for a substantial number of them (over 40 per cent.) had no ties with the Kiangsi Soviet in the South. Both of these groups were elected or re-elected as full CC members at the Eighth Party Congress in 1956, with a few notable exceptions such as the purged Kao Kang and Jao Shu-shih.

In addition to the Groups I and II, another thirty-odd persons were made *full* CC members in 1956. This is Group III, which might best be termed as the near-misses of 1945. It should be noted that this group is predominantly Maoist in the sense that most of them (about 75 per cent.) began their early Party careers in the Kiangsi Soviet. This raises an interesting point in terms of the Party Constitution which suggests that only the *full* members of the CC have a vote.[5] It might be fair to speculate that Mao was packing the full CC membership with his long-term comrades from the early days—remembering that the Eighth Party Congress took place only two years after Kao Kang (originally of the Shensi Soviet) was purged.

Broadly speaking, Group IV may be considered as a category composed of those who began to emerge toward the end of World War II. Finally, Group V is composed of men who began to emerge in the postwar period or even after the Communists gained power in 1949.

In brief, the 187 living members and alternates of the CC have been broken down into five groups, minus fifteen persons deleted because of extreme age, because they are women or for other pertinent reasons. There are doubtless some non-Central Committee members who will emerge to positions of power within a decade, but given the crude tools we must work with, it seems best to concentrate on the large-sized CC in our search for sources of future leadership.

Using these five groupings, the balance of this article is devoted to an examination of them within the confines of selected categories and criteria. These criteria are far from exhaustive, but perhaps they will serve as useful guidelines for further studies.

Age

First is age. This may seem a rather prosaic consideration; in fact it is quite revealing.

AGE (1962)

Group I	—	67
Group II	—	57
Group III	—	57
Group IV	—	55
Group V	—	53

Two facts stand out: Mao's original group (Group I) is quite elderly and, secondly, the remaining groups (II–V) are very close in age.

[5] The 1945 Party Constitution, in Article 33, rather clearly indicates that the alternates are considered non-voting members: they " may " attend plenary sessions where they " have the right to state their opinions." There is no specific mention of the alternates in the parallel article (number 30) in the 1956 Constitution; however, it seems fair to assume that the practice remains the same. In fact, " voting " is probably academic for the present, but recent developments in the Soviet Union suggest that it may not be permanently academic.

From the consideration of age, plus several known cases of infirmity,[6] the following suppositions may be drawn: within the next five to ten years, it is fair to expect a large number of fatalities among Mao's 1945 group, and thereby a full blossoming of leadership from the ranks of the 1945 alternates (Group II). To cite a few familiar names, this is the group that contains such figures as Ch'en Po-ta, Lo Jui-ch'ing, Liao Ch'eng-chih and the Mongol Ulanfu. Secondly, as the next three groupings are so close in age to the 1945 alternates (Group II), it is unlikely that there will be sufficient time for many of them to emerge at the top levels. But even if they do not climb to Politburo heights, these are the men who will be the chief administrators of the policies laid down by the Politburo-level leaders, and are therefore worthy of close scrutiny.

Age alone, of course, is not the only consideration for advancement. That these groupings must not be viewed inflexibly is easily illustrated by noting that Group III alone includes the following: K'o Ch'ing-shih, Li Ching-ch'üan (both already on the Politburo), the Organisation Department Director An Tzu-wen, plus such other notables as Liu Ning-yi, Li Hsüeh-feng and Yang Shang-k'un.

There is a rather remarkable consistency of age when all these categories of men reached the CC. With the exception of the slightly younger 1945 alternates (Group II), all were about fifty years old when placed on the CC as full or alternate members. In others words, all had about twenty-five years of Party experience behind them. And, as we are exactly twenty-five years removed from the outbreak of the Sino-Japanese War, it seems obvious that nearly all future leaders will date their Party membership from that time or after.

PLACE OF ORIGIN [7]

	Central-South	North
Group I	31 (86%)	5 (14%)
Group II	15 (58%)	11 (42%)
Group III	21 (75%)	7 (25%)
Group IV	35 (62%)	21 (38%)
Group V	8 (38%)	13 (62%)
Totals:	110 (66%)	57 (34%)

---

[6] Hsü Hsiang-ch'ien and Cheng Wei-san, for example, are apparently in ill-health. Though now fairly active again, Lin Piao may still suffer from the illness that kept him inactive in the early 1950s.

[7] Information is lacking on the birthplace of five persons in the total sample. North China is loosely defined as Manchuria, Inner Mongolia (including Suiyuan), Hopei,

Place of Origin

The place of origin represents one of the most striking features of the emerging leaders. The reader will recall that the top leaders today are overwhelmingly Southern or Central-Southern in origin, with Mao's native Hunan Province being particularly dominant.

As the Party shifted its base to the North following the Long March, it is natural to expect more recruitment from North of the Yellow River. This supposition is clearly borne out by statistical examination. Broadly speaking, the successive layers of emerging leaders disclose more Northern blood—to the extent that the last cluster (Group V) has more than a three to two ratio of Northerners over Southerners. Shensi and Hopei are especially well represented—Shensi being the locale of Yenan, and Hopei the area from which a number of young intellectuals fled after the Japanese attack in 1937.[8] Hopei is particularly striking—in fact, it is more dominant than Hunan in Mao's 1945 group (Group I), representing a third of the members most recently recruited into the CC (Group V). This transformation is illustrated in the following chart:

PLACE OF ORIGIN—THREE LEADING PROVINCES

	Central-South	North	
	Hunan	Shensi	Hopei
Group I	11	0	0
Group II	9	3	1
Group III	10	1	3
Group IV	9	7	5
Group V	3	3	8

From these facts, it seems safe to predict that the leadership of the future will tend to become more and more Northern in origin. The traditional hostility of Southerners to rule from the North suggests a possible diffusion of authority or even an openly divisive element for the future, one which might well be explored by students of other disciplines to see, for example, if this has affected economic planning.[9]

Shantung, Honan, Shansi, Shensi, Sinkiang, Kansu and Chinghai (though only one is known to hail from Sinkiang, and none from Kansu and Chinghai); the balance of the provinces are defined here as Central-South.

[8] For a recent article depicting—in a romanticised form—this flight to the Communist guerrilla areas, see *Selections from China Mainland Magazines* (SCMM) (Hong Kong: U.S. Consulate-General), Nos. 296 and 297, dated January 15 and January 22, 1962, respectively. These contain an article written by Li Ch'ang (Group V) for *Chung-kuo Ch'ing-nien* (*Chinese Youth*), No. 22, November 16, 1961.

[9] Several years ago, Allen S. Whiting conducted a series of interrogations of Chinese soldiers who refused repatriation to the China mainland after the Korean War (" The New Chinese Communist," *World Politics*, Vol. VII, No. 4, July 1955, pp. 592–605). Among other things, he found a high correlation of what might be termed anti-Soviet attitudes among those from the North-East, as opposed to those from the Central-South or interior provinces. These interrogations were of men with extremely

It is noteworthy that at the grass-roots level this trend towards Northern control is even more marked : eight provinces of the North and North-East, containing but one-third of the total population, now have about one-half of the Party members, and recent figures suggest that this trend continues.[10]

Lest the point has been over-emphasised, it should be recalled that the Central-Southerners still outnumber the Northerners by almost two to one. The point is not that the Northerners *now* have control of the power apparatus; rather, they are on the way to control in the near future.

Family Background and Education

Unfortunately, information on family backgrounds for the rising leaders is sorely lacking—very possibly a deliberate omission by the Communists.[11] Despite the great propagandistic emphasis on proletarian and peasant origins, it appears that the basic core of present-day leaders is on the average far above the poor-peasant or proletariat category. Inferential evidence suggests that this continues to be the case with the up-and-coming leaders. Given the lack of comprehensive data on family backgrounds, the best alternative clues are found in educational backgrounds.

If it is assumed that college-level training implies moderate prosperity, then the majority of the emerging leaders must come from well-to-do peasants or elements of the gentry. Approximately 75 per cent. of the entire CC have had some college-level training [12]—and throughout the five clusters of leaders this remains a fairly consistent figure.

A good number of Mao's original group (Group I) had some education in military academies (especially Whampoa), though more often in regular colleges. The emerging groups of the 1950s are predominantly products of regular Chinese colleges. Of interest is the fact that among

limited educational backgrounds, and while not explicitly relevant to the elite considered here, it is suggestive of attitudes which *may* prevail even at more sophisticated levels.

10 These figures are computed from the statistical information on Party membership contained in *Current Background* (CB) (Hong Kong: U.S. Consulate-General), No. 411, September 27, 1956, pp. 26–27.

11 See, for example, the who's who section in *Hsin Ming-tz'u Tz'u-tien* (*New Terminology Dictionary*) (Shanghai, 1952), pp. 9001–9026, which contains a number of brief biographical sketches. In the rare instances in which family background data is listed, it is almost always something like " poor farm " family. A similar manipulation of data in the Soviet Union is suggested by Herman Akhminov in " Obituaries as a Key to the Soviet Elite," *Bulletin* (Munich : Instititute for the Study of the USSR), Vol. VIII, No. 7, July 1961, pp 37–43. Of the 266 obituaries examined, only eighty-two listed social origin. " If it assumed that wherever the question of social extraction is ignored in the obituaries the person concerned originated from some other class than the peasantry or the proletariat, the conclusion emerges that the proportion of non-working-class origin among the Soviet elite is very high."

12 The term " college-level training " is quite uneven as used here. In a number of cases this means a fairly substantive education, including advanced graduate work. In even more instances, however, " college " is used rather charitably.

the most recent arrivals to the Central Committee (Groups IV and V) there is a fair sprinkling of Tsinghua and Peking University graduates.

COLLEGE-LEVEL TRAINING—CHINESE AND FOREIGN [13]

Group   I   —   89%
Group   II   —   77%
Group   III   —   78%
Group   IV   —   61%
Group   V   —   75%

Foreign Education and Training

While the level of education among future leaders will remain fairly high, there is a marked change in terms of foreign education. As the reader will know, Mao's original group (Group I) has a high percentage of foreign-trained persons. This drops off sharply in the succeeding groups.

FOREIGN EDUCATION AND/OR TRAINING [14]

Group   I   —   60%
Group   II   —   35%
Group   III   —   39%
Group   IV   —   39%
Group   V   —   12%

Though the Soviet Union predominates among Mao's 1945 group (Group I), France ranks as a strong second. But after Group I a French education abruptly halts—of the total 136 full and alternate CC members ranking behind Mao's group (*i.e.*, Groups II–V), only three went to France. In the entire CC today, only a handful have studied in countries other than Russia and France, and these few are fairly well confined to Germany and Japan.[15]

It seems clear, therefore, that a lack of a foreign education will begin to characterise the leaders of the late 1960s and early 1970s. Whether or not this will tend to give these men a parochial outlook remains a moot point, but one which we cannot afford to dismiss.

---

[13] Information for Groups I and II is fairly complete, but is rather inadequate for Groups III through V. The percentages used here are based on those for which information is available.

[14] See note 13.

[15] As noted above in dealing with " college-level training " (note 12), a " foreign educa-tion " must be taken with at least a partial grain of salt. For example it is often rather casually noted that such famous leaders as Chou En-lai are " French-educated." According to the preliminary findings of Dr. Conrad Brandt, who is now preparing a detailed study of the Chinese who went to France in the early 1920s, it is clear that few received more than a smattering of a higher education. According to Dr. Brandt, Nieh Jung-chen appears to be one of the few of the prominent contemporary leaders who clearly profited from a purely educational standpoint.

COUNTRY OF FOREIGN EDUCATION AND/OR TRAINING [16]

	U.S.S.R.	France	Germany	Japan	U.S.A.	Mongolia	Belgium
Group I	18	9	4	4	2	0	1
Group II	9	0	1	1	0	0	0
Group III	5	2	1	1	0	0	0
Group IV	8	1	2	1	1	1	0
Group V	1	0	0	0	0	0	0

Before leaving the topic of education, it is worth noting that this is one area where one can look two decades ahead with some confidence: by 1980 there will certainly emerge another batch of Soviet-trained Chinese leaders. That group, however, will probably be trained more in technology [17] than in military and political affairs and may well resemble some of the present-day technocrats of the Soviet Union.[18] And, of course, this trend towards a technical education will be reinforced by those educated domestically, where the emphasis is also on technology.[19]

Travel Abroad

The subject of a foreign education leads naturally to a related topic: travel abroad either as a student or in an official capacity in the past decade.[20] Here we find a number of suggestive facts. Not surprisingly, the more senior the man, the more widely he has travelled on various missions. This is graphically illustrated in the following chart.

In general, the more junior of the elite have been confined to intra-*bloc* travel. Conversely, a fairly high proportion of the senior leaders have been in technically advanced non-Communist nations, but a strikingly low percentage of the leaders introduced to the CC in the 1950s have

---

16 These figures are overlapping, *i.e.*, a number of these men went to two or more countries.

17 See John M. H. Lindbeck, "The Organisation and Development of Science," *The China Quarterly*, No. 6, April–June 1961, pp. 98–132, especially pp. 111–112. Dr. Lindbeck reports that by May 1957, 7,075 students had been sent to fourteen different countries for study, all but 500 of them to the Soviet Union. By 1960, 3,700 had returned to China following two to five years of study, with an estimated 1,200 to 1,500 having advanced degrees, " most of these in engineering and fields of applied science."

18 It has been estimated that 40 to 50 per cent. of the delegates to the 1961 CPSU Congress were engineers. (See *Science*, Vol. 135, No. 3499, January 19, 1962, p. 204.) It is obvious that not even a fraction of the Chinese counterparts have this sort of background. But it seems equally obvious that there will be a trend in this direction as the years pass and as the stress on industrialisation continues.

19 See Joseph C. Kun, " Higher Education: Some Problems of Selection and Enrolment," *The China Quarterly*, No. 8, October–December 1961, pp. 135–148, especially the table on p. 139.

20 For a more detailed treatment of this subject, see my " Peking's Leaders: A Study in Isolation," *The China Quarterly*, No. 7, July–September 1961, pp. 35–43, as well as the exceptions taken to this article in " Comment," *The China Quarterly*, No. 9, January–March 1962, p. 198.

ever seen a Western industrial nation. The percentages of those who have visited non-Communist industrial countries in Groups I through V are, respectively, 47, 38, 21, 12, and 9.

TRAVEL ABROAD [21]

	Abroad [22]	Never Abroad
Group I	33	3
Group II	24	2
Group III	23	6
Group IV	37	21
Group V	10	13

Obviously, as time passes, more of those who have not been abroad will get their chance for travel. But with the continuing East-West impasse, it is unlikely that many will have the opportunity to visit the West.

Despite much-publicised forays into South-East Asia such as the Bandung gathering, surprisingly few of the elite have been in this area. Specifically, only twenty-two (13 per cent.) of the 172 CC members and alternates in our sample have been there. In the other areas of the world —the Middle East, Africa, and the Americas—travel is negligible by all levels of the elite (nine, or 5 per cent.).

Type and Locale of Work of the CC Members

Two related questions might now be posed: what has been the major field of work of these men and where, since the régime has been established, have they been working?

To begin with a truism, up to 1949 the Party, the Bureaucracy, and the Army were virtually one and the same. Almost all of the full CC members (Groups I–III) once held a high rank in the Red Army. But with the conquest of the mainland in 1949, new problems demanded more than a military solution.[23] Already by 1949 the elite were rather evenly spread between Party, Bureaucracy (or Government) and Army channels, although the military still had a slight edge. As the régime became stabilised in the early 1950s, the elite members were increasingly assigned

21 These figures are based on information through the early days of 1962.
22 The reader will realise that a number of these men (*e.g.*, Chou En-lai) have been abroad a number of times.
23 In Mao Tse-tung's famous report to the Second Session of the Seventh CC, March 1949, he stated: " The 53,000 cadres now ready to leave with the army for the [yet ' unliberated '] south are very inadequate for the vast new areas we shall soon hold, and we must prepare to turn all the field armies, 2,100,000 strong, into a working force. . . . We must look upon the field armies with their 2,100,000 men as a gigantic school for cadres." *Selected Works of Mao Tse-tung*, Vol. IV (Peking: Foreign Languages Press, 1961), p. 363.

to non-military work, until now the Party has a clear numerical superiority, the Government bureaucrats are second, and the " People's Liberation Army " (PLA) leaders a poor third. This is illustrated in the following chart.

ELITE FUNCTIONS BY GROUPS [24]

		Party	Government	Army
Group I [25]	1949–50	11	11	13
	1962	12	16	7
Group II	1945–50	9	8	9
	1962	13	8	5
Group III	1949–50	9	7	13
	1962	17	5	7
Group IV	1949–50	15	19	24
	1962	21	19	18
Group V	1949–50	8	10	5
	1962	10	8	5

Taking the total sample (less one man), we find this breakdown.

ELITE FUNCTIONS—TOTAL SAMPLE

	1949–50	1962
Party	52	73
Government	55	56
Army	64	42

For the purposes of this article, it is probably most significant that in the more junior groupings there is a sizeable proportion—though still less than half—who have *not* held a high military rank.[26] This is rather precisely reflected in the military medals awarded in 1955.[27] In the

[24] Readers will appreciate the fact that for the 1949–50 period, it is virtually impossible to state with certainty the *main* function of any given leader, so overlapping were his tasks at that period. The assigned " functions," therefore, can only be considered a crude reckoning. By 1962, on the other hand, it is relatively easy to identify the chief tasks of the elite members.

[25] One man—Cheng Wei-san—has been deleted from this calculation. He has apparently been in ill-health from the late 1940s and living in semi-retirement.

[26] Though complete information is lacking, of the twenty-three men in Group V, it appears that only four held significant military posts prior to the Long March (1935), twelve held such posts *only* after the Long March, and that seven have no significant military record in any period.

[27] These awards were first given in September 1955. The three awards, together with the era for which they are applicable, are: Order of August 1 (1927–45); Order of Independence and Freedom (1937–45); and Order of Liberation (1946–50). For a detailed analysis of these awards, see CB. No. 368, November 15, 1955.

first four groups, about one-third received at least one medal, but in Group V—those elected in 1958—only one-sixth received awards.

Turning to locale of work, in the 1949–50 period, better than two-thirds of the total sample were working in the provinces rather than in the capital. As might be expected, most of the lower-ranked elite members were working in the provinces, whereas almost half of Mao's 1945 group (Group I) were in Peking. Then, as the period of consolidation ended between 1952 and 1954, many of these men gravitated to Peking, until today 70 per cent. of the CC members and alternates are in Peking. These points are illustrated in the following two charts.

ELITE LOCALE BY GROUPS

			Capital	Provinces
Group	I [28]	1949–50	16	19
		1962	35	0
Group	II	1949–50	11	15
		1962	22	4
Group	III	1949–50	11	18
		1962	20	9
Group	IV	1949–50	10	48
		1962	33	25
Group	V	1949–50	3	20
		1962	10	13

ELITE LOCALE—TOTAL SAMPLE [28]

	1949–50	1962
Capital	51	120
Provinces	120	51

Of course, gravitation to the national capital and away from military work are not characteristics peculiar to Communist China. Projecting into the future, it would seem that junior elite members will mainly get their training in the provinces, but this training will tend to be in non-military rather than military work.

Having made this point—that is, a shift away from the PLA to work in the Party or Government—a contradiction arises. But an amplification of this contradiction suggests the primacy of the Party, which in turn points to the Party as the most frequently used path to power of future

[28] One man—Cheng Wei-san—has been deleted from these calculations. See note 25.

leaders.   In the early 1950s, the top post in the provincial military districts—that of political commissar—was usually held by a Party veteran, who very often doubled as the ranking provincial Party Secretary.[29]   Then, in the more relaxed mid-1950s, the job of political commissar was entrusted to lesser figures who were essentially military men. Or, to put it another way, by the mid-1950s, there was more specialisation —Army figures worked mainly in Army affairs and Party figures in Party affairs.[30]   But since 1958—or the period coinciding with the Great Leap Forward and the communes—there are at least eight instances in which CC members or alternates have been made political commissar within their provinces.[31]   That is not to say that they have been moved *from* Peking to the provinces, but rather they have taken on this post as an additional task *within* their provinces.   Such suggestions of Party primacy are probably not lost on younger elite members in search of ways to advance their careers.[32]

The Military

Previously the point has been made that as the régime has been consolidated, fewer of the elite have been engaged in purely military duties. While this is true in the sense of a nose-count of the CC members, it would probably be incorrect to project from this that the military will play only a minor role.   For one thing, events have caught up with the personalities and power struggles; modern military technology compels all nations to readjust constantly their military strategy and, as capabilities permit, their weaponry.   But there are, apparently, obstacles in China to such readjustments.   Alice Hsieh, for example, has observed that PLA adherence to Maoist guerrilla doctrines has made it difficult for Chinese military and political leaders " . . . to grasp and then to assert

---

29 In the 1953 period at least thirteen political commissars of provincial military districts served concurrently as the ranking Party Secretary.   On the other hand, only two provincial military district commanders served concurrently as the ranking Secretary. It is on this evidence, in part, that the assertion is made that the political commissar was the ranking figure in the provinces.

30 See note 24.

31 Province is used here loosely.   Specifically, the men and the posts involved are as follows: T'ao Chu, Kwangtung First Secretary, as Political Commissar of the Canton Military Region; Yeh Fei, Fukien First Secretary, as Foochow Military Region Political Commissar; Chiang Wei-ch'ing, Kiangsu First Secretary, as Kiangsu Military District (MD) Political Commissar; Wu Te, Kirin First Secretary, as Kirin MD Political Commissar; Huang Huo-ch'ing, Liaoning First Secretary, as Liaoning MD Political Commissar; Chang P'ing-hua, Hunan First Secretary, as Hunan MD Political Commissar; Ch'en P'i-hsien, a Secretary of the Shanghai Party Committee, as Shanghai Garrison Command Political Commissar; and, Liu Jen, Second Secretary of the Peking Party Committee, as Peking Garrison Command Political Commissar.

32 In addition to the partial counter-shift of Party leaders being returned, in part, to military assignments, there are signs of a counter-development to the general trend of gravitation from the provinces to Peking.   In 1954 the Party abolished six regional bureaux which, structurally, stood between the provinces and the Party Centre.   Then in early 1961 these were recreated " . . . to act for the CC in strengthening leadership over the Party committees in the various provinces, municipalities and autonomous

the strategic import of nuclear weapons." [33]   As Mao and the Long Marchers pass from the scene, one might look for a resurgence of the importance of the modern military planners and their close allies, the modern scientists.

There is another aspect of the military establishment which should be mentioned. Noting that by 1970 there will be 3–400,000,000 more Chinese than in 1949, and that food shortages may endanger the security of the régime as a consequence, one might reasonably assume that the role of the public security forces will grow in importance. In general, it seems fair to hold that in the past decade the régime has relied more on persuasion than coercion.[34] Now, however, we may be on the eve of a period where the specialists in persuasion will tend to give way to the specialists in coercion.[35] Perhaps the appointment of Lo Jui-ch'ing as PLA Chief of Staff was a harbinger of things to come. Prior to this Lo doubled as Minister of Public Security and Commander and Political Commissar of the Public Security Forces. In this respect, we may find a reversal of the pattern in the Soviet Union where under Stalin the secret police reigned supreme, only to be replaced in influence by the regular army after Khrushchev came to power.[36]

The above lines border on a prediction of a coming Stalinist period in the dreaded sense of that phrase. Although it would be rash to make such an unqualified supposition, the evidence available does seem to suggest that the Chinese face a period of domestic rigours, to use a rather

regions." (For the text, see *The China Quarterly*, No. 6, April–June 1961, pp. 184–186.) Although the evidence is slim, it is of interest that at least three members of the elite who had been working in Peking have been sent to provincial areas as ranking figures in the regional bureaux. The outstanding example is that of Sung Jen-ch'iung (Group II) who has been made First Secretary of the North-East Bureau.

33 Alice Langley Hsieh, *Communist China's Strategy in the Nuclear Era* (Englewood Cliffs, New Jersey: Prentice-Hall, 1962), p. 9. This quotation may do an injustice to Mrs. Hsieh's overall thesis. She holds, for example, that there has been an awareness of the import of nuclear weapons since at least 1954 (p. 23), and that the debate over the appropriate military posture has been a vigorous one (*passim*).

34 H. F. Schurmann has put it this way: " Though external control systems are important, more important is internal group control through cadre supervision and group indoctrination. Significant is the relatively minor role played by the secret police. The Chinese communists have always held it crucial to manipulate and control an organised group from within, rather than simply to maintain a firm hold on the group through external coercion." (" The Roots of Social Policy," Reprint No. 12, Centre for Chinese Studies, Institute of International Studies, University of California, p. 165; reprinted from *Survey*, No. 38, October 1961.)

35 In the past year, the régime has moved to a more " liberal " position on many fronts, and " persuasion " still appears far more important than naked coercion as a system of control. This writer would be the last to deny the skilled tactical manoeuvrings of the elite, but the acid test might arise if the population outruns the food supply on a grand scale. At such a juncture there is little doubt that open coercion would be used if it meant the security of the régime.

36 For an interesting development of this theme, see W. W. Rostow, " Russia and China Under Communism," *World Politics*, Vol. VII, No. 4, July 1955, pp. 513—531, especially pages 522–525.

mild term.   It remains for us to attempt to consider such a possibility
within the framework of the ruling elite.

Party Cohesiveness after Mao

It is difficult to imagine the continued high degree of cohesiveness of
the Party after Mao's death.   No matter how carefully the succession
may be planned, any form of collective leadership could easily lead to
the rapid rise and fall of top elite members.[37]   To use 1970 as a crude
target date, there will still be many who owe their rise directly to Mao,
but after he passes from the scene they may be less certain of whom to
transfer their personal allegiance, if such is required.[38]

The Purge

There are already signs that the purge may become widespread, and
the historical odds suggest an acceleration following Mao's death.   Despite
the notoriety of the Kao Kang-Jao Shu-shih purge of 1954–55, it is a
fact that there have been more elite-level Party purges or " semi-purges "
in the past six years than in the first seven years of the Communist
régime.   The term " semi-purge " is used for those who were severely
criticised and stripped of some (but not all) of their posts (*e.g.*, Ku
Ta-ts'un).   In a number of identifiable cases, some were given lesser
posts, but their hopes for a future career were probably dashed by their
political errors.

These purges seem to have resulted from policy disputes or personal
power struggles.   Yet it is important to note that *the purge need not be
interpreted as a sign of weakness unless it assumes great proportions.*
It may play havoc with the neat order of elite seniority, but within the
value system of the Communists this has little relevance.   In absolute
numbers, the already huge Party is growing rapidly; correspondingly,
the standards of membership and advancement are rising, thereby allowing the top elite to have a greater range of selection from among the
up-and-coming elite members.[39]   From this viewpoint, the " selective
purge " may represent a mark of efficiency rather than weakness.

[37] Some readers may find comfort in Rostow's suggestion (*ibid.*, p. 531) that it is
" . . . much harder to organise and plan aggression when many voices make high
policy and when command over resources is diffuse."
[38] The necessity of a personal allegiance to Mao can only be guessed at.   One set of
facts urges that Mao put his imprimatur on several leaders raised to the Politburo and
to Central Committee alternate status in 1958.   Over the 1957–58 winter, Mao travelled
extensively throughout China.   Seemingly he came into personal contact with five or
six regional leaders who were subsequently elevated to the Central Committee in
May 1958.   More significant, however, is the fact that he apparently had personal
contacts with Li Ching-ch'üan and K'o Ch'ing-shih, both of whom were elevated
to the Politburo.   The cases of Li and K'o stand out if only because they were jumped
over dozens of other leaders, *including* six alternate Politburo members.
[39] Lasswell has observed that " . . . in crises . . . old ways of doing things rapidly grow
obsolete, and leaders are superannuated at a faster rate than usual."   Harold D.
Lasswell, Daniel Lerner, and G. Easton Rothwell, *The Comparative Study of Elites,*

Unifying Experiences

Not only will the leaders of the 1970s lack *the* unifying man (assuming, of course, that Mao will be dead), but they will also lack the common experiences and hardships shared by so many of the early leaders. Consider, for example, the Long March. An overwhelming majority of Mao's core group of 1945 (Group I) took part in this historic retreat, but only one-third of the most junior elite members (Group V) participated.[40] Although it is beyond proof and quite speculative, it may be that the passing of the Long Marchers may also mark the passing of the remarkable cohesiveness that has so characterised the Chinese Communist Party. This torturous adventure seems to have created a bond between these leaders as no other single event has. In part, this seems borne out by the numerous articles published in the recent past exalting this event. To readers of this journal, one need only mention some of the other dramatic events shared by many of the present top-level leaders: the May 4 Movement, the Northern Expedition, anti-Japanese resistance, and the triumphant victory over Chiang Kai-shek. Probably the most commonly shared event of the elite of the 1970s will be the rather dreary chapter of the Korean War, or the even more dreary lists of production statistics.

Bureaucratic Reshuffling

Domestically, the problems of running an increasingly industrialised nation may create a constant shuffle among the elite as the régime searches for the right persons to make the administrative machinery function properly. There seems to be a widespread impression that the central government bureaucracy—that is, the State Council—has been highly stable. One set of figures suggests exactly the contrary: since 1949, there have been no less than 67 different ministries headed by 101 ministers.[41] Most of these numerous changes have come within the

An Introduction and Bibliography (Stanford Un. Press, 1952), p. 9. See also some interesting observations on the purge by Robert C. North, "Recruiting Policies of the Chinese Communist Party," mimeographed, 14 pages, prepared for delivery at the 1961 Annual Meeting of the American Political Science Association, St. Louis, September 6–9, 1961.

40 Information on those who made the Long March is somewhat lacking in Groups III through V. The estimated percentages for those who made the Long March is 61, 62, 62, 52 and 35 for Groups I through V, respectively. Group I would be raised to 78 per cent. if those who were ordered to stay behind were included, and to 92 per cent. if those then in Moscow were included.

41 The number of ministries over the past thirteen years has averaged about thirty-five; currently there are thirty-nine. From 1949 to 1954, the cabinet was known as the Government Administration Council; after 1954 as the State Council. "Ministry" as used here also includes the "Commissions" which are on the same level. However, bureaus (*e.g.*, the State Statistical Bureau) are not included. Any given ministry will have about five to ten Vice-Ministers. If the constant shuffling of these Vice-Ministers were added to the figure for the Ministers, the total might well approach 1,000 different men in the past thirteen years.

economic ministries. If economic difficulties persist, especially in the
agricultural sector (and this writer holds that they will), then it would
seem fair to assume that there will be a continuing shuffle within the
government machinery that may break many a rising leader.[42]

The Non-Communist Intellectuals

There is still another problem in executive management that will
arise: the passing of the non-Communist Party intellectuals, many of
whom have excellent technical backgrounds. No doubt some have been
purely figureheads, but others apparently have been effectively utilised
by the régime. Li Szu-kuang, an internationally known geologist and
Minister of Geology, is an example of such a man. The reader will
recall that in 1949 the Communists gave a number of important posts to
non-Communists. Specifically, in the 1949 cabinet, eleven of the twenty-
four portfolios were held by non-Communists such as Mao Tun.[43] Now,
however, less than a third (twelve out of thirty-nine) of the cabinet
ministers are non-Communists.[44] Equally important is the fact that
this is an elderly group—their average age being sixty-eight years. It is
unlikely, for example, that the Communists have available from the
Party ranks a man to fill the shoes of the above-mentioned Li Szu-kuang
who is now seventy-three. It will probably be two decades before the
Chinese Communists can efficiently replace a number of such senior non-
Communists who have lent their talents for the past thirteen years.[45]

Conclusion

There is a certain pretentiousness in trying to project some (but many
more unknown) factors a decade into the future. But granting these
shortcomings, one might expect the situation to develop along these
broad lines.

Within the near future there will be a rapid turnover at the very
top levels, with the succeeding echelon being itself rather old. Within

[42] As in the case with the purges (see note 39 above), unless a personal reshuffle assumes
great proportions, it may be possible to interpret any given change as a mark of
increasing efficiency rather than the reverse.

[43] Of the eleven, seven were leaders of the various " democratic parties," three were
intellectuals or " democratic personages," and one was an ex-Kuomintang general.

[44] Technically, only ten of the thirty-nine are non-Communists, two " democratic personages " (Li Szu-kuang and Mme. Li Te-ch'üan) having been granted Party membership in late 1958 as a reward for their steadfastness during the 1957–58 *cheng feng*
campaign. This has been ignored in the basic calculation above as an obvious
gesture having no importance in the higher reaches of Party policy making.

[45] This fact has not been lost upon the Communists. See, for example, " On the Problem
of the Relationship Between Young and Old Intellectuals," in *People's Daily (Jen-min
Jih-pao)*, August 26, 1961 ; translated in *Survey of China Mainland Press* (Hong Kong :
U.S. Consulate-General), No. 2573, September 7, 1961, pp. 14–19. Essentially, the
article is a plea for co-operation between the young and the old, " especially between
the young intellectuals among Party members on the one hand and the veteran
professors and veteran experts who are not Party members on the other."

ten years, there is likely to be a sudden breakthrough with the emergence of a host of younger figures. These newcomers will be the products of the post-Sino-Japanese War, will increasingly hail from the North, and will be fairly well educated. Propaganda notwithstanding, the top elite will (given Chinese standards) continue to hail from families of some means. There will be fewer directly acquainted with the outside world (especially the non-*bloc* nations) either through education abroad or travel in more mature years, and therefore possibly more parochial in outlook.

The Party machinery—as opposed to the Government or Army—will be the most widely used avenue for advancement, though the modern military planners and the police may grow in power. But at this same time—roughly a decade ahead—there will likely be observable signs of emerging technocrats whose allegiance may be more to their disciplines than to Communism or nationalism. Such factors as material reward and public prestige will probably serve as greater incentives to these men than Maoism or whatever ideological shifts may replace Maoism.

The elite will probably lack a unifying or charismatic leader as symbolised by Mao, which could lead to widespread (though not necessarily damaging) purges and a constant reshuffle within the administrative hierarchies. In addition to a unifying leader, a unifying event—as symbolised by the Long March—will be absent. Finally, the elite will also be shorn of the talents of many of the non-Communists who will pass from the scene.

FINAL NOTE AND BIBLIOGRAPHY

A few final words may be in order in terms of research and bibliography. First is the comment that the sharpest cleavage in backgrounds comes between Groups IV and V (those elected to alternate CC membership in 1956 and 1958, respectively). This seems to be a clear breaking point between the fairly familiar past and the uncertain future; it may serve as a useful focal point for further investigation. The problem is complicated, of course, by the fact that it is far more difficult to get information on the younger members of the Central Committee than on the older ones.

In attempting to develop correlations, the writer ran into a number of *culs-de-sac*, a few of which are worth noting. An attempt to find information on the age-old problem of nepotism proved fruitless—very possibly because it may not exist to any important degree. For example, the few wives of any political importance (*e.g.*, Mmes. Li Fu-ch'un and Chou En-lai) seem to be in high places on their own merits. Information on elite offspring is almost totally lacking.

Although it is easy to list those who belong to the national minority groups, there are no indications that this has posed a serious problem at the elite level. Information on language abilities (including Chinese dialects) is sorely lacking. Data on the personal ties that may exist between leaders or factions is a research problem of no small magnitude. An exhaustive study of organisational structures and the personnel involved may be one approach to this difficult problem. A similarly vast study stressing content analysis of speeches needs to be undertaken.

In addition to the lack of much data, there is a serious problem of conflicting information. To cite but one of hundreds of examples, three different birthdates are listed for Liu Shao'ch'i in *Communist* publications dated *within a three-year period*.

In an article which stresses biographical information, it is virtually impossible to footnote each statement in terms of sources, especially when broad correlations are manipulated. Therefore, it would be fitting to close with a listing of the chief sources of information. First and foremost has been the information found in the Chinese press sources and compiled over the years by the writer. In terms of reference works, by far the best single volume (though somewhat dated) is *Gendai Chugoku Jinmei Jiten* (*A Who's Who of Contemporary Chinese*), edited by the Kasumigaseki Association (Tokyo: 1957). Another Japanese source of value is *Chuka Jinmin Kyowakoku Soshikibetsu Jinmei Hyo* (*Organisational Directory of the Chinese People's Republic*), published at intervals by the Research Council of the Japanese Cabinet, the latest edition of which is 1959. A parallel work in English is *Directory of Party and Government Officials of Communist China* (Washington: Department of State, July 20, 1960). A very valuable source is the biographic series published regularly by the Union Research Institute in Hong Kong. Another series of some value is the *Asia Who's Who* (latest edition, 1960), published by the Pan-Asia Newspaper Alliance, Hong Kong. Information found in early " official " Communist sources (*e.g.*, *Hsin Mingtz'u Tz'u-tien*, see note 11 above) has been fairly well incorporated into the various non-Communist sources cited above.

Organisational Principles of the Chinese Communists

By H. F. SCHURMANN

THE countries of Asia and Africa have seen the rise of numerous and powerful socio-political movements during the past few decades, movements which have shaken existing orders and have launched these nations on the road of modernisation. Although these movements have almost always been nationalist in character during the early phases of revolution, subsequently leftist radical movements have arisen; most of these have been Communist.

Both the nationalists and the Communists have shown themselves capable of eliciting great collective response from the peoples on whom they have acted. But in regard to one essential mechanism of political action, the nationalists have shown themselves far weaker and less adept than the Communists. That mechanism is *organisation*.

Almost without exception, where the Communists have arisen, they have established disciplined, effective, structured movements, capable of quick and sustained political action, and, perhaps of even more importance, of moving in and mobilising inert masses of people. In those countries of Asia in which the Communists have seized power (China and her smaller neighbours, North Korea and North Vietnam), they have even further extended this propensity for organisation.

The case of Communist China is perhaps the most extraordinary of all. At the moment of victory, the Chinese Communists were in possession of a powerful, battle-tested army and a highly disciplined party. But they also faced a huge land area, wracked by almost a half-century of war, a poverty-stricken population, disorganised masses of people, and the total collapse of government. Within ten years, Communist China has become one of the most powerful nations on the globe. A programme of rapid industrialisation has been launched. Disorganised masses have been transformed into organised masses toiling at monumental construction projects. And, negatively speaking, there is not the slightest indication that the iron grip of the régime is seriously threatened by internal rifts or internal protest.

If one were asked for the magic key to this phenomenal feat, the answer would have to be *organisation*: the ordered mobilisation, control, and manipulation of people for certain ends. Not only organisation in a limited sense, but *total organisation*: the spread of a tight web of organisation over a land of 650,000,000 people. In this article, we shall examine some of the central principles of organisation of the Chinese Communists, principles which might be termed a practical ideology of organisation.

Despite the massive nature and far-reaching extent of organisation in Communist China, there exists a remarkable uniformity in this great structure, a uniformity possible only in a totalitarian society. This uniformity results not only from the persistence of established structures, but through the operation of certain basic organisational principles. These organisational principles derive from the organisational theories and practices of Lenin and the Bolsheviks. However, there are elements in these principles that are distinctly Chinese, elements which were infused as a result of the concrete experiences of the Chinese Communists during the pre-1949 period when they were the leaders only of a revolutionary movement.

There are two elements which are central to the practical ideology of the Chinese Communists: (1) the theory of contradictions, and (2) the theory of democratic centralism. The theory of contradictions has been elevated to the level of supreme dogma in Communist China. It is regarded as the key to the proper understanding of all phenomena. Chinese Communist theoreticians lay more emphasis than their Russian colleagues on the all-pervasive nature of contradictions in the world. They see action and behaviour as the result of the resolution of these contradictions. The principle of democratic centralism is treated as a derivative of the theory of contradictions. It is the theory of the " contradictory " principles of democracy *and* centralism. The theory of democratic centralism finds direct expression in the organisational structure of Communist China. If the theory of contradictions represents what one might call a metaphysics of organisation, the theory of democratic centralism is the basic theory of organisation itself.

THE THEORY OF CONTRADICTIONS

The theory of contradictions has played a prominent part in the official ideology of the Chinese Communists since the publication of Mao Tse-tung's famous article *On Contradiction*.[1] This article became supremely important in Chinese Communist ideology after the publication of Mao Tse-tung's February 1957 speech *On the Correct Resolution of Contradictions among the People* [NCNA, June 18, 1957]. The reasons behind the original formulation of the theory of contradictions undoubtedly related to the real contradictions which the Communists faced during the early years of their nationalistic United Front policy—

---

[1] See his *Selected Works* (London: Lawrence & Wishart, 1954), Vol. II.

contradictions between the radical revolutionary aims and actions of the Party and the call for a class-transcending alliance against the Japanese.

However, as one reads the literature on organisation which began to appear in China during the Yenan period, in particular the writings of Liu Shao-ch'i, who, much more than Mao himself, deals explicitly with the theory and practice of organisation, it emerges that the theory of contradictions gradually became a device—an ideological device—out of which a complex but highly practical theory of organisation was created.[2] This theory, in almost all essential respects, anticipates the definitive formulation of the theory in the February 1957 speech. There were definite practical considerations—the Hungarian Revolt and the need for a new "rectification" movement—which prompted Mao to make that speech then. But in essence the speech simply outlined in clear-cut terms a theory which had become deeply rooted in Chinese Communist thinking long before that.

Mao stated in the speech that there were two types of contradictions, antagonistic and non-antagonistic. The former are the classic contradictions of Marxist ideology, contradictions between hostile classes and hostile social systems, " the contradictions between the enemy and ourselves." These contradictions cannot be resolved except by force; these contradictions are the very substance of the inexorable process of history.

But non-antagonistic contradictions are of a different sort. They occur within Socialist society. In fact, although this is not stated explicitly, they seem to be a part of the very fabric of Socialist society. For Stalin, the so-called non-antagonistic contradictions were basically technological in nature, contradictions which arose out of discrepancies between the "relations of production" and "the productive forces of society," in other words contradictions due to the "advanced nature" of the Soviet social system and the "backward nature" of its economic structure.

However, the non-antagonistic contradictions of the Chinese Communists are much more than mere technological discrepancies. They are, as Mao puts it, "the contradictions between the interests of the nation and the collective on the one hand, and those of individuals on the other, the contradictions of democracy and centralism, the contradictions between leaders and led, between the bureaucratic tendencies of certain individuals who work in the bureaucracy and the masses."

Contradictions, in the Hegelian-Marxian scheme, demand resolution, and the lineal progression of contradiction—resolution—contradiction makes up the process of history. The mode of resolution for each of

---

[2] Almost all of the known writings and speeches of Liu prior to 1949 deal with problems of organisation, discipline, training, etc.

these two contradictions is different. For the former—antagonistic—it is essentially violent. For the latter—non-antagonistic—it is essentially non-violent, through the process of " discussion, criticism, and education."

There is no question that the timing and the substance of Mao's speech on contradictions related to certain practical problems which had arisen. As we now know, the Hungarian Revolt made a deep impression on the Chinese, particularly the intellectuals, and had led to serious questions being raised on the relations of the leadership to the masses in Communist society. Furthermore, the old, recurrent organisational enemy " bureaucratism " had again shown itself. The beginnings of a " rectification " movement were already apparent in the widespread movement for the decentralisation of cadres (the *hsia-fang*) movement— a movement to transfer urban cadres to rural areas.

But aside from the practical significance of the speech, it also had great theoretical importance, for it expressed formally a mode of thinking already basic to practice. This mode of thinking is perhaps nowhere more clearly expressed than in the writings of Liu Shao-ch'i. In a talk given some time between 1941 and 1945, Liu began a long and detailed explication of principles of organisation and discipline with the statements : " What is the organisational structure of the Party? As with other things, it is a contradictory structure, it is a contradictory unity. . . ." In this speech, Liu applies the dialectic to an analysis of the internal structure and functioning of the Party. The basic contradictory polarisation in Party organisation, he maintains, is that between " centralism " and " democracy," between the leaders and the led. Correct resolution of the contradictions which therefore arise gives life and lineal development to the organisation. Incorrect resolutions—incorrect intra-party struggles, so to speak—would lead to its destruction.[3] The theory of contradictions as applied to organisation thus presupposes a precarious structure in which the opposition of forces and counter-forces produces tension. The structure can only be maintained by a continuous process of correct resolution of the contradictions and removal of the tensions.

Mao Tse-tung entitled his speech *On the Correct Resolution of Contradictions among the People*. We have already spoken of contradictions and resolution, but the word " correct " must not be overlooked. For every contradiction, there can only be a single correct resolution, for the contradictions are objective and the laws of history are objective.

---

[3] One of the most interesting discussions on organisation is this little-known speech by Liu given some time between 1941 and 1945. To my knowledge, this speech, entitled " Training in Organisation and Discipline," *Tsu-chih-shang ho chi-lü-shang ti hsiu-yang*, was never published in China, but was printed and circulated by the Malayan Communists (publication date of April 5, 1952).

Of course, what seems correct today may, in the light of a more exact analysis of the laws of history, prove incorrect tomorrow.[4] Such correctness not only springs out of metaphysical determinedness, but more specifically out of what Mao calls " the fundamental consensus as to the interests of the People." But what is this consensus? It is consciousness of the true interests of the People. Given the Leninist theory of the vanguard, to which the Chinese Communists undeviatingly adhere, it is the Party which emerges as the infallible and supremely competent interpreter of this consensus. The " correctness " of the resolution thus relates to the role of absolute and supreme authority held by the Party. It is natural for contradictions to seek resolution, but only the Party can guarantee correctness.

This syndrome of interacting and counteracting forces in a context of absolute authority is perhaps the most important aspect of the organisational model of the Chinese Communists. It is this syndrome which gives Chinese Communist organisation both flexibility and rigidity, which at times makes it appear monolithic and at other times dynamic. It is an organisational model which expects simultaneously abject submission from all echelons and along with this spontaneity and creativity. In its structure it is dialectical, for it is " contradictory," as Liu Shao-ch'i says. And as such it produces tensions, the benign contradictions of the " non-antagonistic " sort. These contradictions find resolution in the various rectifying actions instituted by the Absolute Authority: mass movements, criticism and self-criticism, " rectification " movements and so on. If in the above sections we have dealt with what may be called the ideology of organisation, we must now proceed to organisation itself. And here the two crucial principles are " democratic centralism." We say two because in the Chinese context " democratic centralism " becomes two nouns, " democracy and centralism," the two contradictory principles of democracy and centralism, as Liu Shao-ch'i says. We must further, in order to understand properly the operations of organisation here, completely lay aside any notions we have as to the meaning of the word " democracy." For the Chinese Communists, " democracy " has real and important meaning, albeit a meaning which has nothing to do with what is understood by this term in the West. For the Chinese Communists, all organisational structure and function must operate according to the principles of democracy and centralism. Let us first discuss centralism, familiar enough in its Soviet context.

---

[4] In the talk " Training in Organisation and Discipline " Liu admits that it is possible even for the majority of the Central Committee to be wrong. As an example, he cites the Sian Incident, where " it was a minority of geniuses and far-sighted men who perceived the march of history " (p. 12).

CENTRALISM

The operation of the principle of centralism has seen the creation of a web of organisation with vertical chains of command which ultimately merge, like the apex of a pyramid, at the very top. Although at a few key points, a certain form of horizontal contact and communication can and does occur, for the most part commands move downward and information moves upward, all along vertical lines. Organisational charts give a graphic picture of the web of organisation for the country as a whole, but the actual operation of centralism may perhaps be seen most easily on the lowest level of organisation, at the point where organisation is in direct contact with the masses. For this purpose, let us consider the organisational structure and function of a " party primary group "— the most basic nucleus of party organisation—in an hypothetical factory. The Chinese Communists (like the Russians) place their nuclei of organisation in some existing organisation, whether social, economic, ecological or other, such as a factory, a school, a military unit, a village and so on. These are known as " primary units of production or terri- tory." Thus in the case of our hypothetical factory, the party primary organisation (also so called in the U.S.S.R.) exists only in the factory; its members are drawn from the factory alone and its activities relate only to the factory. Aside from intra-unit communication, its only official contacts are with higher party echelons.

In a large industrial unit, the party primary group may consist of enough members so that there will be some structuring along echelon lines within the primary group. Such structuring will always follow the principle of centralism. Party branches will be set up in each of the " shops "—below the branches there will be the party small groups, the most basic of all organisational groups. A series of such shop branches will be under the control of a general branch. The cadres of the general branch form the members of the executive committee of the party primary group. Within the party organisation in the factory, supreme control rests in this committee, and ultimately in the hands of the party secre- tary. The only real decision-making power within the context of the party primary group rests with the executive committee. Party rules and organisational handbooks specify periodic delegate meetings at various higher levels. Although there is every reason to believe that no impor- tant decisions are made at these meetings, there is also every reason to believe that these meetings, like mass meetings in general, have other important organisational functions.

If hierarchical structuring is crucial to centralism at all levels, there is another dimension to centralism which is of great importance: leader- ship. Few organisational problems have been discussed more seriously in Chinese Communist literature than the problem of leadership. No society can undergo rapid change without a great corps of leaders to direct and carry out changes. Leaders may be born, but the Chinese Communists operate with the conviction that they can be made. Leadership ability is one of the requisites for membership in the party. Prospective members and candidate members must have demonstrated not only absolute political loyalty, but leadership ability. They must be able to influence and lead the masses in practical tasks such as mass movements, propaganda and agitation, work brigades and so on. The term *kanpu*—cadre—means, in fact, a leader, an organiser, a person who holds command and authority in a given organisational setting. Liu Shao-ch'i has spoken and written at length on " training for leadership." In the specific context of our hypothetical party group, the principle of leadership demands that each party grouping, whatever small group or branch or committee at whatever level, be headed by a defined leader. There must be collective leadership, say the Communists, but there must also be individual responsibility. The group leader is the direct link in the chain between the group and higher echelons. It is from him that higher party directives are transmitted to the group members. As leader and as crucial link in the chain, the group leader possesses immense authority. It is through his authority and through the more " positive " elements around him that control from above extends downward. But, as we shall show, there is a control from below, control of a certain and limited type, of course.

During the early years, both before and after victory, cadres were divided into party and non-party cadres. A large segment of party membership consisted of peasants of low literacy and no technical competence. As a result, the régime was compelled to make wide use of individuals who possessed the requisite competence to act as organisational leaders, but who were not party members. However, through training and education, and through selective recruitment, the general qualitative level of party members has been considerably raised over the past ten years. Therefore, the ratio of non-party to party cadres has been declining. More and more of the top bureaucrats in industry are now party members. The tolerance of minority parties does not seem to involve tolerance of a vast non-party cadre group in the country, such as the technocratic group in the U.S.S.R.

Another example of the tendency to merge organisational cadre with party membership may be cited. When the communes were formed, instructions were issued to place party members in key cadre positions or to recruit leadership personnel into the party. However, this does not mean that in a factory, for example, the director is also head of the party unit. Judging from scattered information, the party secretary usually has a full-time job, and is usually distinct from the directors, either of management or of the " trade union." However, inasmuch as the top people of management and the union are party members, they participate—and in a most important way—in party meetings. Thus, on the one hand, the party maintains an organisation separate from and parallel with the organisational lines of management (which are subordinate to the relevant ministry) and with the unions (which are linked with a given " industrial union "); but on the other hand, the frequency of what the Chinese Communists call " double roles " (holding party membership and at the same time some other position in organisation) has brought about an important meshing of the three organisational sectors of our hypothetical factory. It is in the party meeting that top party people, top management people, and top union people meet together. It is undoubtedly at such meetings that the most important decisions are made.

DEMOCRACY

If the operation of the principle of centralism has created hierarchical structurings with defined leadership at all levels—the skeletal framework of a totalitarian society—the dialectical opposite of centralism, " democracy," also has great organisational functions. As a whole, in the organisational handbooks, a straightforward definition of " democracy " is avoided in favour of a more elliptical treatment in terms of yet another duality of principles: " centralism on a democratic basis " and " democracy under centralised leadership." This, of course, avoids the obvious embarrassment of dealing with " freedom " without the qualification of " necessity." However, despite the tortuous road which the Communist ideologues follow in treating these principles, " democracy " plays an important part in Chinese Communist organisational thinking and practice.

In one organisational handbook, three important functions of active intra-party democracy are singled out. First, sufficiently broad intra-party democracy will permit individual party members and local party organisations to develop " positivism " and " creativity." The development of these qualities is important for they are requisites for leadership capacity. Secondly, the broad development of intra-party democracy will strengthen ties between the party and the masses. If the active participation of all party members in party life is assured, in particular if " criticism " of party cadres is permitted, then this will act to counter the tendencies of " subjectivism " and " bureaucratism." Furthermore, such close ties between party and masses will assure that the " opinions and demands " of the masses are " reflected " at all times to the party organisation. Thirdly, broadening of intra-party democracy permits regional party organisations to solve problems " according to the special conditions in their own particular work areas." This independent problem-solving makes it possible to adapt party directives " to all kinds of dissimilar conditions of time, place, and circumstance." [5]

In a typically concise way, the organisational handbook has explained the three major functions of " democracy." Before going on to an analysis of the actual nature of " democracy," let us consider these three functions. " Positivism " and " creativity " are favourite terms in organisational literature. " Positivism " in many ways is the Chinese counterpart of the Soviet " *aktivnost*." However, there seem to be differences, which become more apparent when one considers the paired term " creativity." " Positivism " and " creativity " demand not only enthusiastic, absolute obedience from individuals, but demand what might be called creative obedience, the capacity to make decisions of an independent nature but absolutely in accord with the intent of a party resolution. In other words, initiative, spontaneity, willingness to make decisions are attributes of " positivism " and " creativity." Blind obedience, as Liu Shao-ch'i has stated, is not what the party expects from its members.

The second point stresses participation in party life and criticism of cadres as important mechanisms for combating " bureaucratism." In a sense, every one of the party's many " rectification " movements has been directed to the problem of " bureaucratism." Bureaucratism may be described as the over-perfect functioning of centralised control—excessive centralism as it has been described in the literature. The party bureaucrat functions in perfect accord with the directives of the party, but in the process his work becomes mere routine and he loses his ability to make independent decisions. He depends increasingly on his position of power and on the formal rules of his office to enforce his will.

In such situations, the party senses trouble: alienation of the party from the masses, stagnation of party work and so on. Through clever manipulation, a programme of " criticism and self-criticism " is launched against the offending bureaucrat. In the regularly scheduled party meetings, certain individuals will arise and commence the criticism. Usually, the target will know that the criticism has been arranged. He cannot fight it, not only because the party at higher echelons is immediately behind it, but because criticism and self-criticism are legitimate institutions within the system (" everybody is subject to criticism "). The process of criticism may proceed for a short or long period. Either the critics will be able to arouse their target from his bureaucratic stupor and reinvigorate him with the spirit of " positivism " and " creativity "; or the erring bureaucrat will be dismissed. Though

[5] *Questions and Answers on the Program of the Chinese Communist Party* (*Chung-kuo Kung-ch'an-tang kang-ling wen-ta*) (Peking, 1957), pp. 80–84.

the Chinese Communists have never been involved in the bloody purges of party and bureaucracy which were instituted in the U.S.S.R. in the 1930s, in a sense a continuous purge goes on all the time. These are periodically interspersed with large-scale purge movements, the so-called "rectification" movements. Though rectification sometimes aims at cleaning out politically unreliable elements, more often its aim is to stir up bureaucracies become stagnant through routine.

The third point made by the handbook stresses the importance of "democracy" in allowing regional and local party organisations to make independent decisions in the framework of the particular problems which they encounter. Here again, not "blind obedience," but initiative, is demanded from party cadres.

One of the extraordinary characteristics of organisation in Communist China has been its flexibility, a flexibility apparently greater than that in the bureaucracies of the U.S.S.R. The source of this flexibility is "democracy," just as "centralism" is the source of rigidity. This flexibility manifests itself in the expectation of considerable independence on the part of local cadres, though, of course, on a basis of absolute commitment to the party. The Communists stress that "democracy" means the rights of individual organisation members to express their opinions, to criticise, to participate in party meetings, to take part in collective decision-making and so on. The common thread which runs through all these "rights" is the "right" to participate, to be present at all meetings. This is in fact the crucial requisite of "democracy." For it is through participation that the full effect of indoctrination, group pressure, involvement through work—all the various devices through which an individual can be bound behaviourally, ideationally, and emotionally to a group and a cause—exert their full force on the individual member. The Chinese Communists work on the assumption that if one can force a person to participate in some organised and controlled group, then, whatever the personal inclinations of the individual involved, the proper use of the techniques of "discussion, criticism, and education" will enable one to secure his commitment of one degree and kind or another.

Furthermore, the Chinese Communists never permit participation in group activity to be simply verbal. In most instances "study groups" and "work groups" are one, so that an individual subjected to verbal pressures in one group context will find himself being tested by his concrete work in that same group context. In other words, the party member not only engages verbally with his comrades, but finds himself sent out to do practical party work, like organising, lecturing, interviewing and so on. Both work and talk are forms of participation, and coming together they compound the pressures to involve an individual in the

" cause " or organisation in question. It is through the " broadening of democracy " that the party feels it can rely on local party people to make correct decisions, even when an explicit party directive is not forthcoming, or when a party directive is so loosely formulated that the situation explicitly calls for local adaptation. The operation of the latter procedure was seen clearly in the programme of commune-isation. The decree of August 29, 1958, in no way spelled out in minute detail how communes were to be established. Communes of different types and dimensions arose in various parts of the country. The format of each commune was more often than not the work of the local party cadres. Only in December was there introduced the programme of *Gleichschaltung* which gave the communes a more uniform appearance.

ORIGINS

One might ask what is the historical source of this flexible, " dialectical " organisational structure? An organisational history of the Chinese Communists has not yet been written, but there are strong indications that these practices, this mode of thinking, arose in the Yenan period. One has direct indications of this in the writings of Mao Tse-tung on guerrilla warfare. One of the central problems which the Communists faced during that period was the control and manipulation of scattered bands of guerrilla fighters in an overall context of military co-ordination. Actual military conditions did not permit the transformation of these units into regular armies, but on the other hand there always remained the danger of " mountainism," the loosening of central control. Furthermore, both regular and guerrilla warfare had their positive functions. The problem posed itself in terms of " contradictions " and the practices which developed had a " contradictory," " dialectical " character. The intensive use of group pressures—the use of thought control—seems to have developed during the Yenan period. And thought control inculcated the contradictory ideas of centralism and democracy, or, interpreted in military terms, absolute obedience to supreme command coupled with the maximum of independence in guerrilla action.[6]

Contradictions demand resolution, as the ideology of the Chinese Communists teaches. Therefore, one must ask: what are the institutionalised forms of the resolution of contradictions, of the management of intra-organisation tensions? On the everyday level, criticism and self-criticism, and denunciation are mechanisms for resolving intra-organisation tensions. As Mao Tse-tung and Liu Shao-ch'i have repeatedly stated, and as is quite simple to imagine, tensions are generated

---

[6] Compare the very illuminating discussion by Boyd Compton on the organisational significance of the " rectification " movements of 1942–44; Boyd Compton, *Mao's China—Party Reform Documents, 1942–44* (University of Washington Press: Seattle, 1952), pp. xv–xxxiii.

in the typical organisational setting in which there is a person who leads and people who are led. These tensions have their positive aspects if they induce sufficient anxiety and insecurity in the individual to work out his tensions positively, in work, in study, and in struggle—all sanctioned forms of releasing tension in Communist China. On the other hand, the "contradictions" may begin to impede the orderly functioning of the organisation. Here the mechanisms of denunciation and criticism come in. A cadre is reported to the party through one or another channel. Such reporting is openly encouraged and in many instances denunciation has become a legitimate part of organisational life. Such denunciation will probably be followed by a criticism and self-criticism session in which the denounced becomes the target of criticism.

Aside from the day-to-day programmes of orderly "resolution of contradictions," periodic large-scale movements—"mass movements"—are launched. Mass movements can be launched for many purposes, to implement whatever internal policy the régime wishes carried out. But the "rectification" movements are aimed at solving intra-organisation "contradictions" on a grand scale. Mao's speech of February 1957 ushered in a "rectification" movement. The present, somewhat veiled campaign against rightists in the party seems to be directed against party members who opposed the radicalism of many of the local cadres in the great leap forward and in communisation. Here more is involved than simple elimination of intra-organisation tensions. However, whatever the specific aim of the mass movements, their consequences are usually manifold. In building the party (*chien-tang*), the Communists have always stressed the tremendous importance of participation in mass movements as a training ground for party work. Such participation increases the "democratic aspects" of the party, infuses life and dynamism into its members. In this sense, all mass movements tend to push the pendulum of the dialectic from "centralism" toward "democracy." There is considerable evidence that the present leadership intends to continue to emphasise the importance of "democracy." More than a year ago, voices which suggested the abolition of mass movements in advanced industrial sectors for the sake of rationalised, ordered production were severely attacked by the organs of the Central Committee. The present campaign against the rightists also seems to be directed against those who are calling for moderation or change in organisational methods. However, it seems that Mao Tse-tung and Liu Shao-ch'i are holding fast to those methods and practices of organisation which they helped bring into being during Yenan times and with which they won China and have succeeded in transforming a prostrate, disorganised mass into one of the most powerful, organised, and dynamic countries in the world.

Rural Administration in
Communist China

By ROY HOFHEINZ

SINCE the Ch'in dynasty first divided the area under its control into forty administrative districts, the Chinese countryside has experienced a bewildering variety of units of local organisation. Although beneath this variety there is a discernible continuity (for example in the maintenance of the provincial level of organisation since Han times), the student is often hard put to give adequate explanations of the changes which have occurred.[1] This is particularly true of the Republican period, when local governmental organisation was not only a topic of heated discussion but also a focus of considerable explicit experimentation.[2]

The Chinese Communists, when they came to power in 1949, sought to improve on the Republican system of local administration by applying their own experiences of border governments and the knowledge of thirty years of Soviet administrative history. It is the purpose of this essay to describe and to attempt to explain the changes in the system of rural administration in China from the formation of the People's Government to the initiation of the new administrative system based on the people's commune in 1958. Such a description must perforce examine the policy motives behind changes. In a Communist society such as China's, the formation of policy is often obscured from view by a controlled press and a notorious lack of internal documentation. We are therefore forced to *reconstruct* rather than simply to describe the motivations of the Party leadership in instituting given administrative changes.

Obviously the scope of local administration is so broad that some point of focus must be selected in a paper of this size. I have decided to single out the issue of the size and articulation of local organs of administration largely because it is more manageable and better illustrates the changes of administrative policy than others. I have selected it also because it incidentally provides considerable insight into the policy background of the commune phenomenon, although it hardly exhausts that background. Other, more interesting, issues such as the selection

---

[1] See, for example, Chin Ta-k'ai, "The Problem of Administrative Divisions on the Mainland," *Min-chu P'ing-lun,* September 1955, who argues that changes in the size of local organs made little real historical difference anyway.

[2] Ku Tun-jou, "Experiments in Local Government," *Yenching Journal of Social Studies,* July 1939.

and employment of personnel, the lines of authority and the degree of overlap of local organs are unfortunately less often discussed in the Communist press and are less clear-cut. Even less answerable are such questions as the impact of rural administration on the countryside, the " success " of the régime, etc., however fascinating it may be to speculate on them.

However, despite the fact that the present research is not armed nor aimed to attack major questions, it may still help us to bring down some of the smaller ones. For example—what *are* the changes in administrative organisation in the Chinese countryside following the formulation of the Communist régime? Can these changes be related to more general shifts in the " Party line?" Do they tend to follow any patterns set by the Soviet Union? Is there a trend towards more efficient forms of rural organisation? These are the questions that will be examined in this article.

THE CREATION OF THE STATE ADMINISTRATIVE SYSTEM

The month of October 1947 marks the beginning of an independent policy of rural administration by the Chinese Communists following their final break with the United Front and the announcement of a new offensive against the Kuomintang (KMT). Whereas during the period of co-operation with the Chiang government the standard seven level KMT pattern of local organisation based on the *pao* and the *chia* was applied to the Border Region under Communist control,[3] according to the declaration of October 10, 1947, the organisation of the countryside was to be managed by the People's Liberation Army.[4]

As various areas were gradually " liberated " in the course of the civil war, the army left behind cadres whose job it was to liquidate all traces of the previous administration and to build up the foundation of a new " People's Government." This involved the immediate elimination of the *pao-chia* and the formal village governments, and the gradual disarming and discrediting of the former informal centres of power such as the local clans, crop protection associations, and athletic clubs. In their place the so-called Military Control Commission would set up a village " peasant's association " to organise village activities and would have it elect a " progressive " village headman who was responsive to the demands of the military cadres. In addition, by encouraging hatred of landlords and participation in newly-organised associations (such as the youth league, women's league and militia), the cadres attempted to

---

[3] The several levels were region, sub-region (*fen-ch'ü*), *hsien, ch'ü, hsiang,* administrative village (*hsing-cheng ts'un*) village (*ts'un*). Hsü Lung-ying, *A Survey of the Shensi-Kansu-Ninghsia Border Region,* Part I, p. 47.

[4] Peter Tang, *Communist China Today* (London: Thames & Hudson, 1957), p. 268.

create a new sense of participation in the government, and thus to increase the responsiveness of the village to the policies of higher administrative echelons.[5]

At the same time as the population was being organised at the local level, a new system of state administration was being developed to manage them. At first, following Article 14 of the Common Programme of the Chinese People's Political Consultative Conference (CPPCC),[6] the Military Control Commissions selected " All-circles' People's Representative Conferences " at the local level. Eventually these became "People's Congresses " when elections were held, as they were in the majority of rural districts after 1951.[7]

Following the establishment of the system of people's congresses and the holding of general elections in 1953,[8] a Constitution and an Organic Law of Local People's Congresses were promulgated (September 20 and 21, 1954) which called for, or rather recognised the existence of, a state system of administration closely resembling that of the Soviet Union. This system was characterised by an ostensibly simple hierachy of administration which (in theory) comprised only the central (*chung-yang*), provincial (*sheng*), county (*hsien*), and village (*hsiang*) levels, but which allowed in practice the creation of two additional levels: the Special Region or *Chuan-ch'ü* between the provincial and county levels, and the District or *Ch'ü* between the county and the village.[9] Completely abolished in the course of 1954 were the six large Administrative Regions (*Ta-hsing-cheng-ch'ü*) between the central and provincial levels which had been created in 1949, and in order to make up for their loss the number of units at the provincial level was sharply reduced from 35 in 1949 to 27 in 1954.[10]

But whereas the upper structure of administration was consciously being streamlined and simplified, during the first five years of the régime, administrative organisation at the village level was left deliberately atomised. In fact, during the period of land reform directives were issued

---

[5] An excellent description of this process in a particular village is found in C. K. Yang, *A Chinese Village in Early Communist Transition*, Part 2.

[6] Adopted September 29, 1949. For excerpts see Chao Kuo-chün, *Agrarian Policies of Mainland China: A Documentary Study (1949–1956)* (Harvard Un. Press, 1957), pp. 6–7.

[7] S. B. Thomas, *Government and Administration in Communist China* (New York: I.P.R., 1955), p. 84.

[8] Only 85 per cent. of those elegible to vote participated in this election, indicating a certain difficulty in explaining the electoral process to the population. L. M. Gudoshnikov, " Development of the Organs of Local Government and Administration in the PCG," *Sovetskoe Gosudarstvo i Pravo*, No. 10, October 1957, (JPRS 342D, U.S. Govt. Publication 17043/1958 microtext.)

[9] " Organic Law of the Local People's Congresses and Local People's Councils of the PGS," Article 42, in *Documents of the First Session of the First National People's Congress of the PRC*, p. 231.

[10] Theodore Shabad, *China's Changing Map* (London: Methuen, 1956), p. 25.

to *reduce* the size of the *hsiang* to " forge closer ties between the government and the masses." [11]   And whereas the state system was shaped
formally according to the Soviet model, it did not adopt the Soviet principle of arranging administrative units according to economic functions.[12]
The first policy was to be changed in the course of the collectivisation
drive; the second with the introduction of the people's communes.

COLLECTIVISATION: THE ECONOMIC ADMINISTRATIVE SYSTEM

After the establishment of the system of state administration, the Chinese
Party leadership embarked on a policy of wholesale collectivisation, and
thus created a second, rival economic system of administration in the
countryside. We must now examine that system.

Just as in the U.S.S.R., there was a period of voluntariness in agricultural co-operation in China following land reform.[13] In this period the
form of co-operation which had been used in the Yenan period was
encouraged: it consisted of very small-scale mutual aid teams (*hu-chu-
tsu*) which shared manpower and draught animals for specific tasks. The
principle of organisation was that ownership of land, animals and farm
implements remained in the hands of individuals. Co-operation could
be only seasonal, although permanent teams were encouraged as " more
advanced." The size of these teams was usually restricted to a few
families, often closely related.[14] From 1950 to 1952 the percentage of
total agricultural households organised in mutual aid teams rose steadily
from 10·7 per cent. to 40 per cent., but the average number of families
in each group remained between four and six.[15]

Beginning in 1953 a second, higher form of co-operative farm was
introduced, called the Agricultural Producers' Co-operative (" APC "—
Nung-yeh sheng-ch'an ho-tso she). A tiny handful of such co-operatives
had been set up in the Yenan period.[16] Their organisation corresponded
to the form of co-operation known in Russia as the TOZ (standing for
" society for land cultivation "), wherein land was held collectively but
still yielded dividends to the former owner. According to the directive

---

11 Chang Li-man, " Special Features in the Changes of Administrative Areas in China."
   Cheng-fa Yen-chiu No. 5, October 2, 1956. In *Excerpts from China Mainland
   Magazines* (ECMM) (Hong Kong: U.S. Consulate-General), No. 57.
12 Shabad, *op. cit.*, p. 30. The process of administrative simplification at the upper
   levels had its parallel in Russia in the merger of the *guberniya* into larger units during
   the 1920s (p. 29).
13 See for example Article 38 of the Common Programme. (Chao, *Agrarian Policies*,
   p. 7.)
14 Hsu, *Survey*, Part II, p. 132. In Yenan about 27 per cent. of the population of the
   border region was organised in co-ops, and these were mostly in consumers' co-
   operatives.
15 Chao, *Agrarian Policies*, p. 56.
16 The model co-operative of this form was the " South District Co-operative." Hsu,
   Survey, Part II, p. 120.

which prescribed this form of organisation (February 15, 1953), it was to be instituted in areas " where the masses have accumulated relatively rich experiences in mutual aid and where comparatively strong leading activists have emerged." [17] Following this directive the number of APCs rose steadily from 15,000 (1·2 per cent. of households) in 1953 to 633,000 (13·5 per cent.) in 1955, maintaining an average size of 20–30 households each.[18] By mid-1955 the APC was clearly on its way to becoming the favourite form of economic organisation in the countryside, much as the TOZ had become in the Soviet Union in the 1920s.

This was the situation when in late autumn 1955 a new form of rural collectivisation was announced. The decision to press forward with a higher form of organisation was the result of sharp debate within the Party. In July of 1954, the CCP Secretary in charge of the Rural Work Department, Teng Tzu-hui, had argued that collectivisation using the " semi-socialist " (*i.e.*, TOZ) form of APC could not be complete until sometime in the Second Five-year Plan (around 1958). Under the then prevailing conditions, Teng claimed, the semi-Socialist APC was better suited since it was more likely to have the support of the peasants, who have " harboured the conception of private ownership of land for a long, long time," and hence were not likely to be easily divested of it.[19] Although Teng declared the ultimate aim of collectivisation to be to move towards larger forms of organisation, still " at the start, the size should not be too large, because the peasants' ability is limited and because we are not in a position to assign cadres to lead every co-operative." [20]

In his speech of July 31, 1955, " On the Co-operativisation of Agriculture," which was significantly kept secret until October of that year, Mao Tse-tung argued that such critics of faster collectivisation as Teng were simply adopting the " rightist mistake of resolute shrinkage," and suggested that local cadres discuss the question and report after the harvest. The reports which came to Peking from the field in September and October of 1955 not only indicated the most abundant harvest since the beginning of the régime, but also showed a massive increase in the rate of collectivisation; from July to the end of the year over 50 million peasant households had entered semi-Socialist co-operatives.[21] With the

[17] Central Committee, Chinese Communist Party; " Decisions on mutual aid and co-operativization in agricultural production," in Chao, *Agrarian Policies*, p. 61.
[18] Chao, *loc. cit.*
[19] Teng Tzu-hui, " Report to the Rural Work Conference of the Central Committee, New Democratic Youth League," July 15, 1954, Chao, *Agrarian Policies*, p. 74.
[20] *Loc. cit.*, p. 78. Teng later was to accuse himself of " rightist opportunism," presumably because of this and similar speeches. (See his speech to the Eighth National Congress of the CPC, in volume II of the documents of that congress, p. 182.)
[21] Preface to *Socialist Upsurge in China's Countryside* (Peking: Foreign Languages Press, 1957), p. 8.

rightists thus rebuked by successes in the countryside, the Party was moved to declare that " higher stage " (*kao-chi*) co-operatives were called for, and announced in the Twelve-year Draft Outline for Agricultural Development presented in January 1956 that the whole nation would by 1957–58 be organised into these advanced co-operatives.

The form of co-operativisation advocated in the Twelve-year Plan, described in glowing terms in the book *Socialist Upsurge in China's Countryside* (published January 1956),[22] and finally codified in the " Model Regulations for Advanced APCs " (adopted June 30, 1956) was the " fully socialist " form in which the peasants relinquish all claims to individual profit from their land and earn their living by wages based on work-points. This was the form of organisation known as the *artel* in Russia, where it became the standard type of collective farm after 1930. But, aware of the unfortunate episode of forced collectivisation in Russia from 1930–32 (which Stalin later styled a period " dizzy with success "), the Chinese deliberately patterned their artels on the Russian " Model Regulation for Kolkhozy " of 1935, which was considerably more permissive than earlier Soviet forms.[23]

In the course of the first half of 1956 advanced collectivisation proceeded at a rate which even the sanguine Twelve-year Plan had not foreseen, so that by March 90 per cent. and by September 96 per cent. of the country's agricultural households had joined collective farms of the socialist type. These farms differed from their predecessors not only in the principle of ownership and distribution, but also in size and complexity of administration. Whereas the semi-socialist co-operatives averaged thirty households and covered some ninety acres of land, each of the new farms averaged over 100 and covered 290 acres.[24] And whereas the ordinary APCs concerned themselves almost entirely with farming, the new higher-level farms had to deal with subsidiary occupations such as forestry, animal husbandry and pisciculture as well as with large-scale agro-technical projects and culture and welfare services. In order to cope with this new scale and variety of activity, each co-operative was required to establish production brigades (*sheng-ch'an-tui*) built on the former lower APCs and mutual aid teams as permanent units of organisation.[25] By mid-1956 a new network of rural administration, this time economic in nature, had been created and would have to be integrated into the network already existing.

---

[22] *Op. cit.* See for example the article " The Superiority of Large Co-ops.," pp. 460–476.
[23] For this foresight Mikoyan was to congratulate the Chinese. See his speech to the Eighth National Congress, *Documents of Eighth National Congress*, Vol. III, p. 18.
[24] Chao, *Agrarian Policies*, p. 55.
[25] " Model regulations for Advanced APCs," article 31.

COLLECTIVISATION: ADMINISTRATIVE EFFECTS

Merger and Simplification of State Organs: On December 27, 1955, the same day as Chairman Mao signed the preface to *Socialist Upsurge in China's Countryside*, the State Council issued a directive " On further Improving the Simplification of Governmental Organs." Two different kinds of simplification were declared necessary in order to save administrative man-power and expense: (1) the relative importance of the *chuan-ch'ü* and the *ch'ü* must be reduced, and (2) the size of the *ch'ü* and the *hsiang* must be increased. In the words of the directive, " The system of small *ch'ü* and *hsiang* administrative areas no longer meets the new situation following the rapid development of agricultural co-operativisation, and so they should be gradually adjusted." [26] Following these instructions, in the course of 1956 the total number of *chuan-ch'ü* was reduced from 157 (around which figure it had hovered for several years) to 140, the total number of *ch'ü* in agricultural areas fell from 19,000 to 9,000 and the total number of *hsiang* from 210,000 to under 100,000.[27] The rule of thumb applied in merging *hsiang* areas was to combine two or three into one (in Manchuria, because the average size of *hsiang* before merging was small, four or five were combined into one new unit).

It seems clear that the widespread merger of *hsiang* throughout the countryside was thought necessary in the light of successes in collectivisation. Once again Soviet experience had a bearing: in the early 1950s N. S. Khrushchev's agricultural reforms had resulted in a drastic reduction in the number of *kolkhozy*: from 250,000 to 100,000 between 1950 and 1952. In fact, there were cases reported in 1953 wherein a single *kolkhoz* contained as many as four village soviets (the Russian equivalent of the *hsiang*). To correct such anomalies, Khrushchev reduced drastically the number of village units beginning in 1954. Reorganisation was called for in China for similar reasons. An article in *Shih-shih Shou-ts'e* (*Current Affairs Handbook*) in July 1956 summarised the case for one:

> With the rapid development of the agricultural co-operative movement since the second half of last year, the former administrative division of *ch'ü* and *hsiang* areas could no longer meet the requirements of the situation. As a result of amalgamation, a number of agricultural co-operatives have broken through the *hsiang* boundaries. In addition, the small *hsiang* system renders it inconvenient to make overall plans for rural construction work. Hence the necessity for enlarging the *hsiang* areas.[28]

---

26 *Jen-min Shou-ts'e*, 1957.
27 Hsieh I-yuan, " Delineation of Administrative Regions of the PRC," *Acta Geographica Sinica*, No. 1, February 1958 (JPRS 650D, U.S. Govt. Publication 17043/ 1958 microtext).
28 " Changes in the Administrative Division of *ch'ü* and *hsiang* areas," *Shih-shih Shou-ts'e*, July 25, 1956. (Chao, *Agrarian Policies*, p. 258, or ECMM, No. 48.)

The streamlining of the local administrative apparatus thus resulted from a desire to increase its efficiency. As one geographer put it: " (When) the *hsien* takes over leadership of the *hsiang* directly, policy directives find it easier to meet the masses." [29] It is also probable that the onset of collectivisation placed a severe strain on the number of available trained personnel; the simplification of state organs would probably have freed a large number of cadres for work in the new economic apparatus of the APCs.[30]

The Confusion of Administrative Functions: Whereas in principle the organs of state power and the collectives were separate administrative units with separate membership, the shortage of personnel and the desire to maintain a high rate of collectivisation caused these distinctions to be blurred in practice. This blurring was not so much a result of jurisdictional disputes such as those which marred the early stages of collectivisation in the Soviet Union, but rather seemed to be due to a basic lack of precision as to what the functions of the different offices were. An article in *Hsüeh-hsi* (*Study*) in August 1956 summed up the problem:

> Following the major development of co-operativisation, cadres of some areas, who are unable to distinguish the character and function of state power from the character and function of APCs, assign many administrative tasks which should not fall within their competence to the APCs. The result is that the *hsiang* state power has little to do, whereas the APCs shoulder much non-productive business. . . . Some people get the impression that co-operatives may take the place of the *hsiang* organs.[31]

One result of this over-concentration on economic administration was the apparent atrophy of the *hsiang* people's congresses. Not since 1954 when the requirement was set had the number of *hsiang* congresses per year reached the standard of four, and meetings were spaced wider and wider apart.[32] Tung Pi-wu complained at the Eighth National Congress of the CCP in September 1956 that " a few of our Party members and government personnel do not attach much importance to the legal system of the state, or do not observe its provisions." [33] But regardless of the tendency in practice to allow state organs to lapse into disuse, there was no lack of theoretical support for the separation of functions. The editors of *Hsüeh-hsi* left no room for doubt on this question:

---

29 Hsieh, *op. cit.*
30 The State Council directive on simplification of December 27, 1955, also urged that all " non-productive man-power " be removed from administrative organs of state and sent down into the fields.
31 " Is *hsiang* State Power Organisation Still Required for a Co-operativised *hsiang*?" *Hsüeh-hsi*, No. 98, August 2, 1956. (ECMM, No. 54.)
32 *Kuang-ming Daily*, December 14, 1956. Quoted in *China News Analysis* No. 254.
33 *Documents of Eighth National Congress*, Vol. II, p. 88.

We consider that the *hsiang* state power is the basic level of state power organisation, that the *hsiang* people's congresses are the local state organs in the *hsiang* areas, and that the *hsiang* people's councils are the executive organs during the recess of the congresses as well as the administrative organs of the state in *hsiang* areas, and that APCs are merely collective economic organisations of the working peasants. The two being basically different in character, their functions cannot be interchanged.[34]

The Return of the Smaller Co-operative: Events in 1956 and early 1957 caused the Party to undertake a reassessment of the collectivisation programme. Firstly, and predictably, the rapid programme of collectivisation had met with widespread passive peasant resistance which took the form of slaughter of livestock (rather than surrender of it to the state)[35] and a mass exodus from the villages to the cities.[36] Secondly, and unexpectedly, the policy of collectivising and mechanising simultaneously, which had been one of the main arguments of the Leftists in the discussions of 1955, proved highly doubtful as a result of the colossal failure of the " double-wheel, double-share plough." The Twelve-Year Plan of January 1956 had proposed that six million of these instruments, which had been used to tame the new lands of Siberia, be " popularised " within the next three to five years.[37] In the first half of 1956 about 1·4 million were produced, using a large amount of valuable steel, but only 10 per cent. of them were distributed and only 5 per cent. actually put to use; the ploughs were too heavy to be pulled by draught animals through the wet soils of China.[38] Such a fiasco, bringing into question as it did the validity of the Soviet model of mechanisation, was bound to have some effect on administrative policy.

Thirdly, the system of collective farms suffered from major inefficiencies of administration. Perhaps the greatest lack was of trained accountants, which was declared to be the " weak link in the APC movement." [39] The Party was required in the early part of 1956 to take in large numbers of recruits to manage collectives, but it found the literacy

---

34 *Hsüeh-hsi, loc. cit.*

35 For some vivid examples of this practice, see *Union Research Service*, Vol. 2, No. 6. The basic economic reason for the slaughter seems to have been that a dead cow was worth more than a live one. This was of course caused by a flooded market for live cattle. The state council was forced to issue a directive on this subject on December 30, 1955.

36 During the first five-year plan (1952–57) some eight million peasants made the move (Chao Kuo-chün, *Economic Planning and Organisation in Mainland China: A Documentary Study (1949–1957)* (Harvard Un. Press, 1959), Vol. 1, p. 144).

37 Chao, *Economic Planning*, Vol. 1, p. 120.

38 See *Union Research Service*, Vol. 5, No. 20, and Chou En-lai's speech to the Eighth National Congress on the Second Five Year Plan, *Documents of Eighth National Congress*, Vol. II, p. 275.

39 Liu Jui-lung, " Conclusions at the conference on financial and accounting work of the APCs," *Chung-kuo Ching-nien Pao*, No. 21 (1955). (Quoted in Chao, *Agrarian Policies*, p. 117.)

rate so low among them that many were incapable of keeping records at all.[40]

The combination of discontent, failures of planning and inefficiency was brought home to the Party by the inadequate harvests of 1956 and 1957.[41] Gradually the leadership came to realise that the nation's industrial growth was directly dependent on agricultural output,[42] and that the rate of increase of food production would have to exceed the rate of population growth—as it had not in 1956.[43] Beginning in April of 1956 (with a State Council directive on "The Running of Agricultural Co-operatives Industriously and Economically")[44] the Party, allowing its conservative elements to take the lead once again, began a long struggle to rationalise the implementation of planning and to relax the pressure of collectivisation. From May to August of 1956 a long series of meetings of the State Council were held to examine the state administrative system. The Council recommended and the Eighth National Congress of the Communist Party (September 16–27, 1956) adopted a condemnation of the "existing situation of excessive centralisation," and urged greater leniency in enforcing collectivisation.[45] In the early part of 1957 a larger amount of freedom and consultation in planning was introduced in the hope that this would encourage the elimination of extravagance and waste. However, an equally poor harvest in 1957 put the conservatives on the spot. They therefore in mid-September initiated a large-scale overhaul of the agricultural co-operatives.

The directives of September 1957 are the first public indication of a feeling on the part of the Rightists that the co-operatives were being allowed to grow too large and inefficient.[46] In addition to reiterating the demands for decentralisation of planning and for increased incentives and guarantees to peasants, the State Council declared that "some co-operatives which have grown to huge and unwieldy proportions should be properly readjusted according to the demand of the masses."[47]

40 *JMJP* July 6, 1956, reported that in Kirin 30–50 per cent. of APCs either keep books faultily or not at all. (*China News Analysis*, No. 164.)

41 On this inadequacy see Li Choh-ming, *Economic Development of Communist China* (Berkeley: Un. of California Press, 1959), p. 58.

42 Speech of T'an Chen-lin, *Documents of Second Session of the Eighth National Congress of the CPC*, p. 92.

43 Li Choh-ming, "Economic Development," *The China Quarterly*, No. 1 (January–March 1960), p. 42.

44 Survey of the China Mainland Press (SCMP) (Hong Kong: U.S. Consulate-General), (No. 1268, April 4, 1956 summary). New China News Agency (NCNA).

45 Speech of Chou En-lai, *Documents of Eighth National Congress*, p. 310.

46 That the Party was wary of over-expansion was learned by a visiting Indian delegation as early as summer, 1956. See their *Report of the Indian Delegation to China on Agricultural Planning and Techniques* (New Delhi: Government of India, Ministry of Food & Agriculture, 1956), p. 121.

47 September 14, 1957. Directive "On Overhauling Co-operatives," SCMP, No. 1618, p. 21.

Another directive, entitled " On the Improvement of Production Administration in APCs," argued for smaller farms as follows:

> The size of co-operatives and production teams has much to do with the administration of agricultural production. Agriculture has its peculiarities, and the level of technique and management in APCs is low. As a result of practice in the past years, it has been proven that big co-operatives and big teams are generally not suited to the present conditions of production. . . . Therefore, except for a few big co-operatives which are really run with success, all the existing co-operative farms which are too big . . . should be appropriately reduced in size." [48]

The standard size recommended by this document was 100 families. Since the average size of co-operative at the time was 171,[49] this therefore meant that the Party was willing to allow a large number of its APCs to split up and revert to a previous level of organisation. And to show their firm intention not to waver from this decision the directive added, " Once the size of the co-operative farm has been fixed, an announcement should be made that there will be no change for the next ten years."

However, the acute reader of Party pronouncements would have discovered within a month that, far from a decade of rest, the harassed peasant was likely to receive only renewed demands in the months to come. At the end of October a speech by Teng Hsiao-p'ing made on September 25 was finally made public condemning " a serious rightist deviationist ideology " in rural development. On October 25 a new revision of the old Twelve-year Plan for agricultural development was issued, with a new preamble full of confidence about collectivisation.[50] And on November 6, at the celebrations on the anniversary of the Bolshevik Revolution, Liu Shao-ch'i gave a speech containing in embryonic form the slogans and concepts of the " great leap forward." It was clear that by winter of 1957–58 a radical shift in agricultural policy had been made, and that some sort of new answer to the problem of agricultural growth was being sought. The answer which the Party ultimately arrived at was the creation of a revolutionary new system of administration in the countryside: the people's communes.

BACKGROUND OF THE PEOPLE'S COMMUNE: THE CASE OF HONAN

In order better to understand the reasons for the administrative revolution in China in 1958, it is helpful to focus on the administrative policy of a given region. I have selected Honan province in the North China plain for a case study in the background to the communes partly because

---

[48] SCMP No. 1618, pp. 24–25.
[49] Y. C. Yin and Helen Yin, *Economic Statistics of Mainland China (1949–1957)* (Harvard Un. Press, 1960), p. 38.
[50] Chao, *Economic Planning*, Vol. I, p. 157 *et seq.*

it demonstrates that background clearly, and partly because the Party selected it as its model province in the movement.[51]

No doubt just as in most provinces, the Honan Party line described a cycle similar to the national one. During the " high tide " of collectivisation there was a " major overhaul " of the majority of Honan's 15,000 APCs, in which a " state of confusion in labour organisation and utilisation " was cleared up and " order established in production " [52]; and there were conferences called to criticise the conservatism of cadres who underestimated the abilities of co-operatives.[53] In the campaign to increase administrative efficiency, the Provincial Committee issued a directive to send cadres down into rural areas, to abolish superfluous offices, and to reduce unnecessary expenditure to a minimum.[54] When the line made its swing back to the right, a cadre conference was called to denounce the " deviation of hasty adventurism " and the " colossal machinery " of bureaucratism.[55]

However, Honan differed from other provinces in 1956 and 1957 in the number and severity of its natural disasters. Because it is traversed by five rivers and receives its peak rainfall during the harvest season, Honan is in constant danger of devastating floods. In June 1956 a flash flood hit just at the time of the wheat harvest, and would have eliminated the crop had it not been for a massive mobilisation of manpower organised by telephone by the Provincial Committee. As it was, with millions of workers organised in the fields, only 60 per cent. of the crop was saved.[56] Again in August the Chang and the Wei rivers overflowed

---

51 In adopting this method, I am aware that it has major pitfalls. (a) In this paper no original provincial sources are used. I am therefore forced to rely on stories from the province which are picked up either by NCNA or the Hong Kong translation services. (b) Each province has peculiarities of its own which make generalisation from it to the national scene difficult. (c) Policy generally comes from above (especially after the moving of regional bases of power to the centre in 1954), but it is convenient to make it appear spontaneous.
   At the same time, if one avoids these possible sources of error, the method may shed light on the detail of realities which affect central policy and particularly on the problems faced by local authorities in implementing policy.

52 SCMP, No. 1262, NCNA, Chengchow, March 24, 1956.

53 For example the First Provincial Party Congress of July 1956 (SCMP, No. 1336, NCNA, Chengchow, July 22, 1956). Nine other provinces held congresses at the same time. Note that the criticism of conservatism was still fashionable after the April decrees from the centre urging nationalisation. The cry of " leftist adventurism," heard in the autumn, was probably a product of the Eighth Congress.

54 SCMP, No. 1448, NCNA, Chengchow, December 26, 1956. Two interesting details of this communiqué are (a) the order to rural party headquarters to cease posting armed guards at the entrance to the party office, so as to " forge closer ties with the masses "; and (b) the order to cease undertaking construction of new buildings, purchase of new furniture, automobiles, entertaining of guests (except foreigners), and to cut back telephone and other miscellaneous expenses. Obviously a radical programme of saving was necessary to reduce administrative expense to a minimum.

55 SCMP, No. 1416, NCNA, Chengchow, November 9, 1956.

56 SCMP, No. 1319, NCNA, Chengchow, June 12, 1956.

their banks, inundating some 1,700 villages.[57] And finally in mid-November a severe drought caused only 80 per cent. of the planned wheat acreage to be sown.[58] In recognition of the severity of these disasters, the central government sent 81 million catties of grain as relief,[59] and further granted all male citizens of Honan exemption from military service for the next year.[60] But next year, too, was unlucky: a two-month-long drought in late summer caused great damage to crops, and drove peasants to water their fields using washbasins to carry water and electric lighting to show them the way at night.[61] It was therefore clear by autumn of 1957 that some drastic steps would be necessary to reduce the damage to crops in the future.

Probably in answer to the joint Party Central Committee and State Council directive announcing a campaign for more irrigation projects (September 25, 1957),[62] Honan held a series of provincial conferences in winter 1957–58 concentrating on the problem of water conservancy.[63] Present and speaking at each of these conferences was T'an Chen-lin, a recently elected member of the Secretariat of the Central Committee. The conferences, presided over for the most part by the then governor of Honan, Wu Chih-p'u, passed resolutions condemning " Rightist Conservatism " and projecting a threefold increase in irrigated acreage in the coming year.[64] As one of the resolutions pointed out,

> If we got the problem of water conservancy straightened out, we could expect a wheat production increase of 1,000 per cent. . . . Only the construction of small irrigation facilities as the main portion of the programme could develop into a mass movement. And only such a movement could extirpate the threats of flood and drought.[65]

The campaign for mass conservancy projects lasted throughout the winter; at one time it was declared that an army of 10 million peasants had been organised to work on minor irrigation and flood control projects.[66] In April, the New China News Agency (NCNA) could declare that " Honan, in Central China, is the province that has made the most rapid progress in the current mass water conservancy programme." [67]

[57] SCMP, No. 1362, NCNA, Chengchow, August 14, 1956.
[58] SCMP, No. 1433, *People's Daily*, December 1, 1956.
[59] SCMP, No. 1433, NCNA, Chengchow, November 30, 1956.
[60] SCMP, No. 1696, *Honan Daily*, December 13, 1957.
[61] SCMP, No. 1636, NCNA, Chengchow, October 13, 1957.
[62] SCMP, No. 1628, *Kuang-ming Daily*, September 25, 1957.
[63] The meetings were:
" Water Conservancy Conference " October 21–27, SCMP, No. 1650.
" Water Conservancy Forum " November 14, SCMP, No. 1659.
Second Session of First Party Congress of Honan November 12–December 2, SCMP, No. 1671.
[64] *Loc. cit.*
[65] SCMP, No. 1650, NCNA, Chengchow, October 29, 1957.
[66] David Rousset, " The new tyranny in the countryside," *Problems of Communism*, January–February 1959.
[67] SCMP, No. 1760, NCNA, April 24, 1958.

Although the national newspapers of April carry no hint of what was later declared to have happened in Honan in that month, in May there were indications that an unusual degree of organisation had been introduced into the countryside in preparation for the harvest. In the first week of May another flood prevention work conference stressed the need to *man* the thousands of flood control projects built in the last six months, and particularly to pay attention to projects in under-populated mountainous areas where floods were likely to begin.[68] This implied, of course, a much greater degree of co-operation among APCs and *hsiang* in mass labour exchanges. On May 9, a joint conference of the Party's Honan Provincial Committee and the Provincial People's Council ordered:

> Collaboration shall be worked out between *hsiang* and *hsien*, among APCs and brigades and teams, between mountainous regions and the plains, and between cities and villages. . . . All APCs shall make due arrangements for living requirements of their members during May and June. . . . Headquarters for directing the summer harvest and cultivation shall be established in all administrative districts, *hsien* and *hsiang* to unify the forces available and to bring about concerted action.[69]

In response to this directive it was reported on May 20 that " organisations have been set up in all parts of the province to direct the summer harvesting and sowing work. . . . Creches, baby-care groups, sewing groups, temporary mess halls, and centres for old people have been set up to enable more peasants to be free from domestic chores." [70] It was clear that by wheat harvest time in late May the countryside of Honan had been turned into a veritable honeycomb of local organisations.

On May 17, T'an Chen-lin, who had been the inspiring force behind the organisation of water conservancy projects in Honan, delivered the explanatory speech on the Second Revised Draft of the Twelve-Year Plan to the same Second Session of the Eighth National Congress which heard Liu Shao-ch'i's proclamation of the " general line of socialist construction " and the " great leap forward." In addition to affirming Liu's rabid optimism about China's ability to grow agriculturally *without* the assistance of state investment (*i.e.*, relying on the organisation of masses of peasants to produce the surplus necessary for growth), T'an noted that there were many Rightists in the country who were " still waiting for the autumn harvest ' to settle accounts '." [71] " Well, let them wait," he challenged. " They will lose out in any case."

[68] SCMP, No. 1781, NCNA, May 13, 1958.
[69] SCMP, No. 1781, NCNA, Chengchow, May 12, 1958. It is interesting that one of the important advantages claimed for the first " model commune "—Weihsing—in Honan was that it encompassed both hilly and flat areas and thus could direct economic co-operation between these two ecologically different areas. (*Ts'ai-ching Yen-chiu*, No. 16, September 15, 1958—ECMM, No. 148.)
[70] SCMP, No. 1780, NCNA, Chengchow, May 20, 1958.
[71] *Documents of Second Session of Eighth National Congress*, p. 82.

In fact, the Rightists did lose out, but sooner than they might have thought: in mid-July T'an paid a visit again to Honan, this time to witness the purge of the former provincial Party Secretary, a man named P'an Fu-sheng. P'an was indicted for having advocated easing pressures on the peasants and for having successfully urged the splitting up of co-operatives into smaller units.[72] Wu Chih-p'u, the former Governor and now P'an's replacement as Provincial First Secretary, summed up the story of Honan in the following way:

> In Honan, when co-operativisation at the higher stage was realised in 1956, there were in all 26,211 co-operatives with an average of 358 households in each [*i.e.* more than twice the national average]. . . . By the spring of 1957 the co-operatives throughout the province had been initially overhauled and basically consolidated. . . . At that time, individual Right opportunists in the Honan Provincial Committee of the Party, without the least regard for the situation in the province . . . forced all the large co-operatives to be split, so that the number of APCs in the whole province came to more than 54,000, with an average of 180 households to each. . . .[73]

From this account it can be seen that the crime of P'an Fu-sheng consisted simply in having followed the directive of September 14, 1957, too well: he had tried to reduce the size of the co-operatives to the required level. Whether his demise was due to a personal feud with Wu, a fatal delay on his part in recognising the shift in line, or simply the need of the Central Committee for a scapegoat, the fact remains that his conservative position on rural organisation had been thoroughly rejected. Immediately after the purge, at a cadre conference in North China, T'an Chen-lin announced that " the administrative methods and the remuneration system of the APCs is outmoded " and that a " commune-like form " (*kung-she-hsing-te hsing-shih*) of organisation was being experimented with.[74] When Chairman Mao made an inspection trip to Honan in early August, he was moved to declare, " It is better to run people's communes," [75] and so a new system of rural administration, based on this experimental unit, was born.

[72] The Party's case against P'an (as found in SCMP, No. 1838 *passim* and *Current Background* (CB) (Hong Kong: U.S. Consulate-General), No. 515 *passim*) was essentially that he was guilty of localism—*i.e.* of attempting to protect the citizens of his province from national pressures. One of the prime examples of this was that he, according to the indictment, claimed that " peasants get no grain for the next day " and were forced to eat stone powder. The Honan papers went to great pains to prove " scientifically " that in fact it was only disguised *rich* peasants who were pretending to eat stone powder in order to embezzle the government, and that P'an was in collusion with them (*Honan Daily*, July 25, 1958, SCMP, No. 1838).

[73] Wu Chih-p'u, " From APCs to People's Communes," *Red Flag*, No. 8, 1958 (in *People's Communes in China (PCIC)*, p. 32).

[74] *Hsin-hua Pan-yüeh K'an*, No. 15, 1958, pp. 113–114; quoted in *China News Analysis*, No. 26.

[75] Wu, *op. cit.*, in *PCIC*, p. 34. The earliest mention of the term " people's commune " (*Jen-min Kung-she*) that I have discovered is in an article in *Red Flag*, No. 3, 1958,

But before describing that system one must first ask why Honan became its cradle. Firstly there are geographical reasons: Honan, by virtue of its large population (with over 44 million it is third after relatively backward Szechwan and Shantung in size), its relatively high incidence of natural calamities, and its varied terrain (from the floodplain of the Yellow River in the north to the Funiu mountains on the south-west), is a sizeable microcosm of agricultural China and a paradigm case of its problems. It, as much as or more than any other province, stood to gain from concerted organisation and planning. Secondly there are political reasons: apparently the Honan representatives of the more radical faction of the Party were more active than those of other provinces, since already by April they had begun the large-scale merger of APCs [76] and had made the province the leader of the country in water conservancy. The purge of P'an Fu-sheng and his colleagues, the most serious struggle since the elimination of Kao Kang and Jao Shu-shih in 1954, and the elevation of Comrade Wu Chih-p'u was a reward for this faction's precociousness.[77]

THE PEOPLE'S COMMUNE SYSTEM OF ADMINISTRATION

The people's commune, although specifically compared by the Chinese to the Paris Commune of 1871 to which it bears little resemblance,[78] is in principle the third of the three forms of collective organisation tried by the Russians in the 1920s and known to them as the *kommuna*. In it all property is owned communally and distribution is to be according to need. But however important the similarity of principle (in this case particularly important since it is actually the foundation for the claim that the people's communes represent a " communist " stage of develop-ment), the differences in administrative practice from the Russian model are striking. Firstly, the people's commune did not, except in its early, apocalyptic phase, actually communalise all property, forbid private production, force communal living or eliminate distribution according

by Ch'en Po-ta entitled " Entirely New Society, Entirely New Man " (" Ch'üan-hsin-te She-hui, Ch'üan-hsin-te Jen "), p. 10.

[76] Wu, *op. cit.*, p. 34.

[77] These purges were not, of course, restricted to Honan. They also occurred in Kansu, Liaoning, Yunnan, Shantung, Kwangsi and Chekiang (A. V. Sherman, " The People's Commune," in Geoffrey Hudson *et al.*, *The Chinese Communes* (London: *Soviet Survey*, 1959), pp. 16–17. For the Chekiang case of Sha Wen-han, the Governor of Chekiang accused of " localism " in December 1957, see *Union Research Service*, Vol. 10, No. 7). But P'an held the highest rank in the National Party (alternate mem-ber of the Central Committee) of any of the lot purged. There may also be some connection between the purges in the provinces and the drive to decentralise authority in late 1957. At any rate, since then a number of provincial figures such as Wu Chih-p'u, Ko Ch'ing-shih of Shanghai, and T'ao Chu of Kwangtung have risen to national prominence.

[78] *e.g.*, by Governor Wu in an article for *Chung-kuo Ch'ing-nien Pao*, September 16, 1958, entitled " On People's Communes " (CB, No. 524).

to work (although these are declared the ultimate aims of policy). Secondly, whereas the Russian *kommuna* was a completely agricultural collective reminiscent of the *mir,* the people's commune is an administrative unit of vastly wider competence: it claims to unite the administration of industry, agriculture, commerce, education and the military (*kung-nung-shang-hsüeh-ping*). Finally, the people's commune completely absorbs the functions of the local state organs; it is therefore not merely a form of collective farm as in Russia but rather an all-encompassing organ of local administration.

But given the principle of the commune, its practice is yet another thing. Rather than try to boil down its variety into a few paragraphs, it is better to concentrate on those aspects of its administration which bear on the central focus of this paper: its size and relation to the state administrative system. For this purpose, it is the principle of the unity of the state and the commune (*cheng-she ho-i*) that is of paramount interest.

From the beginning, an important subject of discussion and experimentation was *which* level of government was to be absorbed into the commune; that is, just how large were the units to be. Much flexibility in the solution of this problem was allowed. The *People's Daily* declared on September 3: " The development of people's communes will doubtless be different in time, scale, pace and method in different places. Uniformity should not be imposed." [79] As to the size of communes, the first resolution of the Communist Party's Central Committee (the Peitaiho resolution of August 29, 1958) declared:

> Generally speaking it is at present better to establish one commune to a township with the commune comprising about two thousand peasant households. In some places, several townships may merge and form a single commune comprising about six or seven thousand households, according to topographical conditions and the needs for the development of production. As to the establishment of communes of more than 10,000 or even more than 20,000 households, we need not oppose them, but for the present we should not take the initiative to encourage them.[80]

The size of the commune to be created was naturally a determining factor in deciding which level of government it was to replace. The original model commune, the Weihsing (Sputnik) People's Commune of Hsinyang *chuan-ch'ü,* Honan, was designed to replace the *hsiang* government and had a size of some 9,000 households.[81] But the Peitaiho

---

[79] " Hold High the Red Flag of People's Communes," *People's Daily* editorial, September 3, 1958, *PCIC,* p. 24.

[80] " Resolution of the CC CCP on the establishment of people's communes in the rural areas " (August 29, 1958), *PCIC,* p. 3.

[81] " How to run a people's commune," *People's Daily* editorial, September 4, 1958, *PCIC,* p. 82.

resolution also provided for " *hsien* federations of communes " (*hsien-lien-she*), and by the end of September there were 134 of these units.[82] A third form of organisation was the *hsien* commune, of which a good example is the Chaoyuan *hsien* People's Commune (Heilungkiang) with its 39 *hsiang* and population of 260,000.[83] The difference between the last two forms of organisation was simply that the *hsien* commune was able to distribute free supplies equally throughout the *hsien*, whereas the federation could not afford to. As a vice-chairman of the State Planning Commission, Lo Keng-mo, put it,

> If a commune is to be set up for each *hsien*, economically the level of production must be so high as to insure that, in addition to providing the necessary accumulation funds, the *hsien* committee will maintain the consumer funds for members of its subordinate basic-level communes with unsatisfactory production conditions at the same level as those basic-level communes whose production conditions are better.[84]

It was therefore concluded that at the present time the proper level for the commune was the *hsiang* level, with the exception of those giant communes which could afford equitable supply over a whole *hsien*.[85]

By the end of the period of experimentation 740,000 APCs had been merged into 24,000 people's communes with an average size of 5,000 households in each Since the summer of 1958 there had been some 1,750 *hsien* and some 80,000 *hsiang* in the country, each *hsien* encompassed some 14 communes on the average, and each commune represented a merger of 3–4 former *hsiang*. These averages do not, however, reveal the extent of actual merger of *hsiang* to form communes. In more advanced areas such mergers undoubtedly did occur; Liaoning is an example, where an original 2,854 *hsiang* were merged into 1,226—of which 86 per cent. contained single communes.[86] But it is also possible that the average was raised by the formation of *hsien* level, multi-*hsiang* communes, rather than by any extensive merger of existing *hsiang* units.

From the point of view of administrative organisation, the observer is struck by the degree of continuity with previous institutions. The Party itself approached this question with remarkable cynicism. It declared in the Peitaiho resolution that, in order to disturb current production as little as possible, " in the early period of the merger (of APCs), the method of ' changing the superstructure while keeping the lower

[82] Lo Keng-mo (vice-chairman, State Planning Commission), "*Hsien* Federations of People's Communes," *Ching-chi Yen-chiu*, No. 1, 1959. (ECMM, No. 159.)

[83] Chao Fu-chi, "The System of One Commune for One *hsien*," *Ts'ai-ching Yen-chiu*, No. 9, 1958. (ECMM, No. 156.)

[84] *Ibid.* (Italics mine.)

[85] Wu Shan and Sheng Kang-hou, "The Unification of the State and the Commune," *Cheng-fa Yen-chiu*, No. 1, 1959, pp. 4–8.

[86] Liaoning Province Rural Work Department, "The Experience of Liaoning Province in Merging Co-operatives," *People's Daily*, September 2, 1958.

structure unchanged' may be adopted. . . . The original organisation of production and system of administration may, for the time being, remain unchanged and continue as before." [87] As a result, in the period of experimentation there was considerable discussion over just what might legitimately be termed a " people's commune." In one case, the problem of what to term a former large APC in Liaoning, the problem was resolved by calling it a commune " in consideration of the mass character of the present revolutionary movement "—*i.e.*, because it sounded better.

The internal administration of the commune, though showing great variation, likewise was fairly directly inherited from former organisations. In the case of Weihsing People's Commune, the administrative branches of the commune were made up of the former organs of the *hsiang*: a congress, a managing committee and a set of departments.[88] The operative units at lower levels were the former APCs, now called " production contingents " or " production brigades " (*sheng-ch'an lien-tui*), and their constituent " production teams " (*sheng-ch'an-tui*). A *hsien* commune such as Chaoyuan would have in addition " work districts " (*tso-yeh-ch'ü*) at the former *hsiang* level. And as time wore on and more emphasis was placed on efficiency at the lower levels, smaller units were organised and titled " small team " (*hsiao-tui*) or " work group " (*tso-yeh-tsu*). The proliferation of organs and levels of organisation, therefore, tended to approach the complexity of the pre-commune period as more and more emphasis was laid on the consolidation of the existing administrative organisation built on the commune.

CONCLUSIONS

The short history of Communist administrative rule in China might be summarised as follows: from 1949–54 the Party sought to create a state structure that would have roots in every village of the countryside. It therefore simplified the chain of command of the superstructure and deliberately left the size of local organs small. Beginning in 1953 and gathering speed after 1955 a second system of administration, the economic system of collective farms, with local organs of ever-increasing size and competence was created. In 1957 there was a serious attempt to block and set back the growth in size of APCs, but in the end the necessity of greater mass organisation for agricultural growth thwarted it and caused to be created a new system of very large units combining state and economic authority.

In this history the model of the Soviet Union looms large. The state system established in 1954 bore a marked resemblance to that of the

---

[87] *PCIC*, p. 5.
[88] " Tentative Regulations (Draft) of the Weihsing (Sputnik) People's Commune," August 7, 1958, *PCIC*, p. 68.

U.S.S.R. under the constitution of 1936. The process of collectivisation seemed to repeat in almost ontogenic fashion the same process in the U.S.S.R. But increasingly after the realisation in 1956 that the Soviet pattern of agricultural mechanisation was not applicable to China, the Chinese struck off in directions of their own—in the substitution of water conservancy for mechanisation, and finally in the elimination in principle of the cherished Soviet socialist distinction between the state and the economy.

If there is a central theme to this history, it is that the size and articulation of local organs of administration were adjusted at will by the Party to meet their criteria of efficiency. The goals of efficiency determined the ideal configuration: during the period of consolidation to 1955 it was the administrative *integrity* of the units that was desired, and therefore they were kept small to facilitate their internal order. During the period of concerted growth after 1955 it was the administrative *amenability* of local organs to central demands that was desired, and therefore they were expanded to the maximum size consistent with internal order. The balance between integrity and amenability was determined, often after considerable intra-Party discussions, by the nature of administrative business (*i.e.*, whether large-scale or small scale activities) and by the availability and capability of personnel. It is likely that the problem of balancing these factors of area and power will continue well into the future.

Some Problems of China's Rural Communes

THE rural people's communes, launched in the summer and autumn of 1958, purported to be a grand new social, political and economic organisation. They were supposed to be like " a fine horse, which having shaken off its bridle, is galloping courageously directly towards the highway of Communism." [1] An organisation had been created where collective living was actively promoted and the " Five-togethers " practised,[2] where women were " freed from the drudgery of home life " and drawn into full time participation in the commune production, where labour could be shifted from area to area or even occupation to occupation according to needs and requirements, where the rural areas were not only the scene of agricultural production, but were also new centres of workshops producing steel and machine tools, and where the previous village, township and even county administration was now merged into the new commune administration, which thus undertook multifarious activities.

But hardly had a few months passed when the need for exercising some restraint on that " gallop " was felt, and the Communist Party's Central Committee passed the famous December 1958 resolution in an attempt to rectify the excesses. Obviously, despite the claims of fantastic increases in agricultural production, the Party leadership became somewhat concerned with the impact of the changes on production.[3]

The December 1958 resolution criticised excessive centralisation, commended greater distribution of income according to work in order to provide some incentives to the peasantry, stressed the strengthening of labour management and the fixing of responsibility for various production tasks, and in general called for moderation. Yet neither the leadership nor a number of high-level cadres seemed to be in a mood for real moderation and for a correct perspective of the problems that had been

---

[1] *Kiangsi Daily*, Nan Ch'ang, November 26, 1959, p. 3.

[2] The " five-togethers " were working together, eating together, living together, studying together and drilling together.

[3] For a background to the formation of the communes, the changes that were introduced, the adverse effects they had on the peasantry, and the details of the 1958 resolution, see the author's article, " The Rural People's Communes of China," *International Studies*, New Delhi, Vol. III, No. 1, July 1961, pp. 45-64.

created by the new system. It was only when the misfortunes of 1959 were followed by the disastrous harvest of 1960 that Peking finally woke up to the realities of the situation and implemented the serious and drastic measures to check the rapidly deteriorating conditions. This paper deals mainly with the situation and changes introduced from late 1959 to recent times in the status and working of the rural people's communes. These changes relate to the whole gamut of organisation, social, economic and technical fields, and an attempt has been made here to touch upon the most important ones.

While the human and organisational problems were to prove more and more vexing in the next two years, some of the economic and technical problems were being realised by agricultural experts and technicians even at an early stage. The attempt of the communes to start developing in every direction regardless of resources and capacities, the attempt to grow into self-sufficient units, to become more or less states within the state, was already worrying the experts in early 1959. They were concerned with the fact that the role of economic geography in the plans of development of a particular area was being completely forgotten. A group of twenty experts of the Geography Department of the Peking Teachers' Normal College, for instance, found in a survey of many communes that not enough attention was being given to natural conditions, characteristics and economic geography of the area in laying down its plans of development. In the drive for self-support, the communes did not stop to weigh carefully to what degree the communes should achieve self-sufficiency, in what products could the commune feasibly achieve self-sufficiency, and what agricultural and industrial operations could the commune possibly undertake.[4]

They cited the instance of a commune only ten kilometres from Foochow in Fukien province, with a population of 40,300 and farm land of only 25,000 mow of land—a typical overpopulated area—the traditional crops were rice and citrus fruit, followed by wheat, rapeseed and vegetables. The production programme mapped out in October 1958, however provided for a " multi-product " economy and demanded the planting of 1,000 mow of cotton to meet the consumption needs of the commune members. In fact the area had never grown any cotton and natural conditions were not favourable for the production of cotton. The plan also called for the construction of an iron smelting plant with an annual capacity of 2,000 tons and a machine factory; the area actually produced neither iron nor limestone.[5] Another commune in the same province was situated in a hilly area and was in a well-known forest

---

[4] *Ti-li hsüeh-pao*, Vol. XXV, No. 1, February 1959.
[5] *Ibid*.

district [of its total land area of 550,000 mow, forest-area accounted for 421,000], but in pursuance of the Party policy of self-sufficiency, it placed all its emphasis on rice production, although climatic conditions did not suit rice planting here.

The experts decried such " irrational development " and called for due attention to " natural conditions, historical background, labour force and economic characteristics " of an area while shaping plans for its economic development. It is doubtful, however, whether the experts were taken very seriously at the time. Moreover, at that time even they either did not have the courage to point out the extremely unsettling effect of the recent changes or were themselves swept away by the propaganda of the big leap and talk of huge armies of labour moving up and down to perform Herculean acts of labour. They too had grandiose plans of merging villages and moving populations and developing new centres of population in the communes so as " to coordinate farming, forestry, animal husbandry, subsidiary production and fishing, to facilitate the leadership and administration of production and to mobilise and allocate the labour force." Such concentration points should, in their opinion, be determined according to general investigation of the characteristics of the area, the needs of the commune people, and use of all favourable conditions for maximum development of production.[6]

Indeed, Peking had as yet a very insufficient understanding of the problems that had been raised and had no intention of making any but the minimum concessions to keep the peasant galvanised into intense labour activity. It was apparently the hope of Mao and his colleagues that by a little " tidying up " and by giving some small concessions they would be able to meet the demands of the peasantry and the interests of production and still retain essentially the same policies. The " gallop " would be curbed a little bit, but not allowed to degenerate into a slow trot. The leadership had to do a great deal of tight-rope walking by arresting the excesses and preventing the situation from getting out of hand [7] and at the same time keeping the movement going ahead at a fast speed. As a result there was considerable confusion both at the top and the lower levels, and many of the readjustments envisaged in the 1958 December resolution were not genuinely implemented, an act of omission for which the cadres were, of course, duly rebuked later.

STRUGGLE AGAINST THE " RIGHTISTS "

But once it was admitted that " some mistakes " had been made and that " readjustments " were necessary, the working of the people's

---

6 Article by Lien I-tung, *Ti-li chih-shih*, No. 9, 1959, pp. 390–392.
7 The Communist Party issued directives in February 1959 as well as in August 1959 regarding " readjustments."

communes ran into a spate of criticism in the countryside during 1959. In fact, the Party machinery had to be geared into action to put down this criticism and defend the Party policies. This criticism was further reinforced when the admissions regarding 1958 output claims were made. It was all the more serious because it appeared within the Party too. " In the past several months inside our Party, a rightist opportunist ideological tide has risen from the horizon. A small group of rightist opportunists are associating themselves with the slander-mongering campaign launched by the enemy both within and without the country." [8] In an article on October 1, 1959, marking the tenth anniversary of the People's Republic, Liu Shao-ch'i, Chairman of the Republic said that the critics of the Party policies maintained that the communes were " in a mess " and had " outstripped the level of social development and the level of the people's consciousness." [9] The critics described people's communes, it was alleged, as " the result of the subjective wishes of a few people and did not reflect the desires of the peasant masses," said " no early shoots of Communism could exist in a socialist society," that the " combination of the wage and free supply system was harmful," that " community dining rooms were imposed on the peasant " and so on.[10] There was also criticism of the Party's agricultural policies, particularly of the Eight-point Charter [11] of mess halls,[12] and of commune ownership.[13]

The Party leadership launched a strong counter-attack on the " rightist " critics of the commune developments both inside and outside the Party. In the autumn and winter of 1959 a severe rectification campaign was afoot to defend the communes and their various features and to silence the critics. The rightist critics of the communes were, of course, weeded out but the rightism of cadres who were " cautious " and wanted to " go slow " was also condemned. The *People's Daily* complained about those cadres who thought that it was better to " go slow " and fix " low targets " [obviously these cadres wanted to avoid the experience of the false claims of 1958] and stressed that there was a rightist danger on the economic front." [14] Even many of the features that were later discarded were defended at this time.

For instance, although the December 1958 resolution laid down the principle of three level ownership (those of the commune, brigade and the team) in order to boost peasant enthusiasm, in late 1959 emphasis was still being laid on ownership at the commune level as the most fundamental

[8] *Nan-fang Daily*, September 15, 1959.
[9] *People's Daily*, October 1, 1959.
[10] *Red Flag*, No. 20, 1959, *Peking Review*, December 1, 1959, p. 6
[11] *People's Daily*, October 19, 1959.
[12] *Kiangsi Daily*, August 20, 1959.
[13] *Ibid*. Editorial, November 24, 1959.
[14] *People's Daily*, August 6, 1959.

and significant aspect of the new organisation and hope was being expressed that this would soon develop to an extent that it would dominate the economy of the whole commune and thus bring the peasantry closer to the Communist stage of collective economy. It was emphasised that the economy of the commune was revolving around the system of commune ownership [15] and that " Socialist and Communist education " of the peasants must be vigorously developed so that they could switch over from " small-scale collective ownership " to " grand scale collective ownership " and thus progress towards the " people's ownership." [16] Liu Shao-chi in his article on October 1, 1959, declared that commune ownership had elements of ownership by the whole people and envisaged that as this ownership developed (as against brigade and team ownership) and when it became the basic form of ownership, " a reliable foundation will have been laid for transition to Socialist ownership by all the people in the countryside." [17]

In the struggle against the critics all the old advantages associated with the establishment of the communes in 1958 were recounted (thus indirectly revealing the dichotomy of thinking in the Communist councils by which the Party wanted to " tidy up " the communes and yet retain the essentials of the original features of the people's communes). The commune had brought about " startling changes " within one year by combining " industry, agriculture, commerce, education and militia." It was once again emphasised that the commune could undertake basic agricultural reconstruction which was beyond the resources of the agricultural co-operative because of limited manpower and insufficient funds. Now the commune with its " strong economic power " could use its resources " in a unified way." Land potentialities could now be thoroughly developed. Although land, draught animals, farming instruments, etc., belonged to the brigades, the commune still had the right to make " partial and appropriate adjustments under conditions advantageous to both sides." Moreover, it was said, the commune served as " social insurance " for the poor peasants, as it was better able to help them out during their lean days than the old co-operative could. A " section " of the farm families, on account of " insufficient working power or labour power," with a large number of mouths to be fed or other " social reasons " lived in poverty—so it was said. They regularly overdrew money from the co-operative. In 1957, for example, in Chiang-hsiang commune in Nanch'ang *hsien* of Kiangsi province, there were about 62·2 per cent. of such peasant households. As a result, it was stated that a " section " of peasant households who should have received their income

[15] *Kiangsi Daily*, November 29, 1959, p. 3.
[16] *Ibid*. October 24, 1959, p. 2.
[17] *People's Daily*, October 1, 1959.

were unable to " get it in full "—there were the " empty shareholders,"
who said " looking-glass money can be seen but not touched, it is
alright to earn just sufficient money to feed yourself but no more." Now,
it was claimed, the commune could assure adequate rations to everyone
and pay their share of income in cash, and that the communes
had created conditions for the poor brigades to catch up with the richer
ones.[18]

It was thought conceivable that after completion of the rectification
campaign in the communes " this winter or next spring " the " revolutionary strength " of the broad masses would have been greatly increased, and that after persistent effort the goal of the struggle [complete
communal ownership] would be reached.[19] This " rectification " movement was in effect a sharpening of the class struggle in the countryside,
which the Chinese Communists resort to every time they change the
existing social and economic organisation in the villages. During the
early land reform period, the leadership asked the Party cadres to " isolate " the landlords, " neutralise " the rich peasants, and unite with the
poor and middle peasants; at the time of the formation of agricultural
producer co-operatives, it was the rich peasants who were to be isolated,
middle peasants who were to be neutralised, and the poor peasants who
were to be united with; now with the formation of the commune, the
cadres were advised to rely mainly on poor peasants and lower middle
peasants and struggle against the rich and middle peasants.[20] While the
object of reliance, the poor peasantry, has remained constant, the
" enemy " has been eliminated one by one—the landlords, then the rich
peasants, and now—though not quite (because of agricultural difficulties)
—the middle peasants.

In any case, the critics were counter-attacked and the supremacy of
the commune system was asserted. In January 1960 Li Fu-ch'un, Chairman of the State Planning Commission claimed that " although China had
in 1959 suffered from the most serious natural calamities of the past few
decades and the farm lands affected exceeded 600 million mow, that is
more than one third of the land under cultivation, we still succeeded in
scoring outstanding achievements. The total value of agricultural output
is far greater than the planned targets." [21] It was claimed that grain
production reached the 270 million tons mark.[22] It was also asserted that

---

[18] *Ibid. Red Flag*, No. 20, 1959.

[19] *Kiangsi Daily*, Editorial, November 24, 1959, p. 1.

[20] Mobilisation of the poor peasantry and concentration on development of poor
brigades and teams to meet the challenge of the " rightists " was an insistent note
in the Communist Party writings during this time.

[21] *Red Flag*, No. 1, 1960; *Peking Review*, No. 1, January 5, 1960, p. 9.

[22] Press communiqué on the growth of China's economy, January 22, 1960, *Peking
Review*, No. 4, January 26, 1960, p. 10.

in 1959 there was an "integrated, all-round development in farming, forestry, animal husbandry, side-occupations, fishing, grains, cotton, oil bearing crops, silk, fruits, vegetables, medical herbs, miscellaneous farm products." And that "with the exception of Tibet, the various provinces, municipalities and autonomous regions have all built up their own iron and steel industry, engineering industry and other heavy industries and light industries.[23]

There is little doubt, however, that some of these claims were highly exaggerated. Apart from the fact that many of the blast furnaces had to be scrapped as the so-called pig iron that they were producing was totally useless, the figure for grain production was also incorrect, particularly in view of the admission that one third of the cultivated land was badly affected by inclement weather. Moreover, the Chinese authorities themselves admitted in 1962 that they had had three successive bad years in agriculture, and included 1959 in it.[24] What is perhaps true is that the damage in 1959 was not as great as in the next year and consequently a thorough readjustment in organisation and techniques was not undertaken until 1960 proved to be even more disastrous than 1959 and showed beyond any doubt that it was not only the weather which was unkind but that human, organisational and technical problems were also responsible for the increasing difficulties in agriculture.

"STRENGTHENING" OF PARTY LEADERSHIP

The dilemma of the Chinese authorities—the contradiction in fact—was that they wanted to keep the leap forward movement going at full steam and yet, disturbed by reports about peasant disaffection, had to take steps to curb the "excesses" and provide some incentive to the peasantry. Following upon a resolution by the Central Committee in December 1958 and a number of directives issued as a result of a Central Committee meeting in February 1959, a series of measures were outlined in an attempt to keep the economic progress from being derailed and contain both the disenchantment of the peasants and the enthusiasm of some cadres who were becoming "giddy with success." [25] A few of the important directions have been mentioned above. Apart from the measures designed to reassure the peasantry, the Communist Party also seemed to lay great store by the "strengthening of leadership" in the communes. It was believed that many of the problems would be resolved if more direct and

---

23 Li Fu-chun, *op. cit.*
24 See for instance, Chou En-lai's speech at an anniversary reception on September 30, 1962. *Peking Review*, No. 4, October 5, 1962, p. 6.
25 For a full text of the December 1958 Resolution see the pamphlet entitled *Sixth Plenary Session of the Eighth Central Committee of the Communist Party of China*, Foreign Languages Press, Peking, 1958, pp. 12-49.

firm leadership was provided in the villages. For this it was considered essential for the cadres, particularly those at the higher level (in the commune secretariat, for instance) to reinforce their ties with the peasants, take part in day to day work themselves, and provide greater attention and direction to the problems of production at lower levels.[26]

The case of the Ever Green Commune in Shensi province was cited by the *People's Daily* as an example of how leadership should be improved in the communes. There, it was reported, the Party cadres shed their routine work and began spending most of their time in the fields and re-invigorating the work in " political-ideological education as well as in organisation." Whereas formerly the first secretary of the commune Party committee could only spend six or seven days in a month in the villages, now he could live as many as twenty days among the commune members, " working together with them on the one hand and conducting investigation on the other." So, under the " concrete assistance " of the Party committee, the Party branches in various brigades and teams also changed their working methods and began giving more thorough and on-the-spot guidance.[27]

In 1960, and particularly in the latter half of the year, a relocation of the duties and functions of the cadres took place in order to bring about greater supervision by them at the team and brigade levels. For instance, in June 1960 the *People's Daily* gave publicity to the so-called " two-five " system, first practised in Wu-ch'iao *hsien* of Hopei province, by which two days out of a week were given by the cadres to " studies, conferences and research projects " and for the rest of the five days they joined small production teams, participating in and taking charge of production and " substantially assisting " in the resolution of the problems of the teams.[28] After this experience various other systems of leadership programmes were devised. Reports came from Kirin province about the " three-seven " system. The three levels of cadres—*hsien*, commune and brigade—reportedly conducted " study," " investigation " and allocation of work for the first three days in ten days and in the remaining seven days they engaged in production work.[29]

The essential purpose of these or a variety of these systems was to provide for greater supervision by the cadres of the basic production units. It was, to take one instance, reported from Hopei's Shang-tu *hsien* that " high-level " cadres of all departments at the *hsien* level were appointed assistant secretaries of the brigades or assistant brigade leaders

---

[26] See, for instance, the example of Ever Green People's Commune lauded by the *People's Daily*, August 14, 1959.
[27] *Ibid.*
[28] *Ibid.* June 16, 1960.
[29] *Ibid.* June 29, 1960.

and that the " general " cadres of the *hsien* and the commune functioned as assistant secretaries of production teams or assistant team leaders.[30] Another report from the Chinghai province stated that in each of the six people's communes in Kung-ho *hsien* at least one member of the Communist Party *hsien* committee was sent to the commune in a position of leadership and that a cadre of the *hsien* " leadership class " was stationed in each production brigade in some responsible position. Lower-level cadres from the *hsien* and commune Party committee were suitably posted among the production teams.[31]

Thus, it was hoped, the problems could be solved, the pitch of high labour activity and enthusiasm derived by the Party leadership and witnessed during the first year of the Big Leap maintained, and agricultural production increased at a fast rate. The concessions in organisation and distribution of income were calculated to mollify the peasants somewhat, and it was confidently hoped that these would be sufficient to keep the agricultural economy going at a fast tempo. The setback in 1959, which was attributed entirely to bad weather, produced no basic change in the Politbureau's thinking and policies. There was greater stress on agriculture with " priority to heavy industry," [32] but essentially the old policy of giving small concessions but preserving the main features was continued. The year 1960 proved to be one of the most disastrous years in Chinese Communist agricultural history. According to one visitor to China with high-level contacts, grain production slumped down to 150 million tons [33] (and it may be remembered that this included coarse grains and sweet potatoes). Chinese agriculture was in the throes of a serious crisis and it was obvious that a thorough overhaul of Party policies however agonising must be undertaken to stop the rapid downward trend and get the economy back on an even keel; it was equally obvious that this would require major and sustained effort.[34] There were political problems, organisational problems, economic problems, technical problems, all of which required a thorough shake-up of old policies and methods.

DISLOCATION OF THE SYSTEM AND REORGANISATION OF THE COMMUNES

First of all, and in general, it may be said that the Chinese effort at fast agricultural expansion through mere socio-economic reorganisation without comparable capital investment by the state had failed. The aim of

---

[30] *Ibid.* October 21, 1960.
[31] *Ibid.* July 3, 1960.
[32] *Ibid. Editorial*, August 25, 1960.
[33] Lord Montgomery's article in *The Sunday Times*, Magazine Section, October 15, 1961.
[34] How serious the crisis has been can be seen from the fact that the authorities have yet to release production figures for the last three years.

all Communist countries has been to achieve rapid industrialisation and the policy of each has been to put all the funds in industry and starve agriculture. The Chinese thought that they had found their salvation in the commune organisation which would enable them to develop both industry and agriculture at the same time at an almost equally fast tempo. They now had to learn the bitter lesson that no amount of structural changes were a substitute for capital investment in agriculture— structural changes had meaning only if accompanied by large capital investment in agriculture. In what must have been a painful decision, Mao gave up the hitherto accepted principle of Communist development, made agriculture genuinely the " foundation " of the economy, cut back industrial investments and substantially trimmed industrial expansion, and gave the slogan of making industry " serve " agriculture.[35]

Apart from the basic problem of lack of adequate investment in agriculture, there were other fundamental problems afflicting the Chinese communes. One of the most important was that the commune had upset the peasant routine far too much for production to be maintained even at earlier levels. The peasant's life had been dislocated and he was pulled away from his roots. The notion of vast peasant armies moving up and down the land to perform great feats of labour to " transform nature " and of the peasant alternating for different kinds of jobs and skills, becoming both a worker and a peasant, not to speak of being a student, soldier and technician all lumped into one, played havoc with agricultural production. The changes were too great, too sudden and too startling. Not only did the peasant lose his moorings, but the whole system of agricultural production became dislocated. It had to be put back into shape, and a thorough reorganisation effected before the situation could return to normal.

People who had one kind of skill were sent to jobs requiring a different kind of skill; those who had spent a lifetime in farming found themselves suddenly smelting iron. The peddler, who knew the needs of the villages and the requirements of the small towns nearby, thus providing a useful economic link between the two, disappeared. The village blacksmith and mason too, vanished in many cases. Consequently, not only did farming suffer but there were no adequate substitute organisations to repair the implements and do the semi-skilled jobs in the villages and function as economic links between the towns and villages. Those who were familiar with the lay of the land and the conditions in one area were often sent to work in other areas where they were strangers both to the area and to the agricultural conditions prevailing there. It was this

---

[35] See the resolution of the Ninth Plenum of the Central Committee of the Chinese Communist Party, January 14-18, 1961. *Peking Review*, No. 4, January 27, 1961, pp. 5-7.

general dislocation of the system, perhaps more than anything else, which greatly contributed to the magnitude of agricultural failures of 1959 and 1960. It became imperative that the Communists restore the normalcy of life and of agricultural operations as a first step towards rehabilitating sagging agricultural production. No doubt, the Communist difficulties were substantially compounded by natural calamities,[36] but the latter can by no means be made to explain away the troubles of the last three years.[37]

Conditions had to be recreated in which the peasants' normal routine and sense of belonging was the primary object of attention, in which skills were respected and used rationally and in which the system could function without unbearable tension, ferment and uncertainty. Economically, the people's communes, it was now declared, were an " aggregate organisation of our production brigades; therefore it is a socialist organisation one grade higher than the advanced agricultural co-operatives." [38] Since the production brigades were approximately the same as the old agricultural co-operative, the peasant was once again to function in the environments that he was so accustomed to. " Centralised guidance " and " separate management " were now asked to " coexist." It was, however, explained that there was a big difference between the old co-operative and the new system, because the farmer was now a constituent of the aggregate organisation of the people's commune, " guided " and " assisted " by the commune committee and " supported by sister brigades." When necessary and on the basis of needs and possibilities, the commune committee could " rely on the co-operation of the production brigades " for working anywhere on commune projects and other " basic construction beneficial to agriculture," but the production brigade was an " independently managed and basic budgetary unit in the aggregate organisation of the people's communes." [39]

To begin with, the economic relationships within the commune were reorganised so as to provide greater incentives for hard work. A policy of " three-level ownership " and " four fixes " was emphasised, by which labour power, land, draught animals and farm tools were owned by the production brigade but " fixed " for the use of the production team, and the commune administration could no longer withdraw them, withhold them or tamper with them at will.[40]

[36] NCNA reported on December 29, 1960, that in that year one-half of the total arable land, or 900 million mow (60 million hectares) were affected and that the damage was heaviest on 20–27 million hectares.

[37] Chou En-lai in his speech on the 13th anniversary admitted that the agricultural difficulties were caused both by serious natural disasters and " shortcomings and mistakes in our work." *Peking Review*, No. 40, October 5, 1962, p. 6.

[38] *Chung-kuo Ch'ing-nien*, No. 8, April 1961.

[39] *Ibid.*

[40] *Red Flag*, No. 3–4, February 1, 1961, pp. 26–32.

Management, use of labour power and ownership of basic implements were thus decentralised to allow for both greater efficiency and harder work, and a small unit like the production team once again became the basic economic unit in the commune.[41] The production team was ensured the right to plant according to soil conditions of its land, the right to change its planting system according to the soil conditions, the right to determine technical measures and labour man hours in accordance with the ability of the team, the right to decide the order of the work, the right to control manpower, cattle and farm tools, the right to disburse wage funds possessed by the team and the right to conduct a minimum of side occupation. In other words, so far as the daily life and occupation of the peasant was concerned, some of the old familiarity and old routine was returning.

Whatever the advantages of mobility of labour in agriculture in large economic units theoretically might have been, in practice such attempts to move peasant labour from one place to another were found to disrupt agricultural production. Labour was, therefore, " fixed " and its deployment determined by the brigades and teams, which in effect, as mentioned above, substantially recreated the old pattern of agricultural activity for the peasant. Apart from the psychological impact of the mobility of labour in agriculture as envisaged in the earlier phase of communisation, the organisational and technical impact was no less deleterious. Since there was so much uncertainty about the availability of labour at particular times to particular areas, production targets could hardly be planned with reasonable assurance. Decisions at the commune level were frequently divorced from actual conditions and tended to disregard the specific requirements and local peculiarities which play a very significant role in agriculture production. The cadres had to be reminded of local " feasibility " and local " conditions." It was now warned that areas which observed and adhered to the principle of local " feasibility " " usually score faster and better agricultural production." [42]

EXCHANGE AT " PAR VALUE "

With agricultural production as the focal point of all activity, a new stress came to be laid on " exchange at par value." This had wide significance in the Chinese context. This affected exchange relations between industrial and agricultural produce, exchange between communes and other " collective " units, between brigades and the commune and between teams and the brigades.[43] Obviously since agriculture was being made to pay for

[41] *Chung-kuo Ch'ing-nien*, No. 8, April 1961.
[42] *People's Daily*, September 1961, September 13, 1961 and March 22, 1962.
[43] Article by Kung Shih-chi and Wu-chien, *Jen-min Jih-pao*, May 20, 1961, p. 7.

rapid industrialisation, agricultural prices were at a disproportionate disadvantage to industrial prices. Now the Party promised the peasantry more equitable terms of exchange between agricultural and industrial products, thus providing the peasants with larger income to compensate for their hard work. To what extent the imbalance was rectified is not known, but the Party did not really envisage a major change in the price structure of industrial and agricultural sectors, and the instructions were that the proportionate price of the industrial and agricultural products should neither be lowered too much nor enhanced too much.[44] At the same time the communes were assured better terms when exchanging goods with other state-managed enterprises.

However, the significance of " parity exchange " went beyond the fixing of equitable ratio between industrial and agricultural prices. Apparently in the first phase of communisation, the commune administration would take over the produce from the brigades at unfair terms and the teams parted with their produce at equally unfair terms dictated by the brigades. Not infrequently, the labour of a production brigade would be requisitioned for work at a different place—maybe for some large scale water conservancy project or for setting up some industrial enterprise—without proper payment and compensation for labour thus employed. It was now conceded that if " exchange at par value " was not practised, then one party would have encroached upon the ownership rights of the other party and occupied the latter's " property and the fruits of its labour without compensation." This " cannot be allowed " because of its " direct effect on production in the socialist stage." [45] So full compensation must be made for acquisition of material or labour by the commune from the brigade, by one brigade from another brigade, by the brigade from the team and by the team from its members. And if somebody's " socialist consciousness " rankled, he was assured that this system would promote " socialist co-operation " by " realising the principle of voluntariness and mutual benefit."

All this was, of course, tied up with the central question of ownership, distribution and exchange. Although the 1958 resolution had envisaged three-level ownership (partly owned by the whole commune, partly by the brigade, and partly by the teams), we have seen above how the emphasis in late 1959 was still on commune ownership and it was hoped that very soon commune economy would dominate that of the brigades and the teams. Now, after the agricultural failure of 1960, more serious implementation of the concept of three-level ownership with brigade as the foundation was undertaken, and it was conceded that " the transition from

---

[44] See, for instance, an article on " Some Problems of Procurement of Agricultural Products." *People's Daily,* October 26, 1961, p. 7.
[45] *People's Daily,* May 20, 1961, p. 7.

basic ownership by brigade, to basic ownership by the commune is a thing of the future." [46]   Furthermore, the assurance was given that even in the future commune ownership would not be developed by confiscating the property of the brigades and teams, which immediately affected the peasants, but by modern agro-technical developments at the commune level, like " commune-operated tractors and pumps, etc."; but as for the draught animals and farm implements owned by production brigades, the forests, fruit trees and perennial crops cultivated by the production brigades, and the enterprises operated by production brigades, they were not to be taken over and placed under commune ownership, but were to be developed by the production brigades and operated and used by them. [47]

With the ownership rights of the brigades and the teams thus confirmed, the organisation and management of production as mentioned above briefly had also been changed. A gradual system of responsibility from the production brigades to the teams was instituted under a system of " three guarantee-one reward." [48]   The communes entered into contracts for fulfilling production targets with the production brigades, and the brigades with the teams, and the teams with the team members, either individually or in groups, and rewards were awarded for overfulfilling of the quotas. At the same time responsibility was fixed for each chore of work either group-wide or individually, [49] and emphasis in agricultural production was in fact shifting not only from the commune to the brigades, but from the brigade to the team, and even to smaller groups within the team.

A NEW WAGE SYSTEM

Essentially, the Party had to re-establish a pattern of incentives to rehabilitate peasant enthusiasm, and abjure the criticism of wages as a bourgeois concept. The wage system had to be refurbished on the principle of he who does not work, neither shall he eat, and he who works more shall get more. Basically, the Party had to recognise that differences would exist between different brigades, and between different teams even within the same brigade, not to speak of individuals. These differences, it was now acknowledged, stemmed from different degrees of fertility of land, different distances between farm lands and community markets, different amounts of money invested in land, and different amounts of labour used. [50]   Agricultural production could not be promoted by punishing the

[46] *Red Flag*, Nos. 3–4, February 1, 1961, pp. 26–32.
[47] *Ibid.*
[48] See the report of Tung-Ying brigade of Lu Pu commune in Kiangsu province. *People's Daily*, May 20, 1961, p. 2.
[49] See, for instance, the report on the Min-Chi commune in Ma-Cheng *hsieh*, Hopei province, *People's Daily*, June 30, 1961, p. 4.
[50] *People's Daily*, July 26, 1961.

richer brigades or teams or by developing the poor brigades and teams at the expense of the rich ones, but by trying to lift the poor ones through better organisation and efficiency and through commune and state aid. The differences in income and standards of living created by this kind of inequality must be recognised.[51] A complicated hierarchy of wage structure was evolved, which differed sometimes in different places, but was at bottom the piecework wage system. The wage points for each commune member were appraised on the basis of diverse farm chores and the quantity of daily labour performed. According to an authoritative article in the *People's Daily*, basically there were two methods adopted for wage appraisal. The first one was work calculated by time (by hours or days). A " labour point " was fixed for a member after taking into account the labour force, his techniques and his labour " attitude." The other method was wage by piecework, wherein labour norms for various kinds of work were set beforehand and wage points were calculated according to the amount and quality of work of each member.[52]

The article said that wage by piecework was " preferred " in the present stage when communes were implementing the principle of distribution in accordance with labour. It raised the " labour efficiency " of the members and provided greater scope for the use of auxiliary labour (for instance, it " encouraged " the aged and the children to take part in the work, such as weeding of grass and tidying up of trees). However, the cadres were exhorted that labour norms must be fixed " fairly and rationally " and that in this process due attention must be given to nature of the farm chores, their technical requirements, the degree of hard labour involved and their importance in production, heavier work being assigned more labour points than lighter work, skilled work more than unskilled, and in general higher remuneration fixed for busy season as against off season.[53]

The complex nature of the wage system that was being evolved may be gauged from a report on the Ming-hsing production team of Wo-lung commune in Hsiang-yang *hsien*, Hupei, where the work of the " labour norm control " and " wage appraisal " had been " revamped " and labour organisation " readjusted," thus streamlining the production responsibility system and better enforcing the policy of whoever works more gets more. According to the report, there were in this team throughout the year 314 kinds of chores, among them 158 chores for the lunar calendar's fourth, fifth, sixth, seventh and eighth moons, which constituted the busy season, and 93 chores in third, ninth and tenth moon which formed the " fair "

[51] *Chung-kuo Ch'ing-nien*, No. 8, April 1961.
[52] Article by Liu Kang, *People's Daily*, August 4, 1961, p. 7.
[53] *Ibid*.

season, and 63 chores in the eleventh, twelfth, first and second moon which fall within the off season.[54]

In order to reassure the peasantry on the policy of distribution according to labour and to " stimulate " the people's " positive qualities " towards production, the " economic handbook " was popularised. The economic handbook was described as " certificate of all economic transactions between the commune members and the production brigade." It consisted of two parts, the first part recording the labour contribution of the member and the second part containing the record of all economic transactions of the member, such as periodic and advance payments of wages and their financial accounting, charges for food, and accounting for the transactions between the member and the brigade, etc. Thus each member knew the amount of labour he had put in, the sum of money that he might have drawn, and his final share in the income.[55]

A great deal of experimentation in evolving the wage system went on all over the Chinese countryside and in April 1962 the *People's Daily* wrote that " all remuneration methods adopted by different localities were good as long as they conform with actual local conditions, satisfy the masses and are continually given attention and study so that they can be continually improved." [56] A vastly complicated system, if the educational level in the villages and the other burdens of the cadres are kept in view, was being evolved. The amount of bookkeeping itself was enormous, and then the fixing of labour norms for different chores of work [which ran into hundreds], and even within one kind of work the determination of labour points for each member according to the quantity and quality of work—all these were extremely complicated tasks on whose correct handling depended whether the peasant would feel generally satisfied or not. To take only a few scattered instances of the kinds of problems that could arise, the sixth production team of the sixth production brigade of the Min-Chi commune in Hopei province had originally assigned thirty-five points for planting one mow of rice seedlings in the seed beds, and one point for removing thirty bunches of rice seedlings from the seed beds. This led to much dispute among the commune members engaged in the removal of seedlings. They said that the seedlings were small and labour consuming and that they would be better off by planting (which would bring them higher labour points) than removing seedlings. A commune representative, in an on-the-spot survey, found that the assignment of one point for removing thirty bunches of rice seedlings was unfair and that members who really worked fast could only earn eight points, while in the

---

[54] *Ibid.* August 19, 1961, p. 5.
[55] *Ta Kung Pao*, March 20, 1961.
[56] *People's Daily*, April 25, 1962.

planting of seedlings even the very slow workers could earn more than ten points a day.[57] In another kind of example in the ninth production team of the same brigade it was observed that some female members out-performed their male colleagues in speed and quality in planting rice seedlings; consequently the male members were unwilling to have female members plant rice seedlings and they were not given the points due to them. The commune Party Secretary when conducting a survey found that such discrimination against women was not uncommon.[58]

"PRIVATE PLOTS" AND RURAL MARKET FAIRS

In another step in the process of recreating a pattern of incentives, since the end of 1960, the " private plot " was restored and the peasants were allowed to engage in small private production and subsidiary occu-pation.[59] The plots allotted were tiny, as only 5 per cent. of the average cultivated land could be set apart for such private cultivation, and the peasants could work on them or any other private sideline occupation only in their spare time; but the psychological and material value of this step was not insignificant, and it helped in shortening the gap between supply and demand of many commodities.[60] At the same time the autho-rities encouraged the holding of rural market fairs where the private produce could be sold under control and supervision of the administra-tion. These rural fairs were popularised by extensive coverage in the press,[61] and were soon developed not only as a medium of exchange between individual peasant and state stores but also between villages and towns and significantly between communes and other production units. It was stated that in order to " strengthen economic intercourse between urban and rural areas as well as between different rural areas," various departments of business, light industry and handicraft industry were holding commodity exchange exhibitions in which " large quantities of industrial products were sold to rural districts and industrial raw materials and subsidiary foodstuffs were supplied to the urban areas." [62]

In holding these fairs mostly the representatives of neighbouring dis-tricts, cities and people's communes were invited to take part, but " some-times " the representatives of other provinces were also invited, and it

[57] *Ibid*. June 30, 1961, p. 4.
[58] *Ibid*.
[59] For the régime's new approach towards private plots see article by Yao Fang-yu in *Ta Kung Pao*, June 12, 1961.
[60] According to an instance quoted in *People's Daily* in one production brigade the income from sideline occupations constituted 14·7 per cent. of the total *per capita* income of the brigades, *People's Daily*, February 2, 1961.
[61] See, for instance, *People's Daily*, June 2, 1961, June 21, 1961, July 18, 1961, August 17, 1961, and March 9, 1962.
[62] *People's Daily*, August 16, 1961, p. 2.

was claimed that at such fairs " traditional channels of commodity exchange " were developed and " new economic relations " were brought into being. A report on such a fair in Szechuan province stated that Chengtu completed transactions with seventy-four *hsiens* and towns and that Chungking signed a contract with neighbouring areas valued at Y5,870,000. In exchange the two cities sold about Y9 million worth of indigenous products to such areas.[63] Warehouses were established by the government agencies like the State Department Store for storing the produce of the subsidiary occupation of the communes, the brigades and the teams [64] and rural " service departments " mushroomed whose function it was to engage in buying and selling, to find customers for both sides and to introduce business transactions, and at the same time it sent staff members to visit the production teams, to understand their needs and their capacities and to " organise " direct hook-ups between the producers and the markets," [65] as a result of which " forward trading " also took place and the teams often produced goods on contract.

As regard to what products could or could not be thus exchanged, all agricultural products are classified into three categories. The first category comprised grain, cotton and oil seeds for which centralised purchasing at fixed prices was enforced. Then there was a second category consisting of " important industrial crops and animal products " and products constituting " resources for exports " and for these " consultations were held between the State and the peasants " and " contracts " for consigned purchases signed in accordance with planned prices. All other types of products, not covered by the first two, fell into the third category, and for such products " consultations " were held with the peasants by " State Commercial Agencies " or " Consumer Co-operatives " and in accordance with " planned or arranged prices " contracts for arranged or negotiated purchases were signed.[66] Obviously contract production and rural market fairs were allowed only for the third category of goods. In signing the contracts the two parties were urged to take into consideration the needs of the state and the peasants and to treat the contract both as an economic and political relationship. The communes, the brigades and the teams should arrange their production in accordance with the contracts, and the commercial departments were similarly advised to observe the provisions of the contracts and organise supplies of industrial goods to the peasants.[67]

[63] *Ibid.*
[64] *People's Daily*, August 17, 1961, p. 3.
[65] *Ibid.* June 21, 1961, p. 2.
[66] Article by Kuan Ta-t'ang, *People's Daily*, March 9, 1962.
[67] *Ibid.*

SOME OTHER ORGANISATIONAL CHANGES

With the slump in agricultural production, the " most central task " set by the Party for the people's communes was the development of agricultural production, " chiefly grain production." The communes were asked to readjust their utilisation of labour power so that during the busy season at least 80 per cent. of the working population would be used " on the front line of agricultural production." All undertakings of the communes must be carried out according to the farming season and the communes were advised to curtail their other operations during the busy seasons, stop these operations when the farm work was too heavy, and to resume them only in the slack season. It was reported that since the autumn of 1960 over 20 million people had been transferred from various fields to agriculture, and that the majority had been shifted from within the people's communes, but it was believed that " further adjustments " were still necessary.[68] Commune industry took a back seat and it was to be developed only when feasible and where feasible. Although commune industry was relatively speaking pushed to the background, subsidiary production in the communes which plays a vital role in village economy was given special importance. And it was in the field of subsidiary production that a controlled free market was allowed.

Apart from grain production, one of the chief problems of the people's communes was that of livestock. In the first phase of communisation, the cadres had forgotten to make adequate arrangements for livestock breeding (problems like land for grazing and growing of fodder, etc.), and many heads of livestock were eaten up by the commune members in the fear that their livestock would be communised. As a result there was an acute shortage of livestock, only a little different from the one that was felt in the Soviet Union after collectivisation. Now in the period of tidying up the cadres were told to place equal emphasis on farming and livestock breeding.[69] The example of Wu Ch'ang commune in Honan province came in for special mention by the *People's Daily*. As a result of " drought " it was short of 2 million catties of fodder for its 2,884 animals, and so the commune organised a drive for the purpose of collecting and storing up as much fodder as possible. Special organisations were set up and special persons were appointed to take charge of storage and management of fodder. The production groups collectively collecting grass were given work credit on a quota basis and members doing it individually received in return cash or coal or wheat straw to mend their houses with, and " after work hours " or " rest period " were generally used for this

[68] *Red Flag*, No. 5, March 1, 1961.
[69] *People's Daily*, August 23, 1961, p. 1.

purpose. Thus animal husbandry was to be given prime importance and attention.[70]

Among some of the other organisational problems that needed adjustments were those resulting from centralisation and absence of immediate touch with local needs. For instance after the almost total elimination of the middle man the industrial enterprises would arbitrarily send their products to the villages regardless of whether there was need or demand for them. The Peking General Goods Wholesale Company sent its inspectors to nearby rural areas and they found that as married girls combed their braids into knots, they needed hair nets, and that as they reared cocoons in those areas, they wanted large bags for holding mulberry leaves; but what did the state store offer: electric scissors, plastic bags and high heel ladies' shoes![71] The department stores started appointing agents in rural areas in order to get informed about the requirements of the peasantry in various areas. Then again as the brigades, and sometimes even the communes, purchased tools and small machinery and other things required for production work in the villages, the cadres at that level often purchased goods not actually required locally. As a result in many places the commune members were asked to handle their own purchasing work so that it could be done more efficiently or economically.[72]

SOME TECHNICAL PROBLEMS

Many technical problems had arisen because of blind adherence to the policies of the Big Leap. For instance in the drive for rapid increase in agricultural production, inadequate attention was paid to problems of soil conservation and soil fertility. It was admitted that in recent years " owing to the comparatively fast development of production," which had rapidly changed "farming systems," and the "effect of natural calamities," the work of soil conservation had been done " rather poorly." This was evident in the " undue increase in the repeat planting index," in " improper crop rotation system," and in the " limited application of fertilisers." Consequently, " soil strength " had shown " signs of decline in some places." [73] The Party's Eight point Charter for cultivation called for close planting and deep ploughing. The instructions were carried out blindly with great harm and expense to areas where the soil was not suitable for the application of this policy. Similarly the Party policy had earlier favoured a " double crop " policy rather than a single crop one.

70 *Ibid.*
71 *People's Daily*, July 15, 1961, p. 3.
72 *Ibid.* June 20, 1961, p. 2.
73 Article by Liu Hsun-ho, *People's Daily*, November 15, 1961, p. 5.

Not unexpectedly, this policy applied without consideration to local feasibility harmed the soil and raised the expenses of production in many cases. It was later conceded in the period of readjustment that in recent years soil had a " tendency to become less fertile " because more wheat and double crop rice were planted, and it had to be emphasised that crops must be arranged so as to suit local conditions.[74]

Vast conservancy projects were undertaken in 1958 and 1959, which normally should have yielded highly beneficial results, but serious mistakes were made in doing this work for lack of attention to soil and climatic conditions. The emphasis was on huge projects, ignoring the less grandiose but highly useful and effective work of small ditches, wells, etc. The *People's Daily* chided those who believed that small conservation projects could not solve their problems and lauded those areas which were not " greedy " and which finding that mammoth projects were beyond their resources concentrated their attention on smaller ones.[75] While new projects would be taken in hand, the work of maintaining and repairing the work that had already been done was frequently forgotten. According to an investigation of nine irrigation areas in the north by the Ministry of Agriculture, the potentialities of all the projects built in the last few years had not been fully developed. In those nine areas only 56 per cent. of the area was actually under irrigation while 44 per cent. of the area that could have been irrigated was not brought under actual irrigation. The " head ditch " and the " branch ditches " were " basically completed," but only 30–70 per cent. of the " sub-ditches " and farm projects were completed and with the exception of certain irrigated areas, no drainage ditches had been completed.[76] In another report on the Kwangtung area, it was complained that whereas some 210 water reservoirs (large, small and medium) had been built, only 160 were " effective "; only 20 per cent. of the projected area meant to be irrigated was actually served by large reservoirs and only 40 per cent. of the envisaged area by medium reservoirs.[77]

Learning from the experience and many unnecessary mistakes new instructions were that all agricultural planning and work in a given area must conform to three criteria. First, natural conditions must be taken fully into account, including the area of tillable land, condition of the soil, topography, sunshine and rain, water resources, etc. Secondly due weight must be given to " economic conditions," which encompassed labour

---

[74] *People's Daily*, September 15, 1961, p. 2.
[75] *People's Daily*, Editorial, January 18, 1962.
[76] *Ibid*. Editorial, November 23, 1961.
[77] *Ibid*.

force, animal power, tools and fertilisers. Finally, the "subjective conditions"—technical strength, production experience, etc. All the three conditions were interrelated and, it was conceded, on their comprehensive understanding depended the success or failure of the plan.[78]

THE CADRES: PROBLEMS AND DIFFICULTIES

Once again the Party turned its attention towards "strengthening" the "work of leadership" of the communes and of raising the political and ideological level of the cadres who included both Party members and those holding any official position in the communes, brigades and teams. Once again there was rectification and once again stress on closer links between the cadres and the masses. In the winter of 1960 and early 1961 there were reports of a fresh rectification campaign with the attention on the political education of cadres and of the purging of some of the "dead wood" among the cadres as well as of special recruitment from among the "poor peasants." In the I-tu-ho production brigade of Chiao-tzu commune in the Peking municipality, the Party branch "insisted" on holding Party classes every Saturday evening with the Secretary and Deputy Secretary as instructors, and called a conference of Party cells every Sunday evening as well as joint conferences of branch committee members and leaders of Party cells each month to examine and study the progress of Party members in executing the Party policies and resolve any problems that might have arisen.[79] The Party Committee of the Ma-Yun *hsien* near Peking decided to open on an experimental basis a small Party school in a production brigade for cadres at the "front line of production," where Party policies were explained and discussed.[80]

From Anhwei came the report that in the Ta-kuan commune after rectification campaign and reorganisation of the commune, 20 per cent. new cadres had been added and that as 79 per cent. of the cadres were originally poor peasants, they were urged to recall their miseries under the old dispensation and thus raise the consciousness and enthusiasm of the people.[81] Still another report from Kwangtung said that the Nan-tou commune after the rectification movement had the cadres in its production brigades "elected" anew. In one of the brigades, of the original seventy-four cadres sixty-one were retained and thirteen "elected" from the "active elements" of the lower middle and poor peasants groups.[82] The peasants were advised to be particularly careful and watchful in

78 *Ibid.* Editorial, April 22, 1961, p. 7.
79 *Ibid.* April 28, 1961, p. 4.
80 *People's Daily*, May 4, 1961, p. 4.
81 *Ibid.* April 28, 1961, p. 4.
82 *Ibid.* March 29, 1961, p. 4.

" electing " cadres of their teams and brigades which was likened to selecting a " son-in-law." " We must be earnest in our selection just as a girl chooses her husband." And the advice was to elect poor peasants and lower middle class peasants.[83]

For the cadres, the Party press was full of exhortation to go deep among the masses, to investigate and study problems and to forge closer links with the peasants. There were admonitions for " some comrades " who did not go deep into the basic level and who sat in their offices and issued many impractical and empty decisions. In dealing with " directives from the higher levels " or " advanced experiences of other localities " they did not " first investigate local conditions or carried out necessary experiments at test points " and then " proceed from actualities to thoroughly implement these directives." On the other hand, the cadres were further admonished, that it was not just enough to go around visiting without a thorough understanding of the problems. " Some comrades " were " busy the whole day, visiting here, looking there," but not prepared to go deeper to carry out the " penetrating and intensive investigation and study of things." They failed to overcome " routinism." The directives and policies of the Central Committee, the cadres were told " reflect the objective laws " and must be made " guides " to the analysis of things, but cadres must " join the masses in seeking reasons for the problems and measures for their solution." It was a mistake to say, " you (the masses) supply the facts and we supply the measures." [84] At the same time the cadres were advised to profit from the experience of veteran peasants and learn their method and make them their advisers. The experience of the veterans had accumulated during a long period when agricultural production was done by manual labour. This experience was still very useful because " our agricultural production still relies basically on manual labour." Old techniques were not to be discarded until the new ones were fully established and thus " avoid the chaos caused by the gap that might occur as a result of premature actions of transformation, which could lead to a decrease in agricultural production." [85]

The problem of the cadres and with the cadres in the countryside was that while their general educational level was not very high, they were expected to deal with complex and difficult issues in a most prescient manner. After a " correct policy " had been formulated (by people at the top), the cadres became " the keystone to the success or failure of work." [86]

---

[83] *Ibid.* May 20, 1961, p. 2.
[84] *Ibid.* April 29, 1961, p. 7.
[85] *Ibid.* April 4, 1961, p. 7.
[86] *Ibid.* October 27, 1961, p. 7, Reproduction of the Editorial of *Front Line*, No. 20, 1961.

The cadres had on the one hand to faithfully carry out Party directives (whether they were in time or out of time, feasible or not, popular or otherwise), and, on the other, would have to take the blame if Party policies failed. They had also to function as a pipeline between the peasantry and the Party high command; the higher echelons of the Party were almost completely dependent on reports that percolated from the lowest level cadres to the middle-level ones. If these reports departed too greatly from Party policies the axe could easily be applied against them on the charge of " rightism " or " sectorianism," but if they did not reflect properly the mood of the masses and report the actual conditions, the formulation of Party policy itself became vitiated. Often very finely balanced and intricately formulated policies and directives would be handed down to the cadres who had first to fully comprehend the policies themselves (by no means an easy task) and then, in a manner of speaking " sell " them to the peasantry. The dilemma—at least one aspect of it—was clearly evident in the instructions emphasised by the *People's Daily* which stated that the cadres could " neither alter the resolutions of the Party committee without asking for instructions," nor could they " observe the rules to the letter without regard to the actual situation." [87]   At the same time since the cadres exercised tremendous power and influence in their own places of work, they could twist Party policies to some extent and otherwise abuse their power. The Chinese press every now and then prints cases of such abuse of power.

CONCLUSION

The basis of this comprehensive reorganisation of the commune system was laid in late 1961 and all the changes outlined above have continued to be implemented in 1962 and 1963. The importance of agriculture as the foundation of the economy; the investment of substantially increased sums in agriculture; the partial diversion of industry towards the production of agricultural machinery; the recreation of the wage system and the abandonment of the supply system; the decentralisation of agricultural operations with the production team as the most important unit; the private plot and rural fairs—all these and other changes have continued to be stressed in the last two years. The dilemma of the regime is that while on the one hand it has been compelled by objective circumstances to make a substantial retreat on the agricultural front in order to rehabilitate agricultural production, it is at the same time afraid of going too far on the road towards concessions to individual initiative lest it should revive capitalist tendencies in agriculture. This dilemma

[87] *People's Daily*, December 14, 1961.

does not lend itself to any easy solution and the Chinese agricultural policies as well as agricultural development will continue to follow a tortuous path.

Looking at the brighter side of things, the difficulties of the last three years have brought about a radical change in the attitude of the leaders towards agriculture. The new notes introduced are the primacy of agriculture and industry being made to serve agriculture, rather than vice versa. There is a new stress on providing agriculture with adequate funds as well as small machinery. "Mechanization" in the sense of a large scale use of small and medium sized tools, which it is the duty now of industry to provide, is an important element of the new policy. At the same time letting the peasant work somewhat the same way as he used to do with due regard to local conditions and peculiarities and without an immediate and inveterate drive to transform nature—this being the essence of the reorganisation since the middle of 1961—will help restore agricultural production. Some of the advantages of the commune system may now be expected to play a more positive role. The communes have greatly expanded opportunities for technological education and can also provide greater resources for undertaking the technological improvements. It will take considerable time to speed up the development of agriculture but the very major effort that is being put in may be expected to yield results over the long run.

Economic Development

Economic Development

By CHOH-MING LI

IN the ten years of Communist rule since late 1949 a thoroughgoing revolution has taken place on the Chinese mainland in economic organisation, savings and investment, and distribution, with profound effects on the daily lives of the people. Peking has claimed that immense progress has been made on all economic fronts, including the real income of industrial and agricultural workers. It has felt confident enough to shorten from fifteen to ten years (beginning 1958) the target period at the end of which its output of electric power and certain major industrial goods would match or exceed that of Britain. In the non-Communist world, commentators vary greatly in their judgments; they range from those who reject all the official statistics and consider no important progress to have been made during the period, to those who not only accept the claims *in toto* but have advanced all sorts of arguments to defend even those claims that Peking has later had to repudiate.

There are, indeed, serious problems connected with the official statistics, and the early claim of a 105 per cent. increase in food output for 1958 over 1957 was so unreasonable as to cast grave doubt on the reliability of all official data in the minds of objective investigators. But, despite the domestic and international fanfare given to these " Great Leap Forward " achievements, Peking later saw fit to announce a drastic downward revision of them as well as of the targets for 1959. This lends strong support to the view that the régime has not been operating with two different sets of statistics, one for confidential use and the other for public consumption; that in the need of reliable data for planning purposes it demands accurate information from junior officials whose psychological bias and incompetence are the major source of error; and that provisional data must be sharply distinguished from final figures, which, however, particularly in respect of agricultural statistics, represent at best the considered judgment of the State Statistical Bureau and therefore have to be used with care.[1]

Statistical differences notwithstanding, there can be no doubt that the economy was able to sustain continuous growth in national product during the period under review at an annual rate much higher than the rate of population increase. This performance has greatly impressed many of the underdeveloped countries and has caused India, for example, to shift its emphasis from agriculture in its First Five-Year Plan

[1] For further comment on 1958 statistics, see below.

to heavy industry in the Second, and more recently, to introduce " co-operative farming " on the Chinese model. To the West, the crucial question is whether this growth will continue and China will thus become a World Power. It is important, therefore, to examine the record care-fully: to evaluate the overall rate of growth, to find out how it was achieved, to understand the background that led to the " Great Leap Forward " and the people's communes and their current status, and to realise the sacrifices the people have been called upon to make.

THE FIRST FIVE-YEAR PLAN

The ten-year period falls into three phases, namely, rehabilitation (1950–52), the First Five-Year Plan (1953–57), and the " Great Leap Forward " (1958–59). The first phase saw the rehabilitation of the war-torn, inflation-infested economy, the completion of the land re-distribution programme, and the beginning of socialisation of private trade and industry—a process which was destined to be consummated, together with that of agriculture, in 1956. The cessation of civil strife, Soviet aid towards restoring the industrial base in Manchuria, and the Korean War all contributed to the rapid economic recovery. Deliberate economic development began in 1953 when the First Five-Year Plan was launched. Evaluation of Peking's performance must start from this point. The third phase, covering the first two years of the Second Five-Year Plan, witnessed such a radical change in economic organisa-tion and in the nature of data that it is best treated separately.

How fast did the economy grow from 1953 to 1957? According to official calculations, the net domestic material product (that is, the total values added by all the materially productive sectors minus depreciation) increased from 61·1 billion *yuan* in 1952, 70 billion in 1953, to 93·8 billion in 1957, all at 1952 market prices.[2] This gives an annual rate of 8·9 per cent. with 1952 as the base and 7·6 per cent. with 1953 as the base. It is interesting to note that a recent Western estimate of China's gross national product for the seven-year period from 1950 to 1957, made by William W. Hollister, who made use of official raw data together with independent calculations, gives an annual growth rate of 8·6 per cent. with 1952 as the base and 7·4 per cent. with 1953 as the base.[3] Thus, the choice of the base year makes a great deal of difference to the growth

---

[2] The annual figures for 1952–56 are given by the State Statistical Bureau, Research Department, " A Preliminary Study of China's National Income Produced and Distributed," *T'ung-chi yen-chiu* (*Statistical Research*) 1.11–15, January 1958. The figure for 1957, being provisional, is given by Po I-po, " The Tasks and Functions of Statistical Work in China's Socialist Construction," *ibid*. 4–10. (The exchange rate between *yuan* and £ sterling is 6.9—£, and between *yuan* and $ U.S. is 2.5—$.)

[3] William W. Hollister, *China's Gross National Product and Social Accounts 1950–1957*. (Glencoe, Illinois: The Free Press, 1958), p. 2. The rates are computed from the data given in his Table 1.

rate. It is important to realise that 1952 is not a representative base, because for a good part of the year trade and industry were at a low ebb due to the dislocation caused by the " three anti " and " five anti " movements. For this reason, 1953 is a much better choice as the base year.

Taking 1953 as the base, the 7·6 per cent. annual rate as obtained from official statistics is still an exaggeration. Among the factors contributing to the exaggeration are the pricing of new products in industry, the low pricing of agricultural products on the constant price list, and above all, the understatement of the gross agricultural value product from 1952 to 1954 and overstatement in the subsequent three years.[4] What the actual growth rate was during this period has not yet been satisfactorily determined. Professor Ta-chung Liu of Cornell University has recently published the summary results of his estimation of China's net domestic product (that is, the net domestic material product plus the values added by government administration and other service sectors).[5] They show an annual growth rate of 6·8 per cent. with 1953 as the base.[6] The details of his calculation have not been published, but when computed in 1952 prices, a growth rate of this magnitude is probably closer to reality than any of the others.

Be it 7, 6·5, 6 or thereabouts, China's rate of growth during this period was quite high—more than double, if not three times, the average annual rate of natural increase of the population, officially estimated at 2·2 per cent. One is tempted to compare it with those of other countries which were or are at a similar stage of development. But such a comparison is fraught with difficulties; for example, methods of estimation, bases of calculation, length of period, and degrees of accuracy, all vary a great deal among different national estimates. For general interest, however, the following annual growth rates (all computed in constant prices) may be cited: for the Soviet Union, about 7 per cent. during the period 1928–37; for Japan, 4·6 per cent. during the period 1898–1914 and 4·9 per cent. from 1914 to 1936; and for India, 3·3 per cent. during its First Five-Year Plan period from 1950–51 to 1955–56.[7]

---

4 See Choh-ming Li, *Economic Development of Communist China* (Berkeley: University of California Press, and London: Cambridge University Press, 1959), pp. 53–74.
5 See his " Structural Changes in the Economy of the Chinese Mainland, 1933 to 1952–57," *Papers and Proceedings* of the American Economic Association, xlix: 84–93, May 1959; particularly p. 93.
6 Interestingly, his figures yield a rate of 6·9 per cent. if 1952 is taken as the base.
7 For the Soviet Union, see Gregory Grossman, chapter on " National Income," in A. Bergson, ed., *Soviet Economic Growth* (Evanston, Illinois: Row, Peterson & Co., 1953), pp. 1–23, especially p. 8. For Japan, see K. Ohkawa and others, *The Growth Rate of the Japanese Economy since 1878* (Tokyo: Kinokuniya Bookstore, 1957), p. 248. For India, see Government of India, Planning Commission, *Review of the First Five Year Plan* (New Delhi. 1957), pp. 7–8.

Soviet Aid and the Rate of Investment

What made this growth possible was a massive investment programme which was financed almost completely through compulsory savings in the form of taxes, profits and depreciation reserves of state-controlled enterprises and reserve funds of the farm units. In Peking's national income accounting, the total savings (net of current replacement costs) of the economy are designated as " accumulation " and may be regarded also as that part of net national material product (that is, net domestic material product, adjusted to international balances) devoted to increasing fixed capital assets in the entire economy, working capital of the materially productive sectors, commercial inventories, and stock-piles of the state. According to the latest official data, the rate of accumulation at 1952 prices had increased from 19·7 per cent. of the net national material product in 1952 to 23·7 per cent. in 1957, with an average rate of 23 per cent. for the five-year period.[8]

Although the underlying concepts are different, it may be pertinent to mention three other estimates, all based on 1952 prices. Hollister found the rate of gross domestic investment to gross national product to be 18·5 per cent. for the five years; and Liu gave the rate of net domestic investment to net domestic expenditures to be 21·8 per cent.[9] Taking only fixed capital investment and working capital for industry and agriculture into account, I have estimated that for the same period the rate of capital formation to net capital product averaged 11 per cent.[10]

Whatever the precise rate of investment was, it is certain that virtually all investments were made with internal savings. Financial assistance from abroad was not substantial. Since 1950, only two Soviet loans for economic development purposes have been announced; one, contracted in 1950, was for 1,200 million roubles, and the other, in 1954, was for 520 million. Together they were only enough to pay for 31 per cent. of the necessary equipment and supplies for the original 156 industrial and other projects which the Soviet Union agreed to help China construct, or to cover but 11 per cent. of China's total imports for the eight years from 1950 to 1957. During the First Five-Year Plan, the amount of Soviet credit available for new investment (1·57 billion *yuan*) constituted merely 3 per cent. of the total state investment (49·3 billion *yuan*). By the end of 1957, all outstanding Soviet credit was

---

[8] Yang Po, " The Relationship between Accumulation and Consumption in China's National Income Account," *Jen-min Jih-pao* (*People's Daily*), October 13, 1958.

[9] Hollister, *op. cit.* pp. 128–129 ; Liu, *op. cit.* p. 93. Again it may not be amiss to cite here Professor Henry Rosovsky's recent findings on Japan's rates of capital formation: the rate of gross investment to net national product at current prices averaged 10 per cent. from 1889 to 1914 and 18 per cent. from 1914 to 1936. See his " Japanese Capital Formation: The Role of the Public Sector," *Journal of Economic History*, XIX: 350–375, September 1959 ; the average rates cited are computed from Table 2, pp. 354–355.   [10] Li, *ibid.* p. 138.

exhausted, and since then no new loan has been announced. Meanwhile, amortisation payments have been mounting since 1954.

Of course, the Soviet contribution cannot be evaluated in terms of financial assistance alone. In respect of the Soviet-aid projects, not only the supply of machinery and equipment is assured, but all ancillary services are made available, including installation and operation of the plants and training of personnel. At the end of 1957 the total number of these projects already agreed upon came to 211, a figure which was subsequently increased by 125 through the agreements of August 1958 and February 1959. Equally important, if not more so, is the Soviet supply, virtually gratis, of whole sets of blueprints and related technical materials giving direction for the layout of a plant, its construction, and pilot manufacturing in various heavy and light industries. From 1954 to 1957, over 3,000 items of such information were provided. In the field of training, during the period from 1951 to 1957, some 6,500 Chinese students were sent to the Soviet Union for higher education and 7,100 workers for acquiring experience in Soviet factories. For basic research, significant Soviet assistance has been given in both personnel and equipment, the latter including such facilities as electronic computers and a 6,500 kw. atomic reactor pile and rotating accelerator.[11] Indeed, Soviet experience and experts were made readily available to Peking in perhaps all state endeavours. Premier Chou En-lai revealed in a tenth anniversary article in the *People's Daily* on October 6, 1959, that the Soviet Union had sent over 10,800 experts and the East European satellites over 1,500 to China during the previous decade.

Technical assistance of this scope must have contributed greatly to the efficiency of investment—which probably meant as much to the country as capital supply, especially in view of the shortage of engineering and management personnel. But the fact remains that for the five-year period, 97 per cent. of the investment for basic development came from the Chinese people themselves.

PHENOMENAL INDUSTRIAL GROWTH

The investment programme centred around 156 Soviet-aid engineering projects. In the words of the Chairman of the State Planning Commission, the underlying objective of economic development is " the marshalling of all efforts and resources for the development of heavy industry so as to lay down a foundation for an industrialised state and a modernised national defence." [12] It is anticipated that by the end of

[11] The research plant, located in the outskirts of Peking, has been in operation since September 1958.
[12] Li Fu-ch'un, " The First Five Year Plan," *Ta Kung Pao* (*Impartial Daily*), Tientsin, September 16, 1953.

the Third Five-Year Plan the country will be capable of producing all machinery and equipment needed for further economic development. This objective gives overall guidance to the allocation of state investments. From 1953 to 1957 the total amount of realised state investment for basic development came to 49·3 billion *yuan*, of which three-quarters went to industry (56 per cent.) and transportation and communications (18·7 per cent.), and only 8·2 per cent. to agriculture, forestry and water conservation.[13] And out of the 27·6 billion *yuan* of investment in industry 87 per cent. was for heavy industry, leaving 13 per cent. for light industry.

As a result, heavy industry grew at a phenomenal and sustained rate. To cite a few examples: rolled steel output increased from 1·1 million metric tons in 1952 to 4·5 million in 1957, coal from 64·7 million tons to 130 million, electric power from 7·3 billion kilowatt hours to 19·3 billion, and cement from 2·9 million tons to 6·9 million. For the first time and in quantity, the country was able to produce trucks and automobiles, merchant ships, tractors and jet aeroplanes, and to export whole sets of cotton textile machinery, sugar-refining machinery and paper-making machinery. By the end of 1957, expansion of the iron and steel complex in Manchuria was virtually accomplished, and new centres of comparable size were being built at Wuhan in central China and Paotow in Inner Mongolia. In light industry, production capacity was also rapidly enlarged, especially in the paper, textile and sugar industries, but production was repeatedly held back by shortages of raw materials.

To support this development, the educational system was completely revamped to give primary emphasis to technical subjects. Polytechnical schools and short courses for industrial and agricultural techniques were introduced everywhere. On-the-job training and apprenticeship were introduced on a national scale. It is reported that the engineering and technical personnel in industry had increased 200 per cent. from 58,000 in 1952 to 175,000 in 1957, while industrial employment (including mining and construction) grew 66 per cent. from 6·15 million to 10·19 million.[14]

The development of agriculture presents a different picture. It is true that in addition to state investment, the independent peasants, the agricultural co-operatives and collectives did set aside, as required, a small percentage of their annual output for expansion. But this amount, together with the state investment, was, at best, equal to about one-half of the state funds spent for industry. During this period, mobilisation

---

[13] State Statistical Bureau, " Communiqué on the Results of the Frst Five Year Plan for National Economic Development," *Jen-min Jih-pao* (*People's Daily*), April 14, 1959.   [14] *Ibid.*

of the masses for construction was practised every year, but never on such a gigantic scale as in the spring of 1958. This neglect of agricultural development was reflected in agricultural output.

According to official statistics, the output of food grains (not including soyabeans) increased from 154·4 million to 185 million tons over the five years, at an annual rate of increase of 3·7 per cent. If this rate of increase were correct, there would have been an ample supply of food for various purposes. But by the beginning of 1956, the number of draught animals, essential for farm work, had been drastically reduced, owing, among other reasons, to the lack of feed. It is certain that the rate of increase in food production was exaggerated in official data, due to underestimates of output from 1952 to 1954 and overestimates from 1955 to 1957. One cannot help drawing the conclusion that " the average annual rate of increase in food production during the First Five-Year Plan was very close to but perhaps somewhat higher than the natural rate of population increase." [15] In this connection, it is of interest to note that Hollister, in his estimate of the output of basic food crops and animal products, came out with an annual rate increase of 2·65 per cent.—which is much closer than the official rate of 3·7 per cent. to the natural rate of population increase (2·2 per cent.). [16]

Thus, as one might expect from the shape of the investment programme, it was " the marshalling of all efforts and resources for the development of heavy industry " that accounted mainly for the economic growth of this period.

PROBLEMS OF COLLECTIVISATION

The " high tide " of collectivisation of agriculture and socialisation of all other sectors of the economy came after the autumn harvest of 1955, when a nation-wide movement for the " liquidation of counter-revolutionaries " had just concluded with huge numbers of people either executed or put in labour camps. The change in economic organisation was so sweeping that although the changeover was successfully completed by the end of 1956 as the authorities claimed, it would have been logical for them to devote the next few years to consolidating these new gains in the interest, at least, of economic development. How then can one explain the " Great Leap Forward " movement that began in the winter of 1957 and the people's commune system which was introduced in the summer of 1958? Could it be that the changeover had not been

---

[15] Li, *op. cit.* p. 73.

[16] Hollister, *op. cit.* pp. 23–24. The rate is computed from his production index, adjusted " for probable overstatements in trend for 1950, 1951 and 1953–54 resulting from changes in statistical coverage." He did not make any adjustment for the subsequent years.

as successful as claimed and that it was felt that if the resultant difficulties were not promptly corrected, economic growth and perhaps
political stability would be jeopardised?

What were these difficulties? I believe the key to this question lies
in the agricultural situation, which, contrary to Peking's expectations,
deteriorated rapidly because of collectivisation. Slaughter of farm
animals and destruction of farm implements were widespread.[17] Many
collectives existed only in name because the members were attracted to
trading in the " free markets." As a result, even though the cultivated
area affected by natural calamities was only 14·7 million hectares in
1957 against 15·3 million in 1956, the total cropping area was reduced
by 2 million hectares, and the cropping area for food by 3·4 million
hectares. The multiple cropping index also fell from 141 to 139; the
amount of fertilisers collected was smaller; and the rate of increase in
irrigated areas stood lower than that of 1956.[18] What was even more
alarming was that food output increased only 1·3 per cent., from 182·5
million to 185 million tons, over the year, a rate which was far below
the natural rate of population increase. Collectivisation thus turned
out to be a great failure—more so than the provisional statistics had
led one to believe. When collectivisation was first introduced nationally,
there was already strong opposition to it within the Chinese Communist
Party on the ground that the step was too hastily taken. Now
the architects of the plan had to find an immediate solution for both
political and economic reasons.

The situation was all the more serious because agricultural development could no longer be neglected in favour of concentrated development
of heavy industry. By the end of 1956 it had become increasingly clear
that economic growth was closely tied to agricultural output. The
amount of savings from which all industrial and other investments are
made depends heavily on the harvests of the preceding year. A good
crop permits large capital investments in the subsequent twelve months
while a poor crop reduces them. In fact, the whole economy follows
closely the fluctuations in agricultural output with about a one-year
time lag.[19] But this was not appreciated by the leaders in Peking until
the latter half of 1957 when the summer and winter harvests fell far
short of what the proponents of collectivisation insisted that they should
be.

Recognition of the basic importance of agriculture immediately raised
the issue of whether the state investment programme for the Second

---

[17] Yueh Wei, " The Problem of Accumulation in Agricultural Co-operatives," *Hsueh-hsi*
    (*Study*), 7 : 23–24, April 1958.
[18] Liao Lu-yen, " Strive to Realise the Goals of the National Agricultural Development
    Programme," *Hsueh-hsi* (*Study*), 3 : 2–8, February 1958.
[19] See Li, *op. cit.* pp. 135–136 and 219–220.

Five-Year Plan be changed to favour agriculture at the expense of heavy industry. Such a change would, of course, have run completely counter to Peking's primary objective in economic development and also to the ideological tenets of the Communist world. What could Peking do?

To deal with the situation, a series of directives were issued in the name of the Central Committee of the Party.[20] Two stood out as the most significant. One, dated September 14, 1957, concerned improving the management of agricultural collectives. It said, in part (Article 6):

> The size of collectives and production teams is crucial to the success of management. Because of the various characteristics of agricultural production at the present and because the technological and managerial levels of the present collectives are not high, experiences in different localities during the last few years have proved that large collectives and large teams are generally not adaptable to the present production conditions. . . . Therefore, except the few that have been well managed, all those that are too big and not well managed should be divided into smaller units in accordance with the wishes of members. Henceforth, a collective should generally be of the size of a village with over 100 households. . . . A much larger village may become one collective or be organised into several collectives. . . . As to the size of production teams, twenty neighbouring households is the proper number. . . .
>
> After the size of the collectives and production teams has been decided upon, it should be publicly announced that this organisation will remain unchanged in the next ten years.

Thus, one of the immediate steps taken was to reorganise the collectives and production teams by reducing their size. The ten-year period of no further change was obviously intended as a device to appease the peasants and to give the régime a chance to consolidate its position in the rural areas. The reasons given for the reorganisation were based on practical experiences. All this seems to indicate strongly that the later development of " people's communes " was not a preconceived, ideological move on the part of the Party leadership, although as early as 1955 Mao did remark on the operational superiority of large co-operatives on the basis of actual observation.

The second was the revised draft of the national agricultural development programme from 1956 to 1967, released on October 25, 1957. This, together with an earlier directive of September 24, seemed to have given rise to the slogan " Great Leap Forward." Moreover, it sparked a national movement to mobilise the farming population to repair and build irrigation works of various sizes (chiefly small) and to collect all sorts of organic fertilisers throughout the countryside and in the hills.

---

[20] They are conveniently collected in *Jen-min Shou-ts'e 1958* (*People's Handbook for 1958*), Peking, 1958, pp. 502–507, 514–525 and 533–539.

It was reported that from November 1957 to well into the spring of 1958 tens of millions of peasants were mobilised every day, often working long hours at places far away from home. This started the establishment of common mess halls. When the time for spring planting arrived, a labour shortage began to be felt. Utilisation of idle labour time as a form of capital formation had reached a limit. Additional manpower had to be found if full advantage was to be taken of the investment. The dispatch of people to the villages from overcrowded cities and overstaffed offices and factories was one expedient. More important was the other—the induction of women into the labour force by freeing them from housework through further development of mess halls and the introduction of tailoring teams, nurseries, old folks' homes, etc. Since peasants working in large groups needed discipline to ensure punctuality and a good work pace, something akin to military organisation was needed. In sum, it was against this background that the communes were developed—with Mao's personal blessings and encouragement.

Although this development was diametrically opposed to the Party's directive issued a few months previously, the chain of events that led up to it seemed to the leadership a justification for taking a bold step which would not only wipe out responsibility for the failure of collectivisation but offer a new and rational solution to the baffling agricultural problem. To them, low man-hour productivity was not so important as high unit-area productivity which was the crucial factor for accelerating industrialisation.

Thus, in 1958, out of a total basic development investment (not including investment by the communes for their own purposes) of 26·7 billion *yuan*, 78 per cent. went into industry (65 per cent.) and transportation and communication (13 per cent.), and only 10 per cent. into agriculture, forestry and water conservation. In the original plan for 1959, which called for a total investment of 27 billion *yuan*, only 7 per cent. was allocated for the latter three related fields.[21]

THE " GREAT LEAP FORWARD "

Just as collectivisation produced a strong psychological bias on the part of the rank and file to overreport the agricultural output of 1956 and 1957, so the harvests of 1958 were grossly exaggerated as a result of the " Great Leap Forward " and the formation of the communes. Whether food output actually increased from 185 million tons in 1957 to 250 million (instead of 375 million) in 1958, as the officially revised statistics show, remains a question to which perhaps even the State Statistical

21 The revised plan for 1959 scaled the total investment down to 24·8 billion *yuan*, with no details given.

Bureau itself is not in a position to give a definite answer. Admittedly, such measures as the building of irrigation facilities and the introduction of various labour-intensification methods (deep ploughing, close cropping, etc.) might have increased unit-area productivity and therefore total output. Moreover, the area devastated by flood and drought—only 6 million hectares as compared to 14·7 million in 1957—was the smallest in five years. It was naturally a bumper crop year. But the reasons officially given for the overreporting in the first instance refer to the methods of estimating which are still being used and in which a high margin of error is always present, regardless of how carefully the results are checked.

If the 35 per cent. increase were accepted, it would be difficult to understand the severe food shortage in both rural and urban areas during 1958 and 1959. Perhaps part of the explanation is to be found in the 1 per cent. increase in food output in 1957, which affected the supply situation the following year. Then there is the question of the composition of the 35 per cent. increase in 1958. According to the original, unrevised claim, a 103 per cent. increase had taken place in food output, reflecting an increase of 70 per cent. in wheat, 73 per cent. in rice, 76 per cent. in coarse grains, and 320 per cent. in sweet potatoes. No such breakdown has yet been given for the revised figures.

Is it possible that sweet potatoes accounted for so much of the 35 per cent. increase in food output that the other food crops did not register any significant improvement? That the population on the mainland have been forced to accept the unwelcome sweet potatoes as their regular diet lends plausibility to this speculation.

Toward the end of autumn harvest in 1958 and at the height of the commune movement, there was another nation-wide mobilisation of the masses, especially in the countryside, for producing pig iron and steel. With the great majority of women drawn into the labour force, the end of the agricultural season brought in its train the pressing problem of how to keep the working population fully occupied without the state having to make any investment. The " backyard furnace " scheme seemed to be the answer. As usual, the cadres carried it too far with a resulting disruption of regular transportation and the neglect of irrigation and other field work. In the meanwhile, a large majority of the so-called furnaces were not able to produce, and most of those that could came up with products so poor in quality that for modern mills raw materials were of more use. Both manpower and materials were misused. The project was finally abandoned in the spring of 1959 as a movement, although industrial production by indigenous methods was allowed to continue to grow in localities where limited success with good prospects had obtained.

For 1958, the régime thus claimed a great leap in industrial output, pointing especially to an increase in the output of steel by 101 per cent., coal by 107 per cent., and pig iron by 130 per cent Only in August 1959 was it made clear that these output figures for 1957 and 1958 were not comparable and that when production from indigenous sources was omitted, the increase in each case was reduced to about one-half of the original claim—a still quite impressive record. It is not clear if the modern factory output and the production by indigenous methods had been properly segregated and if the quality of factory output was as uniform as it was before. However, a substantial increase in factory output was credible because some of the major projects built under the first Five-Year Plan were now bearing fruit.

The downward revision of the official claims for 1958 was accompanied by a scaling down of the plan for 1959. To cite a few examples, the planned increase in the production of food was reduced from 40 to 10 per cent., raw cotton from 50 to 10 per cent., coal from 40 to 24 per cent., metal-cutting lathes from 40–50 to 20 per cent In each of these cases, the planned increase was far less than the increase in 1958 over 1957. According to the definition given by Chou En-lai, the " Great Leap Forward " had now petered off to a " Leap Forward." It was reported that floods and drought had occurred over a large area of the country in the late spring and summer of the year. The drastic reduction in the goals for food and cotton output, made public in August, must have taken their effects into account. Nevertheless, if the innovations, plus excellent weather, had accounted for the 35 per cent. increase in food in 1958, thus advancing the level of output to a new plateau, and if the experience of other countries is any guide, one may legitimately express doubt whether the 10 per cent. planned increase in the output of food as well as cotton in 1959 could be realised—without mechanisation and large-scale use of chemical fertilisers. Perhaps a 10 per cent. increase or a higher rate will be reported, but the 1958 episode should teach us to be extremely cautious in respect of such claims.

DEVELOPMENT AND THE CONSUMER

At the end of the decade of Communist rule, the economy would seem so well launched on the path of development that further growth would be easier. This would have been the case if the process had been carried through under a leadership that inspired popular support or at least consent. But the development programme, calling for heavier and heavier sacrifices, was determinedly imposed upon the people from above. Discontent was growing and widespread. The régime may indeed face an internal situation far more serious than at any other time since 1949.

To be sure, Peking has long instituted certain socio-economic measures designed to gain the support of the workers. As early as 1951, a system of social security was inaugurated by which state enterprises were required to contribute annually an amount equivalent to about 15 per cent. of the wage bill to various welfare purposes such as workmen's compensation, medical assistance, cost-of-living subsidies and trade union activities. Private enterprises, when still in existence, were required to enter into contract with their employees to provide similar obligations. For workers in governmental and educational institutions, a system of free medical benefits was established in addition to welfare and educational benefits. It was reported that from 1953 to 1957 the actual outlay for all these purposes equalled about one-quarter of the national wage bill. Then in 1958 a system of retirement was put into effect for workers in industrial and business enterprises and governmental and civil institutions. All these measures were innovations introduced into the country for the first time on such a large scale.

As against these benefits, however, the workers have completely lost their freedom of choice of jobs. They are subject to deployment from factory to factory and from locality to locality. Direction of labour is practised extensively to support the growth of new industrial cities in the hinterland. Moreover, workers are not secure in their jobs, because especially after 1957 they are liable to be assigned to the countryside to become a part of the agricultural labour force, thus losing a great deal of the benefits accruing to them in the cities. While technical skill enhances security in industrial employment, the determining factor is political attitude and " socialist consciousness."

As was foreseeable, social security benefits have not been extended to the peasants. The early official justification that their position had already improved as a result of land redistribution no longer held true under collectivisation and the communes. They have been required to take care of their welfare collectively out of their own annual output, and even primary education in the countryside is financed out of agricultural taxes. Mass mobilisation projects often take them far away from home. And during the " Great Leap Forward " movement they were driven to labour such long hours that the Party at the end of 1958 had to reaffirm the principle of giving them eight hours of sleep and four hours of mealtime and rest every day except in the busy agricultural seasons. As compared with the urban workers who were also pressed into emulative and overfulfilment-of-the-plan drives, the peasants are the worse off by far because their work is all physical exertion unmitigated by mechanical assistance.

Changes in the real income of workers and peasants are among the subjects yet to be carefully investigated. During the period from 1952 to 1957, " *per capita* consumption of food, cloth and housing services had declined in absolute terms, with the exception of staple food grains, the total consumption of which probably had increased a little for the country as a whole, owing primarily to the growing need for energy work by those not used to work on the farm and to the levelling process of collectivisation." [22] The slight increase in staple food consumption, however, was in terms of weight, and there was strong evidence that the composition of staple food had been rapidly changing in favour of sweet potatoes and coarse grains. In 1958 and 1959, *per capita* consumption as a whole took a deep dive. The severe shortage of staple (rice and wheat) and subsidiary food and cloth was nation-wide.

The situation was particularly bad in the rural areas. According to the many instances reported in the mainland newspapers, in 1958 the communes were generally required to set aside, as " accumulation," 50 to 70 per cent. of their total output, net of production and management costs. Now a survey made by Peking's State Statistical Bureau of 228 collectives in the country reveals that in 1957 consumption accounted for 89 per cent. of the net output, with only 11 per cent. for accumulation. The collectives investigated were better than the average, so that the share of consumption must have been higher for the country as a whole.[23] Assume conservatively that consumption took 90 per cent. in 1957 and that accumulation was raised to 50 per cent. in 1958. It does not take much calculation to see that the net agricultural output must increase 80 per cent. if consumption in 1958 was to be maintained on the same level as in 1957. Obviously the 50–70 per cent. accumulation rate was decided upon in accordance with an expected increase in gross agricultural output of about 80 per cent. However, since the gross agricultural output in fact increased only 25 per cent. (according to officially revised data), if one assumes that the net output had grown at the same pace consumption must have declined by about one-third when one-half of the net output went into accumulation. It is not surprising that the peasants became restive.

The causes of discontent were not confined to economic factors. Many of the national movements, coming on each other's heels, were in the nature of purges. Countless numbers of people were executed, imprisoned, or placed in labour camps. The threat to personal safety was ever present, and the atmosphere of insecurity must have been tense and oppressive. This was enough to generate unrest. A further major

---

[22] Li, *op. cit.* p. 215.
[23] " A survey of the Gross Income and its Distribution of 228 Agricultural Collectives in 1957," *T'ung-chi yen-chiu* (*Statistical Research*), 8 : 8–12, August 1958.

blow was the disintegration of the family system in the communes. It may well be true, as the document issued by the Party in December 1958 stated, that husband and wife had not been forcibly separated in different quarters. But when people had to eat in common mess halls and both husband and wife had to work long hours outside and the children were in nurseries, the family ceased to have any common bond or unity of interest and purpose. It was no longer the place where material rewards were shared together or occasionally with friends; nor was it a place for enriching personal cultural heritage. Even the Soviet Union had never gone this far.

Thus discontent had been growing and widespread. One needs only to read Deputy Premier Teng Hsiao-p'ing's report of September 1957 on the " Rectification Movement " to realise the extent of it among intellectuals, peasants, industrial workers, minority nationalities, armed forces and Party members. The situation deteriorated even further after that date, not only because of the further decline in *per capita* consumption, but because of the " Great Leap Forward " and the people's communes. Resentment was particularly strong among the peasants, as attested by the official acknowledgment that the bumper crop of 1958 suffered heavy losses from poor reaping, threshing, collecting and storing. This feeling was quickly communicated to the armed forces, whose recruits came chiefly from the rural areas. Therefore, it was not unexpected that opposition to the present leadership stiffened within the Chinese Communist Party, as clearly revealed in the *People's Daily* editorial of August 27, 1959.

Peking, of course, had already taken steps to cope with the situation. Since March 1959, many of the radical features of the commune system had been gradually altered. Accumulation in the communes was generally scaled down from 50–70 per cent. to about 30 per cent. for 1959; participation in common mess halls became voluntary; ownership of most of the means of production was reverted back from the commune to the " production brigades "—the old collectives; small plots of land were returned to individual households for private cultivation; " free markets " were partially reopened. Thus by the end of 1959 the people's communes existed very much in name only, although each still retained a share of accumulation funds for developing local industries. On the political scene, perhaps the most important move was the strengthening of the present leadership through an extensive reshuffle of Party personnel in the government, and the appointment of General Lo Jui-ch'ing, who had long been Minister of Public Security, as Chief of Staff of the Army.

How the future will shape up is, of course, a hazardous guess, for much depends on how well the widespread discontent is contained.

There is, however, no indication that the present leadership has any desire to give up the commune system—a step that would vindicate the opposition. Perhaps, for some time to come, the commune will continue primarily as an administrative unit, engaging more and more in industrial activities supported by the farming units operating as collectives. But even under *de facto* collectivisation, the agricultural problem still awaits urgent solution. In the economic picture proper, two developments should ease somewhat the régime's effort in this direction—the extensive construction of irrigation works in 1958 and 1959 which, if properly maintained, will raise agricultural productivity to a new level, and the increasing flow of capital goods from the major projects built in the last few years. Thus, barring a violent outburst of general discontent, a change in Party leadership, or war, continuous and rapid industrialisation of the country may be expected.

Berkeley.   *November 1959.*

Communist China's Agricultural Calamities

By W. K.

COMMUNIST China is entering yet another year of calamities of major proportions. They stem chiefly from its unbalanced farming industry and affect every sector of its economy.

Chinese and Western analysts have come full circle in their assessment within the last three years. In China the exuberance of the Great Leap Forward has given way to the gloom of austerity programmes and emergency regulations. Abroad, the voices praising the miracles of 1958 have been displaced by those reporting disaster and starvation. Those advising caution and moderation in the face of obvious Chinese exaggerations tend to be dismissed now as they were then.

Yet, any assessment of the magnitude of the dramatic changes in economic development and social engineering which are taking place in China today depends on the degree of accuracy with which the fluctuations that occur in farm production and food consumption are measured. In a country where four out of every five inhabitants are villagers and where, for many years to come, three out of every four will continue to be engaged in the production of the nation's food, everything depends ultimately on this largest sector of the national economy.

It is not by accident that there exists a direct correlation between the rate of economic growth, industrial output, capital investment, budget revenue and trade turnover on the one side and the harvest of the previous year on the other. Food provides half the country's retail sales and two-thirds of rural consumption; agricultural raw materials supply one-third of the industrial gross output and four-fifths of the produce of the consumer goods industries; and foodstuffs and other goods processed from farm products contribute nearly two-thirds of the earnings of foreign exchange.

No excuse is thus needed for insisting that efforts should be concentrated on assessing farm output, its utilisation and its susceptibilities to natural and institutional changes rather than the output of, say, steel in backyards, important though this may be in a process of thought formation the like of which the world has hardly experienced since the days of

163

the counter-reformation and inquisition. Assessments of this kind are not easy to put into effect. It is one of the marks of backwardness of a country that its statistical services are underdeveloped, its statisticians are susceptible to persuasion and its statistics are wide open to question. If, added to this, official exaggeration becomes part of a process of public education, the dangers inherent in basing impartial analysis on partial documentation become obvious. Yet, as one is permitted to eliminate from official statistics of steel output the impure iron produced in backyards by cultivators or journalists off duty, so one ought to be able to apply experience and common sense when faced with extreme claims of success or failure in the agricultural sphere.

It must not be assumed that this is an exercise that can be practised with impunity by the uninitiated. The vacillations of Chinese farm policy have been so momentous in the last three years as apparently to call in question all that has ever been known of the country and its people. The efforts of the first Five-Year Plan were followed by a short phase of relaxation which became widely known as the period of the Hundred Flowers. The criticism which it bred in all walks of life became so dangerous that it was brought to an abrupt end; too many weeds had grown to be tolerated. Renewed effort and emulation coincided with natural conditions which by all accounts yielded an all-time record crop.

Experienced farmers will confirm that even under less unstable conditions than those prevailing in China today, cultivators can easily be deceived by an exceptionally favourable crop. How much more must such deception be possible in a country where Party cadres urged constant vigilance and increased effort on all. It is worth recalling in this connection the defeat of the individualists in the statistical controversy between " rightists " and " leftists," *i.e.*, between those adhering to conventional methods of recording and reporting and those open to Party political guidance and persuasion which had been raging ever since the relaxed atmosphere of the Hundred Flowers had brought the conflict between the two concepts into the open.

Conversely an exceptionally poor crop, following a bumper harvest, may well fool crop reporters more experienced than those selected and trained by Communist cadres. The shock of failure must have been very much greater in a country where the populace had been conditioned to accept that the new Son of Heaven could master nature, double the nation's crop within one year and increase it further by one half in the following year.

The magnitude of the exaggeration that was officially permitted, if not manufactured, is on the record. As it has not served as a warning in the face of renewed exaggeration, in the opposite direction, it may be recalled briefly as a reminder of the grossness of the untruth to which

Chinese and non-Chinese were treated in 1958. Following a harvest of 185 million tons of grains (which in Chinese definition include pulses and the grain equivalent of potatoes, but no longer soya beans), the harvest forecast released in February 1958 was 196 million tons.

Thereafter not only was the weather exceptionally favourable, but superhuman efforts were made in the name of the Great Leap Forward to maximise production and supply. By the end of 1957 all cultivators had been organised, ten years ahead of the original schedule, into nearly 700,000 collective farms. Four months later the first communes were founded. Without allowing for the consolidation of the collectives, by harvest-time 1958 they had been merged into some 26,000 communes. In August the grain production was predicted to be going to reach 300–350 million tons and in December the claim was raised to 375 million tons or twice as much as in 1957. While a harvest of truly stupendous proportions was reportedly gathered, a programme of social and economic engineering was carried out in the communes which must have affected the life of every Chinese family even if dormitories still lay ahead.

Disregarding the dislocations which the introduction of the communes was bound to cause, Western observers fascinated by the magnitude of the harvest claim were only too ready to accept it uncritically. " Nothing convinces more than success," wrote Dr. Biehl of the Institute of World Economics of Kiel University who had travelled extensively in China. " The burden which the Chinese cultivator had to accept in accordance with the Party's doctrine was immense. Now the results are there for everyone to see. Any resistance that may have existed among the rural population is thus likely to have lost its ground." [1] Even in 1959 when signs had become plentiful that all was not well in China's food economy, Dr. de Castro, once closely connected with the Food and Agriculture Organisation of the United Nations wrote that " New China's victory over the eternal plague of hunger is as startling an event as the conquest of interplanetary space." [2]

Western statements of this kind are inexcusable even if the ultimate responsibility for the exaggerations rests with the Chinese Government and Party. It is sometimes reasoned that they were misled by enthusiastic statisticians reporting yields that did not exist.[3] This is hardly likely in view of the evidence available. Though limited and at times conflicting, it suggests that the exaggeration formed part and parcel of the

---

[1] Dr. M. Biehl, China in " World Economy," Half Yearly Report of the Institute of World Economy, Kiel, December 1958.

[2] As quoted by Reed J. Irvine in " Phantom Food in Communist China," *Asian Survey*, Vol. I, No. 1, Berkeley, California, March 1961.

[3] Non-food crops and livestock numbers were similarly affected by statistical exaggerations.

Communist Party programme of moulding the countryside, in a matter of a few months, into a society ready to accept burdens unheard of, in the expectation of returns that were to show results almost immediately.

We may never know for certain whether the setbacks of 1959 were partly caused by a disillusioned peasantry. The fact remains that the claim that grain output had doubled in 1958 was withdrawn in August 1959. The harvest estimate was scaled down from 375 to 250 million tons, but in the course of the adjustment statements were made which were hardly any more credible than the ones withdrawn. Allegedly the amendment was the result of two recounts carried out in the spring of 1959 when doubts were raised by some of those who had been among the " rightists " on earlier occasions. As nearly two-fifths of the crop must have been dispersed at that time, there is no reason to accept the revised estimate any more than the original one. As the weather had been quite exceptionally favourable throughout 1958 in all parts of China, a harvest of 220 million tons or nearly 20 per cent. above that of 1957 can be accepted as probable; but as the dislocations caused by the creation of the communes are likely to have been on a vast scale, the waste, like the harvest, can be assumed to have reached an all-time record.

New exaggerations were allowed to blur the harvest estimate of 1959. Although the weather was less favourable than in the previous year and almost one-third of the sown area had suffered from drought or floods (against one-sixth in 1958), the harvest was said to be 10 per cent. larger than the all-time record of 1958. Allowing for the hazards of nature, a grain crop of 200 million tons was probably the most that was gathered, though it may well have been a little less. Consumption was kept stringent. Shortages were reported from both towns and rural areas where cultivators were engaged in much heavy work outside the farms.

The year 1960 brought further deterioration in farm output and food production. The grain target was set, once again, 10 per cent. above the harvest claimed for the previous year. In the event, no results were published, but the sombre official pronouncements left no doubt as to the seriousness of the situation. This was supposed to be the worst year in a century. Drought affected almost every province of China proper, worst of all Hopei, Honan, Shantung and Shansi. Floods and typhoons hit twenty provinces, in particular the coastal areas of Kwangtung, Fukien, Kiangsu and Shantung, and also some parts of Manchuria. In all some 60 million hectares of land were said to have suffered. Against this, the acreage under grain crops was increased by 11 million hectares or over 10 per cent. and it was thus as large as in 1958 before the bumper crop had led to untimely reductions in acreages.

Whereas the harvest was seriously affected by natural hazards, there is some ground for doubt as to its extent. Nothing was said earlier in the season to suggest disasters of such magnitude as were in fact reported in the Chinese press. The summer crops were said to have yielded, according to plan, 10 per cent. more than in 1959. The possibility can thus not be ruled out that exaggeration blurs once again the true situation. After two unquestionably poor crops, Government and Party may have seen no other way to stimulate to renewed effort a population, increased by over 40 millions in three years, overworked in heavy capital projects, and disillusioned with the way land distributed by reform had reverted to the state and individual farming had deteriorated into communal life.

Western observers, on the basis of accounts given by refugees from Kwangtung and Fukien, have been quick to report conditions of starvation on a nationwide scale. They have taken China's contracts for large-scale shipments of Canadian and Australian wheat, barley and flour as supporting their contention; but in fact, the evidence available, though limited, does not wholly bear out their pessimism. The only statement as to the size of the 1960 harvest is attributed to Chou En-lai. When interviewed by Edgar Snow, Chou is said to have described the harvest of 1960 as less than those of 1958 and 1959, but more than in 1957.[4] This would point to something of the order of 190 million tons, a crop which, if evenly distributed, should be sufficient to feed a population of some 650 million people.[5]

Against this, there are the refugee reports which quote lack of essentials and rations substantially lower than in previous years. Rations, though varying according to locality and not always honoured, are a useful check on reports from official sources. Introduced informally at the end of 1953, rationing was regularised in the autumn of 1955 and has been in force, in one form or another, ever since. At the height of communal feeding food allocations were made to communes rather than families, but in essence rationing according to age and form of occupation has remained in force.

In 1959 monthly rations of grains were said to provide 40–60 lbs. for working men, with white-collar workers drawing approximately 30 lbs. In 1960, reports reaching Hong Kong and referring mostly to conditions in Kwangtung quoted rations of 40 lbs. for heavy and 25 lbs. for light workers. Later in the year they were apparently reduced further. Cases of malnutrition, *e.g.*, peripheral oedema, beri beri, night blindness and inflammatory disorders of the liver have been reported from various parts

4 Edgar Snow, A Report from Red China. *Look*, January 31, 1961.
5 As given by Ho Wio-Yang and Ch'un-Lsü in " distribution and exchange of China's agricultural products," Kuang-ming Jih-Tsao, February 27, 1961. See Survey of China Mainland Press (Hong Kong: U.S. Consulate-General), No. 2515. Figures as high as 700 million are sometimes quoted, but these seem unduly inflated.

of China. These reports naturally leave out of account non-rationed foodstuffs; nor do they say anything in quantitative terms of supplies in the villages or the frequency of malnutrition. There is no telling whether the rural population live better or worse than the town dwellers. The usual assumption that villagers suffer most in a year of scarcities is not supported by the evidence available in Asia and Europe during the Second World War. Also in 1956 food consumption in Chinese urban and country areas was known to be of identical calorie content, though more varied in towns than in villages.

The diet of the Chinese is of course such that any departure from normal standards is likely to cause hardships. Grains, pulses and potatoes provide almost nine-tenths of the calorie intake, and the diet is thus deficient even in normal circumstances in sugar, vegetable fats and protective foods, and in particular in animal proteins and vitamins. Before the calamities of the last year made themselves felt the diet provided approximately 2,000 calories which was 10 per cent. less than in the years before the Japanese invasion nearly a generation ago. In 1958 that level of consumption was reached again for the first time. Even so, bearing in mind the climatic conditions, body-weights and age composition of the population, the Chinese diet of the last few years has hardly been worse than that of many countries in Asia and possibly better than in some of them.

The situation has been far from satisfactory since the harvest of 1960. Taking all available information into account, and allowing for such non-food uses as seed, waste, feed and industrial requirements, a food balance may be constructed which eliminates the impossible and reveals the probable. It suggests a national average consumption in 1960–61 of 1,850–1,900 calories per head per day. It may be more.[6] Behind this average there are hidden, side by side with ample food for the privileged, certain cases of malnutrition in deficit areas, particularly during the last months of the consumption year. These conditions have given currency to the erroneous view that the whole of China is suffering from conditions of starvation. There is no evidence to support such a contention.

The Chinese Government has not taken the situation lightly; in fact it has acted with foresight in placing promptly large-scale orders of grain with overseas surplus producers, principally with Canada and Australia. Within the last six months or so orders for close on 10 million metric tons of grain have been placed for supply between the beginning of 1961 and the middle or end of 1963. This means an average of approximately 2·5 million tons per annum at the cost of U.S. $150 million or so. In addition China has accepted an advance of 500,000 tons of sugar from

---

6 If the population were in fact 700 million, supplies as calculated for 1960–61 would provide only 1,700–1,750 calories per head per day.

the Soviet Union at the cost of nearly U.S. $50 million to be repaid in kind at some future date. These imports represent a dramatic departure from recent Chinese practice, but the orders of magnitude are not substantially larger than they were before China embarked on a policy of domestic self-sufficiency in foodstuffs. The imports will suffice to meet the requirements of the annual increase in population and a portion of China's export commitments to countries of the Soviet *bloc*. They will add to the average daily diet no more than 2 per cent. or 40 calories, but allocated to towns and industrial areas along the coast these shipments may well improve substantially the urban diet.

The diversion of precious foreign exchange to the purchase of food-stuffs is bound to slow down the pace of capital construction in industry; all the more so as agriculture will be less of a source of domestic capital formation than in previous years. It is thus not surprising that the emphasis is on consolidation rather than advance in all current public pronouncements.

It would be erroneous to assume insuperable difficulties in the way of China's meeting her overseas commitments. An intensified export drive in South-East Asia and elsewhere, increased sales of silver and renewed appeals for remittances of Chinese savings overseas are likely to yield the foreign exchange required to pay for the food imports of the next three years. The supply of foreign capital equipment, however, will depend largely, if not exclusively, on the availability of credit facilities. The Sino-Soviet trade agreement of May 1961 allowed for deferred payment, over the next four or five years, of China's debt on current account, possibly equivalent to as much as U.S. $200 million. The conclusion of the 1961 protocol of the Sino-Soviet economic assistance pact of 1959 is still outstanding. It is apparently being negotiated in Moscow at this moment; on its terms will depend the size of China's import this year of Soviet capital goods.

It may take anything up to three years before China can hope to recover from the setback caused by two unsatisfactory harvests. In the meantime the number of consumers will have increased by nearly the size of the population of Great Britain. As matters stand at the moment, the prospects are far from satisfactory for the crop which is due to be gathered in a month or so. Again the possibility of exaggerated accounts of crop failures cannot be dismissed, but a large crop can almost certainly be ruled out. Drought has been reported from Shantung, Honan and Hupeh, typhoons and torrential rains from Kwangtung and Fukien, and hail and snow from a wide area between the Yellow and Yangtze Rivers.

In these circumstances the Chinese Government may be obliged to review its long-term farm policy which was adopted as recently as in

April 1960. The Twelve-Year Agricultural Programme, covering the period from 1956 to 1967 was conceived early in 1956, a few months after the first Five-Year Plan (1953–57) had been published belatedly. At that time long-term planning was being considered throughout the Soviet orbit as an alternative to planning for periods of five years only. The Chinese agricultural programme was designed as a master plan for the period terminating with the end of the third Five-Year Plan. It represented little more than an expression of intent and was considerably cruder than the plans formulated before the last war under the auspices of the National Agricultural Research Bureau. The targets set for 1967 were over-ambitious and unrealistic.

Food output was to increase by 150 per cent. and cotton production was to treble within twelve years. Grain harvests were to increase from little more than 180 million tons in 1955 to over 450 million tons in 1967, an utterly unattainable task. The optimism displayed by the authors of the programme rested on the erroneous assumption that accumulated gains could be derived from a programme of various improvements the success of each of which in fact depended on the simultaneous application of modern methods in several spheres. Irrigation and flood control ranked highest on the list of measures to be taken, and as distribution canals and ditches had been neglected badly during the years of war and civil war considerable improvements were indeed possible. Other measures such as mechanization, seed multiplication, pest and disease control, land reclamation, multiple cropping and the application of fertilisers could be expected to contribute modestly to increases in yields, if they were applied side by side with one another.

As it stood, the programme lacked co-ordination and integration. As it began to be implemented it revealed its principal weakness, an appalling lack of funds. Less than one-tenth of all public investment was set aside for agriculture, water conservancy and forestry together, and two-thirds of this small amount was devoted to water conservation and irrigation. No wonder yields remained in essence dependent on the hazards of nature the impact of which was in no way alleviated, in spite of all official manifestations to the contrary, by the introduction of such farm requisites as fertilisers or mechanical drought power.

As the prospects of progress varied with the change in the weather and the controversy vacillated between "rightist" and "leftist" elements in the Party, so the Twelve-Year Agricultural Programme suffered its downward and upward changes in 1957 and 1958. In the end it was adopted by the National People's Congress without any serious amendment in April 1960. An abridged version was issued in the autumn of 1958 when the campaign in favour of merging collectives into communes was at its height. It was allegedly drawn up by Mao Tse-tung himself and was described as a Charter for Agriculture. In his report to the National People's Congress T'an Chen-lin, member of the Party's Politburo, described it as even richer and more complete in content than the Agricultural Programme. Its chief innovation was the inclusion of " close planting " as one of the means of achieving increased yields. This method had been abused so much in 1958 that it was exposed to serious criticism by farm specialists, later branded as " rightists." Little is heard of it nowadays.[7]

The setbacks of 1959 and 1960 have made it abundantly clear that the future development of China's main industry does not lie with amateurish plans of this kind. Not unnaturally the emphasis of Government action has shifted in face of the emergency to remedies more in tune with current requirements. The most authoritative statement in this respect was made by the Minister of Agriculture, Liao Lu-yen in an article published early in 1961 in *Red Flag*. In place of the communes, the production brigade (formerly the collective) is to form the basis of farm management at the present stage of development. " Draught animals, farm tools and the other principal means of production belong to the production brigade and the products of the brigade are at its own disposal." " The transition from the present system of commune ownership is a matter for the future." [8] At the same time members of communes are encouraged to engage in family sideline production supplementary to the state-controlled economy, and to keep animals and poultry. The private plot of the members of communes is left for family use and a private trade in farm products is to be permitted where prices may be fixed as a result of bargaining by both parties. Finally, bonuses are to be issued in kind so as to encourage additional efforts on the part of production brigades.

The position of the communes is thus seriously undermined. China's political leaders have realised (like Stalin at the height of his campaign to eradicate the peasantry as an independent economic and social entity) where " dizziness with success " leads. Like Stalin, they have sounded a temporary retreat. The Chinese cultivator has often been described as a contented member of the Communist state. It is of course hardly possible to assess the extent to which he may have succeeded in expressing his dissatisfaction with the way his affairs have been handled on his behalf by Government and Party. It stands to reason, however, to assume that a villager whose desire to own his own piece of land was fulfilled in 1950 became somewhat critical when he was induced five

---

[7] Reference has been made to this question in the March and April (1961) issues of *Jen-min Jih-pao* and *Kuang-ming Jih-pao* discussing a critical article on the " group concept in agricultural production " by Yin Hung-chang, published in *Jen-min Jih-pao* June 13, 1960. See *Current Background* (CB) (Hong Kong: U.S. Consulate-General), No. 652.   [8] *Hung Chi* (*Red Flag*), third and fourth issues, Peking, February 1961.

years later to abandon it again in the interest of the agricultural production co-operative of the higher grade, commonly known as collective. He may even have become hostile towards the régime when another three years later he was persuaded to eat in mess halls, sleep in dormitories and work without reward.

Like peasants elsewhere, the Chinese cultivators are unlikely to turn actively against higher authority, but they are likely to resent the Communist version of farm policy as much as the Russian peasants still do more than forty years after their abortive agrarian reform. In Russia where nature was probably more responsible than men for last year's crop failure, Mr. Khrushchev has demoted senior agricultural experts and Party secretaries. Conversely in China nature has been blamed for calamities which may have had less serious effects had it not been for a deadly conflict between rulers and ruled. Here then may lie the explanation of the dislocations caused for two, possibly even three, years in succession, in the wake of the cruel experiment in social engineering that goes in the name of Communism by way of the communes.

Table 1

CHINA.—FARMS AND FARMERS

	1950	1955	1956	1957	1958	1959	1960
Peasant Households (millions)	105·50	119·20	120·00	121·50	123·20	(125·00)	n.a.
Mutual Aid Teams (millions)	2·70	7·15	n.a.	none	none	none	none
Agricultural Producers "Co-operatives" (000)	0·02	633·70	764·00	784·00	negl.	negl.	none
lower level ...	0·02	633·20	276·00	84·00	none	none	none
higher level ...	0·00	0·50	488·00	700·00	negl.	negl.	none
People's Communes (000)	none	none	none	none	26·00	24·00	(24·00)
Households in Mutual Aid Teams (millions) ...	11·30	60·40	n.a.	none	none	none	none
Agricultural Producers "Co-operatives" (millions)	0·00	16·90	117·80	119·50	negl.	negl.	none
lower level ...	0·00	16·90	10·40	4·50	none	none	none
higher level ...	0·00	0·00	107·40	115·00	negl.	negl.	none
People's Communes (millions)	none	none	none	none	(122·00)	(124·00)	n.a.
State Farms (000) ...	1·20	2·24	2·25	n.a.	n.a.	n.a.	n.a.
Sown Area of State Farms (000 hectares) ...	155·00	394·60	587·50	n.a.	n.a.	n.a.	n.a.
Employed on State Farms (000)	43·00	134·00	206·00	n.a.	n.a.	n.a.	n.a.
Tractors (15 h.p.) on State Farms (000)	1·20	2·80	4·40	n.a.	n.a.	n.a.	n.a.

Sources: Official Chinese Statistics.　　　( )=estimated.　　　n.a.=not available.

Table 2

CHINA.—LIVESTOCK POPULATION

	1949	1955	1956	1957	1958	1959	1960
				millions			
Horses, Donkeys and Mules	15·8	21·4	20·8	19·8	n.a.	20·0	n.a.
Cattle and Buffaloes	43·9	65·9	66·6	65·8	(65·5)	65·4	n.a.
Pigs	57·8	87·9	97·8	145·9	160·0	180·0	243·0
Sheep and Goats ...	42·3	84·2	92·1	98·6	108·9	112·5	n.a.

Table 3

CHINA.—CROP ACREAGES, PRODUCTION AND YIELDS

	1949	1955	1956	1957	1958	1959	1960
Acreages			million hectares				
Rice	25·7	29·2	33·2	32·3	32·7	29·4	31·0
Wheat	21·5	26·7	27·3	27·6	26·6	24·1	27·5
Other Grains and Pulses	47·4	52·4	52·7	50·6	45·7	49·2	44·0
Potatoes	7·0	10·0	11·0	10·5	16·3	16·3	(17·5)
Total Grains and Potatoes	101·6	118·4	124·3	120·9	121·3	109·0	(120·0)
Soya Beans	8·2	11·4	12·0	12·6	12·9	(13·0)	(13·0)
Total Foodcrops ...	109·8	129·8	136·3	133·5	134·2	(122·0)	(133·0)
Non-Foodcrops ...	(21·2)	21·3	22·9	23·7	22·1	(20·5)	(21·0)
Total Area sown ...	(131·0)	151·1	159·2	157·2	156·3	(142·5)	(154·0)
Total Area cultivated ...	98·0	110·2	111·8	111·8	107·8	105·0	(110·0)
Multiple Cropping Index	133·8	137·2	142·3	140·6	145·0	135·3	(140·0)
Harvest			million metric tons				
Rice	48·6	78·0	82·5	86·8	113·7	n.a.	n.a.
Wheat	13·8	23·0	24·8	23·6	28·9	n.a.	n.a.
Other Grains and Pulses	35·8	54·9	53·4	52·7	62·0	n.a.	n.a.
Potatoes*	9·8	18·9	21·8	21·9	45·4	n.a.	n.a.
Total Grains and Potatoes	108·0	174·8	182·5	185·0	250·0	270·0	297·0
Soya Beans	5·1	9·1	10·2	10·0	10·5	11·5	(12·5)
Total Foodcrops ...	113·2	183·9	192·7	195·0	261·5	281·5	(309·5)
Yields			metric tons per hectare				
Rice	1·90	2·67	2·47	2·70	3·47	n.a.	n.a.
Wheat	0·64	0·86	0·91	0·86	1·09	n.a.	n.a.
Other Grains and Pulses	0·76	1·05	1·02	1·04	1·35	n.a.	n.a.
Potatoes*	1·40	1·88	1·99	2·09	2·80	n.a.	n.a.
Total Grains and Potatoes	1·06	1·46	1·42	1·54	2·03	2·48	(2·47)
Soya Beans	0·62	0·80	0·88	0·80	0·81	0·88	(0·96)
Total Foodcrops ...	0·86	1·22	1·21	1·24	1·67	1·97	(2·01)

Sources: Official Chinese Statistics.
      * in grain equivalent.   n.a.=not available.   ( )=estimated.

Table 4

CHINA.—FOOD RATIONS 1960-61

| | per month | | per annum | |
| | light | heavy | light | heavy |
		workers		workers
Grains	25 lbs.	40 lbs.	135 kilos	218 kilos
Sugar ...	4 oz.	4 oz.	1.35 kilos	1.35 kilos
Meat ...	12 oz.	12 oz.	4·10 kilos	4·10 kilos
Vegetable Oil	12 oz.	12 oz.	4·10 kilos	4·10 kilos

Table 5

CHINA.—GRAIN IMPORTS 1961-63

| | 000 million metric tons | | | | Total (Commodity Weight) |
	Rice	Wheat	Barley	Flour	
from Burma ...	0.35	—	—	—	0.35
from Canada ...	—	5·89	1·28	0·03	7·20
from Australia ...	—	2·08	0·30	0·04	2·42
from Europe ...	—	0·03	—	—	0·03
Total	0.35	8·01	1·58	0·07	10·00

Table 6

CHINA.—FOOD BALANCE 1960-61

| | Gross Domestic Production | Non-Food Uses | Net | Food | Supplies |
| | | | | Kilos per head | Calories per head per day |
	million metric tons				
Grains	140·0	46·0	94·0	145·0	1,430
Potatoes	40·0	17·0	23·0	35·0	90
Pulses	10·0	6·8	3·2	5·0	50
Soya Beans	8·0	4·8	3·2	5·0	50
Sugar	1·5	0·2	1·3	2·0	20
Fruit and Vegetables	80·0	40·0	40·0	60·0	50
Meat and Poultry ...	5·7	0·5	5·2	8·0	65
Eggs and Fish ...	5·0	1·1	3·9	6·0	15
Fats and Oils ...	3·0	0·4	2·6	4·0	90
Total Domestic					
Imports ...	—	—	—	—	1,860
Grains	2·5	0·5	2·0	3·0	30
Sugar	0·5	—	0·5	1·0	10
Grand Total ...	—	—	—	—	1,900

Sources: Official Statements.
         Estimates.

The figures in these tables have been compiled from numerous sources over the years.

China's Industrial Development, 1958-63

By CHOH-MING LI

CHINA had no Second Five-Year Plan (1958–62) only five *ad hoc* annual plans during that period. In basic construction and industrial production a great leap forward did take place in the first three years, only to be followed by collapse and readjustment in the last two years. In agriculture, the period started with an unprecedented bumper crop in the first year, after which there commenced an agricultural crisis that grew in intensity from year to year until 1962 when the output of food grains and green vegetables began to show recovery. This was in sharp contrast to the First Five-Year Plan period which concluded with spectacular achievements in heavy industry, moderate success in light industry and slow but steady improvement in agriculture.

The accomplishments in industry during the Second Five-Year period have been officially assessed in different ways. A general evaluation was given by the chairman of the State Economic Commission.[1]

> We have now built an industrial system of some size ... Now we have progressed from copying to independent designing ... We are able to make some big precision equipment ... We are able to design independently and to build with our own technical forces many important construction projects ...
> During the First Five-Year Plan China could make about 55 per cent. of the machinery and equipment she needed. During the Second Five-Year Plan, this level was raised to about 85 per cent. Our level of self-sufficiency in steel products climbed from about 75 per cent. in the First Five-Year Plan period to around 90 per cent. in the Second Five-Year Plan period ...
> Nowadays, not only has the industry in these coastal cities been greatly expanded but every province and autonomous region in the country has established modern industry to some extent or other. ... Now we have not only thoroughly built up the [large-scale Anshan iron and steel industrial] base but also constructed new iron and steel bases at Wuhan, Paotow and elsewhere ... now all the big, small and medium-sized cities and quite a number of villages too have power stations of various sizes ... now many provinces of the country have established up-to-date textile mills.

[1] Po I-po, " The Socialist Industrialisation of China [written for *Cuba Socialista* of Cuba]," *Peking Review*, No. 41, October 11, 1963.

The National People's Congress in November 1963 was told that "since 1958 China's industry has progressed satisfactorily both in the scale of production and in quantity; there has been a leap forward development especially in the variety and quality of products." [2] In comparing 1962 with 1957, the varieties of steel, rolled steel and non-ferrous metals produced in the country were more than doubled, varieties of petroleum products increased by nearly 200 per cent., and varieties of machine tools grew by nearly 150 per cent. The country was used to importing the great bulk of the petroleum products she needed; now she is in the main self-sufficient. [3]

According to another official evaluation, the readjustment since 1960 had produced a better balance within the industrial structure. From 1953 through 1960 China's metallurgical, chemical and other heavy industries showed tremendous growth, but the mining industries (coal, ferrous and non-ferrous metals)—the foundation of all heavy industries—failed to keep apace. Since 1961, priority has been given to the development of the mining industries, and their growth accelerated accordingly. Likewise petroleum, timber, chemical fertiliser, and special steels—the four weak links in the industrial system—have also been strengthened. All this, together with the establishment of new industries producing synthetic fibre, plastics, synthetic fatty acid, etc., during the Second Five-Year period, lays a basis for further industrial growth. [4]

Finally, it was officially claimed that by the end of 1962 the number of scientific and technical personnel in various fields increased by 70 per cent. when compared with 1957; that they had higher scientific and technical standards. As a result, the number of big and medium-sized industrial projects, designed and equipped with installations made by the Chinese themselves, had increased from 413 in the First Five-Year Plan period to 1,013 in the second. [5] China, therefore, is growing more and more independent in technological matters. [6]

These official claims of accomplishments actually cover up many developments of basic importance to the economy during the last five years.

2 " Continue Striving for the Construction of an Independent, Comprehensive and Modern National Economic System," *People's Daily* editorial, December 4, 1963, p. 2; translated in *Peking Review*, No. 49, December 6, 1963. It is, of course, possible that the country is self-sufficient because of a drastic reduction in consumption.

3 " Press Communiqué of National People's Congress," *People's Daily*, December 4, 1963 ; translated in *Peking Review*, No. 49, December 6, 1963.

4 " Situation in Industry—Good," *Peking Review*, No. 31, August 2, 1963.

5 " Press Communiqué . . .," *op. cit.*

6 A technical note is in order. The official statistical figures quoted in this paper are taken from Chinese and Russian official publications familiar to all those working in this field of study. They will not be cited in the interest of space. All rouble figures have been converted in terms of the 1961 rouble, which is equivalent to $1·10 or 4·44 roubles of the 1950 variety. The official exchange rate of the yuan is 2·617 to the U.S. dollar, but the market rate in Hong Kong, according to one report, was about 5·5 yuan to the U.S. dollar in 1958, 7·7 in 1959, 7·9 in 1960, and 8·0 in 1961 and 1962.

The following discussion starts by examining the nature of the so-called Second Five-Year Plan and tracing the changes in over-all development policies with particular reference to industry. This is followed by an analysis of the course of industrial development during the period, and the consequent structural changes in industry and in the economy as a whole. Then comes a discussion of the internal factors underlying developments for the period; they include the investment programme, the small-industry experiment decentralisation and planning, industrial management and Soviet aid. This discussion will be concluded with the developments of 1963 and the trends which are emerging.

THE SECOND FIVE-YEAR PLAN AND DEVELOPMENT POLICIES

By the middle of 1956, the fourth year of the First Five-Year Plan, socialisation of the whole economy had practically been achieved without serious resistance from the people. Industrialisation based on the development of heavy industry around a nucleus of Soviet-aid projects was proceeding with satisfactory speed. A major wage reform was introduced at this time and the income of industrial and other urban workers rose on average by 14·5 per cent. Basic-construction planning and control, material balances and allocation, comprehensive planning of state budgets, business finance and bank credit had all been systematised for some years and were being improved with practice. The number of engineers and technicians in industry was increasing rapidly, and as a result of Soviet help the Chinese were able to do more and more surveying, designing and installation by themselves. It was against this background that the Central Committee of the Chinese Communist Party decided in July 1956 to convene the Party's Eighth National Congress that September to discuss, as one of the four major items in the agenda, a proposal concerning the Second Five-Year Plan for national economic development.[7]

The proposal aimed to make China 70 per cent. self-sufficient in machinery and equipment, including some heavy and some precision machines which would be needed for national development plans by 1962, and to ensure that by 1967 China would be transformed from a backward agricultural country into an advanced industrialised nation.[8] According to the resolution passed by the Party Congress, the basic tasks under the Second Five-Year Plan included, among others, " continued development of various industries with heavy industry as the core," and

---

[7] *People's Daily*, July 7, 1956.
[8] Liu Shao-ch'i, " Political Report to the Party's National Congress," *People's Daily*, September 17, 1956, and " The Party's National Congress Approves ' The Proposal Concerning the Second Five-Year Plan (1958–62) for National Development,' " *People's Daily*, September 29, 1956.

" further promotion of industrial, agricultural and handicraft production with concomitant development of transportation and trade." The industries to be given special emphasis were the expanding industries such as metal processing, machine making, electric power, coal and building materials, together with weaker industries such as petroleum and radio, and the yet-to-be-established industries of synthetic chemicals and nuclear power.[9] In comparison with the First Five-Year Plan, the amount of basic investment during the second five years was expected to double, with the share for industry increasing from 58·2 per cent. to about 60 per cent. and that for agriculture, water conservation and forestry from 7·6 per cent. to 10 per cent. Target figures for major commodities and other items of special importance were listed.

In February 1957 the State Council accepted the proposal and instructed the State Planning Commission to work out as soon as possible, with various central ministries and commissions and local governments at the provincial level, a draft of the Second Five-Year Plan to be submitted to the State Council and through it to the National People's Congress for approval. The official record, however, shows that no such draft plan was ever submitted to the State Council let alone the National People's Congress.

The proposed targets for the Second Five-Year Plan, together with later revisions, are presented in Table 1, which also gives the official output data for 1957 through 1959 as part of the statistics with which the planning authorities had been working. Several observations may be made about the table. In the first place, even after endorsement by the Party's National Congress, the proposed 1962 targets were still questioned by some Party Members and government officials on the grounds that they were set too low. To answer these objections an article was published in the official journal of the State Planning Commission in October 1956 which pointed out that the proposed basic investment, already more than twice as much as that for the First Five-Year Plan, was based both on a maximum supply from domestic sources, with China producing as much as 70 per cent. of the heavy machinery and equipment required, and on the half a million new graduates from colleges and universities that the country could possibly produce during the period. Hence, it would be inappropriate either to increase the proposed amount for basic investment or to step up the rate of industrial growth.[10] In fact, at the end of the First Five-Year Plan when the economic shape of 1957

9 Chou En-lai, " Report on the Proposal concerning the Second Five-Year Plan (1958–62) for Economic Development," *People's Daily*, September 19, 1956.

10 Chia Fu, " On the Growth Rates for the Period of the Second Five-Year Plan," *Chi-hua Ching-chi (Planned Economy)*, No. 10, October 23, 1956. Also reprinted in *Hsin-hua Pan-yueh-k'an (New China Semi-Monthly)*, No. 24, December 21, 1956, pp. 40–42.

Table 1

OFFICIAL DATA RELATING TO THE PROPOSED TARGETS FOR THE SECOND FIVE-YEAR PLAN

Item	Unit	Proposed target 1957 (FFYP)	Proposed target 1962 (SFYP) proposed 9/56	1962 target, revised 12/57	Actual output (official) 1957	Actual output (official) 1958	1962 target, revised 8/59	1959 output (official)
A. Heavy industry:								
1. Coal	million tons	113·00	190–210	230·00	130·00	270·00	335·00	347·80
2. Crude Oil	million tons	2·01	5–6	" Less "	1·46	2·26	—	3·68
3. Electric power	bil. kw-hrs	15·90	40–43	—	19·34	27·53	—	41·50
4. Steel	million tons	4·12	10·5–12·0	12·00a	5·35	8·00	12·00b	8·63
5. Aluminium ingot	thous. tons	20·00	100–120	—	—	—	—	—
6. Ch. fertiliser	thous. tons	·58	3·0–3·2	7·00	·63	·81	—	1·30
7. Metallurgical equipment	thous. tons	8·00	30–40	—	—	—	—	205·00
8. Metal-cutting machine tools	thous. units	13·00	60–65	" Less "	28·00	50·00	—	70·00
9. Power generating equipment	million kw s	·16	1·4–1·5	—	·20	·80	—	2·15
10. Cement	million ton.	6·00	12·5–14·5	12·50	6·86	9·30	—	12·27
11. Timber	mil. cub. m	20·00	31–34	—	27·90	35·00	—	41·20
B. Light industry:								
1. Cotton yarn	mil. bales	5·00	8–9	—	4·65	6·10	—	8·20
2. Cotton cloth	bil. metres	5·58	7·25–8·00	—	5·05	5·70	—	7·50
3. Salt	million tons	7·55	10–11	—	8·28	10·40	—	11·04
4. Edible vegetable oil	million tons	1·79	3·1–3·2	—	1·10	1·25	—	1·47
5. Sugar c	million tons	1·10	2·4–2·5	—	·86	·90	—	1·13
6. Machine-made paper	million tons	·66	1·5–1·6	—	·91	1·22	—	1·70
C. Crops								
1. Food grains	million tons	181·60	250·00	240·00	185·00	250·00	275·00	270·00
2. Ginned cotton	million tons	1·64	2·40	2·15	1·64	2·10	2·31	2·41
3. Soybeans	million tons	11·22	12·50	—	10·05	10·50	—	11·50
D. Livestock:								
1. Cattle	million head	73·61	90·00	—	63·62	—	—	—
2. Horses	million head	8·34	11·00	—	7·30	—	—	—
3. Sheep and goats	million head	113·04	170·00	—	95·58	108·86	—	—
4. Pigs	million head	138·34	250·00	220·00	145·90	160·00	—	180·00d

Note: a   Presumably both factory-produced and indigenous steel
       b   Factory-produced steel only
       c   Including both factory-produced and indigenous sugar
       d   Preliminary
       —   Not available

began to emerge, the chairman of the State Planning Commission announced that " with two more years of experience after the Party's proposal in 1956 for the Second Five-Year Plan, the proposed targets for 1962 had to be readjusted." [11] The few revised figures that were released indicate that except for coal, steel and chemical fertilisers, the proposed targets were scaled down either to the original lower limit, as in the case of cement, or further below it as in all other cases. The reduction in the quota for the critical petroleum industry was explained as a

11 Li Fu-ch'un, " On the Achievements of China's First Five-Year Plan and the Tasks and Directions of Socialist Construction in the Immediate Future," *People's Daily*, December 8, 1957. This was a speech given at the Eighth National Congress of All-China Labour Unions.

result of limitation of natural resources, and the reduction in metal-cutting machine tools, as a result of limited demand. Significantly, in the same speech where these downward revisions of 1962 targets were made public, the slogan of " surpassing Britain in the output of steel, coal, machine tools, cement and chemical fertilisers by 1972 " was advanced. And this was shortly after the release of the revised Draft of the Outline for Agricultural Development from 1956 to 1967.

Secondly, although in the latter half of 1957 the planning authorities began to realise the importance of agriculture to industrial development, and the proposed output of chemical fertilisers for 1962 was substantially raised at the end of 1957, the theme underlying the proposal concerning the Second Five-Year Plan remained unaltered, as was evident in Li Fu-ch'un's statement in December 1957: " Heavy industry should constitute the centre of the plan with priority in development " over all other sectors. It must have also been realised at that time that agricultural output could not increase rapidly without a substantial increase in state investment in agriculture. Hence, the proposed 1962 targets for food grains, raw cotton and pigs were scaled down while the target for chemical fertiliser was raised by over 100 per cent., along with the introduction of farm implements as a major item in the national plan. Since both chemical fertilisers and farm implements come under heavy industry, the attention given to agriculture made the " priority development " of heavy industry all the more inevitable.

Mass mobilisation in the winter of 1957 to launch both the national agricultural development programme and the campaign to surpass Britain in major heavy industrial output probably set off the Great Leap Forward movement in 1958. The objective of the movement was formulated by the Party's Central Committee as the " General Line of going all out and aiming high to achieve greater, quicker, better and more economical results in building socialism." [12] As a result, all the caution that had been taken in setting up the growth rates and targets in the 1956 proposal concerning the Second Five-Year Plan was now swept aside. Politics were in command everywhere. Statistics were reported by the cadres in the field according to their " enthusiasm in socialist revolution " rather than on the basis of fact. [13]

Speaking before a joint meeting sponsored by the Metallurgical Ministry and the Ministry of Finance in July 1958, Li Hsien-nien, the Finance Minister, described succinctly the differences of planning then prevailing: "At present the central authorities are compiling targets for

---

[12] Liu Shao-ch'i, " Report on the Work of the Chinese Communist Party's Central Committee to the Second Session of the Party's National Congress," *New China Semi-Monthly*, No. 11, June 10, 1958, pp. 1–11.

[13] See my volume, *The Statistical System of Communist China* (Berkeley: University of California Press, 1962), especially Part II.

the Second Five-Year Plan, but have not been able to catch up with the swift changes in practical conditions that require upward revision of the targets almost every day." [14] These difficulties multiplied as long as the Great Leap Forward movement continued.

When the Eighth Plenary Session of the Party's Central Committee came in August 1959 to deflate the earlier fantastic claims of economic accomplishments, it singled out coal and factory-produced steel in industry and food grains and cotton in agriculture as the most important of all items in the Second Five-Year Plan and revised upwards their targets for 1962. Yet, five months later when the annual economic plan for 1960 was submitted, it was discovered that by the end of 1959 two (coal and cotton) out of the four revised targets had already been surpassed, one other (food grains) had almost been reached, and only the item of factory-produced steel trailed behind. Either the statistical information available to the planners in August 1959 was faulty or the statistical reports at the end of the year were false. Planning had clearly become impossible.

Table 1 also shows that by the end of 1959, the quotas for 1962, as originally set forth in September 1956, had been fulfilled in the case of thirteen out of the twenty-four items and not fulfilled in the case of eleven others. This called for a " Supplementary Plan for the Last Three Years of the Second Five-Year Plan," which may have been prepared and submitted by Li Fu-ch'un to the National People's Congress in March 1960, but which has not been published. The report of Li Fu-ch'un that was published at the time, concerned the draft economic plan for 1960, in which the idea of regarding agriculture as the foundation, with industry taking the lead in economic development, was advanced.[15] But no indication was given yet that the basic policy of priority development of heavy industry had been changed.

The change began to develop in the autumn of 1960 when the harvest turned out to be much worse than expected. In late September, a movement of " all people to agriculture and food grains " was brought to a peak by cadres all over the country.[16] This represented a complete turnabout from the nation-wide movement of " all people to iron and steel " that took place in the late summer of 1958. Then, in November 1960, an editorial appeared in the Party's journal *Red Flag* under the title " Simultaneous Development of Industry and Agriculture is an Important Law in China's Socialist Economy," in which Mao was credited with formulation of the policy of placing agriculture at the top

[14] *Ts'ai-cheng (Finance)*, No. 8, August 5, 1958.
[15] *People's Daily*, March 31, 1960, pp. 2–3.
[16] *People's Daily*, September 27, 1960.

position in the economy—a policy, observed the editorial, "not incompatible with that of priority development of heavy industry." The importance of agricultural development was clearly realised, but there was to be no change in priority in terms of resource allocation when compared with heavy industries.

The sharp change occurred in January 1961 when Li Fu-ch'un, in his report to the Eighth Plenum of the Central Committee, admitted that the planned agricultural output for 1960 had not been attained because of " severe natural calamities in 1959 " and " natural calamities in 1960 that were unprecedented in 100 years." This led the Plenum to reaffirm the movement of " all the party and all people to agriculture and food grains." The Plenum decided further that " since there had been tremendous development in heavy industry in the last three years, its output of major products already far in excess of the planned level for 1961 and 1962, the scale of basic construction should therefore be appropriately reduced." As to light industry, in order to ease the severe shortage of supply of consumer goods, assistance was to be given to " further development of light industry, rural and urban handicrafts, family side-line occupations and suburban agriculture, and to the revival of primary markets in rural areas." [17] In spite of this lip service paid to the promotion of light industry, the general industrial policy was known to be that of " readjustment, consolidation, reinforcement and improvement." [18] The Great Leap Forward movement was thus officially brought to an end.

The year 1961 saw the agricultural crisis deepen. China began to import food on a huge scale. From December 1960, when the first shipments arrived, up to the end of 1963, about 16 million metric tons of grain have been purchased largely from Canada and Australia. The total includes 5·6 million tons in 1961 (mainly wheat, flour and barley), 4·7 million tons in 1962 (mainly wheat and corn), and 5·5 million tons (mainly wheat) scheduled for delivery in 1963 (about 3·5 million tons for the first half of the year). [19]

When the autumn harvest of 1961 was no better than that of 1960, it was clear that the mere reduction in the scale of basic construction was not enough. In December 1961 the Party issued secretly to the cadres in the field a document known as " Seventy Articles of Industrial

---

[17] *People's Daily*, January 21, 1961.
[18] Kung Hsiang-cheng, " Produce More and Better Light Industrial Products for Daily Use," *Red Flag*, No. 89–90, February 10, 1962.
[19] " A Report on World Grain Exports to Red China," *Foreign Agriculture*, I, No. 18, May 6, 1963, and " Australia Sells Communist China more Wheat," *ibid*. No. 26, July 1, 1963. These estimates by the United States Department of Agriculture differ somewhat from other estimates, such as those published in this journal; see Allan J. Barry, " The Chinese Food Purchases," *The China Quarterly*, No. 11.

Policy." [20] In essence, it directed that unless special authority was given, all basic construction should be suspended, all those enterprises that had been operating regularly at a loss be shut down, and the practice of recruiting labour from rural areas be abandoned for at least three years. But at this time warnings were still voiced in the official journal of the Party against one-sided emphasis on agriculture at the expense of the simultaneous advance of industry, transportation, culture and education. [21]

Most probably the " Seventy Articles " furnished the basis for Chou En-lai's formulation of " The Work of Readjusting the National Economy and Our Immediate Tasks," which took a whole section in his report on the work of government to the National People's Congress on March 27, 1962. Here he stressed that " the core of readjustment " consisted in carrying through the policy of readjustment, consolidation, reinforcement and improvement, and entailed ten immediate tasks, three of which were of direct concern to industry. [22]

> Task 3. Contract further the basic construction front, and redirect the materials, equipment and manpower to the most urgent areas.
> Task 4. Properly reduce urban population and workers and function-aries, the first move being to send those workers and functionaries who came from the rural districts back to take part in agricultural production, so as to strengthen the agricultural front.
> Task 10. Improve further the work in planning and try to attain a comprehensive balance among different sectors in the national economy in accordance with the [declining priority] order of agri-culture, light industry, and heavy industry.

The extent to which these measures were applied may be gathered from the fact that the sudden exodus of Chinese refugees (which included many unemployed from urban areas) from the mainland to Hong Kong took place in May of that year.

The change from the priority development of heavy industry to " agriculture first " was complete when the Tenth Plenum of the Party's Central Committee, meeting in September 1962, resolved that " as the immediate urgent task of the people, the development of agriculture, itself the foundation of the national economy with industry as the

---

[20] It has been widely reported that during this period of economic crisis several other policy documents were also issued, namely, " Thirty-five Articles of Handicraft Policy " issued by the State Council in December 1960, and " Sixty Articles of the By-laws (Draft) for Rural People's Communes " and " Seventy Articles of Cultural and Educational Policy " issued by the Party's central authorities in about May 1961. Copies of these have been smuggled out to Hong Kong. The Union Research Institute, for example, has records of them. Extracts have been published in several issues of the Institute's journal, *China Weekly*.

[21] Wen Shih-jun, " Centralise all Effort to Seek Solutions for Industrial Problems," *Red Flag*, No. 24, December 16, 1961.

[22] *People's Daily*, April 17, 1962, p. 1. The official translation of the ten immediate tasks in *Peking Review* is too abbreviated to convey the full meaning of the original.

leading factor, must be given the topmost position." The resolution made it clear that what was required under this policy was " to re-locate resolutely our work from the industrial departments to the sphere where agriculture is the foundation." In concrete terms, this called for further readjustment of industry without straining existing resources—through better management, greater variety of products, and higher quality of output—in order to meet the needs of the technological reform of agriculture.

The earlier policy changes in 1961 and 1962 had already necessitated the drafting of an " Adjusted Plan for the Last Two Years of the Second Five-Year Plan," a step approved by the National People's Congress as late as April 1962. This " adjusted plan " has not been made public, although at its meeting in July 1963 the Standing Committee of the National People's Congress gave its approval to Li Fu-ch'un's report on the " adjusted plan " and its results as well as to Li Hsien-nien's report on the final state accounts for 1961 and 1962.[23]

Hence, except for the brief statement of intentions and output targets in September 1956 and a few subsequently revised target figures, there has not been any formulation of a Five-Year Plan for the period from 1958 to 1962. The Great Leap Forward made any long-term planning—or any planning, for that matter—impossible, and the deepening of the agricultural crisis since 1959 has rendered the annual plans for the following three years entirely *ad hoc* affairs. There has never been a Second Five-Year Plan in any real sense of the term. As regards development policies, the first three years of the period continued, rather unswervingly, the policy underlying the First Five-Year Plan of focusing on the rapid growth of heavy industry, while the last two years of the period saw an increasingly severe application (at least up to the second or third quarter of 1962) of the measures of " readjustment, consolidation, reinforcement and improvement " in basic construction and industry, with agriculture finally gaining over-riding priority in " development by modernisation " towards the end of the period.

THE COURSE OF INDUSTRIAL DEVELOPMENT AND STRUCTURAL CHANGES

Given the *ad hoc* policies of the Great Leap and subsequent retrenchment during the period from 1958 to 1962, what was the picture of industrial development? It is not easy to give a satisfactory answer because even the officially finalised statistics are of dubious validity for the first two years and are virtually unavailable for the last three.

---

[23] This seems to imply that official statistics for 1961 and 1962 were not finalised until July 1963.

Serious attempts, however, have been made by several scholars to estimate the development in quantitative terms. The most elaborate is certainly the study of China's national income for 1933 and 1952–59 by T. C. Liu and K. C. Yeh, in which a great deal of attention inevitably was paid to industrial growth.[24] Another scholarly study is Alexander Eckstein's, which, however, is concerned with the national income for 1952 alone.[25] W. W. Hollister's early estimates of China's national income since 1950 are being extensively revised.[26] A study of China's economic potential by Y. L. Wu, F. P. Hoeber and M. M. Rockwell has been published, in which China's national income from 1950 to 1962 was "reappraised."[27] Their estimates, based heavily upon the Liu-Yeh study up to 1958, are noteworthy because the estimates were brought up to 1962. For industrial output alone, Kang Chao's index from 1949 through 1959 merits special mention; it is based primarily on official figures without independent adjustment.[28]

All these estimates are beset with technical difficulties generally known as index-number problems, many of which cannot be avoided; and, because of the very nature of the source material, perhaps it is not unfair to say that all the estimates for the period under discussion cannot claim to be more than "educated guesses."[29] Nevertheless, several of them are of interest to students of China's industrial development and deserve a summary presentation here—without a technical discussion of their difficulties or any critical evaluation of them.

Their comparability need not be seriously questioned, as long as they are compared not in absolute magnitude but in general tendencies. For purpose of comparison, it may be noted that "industry" includes manufacturing, mining and utilities, and that within industry the distinction between modern (factory) industry and handicrafts generally depends on whether mechanical power is used in the main working

---

24 Ta-chung Liu and Kung-chia Yeh, *The Economy of the Chinese Mainland: National Income and Economic Development, 1933–59* (Santa Monica, California: The RAND Corporation, Memorandum RM-3519-PR, April 1963), two vols.

25 Alexander Eckstein, *The National Income of Communist China* (Glencoe, Illinois: The Free Press, 1961).

26 William W. Hollister, *China's Gross National Product and Social Accounts, 1950–57* (Glencoe, Illinois: The Free Press, 1958); also his "Estimates of the Gross National Product [of China], 1958–59," in Yuan-li Wu, ed., *The Realities of Communist China* (Milwaukee, Wisconsin: Marquette University, October 1960). See also his article below.

27 *The Economic Potential of Communist China* (Menlo Park, California: Stanford Research Institute, Technical Report No. 2, October 1963), two vols. The national income estimates given in this work apparently supersede an earlier estimate by Y. L. Wu which appears in his volume *Economic Development and the Use of Energy Resources in Communist China* (New York: Praeger, 1963).

28 Kang Chao, "Indices of Industrial Output in Communist China," *Review of Economics and Statistics*, XIV, No. 3, August 1963. For an estimate by Hung and Wu according to a short-cut method, see their joint article.

29 Thus Lin and Yeh regarded their estimates for 1958–62 as "conjectural."

process, irrespective of the number of workers employed. These definitions have been used by Peking, and are therefore adopted to facilitate the recalculation of growth by sub-aggregates. Gross value product is generally much larger than net value product because the former takes into account the cost of materials used in production and therefore one is confronted with the problem of double-counting.[30] In all the estimates, either 1952 or 1957, prices were employed in order to compute the value of aggregates at constant prices. Because of differences in price structures between those two years, a given time series would show higher rates of growth when computed at 1952 prices than when computed at 1957 prices.

THE COURSE OF INDUSTRIAL DEVELOPMENT

Table 2 summarises different estimates of the value of output for the whole of industry in relative terms. It will be observed that all the four estimates agree that there was a "great leap forward" in industrial growth from 1957 through 1959 or 1960 when the growth rate for these two or three years is compared with that in the preceding five years. Although the growth rate shown in official statistics for either one of these periods is much higher than that arrived at by any one of the

Table 2

DIFFERENT ESTIMATES OF INCREASES IN INDUSTRIAL VALUE PRODUCT OVER SPECIFIED PERIODS, 1952–60

(In per cent.)

Source of estimate	Nature of value product	Total increase over			Increase in		
		1952–57	1957–59	1957–60	1958	1959	1960
Liu-Yeh	net (1952 p.)	94·2	51·9		19·6	27·0	
Wu *et al.*	net (1952 p.)	89·2	58·1	82·9	19·5	32·3	15·7
Chao	net (1952 p.)	85·9	71·3		30·3	31·5	
Official	gross (1952 p.)	128·4					
Official	net (1957 p.)		131·5	177·3	66·3	39·2	29·0

three private studies, the official data and Chao's estimate give a steadily declining annual rate of increase in 1958 and 1959, whereas in the other two studies the growth rate was increasing during these two years. But both official data and private estimates agree that the rate of increase fell in 1960, although the absolute magnitudes still

---

[30] Discussion of this problem can be found in many publications. See, *e.g.*, my volume *Economic Development of Communist China* (Berkeley: University of California Press, 1959), pp. 30–35.

showed an increase. Not given in the table, the complete series of Wu *et al.* further displayed a precipitous decline in absolute magnitudes by 74 per cent. in 1961 and levelled off with a slight further drop of 3 per cent. in 1962. In their joint article below, Hung and Wu have tentatively concluded that the economic downswing of 1961 and 1962 had probably come to an end by the second part of 1962 and that the second half of the year was probably marked by a vigorous rebound in the industrial sector.

MODERN INDUSTRY VS. HANDICRAFTS

Table 3 presents different estimates of changes in the value output of modern industry and handicrafts in different periods from 1952 to 1960. As expected, modern industry showed a much higher rate of increase than handicrafts, the difference being much more glaring in the private estimates than in official data. All the estimates agree that in the case of modern industry the rate of increase was greater from 1952 to 1957 than from 1957 to 1959, but the disparity between growth rates was much less according to Chao's estimate and the official series than it was according to the other two studies. During the first two years of the Great Leap Forward, official data showed a declining rate of growth in modern industry whereas the study of Wu *et al.* gave an increasing rate. The latter study also painted a picture of a declining rate in 1960, and a sharp drop in absolute terms by 71 per cent. in 1961 and by 4 per cent. in 1962. (Not shown in table).

Table 3

DIFFERENT ESTIMATES OF INCREASES IN THE VALUE OF OUTPUT OF MODERN INDUSTRY AND HANDICRAFTS OVER SELECTED PERIODS, 1952–59

(In per cent.)

Source of estimate	Value product (in 1952 prices)	Increases over 1952–57 Modern	Handicrafts	Increases over 1957–60 Modern	Handicrafts
Liu-Yeh	net	140·2	14·0	60·4	20·4
Wu *et al.*	net	134·1	12·5	71·9	9·3
Chao	net	95·9		89·6	
Official	gross	152·3	85·4	144·8[a]	99·7[a]

[a] My interpolation from the official data in 1957 prices.

For handicrafts, there is a sizable difference between the official and private estimates in regard to the rate of growth. But the Liu-Yeh study agrees with official data in showing that the growth of handicrafts was greater during the first two years of the Great Leap

Forward than it was during the preceding five years. The study of
Wu *et al.* arrives at a reverse result, and indicates further that because
of the agricultural crisis the handicraft value product actually dropped
8·5 per cent. in 1960 and another 11 per cent. in 1961, with the fall
halted in 1962.

STRUCTURAL CHANGE IN INDUSTRY

Table 4, compiled entirely from official data, presents the changing
composition of industry according to different criteria, namely, method
of production, nature of product, operating organisation and level of
control. The figures for 1960 were those of the plan for the year; the
gross value of industrial output has since been officially estimated at
195·25 billion yuan, that is, 7 per cent. short of the planned figure,

Table 4
OFFICIAL DATA ON CERTAIN ASPECTS OF INDUSTRIAL STRUCTURE, 1957–1960
(In 1957 prices)

Item	1957	1958	1959	1960 planned
Gross value of all-industry output (in billion yuan)	70·4	117·1	163·0	210·0
Composition:	In per cent.			
A. By production method				
1. Modern	70·6	74·5	74·6	—
2. Handicrafts	29·4	25·5	25·4	—
B. By nature of product				
1. Heavy industry	48·4	57·3	58·7	60·5
2. Light industry	51·6	42·7	41·3	39·5
C. By operating organization				
1. Industrial departments ..	100·0	94·7	92·7	91·0
2. People's communes ..	0	5·3	7·3	9·0
a. Rural	*0*	*5·0*	*6·1*	*7·1*
b. Urban	*0*	*0·3*	*1·2*	*1·9*
D. By level of control				
1. Central	46·0	27·0	26·0	—
2. Local	54·0	73·0	74·0	—

but no other details are available. Heavy industry includes, of course,
defence industries. Consolidation and retrenchment since 1960 must
have eliminated a large number of the workshops operated by the rural
and urban communes.

The changes in the proportion between local and central industries did reflect somewhat a wider dispersion of industrial location than ever before, as is well demonstrated in the case of the iron and steel industry by Ronald Hsia's article below; but the main reason was the decentralisation move started in the winter of 1957. On the whole, the central authorities controlled all the large and strategic industries, mostly in the category of heavy industry. It should be pointed out that in 1959, since modern industry produced about three-quarters of industrial output and the centrally controlled sector produced a little over one-quarter of industrial output, about one-half of the modern industrial output must be in the hands of local authorities. By the same reasoning, over a half of the heavy industrial output must be out of the hands of the central authorities.

As expected, heavy industry grew much faster than light industry; this was as true in the first two years of the Great Leap Forward as it was in the preceding five years. It is interesting to find that in both periods heavy industry developed faster than modern industry while light industry fell behind the handicrafts.

According to Wu *et al.* modern industry reached the height of its relative importance in 1960 when it accounted for 88 per cent. of the industrial value product, leaving only 12 per cent. for handicrafts; but the proportion between them changed to 69 per cent. for modern industry and 31 per cent. for handicrafts in 1962.

CHANGES IN THE STRUCTURE OF THE ECONOMY

The rapid growth of industry may be viewed in terms of the change in its relative position in the whole economy. Table 5 summarises two different estimates of the changes in national income and its composition from 1952 to 1962. It should be recalled that Wu and his associates relied heavily in their estimates up to 1957, if not up to 1959, on Liu-Yeh's work. The similarity between the two estimates for 1957 is striking.

According to Liu and Yeh, in the space of three years from 1957 to 1959 modern industry increased substantially its contribution to the net domestic product from 21 per cent. to 25 per cent., while handicrafts' share declined slightly from 6 per cent. to 5 per cent. But as a result of the economic crisis that induced a series of policy shifts since the end of 1960, the share of modern industry dropped drastically and that of handicrafts increased in 1961 and 1962, as shown in the findings of Wu and his associates. Their findings also suggest that the sectoral structure of the economy at the end of 1962 had changed little from that at the end of 1952 (not shown in the table). This, of course, does not represent any basic change in structure, since the decline in the relative importance of modern industry was not due to any significant destruction of productive capacity, but rather to the temporary shutting down of many factories and mines.

Table 5

TWO ESTIMATES (IN 1952 PRICES) OF THE CHANGES IN ECONOMIC STRUCTURE, 1952–62

Item	Liu-Yeh estimate of Net Domestic Product			Wu *et al* estimate of Gross National Product		
	1952	1957	1959	1957	1959	1962
Aggregate in billion yuan	71·41	95·34	124·52	95·2	110·5	82·7
Composition:	In per cent					
1. Agriculture	47·9	39·0	33·9	39·2	32·2	47·1
2. Modern industry	11·5	20·7	25·0	20·3	29·5	14·5
3. Handicrafts	6·6	5·6	4·8	5·7	5·3	6·4
4. Construction	2·6	4·8	6·5			
5. Others	31·4	29·9	29·8	34·8	33·0	32·0
Total	100·0	100·0	100·0	100·0	100·0	100·0

FACTORS UNDERLYING THE CHANGES IN INDUSTRIAL DEVELOPMENT AND POLICY

Given the policies of the Great Leap Forward, what were the factors within industry that made possible the course of industrial development from 1958 through 1960? What accounted for the momentous change in policy at the end of 1960 from priority to the development of heavy industry to the overriding priority for agriculture?

The agricultural crisis, with growing intensity from 1959 through 1961, must be accorded the most prominent place among all the factors that had shaped the economy during the five-year period from 1958 through 1962. As far as industrial development is concerned, however, the crisis was an external factor. The subject has been commented on earlier in the discussion on general economic policies and need not be taken up here.[31]

The internal factors, however, have to be examined. They include the investment programme, the small-industry experiment, decentralisa-

[31] For more details, see Leslie T. C. Kuo's article below. I have commented on the subject in a chapter entitled " Communist China's Economy and its Impact on Afro-Asia," in Kurt London, ed., *New Nations in a Divided World* (New York: Praeger, 1964); a popular version appears as " What Happened to the Great Leap Forward," *Challenge* (New York University), XI, No. 10 (July 1963).

tion and planning, industrial management, and Soviet aid. Each of these subjects will be discussed in turn.

THE INVESTMENT PROGRAMME

The Great Leap Forward policies of 1958 would not have produced concrete results unless the productive capacity of industry had been expanded accordingly. The plants that were brought into operation for the first time in 1958 accounted heavily for the leap forward in production that year. During the period of the First Five-Year Plan, 537 above-norm industrial projects had been completed. But during that period the heaviest investment was made in the last two years, a time span that was generally required for the completion of one of these projects. Hence, in 1958 alone, 700 industrial projects came to completion and were immediately placed in the production front.

As early as September 1956, in his presentation of the proposals for the Second Five-Year Plan, Chou En-lai estimated that the industrial enterprises newly constructed or reconstructed during the period from 1953 to 1957 would contribute 15 per cent. to the gross industrial value product during the First Five-Year Plan period, and that those built or rebuilt during the period of the first two five-year plans (1953–62) would contribute 50 per cent. By the end of 1957, however, it turned out that the new plants and mines contributed about 30 per cent. to the gross value product of modern and co-operative factories.[32] The increase in new productive capacity in 1958 was given in a study which showed that if the value of industrial output of factories derived from the newly increased productive capacity during the year was 100 in 1954, it would be 103 in 1955, 184 in 1956, 179 in 1957, and 449 in 1958.[33] One may, therefore, surmise that new enterprises accounted for 26 per cent. of factory output in 1954, 25 per cent. in 1955, 34 per cent. in 1956, 30 per cent. in 1957, and 50 per cent. in 1958.

Officially it was claimed that there was an improvement of 8 per cent. in the over-all productivity of industrial labour in 1958. Some such improvement must have taken place because of the sudden large-scale increase in plant capacity. Nevertheless, the other major factor, in addition to the increase in plant capacity, responsible for the great leap in industrial output was doubtless the large expansion of the industrial labour force in 1958 and 1959. Shortage of labour was, in fact, felt from the start of the Great Leap. In July 1958, Li Hsien-nien, Minister of Finance, dwelt at length on the lack of labour for basic investment

[32] Lin I-fu, " Seek all effective Means to Develop fully the Productive Potential in Existing Industrial Enterprises," *Planned Economy*, No. 3, March 9, 1958.
[33] Fang Chung, " High Speed and the Wavy Course," *Chi-hua yü T'ung-chi (Planning and Statistics)*, No. 10, July 23, 1959.

projects, and stressed the urgency of "liberating" housewives from domestic chores for socialist construction.[34] The development of local and commune industries soon aggravated the labour-supply situation. The result was a heavy drain from the working force in agriculture. The problem was publicly admitted by Chou En-lai in August 1959 before the Standing Committee of National People's Congress.[35] According to an editorial in *Red Flag* in November 1960, much of the increase in the output of local industries at the *hsien* level and above since 1958 had been dependent entirely on a continuous increase in the size of the labour force, and not on any improvement in labour productivity.[36] It was late in 1960 that the communes were required to allocate, as much as possible (over 80 per cent. in most cases), of their manpower to participate in agricultural production—at the expense of all other activities, industry included.[37]

If heavy investment in 1956 and 1957 and substantial increases in the labour force accounted for the great expansion in industrial output from 1958 to 1960, the investment programme during these three years was a major factor bringing about the end of the Great Leap Forward. The 1956 proposal concerning the Second Five-Year Plan called for a doubling of state investment as compared with the first plan; this would mean raising the ratio of state investment from 36·5 per cent. of the state budget to about 40 per cent. During the Great Leap Forward, however, state investment jumped from 12·64 billion yuan (41 per cent. of state budget) in 1957 to 21·4 billion (51·5 per cent.) in 1958 and to 26·7 billion (49·2 per cent.) in 1959. When extra-budgetary investments were included, the total for 1958 and 1959 was 58·4 billion yuan, as compared to a total of 55 billion for the five years from 1953 to 1957. The planned investment for 1960, the latest data available, was 38·5 billion yuan, including 32·5 billion (46·4 per cent. of state budget) from the state and 6 billion from sources outside the budget.

These massive investments resulted in the production of large quantities of capital goods which could not be readily used in the economy for lack of complementary factors. This, of course, differs from the case of producing defective goods. But in both cases national income would be boosted, giving a picture of growth that is entirely illusory. William Hollister, in his article on capital formation below, puts forth the interesting thesis that the sharp increase in investment during the three years of the Great Leap Forward represented a case of "over-investment," defined as the situation where capital goods are

---

[34] *Finance*, No. 8, August 5, 1958.   [35] *People's Daily*, August 29, 1959.
[36] "Simultaneous Development of Industry and Agriculture is an Important Law in China's Socialist Economy," *Red Flag*, No. 22, November 16, 1960.
[37] "Explore the Labor-Supply Potential in the Communes," *People's Daily* editorial, September 27, 1960.

added to the economy more rapidly than can be absorbed into the existing system of production in heavy industry and agriculture.

Borrowing Lord Keynes' concept of a " sudden collapse in the marginal efficiency of capital " at the last stage of the boom in the trade cycle, Hollister postulates that even the Chinese planners, in the grip of the Great Leap psychology, would base, like the entrepreneurs in a market economy, their investment decisions on expectations of an increase in production of capital goods which would offset their growing abundance (and growing quantities of investment goods of poor quality or without a market) and rising real costs involved in diverting labour from other productive sectors to construction activities. These optimistic expectations did not materialise. Substantial parts of the investments from 1958 to 1960, especially those in small-scale heavy industry and in agriculture, were ineffectual, resulting in sheer waste of resources. This alone, according to Hollister, would have induced the Chinese planners to reduce heavily the investment programme in 1960. And when the effects of crop failures in 1959–60 and the Sino-Soviet dispute were added, the decline in the marginal efficiency of capital was very large—probably to the same level as in 1957 before the Great Leap. The policy of consolidation, introduced toward the end of 1960 was, therefore, inevitable. Indeed, according to another study, the rate of investment (the proportion of gross investment to gross national product) rose from 28·8 per cent. in 1958 and 35·9 per cent. in 1959 to 43·7 per cent. in 1960, only to drop sharply to 21·6 per cent. in 1961 and 21·3 per cent. in 1962, a level far below that of 1957 and only comparable to that of 1953.[38]

It will be observed that " over-investment " is not over-abundance of capital or investment funds, but misallocation of investment resources. For example, the small-enterprise experiment, especially in heavy industry, was a disaster. Moreover, there was a clear lack of balance within and between the sectors of the economy.[39] Nevertheless, agricultural crisis and the Soviet withdrawal of assistance aside, the collapse of marginal efficiency of capital in 1960 could have been avoided if there were sound or reasonable planning. In fact, as we have seen, during the Great Leap Forward years, economic planning was decentralised, national plans were based on completely erroneous reports from the field, and local plans ran wild with their extra-budgetary investment funds. The return to professionalism in planning and factory management since the beginning of 1961 was probably as inevitable as was the collapse of the investment programme in 1960.[40]

---

[38] Wu *et al.*, *ibid.* p. 340, Table 80.
[39] See the article by Hung and Wu below.
[40] For a discussion of return to professionalism, see a later section in this article and also Franz Schurmann's article below.

THE SMALL-INDUSTRY EXPERIMENT

Among the basic points of the General Line put forward by the Party in May 1958 were, first, " to develop industry and agriculture simultaneously while giving priority to heavy industry " and, second, " to develop, under centralised leadership and with over-all planning, proper division of labour and co-ordination, centrally controlled industries simultaneously with local industries, large enterprises simultaneously with medium-sized and small enterprises," and, as was added later, " foreign methods " of production simultaneously with indigenous methods. Both of these points were said to constitute the whole set of policies for balanced national economic development known as " walking on two legs," which is best explained as follows [41]:

> If there were only one leg, that is heavy industry, without the other leg, that is, agriculture and light industry, or if the other leg is too short, it will be impossible to develop national economy at top speed. For this reason, particular importance must still be attached to agricultural development during the Second Five-Year Plan period.

To implement this policy, all people and all *hsien* in the country were told to build up industries. This was the proper, correct road for China to take in her attempt to bring about a great leap forward in industrial development.[42] Decentralisation of control over finance and enterprises since the end of 1957 gave the local Party authorities the necessary means to carry out this new policy.

As a result, manufacturing plants of all sorts sprang up all over the countryside. Preponderantly, they were small handicraft workshops. A report of Kiangsu province in June 1958 revealed that the so-called new industries in the process of establishment in the province were instituted by the various following ways: (a) completely new investment and construction; (b) independent operation of individual workshops in an existing factory; (c) merging of a handicraft producer co-operative with a locally controlled state enterprise or state-private joint enterprise; (d) expansion of a handicraft producer co-operative or group; (e) transformation of certain service trades; and (f) merging of a handicraft producer co-operative with the by-employment group in an agricultural producer co-operative.[43] By the autumn of 1959, some 700,000 workshops were found in operation among the 26,578 communes.

Table 4 shows that the industrial output of the communes contributed 5·3 per cent. to the national industrial output in 1958 and 7·3 per cent. in 1959. The total share for local industries, of which the commune

[41] Hsueh Mu-ch'iao, Su Hsing and Lin Tse-li, *The Socialist Transformation of the National Economy of China* (Peking: FLP, 1960), p. 256.

[42] Liang Ying-yung, " Which is the Correct Road for China's Industrial Leap Forward," *Hsueh-hsi (Study)*, No. 8, April 18, 1958.

[43] Yen Chuan and Chiang Chieh, " Certain Views on Statistical Work for Newly Developed Industries," *T'ung-chi Yen-chiu (Statistical Research)*, No. 6, June 23, 1958.

workshops formed a part, however, did not show any important advance. This does not mean that the development of local industries was arrested, but rather that local industries were growing apace with centrally controlled industries. State investment funds were allocated to local as well as to centrally controlled industries. It has been reported that state investment in 1959 represented an increase of 16 per cent. over the preceding year in the case of local industries against an increase of 39 per cent. in the case of centrally controlled industries.

The best proof that this expansion of local industries had gone too far, involving great waste of manpower and materials, can be found in the disastrous so-called " backyard furnace " movement to produce iron and steel toward the end of 1958. This " small-industry " sector has since been reorganised and much reduced, with reasonable cost and profit as the acid test of continued operation. Moreover, as the economic crisis in the country deepened, the resilience of handicraft production became more and more appreciated by the planners. As recently as March 1962, the Party authorities made clear that in the handicraft sector private ownership would be allowed and expected to co-exist with state and co-operative ownership for a long period to come.[44] And for the first time the supply of major raw materials for handicraft production was incorporated into the state plan for 1962.[45] It has also been reported that about one-quarter of the volume of handicraft production, covering the output of a small number of important products, were now under the direct control of central authorities, leaving the other three-quarters in the control of local governments.[46]

Different interpretations may be given to this experiment of " walking on two legs." Peter Schran maintains in his article that the encouragement given to handicrafts in economic development might result from the realisation that handicraft as a traditional sector should generate a surplus to support industrialisation. Another interesting interpretation has been advanced by Shigeru Ishikawa of Hitotsubashi University (Tokyo). He regards China's effort in this area as a novel undertaking to decide to choose to allocate resources between establishments using different techniques (capital intensity) and of differing scales of production (size)—and, one may add, geographical dispersion—instead of only between different sectors or industries, as is generally the case.[47] To him

---

[44] " Carry out Correctly the Party's Policy and Develop Handicraft Production," *People's Daily*, March 2, 1963.

[45] Chi Lung, " Use the Raw Materials for Light Industry and Handicrafts Properly," *People's Daily*, February 21, 1962.

[46] Chen Hung-yung, " Planning and Flexibility in Handicraft Production," *Ta Kung Pao*, March 23, 1962.

[47] Shigeru Ishikawa, " Choice of Techniques in Mainland China," *The Developing Economics*, Preliminary Issue No. 2 (September–December 1962), pp. 23–56. This is a publication of the Institute of Asian Economic Affairs in Tokyo, Japan.

the failure of the Chinese experiment seemed to indicate that the most effective way to maximise the rate of economic growth is still the application of the large-scale production method.

DECENTRALISATION AND PLANNING

Decentralisation of control over industry, trade and taxation, initiated in the winter of 1957, enhanced immeasurably the authority of Party committees and secretaries at the local and enterprise levels. As shown in Table 4, the share of the locally controlled enterprises was promptly raised from 54 per cent. of the industrial value produce in 1957 to 73 per cent. in 1958, with the share of the centrally controlled enterprises declining correspondingly from 46 per cent. to 27 per cent. Decentralisation was one of the several strategic developments that made the Great Leap Forward possible.

The effect of decentralisation on planning was profound, not to mention the fact that planning itself was also decentralised. The subject is taken up by Audrey Donnithorne in her article, which is primarily concerned with the mechanism and mechanics of planning. Up to the drafting of the 1959 plan, the process of drafting annual plans was known as the "single track" system, which was, in essence, a scheme of centralised planning mainly for the benefit of the centrally controlled state enterprises—in virtually complete neglect of the interests of the locally controlled state enterprises and other local enterprises.[48] The "double track" system devolved upon the local authorities to draw up a co-ordinated plan for all the enterprises in their locale. As Donnithorne points out, the local plan, depending on the level of government, would have to tackle the problems of balancing needs between different enterprises, different economic sectors, and different areas, of defining targets and scopes of planning, and of maintaining proportionate development between different sectors. Plans were controlled and supervised by various government agencies and committees (many coming into existence in 1958 for the first time) and the People's Bank. The whole system was described as "centralised planning and decentralised control."

Under this system the planning unit was a geographical area—a *hsien*, a special administrative district, a city, a province or even an economic region; and every unit aspired to become as self-sufficient as possible and thus tended to ignore the needs of other units. The resulting disruption of the regular flow of supplies between areas or regions was extremely serious for a long while.[49] This kind of development of localism and "base-ism" was not unanticipated, but, according

---

[48] Liao Chi-li, "The Double Track System," *Planned Economy*, No. 8, August 1958.
[49] Wu Hsia, "Enhance the Nature of Organisation and Planning for Inter-Provincial Economic Co-operation," *Planning and Statistics*, No. 6, April 8, 1959.

to a member of the State Planning Commission, this tendency could be overcome by " strengthening the Party's leadership." [50]

But decentralisation could easily be carried, as it was, to a point where even any pretence of unity in national planning and national economic development was destroyed. This danger was real during the years of the Great Leap, when extra-budgetary funds became significant for the first time. They were derived chiefly from a part of the profits retained by different enterprises, major repair reserve funds, supplemental wage funds, and local surtaxes. Whereas the investment funds outside the state plan totalled 5·73 billion yuan from 1953 to 1957, they amounted to 5·26 billion in 1958, 5·00 billion in 1959 and 6·00 billion expected for 1960. And they were invested in new projects without prior central approval, and, worse still, in keen competition with the state's vital basic construction projects for bank credit, materials and manpower. Hence, a return to central control over fiscal and financial plans was ordered by the State Council as early as January 1960. Later it was realised that the financial control system, which dealt, among other things, with extra-budgetary funds, circulating capital and short-term loans of various enterprises, had to be more centralised than the system of fiscal control.[51]

Hence, the slogan of " the whole nation as one chess game," introduced as early as January 1959, has since been re-emphasised from time to time throughout the rest of the period under discussion.[52] The establishment of six regional " central bureaux " in the country to exercise control on behalf of the Party's Central Committee in January 1961 may well be regarded as a move towards centralising control once more. But co-operation between economic regions (mainly provinces) continued.[53]

INDUSTRIAL MANAGEMENT

It was pointed out above that at the beginning of the decentralisation move in late 1957 and early 1958 the tendency on the part of local governments and enterprises towards localism and base-ism was not unforeseen but the strengthening of Party control at these various primary levels was counted upon to overcome it successfully. Basic organisations of the Party have long been established in all industrial

---

[50] Liao Chi-li, *ibid.* " *Base-ism* " (" *Pen-wei chu-i* ") refers to the principle of putting the interests of one's own base (workshop, factory, production team, commune, department, *hsien*, or any other) ahead of and giving them priority over the interests of all others, the national or collective interests in particular.

[51] Ko Chih-ta and Wang Cho, " Several Problems of Relationship in Fiscal and Financial Work," *Ta Kung Pao*, November 17, 1961.

[52] See, *e.g.*, Yang Ch'un-hsu, " The Problem of Centralisation in Socialist Economic Control," *Ta Kung Pao*, April 11, 1962.

[53] See Franz Schurmann's article, especially the section on the rise of regional economies.

enterprises. Decentralisation provided the Party committees in enterprises with the opportunity to take over management by shoving the professionals aside—with disastrous results.

Back in 1950 when the Party had to rely on the industrial workers for uninterrupted operation of factories and mines and for fighting the enemies of the state, a system of democratic management was instituted whereby workers' representative conferences, establishd in all state enterprises, were consulted on all major issues. Trade union organisations, also set up in these enterprises, served as the permanent secretariat for these conferences.

This close relationship between management and workers gradually gave way to centralised control. Complaints about authoritarianism were often voiced by workers. In 1956 the Party's Central Committee decided to adopt, as the basic form of industrial management for the country, a system whereby the manager assumes full responsibility for carrying out all production and management functions under the leadership of the enterprise's Party committee, which would consider and decide on all major policies. This in effect upheld the authority of management. In the meantime the workers' representative conference was reorganised into what is known as the workers' representative general conference with standing representatives in between conferences. The conference was given the authority to receive and discuss reports from the management concerning the various plans of the enterprise (production, finance, technology, wages, etc.) and the disposal of its welfare funds, and to recommend to higher authorities the discipline or dismissal of personnel in the enterprise's leadership if necessary. The trade union organisation in the enterprise continued to be responsible for preparing (by way of agitation, for instance) for the conferences and for seeing to it that resolutions adopted were carried out by management.[54]

Its authority thus defined, management began to exert itself, with the acquiescence of the enterprise's Party committee. As a matter of administration, various rules and regulations were introduced, setting forth for each category of workers duties, work norms, pay scales, promotions, penalties, etc. In the course of time these rules and regulations tended to grow and became the centre of workers' grievances.[55] The relationship between worker and management grew more formal and distant. The workers' representative general conference was reduced to " a mere vehicle for management and the Party committee

---

[54] Teng Hsiao-p'ing, " Report on the Rectification Movement," *People's Daily*, October 19, 1957.

[55] According to a report published in the *People's Daily*, September 27, 1958, a diesel-engine factory in Shanghai had been operating with 133 sets of rules and regulations up to the early part of the year.

to make speeches." [56] The *raison d'être* of trade union organisations was seriously questioned.

The situation changed radically in 1958 when the decentralisation programme enhanced the authority of Party committees at the local and enterprise levels. Mass enthusiasm, whipped up by the Party cadres for the Great Leap, let off a severe attack on commandism and bureaucratism of management in general. As a result, three reforms of the management system were instituted in 1958. First, the various sets of rules and regulations were to be extensively revised to take into account " the interests of the masses." Second, workers were to be organised to participate in management at different levels of the enterprise, while management was required to join the workers in physical labour. Third, a system of " close co-ordination among management, workers, technical personnel and administrative staff under the leadership of the enterprise's Party committee " was inaugurated.[57] The secretary of the committee, for all intents and purposes, became the chief executive of the enterprise. The workers' representative general conference, together with the trade union organisation, was revitalised under his direction.

That was the development in 1958. But it was soon apparent that no one in management was willing to assume any responsibility—even on the production and administrative side. In fact, many of the managerial staff preferred to be sent down to work in the workshops than to be responsible for assigning tasks to various units or for fulfilling planned quotas.[58] Moreover, after the old rules and regulations were discarded, no new ones were adopted to take their place.[59] The administrative machinery in enterprises was fast breaking down. If production were to continue, it would have to rely on mass emulation drives which could only result in a one-sided emphasis on quantity of output, to the virtual exclusion of variety and quality which after all were difficult to measure. The situation on a nation-wide scale became so grave that Chou En-lai, in his report in April 1959 on the work of government, warned.[60]

> Every industrial enterprise must carry through the system of the manager's taking up full responsibility under the Party committee's leadership and must abide by the indispensable system of reasonable rules and regulations. It is intolerable to find in production and basic

[56] Li Ch'un, " Why is it Necessary to Broaden Management of Various Enterprises?" *Chung-kuo Kung-jen* (*Chinese Worker*), No. 6, March 27, 1957.

[57] Liu Shao-ch'i, " The Triumph of Marxism-Leninism in China," *People's Daily*, October 1, 1959.

[58] Li Pao-k'un, " Problems of Plan Management in Hangchow Machine-Making Factory," *Tsai-cheng Yen-chiu* (*Financial Research*), No. 8, November 15, 1958.

[59] Hsu Hsin-hsueh, " Strengthen further the System of Responsibility in Industrial Enterprises," *Red Flag*, No. 20, October 16, 1961.

[60] *People's Daily*, April 19, 1959.

construction that no one takes up any responsibility and that all necessary rules and regulations are being violated.

After this statement, great effort was made to restore the integrity of
the administration system in enterprises. What was to be restored was
clearly stated by the Party secretary of the Municipality of Shanghai.
After stressing that mass movements (like the Great Leap Forward)
were not feasible without the Party's centralised leadership, he went on
to point out three " questions of principle " in relation to industrial
management. First, the system of the manager taking full responsibility
entailed not only his being responsible for the enterprise's administration,
but also proper division of labour between the Party committee and
enterprise administration, and full development of the role of trade
union organisations and Communist Youth League in the enterprise.
Second, the system of rules and regulations was absolutely necessary,
but they should be revised to meet new developments in production.
Third, workers should be given explanations of administrative methods
and be urged to make recommendations in regard to certain administrative problems.[61]

The struggle between management and the Party committee for
authority was not easily resolved. The collapse of the Great Leap
Forward toward the end of 1960 had a great deal to do with the
re-emergence and recognition of the manager as " head of the enterprise." [62] The development since then is well analysed in Franz
Schurmann's article. According to him, it was the severance of Party
control over the financial system which contributed one of the most
serious blows to Party power during the 1961 reforms. Intellectuals
(that is, educated professionals who are graduates from higher middle
school on up)—accountants included—were given proper roles to play;
and they appeared to be firmly committed to professionalism, expertise
and technical knowledge. The Party committee was driven to confine
its major interests to ideological work. Schurmann further observed
that the tasks of management also changed. The goal had been shifted
from production to " accumulation " (in the sense of economy—with
profit, cost, and labour productivity as the major targets. This was made
possible by the régime's relaxation of control over open market activities
and by the growing practice of direct contracting among enterprises
themselves.

Like the authority of enterprise managements, incentive policy for
industrial workers as well as for members of agricultural producers'
co-operatives and the communes was also subject to sharp changes

[61] Tsao T'i-chiu, " Mass Movement and Centralised Leadership in Industry," *People's Daily*, October 24, 1959.
[62] Hsu Hsin-hsueh, *ibid*.

during the period under discussion. This has been documented in Charles Hoffman's article below. The major wage reform in 1956 laid emphasis on material incentives; at that time the piece-rate system had already been applied to between 30 to 40 per cent. of industrial workers in the country. The changes in the " system of wages and welfare " during the Great Leap Forward were well summarised by the chairman of the State Planning Commission as follows: (a) co-ordination of political and ideological education with material incentive with the former playing the predominating role; (b) co-ordination of collective welfare with individual money income, with the former to grow in proportion over time; and (c) adoption of the time-wage rate as the general practice, with piece rates and bonuses as auxiliary methods.[63] This policy of extreme emphasis on non-material incentives was abandoned only in late 1960 when the Great Leap Forward movement came to an end. Since then, the renewed importance of piece-rate systems, renewed emphasis on distribution according to labour, and the playing down of non-material incentives have become widespread.

It may be noted that shifts between material and non-material incentives probably have to coincide with shifts in authority between enterprise managements and Party committees, since only the latter are able to organise, conduct and lead mass movements that make non-material incentives effective. The piece rate is as much a material incentive for industrial workers to increase production as the profit target is for management to increase output, expand sales, improve product quality, multiply variety, and reduce costs.

Thus, in industrial management the turn of events since the end of 1960 has been in favour of the professionals at the expense of the Party committees in enterprises. The impact on the operation of the whole economy has been far-reaching. Hence, the rise of what Schurmann has called the Great Debate, which began late in 1961, and in which one school favoured a return to greater state direction and control of the economy and the other favoured greater autonomy for individual economic units. That such a debate was sanctioned and encouraged by the régime must have been largely due to the fact that its self-confidence had been badly shattered by the collapse of the Great Leap Forward and the deepening of the agricultural crisis. Economic recovery since the autumn of 1962 has rapidly restored its self-confidence. The issues of the debate have not yet been resolved, and discussion is still going on, although much subdued in tone.

[63] Li Fu-ch'un, " Report on the Draft Economic Plan for 1960," *People's Daily*, March 31, 1960.

Soviet Aid

Soviet aid to China has taken many forms. According to official announcements, only two development loans have ever been granted by the Soviet Union to China since 1949; namely, the $300 million in 1950, equivalent to 270·2 million roubles (to be repaid in ten equal annual instalments from the end of 1954 to the end of 1963), and the 117·1 million rouble loan in 1954 (terms unknown). Other long-term debts incurred by China that have been made public include the Soviet shares in four Sino-Soviet joint stock companies and the Soviet military supplies at the Port of Dairen, both of which were transferred to China in 1955; mention should also be made of the Soviet diversion to China in 1961 of 500,000 tons of Cuban sugar as an " interest-free loan " repayable in 1964–67. From various Chinese publications one also gains the impression that Peking's annual debt services have included payments for the supply of Soviet military weapons during the Korean war and probably also thereafter.

The first development loan was used up by 1953, and the second, by 1956—all against Soviet deliveries of industrial equipment and technical assistance. Since 1957 the Soviet supply of capital goods had been largely dependent on China's export availabilities.

Another form of Soviet assistance is the assurance of Soviet supply of complete sets of equipment and technical aid for a number of large industrial projects. From 1950 to 1957, a total of 211 projects had been agreed upon at a cost of 1,824·3 million roubles[64]; the number of projects was subsequently consolidated to 166. This, when added to 47 more projects agreed on in August 1958 (value unknown) and another 78 in February 1959 (at a cost of 1,126·1 million roubles), gives a grand total of 291 Soviet-aid projects since 1950, not including 59 separate workshops and important installations to which Soviet assistance has also been given.[65]

These projects constitute the backbone of China's industrialisation programme. The entire industrial investment plan was built around them during the period of the First Five-Year Plan, and their completion would make a tremendous contribution to the productive potential of the economy.[66] From 1950 through 1957, only 68 had been completed.[67] In 1958 alone, 45 were completed, and their operation accounted

---

[64] I. Andreyev, " Friendship and Co-operation between China and the USSR," *Vneshiaia Torgovlia (Foreign Trade)*, No. 2, February 1959.

[65] " Soviet Technical Assistance to Foreign Countries," *Foreign Trade*, No. 6, June 1961. Aid has also been extended to China in the form of 60 industrial projects by East Germany (41 projects), Czechoslovakia, Poland, Hungary, Rumania and Bulgaria.

[66] Li, Choh-Ming, *Economic Development of Communist China*, pp. 10–12.

[67] In addition, 33 of the projects aided by the six Eastern European countries had been completed.

significantly for the great leap forward in modern industrial output.[68] At the end of 1960, 41 more projects had been constructed, making a total of 154 projects (and 24 workshops) completed since 1950, with 137 to be finished at the latest by 1967. On July 14, 1963, a Soviet statement published in *Pravda* indicated that 198 industrial enterprises, shops and other projects equipped with up-to-date machinery had been built in China with active Soviet assistance, and that " the Soviet Union continues rendering technical assistance to the Chinese People's Republic in constructing 88 industrial enterprises and projects." [69] Apparently, therefore, 44 more projects were completed in 1961 and 1962 (if not up to the middle of 1963), and the total number of projects had again been consolidated from 298 to 286.

It is important to note the difference in the nature of Soviet aid between the projects built during the period from 1950 to 1957 and those built ever since. In the earlier period all the projects were dependent on the Soviet Union for supply of complete sets of equipment and on Soviet specialists for surveying, designing, installation and first-stage operation. In the latter period, except for a few ultra-modern projects for which Soviet aid had to be as thoroughgoing as before, the Chinese undertook the surveying and designing by themselves, relying on the Soviet Union for principal equipment instead of complete sets and for the supply of the most up-to-date design and product blueprints and other technical materials. The Soviet Union still had to send specialists to help in installation and first-stage operation.[70] It has been reported under these and other arrangements (concluded in October 1954 and January 1958) of Sino-Soviet technical co-operation that the Soviet Union supplied more scientific and technical information in 1958 and 1959 than during the previous five years. In 1960, more than 60 per cent. of all machines and equipment produced in China were based on Soviet blueprints.

Between 1949 and 1958, a total of 10,800 Soviet specialists were in China at one time or another to assist China in economic construction.[71] In the same period the Soviet Union had accepted 14,000 Chinese

[68] See *supra*, 23–24.

[69] The *Tass* English translation, published in *The New York Times*, Western Edition, July 16, 1963.

[70] Sun Hsiang-ch'ing, " Brilliant Achievements and Selfless Assistance," *Economic Research*, No. 11, November 17, 1959.

[71] About 1,500 specialists had also come from the six Eastern European countries. The services of Soviet specialists were probably paid for with regular Chinese exports to the Soviet Union. In his *Ocherki ekonomicheskikh otnoshenii SSSR s Kitaem* (*Essays in Economic Relations of the USSR with China*) (Moscow: Foreign Trade Publishing House, 1957), M. I. Sladkovskii remarked, " China was paying with her commodity exports to the Soviet Union not only for the Soviet exports to China, but also for Soviet technical assistance (survey works, projecting, installation of equipment). This kind of expenses was rapidly increasing, particularly since 1954 " (p. 333).

students in Soviet schools and universities, and 38,063 Chinese as apprentices in Soviet factories and plants. At the beginning of 1960, as reported by the Soviet trade journal (February 1960), there were 7,500 Soviet specialists working in China and 6,500 Chinese receiving training in the Soviet Union.

The withdrawal of the Soviet experts in the summer of 1960, who reportedly took with them the industrial blueprints and technical specifications, must have been an important factor in bringing the Great Leap Forward in industrial development to a close at the end of the year. Much speculation has been given to the nature of the agreements and contracts that according to Peking were torn up by the Soviet Government. Clarification has now been given by an editorial in the *People's Daily* on December 4, 1963:

> In July 1960, the Soviet authorities . . . suddenly and unilaterally decided on a complete withdrawal of the 1,390 experts who were in China to help in our work, they tore up 343 contracts for experts and the supplements to these contracts and abolished 257 items for scientific and technical co-operation and since then, they have reduced in large numbers the supplies of complete sets of equipment and key sections of various other equipment. This has caused our construction to suffer huge losses, thereby upsetting our original plan for the development of our national economy and greatly aggravating our difficulties.

On another occasion the withdrawal of Soviet aid was described as having " inflicted incalculable difficulties and losses on China's economy, national defence, and scientific research." [72]

The Sino-Soviet dispute has produced another noteworthy development in the economic relations between the two countries. On April 7, 1961, Moscow announced that due to natural calamities that occurred in China in 1960 the Chinese were unable to fulfil their export quota to the Soviet Union in foodstuffs, thereby creating a deficit of 288 million roubles—presumably in their international account with the Soviet Union for 1960.[73] This deficit, continued the announcement, was to be repaid by Chinese exports, apparently without interest charges, in four instalments beginning 1962, namely, 8 million in 1962, 50 million in 1963, and 115 million each in 1964 and 1965. Since at the time Peking had already embarked on a large-scale purchase programme of food on the international market, the arrangement implied that Moscow had no intention of assisting Peking in facilitating the latter's handling of the severe economic crisis at home. Later, when Sino-Soviet trade in 1961

---

[72] Fan Chung, " All-Round Improvement in China's Economy," *Peking Review*, No. 34, August 23, 1963.

[73] Presumably a deficit in China's international balance of payments with the Soviet Union since there was a trade surplus of 27·9 million roubles in China's favour for the year.

netted a surplus of 165·7 million roubles for China, Peking was allowed to repay " part of her debt " ahead of schedule.[74] In a communiqué issued at the close of the National People's Congress in December 1963, Peking announced that all its debts to the Soviet Union, interest included, would be repaid by 1965.

Table 6

COMMUNIST CHINA'S TRADE WITH THE SOVIET UNION, 1958–62

Item	1958	1959	1960	1961	1962
	(in million roubles)				
A. China's imports from USSR ..	571	860	735	331	210
Composition:	(in per cent.)				
1. Complete industrial plants	26	42	46	21	4
2. Other equipment	24	21	16	9	8
3. Petroleum and products ..	14	12	12	33	35
4. Ferrous metals	6	3	5	5	7
5. Others	30	22	21	32	46
Total	100	100	100	100	100
	(in million roubles)				
B. China's exports to USSR ..	792	991	763	496	465
Composition:	(In per cent.)				
1. Agricultural products ..	44	41	31	9	10
(a) Foodstuffs	26	19	15	3	7
(i) Animal origin (meat, fish)	10	5	3	1	a
(ii) Vegetable origin (rice, fruits	16	14	12	2	7
(b) Raw materials	18	22	16	6	3
2. Fabrics, clothing and footwear	25	36	44	58	62
3. Nonferrous metals	14	11	13	15	12
4. Others	17	12	12	18	16
Total	100	100	100	100	100
	(in million roubles)				
C. China's export balance ..	221	131	28	165	255

a Less than one-half of 1 per cent., amounting to 830,000 roubles.

Sino-Soviet trade is a complicated subject to study. The article by Chao and Mah on the rouble-yuan exchange rate below arrives at the conclusion that Peking's official foreign trade returns, while not available since 1958, present a distorted picture because the exchange rate used

[74] *Pravda*, April 20, 1963.

is not realistic. If more realistic rates are used, the total volume, regional distribution, and other aspects of the trade picture, would become very different. These same comments apply, if not with equal force, to Soviet trade returns. This is a point worth remembering in discussing the trade picture of any Communist economy.

Table 6 presents the salient changes in Sino-Soviet trade from 1958 through 1962 according to Soviet statistics.[75] The substantial export surplus in China's favour represented Peking's determined effort, especially since 1960, to maintain her export volume to the Soviet Union while reducing her imports from the Soviet Union to less than a quarter of the 1959 level in 1962. The most drastic change in China's imports is found in the sharp drop in both the volume and the relative importance of complete industrial plants and other machinery and equipment in 1961 and 1962; for the first time since 1950 petroleum products topped the import list during those two years. In China's exports the precipitous fall of agricultural products, especially since 1960, mirroring the gravity of the agricultural crisis at home, is as dramatic as the phenomenal rise in textile manufactures and clothing, which Peking in all likelihood would have found it difficult to sell at reasonable prices in comparable quantities in other world markets.

In his interesting study of the terms of trade between China and the Soviet Union, based on trade for the period from 1955 through 1959, F. H. Mah reaches the conclusion that Communist China could realise some economic gains by shifting from the Soviet Union to free and closer markets.[76] It would be interesting to find out whether the conclusion applies equally to the trade in 1960 and 1962 in view of the radical changes in trade composition.

CONCLUSIONS

What will be the economic and industrial policy during the period of the Third Five-Year Plan (1963–67)? No information has been made available concerning the outline of the plan, not even a proposal of major targets as was the case with the Second Five-Year Plan. According to a vice-chairman of the State Planning Commission, the "gravitational centre" of policy has been shifted from the development of the metallurgical and machine-making industries in the First Five-Year Plan period to the development of agriculture "at present and for a long time to come." [77]

[75] For a year-to-year discussion, see Oleg Hoeffding, *Sino-Soviet Economic Relations, 1958–1962* (Santa Monica, California: The RAND Corporation, August 1963).

[76] See his article below. The detailed exposition of his study is given in his *Communist China's Foreign Trade: Price Structure and Behavior 1955–1959* (Santa Monica: The RAND Corporation, October 1963).

[77] Yang Ying-chieh, " On the Problem of Comprehensive Balance in National Economic Planning," *Economic Research*, No. 73, November 17, 1962.

The programme for agricultural development has been included under the catchword of "modernisation," to include mechanisation, electrification, chemical fertiliser, and irrigation.[78] Under this reorientation, the overall policy of taking agriculture as the foundation of the national economy with industry as the leading factor actually creates better conditions for the development of heavy industries, for the policy has been authoritatively interpreted as imposing two requirements on the programme of industrial development. First, the size of the labour force needed for industrial development must be basically proportioned to the amount of marketable grains and other means of subsistence that can be provided by agriculture.[79] This is one of the lessons drawn from the Great Leap Forward, since the drain of agricultural labour for industrial construction seriously hampered agricultural production. Second, the state investment plan will have to be readjusted to the new priority scale with agriculture at the top, heavy industry at the bottom, and light industry in the middle. The share of investment going into agriculture will be raised. But the biggest share will doubtless still be spent in the development of heavy industry, inasmuch as investments for effecting technological reform in agriculture have to be made in such fields as agricultural implements, irrigation equipment, chemical fertilisers, electric power, modern transportation facilities, and insecticides—all of which come under the scope of heavy industry. Moreover, to increase their output also requires investment in the coal, non-ferrous metals, iron and steel, and basic chemical industries. What distinguishes this type of investment programme from that in the First Five-Year Plan is that " in the earlier period heavy industry was developed for the sole purpose of serving heavy industry, while now it is developed for the sake of serving agriculture." [80]

This does not mean that no new heavy industries will be built for the sake of developing heavy industry. One of the vice-chairmen of the State Planning Commission has made clear that given the present overall economic policy the direction for the development of heavy industry should be " to make full use of the existing productive capacity, improve product quality, increase product variety and co-ordinate production of parts and equipment [among different plants] so that we will establish new industries not now in existence in the country." [81] Furthermore, another major factor determining the direction of industrial development is the requirements of national defence. From all indications, the priority

[78] See Leslie T. C. Kuo's article.
[79] Po I-po, *op. cit.*
[80] Yang Po, " On the Problem of Accumulation and Consumption," *Red Flag*, No. 21, November 1, 1962.
[81] Yang Ying-chieh, *op. cit.*

accorded to national defence must be on parity with agriculture, if not higher. Thus, the growth in heavy industry will not be hampered. This speculation seems to have been substantiated by the 1963 establishment of three more machine-building ministries in the central government in addition to the three already in existence since September 1960. It has been reported that capital construction was on a larger scale in 1963 than in 1962.[82]

The agricultural recovery beginning in late summer, 1962, had progressed to a point in April 1963 that the market supply of consumer goods was substantial enough to result in a gradual fall of commodity prices. On rural organisation the official line still is that the commune system will always remain " the basic social organisation both for the entire historical period of socialism and for the future period of communism." [83] But, of the 74,000 people's communes in the country today, some " are bigger with production brigades and production teams under them, while other smaller ones have only production teams." [84] That many communes have existed with only production teams under them is a significant piece of information, for it signifies that the organisational retreat from the original commune system has been much greater than expected.

The basic issues of the great debate, however, between a return to Party control over economic and industrial management and the maintenance of professional independence and open-market activities is still unresolved. Significantly, in planning mechanism a nation-wide machinery known as National Commodity-Price Commission was created in September 1963, with Hsueh Mu-ch'iao as chairman. As may be recalled, Hsueh was the founding director of the State Statistical Bureau, created in 1952, but was dismissed from the directorship at the height of the Great Leap Forward in 1959 for his staunch defence of the professional character of statistical and planning work. The establishment of the new machinery under his leadership seems to augur for a much more flexible state pricing policy than before, which would take into account the effects of prices in both the state trading channels and the uncontrolled rural markets on production and market supply.[85]

The cleavage between Peking and Moscow seems beyond rapprochement within the foreseeable future. Peking has disclosed that during the period of her severe economic difficulties China not only did not borrow

82 " Press Communiqué of National People's Congress," *op. cit.*
83 Liao Lu-yen, " Collectivisation of Agriculture in China [written for *Cuba Socialista* of Cuba]," *Peking Review*, No. 44, November 1, 1963.
84 *Ibid.*
85 See Hsueh Mu-ch'iao, " The Law of Value and Our Price Policy," *Red Flag*, Nos. 7–8, April 16, 1963. His underlying viewpoint was that because pricing policy is subjective and man-made while the law of value is objective, " unchangeable at man's will," the former would have to be adjusted to the latter.

a penny from foreign countries, but had in fact paid off on time most of the debts and the interest owed to the Soviet Union since 1950.[86] At present, trade and economic relations between the two countries are under increasing strain. The British Council for the Promotion of Foreign Trade reported in October 1963 that the Soviet Union had placed an embargo on exports to China of equipment that embodied advanced technique and of petroleum products.[87] Reference has been made earlier here to the fact that at the end of the National People's Congress in early December 1963 Peking declared its firm intention of repaying the whole of the small remaining portion of its debts, plus interest charges, to the Soviet Union by 1965 according to schedule. Thus, with little prospect for any long-term development loan from the Soviet Union, China has turned to the free world in earnest for trade development. The contracts placed by China for a vinylon plant in Japan and for a urea plant in the Netherlands represent the first orders for complete industrial plants by Peking from the non-Communist world since the establishment of the Chinese Communist régime. The wheat-purchase contracts with Canada and Australia have served as an effective introduction of Peking to non-Communist markets.

Peking was probably not entirely unprepared for the adverse effects of such a dispute with Moscow on Chinese economic development. It has been officially reported that the central authorities of the Chinese Communist Party " foresaw that if we criticised the errors of the leaders of the CPSU, they would certainly strike at us vindictively and thus inevitably cause serious damage to China's socialist construction." [88] Now the keynote is self-reliance, adopted as the theme of the National People's Congress that met from November 17 to December 3, 1963. In preparation for this new turn in policy, three mass movements had been initiated in the summer of 1963 to conduct a nationwide re-education on class struggle, a full-fledged deployment of cadres to the production front, and a concerted drive to persuade the intellectuals to go into scientific pursuits and experiments.[89] The first movement, in particular, regarded by the Congress in December 1963 as " of extreme importance," was unfolding " throughout the country on a large scale " at the end of the year.[90]

Effort has been intensified to produce more technical personnel, factory foremen, and managerial staff. For example, according to a report, throughout 1963 more than 10,000 people, chosen from various industrial

[86] Editorial, " Continue Striving . . .," *op. cit.*
[87] " Far Eastern Round-Up," *Far Eastern Economic Review*, XIII, No. 42, October 17, 1963.
[88] Editorial Departments of *People's Daily* and *Red Flag*, " The Origin and Development of the Differences Between the Leadership of the C.P.S.U. and Ourselves," *Peking Review*, No. 37, September 13, 1963, p. 20.
[89] *People's Daily* editorial, June 2, 1963; and *Red Flag* editorial, July 10, 1963.
[90] " Press Communiqué . . .," *op. cit.*; and editorial, " Continue Striving . . .," *op. cit.*

enterprises all over the country, were organised into study groups to visit Shanghai, China's oldest and biggest industrial centre, for the purpose of learning Shanghai experience " to improve production techniques and streamline management." [91]

What with all the internal and external difficulties of the régime, Communist China has not wavered in her determination to industrialise as rapidly as conditions permit. This article may appropriately be concluded with an official restatement of the goal for national economic development—after five years of economic trial [92] :

> The socialist industrialisation of our country entails building an independent, comprehensive and modern industrial system and putting the whole of our national economy, agriculture included, on to a modern technical basis in a comparatively short period of time. In other words, we must ensure that the raw and other materials and all kinds of machinery and equipment produced by our heavy industries are able to meet the needs of socialist expanded reproduction, the needs of the technical transformation of all sectors of the national economy, and of the modernisation of our national defence. We must also see to it that our light industries are able to produce various kinds of consumer goods to satisfy appropriately the requirements of the continuously rising standards of living of the people.

This is a great deal more balanced, more tempered goal than that put forth in 1953, which was to build up within about fifteen years a complete heavy-industrial complex in the country capable of producing virtually all machinery and equipment needed by industry and national defence. The restatement is more balanced, because heavy industry and national defence aside, agriculture, light industry and other sectors are all explicitly included and integrated into the goal. It is more tempered, because the goal is expected to be achieved, not in about fifteen years, but in a comparatively short period of time without specifying how long it is going to be.

Eleven years of planned development, including five years of economic trials, have driven home some valuable lessons. To build up and expand heavy industry for the sake of further expansion of heavy industry has proved to be an unsound development policy. And undue haste in development makes irreparable waste which the country cannot afford, and will only result in increasing the suffering of the people and delaying considerably the time schedule of development.

91 " Emulating Shanghai," *Peking Review*, No. 48, November 29, 1963.
92 Po I-po, *op. cit.*

China's "New Economic Policy"—Transition or Beginning

By FRANZ SCHURMANN

POVERTY, ISOLATION AND DEFIANCE

UNTIL a short time ago, it appeared that much of what was going on in China could be characterised by the cynical aphorism *plus ça change plus c'est la même chose*. Many things became manifest in the country that were reminiscent of themes centuries old. China had gone through two radical phases, one during the First Five-Year Plan period when the Chinese Communists tried to repeat the Soviet experience of industrialisation, and the second during the Great Leap Forward when they used their own mobilisational means to try to achieve economic breakthrough. The ninth Plenum in January 1961 called a dramatic halt to the extreme policies of the Great Leap Forward, and launched a period that bears strong similarities to the N.E.P. (New Economic Policy) period of the early 1920s in the Soviet Union. Many traditional patterns that were effaced during the years of radicalism began to reappear. There was talk of the need " to study very well traditional economic relationships." [1] It seemed that for a while the leadership had decided that only a truly voluntary response from below, and not coercion of any sort, could rescue China from the morass in which it found itself. But as of the time of the writing of this article, there are ominous signs that China may be approaching another " 1928." The Party drums are rolling once again, and the themes are not those of the N.E.P., but more like those which preceded the great Soviet collectivisation drive of 1928. During the last few years, the leadership made no attempt to hide the facts of China's poverty and isolation. But now a new note of defiance, of toughness has crept out. Where it will lead is hard to say.

There was never any reluctance on the part of China's leaders to admit the country's backwardness, but the attitude toward it has changed over the years. During the period of the First Five-Year Plan, the leaders were confident that they could give China a heavy industrial base equal to that of any modern nation, and in time carry through an economic revolution in agriculture. During the mid-1950s serious doubts began to set in, but there seemed to be a way out. Backwardness was the theme

[1] Kuan Ta-t'ung, " Our Country's Socialist, Unified Domestic Market," *Red Flag*, No. 6, 1963, p. 34.

underlying the Great Leap Forward, but also a supreme confidence that with organisation and energy China could overtake England in a short period of time, and within a few more years reach the level of the Soviet Union. Much of the earlier confidence has gone, and the theme of backwardness and hard work, and the admonition that it will take decades before China can escape its traditional curse of poverty, comes out again and again in the statements of its leaders. It is the theme of poverty, and the strength which comes from consciousness of poverty, rather than race or colour, which makes the Chinese sense a common cause with all the poor and oppressed nations of the world. Chinese often say that it is their lot in life to suffer. This is said, not in resignation, but as a spur to work, like the dual implication of suffering and work in the expression *ch'ih-k'u*. Mao Tse-tung once said that " we want to carry out construction on a very vast scale, but we are still a very poor country—this is a contradiction." [2] This sums up the attitude prevailing today in China.

Along with the theme of poverty, there is that of isolation. The bitterness against the Soviet Union runs very deep in China. There has been anger against the Party and its leaders over the fanaticism and failures of the Great Leap Forward, but even greater anger against the Soviet Union for abandoning China during the years of its greatest economic difficulties. China wanted equality among the fraternal socialist nations, but not in terms of Khrushchev's attitude of " prosperity for the Soviet Union—and good luck to the rest of the comrades." [3] While the remainder of the " third world " benefits from foreign economic aid from one side or another or both, China, the largest of the poor countries, must go it alone. One of the taunts most often levelled against India is that India is dependent on assistance from imperialist nations, as well as from the Soviet Union. Though it has never been reported officially, most informed Chinese are aware of the fact that wheat purchased from abroad had to be paid for in hard foreign exchange. [4]

---

[2] Quoted in an article entitled: " Since You Calculate the Big Account, You Also Have to Calculate the Small Account," *Workers' Daily*, April 13, 1963.

[3] Edward Crankshaw, " The Changing Mask of Marxism," *San Francisco Chronicle*, August 11, 1963.

[4] Note the statement in a recent issue of *Red Flag*:
Everybody knows that our country's socialist capital accumulation, just as Stalin has said, cannot be carried out through methods imperialism uses in robbing colonies, cannot be carried out through methods capitalism uses to carry out foreign aggression and extort reparations, nor can it be realised by methods of relying on enslaving foreign loans. Imperialism will not make us any loans. The running dogs of imperialism and foreign reactionaries will also not make us any loans. We also have no intention of accepting any kind of unequal conditions to obtain loans from imperialists, foreign reactionaries, or anyone else! *Red Flag*, No. 13–14, 1963, p. 11.

Poverty and isolation have gone together to breed defiance and not resignation. The Tenth Plenum in September 1962 came when a campaign had started to rebuild the morale of the Party and restore its image in the eyes of the people. In the late spring of 1963 the leadership launched another campaign to get cadres out of their offices and work alongside the people. Though industry too has been affected by orders to engineers and technicians to move onto the production floor,[5] the main target is agriculture. Cadres from the production brigade level on up to county administrative levels have been told to do physical labour alongside the peasants to assure a good summer harvest. Increase agricultural production and greatly accelerate the speed of socialist capital accumulation—these are the main policy themes of the spring and summer of 1963. The similarities to the kind of talk that went on in the Soviet Union in 1927 and 1928 are striking. Whereas just a short time earlier, the leadership had shown N.E.P.-like tolerance for administrators and technicians, the old anti-bureaucratic hatred has reappeared with vituperations against those who " love idleness and hate work, eat too much and own too much, fight for status, act like officials, put on bureaucratic airs, do not care about the sufferings of the people, do not care about the interests of the country."[6] What makes the present truculence even more ominous is its association with the idea of isolation, of the fatherland in danger. Sense of crisis, national isolation, poverty, the need to secure more savings from agriculture—all these were elements behind the Soviet collectivisation drive of the 1920s. Is it possible that the Chinese have already passed through their N.E.P. period, and are plunging into their own " 1928 "? This article deals with the period which began early in 1961 and lasted through 1962 and early 1963, and one which can roughly be described as a Chinese N.E.P. Whether the Chinese N.E.P. is simply a transition to another " 1928 " or the beginning of a really new and different period of economic development is something which only events will tell.

THE LINKAGE OF INDUSTRY AND AGRICULTURE

One traditional theme that has emerged is the over-riding stress on agriculture. Ever since the Ninth Plenum, the bulk of economic articles in the country's newspapers have been devoted to the subject of agriculture. In ancient China the primacy of agriculture and the derivative nature of commerce were expressed in the phrase: agriculture is the root and commerce the branch. The old saying has been altered to read: agriculture is the root and industry the guide, a phrase which is linguistically awkward, but leaves little doubt as to which of the two is primary.

5 See, for example, *Workers' Daily*, July 18, 1963.
6 *Red Flag*, No. 13–14, 1963, p. 11.

Actually, the shift toward agriculture in economic strategy took place in. 1957 when the plans for the Great Leap Forward were being drafted.

During the First Five-Year Plan period, agriculture was the ultimate source of savings with which the programme of industrialisation was financed. Savings in tangible form were not directly generated by agriculture, but rather through industrial enterprises which acquired raw materials from the agricultural sector at low prices and produced goods sold at high state-set prices, thus generating a sizeable profit for the state. In contrast to the Soviet Union, enterprise profits have formed the major source of savings in China, so much so that in the 1960 draft budget, 93·4 per cent. of total budgetary revenue was accounted for by profits and taxes from state enterprises (of which profits accounted for 64·7 per cent. of the total).[7] Within the state-owned sector, however, there was an implicit division of labour between the large modern enterprises and smaller regional industries. Whereas the former were allowed to be wasteful with capital and expected to concentrate mainly on output, the main role of the latter was to generate savings for the state. Since light industry in China is 80 per cent. dependent on agriculture for its raw materials, and has played such a major role in generating savings for the state,[8] it is not difficult to see that, in the absence of outright foreign aid, a leap forward in the modern industrial sector would require a concomitant expansion of light industry, which in turn was only possible if there was a sizeable increase in agricultural output. Furthermore, since imports of capital goods from the Soviet Union were to be financed with massive export of food products, agriculture was faced with a double burden: to produce more food and raw materials for urban consumers and industries, and more food and raw materials for export to the Soviet Union. If one looks at the economic statistics for 1957, one sees a uniform pattern: lower rate of industrial output (particularly of consumer goods), lower rate of state revenue (particularly of enterprise profits), and a decline in trade with the Soviet Union.[9]

The Great Leap Forward, with all that it involved, was conceived of as the answer to the problem. There was no change in the view that agriculture still was the basic source of savings for China's programme of industrialisation, but there was a new realisation that " industry and

[7] *Chukyo no zaisei* (*Chinese Communist Finances*), published by the China section of the Asian Bureau of the Japanese Foreign Office (Tokyo: 1961), p. 44.

[8] *Fei-ch'ing Yüeh-pao* (Taipei), May 20, 1962, p. 4. To my knowledge there are no statistical breakdowns for budgetary receipts from different branches of the state-owned industrial sector. Such a breakdown would indicate the extent to which light and regional industry have contributed to the national investment programme.

[9] Ta-chung Liu and Kung-chia Yeh, *The Economy of the Chinese Mainland: National Income and Economic Development, 1933–1959* (Santa Monica: Rand Corporation, 1963), Volume I, pp. 160–227; see also Robert F. Dernberger, " Communist China's Foreign Trade, Sources of Investment Funds and Rate of Growth " (unpublished paper), p. 21.

agriculture had to develop simultaneously." This meant in effect that the economic revolution had to take place throughout the economy.

The failure of the Great Leap Forward did not change the view that industry and agriculture were inextricably linked together. The key to China's further development is still seen as lying in agriculture. However, the failure of mobilisation to elicit greater output from the peasants forced the state to revert to different methods. Aside from organisational liberation, the state resolved to provide material incentives for the peasants. This meant not only greater freedom to tend their private plots, but higher prices for farm products, and assurances to the peasant that he could purchase industrial goods with the larger amount of cash in his pockets.

To meet this new source of demand, the government resolved on a far-reaching programme to re-orient industrial production more and more in the direction of satisfying consumer demand, both urban as well as rural. This was not an easy task to accomplish. With the sharp cutbacks in industrial investment carried out since 1961, major industries had fewer resources with which to meet state output targets. But at the same time, they were expected to broaden their assortment of products to meet the new demand for industrial goods coming from the rural areas. Heavy industry, which still remains capital favoured, has had a somewhat easier time than light industry. Many small plants, set up in haste and in defiance of economic rationality during the Great Leap Forward, were closed down altogether, or had to reduce their operations sharply. Those that remained, however, saw themselves faced with new burdens. Not only had they to fulfil plan targets, particularly profit targets, and meet rising consumer demand, but they had to do this under increasingly adverse conditions, foremost among which were shortages of materials and higher prices for agricultural raw materials. In fact, as during the Great Leap Forward, the smaller industries still had to carry the burden of accumulation, except that now Party organisation was no longer able to dictate and control the conditions under which production took place.

W. W. Rostow, in discussing the preconditions for industrialisation, stresses the role of agriculture as a supplier of food and materials, a market for industrial products, and as a source of savings for the modern sector.[10] Communist economic planners have regarded agriculture as a supplier of food and savings for the modern sector. However, as long as agriculture's task was essentially to bear the burden of the costs of industrialisation, it was idle to conceive of it as an expanding market for the products of the modern sector. Rostow argues that rising real

---

10 W. W. Rostow, *The Stages of Economic Growth* (Cambridge University Press, 1962), pp. 22–24.

incomes in agriculture, rooted in increased productivity, can act as an important stimulus to new modern industrial sectors. Essentially the same argument was made by Bukharin during the industrialisation debates in the Soviet Union during the 1920s. He argued that improving the peasant economy and increasing peasant demand for industrial products could stimulate industrial advance.[11] At a time when the Chinese are in a N.E.P. period of their own it is significant that Chinese theorists are now making the same argument.[12]

If one were simply looking at present reality and for the moment forgetting history and ideology, that seems to be what the Chinese Communists are doing at the moment. Although there are no statistics, official reports and refugee accounts all indicate an upward turn in peasant income, even to the extent of causing considerable worry in official circles. The question is, of course, whether this is only temporary expediency designed to muddle through present difficulties, or whether there has been a real change in economic strategy. Many feel, perhaps rightly, that a Communist system cannot change its spots, like the proverbial leopard. Maybe they are right, in view of the harsher tone that has come out of Peking in the last few months. But one can at least say that individuals in very high places in China have been giving serious thought to a basic approach to economic development that is neither a return to the Soviet model of centralised planning nor a return to the Great Leap Forward approach of guerrilla type mobilisation and production.

THE SHIFT FROM PRODUCTION TO ACCUMULATION GOALS

In 1956 and 1957, Chinese writers began seriously to question the production mania which governed industry, and suggested that the so-called " gross output value " target be scrapped in favour of other targets that would bring about greater efficiency in production. Already at that time it was suggested that profit be made the main success

---

11 Alexander Erlich, *The Soviet Industrialisation Debate*, 1924–28 (Cambridge: Harvard University Press, 1960), pp. 8–23.

12 In presenting the views current in their economic debate, the Chinese usually do it by listing pairs of juxtaposed opinions. Thus the more conservative position argues that low peasant purchasing power must be accepted as a necessary fact, with the state rectifying inequity through financial credit and price policies. What might be called the Bukharinite position argues that industrial support of agriculture must take the form of commodity exchange, which means that the size of peasant purchasing power is the main factor determining the saleability of industrial goods in the rural market. " Summary of the Main Problems Discussed by Shanghai Economists During the Year 1962," *Ching-chi Yen-chiu (Economic Research)*, No. 4, 1963, p. 64. Another significant similarity between arguments advanced now by the Chinese and earlier by Soviet N.E.P. economists is the acceptance of a priority sequence of agriculture-light industry-heavy industry. *Ibid.*, p. 63; Ehrlich, *op. cit.*, pp. 25–26.

indicator of enterprise operations.[13] During the entire period of the First Five-Year Plan, as is the case now, the current slogan had been: increase production and economise. However, as many Chinese writers have more or less openly acknowledged, these two aims are a bit contradictory, for the nation as a whole as for the individual factory manager. If one looks at economic statistics and political documents for the years of the First Five-Year Plan, it is clear that in years when waste was fought and cost-cutting emphasised, production rose at a slower rate. When production soared, as during the 1955 and early 1956 period, savings increased, but at a much slower rate.[14] In modern state-owned enterprises, managers did not worry much about costs, concentrating entirely on meeting their output figures, as has been the case with their Soviet colleagues. Managers of light industry were in a more precarious position. Having fewer investment resources to rely on than their colleagues in heavy industry, they had to struggle constantly to keep output up while at the same time keep costs down to the barest minimum in order to meet the financial targets of the plan.[15]

During the Great Leap Forward the leadership decided that it needed and desired both maximisation of output and of profits. However, in its formulation of the famous decentralisation decisions of November 1957, it demoted the " gross output value " target from its " commanding " position, and in effect substituted profit.[16] As is obvious, this by no means implied a slackening of the state's interest in maximising output, but it removed something which often was as much a restrictive

---

[13] Sun Yeh-fang, " Speaking of ' Gross Output Value '," *T'ung-chi Kung-tso* (*Statistical Work*), No. 13, 1957, p. 11; Yü I-ch'ien, " Can One Substitute ' Profit ' for ' Output Value '," *Statistical Work*, No. 5, 1957, p. 16.

[14] This can be seen in the following table:

Percentage increases of profits and output over preceding year

	1952	1953	1954	1955	1956	1957
State enterprise profits	0	34·0	29·0	12·4	19·0	5·9
Gross value product	0	32·0	17·0	4·7	38·2	6·9
Producers' goods	0	39·9	21·0	19·5	48·6	18·0
Consumers' goods	0	28·8	15·0	−3·0	31·5	−1·2

Based on T. C. Liu and K. C. Yeh, *op. cit.*, pp. 160–227.
During the years 1953–54, the leadership laid great stress on combating waste and keeping costs down, and so the figures for 1954 and 1955 show a higher savings than output rate. This is even more the case if we compare figures for state enterprise profits as a whole and figures for consumer goods output, in view of the fact that light industry provided a disproportionately high share of national savings. In 1955 the leadership launched its great production drive, and so the figures for 1956 show a reverse picture: output, even for consumer goods, climbs at a faster rate than profits.

[15] On tendencies to beat the output plan without regard to costs in capital-favoured modern industries, see Sun Yeh-fang, *op. cit.*, pp. 8–9. Sun admits quite openly that " light industry must bear the burden of accumulation whereas heavy industry does not " (p. 12).

[16] See *People's Handbook 1958*, pp. 461–462; see also Ishikawa Shigeru, *The Structure of Capital Accumulation in China* (Tokyo: 1960), pp. 72–73.

as a stimulative factor guiding managerial decisions. In the spirit of decentralisation, factory managers (which at that time meant Party secretaries) were given broad discretion to set their own commodity mixes, responding to the changing kaleidoscope of national and local needs. There was no doubt in the mind of the government that all the conditions were present for a production craze, for the Party apparatus, which was now in solid control of the factories, always favoured output over money. Production had a Socialist ring to it, while money seemed to be a capitalist remnant which, in any case, would disappear with the imminent advent of Communism. Profit targets would be assured by maximisation and acceleration of turnover.

The more one looks at the details of the failure of the Great Leap Forward, the more it has the appearance of a depression, such as in the capitalist world: overproduction, underconsumption, drying up of savings, unemployment, decline in business morale, disruption of the market, etc. It is clear from the whole literature of the past few years that, aside from insufficiency in agricultural production, the leadership regards the savings picture as the most serious problem it faces. There has been a continuing emphasis on the need for economy, to meet financial targets, for a correct price policy, for a thorough-going reform of the banking system, for financial authority and responsibility in enterprises and in the country as a whole. The counterpart of the drastic cutback in industrial investment was a campaign launched to create new sources of investment funds. The discussion on how to do this has ranged over the whole framework of the economy. There has been discussion on how to set prices in order to satisfy interests on all sides, how to make commodity turnover more efficient, how to accelerate the circulation of capital, how to increase labour productivity, how to save on this and that. But in all this, one thing has become clear. The main targets that are given by the state to enterprises to meet are not output targets but profit targets. There have been Chinese Libermans arguing for the acceptance of profit as the one main goal for state enterprises to meet.

Early in 1962, some orthodox economists were still arguing for comprehensive fulfilment of plan targets, including both physical and value targets, but by the summer of 1962 the leadership had apparently come around to the view that the main targets had to be financial: costs and profits.[17] The acceptance of the cost and profit targets as primary has

17 On July 19, 1962, the *People's Daily* published a theoretical article by two economists who are generally identified with the less liberal wing of the economic debate in which the following statement occurs:
    We feel that cost targets and profit targets are the main indicators for evaluating the economic effectiveness of an enterprise.
However, it is hardly necessary to cite a theoretical article to show that the

not meant a complete conversion of the leadership to the profit principle. More conservative voices still argue that the main concern of a factory manager should be cutting of intra-enterprise costs with the implication that factory managers should continue to be restricted in their scope for selection and preference. Nevertheless, whatever the real situation—and all signs indicate that it fluctuates—the leadership has inaugurated a sharp change through its clear de-emphasis of output targets. This does not mean that production is being discouraged, although there was a real decline in production during the years of severe crisis, but rather that the leadership attaches paramount importance to accumulation, with which to finance its future programmes of expansion.

THE RISE OF REGIONAL ECONOMICS

When the Chinese Communists first came to power, they had to admit what was obvious fact: the country did not constitute an economic entity. For five years, the country was administered as seven large regions. By 1954, the political difficulties obstructing complete unification (notably in Manchuria) had been overcome, and China, for the first time in decades, became truly unified. Political unification was an indispensable prerequisite for carrying out the First Five-Year Plan, which envisaged a steadily expanding modern sector cutting across regional lines and directly administered by the central authorities. The far-reaching decentralisation put through in November 1957 was a tacit recognition of the fact that the Chinese economy could not be directed as a single entity, that regional planning and co-operation would play a vital part in propelling the economy forward. This gave rise to the ideas of " economic co-operation zones " discussed in the literature during 1958.[18]

Regional economic co-operation meant that industries should rely mainly on materials deriving from the given administrative region rather than on materials that had to be transported from some distant source. If the needed materials were not available, they were to be developed or substitutes found. Under the earlier régime of centralised administration, regional economic co-operation would have encountered great administrative difficulties, but with new power and authority vested in the provincial authorities, intra-region allocation of materials could be greatly

leadership has come around to accepting cost and profit targets as the main success indicators of enterprises. The press has been full of articles urging an all-out effort on the part of factory employees to meet cost and profit targets, with only secondary mention of output targets.

[18] Liu Tsai-hsing, " On Problems in Establishing Complete Industrial Systems in Economic Co-operation Zones," *Hsin Chien-she* (*New Construction*), No. 10, 1958, pp. 45–57; Wang Shou-li, " Consideration of the Principles in Outlining Economic Zones Within Provinces," *Economic Research*, No. 1, 1958, pp. 18–21.

simplified. What precisely an "economic co-operation zone" was supposed to be was a matter of dispute. Some of the articles revived the old idea of seven major regions. The decentralisation measures did not provide for any administrative mechanism between centre and provinces, and handed decision-making authority over to provincial governments, thus laying the groundwork for making the provinces the units of economic co-operation. The idea of a regional autarky reached its extreme and most absurd point with the formation of the communes. But by late 1958 it was amply clear to the planners that decentralisation had gone too far, and a swing of the pendulum backward was demanded. In the following year the planners called for a renewed emphasis on national co-operation in the programme metaphorically called: "all the country is a single chessboard." The 1959 attempt to counteract the adverse effects of excessive decentralisation did not work. When the leadership decided to reverse the policies of the Great Leap, it did not call for a massive effort at recentralisation, but changed the conditions which had been largely responsible for the mess: excessive Party control of the production apparatus.

Since January 1961 the leadership had made efforts to reorganise the whole system of economic administration. This has been particularly true of the financial and statistical systems. The banks, which had been under excessive local Party control, have once again acquired authority over financial transactions, as have financial officers in enterprises and state organs. Although one hears little about it, there must be considerable improvement in ministerial work at all levels. However, while there has been a definite recentralisation of financial functions, there is as yet no clear-cut evidence that production administration has been recentralised. Factory managers apparently still have a fairly wide range of discretion in determining concrete production policies at the enterprise levels, and are essentially only held to fulfilment of their financial targets and delivering to the state a particular line of products which the state has ordered from them. During the Great Leap Forward management at the factory level had a similar range of discretion, except that everything was run by the Party cadres, in close liaison with Party cadres who dominated the various levels of local government. It is apparent from a number of indicators that, while some recentralisation has gone on, in other areas the leadership has continued the decentralisation policies introduced in 1957.

One of the emphases that continues is that on regional co-operation. Enterprises have been told that they must try to purchase their materials and equipment within the given administrative area and wherever possible sell their products in the same area. To facilitate this type of local exchange, the government has even suggested that exchanges take place directly between sellers and buyers, bypassing the state-controlled commercial network. Despite the recent expansion of the use of advertising media to find more distant markets for inventories (and also to solicit orders for goods), enterprises have been urged to try to confine their economic relationships as much as possible within the given region, " not to go outside the area to seek objects for economic co-operation." [19] The fostering of direct exchange relationships between economic units means that the state, in regard to a very broad line of goods, has surrendered one important means of control over allocation, namely, the requirement that all factory products be turned over to the state purchase and procurement agencies. It is not uncommon to find references in the literature to " historical " or " traditional " economic relationships, which often is another way of stressing the importance of the regional as opposed to the national economy.

One of the persistent complaints against the idea of regional economies was that it would lead to inequities and gaps. The advanced regions would move ahead faster, while the backward regions would remain behind. The Great Leap Forward policy of the simultaneous development of the entire economy was, among other things, designed to overcome the inequities that had arisen during the First Five-Year Plan period as a result of the favoured treatment of the modern sector. However, the Ninth Plenum ended the levelling tendencies of the Great Leap Forward. The existence of inequity has not only been admitted, but actively encouraged. In fact, regional differences are now regarded as a spur to the less advanced regions to catch up with the more advanced. As in so many other cases, a policy once applied in one sector sooner or later becomes generalised for the system as a whole. Thus the recognition of inequity can be found in agriculture as well. Advanced production brigades are no longer penalised by levelling as they were during the Great Leap Forward. With the stress on material incentives, productive workers are once again regarded as models for their less productive brethren to follow—and are duly rewarded in material terms. As refugees will testify, the standard of living varies sharply from one area to another in China, it generally being highest in the cities, and among the cities highest in Shanghai—as it always has been. The effect of the present policy of encouraging regional co-operation must be to further widen the gap between the advanced and the backward areas. However, at a time when the leadership is deeply concerned with getting the economy moving again, it cannot afford to overlook the fact that the advanced regions add proportionately more new value to the country's economy than the poor regions.

[19] *People's Daily*, April 2, 1963.

INDEPENDENT MANAGERIAL AUTHORITY

One of the complaints that was already made in 1956 against the Soviet system of centralised planning and control was that it left too little room for flexibility at lower echelons of the system. The factory manager was hamstrung by a web of bureaucratic controls which often left him with little choice other than trying to beat the output plan, with all the obvious consequences of waste, inefficiency, and poor product quality. The decentralisation measures of 1957 were designed to change this situation, and give managers much more flexibility in making economic decisions. The principle was fine, but the question was: who actually made the decisions at the enterprise level? During the three years of the Great Leap Forward there was little doubt that it was the Party committee. Given official encouragement to leap forward in production, factory Party cadres started on a production craze that turned out to be one of the causes of the economic crisis of 1960–61. The decisions of the Ninth Plenum changed that, and as became apparent from subsequent publications, authority returned to the hands of the administrators. One might think that Party and management had fairly well coalesced by this time, but judging from repeated attacks levelled against management cadres during the Great Leap Forward, it appears that this was not the case. But in returning authority to administrators and technicians, the leadership could not afford to go back to the practices of bureaucratic centralisation that had prevailed during the First Five-Year period. What this meant was that factory managers for the first time were in a position to exercise the flexibility which the 1957 decisions had granted them.

In both the Soviet and Chinese literature on the subject of " economic accounting," it was always pointed out that enterprise management had the right to make autonomous use of the capital furnished it by the state, as long as the requirements of the plan were fulfilled. In Russia as the forces of centralism grew stronger during the 1930s, such autonomy became increasingly meaningless, as more and more real decisions were made by the *glavks*, the local arms of the state ministries. However, since 1961, the Chinese have once again stressed the aspects of " independent managerial authority " that are inherent in the concept of " economic accounting," and have made it clear that it is up to the enterprise manager to make the correct economic decisions with the capital furnished him and the tasks which the state assigns him.[20]

What are the tasks enterprise management must fulfil today? It is probably impossible to generalise inasmuch as the situation differs from

20 Chin Li, " Discussions in the Very Recent Period by Our Country's Economists on Problems of Socialist Economic Accounting," *Ching-chi Yen-chiu* (*Economic Research*), No. 11, 1962, pp. 66–67.

industry to industry. Yet, judging from consistent lines of discussion in the official literature, it seems that his main tasks are to meet the financial targets given him by the authorities. He must periodically remit to the state the profit targets set. He is enjoined to repay on time and with interest loans that he has received from the state banks. Furthermore, inasmuch as all investment quotas are now furnished in the form of bank loans, he must be able to generate sufficient profit to pay back on time what he has " borrowed." Furthermore, given the present stress on material incentives, he must also generate enough of an above-target profit from which his premium and reward funds derive. In addition to the profit targets, he must satisfy the state in regard to cost-cutting and productivity targets. In the last few months, there has been considerable stress on these intra-enterprise targets, the implication being that the manager should not rely on a favourable price situation to generate his profits, but rather on " subjective efforts " to improve the performance of the firm. However, what goes on within the enterprise is much harder to check on than the size of the profit remittance. He is also obligated to furnish the state a set volume of goods which the state has ordered from him, and which he must deliver on time. But inasmuch as the state no longer sets a high " gross output " target, there is a considerable gap between the large volume he must produce in order to get a satisfying profit, and the smaller volume of output which the state has ordered from him.

For the rest, he is allowed a considerable range of discretion in determining what the enterprise shall produce. He is urged to accept orders from other factories, retail agencies, and from communes and production brigades. Such ordering is nowadays widely solicited through the medium of advertising. Once an order is placed, it is put in the form of an " order agreement." Agreements or contracts, *ho-t'ung*, have played an important role in the workings of the economy in China ever since the early days of the Liberation in Manchuria.[21]

As in Russia, they were regarded as devices for overcoming defects in the planning system, by allowing firms to conclude agreements with each other, and then working the agreements into the over-all planning system. Whereas in Russia, the contract system was taken over by the *glavks* in the form of what was called " general contracts " for a range of industries, in China the planning mechanism never worked well enough completely to replace relatively autonomous contracting by individual firms. Since 1961 the emphasis on " direct contracting " has grown. What this means in effect is that two economic units agree on the exchange of goods for such and such a price at such and such a date,

---

[21] See Kao Kang's speech to the first congress of the CCP Manchurian region, *People's Daily*, June 5, 1950.

much in the manner of capitalistic enterprises. All this, of course, is supposed to take place within the framework of the plan and according to prices set by the state. However, at this point it is hard to say what the state of planning is, how much in the way of real production, materials, and commodities the plan actually covers. And furthermore, given the continuing discussion of price policy, the least one can say is that there is considerable fluctuation in the price picture. There are even some indications that factory managers have some initiative in setting prices for their products.[22]

What this means is that the factory manager must hunt up customers, find out what they want, and then try to produce what he has agreed to produce for them. But isn't he hampered in determining his assortment by state control over supply and materials allocation? There are many indications that the state has surrendered allocational controls over many goods, more or less allowing them to change hands through the market.[23] It must be recalled that it was already in the decentralisation decisions of 1957 that the government surrendered many of its allocational powers to provincial governments. Since then there are indications that these powers have lessened even further, obviously not in

---

[22] This is, of course, a very delicate area inasmuch as all prices are supposedly subject to one or another form of state control. The following story, however, seems to indicate that factory managers, upon pressure from their customers, were able to lower their ex-factory prices:

> ... last year, the Tientsin Machine Casting Plant cast some sewing machine frames for the North China Sewing Machine Plant. Because casting costs were high the latter lost money on its sewing machines. Subsequently, the workers of the Tientsin Plant tried hard to raise quality and productivity, and cut down on the wastage rate. Three months later, costs for casting sewing machine frames were greatly cut, and they were able on their own to reduce the unit price. This way the North China Plant was able to save about 20,000 yuan each month, and solve the problem of losing money on its sewing machines.

People's Daily, April 2, 1963. One can only conjecture at what lies behind this story, but it is reasonable to reconstruct it as follows. The North China Sewing Machine Company refused to renew its contract with the Tientsin plant unless they could reduce their unit price. Since the authorities could not be persuaded to make the North China " take " the goods nor presumably lower their financial targets, the only way out was to cut costs. That this is the procedure is indicated by a remark in the same article that a Kweichow factory sent its representatives to Tientsin, found the price right, and concluded an ordering agreement. See also Yang Fang-hsun, " Consider Price on the Basis of Quality—the Better the Quality the Better the Price," *Ta Kung Pao*, July 16, 1962.

[23] It is hard to find any hard and fast statements on what types of goods are still subject to strict state allocational controls, and what types can be freely exchanged. Writers stress that the state maintains unified allocational controls over all " major " and " important " agricultural and industrial goods, but allows " a certain number of secondary goods to be freely produced and freely sold." Current policy on commodity exchange is described as a combination of " planned allocation " and " selective buying." See Kuan Ta-t'ung, " Our Country's Socialist Unified Domestic Market," *Red Flag*, No. 6, 1963, pp. 33, 35. However, already in 1957, Hsueh Mu-ch'iao admitted that of the thousands and tens of thousands of goods on the market only a few hundred were " plan (controlled) commodities "; " Some Preliminary Opinions on Carrying Out the System of Plan Administration," *Economic Research*, No. 9, 1957, p. 23.

regard to materials that are regarded as critical, but over a range of materials that are generally called " secondary." Once he has produced a line of goods, the manager often still faces the problem of disposal. I gather from refugees that contracts are frequently broken, leaving the manager with undisposed inventories. State purchase and procurement agencies no longer automatically take over inventories, which earlier meant simply transferring the burden of storage from the factory to the commercial warehouse. Again advertising is resorted to, as well as the traditional device of sending out " representatives," *ch'u-ch'ai*, as they are called in China (somewhat like the Russian *tolkachi*), to various places, to secure takers.

The scope of " independent managerial authority " for the factory manager is real only to the extent that the planning mechanism does not function well, and there is nothing to indicate that it does now, or ever has, in China. The financial side of things is apparently still rigorously controlled by the state banks through the system of " current accounts " (the equivalent of the Soviet *rasschëtnyi schët*), and neither money nor credit is supposed to move directly between economic units. But in regard to purchase-sales and production agreements, the manager appears to enjoy considerable autonomy. What, one may ask, is then the incentive for the manager to produce? Here the answer seems to be simple. He must meet the high and stringent financial targets which the state sets for him. He can argue with the authorities about prices, argue out contracts with other units, press for greater savings within his factory, but when the time comes he must pay over the set profit sum to the state. But there is also a material incentive element. Another aspect of the decentralisation policies of 1957 was the so-called profit sharing system. Earlier, all above-target profit was taken by the state, but a portion of it was returned to the enterprise to use for premiums. However, under the profit sharing system, the enterprise was allowed to retain a fixed percentage share of all above-target profit. Obviously, the more profit it could generate, the greater its absolute share. That this proved to be a great boon to the enterprises is already attested to by outcries from the planners as early as the end of 1958 that enterprises were wasting their new source of income on irrational construction projects and workers' welfare.[24] Though there has apparently been some reduction in the size of the enterprises' profit share, the system remains very much in effect. Ever since early 1961 enterprises were ordered to cut down employment, keeping only the best of their workers. There also has been a return to a system of individual material incentives. Thus the premium fund is of great importance to the manager in giving him a

[24] T'ao Sheng-yü, Tan Ya-sheng, " Revised Opinions on the Enterprise Profit Sharing System," *Ts'ai-chang (Finance)*, No. 15, 1959, pp. 13–14.

source of rewards for his workers, now fewer in number than before, but who can thus expect a more substantial " bonus," or *fen-hung* as it is called in Chinese.

Is There a Chinese N.E.P.?

When war Communism failed in Russia, the Soviets started their New Economic Policy which turned out to be a temporary return to market mechanisms in order to get the economy on its feet once again. When the Russians started criticising the Chinese communes, they said sarcastically that they had already tried something similar during the War Communism period. Perhaps they were right and the Chinese are repeating history by moving from War Communism to their own version of the N.E.P.

There are plenty of grounds on which one can argue from internal evidence that the Chinese are indeed in a N.E.P. period, but there are some scriptural references from the Chinese side that indicate that the Chinese see it that way themselves. The most frequently quoted saying of Lenin applicable to the economy today is a statement he made in 1922: " I think that trusts and enterprises have been put on a basis of economic accounting precisely so that they themselves be responsible, and furthermore completely responsible that their enterprises not incur losses." [25] Chinese know their Soviet history well and are not unaware of when Lenin made this statement and in what context.

The main question, from an economic point of view, is to what extent the open market functions in China today. Professor C. M. Li has indicated that an open market of one sort or another existed throughout the period of the First Five-Year Plan.[26] There are indications that the open market was broadened during the Great Leap Forward because of reduced state control over commodities. However, the power and arbitrariness of Party control interfered greatly with the free working of the market mechanism. Since 1961 the leadership has made a number of significant concessions to the open market. Open markets for agricultural products, the so-called *chi-shih*, started to develop, supported by growing amounts of garden crops brought by the peasants to market.

---

[25] One of the earliest references to this quotation from Lenin that I have come across is in an article entitled " All Enterprises Must Strengthen Economic Accounting." *People's Daily*, December 24, 1961. It is significant that it was just around that time that the economic debates started. It would appear, therefore, that it was around the end of 1961 that the Chinese began to see themselves as in a new N.E.P. period. The passage is from a short memorandum, dated February 1, 1922, which Lenin sent to the Commisariat of Finance urging severe judicial action against enterprises that constantly incur losses. Lenin adds: " if we can't assure our own interests in full in a business-like, merchant-like manner, then we are complete fools! "; Lenin, *Sochineniia*, XXXV (Moscow: 1951), p. 468.

[26] Choh-ming Li, *Economic Development of Communist China* (Berkeley: University of California Press, 1959), pp. 19–24.

Judging from the weakening of state control over a wide range of manufactured commodities and the present emphasis on producing consumer goods, it can be surmised that the open market for manufactured goods has been considerably broadened over preceding years. There is no doubt that the leaders are disturbed by the extent of open market phenomena. Hsueh Mu-ch'iao, recently published an article in Red Flag calling for more stringent measures to keep open market prices in line. However, what is significant is that Hsueh Mu-ch'iao admits that the open market exists alongside the planned market as a valid mechanism of exchange. Though he calls for greater price controls, he is against " simple administrative measures to freeze prices." [27]

The price picture is immensely complex in China today, among other reasons, because the state is using its price powers to spur on this or that area of the economy. For example, as one writer admits openly, if factories manage to improve the quality of their output, " they are rewarded price-wise." But is it always the authorities who have the final say on prices? The same writer implies indirectly that ex-factory price changes are often simply authorised in an *ex post facto* way by the state agencies. [28] I get the impression that the Chinese have come up with another of their famous contradictions, this time one between the planned market and the open market. The problem is how to find some kind of Hegelian resolution between the two.

It is quite clear that if the state does not move in with new controls, open market phenomena will continue to grow. Judging from refugee reports, the release of a range of " top class goods " to retail outlets unleashed a buying spree somewhat reminiscent of the one that followed the German currency reform in the summer of 1948. More consumer goods came on to market with the explicit approval of the state, thus strengthening open market tendencies. There is clear awareness of strong inflationary pressures, and much discussion has been published on ways to combat inflation. The state presumably could move on to the open market in two ways. It could either re-institute the whole planning system and try to do what it did during the First Five-Year Plan period, or it could accept the workings of market mechanisms, ranging from completely tolerated functioning of the open market to discreet tolerance of market mechanisms within the so-called planned market, and try to use its enormous administrative and financial powers to obtain leverage over the workings of the price system. I see no indication that the leadership has as yet opted for the first course, and at present seems to

[27] Hsueh Mu-ch'iao, " The Law of Value and Our Price Policy," *Red Flag*, No. 7–8, 1963, pp. 1–9.

[28] Yang Fang-hsün, " Consider Price on the Basis of Quality—the Better the Quality the Better the Price," *Ta Kung Pao*, July 16, 1962.

be trying to muddle through in the manner suggested by Hsueh Mu-ch'iao, *i.e.*, somewhere between the two extremes of using administrative power to fix prices and of completely allowing supply and demand to determine prices.

What the Chinese N.E.P. suggests is that internal conditions have been more similar to what exists in the country of their arch-enemy, Yugoslavia, than their anti-Yugoslav vituperations would let one think. In September 1962, when the Tenth Plenum was meeting, *Red Flag* published an article excoriating the Yugoslavs for their return to capitalism.[29] However, since then, the Chinese Communists have preferred to republish attacks on the Yugoslav economy originally published in some of the fraternal newspapers, e.g., Albania, North Korea, North Vietnam. The reason is quite obvious. There is already too much in the September article which must have set Chinese minds to wondering how different Yugoslav " capitalism " was in fact from some of the things going on in China. The Tenth Plenum was devoted to the problem of the Party. The rectification campaign waged against the Party during much of 1961 had gravely weakened Party control in some areas and had resulted in a lowering of Party morale, quite understandable considering the sudden comedown from the Great Leap Forward period. Since September 1962, there has been a gradual re-emphasis on the Party, on the collective economy, on the role of the Party in the life of the country. But the course launched in 1961 still appears to be the dominant line in the country. Despite the September 1962 communiqué, only a few months later the government issued new regulations on the position of accountants, which gave accountants far-reaching financial authority in enterprises and agencies. The accountants were the arch-enemies of the Party cadres during the Great Leap Forward, for the accountants, like most financial people everywhere, were appalled by the free-spending tendencies of the Party cadres. It was the severance of Party control over the financial system which constituted one of the most serious blows to Party power during the 1961 reforms. Given the continuing pervasive emphasis on accumulation goals, it was hardly likely that the leadership could once again be persuaded to open the doors of the nation's coffers to the Party cadres.

In early 1963 the N.E.P. policy was still in effect. A third five-year plan period has begun, yet little has been said about it beyond that it has begun. Economic conditions have been improving, so the sting of severe crisis has passed. The leadership, for the last few years, had been following Bukharin's famous slogan, " enrichissez-vous," and there has been a payoff in improved living conditions. But microeconomic getting

---

[29] Ch'en Mao-i, " Let Us Talk About the Worsening of Economic Conditions in Yugoslavia," *Red Flag*, No. 17, 1962, pp. 24–31.

rich does not make sense in the face of macroeconomic poverty, and the leadership may be contemplating a change. There have been recent rumours of a 10–20 per cent. wage cut in the cities, which may presage a new wave of austerity. The accent on accumulation is still strong but the N.E.P. approach may not provide dividends fast enough. If China is going to industrialise fast, as Russia did under Stalin, the peasant and the worker will have to bear the burden of sacrifice.

THE RE-EMERGENCE OF THE PROFESSIONAL INTELLECTUALS

As in the Soviet Union, intellectuals in China constitute a social stratum, not quite a class and not just an occupational group. If it is difficult to define precisely what an intellectual is in Marxian class categories, there seems to be little doubt in the minds of the Chinese, judging from the copious literature on the subject and refugee statements, that the intellectuals are the educated professionals of the country. The status of intellectual is acquired through education, graduation from higher middle school on up. In a country in which education continues to act as an important (perhaps the most important) criterion of status, being an intellectual more or less puts one in the ranks of the elite. Although the academic intellectuals are most prominent because of their verbal expressiveness, most of the country's intellectuals are found, not in the universities, but at the management level of organisations. They are the engineers, technicians, administrators, researchers, doctors and teachers of the country. In a factory, though they are to be found at the management level, they do not constitute all of management. Again as in the Soviet Union, lower level management employees, the so-called functionaries, are not accorded the status of intellectuals.[30] They are the true social élite of the country, and are jealous of any encroachments on their hard-earned status, as can be seen in their resistance to admitting skilled workers to the job category of technician, which normally requires a higher educational degree.[31]

The attitude of the Chinese Communists toward the country's intellectuals has fluctuated from time to time. Although the top leadership of the Chinese Communist Party can validly consider itself intellectual, the farther down one goes in Party ranks, the stronger the worker and peasant component. At the factory level, worker membership in the Party predominates, even though most of the top management

---

[30] The conception of what an intellectual is appears to be much the same in both the Soviet Union and Communist China. In the Soviet Union, too, ordinary white collar employees, the so-called *sluzhashchie*, are not considered intellectuals. See Alex Inkeles and Raymond Bauer, *The Soviet Citizen* (Cambridge: Harvard University Press, 1959), pp. 72–73.

[31] K'o Pai, " Preliminary Discussion of the Salary System of Leadership Personnel, Engineers and Technicians, and Functionaries in Industrial Enterprises," *Chung-kuo Kung-yeh* (*China's Industry*), No. 2, 1956, pp. 6–7.

cadres are at least formally within the Party. There can be little doubt, judging from the accounts of refugees who have worked in factories, that there are sharp cleavages between intellectuals and workers. The management-worker gap or the white-collar blue-collar antagonism is well known from just about every country that has gone through a process of industrialisation. It is even more serious during the early stages of industrialisation and perhaps more serious in countries outside the Western world, where cultural and social distance add to the gap. The gap was there in pre-1949 China and has remained to the present time. Whether one can meaningfully speak of a class conflict between intellectuals and workers in Chinese industry prior to 1949 is hard to say. But the constant preaching of the doctrines of class conflict by the Chinese Communists have served, in the end, not to eliminate the gap and assuage the conflict, but to intensify it. Upon Liberation, workers were told that they were now the masters of the factory. This was not empty talk, for large numbers of workers were promoted to leadership positions, some even to positions of factory manager. Top factory cadres, from the earliest days on, were often of worker origin. But it was impossible to proletarianise management, for the simple reason that workers lacked the skills and education necessary to run a factory. The leadership has made continuing efforts to bridge the gap between intellectuals and the workers, by drawing the intellectuals into the Party and mass organisations, by raising the educational level of workers, by trying to create a worker-peasant intelligentsia. But all indications are that this attempt has failed. A goodly number of the country's intellectuals are still of " bourgeois " origin, and the effort to forcibly " reduce the gap between mental and physical labour " has only intensified the antagonism.

During the early 1950s, the leadership was forced by circumstances to make fullest use of the professional intellectuals: managers, technicians, specialists. However, with the intensified production drive and Party recruitment campaign that arose in 1955, the pendulum swung against the intellectuals. But the swing was temporary, and with the " hundred flowers " period, a new period of tolerance set in, that lasted until the abrupt switch in the summer of 1957. By the summer of 1957 the juxtaposition of intellectuals and masses had assumed sharp form, more specifically in the form of conflicts between Party and management, workers and technicians, generalists and specialists. Though the anti-rightist campaign started with denunciations of academic intellectuals, it soon spread throughout the country. In the factories, it took the form of greater Party control over management, of the so-called " send them down " (*hsia-fang*) movement, through which thousands of intellectuals were sent down to the front line of production, of denunciations of managers for demonstrating "conservative tendencies" in the period of the Great Leap Forward, of levelling tendencies between workers and intellectuals with greater equality in pay, of managers and technicians being made to carry out physical labour along with workers, and with workers urged to participate in management (a slogan which was by no means empty, for many crucial economic decisions were "transferred downward" to the production teams). In general, it was a period when the leadership tried to create a single amalgam of cadres, intellectuals, and workers. Force, short of complete extirpation, has never succeeded in reducing status differences that are based on values universally accepted by a population. As long as higher education is still valued in the country (as it is), and as long as higher education remains a scarce commodity, the status of the intellectual is secure. The levelling attempts of the Great Leap Forward failed, and the gap between intellectuals and masses remains.

In the old days, the Chinese scholar-bureaucrat was an amateur, a man of many talents, solidly grounded in the orthodox ideology. Though he had to rely on specialists to conduct his bureaucratic affairs, he despised the status of professional.[32] One of the human reasons for the failure of government-directed early industrialisation in China was the inability for the long-gowned factory administrator to understand the need for expertise; for that, he felt, one could rely on foreign experts. I seem to remember that someone once suggested that one of the results of great social revolutions is that the new ruling class tends to take on the values of the class it has overthrown. There are grounds for arguing that China's present élite of Party cadres is suspiciously like its scholar-bureaucratic predecessors in many respects. The Party cadre is schooled in Marxism-Leninism, he is a man of many talents, rather than a professional (usually a reflection of the type of political education a Party cadre undergoes, with its short courses in economics, politics, theory, technology), and, as became amply evident during the Great Leap Forward, contemptuous of professional expertise. The typical local Party cadre is also a worker (or a peasant if in the villages). On the other hand, China's intellectuals today appear to be firmly committed to professionalism, to expertise, to technical knowledge. All intellectuals I have talked to are admiring of the advanced countries, Russia as well as the United States. They are firmly convinced that only expertise, not political direction, will modernise the country. Expertise is after all their one possession that the Party cannot take away from them, even if it sends them out into the fields to work. The more the Party has tried to convince them of the greatness of improvisation, of

[32] See Joseph R. Levenson, *Confucian China and Its Modern Fate* (Berkeley: University of California Press, 1958), pp. 15–43.

native over foreign methods, of politics over techniques, the more stubborn the resistance. I have found a strong nationalistic streak in the young intellectuals, but no obscurantism, no desire to return to the roots of the past, no love of populism. All these tendencies are what they accuse the Party of wanting to do.

When the Ninth Plenum decided on a radical reversal in economic policy and launched a campaign to pry the Party loose from its totalistic control of the economy, it had to take a further consequent step: once again seek the aid of the country's intellectuals. Factory managers reacquired power. Engineers were once again given control over the production process. Technicians were once again favoured, and their educational status assured. Technical education was once again stressed over political education.[33] Technical accountants were once again given far-reaching powers over an enterprise's finances.[34] Rationality, rather than the mass movement, became the dominant theme of industrial management. The mass movement, in fact, has disappeared as a mechanism of production organisation. Bureaucratic management has superseded worker participation in management. Factory administration has been recentralised, with major decisions once again being made at the executive level, rather than on the production floor. Money is stressed over production. Concern over money somehow seems to be a conservative attitude in almost any society, and much of the talk about economising could come from the mouths of good Republicans in the United States. Concern over money also implies an orientation to some kind of professional or technical élite (bankers, executives, etc.), and so it is not surprising that the present turn toward accumulation goals has gone hand in hand with a return of authority to the country's professional intellectuals. Even the remnant bourgeoisie has benefited from the new atmosphere through promise of continued " fixed interest " payments.

If the Party were suddenly to disappear from the country, and given all the other tendencies we have already described, it is not hard to imagine that China would revert to a kind of state capitalism, politically based on a ruling class of professional intellectuals. But the Party remains with a membership of something around 17,000,000. The communiqué of the Tenth Plenum made amply clear that the leadership was by no means ready to let the Party wither away. On the contrary, there has been a growing campaign to rebuild the image (and power) of

33 See, for example, Shih K'o-chien, " Sufficiently Develop the Capacities of Technical Personnel," *Red Flag*, No. 8–8, 1962, pp. 42–45. There is also now renewed emphasis on the need for Party cadres to have administrative and technical competence; see Chao Han, " Some Questions Concerning Party Cadre Policy," *Red Flag*, No. 12, 1962, pp. 1–13.

34 " The State Council Publishes Tentative Regulations on the Authority of Accounting Personnel," *People's Daily*, December 14, 1962.

the Party in the eyes of the people. Once again, during the summer of 1963, there was a campaign underway to get cadres and intellectuals to work alongside the people. The primary importance of political leadership in the armed forces is once again stressed. There has been a slow toning down of the 100 flowers spirit which, among other things, produced the remarkable economic debates of 1962. Nevertheless, there has been no real attempt on the part of the leadership to subvert the renewed authority that the professional intellectuals gained in 1961. There is no indication that the Party is once again moving into managerial councils, the way it happened earlier. As long as the N.E.P. situation lasts, it is almost impossible for the leadership to let the Party take over the economy once again. All signs indicate that this is a period of tense contraposition of Party and intellectuals, not unlike that which prevailed in 1956 and 1957.

THE PARTY AND THE IDEOLOGY

Of all the organisations that make up the body politic of Communist China, none is in as indecisive a position as the Communist Party. During the early 1950s, the Party was told to stay out of production and let the managers run their factories. However, this was simply a transitional policy. Starting from the great recruitment drive of 1955 (if not earlier), the Party began gradually to expand its leadership functions in industry, as well as in the remainder of society. The Great Leap Forward was the great period of Party leadership. Everywhere Party cadres were in command. Party cadres were young, they were workers and peasants, they were members of a superbly disciplined organisation whose channels of command and communication cut across bureaucratic jurisdictions. It seemed as if the Chinese Communist Party had found the organisational key to social engineering on a scale never before known in the world. Through the cadre-led production team, any problem could be solved. Moral fervour, enthusiasm, the use of group dynamics (to use an American term), leadership which could activate and unite all elements in the society—all this would consumate the economic revolution and push China to the brink of take-off.

When the decisions of the Ninth Plenum gave the order to the Party apparatus to release its hold on the economy, a rectification movement had already started in some parts of the country. Though the leadership was careful not to make the movement too well known, popular resentment against the Party was openly expressed in many areas of the country. There can be little doubt that there was a serious drop in Party morale in 1961 and early in 1962. By the summer of 1962 the leadership decided that Party morale and organisation must once again be strengthened. The Sino-Soviet dispute provided an occasion for intensifying the ideological campaign. The cult of personality, which had been constantly growing, has been more than ever emphasised. The more Mao has retreated from public view, the greater the adulation. The Party held China together in its moments of greatest crisis, and there is no indication that the extraordinary unity and strength of this great organisation has been impaired. However, the Party was taught to lead and not simply to control. Stalin ruled Russia through the secret police, but the whole outlook of the Chinese Communist Party has been opposed to its simply acting as the police guardian of society. All the recent changes in economic policy have put the Party in a difficult position.[35]

Ever since January 1961 management has resumed its old authority in the enterprise. Expertness, not redness, is stressed in the making of economic decisions. Management discussions now deal with technical production and marketing problems, rather than Party policy. Enterprise accountants have complete control over the factory's purse strings. Staff work is once again being emphasised, and the intellectuals who were earlier sent down to the production floor are back in their offices. Within government, there is apparently less to administer than before, with the encouragement of direct relationships between economic units, bypassing state agencies. What is the Party organisation to do under such conditions? Already by the mid-1950s, in some factories as much as 20 per cent. of the total number of employees were Party members. What are all these leaders to do in the absence of mass movements to lead? What does the Party secretary now do in Party committee meetings in enterprises and state agencies? All that can be said is that the situation is very complicated and difficult. In dynastic China, the magistrate usually let his functionaries, who were local experts, run the routine business of the yamen, intervening only if some extraordinary situation demanded his personal decision. Perhaps the same thing goes on today, except that the magistrate was quite content with his role, whereas such a role is something new for the contemporary Party cadre. During the early 1950s, when the Party was instructed not to interfere with production, it was told to concentrate on ideological work and help the unions organise the workers. By now the country is, if anything, over-organised, so not much remains to be done in that area. But it is in the field of ideology that the Party appears to be active today. Without Confucianism, the traditional scholar-bureaucrat was nothing. So today, apparently, the Party holds on to the ideology as its main

---

[35] The situation in China appears to be the opposite of that in the USSR, where since the death of Stalin, there has been a consistent effort to make the Party into an active organisational instrument and give it greater power for making economic decisions at all levels of the system.

weapon in the struggle to maintain the country's unity. Ideology has played a major part in holding China together as a political entity since pre-Christian times, and when the monarchical system collapsed, political failure and ideological erosion went hand in hand. In this context, it may be easier to understand the seriousness of China's charge that the Russians have been guilty of ideological heresy.

But the Chinese Communists have been trained to see ideology and organisation going hand in hand. Today there is a gap. While the ideology remains orthodox, the country as a working system of organisation seems at times suspiciously similar to Yugoslavia. The gap between ideology and organisation existed in Russia during the N.E.P., but at that time Russia was involved in a power struggle. China's leadership and its Party remain, at least on the surface, solidary. Within the country the many gaps that Party leadership was supposed to narrow continue to grow. There are regional gaps, status gaps, economic gaps. The gulf between rich and poor, advanced and backward has not been bridged. The N.E.P. policy has paid off in small but real dividends, but the dividends have been earned by managers, skilled workers, productive peasants without benefit of direct Party leadership. What is the Party to do under these circumstances?

THE GREAT DEBATE ON THE ECONOMY

Before concluding this article, it is well to say a few words about one of the more extraordinary phenomena of recent times in China. This has been the great debate on the economy which began late in 1961 and has continued down to the present time. We have already pointed out that there are interesting parallels between this debate and that which went on in the Soviet Union during the N.E.P. period. Discussions on the economy were held throughout the country in all major academic centres. It is perhaps significant that the local discussions often had as their direct concern economic problems within their own general region. Articles and summaries of the discussions were published in major newspapers and journals, and continue to appear. All the discussants appear to be economists, and only rarely has a person of official prominence, such as Hsueh Mu-ch'iao, entered the debate. The problems discussed have immediate relevance for the course of the economy, but are also problems of a type that would be discussed in any academic circles, east or west. Publications on the discussions which appeared in the spring of 1962 seemed sometimes to reflect a spectrum of views, but by the end of the year, it was clear that there were two main streams of thought. One favoured a return to greater state direction and control of the economy. The other argued for greater autonomy for the individual economic units. It is incorrect, though tempting, to label the former "orthodox" and the latter "liberal," the former proponents of state planning and the latter proponents of a market economy. One must remember that it was the group of political radicals who argued against the planners for decentralisation and greater autonomy at lower levels (of course, under Party leadership). It is hard to say what today constitutes an "orthodox" view in China, inasmuch as the Stalinist approach to economic administration was already attacked during the Eighth Party Congress and scrapped with the decentralisation decisions of 1957.[36]

The debates probably have little relevance for the ordinary factory manager who struggles with day-to-day problems. But they do reflect a similar debate that must be going on in the highest councils of the leadership. Western observers have termed an earlier debate as one between the planners and the sloganeers, the proponents of a centralised planning system and the advocates of a guerrilla approach to economic revolution. The sloganeers won out, as is well known. However, all the articles on the debate point out that issues discussed earlier are not so much discussed now, and that new issues have arisen. Thus, no one seems to question the crucial importance of profit targets as enterprise success indicators, but the question is: what kind of profit target? Should estimation of enterprise success be based on cost-profit ratios or on capital-profit ratios? Should cost targets be emphasised as well as profit targets? What about productivity targets? If the debate is indeed a reflection of a much more significant debate higher up, then it is likely that the issues of the debate are no longer quite the same as they were a few years ago. My own guess is that the two main streams of argument within the leadership are the same as in the economists' debate: should the role of the state be enlarged or should autonomy be further broadened? In their extreme form these arguments could

---

[36] So far four articles have appeared summarising the issues in what might be called the nation-wide debate (there have been several articles summarising the regional debates). All are signed by a man writing under the *nom de plume* of Chin Li. Of these, the third of those listed recapitulates more or less the same issues discussed in the first, indicating some significant changes in views. It would be extremely desirable that a careful analysis of these debates be undertaken, somewhat like Alexander Erlich has done for the Soviet debates in the 1920s.

   (1) "Short Presentation of Dissimilar Viewpoints in the Discussion of Problems of Economic Accounting Under a Socialist System," *Ching-chi Yen-chiu*, No. 3, 1962, pp. 61–67.
   (2) "Dissimilar Viewpoints in the Discussion of Price Problems Under a Socialist System by Our Country's Economists," *Ching-chi Yen-chiu*, No. 6, 1962, pp. 63–69.
   (3) "Discussions in the Very Recent Period by Our Country's Economists on Problems of Socialist Economic Accounting," *Ching-chi Yen-chiu*, No. 11, 1962, pp. 66–67.
   (4) "Discussion in Recent Years of Problems of Socialist Economic Effectiveness by Our Country's Economists," *Ching-chi Yen-chiu*, No. 1, 1963, pp. 60–65.

probably be qualified as Stalinist or revisionist respectively. It is hardly likely that anyone is arguing for either of these extreme positions. One would mean going back to a centralised bureaucratic system; the other going all the way over to the Yugoslav system with its implications for Party control. The argument is one about direction: whereto now?

Heinrich Cünow, a German Socialist commentator on Marx, writes that Marx conceived of state and society as two separate, juxtaposed entities. For Marx, society meant essentially the economy, and state the political community. Whereas the early Marx felt that revolution would arise out of the transformation of society and thereby overcome the state, the later Marx began to assign greater importance to political revolution, *i.e.*, the forcible overthrow of the state, as a means for revolutionising society.[37] One can probably say that the economy in China today is functioning along N.E.P. lines with a broad range of autonomous market tendencies. But the state is governed by different rules deriving from the ideology. Which will transform which? Will the social and economic patterns that now prevail transform the political system, or will the political system once again assert itself and try to fashion society in its own image? China seems to be standing at a kind of crossroad. What it will do internally will probably ultimately be of much greater significance than the role it decides to play on the international scene.

---

[37] Heinrich Cünow, *Die Marxsche Geschichs-, Gesellschafts-, und Staatstheorie* (Berlin: 1923), pp. 252–255, 310–314.

Culture and Society

Communist Education: Theory and Practice

By C. T. HU

PARADOXICALLY, the contemporary phase of China's development under Communism is at once an extreme form of Westernisation and a partial reversion to traditional patterns. The totalitarian character of the present régime is not only reminiscent of the ancient autocratic order but is attributable to that tradition for its acceptance and acquiescence. On the ideological front, the state of confusion of thought, compounded by almost a century's cultural dislocation, has been brought to an abrupt end, with the promulgation of Marxism-Leninism as the state ideology which, though antithetic to Confucian orthodoxy in every essential way, is equally pervasive. Inasmuch as the ideological reconditioning of the Chinese nation is first and foremost an educational task, education has become the exclusive concern of the Communist state. Moreover, within the Marxian ideological framework, the pursuit of concrete national goals requires the education of the Chinese people. Hence there are two major aspects in the study of Chinese education under Communism: Fundamental principles and actual implementation; in short, theory and practice.

There is, strictly speaking, very little in the Chinese Communist educational literature that can be regarded as educational theory as such. What has been labelled by the Chinese Communists as educational theory is no more than the extension and application of certain aspects of dialectical materialism, as expounded by Marx, Lenin, Stalin and Mao, to the direction of educational affairs. Since the Communist doctrine stresses the unity of theory and practice, as well as the importance of " concrete objective conditions," any educational policy or measure can be introduced and promoted or criticised and abandoned in the name of either theory or practice.

THE IDEOLOGICAL BASIS: THE FIRST TRIAD

Of particular significance and relevance to education are three basic concepts of dialectical materialism, as interpreted by the Chinese Communists. The first is the classification of human thought, insofar as the laws of the development of the world are concerned, into the metaphysical and the dialectical, which represent two mutually opposed world outlooks. Mao Tse-tung wrote in his *On Contradiction*:

> " For a very long period of history both in China and in Europe, metaphysics formed part of the idealist world outlook and occupied a dominant position in human thought. In the early days of the bourgeoisie in Europe, materialism was also metaphysical. The Marxist materialist-dialectical world outlook emerged because in many European countries social economy had entered the stage of highly developed capitalism, the productive forces, the class struggle and the sciences had all developed to a level unprecedented in history, and the industrial proletariat had become the greatest motive force in historical development. Then among the bourgeoisie, besides an openly avowed, extremely bare-faced reactionary idealism, there also emerged vulgar evolutionism to oppose materialist dialectics." [1]

In this one short passage one comes across a number of the familiar phrases of Communist jargon: class struggle, bourgeoisie, proletariat, productive forces, capitalism, reactionary idealism and materialist dialectics. No useful purpose can be served by raising philosophical questions about any one of these terms, nor is it relevant to ask if the majority of the Communist followers understand the meaning and implications of these terms. It is, however, exceedingly important to bear in mind that, by categorising all human thought according to such a scheme, there now exists a simple formula by which all thinking and action can be judged. The metaphysical world outlook is equated with idealism, is adhered to by the bourgeoisie, is reactionary, and therefore is opposed to both human progress and scientific truth. On the opposite side is the dialectical world outlook which is founded on the objective scientific truth, represents the irresistible forward running current of history, is supported by the proletariat, and promises the Communist millennium. Thus the line between right and wrong, friend and enemy, progress and reaction is irrevocably drawn, with the party leadership enjoying the exclusive prerogative of interpretation. Ideological rigidity forbids deviation in thought yet allows sufficient tactical latitude for the party itself. The state of confusion of thought in modern China has been brought to an end; education now proceeds in an atmosphere of controlled uniformity.

The second concept concerns practice, with even greater and more direct implications for education. To quote Mao Tse-tung once more:

> " Knowledge starts with practice, reaches the theoretical plane via practice, and then has to return to practice. The active function of knowledge not only manifests itself in the active leap from perceptual knowledge to rational knowledge, but also—and this is the more important—in the leap from rational knowledge to revolutionary practice. The

---

[1] Mao Tse-tung, " On Contradiction," in *Selected Works of Mao Tse-tung* (London: Lawrence and Wishart, 1954), Vol. 2, p. 14.

knowledge which enables us to grasp the laws of the world must be redirected to the practice of changing the world, that is, it must again be applied in the practice of production, in the practice of the revolutionary class struggle and revolutionary national struggle, as well as in the practice of scientific experimentation. This is the process of testing and developing theory, the continuation of the whole process of knowledge." [2]

The nature of knowledge is thus defined. Since search for knowledge is the prime objective of education, any form of education that fails to attain knowledge through practice according to the prescribed formula of production, class struggle, and national struggle is worse than no education at all. If, by classifying human thoughts into two fundamental opposing world views in favour of the dialectical, the Communists seek to create a monolithic pattern of ideological conformity, this emphasis upon practice tends to determine both the nature of knowledge and the meaning of education. Ideologically, the Chinese educational tradition can thus be negated on the ground that it was divorced from practice, hence its failure to lift China out of primitive agrarianism, to eliminate class exploitation, to achieve national power, and to reap the benefits of modern science. The feverish action-oriented form of education in China today can be understood only in terms of this fundamental consideration.

The third part of the triad is the class character of education and culture in general. Culture and education are regarded as concrete expressions of the politics and economics of a given society, and the politics and economics are determined by the class character. With respect to China, there are two aspects in Mao Tse-tung's analysis of the problem of culture. The first concerns his interpretation of China's culture before the Communist revolution, which he described in the following terms:

" There is in China an imperialist culture which is a reflection of the control or partial control of imperialism over China politically and economically. This part of culture is advocated not only by the cultural organisations run directly by the imperialists in China but also by a number of shameless Chinese. All culture that contains a slave ideology belongs to this category. There is also in China a semi-feudal culture which is a reflection of semi-feudal politics and economy and has as its representatives all those who, while opposing the new culture and new ideologies, advocate the worship of Confucius, the study of the Confucian canon, the old ethical code and the old ideologies. Imperialist culture and semi-feudal culture are affectionate brothers, who have formed a reactionary cultural alliance to oppose China's new culture. This reactionary culture serves the imperialists and the feudal class, and must be swept away." [3]

---

[2] Mao Tse-tung, " On Practice," *ibid.*, Vol. 2, pp. 292, 297.
[3] Mao Tse-tung, " On New Democracy," *ibid.*, Vol. 3, p. 141.

The "reactionary culture" must be condemned and swept away because it served only the interests of the exploiting classes which were allied with imperialism and semi-feudalism. This forms the negative aspect of Mao's interpretation. In a positive sense, Mao advocated the new-democratic culture which can only be led by the " proletarian cultural ideology, by the ideology of communism, and cannot be led by the cultural ideology of any other class." [4] It is, in a word, the culture of the broad masses under the leadership of the proletariat.

The Fundamental Principles: The Second Triad

Although there have been tactical retreats on the educational front since the Communist takeover, the three fundamental concepts concerning the dialectical world outlook, the search for true knowledge through practice, and the development of a proletarian culture have remained the very foundation upon which education rests. In this respect, there seems to be a remarkable degree of ideological consistency in the Communist régime, because the educational principles laid down in the Common Programme, which served as the basic guiding rules of the land until the adoption of a constitution in 1954, specifically called for the creation of a culture and education of the New Democracy, " that is, nationalistic, scientific, and popular." [5] These make up the second triad of nationalism, scientism and popularism which, unlike the first, which provides the ideological basis, sets up the educational objectives for the régime to strive for. The achievement of these objectives requires action; now that the Communists are in power, they lose no time in remoulding Chinese education according to the ideological dictates.

There can be little doubt that nationalism has been one of the most pervasive and dynamic forces in modern China which the Communists have manipulated to their fullest advantage. To achieve the nationalistic goal through education, two major strategies have been employed. On the positive side, the Chinese people are taught to cherish their great cultural tradition, reminded of the lasting achievements of their forefathers, the vastness and richness of their land and the tremendous potentials for the betterment of mankind.[6] Negatively, the humiliation of the Chinese nation during the past century, the sufferings of the Chinese

---

4 *Ibid.*, p. 145.
5 Article 41 of the Common Programme, adopted by the Chinese People's Political Consultative Conference which functioned as the highest law-making organ immediately after the Communist seizure of power in 1949. Chapter V of the Programme deals with culture and education; it is translated in *New China: Three Views* by Otto B. van der Sprenkel, Michael Lindsay, Robert Guillain (London: Turnstile Press, 1950), pp. 199–216.
6 See, for example, a collection of essays entitled *Lun Ai-kuo chu-i ti Chiao-yu* (*Essays on Education for Patriotism*), by Hsu T'e-li and others (Peking: The Masses' Bookstore, 1951).

people, and the degradation of China to the status of a semi-colony are ascribed to the unrelenting aggressions on all fronts by the arrogant and vicious imperialists. If the " victory " of the Chinese people in freeing themselves has broken the political bondage of semi-colonialism, the vestiges of imperialist culture and education still present the most serious obstacle to the achievement of the culture of New Democracy.

It is for the " nationalistic " purpose that all Western-sponsored institutions of education were the first ones to be subjected to the fury of educational reorganisation, and in less than three years, from early 1950 to the fall of 1952, all schools with foreign affiliations were " reorganised " out of existence.[7] Labelled as agencies of imperialist cultural aggression, the foreign-supported schools were declared to be hotbeds for the spread of individualism, liberalism, and bourgeois decadence, all implacable enemies of the culture of New Democracy.   Similarly, the Western-trained intellectuals, their repentance and profession of faith in the new order notwithstanding, were subjected to the severest dosages of thought reform.[8]

The " scientific " part of the triad involves two directly related objectives. The first has to do with the acceptance of the Communist definition of knowledge, discussed above, which can be scientific only when it is dialectical and derived through practice.   Within such an ideological framework, scientific education means specifically the development of modern science and technology to expedite the process of industrialisation and national development. Concrete educational efforts in this direction have been both numerous and concentrated and fall under three general categories. On the highest level is the Chinese Academy of Sciences, which has steadily expanded over the past twelve years. The number of its research institutes increased from thirty-one in 1952 to 170 in 1958, with a corresponding increase in trained personnel which for the year 1958 was close to 30,000 strong.[9] The Academy is responsible for the training of scientists in all major fields of specialisation who form the nucleus of an expanding army of scientific manpower. Below the Academy are the institutions of higher and secondary education, the majority of which are devoted to the training of engineers, technicians of all types, medical personnel, and other specialists. On the lowest level are the " broad masses of the people," who are taught not only to read and write but also the rudiments of modern science and technology,

---

7 For further information on the fate of foreign-supported schools of higher education, see C. T. Hu, " Higher Education in Mainland China," in *Comparative Education Review*, Vol. 4, No. 3, February 1961, p. 163.

8 For a thorough and up-to-date analysis of the thought reform of intellectuals, see Theodore H. E. Chen, *Thought Reform of the Chinese Intellectuals* (Hong Kong University Press, 1960).

9 Leo A. Orleans, *Professional Manpower and Education in Communist China* (Washington: National Science Foundation, 1960), p. 111.

consisting, at the present stage, of primarily labour-saving devices. Underlying the whole educational process of scientism is the principle of "walking on two legs," which demands the combination of theory and practice, new and old, Western and Chinese.

The idea of popularism has grown out of the concept of class struggle, and it is in this important respect that it differs from the phenomenon of popularisation of education in non-Communist countries. Concerning the class structure of Chinese society, Mao Tse-tung wrote as early as 1926 an essay entitled " Analysis of the Classes in Chinese Society," in which he classified the Chinese population into five major classes, representing three basically different positions with respect to the Chinese revolution : Those for it, those against it, and those wavering between the two.[10] Since the culture and educational system of China before the Communist revolution were those favoured by the oppressing and anti-revolutionary classes, the culture and education of New Democracy must serve the needs of the masses under the leadership of the proletariat. Needless to say, the Communists are fully aware of the educational needs of the nation at a time of all-out national construction which cannot be accomplished without a literate and technically competent populace. Therefore, from both the ideological viewpoint of class struggle and the practical viewpoint of the nation's educational needs, popularism in education must be held up as one of the major goals. The slogan " intellectualise the proletariat; proletarianise the intellectuals ! " reveals in a nutshell the true meaning of the movement towards popularism.

Different means have been employed to popularise education. Of first importance has been the steady expansion of education on all levels. Enrolment in full-time institutions is reported to have increased by leaps and bounds, with a corresponding increase in the number of schools. In 1958, the government claimed that 85 per cent. of all school age children were in attendance.[11] With the advent of the " Great Leap Forward " in 1958, the informal part of education has received encouragement and attention, resulting in the creation, sometimes almost overnight, of literally thousands of spare-time schools and Red-and-Expert colleges. These schools are undoubtedly far below standard and in some cases exist no more than in name, but nevertheless they are indicative of the extent to which the goal of popularism has been sought.   The class character of the students has also shifted in favour of the proletariat, which by Chinese definition includes both agricultural and industrial

---

[10] Mao Tse-tung, "Analysis of the Classes in Chinese Society," in *Selected Works of Mao Tse-tung, op. cit.*, Vol. 1, pp. 13–20.

[11] A breakdown of the enrolment for 1958 gave 86,400,000 for elementary schools ; 10,000,000 for all types of secondary schools; and 660,000 for higher institutions. See *Wei-ta ti shih-nien (Ten Great Years)* (Peking: People's Publishing House, 1959), p. 170.

workers. According to official reports, the percentage of students of working class origin has increased from 19·1 per cent. in 1951 to 48 per cent. in 1958 for higher education, and that of students in secondary schools from 51·3 per cent. to 75·2 per cent.[12] This is known as " opening the doors of schools for peasants and workers "; in other words, the " intellectualisation of the proletariat." At the same time, the " proletarianisation of the intellectuals " has proceeded according to party dictates, largely through thought reform, intensive indoctrination, and participation in productive labour. By and large, the quality of education in the present phase of development seems to indicate a downward trend, that is, as a result of the heavy demands made upon the students, the Communists have been more successful in bringing the intellectuals down than in raising the proletariat up.

Under Communism, a new generation of " educated Chinese " is slowly emerging. If the earlier phase of modern Chinese education which began about a century ago had created a group of intellectuals with little in common with their traditional predecessors in orientation, outlook and temperament, the present generation has gone even further in renouncing the educational heritage of the recent past. This is the real meaning of popularism.

FOUNDATIONS OF EDUCATIONAL POLICY: THE THIRD TRIAD

By 1958, the Communist Party and the Communist state under its control were sufficiently convinced of the " correctness " of the Party line and satisfied with the progress along the road to Socialism up to that point that an all-out and nation-wide movement known as the " Great Leap Forward " was launched. As education formed an integral and important part of this national assertion, fundamental policy decisions concerning education were proclaimed jointly by the Chinese Communist Party and the State Council on September 19, 1958, in which it was stated that " the policy of educational work of the Party is to make education serve proletarian politics, and to combine education and production labour. In order to carry out this policy, educational work must be led by the Party." [13] Thus there appeared yet another triad, namely, politics, production, and Party control.

To the Communists, the term politics is all-inclusive in its implications. By proletarian politics is meant, therefore, the whole intricate process of establishing a new national polity based upon the leadership of the proletariat, of which the Communist Party is the vanguard. Being aware that the Communist millennium must be created by a people completely immersed in Communist ideology, the Party leadership indeed see

[12] *Ibid.*, p. 178.
[13] Reported in the *People's Daily* (*Jen-min Jih-pao*), September 20, 1958.

no other alternative than to assign to politics the highest priority in all educational tasks. It is significant to note, in this connection, that the Party organisation in China has no educational department as such, and that all major decisions concerning education are made by the Party hierarchy on the recommendations of the Department of Propaganda. In view of the role of the Communist Party in the functioning of the Chinese state, it is clear that the Ministry of Education is no more than an administrative organ through which Party decisions are carried out. The obvious implication is that education, in so far as the Party is concerned, is primarily a propaganda function, with indoctrination of the population as its ultimate aim.

Ideological indoctrination is the essence of the political part of the triad and takes precedence over all other aspects of education. Consequently all persons, and especially educational workers and students, are graded, selected and treated according to their " political consciousness." Academic excellence is, to be sure, desirable and encouraged, but it must be accompanied by political reliability as a result of proper indoctrination. The term " Red and Expert " is, in this sense, particularly pertinent and revealing, for being Red has been, at least until recently, more important than being Expert, and the objective of education is to train a new generation of ideologically trustworthy and technically competent Chinese.

References have been made to the ideological framework when discussing the first triad. Our concern here is with the means by which the political objectives of education are achieved. A variety of methods are in use, ranging from the simple technique of repeating slogans to the highly complex process of thought reform. Broadly speaking, however, these methods fall under two categories, the formal or doctrinal part and the informal or action part, which, according o the Communist scheme, complement each other and unify theory and practice.

On the formal and doctrinal side there are the political subjects of instruction which consist of Dialectical Materialism, Foundations of Marxism and Leninism, History of the Chinese Revolution, Political Economy, and the like. The titles and the manner of presentation of the courses may vary from level to level and from institution to institution, but they are " musts " in all cases, be it the People's University or a rural spare-time school. Moreover, instruction is given, in most cases, by Party cadres operating in educational institutions. Passive acceptance of the doctrines never suffice, and such devices as " Study Groups," " criticism and self-criticism," and " thought struggle sessions " are resorted to from time to time not only to prevent deviation but also to insure complete and absolute belief in the new faith. The informal and action part of indoctrination takes many forms, mostly in organised political activities of one sort or another. Teachers and students have in the past twelve years engaged in several large-scale campaigns, beginning with the first land reform movement in 1950, followed by the Resist-America Aid-Korea movement in 1951, the Three-Anti- and Five-Anti movements of 1952, the Blooming and Contending of 1957, the Great Leap Forward of 1958, and more recently the movement to increase agricultural production. These are political activities of considerable duration and scope, to which must be added a large number of short-term action programmes, such as mass demonstrations against the French and British during the Suez crisis and against Eisenhower's visit to the Far East in 1960.

At the present stage, there is every indication that political indoctrination is receiving the utmost emphasis in all educational activities. The régime seems perfectly aware of the effect of such emphasis upon the quality of education, but as long as the principle of making education serve the needs of proletarian politics is adhered to, political indoctrination will continue to receive the highest priority and constitute the major form of education.

In an article entitled " The Great Revolution and Development in our Country's Educational Task," the Chinese Minister of Education made the following statement concerning the position of politics in education:

> " The great revolution in education further solved the problem of the relationship between education on the one hand and politics on the other. The capitalist class hypocritically chanted ' education for education's sake ' and ' leave the students out of politics.' But we insist that education must be in the service of proletarian politics and that all undertakings must be combined with political thought, because only in this way can we train the type of personnel who are both red and expert. For this reason, we hold up as the soul of all school work the political education of Marxism-Leninism and the political task of the Party. Moreover, we have put into effect the guiding principle of ' let politics be the commander-in-chief ' in all fields of cultural and scientific education." [14]

With respect to the policy of combining education with production, there are two readily discernible reasons by which the policy is justified. One is related to the fundamental ideological consideration of the nature of knowledge and the importance of practice in the acquisition of knowledge. To engage in productive activities is to combine practice with theory, and thus to acquire true knowledge. Also, productive labour is believed to be the surest way to eliminate the class character of education. Through productive labour the socially aloof and ideologically unwholesome intellectuals are made mindful of the dignity and honour of physical

---

[14] *Chien-kuo Shih-nien* (*Ten Years of National Construction*) (Hong Kong: Chi-wen Publishing Co., 1959).

work and are proletarianised in the process. The other reason lies in the actual and acute need of the nation for total mobilisation of human resources for national development. An expanding army of students, particularly on the secondary and higher education level, is an extremely important asset, in that they have considerably more to offer to national construction than the unskilled workers, numerous though they are. Therefore, for both ideological and economic reasons, the school system itself has been adjusted and developed in such a way as to facilitate the combination of education with productive labour.

Within this context, there are now three major types of schools in China, namely, the spare-time schools, half-work half-study schools, and full-time schools. The spare-time schools are designed for the purpose of elevating the cultural level and technical competence of the masses and are, as the name itself indicates, organisationally flexible. Drawing students from the rural communes, industrial plants, and urban residential districts, these schools range from open-air literacy classes to technical training on farms and in factories. Since all participants, including instructional staff, have their regular tasks to perform, these schools represent one form of mass education in which production comes before education. Because the state has encouraged local authorities to assume major responsibility for the organisation and operation of spare-time schools, and because of the diversity in objectives, resources, background of students and other factors, there exist no set pattern or criteria by which the spare-time schools can be properly described or classified. There are, however, common problems besetting these schools both in the mental and physical realms. Over-emphasis upon political indoctrination in spare-time school instruction, often given in addition to regular political meetings of one form or another, has given rise to mental dissipation or resentment, while the compulsory nature of such schools has contributed to physical exhaustion, the working hours being long and arduous.

In the half-work half-study schools students are required to participate in active production in a large variety of fields on a half-day, half-week, or sometimes half-month basis. Both in organisation and in curriculum these schools display a higher degree of articulation and co-ordination. In many cases they are middle schools under the supervision of government agencies which make arrangements with industrial or technical institutions for the provision of technical training and guidance for students, while the regular working force in return receive school instruction when the students are at work. Here education and production receive equal attention.

Forming the backbone of the nation's school system are the full-time schools which are subject to the overall control and supervision of the state in matters relating to organisation, administration, finance, curriculum, admission, graduation, and assignment of work. To combine education with production, different means are employed on different levels of schooling. For children below the secondary level, stress is laid upon the cultivation of the correct attitude towards work. Whenever feasible, children are encouraged to perform manual labour in school, not so much for production as to prepare them for participation in "socialist construction." On the secondary and higher education level, production becomes an integral part of education, and production in this case covers a wide range of activities. University students majoring in Chinese language and literature compile dictionaries; geology students explore parts of the country for minerals; and students in economics or banking work in state operated enterprises. Engineering institutes not only train their students in laboratory plants; they fulfil production quotas assigned by the state. The following report illustrates the extent to which education has been combined with productive labour:

> "Labour has become a formal part of our school curriculum. Schools everywhere have established factories and farms. According to statistics submitted by 323 institutions of higher education, there are now 738 factories and 233 farms, the latter having a total cultivated area of 140,000 *mou* of land. During 1958 and 1959, 386,000 students put in altogether 36,460,000 working days of work, with a total output valued at 1,380,000,000 *yuan*. All that we have belongs to the Party." [15]

It is idle to speculate on the effect of politics and productive labour upon education, although it is generally known that there is deep-seated dissatisfaction with the present state of educational affairs. Inasmuch as there is dissatisfaction and public scepticism, the third cardinal policy calling for party control of education is indeed a necessity, for without it other educational goals would be impossible to reach. The reaffirmation of this policy by no less a personage than Mao Tse-tung himself in 1958 was, therefore, not merely a reiteration of a familiar tune or theme, but an authoritative statement of the official party position concerning education, a position that tolerates no interference in educational matters from other quarters.

The timing of reaffirming party leadership in education was significant. It coincided with the "Great Leap Forward" and signalled the end of the earlier policy of tolerating to a certain degree the so-called old intelligentsia and their limited role in formulating educational policies. With the reaffirmation of this policy, all criticisms directed against various aspects of Chinese education were silenced and positive measures were taken to insure complete and unquestioning implementation of Party

[15] A report by the Chairman of the All-China Students Union, *Hong Kong Times*, February 11, 1960.

directives in the realm of education. These measures included intensified Party work among the students, the strengthening of the power and authority of Party representatives in schools, and the control of academic and administrative affairs by the state through the Party apparatus. In August 1959, one newspaper reported that among the 60,000 or more graduates from institutions of higher education in 1959, the number of Party and Communist Youth League members had reached a record high, with the Peking Normal University claiming as high a proportion as 85 per cent.[16] In virtually all schools, the Party secretary, with the Party machinery functioning at the lowest level and covering all ranges, now wielded absolute power over all essential aspects of school life, ranging from curriculum designing and examination procedures to student selection.

A delegation to the All China Conference of Advanced Socialist Workers in Education, Culture, Health, Physical Education, and Press, held in Peking in the summer of 1960, made the following remarks concerning Party leadership:

> " The educational and cultural task of our country is a task of socialism. It is an instrument for the consolidation of proletariat dictatorship, and it is at the same time an instrument for the Communist education of our people. The fundamental principle is that education and cultural work must serve proletarian politics and socialist economic construction. In order to accomplish this, education must be led by our Party. Within the realm of education and culture, the struggle between the bourgeoisie and the proletariat, and the struggle between capitalism and socialism have manifested themselves in many forms. Over a long time, the focus of contention has always been centred on the fundamental problem of Party leadership. Prior to 1957, despite the fact that we had made great gains in educational and cultural work, we were not able to consolidate, in time, the leadership of the proletariat. As a result, the bourgeois rightists, taking advantage of this condition, began to challenge the party on all fronts, shouting such slogans as ' the Party is incapable of leading educational work,' ' education for education's sake,' and ' separate labour from mental work.' . . . The thorough crushing of the vicious attacks by the bourgeois rightists has firmly established the indisputable correctness of our Party's educational and cultural policy, has paved the way for even greater progress, and has made possible the Great Leap Forward on all fronts." [17]

CONCLUSIONS

The revolt against tradition and the deepening of sweeping changes in modern Chinese education form one important part of the transformation of the most populous nation on earth. The traditional system and pattern of education, like all other facets of Chinese national life, proved totally

16 *Kuang-ming Daily*, August 24, 1959.
17 *People's Daily*, June 2, 1960.

inadequate in the face of an unprecedented challenge from the West. With the abandonment of traditional education came the weakening and later the disintegration of the ideological, moral and political fabric of old China. However valiant the efforts of the educational reformers during the transitional period, the general conditions which prevailed in China since its confrontation with the West prevented the gradual and healthy growth of a new educational system to serve the needs of a nation in transformation. Foreign aggression, civil strife and economic distress combined to render educational development difficult, while confusion on the intellectual front produced cynicism and despair. The Communist revolution is thus the culmination of China's century-long search for a new place in a new world.

In studying Chinese educational development under Communism, the totalitarian character of the new régime must assume first importance. It is precisely because of its totalitarianism that there now exists a government with absolute power, dominated by a disciplined, militant and dynamic political party. Through the government machinery and the Party apparatus, the Communists now control all aspects of national activity, including the re-education of the entire populace. By insisting upon party leadership in education, the régime is now able to pursue its educational goals with remarkable singleness of purpose and a degree of effectiveness and forcefulness that have no precedence in Chinese history. Totalitarianism, moreover, has brought about ideological uniformity and, at least in the present phase, succeeded in suppressing all real and potential challengers to Party doctrine. Through thought control and reform, the Chinese people are being moulded according to the image of the new Socialist Man, made to see the world and its history from the dialectical view, taught to love, hate and work in compliance with Party dictates.

Aggressive nationalism has replaced traditional humanism, and the major objective of education is now the maximisation of national power by means of industrialisation, for which scientism provides the key. Education has become, because of this overriding consideration, an integral part of the gigantic plan for national construction, to be co-ordinated with other phases of development. Thus the types of schools, the number of students, the method of selection, the content of education, as well as the assignment of graduates to jobs are all determined by the state according to a plan which is only a part of yet another larger plan. The political, social, economic and intellectual meaning of education has been rigidly defined by the state which permits no deviation or divergence of view. Education must serve the needs of proletarian politics.

If by totalitarian means the state has achieved complete control over the material and human resources of the nation, and in the field of education has claimed impressive achievements, the very magnitude of the task can cause a mistake or miscalculation to have disastrous consequences. The commune movement resulted in an economic crisis of alarming proportions, and the subsequent mobilisation of man-power for agricultural work dealt a severe blow to education on all levels, if for no other reason than the necessity of reducing the hours of instruction. There is, however, every indication that the régime remains as determined as ever in pursuing its educational goals, and given the organisational advantage of the Party and the dedication of its members, there is little reason to doubt that education will continue to develop according to the Party-formulated plans. The way in which education develops will determine the way in which the whole society develops, and in recognition of this relationship between education and society, it is imperative that we study China's educational developments with the care and attention they deserve.

The Rectification Campaign at Peking University : May—June 1957

By RENÉ GOLDMAN

IN a previous article I outlined briefly the development of the situation on the campus of Peking University (Pei-Ta) before, during and after the momentous events of the spring of 1957, the period of the " rectification campaign." [1]

The sequence of events in the past four years permits us to view the rectification campaign as a dividing date in the history of Communist China. The rectification campaign was the culminating point of a period that had seen the post-revolutionary reorganisation of the country, the assertion by the Communist Party of total control over the political, economic and ideological life of the nation and, following a campaign of liquidation of counter-revolutionary elements in the summer of 1955, a sudden " thaw."

The slogan of " Let a Hundred Flowers Bloom " was first applied in the winter of 1955, when plays previously forbidden were staged again and operas of all provinces were presented in Peking.

On May 26, 1956, Lu Ting-yi, secretary of the Propaganda Department of the Central Committee of the Chinese Communist Party, delivered his historic speech, entitled: " Let a Hundred Flowers Bloom! Let a Hundred Schools Contend! " In this speech he promised the scholars freedom of thought, controversy, creation and criticism. He said China should learn from the entire world, even from her enemies, and not mechanically transplant Soviet experience. The reaction of the intellectuals to this encouraging speech was, however, slow to come; their bitter past experience, and the limitations on freedom of criticism expressed in subsequent speeches of Party leaders and editorials of the *People's Daily*, made them reluctant to air their grievances. It took them a year to become bold enough to accept the invitation.

Following Chou En-lai's report on "The Question of the Intellectuals," delivered at a special conference of the Central Committee on January 14, 1956, the living conditions of the intellectuals were improved: their salaries were raised, they were given better research conditions, more materials were made available, better use was made of their talents and their administrative and meeting assignments were reduced. Although

[1] See " Peking University Today," *The China Quarterly*, No. 7, July–September 1961.

255

Thought Reform remained the ultimate goal, it came to be understood as a long-range process, and the Party decided that coercion was no longer necessary to ensure it.

Meanwhile the walls of Pei-Ta were plastered with slogans like "Think Independently," "Conquer Science," "Storm the Fortress of Science," which permitted the study of the achievements of science in the West and Japan. In the 1956–57 curriculum seminars were included called "Discussion in the Class Room." They were conducted in the form of professors issuing the students with questions to prepare for discussion, following which debates were held in class under the guidance of the professor. Although these questions were formulated in Marxist-Leninist terms and the debates were carefully kept within the bounds of orthodoxy, the very fact that debates were held constituted a marked improvement. University-wide science discussion forums were held by students and professors at the end of the spring term. The students were given a variety of non-compulsory lessons to attend. I still vividly remember the enthusiasm with which my Chinese class-mates started to compile bibliographies on various topics, write papers on the subjects which they had themselves selected and which they now had time to write, since the number of class hours and meetings had been reduced. They were fascinated, almost like children, by *k'a-p'ien* (library cards), which they were taught how to write. Many spent days filling piles of cards with references. Their thirst for learning was admirable and they sometimes dreamed up fantastic plans of research. Throughout the country, new literary and scientific periodicals, sometimes containing heterodox views, began publication.

Some workers' strikes and increasing student unrest in the summer and autumn of 1956 probably caused the Party, especially after the Hungarian uprising, to suspect that it had hitherto underestimated the extent of latent opposition among various sections of the people. The food supply situation was growing difficult, and in order to appease the emerging opposition various measures were taken, like the free distribution of winter clothes to school-teachers in Peking. In addition, a new, more friendly approach to the minority parties was expressed under the slogan: "Peaceful Co-existence and Mutual Supervision." Finally on February 27, 1957, at an enlarged session of the Supreme State Conference, Mao Tse-tung made his famous speech "On the Correct Handling of Contradictions among the People." (Unfortunately the speech was not published at the time, but only in June when the anti-rightist drive was already under way. As officially admitted, it was published with some modifications. In March, Mao's speech was only commented on and interpreted at different levels, inside and outside the Party.)

Mao announced that a " Rectification Campaign " was soon to be launched against the " three evils " in the " style of work " of Party cadres: bureaucratism, sectarianism and subjectivism. By " Letting a Hundred Flowers Bloom and a Hundred Schools Contend " the " three evils " could be uprooted and unity achieved again, on a new basis. " Unity—Criticism—Unity " was the slogan of the campaign. The Rectification Campaign, it was warned, must be earnest and yet like a mild breeze and a thin rain; meetings should be limited to small groups of a few people and assume the form of comradely talks.

Unlike in the 1942 Rectification Campaign, which was an intra-Party movement, in 1957 the minority parties and all the intellectuals were invited to help the Communist Party eradicate the " three evils " plaguing it. From the very moment the Communist leaders had moved into the large urban centres they had been concerned about the corrupting influence these might have on the cadres, who had previously known only the austere conditions of the " Liberated Areas." Besides, Party membership had swollen over sixfold: the bulk of the new members had not been brought up in revolutionary conditions, but had frequently joined the Party for the material and spiritual security Party membership offered or in order to gratify their personal ambitions. The *People's Daily* [2] itself admitted that some Party cadres had contracted the style of work of the ruling classes of the old society: they were dizzy with power and complacent. The intellectuals still had what Fei Hsiao-t'ung called " a feeling of early spring." They were bewildered and hesitating. As Professor T'ao Ta-yung of Peking Pedagogical University said:

> The intellectuals . . . are still not free from misgivings and fear that they might be trapped. They fear that, once their idealistic thoughts appear in print, they might be required to undergo the process of rectification once again in the future . . . they fear that they would be criticised and suffer the loss of prestige and face once their views are found to be unsatisfactory. As a result they have not the courage to contend although they very much want to do so. . . . On the other hand the leadership quarters of some institutions . . . have neither enthusiasm nor regard for the implementation of this line. They refuse to loosen their grip for fear of trouble. . . . [3]

However these feelings of bewilderment were finally overcome when the Rectification Campaign began. The May forums organised by the United Front Work Department of the Central Committee, to which the leaders of the democratic parties and non-party personages were invited, encouraged the movement of criticism against the Party among the intellectuals, and particularly in colleges, all over the country.

[2] See Directives on Rectification, *People's Daily*, May 1, 1957.
[3] T'ao Ta-yung, " The Flowers in Bloom are too Few, The Voices of Controversy are at too Low a Pitch," *Peking Daily*, April 20, 1957.

In Peking University a tumultuous movement started on Sunday, May 19. As in previous student movements in the history of modern China, Pei-Ta came to the fore. The students of Pei-Ta were looked upon by others as leaders, not only because of their school's revolutionary traditions dating from the days of the May 4 Movement, but also because of their location in the capital of the " Party-monopolised country." [4]

There was a stormy outburst of long-suppressed feelings, demands, resentment and frustration. Hundreds of posters were stuck up every day expanding the targets of the movement and attacking the policy of the Party towards the intellectuals. The announced statistics for one single day, May 22, indicated that the number of posters was 264 at 11 a.m. and was increased to 317 by 7 p.m. The rate grew in the following days. The students engaged in a real poster battle. The walls of the dormitories, the canteens and the class-rooms were covered with " *ta-tzu-pao* " or Big Letter Papers (posters). There were posters written by individuals as well as by groups. Many were boldly signed, but some were anonymous, which showed that there were students who strongly suspected that the invitation to " Bloom and Contend " might be a trap planned by the Communist Party to uncover disaffected elements, and this in spite of Party signs fixed up everywhere encouraging boldness: " Speak all you know and speak it fully; no fault will be attached to the speaker, while the listeners will learn a lesson thereof."

Another form of voicing criticism was the open-air meeting. One small plaza on the campus, surrounded by student canteens and dormitories, became the centre of political life: it was called the Democratic "Plaza" (*Kuang-ch'ang*) and a " Democratic Tribune " was erected there from which every evening speakers argued with the crowd, while at times students stood in tight knots around speakers at other places on the campus, creating an atmosphere which reminded one of Hyde Park in London.

One of the persons to speak on the Democratic Tribune was Lin Hsi-ling, a girl-student from the Chinese People's University, an institution for training Party cadres. She denounced the socialism carried out in China as false, because it was undemocratic. She claimed that Mao Tse-tung, in his speech on contradictions, had conceded most of what Hu Feng demanded. She publicly revealed facts which she claimed to know through her connections with important Party cadres, saying, for instance, that, when Mao Tse-tung made his famous speech to the Supreme State Conference, 80 per cent. of the Party members present left the room. This statement attracted an immediate denial from president

---

[4] A formula coined by Ch'u An-p'ing, chief editor of the *Kuang-ming Daily*, in one of his articles.

Ma Yin-ch'u, who had attended the meeting. In reply to this denial, somebody put up a poster entitled—in English: " Please answer the Following Questions." The questions were: " 1.—Did Mr. Ma sit in the last row? 2.—Did Mr. Ma concentrate all his attention in observing whether or not there were people leaving the room? " The answers followed underneath: " 1.—Mr. Ma was not necessarily sitting in the last row and he did not necessarily frequently turn his head backwards. 2.—Mr. Ma was definitely not able to discern whether those going out were leaving or going to the lavatory."

Some meetings actually became accusation meetings but with the roles reversed, with the Party cadres now being denounced for their attitudes and acts. The atmosphere of these open-air meetings was intensely emotional: there were emphatic, over-theatrical gestures, tears and shouts.

Groups were also set up, like the " Hundred Flowers Society " organised by T'an T'ien-jung and several other graduating students of the Department of Physics. The " Society " collected money to print a magazine called *Kuang-ch'ang* (*The Plaza*), the success of which was limited, possibly as a result of an incident with some Party-organised workers who denied members of the " Society " access to the school printing office. T'an T'ien-jung soon became famous, not only at Pei-Ta but all over the country. He usually wrote one poster a day, calling them " poisonous weeds " in a provocative allusion to the differentiation made by the Party between " fragrant flowers " and " poisonous weeds." His first " poisonous weed " started with a famous quotation from Heraclitus: " In Ephesus all adult men should die and government of the city should be handed over to beardless young men." He labelled the *People's Daily* " The Great Wall sealing off the truth." T'an called for bold discussions among students to show the world that, in his words, " besides those ' Three-Good students ' [5] (or morons, model students, ' small nails ' or ' sons and daughters of Mao Tse-tung ' or whatever you call them, it's just the same) who have annihilated their thinking faculties, there are still among Chinese youth thousands of talented and remarkable persons." He signed his poster: " Puer Robustus sed Malitiosus." The " Hundred Flowers Society " attempted to co-ordinate the efforts and goals of all contenders, not only at Pei-Ta, but also in other universities like Tsinghua and Tientsin.

The targets of criticism were many, and there was great variety in the formulations; if many were naive and incoherent, some were remarkable for their boldness, precision of judgment and sharpness of wit. Generally speaking, the targets of criticism of the students were the same as those

---

5 Allusion to the " San Hao " (Three Good) directive of Mao Tse-tung to the youth: " Good health, good study, good work."

of the representatives of the " democratic parties " at the forums, but more concentrated on problems of direct concern to students, and were also, on the whole, more vehement in tone. The criticisms at the forums, coming from older men, were rather carefully worded and always stressed the necessity of the leadership of the Communist Party.

I shall now outline the various questions raised by the students and the way these were treated. I think these reveal to us interesting aspects of the impact of Communist education on Chinese youth.

Perhaps the first issue raised by the students as soon as the movement started at Pei-Ta was the " Su-Fan "—the Movement to Liquidate Counter-Revolutionary Elements in 1955. At the May 22 Forum, Lo Lung-chi, deputy-chairman of the China Democratic League,[6] proposed the establishment of a special United Front organ to inspect excesses committed during such past movements; this was to provide a guarantee that people who dared to " bloom " and " contend " would not be subjected to attack and retaliation. At Pei-Ta, students put up posters asking from the Communist Party a statement as to the fate of Hu Feng, demanding his release and the rehabilitation of all innocent people who had been wronged during the movement, particularly those students and teachers who had committed suicide. Some pointed out that Hu Feng's only crime was to have wanted " blooming and contending " too early. It was claimed that 90 per cent. of the victims were innocent. The experience of the " Su-Fan " was still vivid in the minds of the students; they wanted the Party to take concrete measures to prevent the recurrence of such events. Some posters also demanded an explanation of the case of Kao Kang and Jao Shu-shih. Correlated with these demands were attacks on the police methods employed to suppress opinion, and demands for human and democratic rights.

The question of Party rule in educational institutions was one of the most hotly debated. Students and teachers demanded that the Party committees be withdrawn from educational institutions or limited in power so that decisions in matters of curriculum and education be the sole concern of teachers. Opposition to Party committees running universities had previously been expressed at the May 10 forum for democratic party members by Lo Lung-chi and Ch'en Ming-shu. They denounced the common phenomenon of eminent scholars, some of world fame, being withdrawn from teaching and used solely in purely administrative posts as deans or vice-deans, yet without having the power usually associated with such positions. Actual power was concentrated in the hands of the Party secretaries who sometimes did not rank high in scholastic qualifications. Students felt humiliated and embittered by the fact that

---

[6] Later accused of having headed an anti-Party plot with Chang Po-chün.

sometimes even key courses were taught by lecturers or assistants who had barely graduated, knew little and sometimes had little teaching ability. These young lecturers and assistants were not always drawn from the most capable of the graduates, but primarily from among those who were "ideologically reliable." The President of Pei-Ta, Ma Yin-ch'u, reflected these feelings at one of the May forums when he said that at Pei-Ta, young assistant professors no longer enjoyed the confidence of the students because they were considered to be teaching doctrinairism; he said all students wanted to listen to lectures by old professors.

The application to China of the Soviet educational system even in its minor details, like the grading system (insufficient, sufficient, good, very good), came under sharp attack. Some students denounced the current use in all departments of translated Soviet textbooks, slanted with "Great Russian chauvinism" and depreciation of Western science and culture. This slant was most conspicuous in the curriculum of the departments of literature and history, where in the teaching of foreign history and literature the lion's share was devoted to Russia. On one of the posters put up in the Department of Chinese Language and Literature, a poster entitled "Against Chauvinism in the Teaching of Foreign Literature," one could read:

> On being told that many young people liked to read Romain Rolland's *Jean-Christophe*, the secretary of the Youth League exclaimed: "Don't poison yourself! Romain Rolland is a French writer, of a capitalist country, therefore his work contains poison!" We ask the school: why do you want to seal off Western literature from us? The time devoted to the teaching of Western literature does not even amount to half the time devoted to the teaching of Russian literature. Why do such great masters of world literature as Balzac, Byron and Shelley deserve only a two-hour lecture whereas we had to study Pushkin alone for several weeks? Other excellent writers of world stature like Diderot, Hardy, Stendhal, Rolland, Dreiser, Twain, etc. . . . do not even deserve to have their names mentioned! Alas, these great writers were unfortunate: they were not born in a Slavic nation! We are tired of simple-minded Soviet books filled with chauvinism, propaganda and boasting. We want equal consideration of the whole world literature and not always have some —ski, —ov, —aia, —na, presented as an idol or super-being.

On another poster, put up in the Department of History, and entitled "Oppose Dogmatism in the Teaching of History," one could read:

> Some dogmatists lack the most elementary decency: even products that have nothing to do with Marxism are imposed on us if they carry the trade mark "U.S.S.R." Some say the Russo-Swedish war was a just war because it gave Russia an outlet on the Baltic Sea. It was not aggression because this land belonged to Russia in antiquity, besides

it was necessary for the historical development of Russia. Nelson is presented as a warmonger and a parasite, whereas Suvorov of Russia is presented as a hero who liberated the peoples of Europe from Napoleon's tyranny! Let us not forget that the peoples of Europe greeted Napoleon with bread and salt whereas Suvorov reimposed on them the shackles of feudalism. The reasons for all peasant wars throughout history are presented to us as the same: land spoliation + tax burden + usury, and the main reason of the defeats of the peasant uprisings always was the lack of a progressive class and party to lead them, etc. . . . Long live fighting Marxism!

Science students ridiculed the contention that all major discoveries like photography, the radio, the airplane, etc., were the work of Russians. Biology students criticised the limitation of learning to the theories of Russian and Soviet biologists considered to be materialist while Western biologists were branded as "idealist." Chinese national feelings were also expressed. For instance, the fact that the bust of Lomonosov presented by Moscow University was standing in the main library aroused resentment and many students strongly demanded its removal and replacement with the bust of some eminent Chinese. One poster asked:

> Why was the anniversary of Einstein's death not commemorated when so much noise has been made about the discovery of radio by Popov and so much fuss is constantly made about Lomonosov whose contribution to world science was minimal?

Permission to study more of Western science, to learn from the West was demanded. There was great enthusiasm for reading Western literature, for enjoying artistic works that were not necessarily "filled with ideological content."

Weariness and mockery was expressed at the extreme politicisation of the teaching to a degree sometimes infantile; many students felt Marxism-Leninism dry and boring. As Mao Tse-tung said in his speech on contradictions: "It seems as if the Marxism that once was all the rage is not so much in fashion now." There were posters demanding cancellation of political lessons, especially the "Short Course of the History of the Communist Party of the Soviet Union" which was known from the speeches of Mikoyan and Khrushchev at the Twentieth Congress of the CPSU, to be filled with distortions of the historical truth. Others only wanted these lessons, purged of their dogmatic content, or else to have attendance at them made voluntary. It must be said here that the majority of the students participating in the campaign were not necessarily anti-Marxist. Actually most of them expressed attachment to Marxism, accusing only the Party of having deviated by becoming scholastic and dogmatic. Even T'an T'ien-jung, who was later condemned as the chief rightist of Pei-Ta, did not altogether repudiate Marxism. He accused the Chinese Communists of having no true understanding of dialectics and supported the opinion expressed by Professor Lei Hai-tsung that Marxism had failed to produce any new understanding of human history or new theories of the social sciences after Engels' death in 1895. T'an voiced disappointment at the fact that " Marxism has transformed itself into its own negation, into revisionism and dogmatism." He called for a " negation of this negation " and accused the article " Once more on the Historical Experience of the Dictatorship of the Proletariat " of being filled with " idealism."

Coming to the evil of sectarianism, the students attacked the way of life and the haughty attitude of many Party cadres towards the masses of the people and the intellectuals in particular. They denounced the excessive privileges enjoyed by the cadres which turned them into what Djilas termed " the New Class." Numerous posters appeared describing examples of personal immorality of some cadres who led a dissolute and luxurious life, drove their families on holidays in government cars, coupled their abuse of privileges with high-handedness and authoritarianism towards the people; in a word, they were accused of believing that, as Stalin put it, Communists were made of " special stuff." Many of them were ridiculed on posters and wall-serials, like one entitled *Ju-lin Nei-shih*, a satire of Pei-Ta society modelled on Wu Ching-tzu's novel *Ju-lin Wai-shih*. It was asserted that there were nowadays in China three states: the Party, the Youth League members and the masses, each of them divided in turn into several degrees; Party cadres were labelled mandarins.

In the universities, inequality of treatment was reflected in the allocation of job assignments to graduating students. Innumerable complaints were voiced at Pei-Ta that Party and Youth League members were assigned to choice places in Peking or Shanghai and other major urban centres, whereas others were appointed to remote areas or generally to low-paid posts. Many students attacked the stratification of the people along lines of Party and Youth League membership and the use of " activism " and " political maturity " as criteria for rewards and appointments. Perhaps the most bitter denunciation of the " New Class " came from student Ch'ien Ju-p'ing, who wrote a poster " On the Development of Classes ":

> I come from a poor peasant family and experienced all the bitterness of class oppression. . . . From the time that I went to elementary school I daily dreamed that " there will be a day " when I will enjoy democracy and freedom ; " there will be a day. . . ." Then the experience of the past seven years has proved that it is not so beautiful; a new class oppression is just building up. . . . Following the destruction of the old classes, a new class has emerged, which is naturally different from the old ones, but has nevertheless characteristics of its own. . . . As for the means of production, the main Party, Government and Army people who hold power and represent a very small percentage of the people, own them in

common and embellish this situation by calling it "common ownership by the people." The mandarins back one another and are consciously forming a new social group. . . . Their distrust of the common people is greater than at any time before in history. Even the cruel Kuomintang when they arrested people, did it with at least some factual ground. . . . We can see that at present there are no human rights whatsoever, life and security are constantly threatened. . . . We know from history, that when Chu Yüan-chang conquered the empire, he also strove for the people's support and allied himself with the people. Having brilliantly succeeded, he immediately kicked the people away. . . .

Besides denouncing the disdainful attitude of Party cadres towards the students and the intelligentsia in general, some described how the bestowal of Party membership altered the character of the beneficiary, broke friendships and transformed simple and friendly people into cold and distant officials. Thus lecturer Huang Chi-chung, of the Department of Western Languages, wrote in an article entitled " Boldly Offering my Opinion to the Party and Party Members ":

Shortly after the liberation the Party and Party members enjoyed the highest confidence of the masses. But . . . nowadays relations between the Party and the masses have worsened, a high wall has emerged between the Party and the masses. When the masses see a Party member they have the feeling that they ought to "respect them but keep away from them ". . . . In recent years, from being the most sincere people, Party members have gradually become the most false people. . . . In our department most of the Party members are comrades who graduated two or three years ago and are very young. When they were students they were lively and lovable and naturally friendly. On graduating they were assigned to the department . . . their youthful enthusiasm and energy were buried. . . . In the Party committee of our school, many very young male and female comrades impressed me as little monks and nuns.

Party organisations had exclusive control over the appointment of staff members and graduating students, on the basis of opinion provided by Party members. Knowing the ignorance and the lack of understanding of many Party cadres, their eternal suspiciousness and their habit of relying on confidential reports, one can well imagine the resentment and the indignation of people affected by this system. Many complained that disagreements with Party members had led to political trouble for them, to the accusation of being " politically backward." Some students demanded that the secret files be opened and handed to the people they concerned or burned, as happened in Poland in October 1956.

The selection of students sent abroad, mainly to the Soviet Union, was another aspect of " sectarianism " in the Party " style of work," most violently attacked by the students of Pei-Ta. This selection was made in a manner similar to that of the appointment of graduating students to jobs. China sent an average of 2,000 students yearly to the

Soviet Union and a hundred or so to the East European countries. The basic criterion of selection was their ideological reliability and their social origin. These were determined on the basis of the opinions held by the Party committee. Academic ability and general intelligence were of secondary importance. One poster presented two applications filled by students wishing to study abroad. One of them was the son of a bankrupt merchant who had become a factory worker; his grandfather was an impoverished landlord. This candidate's past record was void, except for the insignificant fact that at the age of thirteen he found himself by accident in a crowd in Shanghai, which he later learned was an anti-Communist gathering. His marks were excellent and his class-mates had the highest regard for him, considered him to be selfless, active and always eager to help. Yet the final decision of the Party committee was that, being by birth a member of the exploiting classes and having a dubious political past, he was unfit to be sent abroad. The second candidate was the son of a cadre who was originally a poor peasant; currently his father was secretary of some Party organisation; his mother was director of some institution. His past was perfectly void. His class-mates had the worst possible opinion about him: that he was haughty, domineering and selfish. In addition, his marks were all bad. However, the opinion of the Party organisation was that his social origin was good, his ideology good and that, being reliable, he could be sent to the Soviet Union for study.

Sometimes anti-Soviet feelings came to be expressed in connection with the criticism of the Party " style of work." Some, following Lung Yün, questioned the " friendliness " of the Soviet Union towards China. There were complaints against " blind adoration of the Soviet Union," the excessively high salaries paid to Soviet experts in China as compared to those paid to Chinese experts and scholars or Western scholars established in China and teaching in Chinese universities. The constant hailing of the " Soviet Big Brother " and the " Progressive Experience of the Soviet Union " was ridiculed. Some even traced the origin of the " Three Evils " in China to the application of the Soviet experience.

Starting from their own problems, students came to take up problems of national importance, such as the duality of Party and government, the one holding power while the other maintained only an appearance of authority; the relations between the Party and the masses; the attitude of the Soviet Union towards China; and naturally also the economic situation. One question brought up was whether or not the standards of living had really been raised, how much the Communist Party had in fact improved the life of the Chinese masses, especially that of the peasants. The student Ch'ien Ju-p'ing already quoted, being himself from a poor peasant family, had this to say on the subject:

> All you can say is: but haven't the living standards of the people been raised? . . . In fact how much have they been raised? When society is in development, the productive forces increase constantly and the living standards also have a general tendency to be raised: this can be seen from history. . . . In fact the incomes of the workers and peasants in our country in recent years have not been raised much. They just get enough to eat and avoid starvation.

The well-known statement of Professor Ko P'ei-ch'i of People's University was even more extreme: he flatly denied that any improvement whatsoever had been made in the living standards of the masses, that it was only the Party cadres who had had their living standards improved.

Posters multiplied beyond any possibility of counting, and it seemed as if the Party had every critical poster surrounded by many others stating the Party viewpoint and attacking the criticisers. Those posters which raised controversial issues usually attracted gatherings of students who reacted to their content by scribbling on these very posters brief remarks. There were various sorts of posters: poems, serials, polemics, cartoons. Some were signed with the names of their authors, some with student identification card numbers, some with pseudonyms; some were anonymous.

More than a week after the beginning of the movement, irritation was growing at the fact that the *People's Daily* remained silent about what was going on in Pei-Ta. Only the *Kuang-ming Daily* and the *Wen-hui Pao,* which had asserted some independence at the time as organs of the democratic parties and the intellectuals, gave favourable accounts of the movement in their reports of May 26 and May 27. In a speech to the Third National Conference of the Communist Youth League, on May 25, Mao Tse-tung said: " Any speech or action which deviates from socialism is entirely wrong." This statement was immediately painted in big white characters on the Democratic Plaza. However, the movement went on unabated.

It was in these late May days that, following repeated demands, Khrushchev's secret speech on Stalin at the 20th Congress of the Communist Party of the Soviet Union, was translated from the abridged version published by the *New York Daily Worker*. The translation was the work of four students of the Department of Physics. For a day or so, crowds gathered around the board where the secret speech had been posted and took notes. This poster was soon removed by the Party committee and other posters replaced it, attacking the four students as " unconscious agents of Allen Dulles " and quoting a remark made by Khrushchev to a Western press correspondent in which he denied ever having made such a speech. The four incriminated students protested indignantly, claiming that they had acted in good faith, that they were sincere young Communists. Nevertheless, when the anti-rightist drive came they were branded as counter-revolutionaries.

It might seem strange that students in physics and mathematics were the most prominent and formed the core of the leadership of the movement rather than students in the humanities. One of the reasons might be that students in the pure sciences had generally a better knowledge of the English language which they were encouraged to acquire in order to study foreign scientific works. Their relative awareness of developments in the outside world was surprising in a country where all media of information are entirely under government control. Also Pei-Ta had a large number of foreign students, some of whom (not necessarily anti-Communist) held heterodox views unfamiliar to the Chinese students. As a rule, foreign students had a better knowledge of developments in the rest of the world, especially the students from non-Communist countries and those from Yugoslavia and Poland. It is no wonder that at the time of the anti-rightist drive, one of the explanations rumoured for the great numbers of " rightists " unmasked among the students of Pei-Ta (800 or 10 per cent. of the student body), was the presence of a large number of foreign students.

To describe the attitude of the average student during this " May 19 movement," whether he approved or disapproved of what the contenders said, or whether he was simply disoriented and confused, is difficult to do. The question is, how many undiscovered rightists were there? In a Chinese student movement, just as in any other movement, there is obviously a leading minority and a mass of followers whose feelings are aroused by the leaders. In Pei-Ta, at the time of the Rectification campaign, there were students openly expressing their dissatisfaction and also some taking the Party stand (probably mainly Party and Youth League members and other activists). However, we can assume that the majority of the students stood somewhere in between, displaying a whole range of feelings from utter confusion and hesitation to semi-approval and unexpressed sympathy, an attitude which might be termed " wait and see." This is indicated by the fact that during the autumn and the winter, many months after the " Blooming and Contending " in May, scores of hitherto " hidden rightists " were " unmasked," while others were criticised for having been indifferent instead of supporting the Party when it was under fire.

The time during which the flowers bloomed and the schools contended was very short; it lasted barely one month. The turning point was June

8, when the *People's Daily* in its editorial " What is this for? " commented on an alleged anonymous letter of intimidation received by Lu Yu-wen, one of the leaders of the Revolutionary Committee of the KMT, after he had made a speech in which he attempted to justify all the policies of the Communist Party. The June 14 editorial of the *Chinese Youth Newspaper* provided an interesting description of the attitude of the students during the period of blooming and contending:

> ... In the ideological storm, not all members of the Communist Youth League and other youths can stand firm; some are sitting on the fence and wavering. Some have compromised [with the enemy] and some have even allowed themselves to be taken captive by the rightists. Some of our young comrades are not yet good enough at distinguishing two kinds of entirely different criticism. . . . Beware of political catarrh! In dealing with reactionary views, we must learn how to refute them skilfully with fact. . . . Do not be deceived by them! . . .

Thus in the second week of June the Party line changed : attention was shifted from the " three evils " in the " style of work " of the cadres to the activities of the " rightists." Officially the Rectification campaign was still continuing and had entered its second stage, described as the " movement against the rightists " which in fact superseded the rectification of the " three evils." The slogans of class struggle, antagonistic ideological struggle directed against " enemies of the Party and socialism " displaced those of " mild breeze," " cool rain," " peaceful solution of contradictions among the people." The " May 19 Movement " at Pei-Ta consequently died down. The number of *ta-tzu-pao* pasted on the walls diminished and the majority of them now attacked T'an T'ien-jung, Lung Yin-hua and other " rightists " and expressed praise of and allegiance to the Party. For a few days " rightist " posters still appeared, but these were isolated cases and mostly anonymous. The nature of their content had changed. Disappointment and bitterness were couched in sharp terms, as in this poster signed " A Group of First Year Students in the Department of History ":

> Intelligent friends! Everybody has been cheated! The goal of the Rectification Campaign of the Communist Party was not the removal of the three evils, the solution of the contradictions among the people or the improvement of the style of work, but the acquisition of even greater power, to be able better to rule over the " stupid " Chinese people. Isn't that clear? Even after the Emperor [*Huang-Shang*] has ordered the Party to mend its ways, the mandarins of all degrees are nevertheless still in place, everything remains just as before. Lately, the Emperor has discovered some " right-wing elements " and he now uses them to frighten the " stupid " Chinese people!

From the samples of opinions expressed by the students of Pei-Ta it can be seen that, although their criticisms were sometimes bolder than those of their elders, on the whole they tackled concrete issues concerning their own life. The essence of their demands was a more liberal cultural and educational policy. Almost none had advocated the overthrow of the Communist Party and a change of régime. The criticisms of the students of Pei-Ta were for the most part expressed in good faith, they were frequently naive, animated by a desire to make Party rule over the universities and national life generally more tolerable; the reforms they demanded were of the nature of those that had already been carried out in Poland and Yugoslavia. Demands were expressed spontaneously, individually; even organised groups like the " Hundred Flowers Society " did not have a clear-cut common programme. This group advocated the preservation of socialist ownership of means of production but changes in other aspects of national life—the sacking of bad cadres and following the Yugoslav path. But while T'an T'ien-jung suggested that these reforms be carried out from the bottom up by means of a mass mobilisation of the youth, his colleague Lung Yin-hua believed that the leaders of the Party could be persuaded to take the initiative in carrying out reforms.

The activities of the students of Pei-Ta and other schools, even linked as they were with the intellectual movement in general, could not possibly have achieved their goals, and not just because they were demanding much more than the Party was willing to grant them. Although organised groups like the " Hundred Flowers Society " existed, the whole movement had no organisational frame, no clearly agreed political programme. Although T'an T'ien-jung did establish some contacts and correspondence with students in other schools, every centre of student agitation was isolated from the other and the isolation was increased by the silence of the Party-controlled press. Moreover the time of " blooming and contending " was so short that many students were not yet aroused from their passiveness. One might wonder why the reaction of the Party was so sharp, why the Party decided to break the pledge that no one would be punished for having criticised? This move was essentially a defensive one, for if this trend of opinion among the intellectuals had not been checked before the rectification of the " three evils " was carried to the broad masses of the peasants, workers and townspeople, in time the widespread distribution of these ideas outside the schools might have provoked far-reaching consequences.[7] Kuo Mo-jo had this to say about the broken pledge:

> This slogan applies only to the innocent speakers and not to the guilty ones. If a man is not charged with guilt, even when he says something

[7] This fear was expressed by Lu Ting-yi in his speech, " The Basic Differences Between the Bourgeois Rightists and Us," delivered to the Fourth Session of the First National People's Congress on July 11.

which undermines the foundation of the state, one might as well scrap the law and discipline of the state altogether. . . . Our land is used for growing food crops. Even common weeds should be eradicated therefrom, not to mention the poisonous ones.[8]

Some of the " rightists " I had the opportunity to talk to were bitter and considered that they had been cheated. The anti-" rightist " movement lasted all through the summer and the autumn and at Pei-Ta did not end till January 1958 with the punishment of the " rightists." Some of them were sent away for " reform through labour "; the majority, however, were allowed to remain at school under supervision. During the summer of 1957 the students did not go home as usual during holidays, but instead took part in endless rounds of " struggle meetings " designed to get the " rightists " to confess their " crimes."

In my opinion the evidence does not suggest that by calling the flowers to bloom, the Party intended to set a trap for critics. Rather the Party leaders discovered that opposition was wider than they had anticipated and that therefore to allow the criticism to continue was hazardous. Careful reading of the editorials of the main newspapers during the summer of 1957 reveals that what really shook the Party was a feeling that it faced the loss of its control over the youth. Young people brought up since childhood under Communist rule had become the loudest in denouncing the Party which had vested its hopes in them. The Party could devise only one means to remedy this failure: more indoctrination. The burden of meetings and labour was increased again and an eight-hours-a-week course of " Socialistic Ideological Education " was added to the curriculum in the autumn.

---

[8] Interview with Kuo Mo-jo, *Kuang-ming Daily*, June 28, 1957.

The Reorganisation of Higher Education in Communist China, 1949–61 *

By IMMANUEL C. Y HSU

WITHIN the short span of twelve years since their rise to power in 1949, the Chinese Communists have completely revamped their educational system. Private institutions of higher learning have been abolished and the number of universities vastly reduced; in their place hundreds of technical institutes have been created, with an unprecedented increase in enrolment and graduates. The faculties of various universities and colleges have been amalgamated in an effort to train more and more scientific and technical personnel. New types of instruction, known as " specialty " (*spetsial'nost*) and " specialisation " (*spetsializatsiia*), have been introduced to accelerate the training of industrial experts. Emphasis on science and technology has completely replaced the traditional respect for the humanities; the highest learned organisation in Communist China today is the Academy of Sciences, and not the Academy of Letters (*Hanlin Yuan*) of Imperial China. A Twelve-Year Science Programme was adopted in 1956 with the avowed objective of producing 10,500 top scientists and some two million technicians by 1967,[1] and towards this end a new University of Science and Technology was established in 1958.

It is noteworthy that whereas in the advanced nations of the West, such as England and the United States, it was industrialisation that generated a natural and spontaneous impact on higher education and influenced the technical and scientific education in the universities, in China, it is the anticipation of economic development and the conscious planning for industrialisation that has brought about a decisive change in the nature and content of higher education. In the West, industrialisation preceded technical education in the universities; in China, technical education precedes industrialisation. In the West, universities establish courses to meet the existing demands of industrialisation; in China, universities and technical institutes train personnel to create industrialisation.

---

* This article will appear in the book *Manpower and Education: Country Studies in Economic Development*, edited by Harbison and Myers, to be published later this year by McGraw-Hill.
[1] John A. Berberet, *Science and Technology in Communist China* (Santa Barbara: General Electric Company, 1960), p. 100.

The philosophy behind the new concept of Chinese higher education is the Marxist belief that education has a class character: the objectives, methods and contents of education reflect the basic nature of the society. With the downfall of the Nationalist Government and the demise of the old society, out must go the old educational system, and in its place a new system, with different objectives, methods and contents, must be born. In a new society under the Communists, education must serve the state and fit into the broad national policy of industrialisation, contributing its share towards the realisation of the national goal. No longer is education a milieu in which man seeks his own highest development, but an instrument of the state designed to provide the personnel needed for national construction. Universities have become training centres for professional engineers and skilled technicians rather than places of learning where knowledge is pursued for its own sake. In this new atmosphere, enrolment in higher education is said to accelerate at the rate of 130,000 students per year. Almost 90 per cent. of China's 254,000 scientists and engineers have been trained since the Communist take-over in 1949. China now produces about 75 per cent. as many graduate engineers annually as the United States and in the next few years it may equal or even surpass the United States, quality of instruction apart. An American physicist estimates that by 1970 China will produce between one and two hundred thousand engineers a year.[2] For better or for worse, the cultural entity that was traditional China is being transformed into a technocratic state, in which higher education is characterised not by dreamy philosophers but by dynamic engineers.

Phenomenal as is the change wrought by the Communists, Chinese higher education had not been static before their assumption of power. In fact, very basic changes had been taking place for many decades, and the Communist reform of education, viewed in this historical context, epitomises the climax of a revolution that had been set in motion by the Western impact in the middle of the last century. For background information it is worthwhile to examine briefly traditional Chinese higher education and its gradual disintegration under Western pressure.

HIGHER EDUCATION IN TRADITIONAL CHINA

The oldest institution of higher learning in China was the Imperial College established by Emperor Wu-ti of the Han Dynasty in 124 B.C., on recommendation of the famous Confucian scholar, Tung Chung-shu. Professors of the Five Classics—*The Book of Odes, The Book of History, The Book of Changes, The Book of Rites,* and *The Annals*

[2] *Ibid.* 3

of Spring and Autumn were appointed to teach the first group of fifty students, who were chosen from the provinces on recommendation of local magistrates for their knowledge and good morals. These students enjoyed exemption from military service during their period of instruction, and those who mastered one of the Classics were rewarded with official posts. So rapidly did this Imperial College grow that by the Later Han period (A.D. 25–220) the enrolment rose to 30,000 and the faculty to 7,000, with a sprawling campus of 240 buildings and 1,850 rooms.[3]

The Imperial Academy, however, was not the only institution of higher learning; there were a number of private academies which came into prominence during the Later Han period. The number of students at these private academies, which were usually under the direction of eminent scholars, ranged from several hundred to thousands of students. The great master, Ts'ai Hsuan, had as many as 16,000 students registered in his academy, and it was not uncommon for the less famous teachers to have several thousand disciples. The massive enrolments made it impossible for the masters to maintain personal contact with their students, and it was common for the more advanced students to instruct for the masters. Story has it that the gifted student, Cheng K'ang-ch'eng, was unable to see his famous teacher, Ma Yung, for three years; nonetheless he managed to become so erudite as to rival his teacher.[4]

The co-existence of the Imperial College and private academies formed the basic pattern of higher education in traditional China, including the Ch'ing period (1644–1911), the last of the long line of imperial dynasties. The Imperial College of the Ch'ing period, however, was much smaller than that of the Han dynasty; there were only two professors, one Chinese and one Manchu, and six assistants to instruct some 300 scholarship students selected on a geographical basis. The national capital and each of the local provinces nominated one candidate a year, each prefecture two every three years, and each county one every two years. A special selection was made every twelve years, with six candidates chosen from the metropolitan capital area, two from each province, and one from each prefecture and county combined. The professors lectured on the recondite meaning of the classics twice monthly, leaving the bulk of instruction to the six assistants, who held

[3] Li Tsung-t'ung, *Chung-kuo Li-tai Ta-hsueh-shih* (*A History of Higher Education in Successive Chinese Dynasties*) (Taipei: 1958), pp. 7–12.
[4] Ch'en Tung-yüan, *Chung-kuo K'o-chü Shih-tai Chih Chiao-yü* (*Chinese Education in the Period of Civil Service Examinations*) (Shanghai: 1935), p. 47.

classes during the first half of each month. The curriculum was over-whelmingly humanistic: the Confucian *Four Books*,[5] the *Five Classics*, history and philosophy. In addition, daily practice in calligraphy was required of all students, who copied several hundred characters from famous models of the past. Quite frequently high officials, famous scholars, and occasionally even the emperor lectured at the college. Examinations were held at the end of each year, and students who excelled were considered for government positions.[6]

In the provinces the highest institution of learning was the academy (*shu-yuan*), a sort of semi-private and semi-public establishment created at the direction of Emperor Yung-cheng in 1733. Every province was asked to provide one or two academies on an initial court subsidy of 1,000 taels each, and some twenty-two such academies were established.[7] The head of each academy was a renowned scholar, whose modest stipend was offset by the high respect his position commanded. All students were carefully selected from the prefectures and counties on recommendation of local magistrates; no tuition was required. In fact, they were given very handsome allowances, sufficient to meet all expenses for themselves and at times even for their families. The budget of the academies was met largely by private contributions, reinforced by official allocations.[8] The primary objective of the academies was to promote research and unrestricted pursuit of knowledge. Unlike the Imperial College, they did not intend to prepare students for civil service examinations or for official appointments, although the graduates could apply on their own. The curriculum consisted largely of anti-quarian research in the classics and literature. The main function of the professors was to advise the students on their readings and to criticise the results of their research; only occasionally did the professors or visiting scholars present formal lectures. Thus, the *shu-yuan* was essentially a centre of independent study and research under expert guidance. The research papers produced compare favourably with graduate theses of European and American universities.[9]

The major criticism of Chinese higher education in the pre-modern era concerns its overemphasis on the humanities. The students studied the classics, literature, history and philosophy but little or nothing about science and technology as understood in the West. It was only by exception that a student included mathematics and astronomy as part of his broad classical education. The Confucianists stressed the exercise

---

[5] These four books are: *The Confucian Analect, The Book of Mencius, The Great Learning* and the *Book of the Mean*.
[6] Li Tsung-t'ung, *op. cit.,* pp. 105–114.
[7] *Ibid.* p. 118.
[8] *Ibid.* pp. 118–123.
[9] Victor Purcell, *Problems of Chinese Education* (London: 1936), pp. 24–25.

of the mind and deprecated the use of the hands. Mencius said: "Those who labour with their minds govern others; those who labour with their strength are governed by others." [10] Applied science and technology, which definitely involved the use of hands, were considered beneath the dignity of the cultured man. But this attitude gradually changed during the latter half of the nineteenth century, when China came into greater contact with the materialistic civilisation of the West.

THE TRANSITION TO WESTERNISED EDUCATION

From its forcible opening by the West in the middle of the nineteenth century, China learned a bitter lesson: in order to survive in the new world which had been rudely thrust upon it, it must change and learn the secrets of Western strength. Beginning in the 1860s, a "self-strengthening" movement was initiated to learn Western techniques of shipbuilding and gunmaking, but before this could be accomplished it was necessary to learn Western languages. In 1861 the Tungwen Language School was established in Peking. It offered instruction in English and French initially, but later also in Russian and German. A variety of other subjects was gradually added to the curriculum—mathematics, astronomy, international law, meteorology, chemistry and natural philosophy—until in 1869 it took on the appearance of a liberal arts college under the presidency of Dr. W. A. P. Martin, an American missionary from Indiana. With the exception of a few Chinese scholars, the faculty was largely foreign.[11]

The college adopted a two-semester system, the first beginning on January 19 or 20 according to the Chinese lunar calendar, and ending about July 20. After a vacation of five weeks, the second semester opened about August 25 and closed on December 20 or 21; it was followed by a vacation of one month. The period of instruction in the Tungwen College was thus longer than that of Western colleges.[12] In 1879 the enrollment stood at 163, with 38 specialising in English, 25 in French, 15 in Russian, 10 in German, 33 in Mathematics, 6 in Astronomy, 7 in Physics, 9 in International Law, 12 in Chemistry and 8 in Physiology.[13]

The full course of study took eight years, with the first three devoted to foreign languages and the next five to scientific and general studies. The curriculum appeared as follows:

[10] James Legge, *The Chinese Classics*, II, *The Works of Mencius* (Hong Kong: 1960), 3rd ed., pp. 249–250. *Mencius*, III, Part I, Chap. 4, verse 6.
[11] W. A. P. Martin, *Calendar of the Tungwen College* (Peking: 1879) pp. 8–9.
[12] *Ibid*. p. 17.
[13] *Ibid*. p. 10.

First Year:	reading, writing and speaking;
Second Year:	grammar and translation of sentences;
Third Year:	geography, history, economics in translation;
Fourth Year:	arithmetic, algebra, translation of dispatches;
Fifth Year:	natural philosophy, geometry, trigonometry (plane and spherical), exercises in translation;
Sixth Year:	mechanics (theoretical and practical), calculus (differential and integral), navigation and surveying, exercises in translation;
Seventh Year:	chemistry, astronomy, international law, translation of books;
Eighth Year:	geology and mineralogy, political economy, translation of books.[14]

Written examinations were given at the end of each month and final examinations at the end of the year, with prizes awarded to outstanding students. The students were given free board and lodging, and beginning with the second year received a stipend for incidental expenses.[15]

The Tungwen College was not only a training centre for Western learning, but also a research institute for the dissemination of knowledge from abroad. A number of translations were undertaken by foreign professors with the aid of their Chinese students, and in 1873 a small printing office was attached to the college as a sort of primitive " university press." Seventeen major publications appeared in the fields of international law, political economy, chemistry, physics, natural philosophy, human anatomy and English grammar.[16]

Apart from Tungwen College, there were several other language schools in Shanghai and Canton and a telegraph school in Tientsin. A Naval Academy was established in 1880 which offered instruction in geometry, algebra, trigonometry, physics, geography and astronomy.[17] Thus Western science and technology began to make inroads into the Chinese system because of their usefulness in the " self-strengthening " movement; Western humanities, on the other hand, were ignored because of their impractical nature. At this point the Chinese still believed that their own classics, philosophy and literature were superior to those of the West. It was not until toward the end of the nineteenth century that greater recognition was given to Western social science and humanities. In 1895 a Sino-Western College, which offered a four-year curriculum in law, mining, engineering, electrical science and mechanics,

---

14 *Ibid.* p. 18.
15 *Ibid.* p. 24.
16 *Ibid.* p. 25.
17 Ch'en I-lin, *Tsui-chin San-shih-nien Chung-kuo Chiao-yü Shih* (*A History of Chinese Education in the Last Thirty Years*) (Shanghai: 1932), pp. 48–49.

was established on recommendation of the moderniser, Sheng Hsuan-huai.[18] Of far greater importance was the Imperial University in Peking created in 1898, with the avowed objective of integrating Western learning with Chinese learning in keeping with the prevailing slogan, " Chinese learning for fundamentals and Western learning for practical application." The curriculum, formulated by the famous scholar-reformer, Liang Ch'i-ch'ao, after a study of the new Japanese educational system, was divided into general and specialised studies. General studies included Chinese classics, philosophy, Chinese and Western history, and introductory courses in mathematics, physics, political science, geography and literature. Specialised studies included foreign languages and advanced courses in the subjects already introduced under general studies. It can be readily seen that under Western influence, Chinese higher education accepted more and more foreign elements.[19]

In 1903 a special educational commission was appointed to prepare a master plan for Western-style higher education in China. The result was the development of a new educational system which called for the establishment of eight colleges within the universities and several departments within each college. These eight colleges were to be Chinese classics, law, literature, medicine, science, agriculture, engineering and commerce. The College of Science, *e.g.*, was designed to include departments of mathematics, astronomy, physics, chemistry, zoology, botany and geology; and the College of Engineering, departments of architecture, mechanical engineering, naval architecture, military technology, electrical engineering, chemical engineering, explosives, mining and metallurgy.[20] China's old humanistic and moralistic education was rapidly being replaced by a much broader and more balanced Western-style education. With the abolition of the civil service examinations in 1905, all formal vestiges of the old educational system were swept away, and a number of Western and Japanese types of universities and colleges came into being.

After the establishment of the Republic in 1912, all institutions of higher learning were organised along Western lines. The prevailing intellectual tendency, especially after the New Cultural Movement of 1919, was to de-emphasise practical, technical training in favour of abstract subjects such as Western philosophy, literature, political theory, music and art. The university became a centre of pure learning, with a dedicated sense of the value of knowledge for knowledge's sake.

---

[18] *Ibid.* pp. 50, 121.
[19] *Ibid.* p. 52.
[20] Ping-wen Kuo, *The Chinese System of Public Education* (New York: 1915), pp. 78, 82.

Ts'ai Yuan-p'ei, President of the influential Peking University, encouraged theoretical subjects enthusiastically and deliberately discouraged professional training. He separated the College of Engineering from Peking University and incorporated it into the technologically orientated Peiyang University. Peking University became identified with pure research and higher learning of a theoretical nature, where principles and theories were emphasised at the expense of applied subjects.[21] Professional schools were regarded as trade schools of inferior status, with the result that the majority of students turned away from engineering and applied science. For instance, from 1928 to 1932, 38 per cent. of the college students specialised in political science and law, 21.8 per cent. in literature and the arts only 10.2 per cent. and 8.3 per cent. respectively in engineering and science.[22] Nevertheless, there was an increasing awareness of the importance of industrialisation and economic development. Enrolment in science and technology in the 1930s and 1940s rose in inverse proportion to that in law and the arts. By 1938–42, engineering and science specialists accounted for 21 per cent. and 11.3 per cent. of the total college enrolment in the country, whereas law and art specialists dropped to 20.2 per cent. and 11.4 per cent. respectively.[23] The trend toward science and technology continued during the ensuing years until the Communists brought it to a climax; in 1957–58 engineering specialists rose to 40.9 per cent. of total enrolment while political science and law majors dropped to 2.1 per cent.[24] The major objective of this study is to show how this drastic change came about.

PRINCIPLES OF EDUCATIONAL REFORM

Although there was an increasing trend towards science and technology in the 1930s and the 1940s under the Nationalists, there was no centralised planning to coordinate education with economic development. The basic philosophy was still the free development of man according to his natural inclination. Students chose their own specialisation and the state exercised no control over enrolment.

When the Communists rose to power in 1949, they immediately set about to change all this. The old educational system and its philosophy were attacked as decadent, feudalistic, reactionary and reflective of Western imperialistic, capitalistic influences. With all their

21 Feng Yu-lai, " Tui-yü Chung-kuo Chin Wu-shih-nien Chiao-yü Shih-hsiang Chin-chan ti T'i-hui " (" An Appreciation of the Educational Thought in China in the Last Fifty Years ") *Jen-min Chiao-yü* (*People's Education*), No. 4, August 1950, pp. 9–10.
22 Leo A. Orleans, *Professional Manpower and Education in Communist China* (Washington, D.C.: 1961), p. 71.
23 *Ibid.*
24 *Ibid.*

revolutionary zeal, they were determined to wipe out the " public enemy of the Chinese people." [25] Education under the new régime must become an instrument of state to serve the needs of national construction. Institutions of higher learning must cease being ivory towers and become training centres for the personnel needed for industrialisation and modernisation. Pursuit of knowledge must be directly useful to the state. In 1949 leading members of the Communist Party openly proclaimed that " at present the Communist Party has no need for pure theoretical knowledge that is found in existing universities. This type of education is wasteful at the present stage. What we need is training classes of one or two years' duration to give (students) some practical knowledge to enable them to engage in work." [26] Ho Kan-chih, Rector of the Communist North China University, on his first visit to the famous Peking University centre of pure research and theoretical learning, asked the pointed question, " Shall we turn Peking University into a cultural salon, or a school for the training of cadres to serve the people?" [27]

Since the fundamental policy of the state is the achievement of an industrialised society, education must contribute its share toward the realisation of the national goal. Ma Hsü-lun, Minister of Education, laid down the principles of reform in a speech before the First National Conference on Higher Education on June 6, 1950:

> First and foremost, our higher education must tie in closely with the needs of economic, political, cultural, and defence constructions of our nation, and it must first serve our economic construction because economic construction is the basis of national construction. Since our higher education has the objective of cultivating high level construction personnel, we must carry out a systematic, scientific education that is at once practical and theoretical, and on that basis put into practice a specialised scientific and technical education. Institutes of higher learning which offer an education that is void of systematic scientific knowledge are inadmissible. Meanwhile, this type of theoretical education must not commit the same old mistake of " knowledge for knowledge's sake," ignoring the needs of the people and the state.
>
> The second important task is this: on the basis of the practical needs of the various constructions, the Ministry of Education shall co-operate with the respective organisations to strengthen the educational process of the Chinese People's University and other types of institutions of higher learning, and to create all types of technical

25 Ch'ien Chün-tuan, " Tang-ch'ien Chiao-yü Chien-she ti Fang-chen " (" A Guide to Our Immediate Educational Construction), *People's Education*, No. 1, May 1950, pp. 10–11.
26 Pai Chih-chung, *Chung-Kung Chiao-yü P'i-p'an* (*A Critique of Chinese Communist Education*) (Hong Kong: 1955), p. 46.
27 Chung Shih, *Chung-Kung ti Kao-teng Chiao-yü* (*Higher Education in Communist China*) (Hong Kong: 1953), p. 1.

institutes. Within the universities and colleges, we should also create necessary departments, specialised subjects and training classes to meet practical needs.[28]

In this way the Chinese Communists hoped to correct the basic defect of the old educational system, namely, the lack of unity between theory and practice, between knowledge and application.[29]

Russian influence was evident in the Chinese educational reform. During the First National Conference on Higher Education in 1950, a leading Russian educator made an all-out indictment against the Nationalist educational system. Universities and colleges were said to have been developed in the unhealthy atmosphere of semi-colonialism. Western imperialists, seeking to discourage industrialisation in China, turned the attention of the educated classes to the humanities and social sciences, with the result that many Chinese professors acquired the colonial habit of lecturing in English rather than in their own native tongue. Many of the libraries had more foreign language volumes than Chinese, and there was no unified translation of foreign technical terms. Chinese higher education exhibited too much dependence on the West. The Russian expert suggested: " Chinese universities should turn out not abstract scholars but practical specialists." In the Soviet Union, it was not the university but the technical institute which exercised a decisive influence on national construction. Of some eighty institutions of higher learning in the Soviet Union, only thirty are general universities and each of them is situated in a proper geographical area. No two universities are located in the same city, in sharp contrast to the situation in China, where most of the larger universities were concentrated in a few big cities along the coast. He concluded by saying that China should benefit from the Russian experience and reorganise her educational system.[30]

On August 2, 1950, the Ministry of Education announced its " Decisions on Implementing Curriculum Reform in Institutions of Higher Learning." Decision four stipulated that the various departments of universities and colleges should reorganise themselves in line with the long-range needs of national economic and cultural construction. Courses that were important and absolutely necessary should be specialised and strengthened, while those that were repetitive and not absolutely necessary eliminated. Courses should not be offered simply

[28] Hsin Chiao-yü She (New Educational Society), ed. *Wen-pu Kai-ke Kao-teng Chiao-yü (Steady Reform of Higher Education)* (Shanghai: 1950), pp. 4–6.

[29] " Ch'üan-kuo Kao-teng Chiao-yü Hui-i ti Ch'eng-chiu " (" The Accomplishments of the National Conference on Higher Education "), *People's Education*, No. 3, July 1950, p. 9.

[30] Hsin Chiao-yü She, ed., *op. cit.*, pp. 74–76. The address of the Soviet expert is reproduced in *People's Education*, No. 3, July 1950, p. 25 *et seq.*

because of the availability of instructors but should be based on the practical needs of national construction. Decision six spelled out the new mission of the universities and colleges as follows:

> To meet the need for a large quantity of construction personnel, the various institutions of higher learning, under the leadership of the Ministry of Education and in consideration of the actual situation, should assist the operational departments in construction work by setting up all types of specialised courses, training classes, or corresponding classes. Their curricula should not be decided until after consultation with the operational departments concerned.[31]

It is thus clear that the new mission of Chinese higher education is to turn out as many technical experts as quickly as possible. Minister Ma succinctly summarised the " Principles and Tasks of Higher Education " in the following words:

> Education must work for economic construction. The emphasis of economic construction is on industry, and the emphasis of industrial construction is on the heavy industry. This clearly indicates that the primary and foremost task of our higher education should be the cultivation of advanced technicians for industries, mines, and transportation.[32]

INSTITUTIONAL AND INSTRUCTIONAL REFORM

With Russian advice and all the zeal of revolutionaries, the Chinese Communists resolutely and rapidly carried out a gigantic and far-reaching educational reform which included the complete reorganisation of all institutions of higher learning and their educational programmes and methods. Institutional reorganisation involved realignment of colleges and departments, *i.e.* similar colleges and schools of different universities were amalgamated into gigantic polytechnic institutes, in which " specialties " replaced departments as academic units of instruction. A Conference of the Deans of Engineering Colleges, called by the Ministry of Education in Peking on November 3, 1951, adopted a " Plan for the Readjustment of Engineering Colleges in China," under which some of the best-known Chinese universities were either abolished or transformed into technical institutes. For instance, the engineering departments of Yenching University and the Engineering College of Peking University were incorporated into Tsinghua University, which became a gigantic polytechnical university. Meanwhile, the Colleges of Arts, Science and Law of Tsinghua University and the corresponding departments of Yenching University were incorporated into Peking University, which retains its status as a general university. Yenching University,

---

[31] Hsin Chiao-yü She, *op. cit.*, p. 36.
[32] Chung Shih, *Higher Education in Communist China* (Hong Kong: 1953), p. 76. This is an English version of his Chinese work quoted earlier, but there are some differences in content.

an American missionary institution, went out of existence. Similar reorganisation went on in nearly all universities: the Schools of Engineering of Nankai University and Chingku University were incorporated into Tientsin University; the departments of aeronautical engineering of Nanking and Chekiang Universities were incorporated into the School of Aeronautical Engineering of Chiao-tung University, etc.[33]

The overriding principle in the reorganisation seems to be " strength " and " location," *i.e.,* lesser departments or schools of some universities were incorporated into stronger universities of suitable location, so that no one area would have an overabundant supply of schools while others suffered from the lack of them. The two areas most affected by this reorganisation were North China and East China, the former having forty-one institutions of higher learning and the latter fifty-four.[34] The immediate result of the reform was the sudden increase in the number of technical institutes and the corresponding decrease in the number of general universities.

The new higher educational system is characterised by the co-existence of general universities, polytechnical institutes, and technical institutes on the same level without distinction in status. General universities consist of several colleges; polytechnical institutes, of many departments and specialities; and technical institutes, of only one type of specialised training, such as the Petroleum Institute and the Geological Institute. The function of the university is to train research and scientific personnel as well as college and high school teachers; those of the polytechnical and technical institutes, to train engineers and technicians of all types.[35] The general universities do not enjoy a status superior to the technical institutes, as they did under the old educational system.[36]

In addition to institutional reform, a new approach to instruction was adopted: the " specialty " (*spetsial'nost*) replaced the department as the new academic unit. Courses offered in the Nationalist educational system were said to have been dictated by departmental needs and availability of instructors. Duplication was inevitable, and worse yet, courses offered by the instructors often bore no relation to the practical needs of the society. The introduction of " specialties " was designed to correct the mistakes of waste, impracticality, and duplication, because they set up clear-cut educational objectives for the training of needed

33 *Ibid.* pp. 43–44.
34 *Ibid.* p. 44.
35 Chung Shih, *op. cit.* (Chinese version), p. 21.
36 Tseng Chao-lun, " Kao-teng Hsueh-hsiso ti ' Chuan-yeh ' She-chih Wen-ti " (" The Question of Setting up ' Specialty ' in Institutions of Higher Learning "), *People's Education*, No. 29, September 1952. p. 6.

personnel in national construction. More and better qualified men could be turned out quickly through this process. The adoption of the "specialty," a proud Soviet contribution to knowledge and education, was hailed as an epochal event in Chinese educational history.[37]

What is a specialty? It is intensive training in a particular subject which prepares a man for a specialised profession. Each specialty has a definite educational programme fixed by the state according to the needs of national construction. All courses within a specialty are required; there is no choice. However, capable and healthy students may take additional courses in specialties other than their own. Each specialty may further be divided into two or more "specialisations" (*spetsializatsii*) for greater concentration on the subject-matter. The difference between the several "specialisations" within the same specialty lies solely in a few different courses in the upper division curriculum.[38]

Several specialties of an allied nature are grouped into a department for administrative purposes. The specialty and specialisation, not being in themselves administrative bodies, have no chairman. Administrative functions are handled by the departmental chairman, but the department does not enjoy a hierarchical superiority over them. The department and the specialty co-exist for the benefit of the division of responsibility. Smaller departments may have only one specialty, and larger ones several but never more than twelve or thirteen. Administratively speaking, there are only two levels: the university or institute president, and the department chairman. The deanship of the old college is dispensed with.[39]

In addition to specialties within a department, there are seminars for advanced research, composed of professors and graduate students. All administrative problems of these seminars are handled by the departmental chairman, allowing the seminar participants complete freedom for research. The structure of an institution of higher learning appears as follows:[40]

University
(or technical institute)—department specialties—specialisations
                      —research seminars

The type and numbers of specialties in each institution of higher learning are decided by the state and cannot be changed locally. The specialties offered in Chinese higher education total several hundred.[41]

[37] *Ibid.*
[38] *Ibid.*
[39] *Ibid.* p. 7.
[40] *Ibid.* pp. 7–8.
[41] Orleans, pp. 209–213.

The defect of the specialty is, of course, its narrowness of training. The graduate of a specialty may be an expert in boiler-making, highway bridge-building, or cement mixing, but he knows relatively little outside his own field. In defence of the new approach, Professor Chou P'ei-yuan of Tsinghua Polytechnical University stated:

> The undergraduate training in English and American universities is very general, and is euphemistically called " high-level general education." I formerly considered it enough to give students only basic knowledge in school, letting them learn about specialised knowledge in factories after their graduation. This type of thinking was doubtless the vestige of capitalistic educational thought, which is incompatible with the society of New Democracy. Let us look at the advanced experience of the Soviet Union. The educational policy of Soviet institutions of higher learning is to train youth on the basis of making practical application from a highly theoretical foundation. What the student learns is very detailed and very specialised in order that after his graduation he may enter a factory at once to take over a certain type of work. The higher education method of New China must develop in that direction.[42]

Professor Chou regretted his earlier attitude of over-reliance on pure science as the basis of industrialisation.

In addition to the specialty, a number of short-term courses were established to meet the immediate needs of industrialisation. An eight-month course on agricultural water conservation was offered at Tsinghua Polytechnical University to train specialists in that field. The whole spirit of the new system was to graduate the maximum number of technicians in the least possible time. Tseng Chao-lun, Vice-Minister of Education, declared in 1952:

> We must create a great number of specialised courses to train a greater number of specialised cadres for construction in shorter time. Our policy for the enrolment of students this year is based on the double consideration of quick training in a fixed period and long-term cultivation. We ought to create a great number of specialised courses, with a more excellent, concentrated, specialised yet simplified curriculum, so that students may complete sooner what needs to be learned, and fulfil the pressing needs of the country for the moment.[43]

After the institutional reorganisation, all private universities and colleges were abolished. General universities dwindled from sixty-five in 1950 to fourteen in 1954, while specialised institutes mushroomed: thirty-nine polytechnical institutes, thirty-one teachers' colleges, twenty-nine institutes of agriculture and forestry, twenty-nine medical schools, four schools of law and political science, six schools of finance and

[42] Chung Shih, *op. cit.* (Chinese version), p. 29.
[43] *Ibid.* p. 39.

economics, eight schools of languages, fifteen schools of art, five schools of physical education, and two schools of minority races.[44]

Administratively, specialties have replaced departments as academic units of instruction. Departments have taken the place of the old schools or colleges, and institutes, the place of the old universities. The character of Chinese higher education has completely been changed.

Reform of educational materials and method was no less drastic than that of institution. Western textbooks, reference works and teaching techniques were considered " unprogressive, mutilated, rotten and reactionary," serving the interests of capitalist-monopolists rather than those of the toiling masses. Western scientific theories and techniques, the Communists insisted, could not promote rapid progress, as is clearly shown in the contest between the West and the Soviet Union. Chinese universities and technical institutes must therefore shun all Western teaching materials and methods in favour of those of the Soviet Union. Faculty members of Chinese institutions of higher learning were urged to reorganise their lecture notes and adopt textbooks of Soviet origin. The People's University mobilised all instructors who understood Russian to translate and edit Russian materials for use in classes. Between September 1950 and August 1955 they completed more than two thousand syllabi, lecture notes and references, which were printed in 7,650,000 copies for distribution to more than a hundred institutions of higher learning. The Ministry of Education decreed that the new lecture notes and syllabi prepared in the various institutions be exchanged to achieve maximum use. In 1953 some 147 lecture notes were circulated, and in the following year the number increased to 441, of which 245 were in the field of technology, 110 in arts and sciences, and eighty-six in agriculture.[45]

The Academy of Sciences and the Central Library collected Russian texts and reference works for translation. Faculty members of eighty-five institutions of higher learning were mobilised to do translations. Those who knew Russian well translated individually, those who did not, collectively. By the end of 1953, more than 281 titles were translated and published, of which 177 were in technology, roughly 62 per cent. of the total number of projects.[46] By 1957 some 12,400 Russian works were said to have been translated and published.[47] As a result, many institutions of higher learning adopted Russian materials, either completely or partially, for class use. In 1954 thirty-four of the sixty-one

---

[44] Li Yu-nung, *Kung-fei Kao-teng Chiao-yü Chih Yen-chiu* (*A Study of Higher Education of the Communist Rebels*) (Taipei: 1957), p. 98.
[45] *Ibid.* p. 74, quoting *Kuang-ming Jih-pao* (*Kuang-ming Daily*), April 3, 1954.
[46] *Ibid.* p. 73, quoting from *Kuang-ming Daily*, January 25, 1954.
[47] Orleans, pp. 12–13.

courses offered in the science departments of Shantung University used Russian materials entirely.[48]

Reform of examination methods was also radical. Classroom examination under supervision of the instructor is considered fascistic and despotic, comparable to a policeman watching convicts. Apart from the question of the students' honour and dignity, the instructor is unnecessarily given the chance to intimidate them. Such a system has no place in the People's Democracy. A new "honour" system has been instituted in which instructors do not attend the examinations and the students agree not to cheat. Prior to each examination, the instructor must be "democratic" about it by pointing out the general pattern and scope of the examination and the essential points to be covered. Collective discussion of these points takes place among the students, who then draft a set of questions for the instructor to approve, after which the questions are sent back to students for examination. Model answers are provided by the instructor for the students to check against their answers after the examination. The instructor usually grades a few typical papers as examples and the rest of the students grade their own papers according to the model answers. The grade given by the student himself is subject to class discussion and vote by majority rule. In case of dispute among students, the instructor intervenes and grades the paper himself. Another "democratic" method of grading is the division of the class into several groups which grade each other's papers.[49]

After all this reform, what is a Chinese college education like, and how does it compare with its counterpart in the United States and the Soviet Union? A typical curriculum of the technical institute in China is as follows:

1. Political studies: 400 hours, about 10 per cent. of total.
2. Basic science: higher mathematics, physics and chemistry.
3. Basic technology: about 34 per cent. of total.
4. Specialised courses: 28 per cent.
5. Russian: three years.
6. Thesis planning: 10–12 weeks.
7. Experiment: 16–28 weeks.
8. Physical education: two hours weekly for first and second year undergraduates.
9. Vacations: six weeks in summer and two weeks in winter.[50]

The leading technical institute in China is the Tsinghua Polytechnic

48 Li Yu-nung, *op. cit.*, pp. 72–73, quoting *Kuang-ming Daily*, April 17, 1954.
49 Pai Chih-chung, *op. cit.*, pp. 150–152.
50 Yang Min-hua, " Kao-teng Hsueh-hsiao Kung-k'o Ni-ting Chiao-yü Chi-hua Chung ti Wen-ti Ho Ching-yen " (" Problems and Experience in Preparing the Educational Programme for Higher Institutions of Technology "), *People's Education*, No. 31, November 1952, pp. 22–23.

University, originally founded as Tsinghua College in 1911 from the United States refunds of the Boxer Rebellion indemnity. In 1957 it had an enrolment of 9,000 and a faculty of 1,000. How does its instruction compare with the leading technical institute in the United States, say, the California Institute of Technology, and a counterpart in the Soviet Union? The following chart provides a comparison of the instructional hours in several major categories [51]:

(In hours)

	Tsing-hua Polytechnical University			Soviet University, 1955	California Institute of Technology, 1956
	1957 (plan)	1955	Pre-1950		
Degree	Engineer	Engineer	B.S.	Engineer	B.S.
Basic courses ...	1,177	1,330	976	1,376	1,167
Technical courses ...	821	893	960	1,082	921
Specialised courses ...	930	1,069	1,072	1,096	367
Average study time per week	26	31	28·5	33	26
Average lecture time per week	17	17·4	18·1	18·7	16

It would appear that except for specialised courses, Chinese training is comparable in hours to that of the United States. But the question is whether the quality of instruction is similar. At Tsinghua Polytechnical University, the first year is devoted to basic courses, and the second to technical subjects. Starting from the third year, classwork is negligible. The Chinese consider this system more " to the point " than the American. At the California Institute of Technology, they pointed out, students in civil, mechanical, electrical and chemical engineering take the same required courses in the first year, and the civil and mechanical engineering students spend 199 hours " unnecessarily " in organic and inorganic chemistry. It is even " worse " at Cornell, where engineering students are required to take such superfluous courses as public speaking, price control and market reports, etc.[52] Of course, the differences between the Chinese and American systems stem from very different educational philosophies: the Chinese want to produce a maximum number of specialists as fast as possible, while the Americans want to produce " well-rounded " engineers, ideally speaking. From the American standpoint, the major defect of the Chinese system is its over-specialisation and narrowness of the scope. A student specialising in railway bridge construction may know everything about the railway bridge, but probably little about the railway

[51] *People's Daily*, February 26, 1957.   [52] *Ibid.*

itself or a highway bridge. In the pre-Communist days when American influence was strong in China, a civil engineering student would have been required to study railway construction, bridge structure and water conservation.

EXPANSION OF SCHOOLS AND ENROLMENT

To meet the anticipated needs of national construction, the Chinese Communists carried out an unprecedented expansion of school building and student enrolment. From 1949 to 1958, the enrolment increased from 117,000 to 441,000.[53] New school buildings were constructed with an area of 1,100 million square metres, which is three times as much as the total area of school buildings in the previous fifty years combined.[54] The enrolment in 1958–59 increased to 660,000, and the graduates to 62,200, as compared with 18,000 in 1949–50.[55]

In reaffirming its objective of developing " engineering colleges and national science departments in universities," the first Five-Year Plan of 1953–57 called for the establishment of sixty new institutions of higher learning, including one general university, fifteen engineering colleges, four colleges of agriculture, forestry and meteorology, two colleges of economics and finance, three colleges of political science and law, nineteen teachers' colleges, six medical and pharmacological colleges, two language institutes, four institutes of physical culture, and four colleges of fine arts.[56] The planned enrolment and graduates in the various fields were as follow [57]:

Course	Planned Enrolment 1953–1957	Percentage of Students Enrolled	Number of Graduates 1953–1957	Percentage of Graduates	Number of Students in 1957	Percentage of Students	Ratio of 1957 to 1952 (per cent.)
Total	543,300	100·0	283,000	100·0	434,600	100·0	227·4
Engineering ...	214,600	39·5	94,900	33·6	177,600	40·9	266·8
Ariculture and forestry	41,800	7·7	18,800	6·6	37,200	8·6	240·7
Economics and finance ...	16,400	3·0	25,500	9·0	12,700	2·9	57·9
Political science and and law ...	10,600	2·0	4,800	1·7	9,300	2·1	242·3
Public health ...	57,600	10·6	26,600	9·4	54,800	12·6	221·4
Physical culture ...	6,000	1·1	2,800	1·0	3,600	0·8	1,107·7
Natural sciences ...	32,600	6·0	13,800	4·9	27,100	6·2	283·4
Arts	29,300	5·4	21,600	7·6	20,400	4·7	150·9
Pedagogy	130,700	24·0	70,400	24·9	89,000	20·5	282·0
Fine Arts	3,700	0·7	3,800	1·3	2,900	0·7	79·3

Enrolment in engineering, which occupied the largest percentage, was further divided in the following thirteen specialised fields.[58]

For footnotes [53] to [58] see p. 146.

Specialised Field	Planned Enrolment 1953-1957	Percentage of Students Enrolled	Number of Graduates 1953-1957	Percentage of Graduates	Number of Students in 1957	Percentage of Students	Ratio of 1957 to 1952 (per cent.)
Total	214,600	100·0	94,900	100·0	177,600	100·0	266·8
Geology and prospecting	17,500	8·1	10,000	10·5	12,500	7·1	219·2
Mining and mine management ...	16,000	7·4	7,600	8·1	12,400	7·0	258·8
Power	15,500	7·2	7,500	7·9	13,300	7·5	232·8
Metallurgy ...	10,000	4·7	3,200	3·4	8,900	5·0	398·4
Machine and tool making	54,100	25·2	19,300	20·4	46,100	26·0	395·2
Manufacture of electric motors and electrical supplies ...	9,400	4·4	1,700	1·8	8,800	5·0	870·2
Chemical technology	10,600	5·0	5,100	5·4	9,100	5·1	219·3
Paper making and lumbering ...	700	0·3	600	0·6	600	0·3	127·1
Light industry ...	4,400	2·0	3,300	3·4	3,600	2·0	138·0
Surveying, drafting, meteorology and hydrology ...	4,600	2·2	2,100	2·2	3,500	1·9	273·0
Building construction and city planning ...	37,400	17·4	25,100	26·4	28,200	15·9	163·5
Transport, posts and telecommunications	9,600	4·5	4,700	5·0	8,500	4·8	200·5
Others	24,800	11·6	4,700	4·9	22,100	12·4	406·2

From these tables one can readily see that the first Five-Year Plan called for the enrolment of 543,300 students and the graduation of 283,000, of which the engineering enrolment and graduates were set at 214,600 and 94,900, respectively. The second Five-Year Plan of 1958–62 called for a further increase of 80 per cent. in enrolment to 850,000 and 500,000 graduates.[59] The rising figures of actual enrolment from 1949 to 1960 may be seen in the following charts [60]:

[53] Joseph C. Kun, *Selection and Enrolment of New Students in Higher Educational Institutions of Communist China*. Mimeo. draft, Center for International Studies, Massachusetts Institute of Technology, July 1961, p. 33.

[54] *People's Daily*, September 19, 1959, p. 2.

[55] The State Statistical Bureau, *Ten Great Years* (Peking: 1960), p. 192.

[56] *First Five-Year Plan for Development of the National Economy of the People's Republic of China in 1953–57* (Peking: 1956), p. 177.

[57] *Ibid.* p. 178.

[58] *Ibid.* pp. 179–180.

[59] Chou En-lai, *Kuan-yü Fa-chan Kuo-min Ching-chi ti Ti-erh-ko Wu-nien Chi-hua ti Chien-i ti Pao-kao* (*A Report on the Recommendation of the Second Five-Year Plan for the Development of the National Economy*) (Peking: 1956), p. 19.

[60] *Ten Great Years*, pp. 192–194; *Jen-min Shou-ts'e* (*People's Handbook*), 1957, p. 583; Orleans, *op. cit.*, pp. 61, 68–69, 71.

School year						Entrants	Enrolment	Graduates
1948–49	...	...	...	...	...	—	—	21,000
1949–50	...	...	...	...	...	—	117,000	18,000
1950–51	...	...	...	...	...	35,000	137,000	19,000
1951–52	...	...	...	...	...	35,000	153,000	32,000
1952–53	...	...	...	...	...	65,900	191,000	48,000
1953–54	...	...	...	...	...	71,400	212,000	47,000
1954–55	...	...	...	...	...	94,000	253,000	53,000
1955–56	...	...	...	...	...	96,200	288,000	63,000
1956–57	...	...	...	...	...	165,600	403,000	56,000
1957–58	...	...	...	...	...	107,000	441,000	72,000
1958–59	...	...	...	...	...	152,000	660,000	62,200
1959–60	...	...	...	...	...	270,000	810,000	—

Higher education: enrolment by field, 1928–58

School year	Engineering	Science	Agriculture and forestry	Health	Political science and law	Education	Finance and economics	Literature and arts	Total
1928–29	2,777	1,910	1,035	977	9,466	1,661	1,695	5,464	24,985
1929–30	3,144	2,191	1,294	1,138	11,431	2,082	1,667	6,171	29,118
1930–31	3,734	2,872	1,419	1,350	15,899	2,561	2,025	7,706	37,566
1931–32	4,084	3,530	1,413	1,800	16,487	4,231	2,156	10,066	43,767
1932–33	4,439	4,159	1,557	1,852	14,523	3,368	2,867	9,372	42,137
1933–34	5,263	4,722	1,690	2,458	12,913	4,004	3,167	8,703	42,920
1934–35	5,910	5,324	1,831	263	11,029	4,059	3,033	7,921	39,370
1935–36	5,514	6,272	2,163	3,041	8,794	2,741	2,951	9,596	41,072
1936–37	6,989	5,485	2,590	3,395	8,253	3,292	3,143	8,364	41,511
1937–38	5,768	4,458	1,802	12,386	7,125	2,451	1,846	4,140	39,976
1938–39	7,321	4,802	2,257	3,623	7,024	3,027	2,809	4,852	35,715
1939–40	9,501	5,828	2,994	4,322	8,777	3,796	3,690	5,137	44,045
1940–41	11,226	6,090	3,675	4,271	11,172	4,823	5,199	5,920	52,376
1941–42	12,584	6,202	4,673	4,607	12,085	5,919	7,231	6,156	59,457
1942–43	13,129	5,852	5,038	5,108	12,598	7,626	7,691	7,055	64,097
1943–44	14,582	6,099	5,599	5,714	15,377	8,804	9,039	8,455	73,669
1944–45	15,047	6,177	6,042	6,343	15,990	10,466	9,742	9,102	78,909
1945–46	15,200	6,480	6,380	6,291	17,774	11,709	9,697	9,967	83,498
1946–47	24,389	9,091	9,364	11,452	28,276	18,389	13,851	14,524	129,336
1947–48	27,579	10,060	10,179	11,855	37,780	21,439	17,698	18,446	155,036
1949–50	30,300	7,000	10,400	15,200	7,300	12,300	19,400	14,600	116,500
1950–51	38,500	—	—	17,400	—	13,300	—	—	138,700
1951–52	48,500	—	—	21,400	—	18,200	—	—	155,600
1952–53	66,600	9,600	15,500	24,700	3,800	31,800	22,000	17,100	191,100
1953–54	80,000	12,400	15,400	29,000	3,900	41,100	13,500	16,900	212,200
1954–55	95,000	17,100	15,900	33,900	4,000	55,000	11,200	20,900	253,000
1955–56	109,600	20,000	21,600	36,500	4,800	63,000	11,400	21,100	288,000
1956–57	150,000	25,000	—	—	—	99,000	—	—	408,000
1957–58	177,600	27,100	37,200	54,800	9,300	92,600	12,700	23,300	434,600

Higher education: enrolment by field as percentage of total, 1928–58

School year	Engin-eering	Science	Agri-culture and forestry	Health	Political science and law	Edu-cation	Finance and eco-nomics	Litera-ture and arts	Total
1928–32	10·2	8·3	3·8	4·0	38·2	7·8	5·9	21·8	100·0
1933–37	14·4	12·8	4·9	10·5	23·5	8·1	6·9	18·9	100·0
1938–42	21·0	11·3	7·3	8·6	20·2	9·8	10·4	11·4	100·0
1943–47	18·6	7·3	7·2	8·0	22·1	13·6	11·6	11·6	100·0
1949–50	26·0	6·0	8·9	13·0	6·3	10·6	16·7	12·5	100·0
1950–51	27·8	—	—	12·5	—	9·6	—	—	100·0
1951–52	31·2	—	—	13·8	—	11·7	—	—	100·0
1952–53	34·8	5·0	8·1	12·9	2·0	16·7	11·5	9·0	100·0
1953–54	37·7	5·8	7·2	13·7	1·8	19·4	6·4	8·0	100·0
1954–55	37·5	6·8	6·3	13·4	1·6	21·8	4·4	8·2	100·0
1955–56	38·1	6·9	7·5	12·7	1·7	21·9	3·9	7·3	100·0
1956–57	36·8	6·3	—	—	—	24·3	—	—	100·0
1957–58	40·9	6·2	8·6	12·6	2·1	21·3	2·9	5·4	100·0

High school graduates who apply for college admission must pass a medical test and an entrance examination conducted uniformly throughout the country by the Ministry of Education. In 1954, for example, seventy-eight examination centres were set up to select 90,000 students. The subjects for examination were divided into two categories: (1) for specialists in science, technology, hygiene, agriculture and forestry: Chinese, political knowledge, mathematics, physics, chemistry, biology and a foreign language, and (2) for specialists in the humanities, social science, law, physical culture and art: Chinese, political knowledge, history, geography and a foreign language.[61]

Applicants of worker or peasant origin receive preferential treatment and those with high political consciousness might even be exempted from matriculation examinations. In 1951–52, of the total 153,000 students, 19·1 per cent. were of worker and peasant origins, and in 1955–56, the percentage increased to 29·2 per cent. of the total 288,000, and in 1958–59, to 48 per cent. of the total 660,000.[62] Other non-high school graduates who entered colleges included active party cadres under thirty years of age with two years of senior high school background, demobilised servicemen, and government employees who had participated in revolutionary activities for three years. Children of revolutionary martyrs, national minorities, or overseas Chinese also received special attention.[63] In 1952, of the 65,893 college entrants, nearly half came from these categories; the party cadres alone accounted for 8,000.[64]

Since 1949, China has graduated an average of 45,000 students per

[61] Li Yu-nung, *op. cit.*, pp. 106–107.
[62] Kun, *op. cit.*, p. 37.
[63] Chu Po-ch'i, *Ta-lu Hsueh-fu Hsin Mien-mu* (*New Appearances of Schools on Mainland China*) (Hong Kong: 1953), p. 8.
[64] Chung Shih, *op. cit.* (Chinese version), p. 40.

year. A detailed breakdown of the graduate figures by fields is as follows: [65]

Graduates of institutions of higher education: number and percentage by field of specialisation, 1949–58.

Year	Engineering		Science		Agriculture and forestry		Health	
	Number	Per cent.	Number	Per cent.	Number	Per cent.	Number	Per cent.
1948–49	4,752	22·6	1,584	7·5	1,718	8·2	1,314	6·3
1949–50	4,711	26·2	1,468	8·1	1,477	8·2	1,391	7·7
1950–51	4,416	23·2	1,488	7·8	1,538	8·1	2,366	12·5
1951–52	10,213	31·9	2,215	6·9	2,361	7·4	2,636	8·3
1952–53	14,565	30·3	1,753	3·7	2,633	5·5	2,948	6·1
1953–54	15,596	33·2	802	1·7	3,532	7·5	4,527	9·6
1954–55	18,614	33·8	2,015	3·7	2,614	4·8	6,840	12·4
1955–56	22,047	35·0	3,978	6·3	3,541	5·6	5,403	8·6
1956–57	17,162	30·6	3,524	6·3	3,104	5·5	6,200	11·1
1957–58	17,499	24·3	4,645	6·4	3,513	4·9	5,393	7·5
Total	129,575	30·1	23,472	5·4	26,031	6·0	39,018	9·1

Year	Education		Finance and Economics		Literature and arts		Others		Total	
	Number	Per cent.	Number	Per cent.	Number	Per cent.	Number	Per cent.	Number	Percent.
1948–49	1,890	9·0	3,137	14·9	2,521	12·0	4,084	19·5	21,000	100·0
1949–50	624	3·5	3,305	18·4	2,306	12·8	2,718	15·1	18,000	100·0
1950–51	1,206	6·4	3,638	19·1	2,169	11·4	2,179	11·5	19,000	100·0
1951–52	3,077	9·6	7,263	22·7	1,676	5·2	2,559	8·0	32,000	100·0
1952–53	9,650	20·1	10,530	21·9	3,306	6·9	2,625	5·5	48,000	100·0
1953–54	10,551	22·5	6,033	12·8	2,683	5·7	3,276	7·0	47,000	100·0
1954–55	12,133	22·1	4,699	8·5	4,679	8·5	3,406	6·2	55,000	100·0
1955–56	17,243	27·4	4,460	7·1	4,025	6·4	2,303	3·6	63,000	100·0
1956–57	15,948	28·5	3,651	6·5	4,294	7·7	2,117	3·8	56,000	100·0
1957·58	31,595	43·9	2,349	3·3	4,131	5·7	2,875	4·0	72,000	100·0
Total	103,917	24·1	49,065	11·4	31,790	7·4	28,132	6·5	431,000	100·0

It is obvious from these tables that because of the national emphasis on industrialisation, engineering, health, and education, graduates multiplied rapidly, while the number of graduates in political science and law as well as arts and literature fell sharply from their pre-war highs. The graduates, whatever their fields, cannot choose their own professions but are sent to specific destinations by the State Economic Commission. For instance, the assignment of the 1956 graduates was made in the following fashion:

1. 15,163 or 24·31 per cent. were sent abroad for advanced training, or to the Academy of Sciences, or to the universities to work as instructors or graduate students, etc.

2. 15,438 or 24·74 per cent. were assigned to the various departments and agencies of the Ministry of Heavy Industry.

3. 8,706 or 13·96 per cent. were assigned to light industry, communication, transportation and agriculture, etc.

4. 1,651 or 2·65 per cent. were sent to the army.

[65] *Ten Great Years*, p. 196; also Orleans, *op. cit.*, pp. 74–75.

5. 21,425 or 34·34 per cent. were sent to the various provinces, etc.[66]

Although the enrolment figure has risen continuously since 1949, a particularly significant increase was recorded in 1958, the Great Leap Forward year in which the government pushed all productive activities to new heights. Education was no exception. Hundreds of " Red and Expert Universities " came into being to train Red experts—in the belief that experts must be Red in order to be good and reliable.[67] As a result, the number of colleges and universities increased overnight to 1,065. These " Red and Expert Universities " gave trustworthy party workers and cadres special training in industry, agriculture, forestry, animal husbandry, fishing and sericulture, etc. Typical of such institutions is the Communist Labour University in Kiangsi Province, which was established in August, 1958, with thirty branches in the province, a planned enrolment of 50,000 and an ultimate goal of 400,000 in the next few years. Students were to divide their time between work and study; regular courses were to run for four years and specialised courses for two. The president of the university is none other than the secretary of the provincial party committee, and the Vice-President is the provincial Vice-Governor.[68]

Needless to say, such spare time " universities " were subject to criticism from the regular institutions of higher learning, but the party defended them from the standpoint of national need: all possible means to hasten industrialisation must be undertaken. The *People's Daily* of June 17, 1958, explained:

We must realise that if our industry is to overtake and surpass Britain in the output of steel and other important industrial products within fifteen years or less, and if our agriculture is to outstrip that of the capitalist countries as soon as possible on the basis of the fulfillment of the national agricultural programme ahead of schedule, development of our culture and our education at a tremendous rate is necessary.[69]

In the spirit of the " Great Leap Forward " movement, a vast number of schools were set up in industries, while a number of workshops were created on school sites. On March 15, 1958, the Ministry of Education decreed that all college students in urban areas must work in factories or plants and those in rural areas must work on farms. Everybody must participate in production. Colleges were instructed to set up factories and farms, while factories and plants were ordered to form schools to integrate work with study. On September 19, 1958, the State

[66] *Jen-min Shou-ts'e,* 1957, p. 587.
[67] Theodore Hsi-en Chen, " Education and indoctrination in Red China," *Current History,* XLI, No. 241, September 1961, p. 163.
[68] J. C., " Higher Education in Communist China: Some Recent Development," *The World Today,* January 1959, p. 39.
[69] *Ibid.* p. 40.

Council ordered that "productive labour must be listed as a regular subject in the curriculums of all schools, and each student must participate in manual labour for a prescribed length of time." [70] The Ministry repeatedly assured the people that this programme would not lower the standards of existing schools but, on the contrary, elevate mass culture. Thus, Tsinghua Polytechnical University's faculty and students set up 61 factories and workshops, a designing company, and an engineering company. The North-east China Engineering College planned to turn out 10,000 tons of iron, 20,000 tons of steel, and 30,000 tons of rolled steel from its own plants annually. The Shenyang Medical College engaged in manufacturing microscopes, medical apparatus and medicine. The workshops of the North-east China Music Academy manufactured musical instruments. [71]

If colleges were proud of their plants and production, factories and farms were no less proud of the "colleges" they set up. The Liming Machinery Works in Shenyang founded a "work-while-you-study" technical institute attended by workers of middle-school background. They worked four hours and studied six hours daily, hoping to reach the standard of a college graduate in three or four years. [72]

With the mushrooming of the "Red and Expert Universities" all over the country, the Chinese Communists boasted of being able to provide education for all who qualify within fifteen years. With everybody engaged in production in one form or another, the distinction between brain workers and brawn workers has disappeared, they said. Everybody is an industrial worker, and hence a proletarian. The Chinese Communists were tremendously proud at the thought that they were marching toward a classless society, and that they were closer to the portals of true Communism than the Russians.

THE DEVELOPMENT OF SCIENCE

While the Chinese Communists lay great emphasis on technology because of its immediate usefulness in economic development, they did not lose sight of pure science as the basis of technology. Premier Chou En-lai stated in his 1956 *Report on the Question of Intellectuals*:

> We are constantly saying that our science and culture are backward, but we seldom stop to consider just where our backwardness lies. Comrades: I want to speak more particularly here about science, not only because science is a decisive factor in our national defence, economy, and culture, but also because during the last twenty or thirty years, world science has made particularly great and rapid progress,

70 Orleans, *op. cit.*, p. 23.
71 J. C., *op. cit.*, p. 42.
72 Orleans, *op. cit.*, p. 23.

leaving us far behind in scientific development. . . . We must catch up with this advanced level of world science. And, bearing in mind that while we are forging ahead others are also advancing rapidly, we must give our best to this task. Only by mastering the most advanced sciences can we ensure ourselves of an impregnable national defence, a powerful and up-to-date economy, and adequate means to join the Soviet Union and the other People's Democracies in defeating the imperialist powers, either in the peaceful competition or in any aggressive war which the enemy may unleash.[73]

Almost immediately after its rise to power in 1949, the Chinese Communist Party sent a trusted member, Ch'en Po-ta, Deputy Chief of the Propaganda Department and Vice-President of the Marx-Lenin Institute, to Moscow to consult with S. I. Vavilov, President of the Soviet Academy of Sciences, on the development of science in China. Ch'en studied the organisation and structure of the Soviet Academy of Sciences and Russian methods of scientific planning. On November 1, 1949, Peking established the Chinese Academy of Science " to direct and promote the development of science," with the noted scholar Kuo Mo-jo as president. Kuo made a personal visit to the Soviet Union, and upon his return, Vavilov's *Thirty Years of Soviet Science* was translated into Chinese.[74]

As an institution the Academy of Science can be traced back to the Academia Sinica established by the Nationalists in 1928 in Peking, Shanghai and Nanking, and the National Academy of Science in Peking. The new Communist Academy of Science began in 1949 with 14 research institutes and 660 members, but it grew rapidly. By 1957 its institutes numbered 68, with a research staff of 5,506 and an estimated 17,336 employees. In 1959 the Academy had 105 institutes, 7,000 researchers, and 40,000 employees.[75] The budget of the Academy is also on a continuously upward curve, rising from $1.22 million in 1950 to $37 million in 1957.[76]

The Academy has five academic departments: (1) Physics, Chemistry and Mathematics, (2) Biology, (3) Earth science, consisting of geology, geography, geophysics and meteorology, (4) Technical science, and (5) Philosophy and social science. Each of these departments maintains a number of institutes, in which most of the research is conducted. For instance, the Department of Physics, Chemistry and Mathematics maintains the Institute of Mathematics, Institute of Mechanics, Institute of Computing Technology, Institute of Atomic Energy, Institute of

[73] Quoted in Hu Chang-tu, *China: Its People, Its Society, Its Culture* (New Haven: 1960), p. 439.
[74] John M. H. Lindbeck, " Organisation and Development of Science," in *Sciences in Communist China*, 1961, pp. 8–9.
[75] *Ibid.* pp. 16–17.
[76] *Ibid.* p. 12.

Physics, Institute of Chemistry and Institute of Macromolecular Chemistry.[77] In 1957 some 254 prominent scientists were made members of the five academic departments, while most of the other leading scientists in the country became members or affiliates of the Academy. In addition to pure research, these departments also accept a limited number of advanced graduate students, for a four-year programme leading to the Associate Doctorate. To be qualified, the student must be a graduate of a university or technical institute, under 40 years of age, and already have had two years of working experience in science and technology. In 1956, 321 candidates were enrolled in the Associate Doctoral Programme.[78]

The Academy of Science also operates a Translation and Publication Department which runs a Science Publishing House. Eighty-nine journals are regularly published and during the period from 1953 to 1957 four million copies of 1,106 books were printed. There is also constant exchange of journals with the Soviet Union. In 1956–57 nine million dollars were spent to secure Western scientific works and periodicals, a sum larger than that spent by Russia, Japan or India for the same purpose in the same period.[79]

By 1956 the compelling needs of economic development led Peking to adopt a Twelve-Year Science Plan, prepared under the direction of Marshal Ch'en I by 200 Chinese scientists and seventeen Soviet scientists under the leadership of A. I. Nikhaylov.[80] A total of 582 problems were identified for research in the following twelve categories: 1. Peaceful use of atomic energy. 2. New electronics techniques. 3. Jet propulsion. 4. Automation in production and precision equipment. 5. Surveying and prospecting for petroleum and other materials. 6. Exploration of mineral resources. 7. Metallurgy studies. 8. Study and development of fuels and heavy machines. 9. Technical problems associated with exploration of the Yellow and Yangtze Rivers. 10. Study of agriculture, with emphasis on mechnisation, electrification, and the use of chemicals. 11. Study of important diseases. 12. Basic theoretical problems in natural sciences.[81]

The Twelve-Year Science Plan calls for the training of 10,500 advanced scientists and two million technical experts by 1967.[82] Toward this end a new University of Science and Technology was created in 1958 to give exceptionally bright students the best scientific education available. The new university has thirteen modern departments: nuclear physics

77 *Ibid.* pp. 35–42.
78 Li Yu-nung, *op. cit.*, p. 95.
79 Lindbeck, *op. cit.*, p. 14.
80 *Ibid.* p. 3.
81 Orleans, *op. cit.*, p. 105.
82 Berberet, *op. cit.*, p. 100.

and nuclear engineering, technical physics, applied geophysics, chemical physics, radio electronics, radioactive and radiative chemistry, thermal dynamic engineering, high polymer chemistry and physics, applied mathematics and computing technique, dynamics, geo-chemistry and rare elements, biophysics and automation.   The president of the new university is also the president of the Academy, Kuo Mo-jo.[83]   The initial enrolment in 1958 was 1,600, and the faculty was largely drawn from the Academy of Sciences.   The best graduates will presumably go to the Academy of Sciences for graduate work leading to the Associate Doctorate, which is the highest degree offered in China.   By 1965 China should be producing 1,000 associate doctors yearly in scientific and technical fields, and this number may be doubled by 1970.[84]

In his inaugural speech at the new university, President Kuo spoke of " Three Basic Principles " and " Five Tendencies."   By the former he meant party guidance of education; unification of learning, teaching, research and productive labour; and service to national construction through mastery of advanced scientific and technological knowledge. By the latter he meant Marxist-Leninist thought, industrialised living, militarised organisation, collective teaching and learning, and versatility in technology.   The school year in the new university is divided into eight months of study, three months of productive work, and one month of vacation.   To realise the principle of unification of study and work, each department operates a small factory and the whole university operates a comprehensive large-scale plant.   The professors and students are advised by the president that they should not only probe into the mysteries of the unknown but also apply what they have learned to economic development and national construction, in order to strengthen defence and elevate the standard of living.[85]   The student spends four hours daily in academic studies, four hours in independent work, four hours of productive labour at a near-by plant, and one hour of physical exercise and military training.   His work is not evaluated through examination alone, but by the combined opinions of Party organisation, instructor and fellow students.[86]   Such is the system at the newest and most modern institution of science, from which China's future leaders in science and technology will come.

NEW TRENDS IN CHINESE HIGHER EDUCATION

Throughout the decade of the 1950s the accent of Chinese higher education was on expansion and growth.   Quantity and political

---

[83] Orleans, *op. cit.*, p. 60.

[84] Berberet, *op. cit.*, p. 101.

[85] " Chung-kuo K'o-hsueh Chi-shu Ta-hsueh K'ai-hsueh " (" The Opening of the Chinese University of Science and Technology ") *K'o-hsueh T'ung-pao* (*Scientia*), No. 19, 1958, p. 604.

[86] Orleans, *op. cit.*, pp. 61–62.

consciousness were stressed over quality and academic achievements. During the " Great Leap Forward " Movement, all too often students engaged in ideological and extra-curricular activities at the expense of academic work, because to be " Red " was considered more important than to be " expert." The inevitable result was the lowering of academic achievements and the poor quality of the graduates. The government learned a hard lesson that there was no substitute for technical know-how and managerial skills. To be Red alone was not enough. Engineers and technicians of quality were needed to restore the momentum of economy. As a result, the decade of the 1960s opened with a new education policy of greater stress on expertise and academic excellence.

In a speech to the graduating college students in Peking on August 10, 1961, Vice Premier and Foreign Minister Ch'en Yi dwelt at great length on the importance of academic standards *vis-à-vis* political activities. Academic endeavours and political " redness " need not be anti-thetical, he said; the two, in fact, should unite, as in the shining examples of Marx and Mao.

> During the early period of liberation, it was absolutely necessary for the Party and the government to stress political training in education. Today it is necessary to emphasise specialised training so as to cultivate large numbers of specialists to transform our country into a great socialist state, with a modern industry, a modern agriculture, and a modern scientific culture. . . . This is our greatest political mission. . . . It is the political mission of the student to master his specialised studies, and it is the political mission of the schools to educate large numbers of specialists.

Ch'en proposed a proper balance between school work and political activity, so that the latter would not cut into the time assigned for the former. He went so far as to say: " It is incorrect for technical schools to spend too much time on political activities and labour movement at the expense of specialised training. If we do not emphasise specialised training, we shall always fall behind in our scientific culture."

He even defended those scholars who had no interest in politics.

> Previously, some organisations criticised those who immersed them-selves in specialised works and seldom took part in political activity as " white experts." This is wrong and should be corrected. . . . We cannot measure a man's " redness " or " whiteness " by the amount of his political activity alone. There are some who need more time for technical work and there are some who have little interest in politics and seldom participate in it; but as long as they can accomplish some-thing in their own fields and contribute to socialist construction, we should not criticise them for engaging in too little political activity.[87]

Nieh Jung-cheng, another Vice-Premier, also told the college students:

[87] *Kuang-ming Daily*, September 3, 1961.

If you do not unite work with study but squander away your time on all kinds of activities, you may seem to be giving a good deal of attention to " redness," whereas in fact you are neglecting your primary duty in socialist construction. The result is that not only will you not become a specialist and a good builder but you are (actually) detached from the reality of work, a fact that makes it impossible for you to be politically red either.[88]

He admonished the students to strive to achieve a unity of work and study, with the implication that while they should not neglect work, their primary duty as students was to master specialised knowledge.

With the opening of the 1961 school year in September, there were endless reports of improvements in academic standards at the various colleges and universities. Libraries were enlarged, new laboratory instruments were purchased, stricter examinations were designed, more basic courses were taught by experienced professors, and political activities for teachers and students were reduced.[89] The catchwords of the year were " elevation of academic standards " and " quality first." There was a conscious effort to swing the educational pendulum toward greater stress on academic achievements, in contrast to the days of the " great leap forward," when quantity rather than quality was emphasised.

PROBLEMS OF CHINESE HIGHER EDUCATION

The biggest problem of Chinese higher education appears to be its overly utilitarian nature. Education has ceased to be the medium for man to pursue knowledge for the sake of knowledge and to seek truth as he sees it. Knowledge, in order to be pursued in Communist China, must be relevant to national construction and consistent with Communist ideology. Academic freedom as understood in the West is forsaken in favour of state control, and spontaneous development of the individual is sacrificed for organised planning. Professors do not teach what they want to teach, but what the state wants them to teach, and students are channelled into subjects the state considers most useful. The drive toward industrialisation has led the state to place top priority on technological training, even at the expense of pure scientific education. The idea behind such an attitude is the pragmatic rationalisation that engineering is more directly useful to national construction than basic science. China, as an underdeveloped country, has much to learn from the more advanced states; until it has mastered all the existing scientific knowledge and engineering techniques, there is no point in delving into basic scientific research. Fundamental theories are a luxury it cannot

---

[88] *Ibid*. September 17, 1961.
[89] *People's Daily*, August 12, 25, 31, September 4, 6, 8, 19, 1961.

afford at present. The state needs a vast number of engineers and technicians for the immediate task of national construction, not pure
scientists who may be potential winners of Lenin or Nobel prizes.
Institutions of higher learning are no longer associated with the notion
of refinement, culture, and elegance, but have been turned into training
centres of robot-like technocrats, whose individuality is totally lost in the
web of state planning and the meshes of economic development.[90]

Another major problem is the extremely heavy curriculum and
demanding school life in Chinese universities. In an attempt to
accelerate graduation the Chinese compressed the five-year Soviet
curriculum into a four-year programme, resulting in an extremely heavy
load of 60–70 hours a week for the student, although the Ministry of
Education prescribed only 36 classroom hours and 18 study hours
weekly.[91] In addition, the student has to participate in numerous
political meetings and labour work during rest hours, weekends, and
even vacations. Because of the exacting demands of school life, as
many as 10 per cent. of the students are said to have developed
tuberculosis.[92] A letter to the editors of the *Liberation Daily* in
Shanghai, February 13, 1953, vividly portrayed the plight of the
students:

> Our mother country anxiously awaits institutions of higher learning
> to cultivate construction personnel, but I witnessed the following
> situation at Fu-tan University. A (woman) student in biology, who is a
> Communist Party member and a member of the Organisation Com-
> mittee of the local (Party) branch, flunked two of the seven examina-
> tions this time, scoring 51 in chemistry and 41 in physics. . . . Since
> the opening of school, she has participated in countless big meetings,
> small meetings, discussion meetings, and report meetings, etc. She
> attends meetings during the day, during the evening, and sometimes
> deep into night, consuming all of her rest hours, and study and class
> time. Of the five chemistry assignments she fulfilled only one, and all
> three physics assignments were neglected. She is physically exhausted
> to sickness, taking medicine and shots regularly. She knows well how
> to learn, but the works ordered by the (Party) leader cannot be declined;
> she has no choice but to attend the meetings.[93]

Rigid state control of education is another problem. The Ministry
of Education centralises the direction and development of all institutions
of higher learning, determines their educational policy and their
" specialties," conducts their matriculation examinations, and assigns
their graduates to work. No room is left for the free development of

90 Chu Po-ch'i, *Chung-Kung ti Hsueh-hsiao Chiao-yü* (*School Education in Communist
   China*) (Hong Kong: 1954), p. 73.
91 F. C. Ikle, *The Growth of China's Scientific and Technical Manpower*. Mimeo. (Santa
   Monica: Rand, 1957), p. 38.
92 Chu Po-ch'i, *op. cit.*, p. 253.
93 *Ibid.* p. 108.

institutions according to local characteristics. After graduation students were often sent to places where they were least welcome. Organic chemistry graduates were sent to inorganic chemical work, and mathematics students to factories to teach Russian. Structural engineering graduates were assigned to engineering units, in which the only available work was to receive telephone calls, cut stencils and perform routine office chores. Some graduates were sent to a construction company, only to discover that it had not yet been established. Over 5 per cent. of the graduates from 1953–56 requested reassignment because of the unsuitability of their work.[94]

Related to the difficulty of proper assignment is the problem of over-specialisation of the student's training. Mathematics is divided into 19 specialties and physics 20. Some institutes of technology boast of 240 departments and specialties, and the graduates of one or two of these specialties certainly cannot be called well-rounded engineers.[95] The narrowness of their training limits their usefulness in places where no such high specialisation is required, with the result that their talent and training are wasted.

The problem of the quality of instruction is also very basic. The large influx of party cadres and discharged servicemen with inadequate preparation into institutions of higher learning definitely lowered the standard of learning. The appointment of new graduates as instructors due to pressing needs for teachers further diluted the quality of instruction. In 1955 some 50 per cent. of the 38,000 teachers were inexperienced instructors. In 1957, only 13 per cent. of the 42,000 college instructors were professors and associate professors[96]—in sharp contrast to the situation at the University of California, Berkeley, *e.g.,* where some 48 per cent. of the faculty are tenure members.

THE FUTURE SOCIETY

Under Communist rule, higher education in China has undergone a radical transformation in philosophy, form, content and method. Chinese higher education today can truly be called an industrial education—a far cry from the classical and moralistic education of traditional China. What was once the land of philosophers and artists has been transformed into a huge throbbing plant of bustling technocrats. Eager engineers, active scientists and busy industrial workers become the mark of New China, while dreamy classical scholars in flowing robes have long since passed into the oblivion of history.

[94] Orleans, *op. cit.,* pp. 94–95.
[95] *Ibid.* p. 93.
[96] *Ibid.* p. 91.

It is significant to note that the changed situation in China is not a spontaneous product of industrialisation, as in most of the Western nations, but a deliberate creation of the drawing board of the economic planners. The single-party state decided that in order to achieve a major breakthrough in industrialisation the central government must assume leadership in organising all national activities toward that end. The Chinese road to industrialisation therefore epitomises the third pattern of economic development described by Kerr-Harbison-Dunlop-Myers:

> The revolutionary intellectuals, self-identified for the task of leadership by their support of what they claim to be a scientific and superior theory of history, set out to pour new wine into entirely new bottles. Their principal new bottle is the monolithic, centralised state. The prime movers of this society demand a rapid forced march toward industrialism, and they mould education, art, literature and labour organisations to their single-minded purpose.[97]

These Communist revolutionary élite asked the inevitable questions: What is the fastest road to industrialisation in China? What should be the priorities in development projects? How can higher education help the cause of economic development? [98] They decided, as we have seen, that education must be reformed in order to turn out the largest possible number of engineers to serve as architects of the desired industrialisation, that technological education must receive top priority over all other types of education, and that the state must assume leadership in *organising and controlling* higher education: from administrating matriculation examinations to enrolment, educational methods, contents, materials, examinations, as well as the placement of graduates to works. In this way they hope to achieve maximum speed of industrialisation.

The Chinese Communists, however, are not communists pure and simple; they are also nationalists because of China's background as a semi-colonial state in the past hundred years. They may properly be called nationalistic Communists, who are determined to catch up with and surpass the West in industrial capacity. They use *national sentiment* to heighten the people's yearning for an improved status for China, and they use *Communist organisation* to channel the people's frenzied enthusiasm into production and industrialisation. The single-party state is their engine of development, nationalism their fuel, and communism their safety valve. The end result is a ruthless, proud and rapid march toward industrialisation, under the efficient leadership of the Communist revolutionary élite.

---

[97] Clark Kerr, Frederick H. Harbison, John T. Dunlop and Charles A. Myers, " Industrialism and Industrial Man," Reprint 165, Institute of Industrial Relations, University of California, Berkeley, p. 5.
[98] *Ibid*. p. 7.

The questions then arise: Will China, once industrialised, become less "communistic" because it is more "technocratic"? Will it become a member of what Kerr-Harbison-Dunlop-Myers call world-wide society of "pluralistic industrialism"? [99] Very possibly the economic planners of Communist China are aware of these possibilities; perhaps it is precisely with an eye to counter these trends that they created the "Red and Expert Universities," in which they train technicians and managers of high political consciousness and reliability. They strive to create a new image of the Socialist Man, who is at once an engineer professionally and a Communist politically, and who owes his engineering or managerial position not only to his professional know-how but also to his political consciousness. Ideally, such a versatile character will not dilute the political contents of the society simply because of his additional technical skill.

Will the future industrialised state of China be "pluralistic," like her Western counterparts? Probably yes, but not to the same degree. The emergence of numerous industrial enterprises is destined to create new pressure groups, exerting a pluralistic influence on the society, but the single-party state will remain the dominant force in the basically monolithic social structure. The powerful arm of state is ever ready to stem the rising tide of pluralism and to crush any divisive influence it may exert, although as the paternalistic welfare state it will make some accommodations and concessions to it. Nevertheless, it will not tolerate harassment and threat by pluralistic industrialism. This is particularly true in China, where there has always been a dominant central government. Little, if any, pluralistic influence existed in traditional China, where the state was much stronger than the society.[100] Individuals and private organisations were always at the mercy of the state, which stressed the duties rather than the rights of man. When this tradition is reinforced by Communist organisation and control, industrial pluralism has a very weak foundation on which to build. Labour protest will be much less than in the West. In fact, it is doubtful whether labour and engineers will take the blunt course of "protest"; more likely they will resort to the polite forms of "request" (*e.g.,* 5 per cent. of college graduates "requested" reassignment of work, as noted earlier) or "passive resistance" and apathy in work.

[99] *Ibid.* p. 3.
[100] Karl A. Wittfogel, "Oriental Society in Transition," *Far Eastern Quarterly*, No. 4, August 1955, p. 471.

The Agricultural Middle School in Communist China

By ROBERT D. BARENDSEN

WHEN the Chinese Communist régime undertook the re-examination of
its educational system in the latter half of 1957 and early 1958, one of
the main conclusions reached by the authorities was that the government,
through its regular political subdivisions, could not afford the tremendous
expenditures that would be involved in achieving its long-range educational goals. These goals included the provision of the opportunity for
junior middle school (7th through 9th grade) education to all young people
by 1967. The régime decided that the only realistic course to follow in
pursuing its goals was to assign the major part of the task of establishing
and running schools in the vast rural areas to the basic socio-economic
units in those areas, mainly, in other words, to the agricultural co-
operatives. Accordingly, the late winter and early spring of 1958 were
marked by the announcement of the rapid establishment of great numbers
of *min-pan hsüeh-hsiao*, or " schools run by the people."

At the secondary level alone, tens of thousands of these *min-pan*
schools were set up within a few months. A report published in the
Chiao-shih Pao (Teachers' Newspaper) on May 2, 1958, stated that more
than 55,000 new middle schools of this kind had been established in
nineteen provinces and had enrolled over 2½ million students. An official
New China News Agency (NCNA) dispatch of June 10 said 61,000 such
schools had been set up between February and May, and figures cited in
mainland sources during the summer of 1958 raised the number in
existence to 68,000. These schools were vocational in their orientation,
concentrating on general agriculture or on related local rural specialties
such as vegetable cultivation, sericulture, tea growing, and animal
husbandry. In some areas the schools reportedly specialised in forestry
or fishing; in others, they concentrated on training for local industries
such as paper-making, ceramics, or wine-distilling.

Most numerous among the *min-pan* middle schools and the most
publicised in their group are the schools which became known in the
spring of 1958 as *nung-yeh chung-hsüeh*, commonly translated as
" agricultural middle schools." The agricultural middle school, a

theoretically self-supporting half-time junior middle school, is not only the predominant type of *min-pan* middle school; it is also the pivotal educational undertaking in the new communes which supplanted the agricultural co-operatives in the summer and autumn of 1958. It embodies in classic form the concept of the close integration of study and productive labour stressed in the educational reforms instituted in 1958, and its success or failure will largely determine the result of the régime's efforts to extend educational opportunity into the rural areas and to surmount the cultural and economic drag of the massive semi-literate and technically unskilled peasant population. For these reasons, an understanding of the agricultural middle schools is the key to comprehension of the Chinese Communists' overall educational philosophy and policy, and to an evaluation of their prospects for success in this field.

ORIGIN, GROWTH AND SPECIAL ROLE

As is the case with the communes themselves, it is difficult for an outside observer to ascertain with assurance just when the " agricultural middle school " in its recent form first appeared on the Chinese scene. There are a few retroactive references in available materials to schools of a similar nature in existence in 1956 and 1957, but the genesis of the idea is usually credited in Chinese sources to the authorities in Kiangsu province, where the first agricultural middle schools were reportedly established in March 1958. In any case, it was apparently the particular form developed in Kiangsu province which first received the stamp of approval of the central authorities. This approval was conveyed by no less a person than Lu Ting-yi, Director of the Propaganda Department of the Communist Party's Central Committee and the Party's main spokesman on educational matters. Lu attended a conference concerning the new schools in Kiangsu in mid-March, and his favourable reaction was immediately reported in Chinese news media.[1]

Pattern of growth

In the wake of Lu's action, many reports of the establishment of agricultural middle schools began to appear in a pattern typical of the early stages of the implementation of any new movement in Communist China. The pace of frenzied activity can best be traced through the record of what happened in Kiangsu, where the course of the movement is best documented. Starting from a base of two such schools in mid-March, Kiangsu was reported to have established more than 2,000 by the end of the month. By April 21, when the authoritative Central Committee journal, *People's Daily (Jen-min Jih-pao)*, gave firm editorial

[1] Chinese Home Service broadcast, March 18, 1958.

support to the campaign, that paper stated that there were already 5,600 agricultural middle schools in Kiangsu. A Kiangsu official later gave the figure for April 1958 as " over 6,000 " schools.[2] Meanwhile, scattered accounts indicated similar activity in other areas. Domestic radio broadcasts reported that Anhwei province had established 2,654 agricultural middle schools by early April, that 608 had been set up in the outskirts of Shanghai by early May, and that by July there were more in Szechwan than in the model province of Kiangsu.

The national rate of growth of the agricultural middle schools during the following year and a half is difficult to trace, as reports for the latter part of 1958 and early 1959 are not available in sufficient numbers to establish a clear pattern. It would appear that during the hectic several months after the mass campaign to establish communes began, in the late summer of 1958, the agricultural middle schools were revamped and adapted to the new organisational framework in rural areas. A domestic news release suggested as much when it later reported that the schools had been " comprehensively overhauled, consolidated, and improved " in the wake of the commune-isation movement.[3] In the spring of 1959 there was again a flurry of publicity for these schools, tied to the first anniversary of their official founding. By the latter part of 1959 and early 1960, the situation had apparently become stabilised to the degree that the first national statistics on the schools and their enrolment could be released.

The first of the new set of statistics, which came in piecemeal in the latter half of 1959, concerned the situation on the provincial level. By April 1960 the following data on the number of agricultural middle schools and their enrolment in various areas were available from Chinese sources :

Provinces, etc.	No. of Schools	Enrolment	Date
Liaoning	930	n.a.	Aug. 1959
Shanghai (outskirts)	220	27,000	Aug. 1959
Hopei	2,125	230,000 +	Nov. 1959
Shantung	1,380	134,000	Nov. 1959
Kwangsi Chuang Autonomous Region	530	46,996	Nov. 1959
Inner Mongolian Autonomous Region	400	31,000	Jan. 1960
Kiangsu	2,174	279,890	Apr. 1960
Szechwan	4,640	385,113	Apr. 1960
Fukien	560	41,200 +	Apr. 1960

[2] Ouyang Hui-lin, " Agricultural Middle Schools in their First Year," *Red Flag (Hung Ch'i)*, No. 7, 1959.   [3] NCNA, March 15, 1960.

Although incomplete, the data is representative of the situation in various dissimilar parts of the country. From these figures it would appear that there was a considerable shrinkage in number of schools, in at least some areas, between the early days of the spring of 1958 and the end of 1959. The later figures for Kiangsu, which are repeated in substantial agreement in several sources, are especially interesting. Whereas the province had been reported as establishing over 6,000 agricultural middle schools in a few months in the spring of 1958, only slightly over 2,000 were mentioned in the spring of 1960. The official explanation of this difference is that during the commune movement the agricultural middle schools underwent a process of "appropriate amalgamation" during which in some cases as many as seven schools were combined into one.[4] Although some consolidation may have been logically called for by the amalgamation of many co-operatives into one commune, it is possible that other factors, such as unrealistic over-extension or exaggerated reporting in the early stages, played a role in the cutback in numbers. It is noteworthy that the late 1959–early 1960 figures reported for the Shanghai hinterland and Szechwan province also suggest a substantial shrinkage from the 1958 accounts.

Toward the end of the period during which the partial figures reported above were being released, the régime issued the first comprehensive national figures for numbers of agricultural middle schools and their enrolment. Unfortunately, the resulting picture is not as clear as one would wish, since two very different sets of national figures were released within a month and a half. On February 2, 1960, the *People's Daily* reported that in the whole country there were "over 20,000" agricultural middle schools with 2,190,000 students. Six weeks later, the official news agency reported that there were "over 30,000" agricultural middle schools with a total enrolment of 2,960,000.[5] A possible explanation of the discrepancy between the two figures is to be found in the fact that in the dispatch giving the larger numbers, NCNA said that the figure was for "agricultural middle schools," but added parenthetically that this included "technical schools," which it later spelled out as being "technical middle schools of forestry, animal husbandry, side-line production, and fishing." It is thus possible that the 20,000 schools represent what might be called the "general" agricultural middle schools, while the 30,000 figure includes about 10,000 "specialised" agricultural middle schools—schools whose vocational speciality is generally the predominant occupational pursuit of the rural locality but not crop-cultivation agriculture. Such a definition could still exclude the *min-pan*

4 Ch'en Kuang, "There is a Great Possibility for Agricultural Middle Schools," *Red Flag*, No. 9, 1959.
5 NCNA, March 15, 1960.

middle schools which specialise in local industrial skills such as ceramics, paper-making, and wine-distilling. And it would presumably not include any of the senior middle school level (10th through 12th grades) " specialised " (technical or vocational) schools which are a separate category in Communist China's school system, since the 2,960,000 students are specifically stated to be of *junior middle* school level. It should be noted, however, that since the release in mid-March 1960 of the 30,000 figure, it has been cited on several occasions in the mainland press as simply representing the number of " agricultural middle schools," without any qualification or indication of the inclusiveness of that term. On the other hand, the 20,000 figure seems not to have been used after March 1960. Since during the past year no new national figures have become available, the report of 30,000 schools and 2,960,000 students remains the latest and best obtainable.

It is immediately apparent that the number of agricultural middle schools averages out at roughly about one such school per commune for the entire country.[6] The distribution throughout the country is uneven, however. The NCNA item of March 15, 1960, which gave the national figure of over 30,000 schools, stated that almost every commune had at least one agricultural middle school, and that some had as many as six or more.

Broadening educational opportunity

The March 15, 1960, NCNA report also discussed the role then being played by such schools in the effort to extend junior middle school education to a larger segment of the population. It said that the 2,960,000 students in agricultural middle schools already represented 27 per cent. of the total enrolment at junior middle level in the whole country, and that these schools were currently " doing a third to a half of the work of universalising junior middle school education." This latter phrasing was apparently a reference to the comparison between beginning enrolments in agricultural middle schools and ordinary junior middle schools. The draft economic plan for 1960, submitted to the National People's Congress in March of that year, stated that the enrolment of new students in ordinary junior middle schools in the fall of that year would be 4,000,000, while another 2,800,000 would enter " agricultural and other vocational middle schools " at the junior middle level. It should be pointed out that the 1960 figures for entering students do not suggest that the Chinese Communists were closely approaching the goal of

---

6 There were about 26,000 communes in China after the initial commune-isation movement in 1958. The figures generally quoted for later years indicate that there are now in the neighbourhood of 24,000. An average commune includes about 5,000 households.

universalising junior middle school education at that time; data from the 1953 census would indicate, for example, that there were probably 12 to 13 million young people of thirteen years of age (the normal age for entering junior middle school) in China in 1960.

The emerging role of the agricultural middle school in expanding the opportunity for middle-school education, as seen in the spring of 1960, was a major one. For example, a Kiangsu delegate, speaking to the National People's Congress in April, reported that his province alone planned to have 1,450,000 students enrolled in agricultural middle schools by 1967. The attainment of such a level of participation on a national scope would enable the régime to approach its goal of universalising junior middle school education, since there will probably be between 40 and 50 million young people in the relevant thirteen-sixteen age bracket at that time.[7] If the goal is to be attained, it will be reached through the agricultural middle schools, and the great majority of students at the junior middle level will be enrolled in schools of this type.

NEED FOR A NEW TYPE OF RURAL SCHOOL

With this brief survey of the role that the agricultural middle schools were playing in the total educational picture in 1960 and the importance ascribed to their future development in mind, one may pause briefly to examine in greater depth the régime's thinking as to the reasons why such schools are necessary and the main purposes the schools are expected to serve.

The need for middle schools in the countryside is clear. Lu Ting-yi, in an article in the February 1960 issue of *Jen-min Chiao-yü* (*People's Education*) acknowledged that prior to the establishment of the agricultural schools, middle-school level education had " failed to penetrate " into the rural areas. The reasons why a special type of junior middle school is deemed necessary in the rural areas are primarily economic. On the one hand, the régime feels it is unable to support an academic-type junior middle school education for the great numbers of primary school graduates now emerging in the countryside. On the other hand, it sees a great need for a vast number of young people who possess a minimal ninth grade general education and who have in addition some knowledge of modern scientific agricultural methods and the ability to handle the tools and machines to be used in the environment of a mechanised and electrified agriculture which the régime is striving to attain. The age group from thirteen to sixteen is not yet adjudged to be

[7] Lu Ting-yi, in an open letter dated March 14, 1959, published on the first anniversary of the founding of the agricultural middle schools, said that there were then about 37,000,000 in the 13–16 age bracket. He added that only a little over 7,000,000 of these could be accommodated in ordinary full-time junior middle schools.

physically mature and capable of carrying a full load in the workaday world. Therefore, it is considered feasible and advisable to allow this group to continue its education to a point enabling it to play a more useful role in society, provided that this schooling will not involve large expenditures of public funds. A corollary of this view is that education for older rural youth at the senior middle level will generally be available only on a spare-time basis, since young people over sixteen are needed for full-time employment.[8]

The need for "junior agricultural technical personnel" in the communes is seen as being very urgent. Lu Ting-yi, in his February 1960 article in *Jen-min Chiao-yü* stated that China would need 1,840,000 agricultural machine operators and 440,000 "technical farming cadres" in order to complete the task of mechanisation and modernisation of agriculture. These are the people who will be counted upon to drive the tractors and combines, maintain the electric motors powering irrigation equipment, perform skilled tasks in local fertiliser and insecticide factories, act as surveyors, veterinary assistants, and bookkeepers, and do similar lower-lever technical work in commune farms and factories.

CHARACTERISTICS OF THE NEW SCHOOLS

Such are the purposes which the agricultural middle schools are designed to serve. But what is the nature of the new type of institution founded to meet these needs, and what kind of educational experience does it offer to the young Chinese students in rural areas?

First of all, it must be remembered that the agricultural middle school is a *part-time* school. It is thus distinguished from the other two types of educational institutions in Communist China considered from the point of view of the daily proportion of the student's time spent in classes: the ordinary junior middle school which is a *full-time* school, and the many *spare-time* (*i.e.*, after a normal working day) schools and classes at all levels which are run by communes and factories. The agricultural middle school is often referred to in mainland sources as "half-school, half-farm," since its students normally devote half their time to classes, and the other half to productive labour, the proceeds from which are used to finance the operation of the schools.

In theory, the students in agricultural middle schools are all in the normal junior middle school age bracket—thirteen to sixteen years. In practice, however, at least in the first year or so, a considerable proportion of the students were apparently over-age. Articles in *Red Flag* by a Kiangsu official in May of 1959 and again a year later made it clear that a sizeable number of students in that model province were over

8 See *ibid.*, in which this line of reasoning is succinctly expressed.

sixteen.[9] At least in Kiangsu, the entrants were described as coming mainly from the families of the poorer peasants and hired farm labourers. It would appear from several accounts of early sceptical attitudes toward the schools [10] that this description of the entrants, in the early years at least, would be more broadly applicable, since many families seem to have held out hopes of getting their offspring into the ordinary schools.

Little data is obtainable on the physical facilities available to the schools for classroom work. Early schools were apparently operated in temples, pagodas and temporarily unused buildings and rooms. The *People's Daily* of April 7, 1958, described the classrooms as having a bare minimum of furnishings, with tables and benches brought in by the students from home or borrowed temporarily from offices. An article in *Red Flag* on May 16, 1960, looking back in retrospect on the early days of the movement in Kiangsu, said that " some of the [schools] were started . . . without fixed premises. The teachers taught . . . in the open, and doors were temporarily used as blackboards with the students squatting and using their knees as desks." Items describing the situation at a later date refer in some cases to new permanent classroom buildings, but offer no details. In view of the considerably greater attention given to describing the installations available for productive labour, this leaves the impression that classroom facilities are minimal.

It is not clear from available data to what extent the students live on the school premises. Probably where housing exists, this practice is generally followed, but there are very few references to dormitories in available mainland sources on the schools. One article concerning the situation in Kiangsu in 1959 took up the question of whether or not the schools should be boarding schools, and said this point was a contro-versial one after a year's experience. The author stated that the living-in system had some clear advantages where facilities existed, but cautioned against large boarding institutions.[11]

The size of agricultural middle schools seems to vary considerably. The national statistics indicate that the average enrolment is about 100 students per school, but enrolment as high as over 600 has been cited in the sources. In Kiangsu, the recommended enrolment is between 200 and 500 per school, with 300 considered an ideal number, but the reported enrolment in the spring of 1960 averaged well below 200 per institution.

Teaching staff

More important than the physical facilties in determining the total educational environment is the teaching staff. In numbers, the teaching

9 In the May 1, 1959, article the author noted that in one school 86 of the 303 students were over 17 at the time of their enrolment. Again, on May 16, 1960, he noted that many students were " relatively advanced in age."

10 See pp. 128–130.   11 Ouyang Hui-lin, *loc. cit.*

force for agricultural middle schools is relatively small. For example, the February 2, 1960, item in the *People's Daily* which gave the national figure of over 20,000 agricultural middle schools with over 2,000,000 students said that there were 60,000 instructors in these schools—an average of less than three teachers for each three-year school and one teacher for each thirty-six students. The reported ratio for Kiangsu and Szechwan (the only areas where provincial-level figures for total teachers are available) is approximately the same as the national ratio.

Teachers are drawn from several sources. When available, graduates of ordinary senior middle schools are taken. Otherwise, the recourse is to ordinary junior middle school graduates, primary school teachers, government functionaries who have been sent to the countryside for experience in " basic-level " work, local Communist Party leaders, and even experienced peasants. The principle behind teacher recruitment is that " every knowledgeable person can teach " and that formal teaching qualifications are not necessary. As a result of this approach and the general shortage of teaching personnel throughout the country, the agricultural middle schools are staffed largely with people who, at the time of their appointment, have admittedly had neither teacher training nor teaching experience.

The nature of this group has posed persistent problems, and has necessitated special training measures which will be discussed later. The problems were apparently not overcome after two years of experience with the new schools. A report on the situation in the Szechwan schools delivered to the National People's Congress in April 1960 stated that only slightly over half of the teachers in that province had had a senior middle school level education, and that inadequate political training and lack of teaching experience were prevalent shortcomings. A speech to the same convocation by a delegate from Liaoning acknowledged that the teachers in that province's schools were " not very good," and cited the difficulties experienced by a fresh graduate of an ordinary junior middle school assigned to teach in an agricultural middle school. According to an article in *Red Flag* in May 1960, teachers in the early days of the Kiangsu schools were often poor: the author cites cases of a female teacher of agriculture who knew nothing of agricultural production, and a teacher of agricultural mechanisation who could not operate a tractor or identify parts of the machine. He claims that conditions in 1960 were much improved, and that 87 per cent. of the teachers in the province had a senior middle school or better level of education.[12]

12 Ch'en Kuang, "The Growth of Agricultural Middle Schools," *Red Flag*, No. 10, 1960.

Time allotments for study and labour

Such, then, is the educational environment into which a student of an agricultural middle school enters. But how does he spend his time while he is enrolled? As indicated previously, the student spends about half his time in classroom study and half in productive labour. Apparently the majority of the schools use a split day, and a minority use alternate days for study and work. Other arrangements, such as alternate-week systems and a system with study in mornings and evenings and work in between, were apparently tried and rejected because of poor academic results or the overburdening of the student.[13] The half-day or alternate-day system is a general practice but is subject to alteration according to the farm calendar. A joint report to the National People's Congress in April 1960 by three Fukien delegates stated that the principle which governs division of time in that province was "less study during the busy farming season, more during slack farming season, occasional study during the busiest season, and all-day study on rainy days."[14] A Szechwan delegate told the same meeting that the work-study schedule in his province varied from month to month and that in busy seasons teachers went to the fields to conduct brief review lessons or introduce new material. Schools in Kiangsu are reportedly in session for eleven months of the year, with either the equivalent of five months given to study and six months to labour or five months for labour and six months for study. In Hopei, on the other hand, schools are apparently in session for virtually the full twelve months, with their overall time divided equally between study and labour.

The Kiangsu schools are variously reported to spend twenty or twenty-three hours per week in classroom study, and one Anhwei school is described as having twenty-four lesson periods per week. The schools presumably operate on the six-day week basis which is the usual system for middle schools in Communist China. No weekly hours are reported for other provinces, but Szechwan schools are said to provide 900 "lesson-hours" per year, a figure which would average out to about eighteen and three-quarter hours per week for an eleven-month (forty-eight-week) year, and less for a longer school session.[15]

Curriculum and academic standards

The curriculum in agricultural middle schools consists of a limited number of subjects. There are four basic courses: Chinese language,

---

[13] See Ouyang Hui-lin, *loc. cit.*

[14] Liu Yung-sheng, Cheng I-mu, and Chou Chü-chen, " Secondary Agricultural Schools Have Struck Root in Rural Areas," *Peoples' Daily*, April 16, 1960.

[15] Chang Hsiu-shu, " Agricultural Middle Schools: More and More, Better and Better," *People's Daily*, April 16, 1960.

mathematics, politics, and a course in agriculture which is most commonly referred to as "basic agricultural knowledge." Language and mathematics are referred to as the two major courses in the curriculum. No specific information on the coverage of the language course is available, other than the general statement that it corresponds to that offered in ordinary junior middle schools. Since most accounts do not mention "literature" specifically, however, it is possible that the course coverage is actually narrower than the scope of the course in Chinese taught in ordinary middle schools. It is not clear whether mathematics as taught in the typical agricultural middle school in Kiangsu includes algebra and geometry; presumably it does. A spokesman from Szechwan listed these subjects as well as arithmetic in the curriculum generally in use in his province. The course on politics includes material on such subjects as important domestic and international current political topics, the programme for agricultural development, and Mao Tse-tung's political thought. The coverage of the "basic agricultural knowledge" course is not well defined in the sources, but it apparently includes such things as basic techniques of crop cultivation, irrigation methods, and fertiliser application. One source states that the teaching materials used in this course are derived from those used in ordinary junior middle school botany and zoology, and give special emphasis to the régime's "8-point charter" for agriculture (a set of guidelines regarding close planting, deep ploughing, fertilisation, etc.) [16] Perhaps the best way to indicate what is included in the basic agricultural course is to note the subjects of some of the courses added to the original four in some schools. Most prominently mentioned among these is a course on agricultural machinery, indicating that this topic is not included in the basic agriculture course. Other special courses which have been added to the curriculum in some areas include animal husbandry, gardening and sericulture. It is claimed that a number of the schools teach physics and chemistry to students in the second or third year of the three-year course, but it is not clear just how widely these courses are offered.

There is unfortunately little indication of the way in which the 20-odd hours of weekly classroom work are divided among the various subjects. The writer has found only one such schedule in the available data, and it pertains to only one agricultural middle school in Anhwei. The schedule covers a class week consisting of 24 "lessons" (presumably equal to class hours), and is divided as follows [17]:

16 *Ibid.*
17 Li Chien, "The Huang-k'ou Agricultural Middle School in the Past Two Years," *Red Flag*, No. 13, 1960.

Language	6	lessons
Mathematics	6	„
Politics	2	„
Biology	3	„
Chemistry	2	„
Cotton cultivation	2	„
Animal husbandry	2	„
Physical education	1	„
Total	24	

Since it is not made clear for which of the three years this plan is designed, and since it does not include a basic agriculture course as such, and does include a course in biology which is not mentioned in the other sources, it is impossible to generalise from this one example. It is probably indicative, however, of a lack of standardisation in the curriculum pattern of such schools.

What standards are achieved in the academic courses in the agricultural middle schools, and how does the record of performance of their students compare with that of students in the ordinary junior middle schools? The general claim repeated frequently in mainland press and periodical articles about the agricultural middle schools is that their students have achieved standards comparable to those of students in the ordinary junior middle schools in the " main subjects " in their curriculum. But more minute examination of the claims reveals that they are often considerably qualified so that this evaluation would apply to only some of the students (or some of the schools) in a given area. A typical example of the resulting vagueness is a statement in a joint article by three officials from Kiangsu in the November 17, 1959, issue of the *People's Daily*. Discussing the schools in Kiangsu, the article says that " the standard of *several* subjects taught in the agricultural middle schools is not lower than that taught in the regular middle schools *in general*, while results achieved by students of *a number of* agricultural middle schools are even better than those achieved by the students of regular middle schools " (emphasis added).

As for achievements in specific subjects, there are several claims of equivalence or near-equivalence to ordinary middle school standards in language and mathematics, and one or two claims of comparable performance in tests on politics; but these claims are balanced by provincial reports which convey a different impression. A Kiangsu delegate to the National People's Congress in April 1960 stated that only about half of the Kiangsu schools inspected equalled or excelled the standards of local ordinary full-time middle schools in language and mathematics. The joint report to the same meeting by the three Fukien delegates stated that in less than one-fourth of the agricultural middle schools in Fukien did the quality of language and mathematics teaching match that in ordinary schools. Tests in three areas in Hopei reported in the *People's Daily* on August 10, 1960, showed that only 50 per cent. of the agricultural schools there had attained the standard of ordinary full-time schools in " cultural studies." It may be noted that whereas there is frequent mention of admirable standards in language and mathematics, standards in physics and chemistry are almost never specifically cited; only one instance of the claim of performance in these sciences comparable to that in ordinary schools has been encountered in the available data.

Perhaps the best evidence of actual nation-wide standards in these new schools is contained in an editorial in the *People's Daily* published March 15, 1960, on the occasion of the second anniversary of the founding of the schools. Although praising the schools and calling for greater numbers of them on a national scale, the editorial says that since they are half-day schools, they " should naturally be regarded as different from the ordinary full-time middle schools in the standards of such fundamental subjects as cultural and scientific subjects." The editorial adds that they " may be able to catch up " with ordinary schools in such " principal subjects " as " language, mathematics, etc." This evaluation was in line with that voiced by a Liaoning delegate to the National People's Congress the following month. He told the meeting that " generally speaking, the students of agricultural middle schools are still somewhat behind the students of full-time middle schools in book knowledge, but their knowledge of productive labour far exceeds that of the latter." [18]

It is clear from the available data that the agricultural middle schools in general offer a substantially watered-down course of study compared to that obtainable in the ordinary junior middle schools in Communist China. It may well be true, as claimed, that by offering only a limited number of basic courses, the schools provide as many hours of instruction in them per year as are offered in the ordinary schools. But it also is evident that the complete absence of the usual junior middle school courses in history and geography, and the indicated lower standard in physics and chemistry where these science courses are offered, would suffice to draw a clear line of distinction between graduates of these new schools and the ordinary schools.

[18] Ch'e Hsiang-chen, " The Promising Future of the Agricultural Middle Schools," *People's Daily*, April 12, 1960.

Schools at senior middle level

Although the original agricultural middle schools and still the over-whelming majority of such schools consist of a three-year course at the junior middle school level, it should be noted in passing that there has been some experimentation with the idea of establishing a continuation of such schools at the senior middle (10th through 12th grades) level. This idea was first publicised in the autumn of 1959, when it was reported that in Kiangsu province a small number of senior agricultural middle schools had been established. The first reports in late November 1959 indicated that fifty such schools with an enrolment of 1,300 students were in existence. The figures released in April 1960 stated that of Kiangsu's 2,174 agricultural middle schools with an enrolment of 279,890 students, 51 were on the senior middle level and enrolled 4,930 students. Thus the proportion of schools and students at senior level was but a minor fraction of the total. An NCNA English-language news release of March 5, 1960, stated that " a number of " senior-level schools had been set up in Kiangsu, Hopei, and " a few other provinces," but no further details on their establishment outside of Kiangsu have been released.

Reasons cited in Kiangsu for the extension of the agricultural middle school system included the claimed successful results of the junior-middle level schools, and the need for more " intermediate-level " technical personnel in the communes. Also mentioned was the desire for further educational opportunities on the part of students in the junior level agricultural schools and graduates of the ordinary junior middle schools who were unable to gain entrance into the limited number of ordinary senior middle schools. The curriculum in the senior-level schools is not given in detail in the sources, but an item in the *People's Daily* on November 27, 1959 indicated that physics and chemistry were definitely being taught and that the mathematics courses included algebra and geometry. A second item in the same issue of the paper said that botany and planting and crop cultivation techniques were being taught in the senior schools. A speech to the National People's Congress by a Kiangsu delegate in April 1960 stated that 30 per cent. of the students in senior-level schools should concentrate on " basic lessons " and be trained to be teachers, while the other 70 per cent. should concentrate on " professional lessons " to prepare to take their places as technical and management cadres in the communes.

The relationship between the new part-time senior-level agricultural middle schools and the full-time technical senior middle schools which specialise in agriculture has not been made clear. Presumably the graduates of the senior-level agricultural middle schools would have qualifications higher than those of junior part-time agricultural school graduates, but lower than those of senior full-time agricultural technical school graduates.

The development of the senior agricultural middle schools will probably remain quite limited. Lu Ting-yi, the Party educational spokesman, gave the existing ones qualified endorsement in his *Jen-min Chiao-yü* article in February 1960, but added pointedly that " it is impossible to set up many half-day senior middle schools at present." A Kiangsu education official was even more specific when he wrote in the *Kuang-ming Jih-pao* on July 27, 1960 that " present economic conditions do not permit more half-day session senior middle schools to be built." It would appear that the régime's basic policy that the vast majority of the physically mature youths over sixteen years of age must further their education in spare-time study after a full working day will preclude any rapid development of senior agricultural middle schools in the next few years.

Productive labour activities

The foregoing material has provided a brief outline of the way in which the student in an agricultural middle school spends that half of his time which is devoted to classroom study. It now remains to consider his use of the other half of his time—that devoted to productive labour. The picture derived from numerous accounts indicates that the student's labour is performed in a variety of enterprises in " production bases " made available to the schools through the local communes. The production bases are of two kinds: agricultural and industrial. Schools have their own crop farms, a part of which are experimental plots. They also often have livestock and poultry farms, orchards and tree nurseries. In some cases they have vegetable gardens, tea plantations, aviaries and stocked fish ponds. The factories run by the schools are generally small, many of them in the nature of handicraft workshops. The two most commonly mentioned types of small plants are those producing local types of fertiliser (both chemical and bacterial) and insecticides. Other shops engage in the processing of economic crops such as soy beans. The *People's Daily* of March 16, 1960, stated that the principal undertakings of productive enterprises run by the schools should be cultivating of high-yield economic crops and making handicraft products of the types produced by rural people as sideline occupations.

There are no national figures available for acreage of farmland cultivated or workshops operated by agricultural middle schools. However, provincial-level figures for three provinces have been reported. In Kiangsu, the 2,174 schools were said to be cultivating 115,400 *mou* (a *mou* equals about one-sixth of an acre) and operating 1,446 handicraft workshops and factories in April 1960. In Fukien at the same time, 560 schools were tilling 16,500 *mou* and running 330 "factories and farms." In August 1959, 930 schools in Liaoning were cultivating 4,532 *mou* and operating 1,016 factories. These figures indicate a rather wide variance in the scope of productive enterprises in the three areas, and suggest that in many schools the students are confined to agricultural labour or work in enterprises that are not run directly by the schools.

The production plans of the schools are incorporated into the overall plan of the commune and the commune assists the schools in obtaining draft animals and large agricultural tools, with arrangements for the supply of raw materials for the workshops, and with the marketing of products. Division of labour within the schools is reportedly based on age and sex, with the older students specialising in agricultural labour and the younger ones in handicraft production. The boys are commonly assigned to heavier work, and the girls undertake lighter tasks such as feeding animals and poultry.

There is little information available on the type and volume of products produced by the school workshops. One account of a school in Anhwei reported that it had trial-manufactured 98 kinds of insecticides and 177 different kinds of chemical and bacterial fertilisers, and that over a period of two years it had produced 5,100,000 catties (a catty is slightly heavier than a pound) of insecticides and 37,000,000 catties of fertiliser for market.[19]

Part of the staff of the school is charged with the special responsibility for supervising productive work. For example, one Kiangsu school with 303 students was reported in the spring of 1959 to have seven "experienced peasants" and "technical workers" in charge of production, in addition to the eleven teachers on its staff.

Degree of financial self-sufficiency

A description of the productive enterprises of the agricultural middle schools leads logically into a discussion of their finances, since the schools are designed to be virtually self-sufficient through their own production activities. The proudest boast concerning these schools has to do with the economy of their operation.

In discussing the economic advantages of the agricultural middle schools, the régime has released some interesting figures on the comparative costs, to the state and to the student's family, of educating a youth in agricultural middle schools and ordinary junior middle schools. The figures used in the discussion are based on statistics collected in the model province of Kiangsu. Three somewhat different versions of these figures are available in the data, but perhaps the most authoritative is

---

[19] Li Chien, *loc. cit.*

the one included in a detailed report to the National People's Congress in April 1960 by a Kiangsu delegate. The figures, on a per student per year basis, are as follows [20]:

	Cost to State	Cost to Family
Ordinary junior middle school	187 yuan	108 yuan
Agricultural middle school	13 „	38 „

The figure for the cost to the state of ordinary middle school study is roughly confirmed by another source, which reports that it costs the state about 500 yuan to put a junior middle school student through his three-year course.[21]

It is not completely clear what is meant by "cost to the state" in the case of agricultural middle schools. Presumably this expense is actually charged to the communes, but it is possible that the provincial or lower-level governmental subdivisions still play a small role directly in the financing of the schools. In any case, it is apparent that the cost of running the agricultural schools borne by the authorities is but a small fraction of the cost of supporting ordinary junior middle schools. The reduction in the financial burden on parents is not so great, but is still equal to two-thirds of the expense of supporting a student in the ordinary schools.

The initial cost of establishing the schools, such as making available school buildings and farm land, is usually borne by the communes out of their welfare fund. From that point on the school is expected to strive as quickly as possible to earn enough to pay its teachers' salaries and its students' tuition, to provide operational funds, and to supply the students with food, books and other needed school supplies.

The extent to which self-sufficiency has actually been achieved by these schools is difficult to determine. There are glowing accounts of individual schools or groups of schools which have paid all their expenses and returned a profit to the communes, and there are frequent statements that "many" agricultural schools are "wholly or partially" self-supporting. But few hard statistics have been released, and those which have become available indicate that the goal of self-sufficiency has proven to be elusive. The case of Kiangsu is again illustrative. In May 1959, after one year's experience with these schools, a Kiangsu official wrote in *Red Flag* that all the agricultural middle schools in his province should be entirely self-sufficient within two years—*i.e.*, by the spring of 1961. About a year later, in July 1960, an enthusiastic NCNA release stated

---

20 Kuan Wen-hui, " Agricultural Middle Schools in Kiangsu," NCNA, April 7, 1960. The other two versions of these figures differ mainly in the cost to the state of the agricultural middle schools, which is variously cited as 10 and 18·20 yuan.

21 Ch'eng Cho-ju, Sun Shui-kuan, and Hsü Wen, " Hail the Success of Agricultural Middle Schools in Kiangsu Province," *People's Daily*, November 27, 1959.

flatly that most of the schools in Kiangsu were already able to cover all their expenditures. But Kiangsu delegate Kuan Wen-hui's speech to the National People's Congress a few months earlier suggests that this report was premature. This speech (in April 1960) stated that at that time only 19 per cent. of the Kiangsu schools were "wholly self-supporting," another 18·6 per cent. were "to a large extent self-supporting," and 31·8 per cent. were "partly self-supporting." The implication left was that the remaining 30·6 per cent. were still wholly dependent on outside sources. In the same speech it was reported that the plan now called upon the schools in Kiangsu to "strive for self-support, partly or wholly," within "two years or a little longer," indicating that full independence was not seen as attainable before 1962 or later.

Reports concerning Fukien in the spring of 1960 suggest a similar situation. Of the 560 agricultural middle schools there, 55 were reported to be able to pay their teachers' salaries fully, and another 61 to be self-sufficient in food. Individual cases of schools which had paid for teachers' wages, food and other expenses were cited, but the impression conveyed was that only a relatively small minority of the schools were able to pay the major part of their expenses.[22]

The best available example of the way in which a typical agricultural middle school seeks to balance its budget is given in an article in *Red Flag* on May 1, 1959. It concerns a school in Kiangsu, and presents the school's balance-sheet of receipts and expenditures in 1958 as follows[23]:

Receipts:

Source	Amount
Agricultural products	13,824·40 yuan
Silkworm rearing	400·00
Wool	76·00
Pig rearing	280·00
Rabbit rearing	11·00
Mfg. of straw ropes	25·00
Mfg. of rush mats	300·00
Mfg. of fertiliser and insecticides	1,100·00
Total	16,016·40 yuan
Expenditures: [not broken down]	18,792·00 yuan

For 1959, the same school planned to attain complete self-sufficiency by earning a total of 30,890 yuan through cultivating 135 *mou* of wheat,

[22] Liu Yung-sheng, Cheng I-mu, and Chou Chü-chen, *loc. cit.*
[23] Ch'en Kuang, "There is a Great Possibility for Agricultural Middle Schools," *loc. cit.*

121 *mou* of paddy rice, and 5 *mou* of soya beans, and by growing vegetables and ramie, raising pigs, sheep, chickens, and fish, and making rush mats.[24] Expenses contemplated for 1959 were as follows:

Item	Amount
Yearly boarding charges (calculated at 6 yuan per capita per month)	22,608 yuan
Wages and salaries of teachers and staff	5,160
School operating expenses	**1,100**
Books and stationery	1,212
Total	30,080 yuan

Research and experimental work

In addition to producing goods for market to achieve self-sufficiency, the agricultural middle schools, like all middle schools and colleges in Communist China, are supposed to give substance to the tripartite combination of learning, labour and research by engaging in various types of experimental work. The schools are generally reported to be devoting at least a part of their agricultural acreage to experimental plots, and there are numerous reports of their achievements in attaining high yields. A number of schools are reported to conduct experimental work in meteorology (weather forecasting) and water conservancy. Some schools apparently also do research on fertiliser, insecticides and soil analysis, and their students design (as well as trial manufacture) new types of farm implements and machinery. In regard to this latter category of investigation, one report stated that senior students in Kiangsu agricultural middle schools had " created " ten kinds of modern agricultural tools, including a mowing machine, a fodder mixing appliance, an insecticide sprinkler, and rice and wheat threshing machines.[25] As has been noted previously, another account stated that students in one school in Anhwei had trial-manufactured 98 different kinds of insecticides and 177 kinds of chemical and bacterial fertilisers.

This kind of activity is considered to be very important. After two years of experience with the schools, the régime emphasised their role as " strongholds for scientific research for the people's communes " and exhorted them to do more in this field.[26] In carrying out experimental work, the schools are urged to focus on problems confronted in current production, and to seek solutions through native methods appropriate to local conditions.

24 The breakdown of income among these several sources was not given.
25 *Kuang-ming Jih-pao*, July 23, 1960.
26 *People's Daily* commentary, May 18, 1960.

Communist Party Leadership

The importance attached to the agricultural middle schools is apparent in the particularly intimate role which Communist Party functionaries play in the daily life of the schools. From the days of their inception, reports from all areas have stressed that the secretaries of the Party Committees in the communes commonly act as heads of the schools. They or other high-ranking local Party functionaries usually are reported to teach the political courses. An unsigned article in the *People's Daily* on February 2, 1960, stated that throughout the country Party Committees at all levels actively supported the schools, included discussions of their work on the agenda of their daily meetings, and inspected them regularly. An editorial in the same paper on March 16, 1960, emphasised strengthened leadership by commune Party Committees as the basic guarantee of the success of the schools, and stressed the familiar dictum that " politics must be in command " and the ideological and political consciousness of both students and teachers must be brought to a high level. Due attention is paid to the fostering of membership in the Young Pioneers and Communist Youth League (for students) and the Communist Party (for teachers).

THE FIRST GRADUATES

Earlier in this article the origin and growth of the agricultural middle schools has been traced and the régime's thinking concerning the reasons and purposes behind their establishment has been examined. This has been followed by a detailed description of the schools and the way they function. Before going on to discuss in summary fashion the advantages seen by the régime in this type of school as compared with the acknowledged problems and criticisms which their launching has engendered, it may be useful to take a close look at the first graduates of these new institutions in order to see what knowledge they are actually claimed to have acquired and to ascertain what plans the régime has for them.

Inasmuch as most of the three-year agricultural middle schools are considered to have been established since the beginning of 1958, it came as something of a surprise to outside observers that a number of graduates of these schools emerged in the summer of 1960. This development seems, incidentally, not to have been expected by even so eminent a personage as Lu Ting-yi, for the Party spokesman stated flatly in his February 1960 article in *Jen-min Chiao-yü* that the first graduates would come out " next year "—*i.e.*, in 1961. Nevertheless, less than a month later articles began appearing with the news that there would be graduates in the summer of 1960. The first of these articles to become available, published in the *Kuang-ming Jih-pao* on March 12, stated that about one-fourth of the students who had entered the third year of the course in one school would be graduated the following summer. It added that the early graduates had been " transferred [into the schools] from a sup-plementary class," thus suggesting that some of the students may have gained advanced standing through spare-time study before their entry into the agricultural schools. Another possibility would be that students had actually been transferred with advanced standing from ordinary junior middle schools.

Kiangsu was not to be allowed an unchallenged claim to the first graduates, however. A speech to the National People's Congress in April by a Szechwan delegate asserted that a school in his province had turned out 34 graduates in 1959, and an article in *Red Flag* later in the year (July 1, 1960) claimed that in 1959 one school in Anhwei had graduated 298 " students with excellent records " ahead of time, to meet the needs of the commune.

Despite these early suspiciously competitive-sounding claims—reminiscent of the earlier apparent competition for the credit for estab-lishing the first agricultural middle school—the main cluster of publicity concerning the " first " graduates came in the late summer of 1960. Between late July and early September scattered accounts revealed that about 50,000 graduates of the schools were turned out that summer in six provinces. Once again Kiangsu came out second best, since Hopei province was reported to have graduated over 37,000 who were said to have studied for three years, while Kiangsu's 6,000-plus graduates were said to have been in school for only $2\frac{1}{2}$ years.[27]

In the fanfare surrounding the emergence of the first sizeable numbers of graduates, their accomplishments were highly praised. The *Kuang-ming Jih-pao*, for example, speaking of the Kiangsu graduates on July 23, 1960, said:

> The half-farming and half-study agricultural middle schools have produced rich fruits. The rural people's communes now begin to have a research force of new-style intellectual and technical cadres trained by themselves. This is a great victory of the thought of Mao Tse-tung and a great victory of the Party's educational programme.

The skills acquired by the new graduates were enumerated in detail. A *People's Daily* commentary of August 10 affirmed that " most " of the graduates had learned how to cultivate farm crops and raise animals, that some of them had learned how to make native-type fertilisers and insecticides and to repair farm implements, and that some had mastered the basic techniques of operating electric motors, diesel engines, lathes, and other machine tools. The article on Hopei's 37,000 graduates in

---

[27] See a group of four items in the *People's Daily*, August 10, 1960.

the same issue of the paper reported that 8,000 of them had learned to drive tractors, 12,000 had learned to operate machines used in irrigation and drainage work, and " quite a few " had learned to make and repair machines, to make soil surveys and plans for water conservancy. Shensi graduates were generally reported to be able to cultivate various crops, control plant diseases and insect pests, irrigate fields, feed and care for domestic animals and fowl, operate agricultural machines, do farm accounting, and make fertilisers and insecticides; " many " among them had learned how to operate special ploughs and weeding and sowing machines. Data on Kiangsu cited the example of one school where all the graduates had learned to cultivate major crops and raise animals, and just under one-third of them had learned either to make native chemical fertiliser and insecticides or to repair farm tools; another group of slightly under one-third of the total had learned such things as weaving, sugar making, and wine brewing, while " some " (apparently a still smaller group) had grasped the main techniques of operating motor-driven machinery.[28] It would appear from these accounts that not all graduates emerged from the schools with the same skills, as a result of either specialisation within the school or differentiation on the basis of ability.

The question of the assignments of these graduates was discussed in the same articles. As expected, the principle was firmly stated that most of the graduates would remain in the rural areas and go to work in the communes. The authoritative *People's Daily* commentary on the graduates said nothing about any of them going on to further study, stating merely that " they will stay in the rural areas to work, as required by the people's communes." The *Kuang-ming Jih-pao* article concerning Kiangsu asserted that 80 per cent. of the graduates in that province would stay in the communes, and the remainder would go on to higher studies. Other reports simply stated that most graduates would take up work assignments, with a small number going on to school.

Graduates were assigned to the communes to work as tractor drivers and mechanics, bookkeepers, workers in weather stations and agricultural experimentation centres, teachers in *min-pan* primary schools, and as holders of a variety of " technical " positions in agricultural machinery, fertiliser and insecticide plants. Some of them were assigned to take further short-term training in such specialities as agricultural technical work, accountancy, chemistry, health work, pedagogy and meteorology before undertaking their jobs.

---

[28] For these details, see the *People's Daily*, August 10, 1960, and *Kuang-ming Jih-pao*, July 23, 1960.

CLAIMED ADVANTAGES AND ACKNOWLEDGED PROBLEMS

Most of the advantages seen by the régime in the institution of the agricultural middle schools have been mentioned in passing earlier in this
article. To summarise briefly, the Chinese Communist leadership views
these schools as a means to satisfy growing popular demands for post-
primary education. It also sees them as a way to train large numbers of
rural youths to serve the communes in a variety of lower-level technical
and administrative jobs requiring a rudimentary form of junior middle
school education plus vocational training in crop-cultivation agriculture
and other related rural occupations. It evaluates the form of the schools
highly because they are at least potentially able to be self-supporting.
They are also able to function with fewer teachers than ordinary middle
schools and to utilise local sources of teaching personnel. It is also
claimed that the integral combination of education and labour in these
half-day schools provides the student with an ideal environment in which
to see more clearly the relationship between theory and practice and,
through opportunities to apply his learning directly and immediately to
practical work, to digest and better understand the things he is taught in
class. The research and experimental work performed by the schools
is considered to be especially valuable because it is closely geared to
current local problems and its results are directly popularised among the
local rural people through the students who live and work among them.

One final advantage of the schools is seen in the political sphere. The
student body is given political instruction and is then used as an organised
young activist group in the furtherance of the various centrally inspired
mass movements through which policy is implemented in Communist
China. One account, for example, notes that because of their active role
in the campaign to establish the communes in 1958, the Kiangsu schools
" were praised as ' political propaganda stations,' while their students
were called ' propagandists '." [29]

Although the agricultural middle schools are highly praised and their
allegedly great advantages have been frequently cited in the available
mainland sources, these same sources also make it clear that the establishment of the schools has elicited criticism from some quarters and
has resulted in a number of admittedly difficult problems. Among the
difficulties mentioned as encountered by the new schools in their early
days were shortages of competent teachers, lack of needed school facilities and equipment, shortages of funds, inadequate provision of production facilities, and poor organisation of arrangements for the division of
time between study and labour. As a result of these problems, there
was apparently considerable early scepticism about these schools on the

[29] Ch'eng Cho-ju, Sun Shui-kuan, and Hsü Wen, *loc. cit.*

part of the masses and some cadres, and these doubts were reflected in low enrolments and, in some cases at least, a serious rate of drop-outs.

As early as July 12, 1958, a few months after the big push to establish such schools began, a domestic radio broadcast reported that some people were saying that the quality of the schools was low, that there were no good instructors in them, and that they were not welcomed by the masses. A Kiangsu official, writing later about the early days of the schools, stated that some people showed a " negative attitude " towards them, asking: " What would be the use for farmers to learn farming? " He added that others predicted that the schools would be failures from beginning to end. The official himself admitted that in the early stages the schools were " inadequate and inferior " in relation to the ordinary middle schools in regard to both facilities and teaching quality.[30]   An article in the *Kuang-ming Jih-pao* on August 14, 1959, stated that after a careful " propaganda campaign," that year's graduates of primary schools in one Kiangsu area were saying that they would " cheerfully apply " to get into the agricultural middle schools if they failed in entrance exams for the ordinary full-time schools—a clear indication that the agricultural schools were considered to be second-rate.

Further criticisms of the early days were belatedly acknowledged in the spring of 1960. An NCNA dispatch of March 15 revealed that some critics had complained that the schools were " supposed to be institutions of education and production but are in fact neither." A Szechwan delegate to the National People's Congress reported in April that ideological problems had been prevalent among both teachers and students. This situation was later reflected in an article in *Red Flag* on July 1, 1960, which stated that at first " the hearts of the teachers and students were not in the school." The author illustrated the point by saying that after early results in one Anhwei commune's school turned out to be " poor," 16 students of an original 80 dropped out in less than half a month and there were " grumblings " among the masses. A Liaoning delegate to the 1960 People's Congress told the meeting that " those obsessed with the capitalist class view of education " said, when the schools were first set up, that since the teachers had not finished senior middle school and the schools were run by the masses, they could not be run well and would not last very long. Perhaps the sharpest early criticism was that reported by Ch'en Kuang in an article in the May 16, 1960, issue of *Red Flag*. The Kiangsu official said that at the beginning " persons with bourgeois viewpoints " derided the agricultural middle school and " called it a school for beggars." He acknowledged that some parents were unwilling to have their children attend.

[30] Ch'en Kuang, " There is a Great Possibility for Agricultural Middle Schools," *loc. cit.*

Apparently the children and their parents were not the only ones who took a dim view of the schools in their early stages. An article in *Red Flag* on April 1, 1959, chastised those cadres who were running the schools " like a spare-time and temporary school." A year later a Kiangsu delegate to the People's Congress criticised " a small number of lower-level cadres " who had felt that attendance at the schools took too much time away from production: " They intended to turn agricultural middle schools into spare-time schools, and . . . would consider these schools as production shock teams." [31]

The majority of the above-mentioned acknowledged criticisms, it will be noted, were publicised only belatedly, and their revelation was customarily accompanied by assertions that the problems which elicited the complaints had been overcome. But some authoritative items in the mainland press published as late as the spring of 1960 indicated that the new schools were not yet accepted as completely successful at that time. For example, an unsigned article in the *People's Daily* on February 2, 1960, made the distinctly qualified evaluation that the agricultural middle schools " have now begun to shape up " and " have fulfilled fairly well their teaching and productive labour plans." An editorial in the same central Party journal on March 16, although calling for more of the schools throughout the nation, admitted that " not everybody is clearly aware of the great significance of the agricultural middle schools. Some say that the agricultural middle schools do not look like schools."

Probably the most persistent single problem faced by the régime in attempting to consolidate the schools has been the recruiting of sufficient teachers with adequate preparation. The existence of this problem is not surprising, since there is abundant evidence of a chronic shortage of qualified teachers in the schools at all levels in Communist China.[32] But the frequent references to the problem and accounts of a variety of stop-gap measures taken to deal with it show that it is particularly serious in the agricultural middle schools. Reference has been made earlier in this article to the calibre of teaching personnel and their level of qualifications. The problem arising out of the recruitment of such people was recognised by the régime. A Kiangsu official, writing in *Red Flag* on May 16, 1960, stated that at the beginning, when the agricultural schools had no full-time teachers and therefore borrowed instructors from the ordinary schools, the policy question arose as to whether it was better to train teachers first, or to set up the schools first. It was decided to establish the schools, obtain a staff, and then train it. This training

---

31 Kuan Wen-hui, " Agricultural Middle Schools in Kiangsu," NCNA, April 7, 1960.
32 In this connection, see Theodore H. E. Chen, *Teacher Training in Communist China*, Studies in Comparative Education series, OE–14058 (Washington: U.S. Office of Education, December 1960).

was given through correspondence courses, short-term special vacation courses organised by normal schools and normal colleges, and in some cases by sending outstanding teachers to attend normal schools. The aid of teachers in the ordinary schools was solicited, and teachers in the agricultural schools visited their classes and learned from them.

There is evidence that not all the teachers were happy with their assignments. Acknowledged " ideological problems " affecting the teachers in Szechwan have already been mentioned. A similar problem was also faced in Kiangsu, where many of the teachers, most of whom were originally from the city, were admitted to have at first disliked the countryside and their appointed tasks there. Their views were reported to have changed as a result of political indoctrination and their salutary experience with labour.[33]

The régime encountered one new problem only in the summer of 1960, when the first sizeable contingent of graduates emerged from the agricultural middle schools. This was the disgruntlement of graduates upon learning that they would not be allowed to continue their schooling. The Director of Education in the Kiangsu Provincial Party Committee acknowledged in an article in the *Kuang-ming Jih-pao* on July 27 that he himself had received a number of letters from " graduates who expressed unwillingness to obey the unified assignments of communes and demanded higher education. Some even expressed reluctance to stay in the countryside and take part in agricultural production." He added that the reasons for going to work in the countryside " are not adequately understood by all graduates. . . . Not a few of them are unable to adjust their thoughts." The Director's answer was to address a stern lecture to the recalcitrant students, telling them that if they were unwilling to take part in labour, it was because they were subject to the " extremely harmful " influence of " bourgeois ideas." He also called upon all the authorities concerned to conduct " penetrating ideological education " among the graduates to explain the necessity for the assignments to jobs.[34] The duty to devote themselves to rural work was also stressed in the commentary accompanying the several reports hailing the graduates published in the *People's Daily* on August 10, 1960.

STATUS OF THE SCHOOLS IN 1961

Despite these problems, the agricultural middle schools were hailed by the régime throughout the first two years of their existence as a highly valuable new educational development. When Lu Ting-yi wrote his

[33] Ch'en Kuang, " The Growth of Agricultural Middle Schools," *loc. cit.*
[34] Ouyang Hui-lin, " Obey Assignments by the Commune, Be Content with Staying in the Country, and Work for the Development of Agricultural Production," *Kuang-ming Jih-pao*, July 27, 1960.

authoritative and widely cited article on the educational reforms of 1958 in the September 1, 1958, issue of *Red Flag*, he said:

> Two measures taken at the end of last year and early this year stimulated the advance in education. One was to apply in all schools the principle of diligent work combined with thrifty study [*i.e.*, the combination of education and labour]. *The other was the opening of agricultural middle schools.* (Emphasis added.)

On the occasion of the first and second anniversaries of the founding of the schools, in the spring of 1959 and 1960, Lu again lent his prestige to them by writing commemorative pieces.

Lu's important endorsement of the schools was seconded by enthusiastic articles in authoritative newspapers and magazines during the same two-year period, as has been noted. There was a significant clustering of publicity for the agricultural middle schools around the March anniversary date in 1959 and 1960, but other items appeared from time to time throughout the period. At the time of the second anniversary of the founding of the schools, in March 1960, the *People's Daily* forcefully repeated its earlier endorsement of them and called for the opening of such schools " at once " in all areas where they did not yet exist. It described the setting up of new agricultural middle schools and the strengthening of the old ones as an " urgent task " in rural educational work.[35] This strong approval voiced by the central Party journal was reflected a few months later in the summer of 1960, when the emergence of the first agricultural middle school graduates was greeted with a fanfare of publicity.

Thus as late as the summer of 1960 there was every indication that the schools had established themselves as an important and highly regarded new feature of the educational system and as the object of continuing favourable comment in mainland media. With the onset of the fall of 1960, however, news of the agricultural middle schools seems to have virtually disappeared from Communist Chinese sources. Throughout the fall and into the spring of 1961 there was no indication in available materials that these new institutions were discussed at any appreciable length in the mass media. Up until March 1961 the absence of such accounts was not particularly noteworthy, as gaps of several months had occurred between earlier flurries of publicity on the subject. But when the third anniversary of the officially celebrated founding of the schools passed in March 1961 apparently without notice, the contrast with earlier anniversaries was rather striking.

There seems to be no particular reason why the third anniversary should have passed unobserved while the earlier two were made the

---

35 *People's Daily* editorial, March 16, 1960.

occasion for considerable publicity featured by comment at authoritative levels. In fact, there was reason to believe, from an earlier high-level statement on the pace with which the schools could be expected to develop, that the third anniversary should have been an especially auspicious one. In the course of endorsing the schools on the occasion of their founding in Kiangsu in March 1958, Lu Ting-yi had predicted that it would take three years to work out their problems and consolidate them.

The conspicuous drop-off in publicity for the schools during the last quarter of 1960 and the first quarter of 1961 raises inevitably some question as to their current status. There is no indication as yet that the schools have been abandoned. As a matter of fact, their continued existence was apparently confirmed in an editorial in the *People's Daily* published on February 28, 1961. This editorial was directed toward the problem of the shortage of personnel capable of handling tractors, irrigation equipment, and other agricultural machines. It mentioned in passing that the opening of numerous agricultural middle schools had been one factor in the training of operators of tractors and other agricultural machines, and it called upon all such schools to set up courses enabling their students to master the skills involved. But the editorial placed no particular stress on the role of the agricultural middle schools in training such personnel, and appeared to take the position that the development of the needed skills was a complicated matter that required more attention than was being given it. In calling upon the agricultural schools to set up effective courses to achieve these goals, it also implied that such courses were not yet generally in operation. This implication was somewhat curious, in view of the fact that the ability to handle tractors and other agricultural machines had been previously reported as one of the main attributes of agricultural middle school graduates. Thus the net effect of the editorial, viewed in retrospect, is to suggest that the esteem in which the agricultural middle schools were held by the régime may have suffered somewhat during late 1960 and early 1961. This in turn might be part of the explanation for the marked decline in publicity for the schools during the same period.

Another possible explanation may be found in the nature of conditions prevailing in the rural areas during the fall of 1960 and early 1961. These months have been marked by the continuation of an acknowledged agricultural crisis which has led the régime to take drastic measures to reinforce the manpower available on the agricultural front. Accounts in the mainland press, for example, have reported that several million people were moved from cities to the countryside in late 1960 and early 1961 to augment the supply of farm labour. It is unlikely that the régime would take such drastic measures until all resources already available on the scene had been utilised. The temporary closing down of schools in such an emergency would not be unprecedented in Communist China. And the agricultural middle schools in particular were designed to adjust their classwork to the necessity for more labour in the " busy agricultural season." All evidence indicates that the period from the fall of 1960 to the spring of 1961 was virtually one continuous " busy season " in the rural areas of Communist China. Thus it is not inconceivable that the operation of the agricultural middle schools has been drastically curtailed or that some of them have even been temporarily suspended during this critical period. Such a situation would serve to explain the absence of publicity for the schools in the spring of 1961.

There is much at stake for the régime in the fate of these new-style institutions which embody their basic educational principles in a striking form. For this reason it is probable that, even if they have been forced to cut back their operations during a period of serious crisis, these schools will be revived, perhaps in a somewhat modified form, once the emergency has passed. To abandon them at this juncture would be to abandon one of the fundamental instrumentalities through which the Chinese Communists hope to achieve their goals in both education and production.

The Organisation and Development of Science *

By JOHN M. H. LINDBECK

WHEN China's Communists came to power in 1949, they began to outline ambitious plans to thrust China into the company of modern, industrial and scientifically advanced countries. They were not prepared with blueprints for the task which fell to them, for national responsibilities came sooner than they had anticipated. Their appraisal of what steps were required, what priorities to assign, the best allocation of resources at hand and to be developed, and the national goals which might be realistically achieved, took time to determine. After an initial period of consolidation and consideration, they set their course of development in the First and Second Five-Year Plans. These were intended to bring about the modernisation of the world's most populous nation at the fastest possible pace in ways which would not jeopardise the state's political control and ideological commitments.

In January 1956, less than six years ago, the compelling scientific needs of national construction finally led the Central Committee of the Communist Party to call for " a march on science." At the State Supreme Council on January 25, 1956, Mao Tse-tung announced that there should be " a long-range plan for the elimination of backwardness in the economic, scientific and cultural fields." Subsequently the State Council, at the direction of the Central Committee of the Communist Party, established a Planning Committee for Scientific Development, under Marshal Ch'en Yi, to prepare a Twelve-Year Science Plan. In the course of seven months 200 scientists, with the assistance for a period of two months of seventeen Soviet scientists, headed by A. I. Nikhaylov,[1]

* Many scholars and specialists contributed advice and information in the preparation of this article. This help, including that of K. I. Kitagawa of the National Science Foundation, R. N. Ross of the Chinese Science Project in the Libraries of M.I.T., and Lawrence (Hao) Chang of Harvard University, is gratefully acknowledged.

[1] *Jen-min Shou-t'se*, 1958, p. 603; I. N. Kiselov, " Scientific Ties Between Two Academies," *Vestnik Akademii Nauk*, S.S.S.R. No. 9, September, 1959, in Joint Publications Research Service (hereafter JPRS): 2139-N (January 13, 1960), p. 5; Kuo Mo-jo, " Development of Scientific Research in China," New China News Agency (hereafter NCNA), June 18, 1956, in *Current Background* (hereafter CB) (Hong Kong: U.S. Consulate-General), No. 400, p. 2.

prepared a draft plan. This was presented to the Eighth Congress of the Chinese Communist Party in September 1956 and endorsed by it on September 27, 1957. It was then sent to the Soviet Union where it was reviewed by 640 Soviet scientists, divided into twenty-six consultative groups. In October 1957 a visiting delegation of 120 Chinese scientists and officials discussed the plan in Moscow and concluded by asking for Soviet co-operation on 100 of the 582 research projects outlined in the plan.[2] Finally, it was forwarded to the National People's Congress for approval. The goal it set for the end of 1967 was " that in those branches of science and technology which are essential to our national economy, we should catch up with the advanced levels in the world." [3] A parallel section of the plan was drawn up for philosophy and the social sciences.[4]

The call for " a march on science " marked a major turning point in the development of science in Communist China. The Academy of Sciences, the main focus of scientific activity, made remarkable growth. Research facilities were expanded and the research staff of the Academy was doubled in one year. Other agencies also benefited in the allocation of funds. From 1955 to 1956 the sums budgeted for science, under the category culture, education and health, underwent over a six-fold increase.

Many factors coalesced to produce this sudden spurt in scientific activity. In general, there was a growing appreciation by the country's rulers that modern industrialism, which they value with determined passion, is the outcome of science. Preparations for the Second Five-Year Plan made the need for a Chinese scientific base evident. Not only engineers, but also scientists in greater numbers were essential if full use was to be made of China's resources. There also was a growing realisation that out of scientific research, new and revolutionary technologies were emerging. Russia's space exploits appear to have made a strong impression on China's leaders. This may have been reinforced by Mao Tse-tung's discussions with Khrushchev and others during his trip to the Soviet Union, November 2-21, 1957, at the time that two major Chinese scientific delegations were conferring about China's Twelve-Year Science Plan with Russian scientists and negotiating for increased scientific and technical co-operation.[5] Moreover, an increase in

---

2 *Novoye Vreruya*, Moscow, No. 50, December 12, 1957, p. 12.
3 Liu Shao-ch'i to the Eighth Party Congress, NCNA, September 16, 1956.
4 Chou En-lai to the Eighth Party Congress, NCNA, September 18, 1956.
5 *Jen-min Jih-pao (People's Daily)*, Peking, November 2, 1957.

China's dependence on other countries for scientific assistance was neither satisfactory nor feasible. Russia had provided the scientific skills and support during the First Five-Year Plan, but could not be expected to meet China's growing needs during future and larger plans. Finally, inferiority in science touched Chinese national pride and ambitions. Seeking great power status, China's leaders expressed determination to match the scientific performance of modern and great powers.

Whatever the reasons for Communist China's increased attention to science, the present scope of Chinese activities requires examination and appraisal of both its potential contributions to science and its international implications. A survey of the general pattern of organisation and trends in the development of science in China will assist analysis. What resources did the Chinese Communists have when they began their "march on science"? How were these resources used? How were scientific capacities developed? What were some of the critical problems? What policies were adopted to promote science? How has research been organised? Answers to many of these questions can only be approximate with publicly available information. Secrecy, which has drawn sharp protests from some of China's scientists, restrictions on international communications, also a cause of complaint by Chinese scientists,[6] and a welter of conflicting claims and statistics obscure many features of the situation. Nonetheless, the main developments seem to be plain.

AVAILABILITY AND USE OF RESOURCES, 1949–56

When the Chinese Communists took major steps to develop science in China, they started with resources inherited from decades of earlier scientific activity and development. These remained basically unchanged before 1956.

Ten years ago China already possessed a small corps of college graduates trained in various scientific and technical fields. Among college graduates there were very roughly 10,000 who had degrees in the natural sciences, 25,000 in engineering, 10,000 in agriculture, 7,000 in medicine

---

[6] Some of these complaints were voiced in a memorandum published by a group of scientists in *Kuang-ming Jih-pao*, June 7, 1957; also see *Opposition Aroused in China by Marxist Planning of Scientific Research* (Oxford: Society for Freedom in Science), Occasional Pamphlet No. 19, December 1959; *Scientia Sinica* (*Chung-kuo K'o-hsueh*), Vol. VIII, No. 10, 1959, p. 1159. Part of the problem was the overzealous interpretation and application by Chinese Communist officials of Article 8 of the "Provisional Regulations Governing the Control of Book and Periodical Publishing, Printing, and Distribution Trades" (promulgated August 16, 1952) which stipulated that publishers "shall not publish words or charts that disclose state secrets." All research, of course, is state business.

and health, and 60,000 in law and the social sciences.[7]   Those with advanced post-graduate degrees were the significant group for scientific progress, both in terms of conducting research and for training new scientists. Since graduate work was nearly non-existent in China, this group was composed almost entirely of those who had studied abroad. In all fields combined, of those who received one or more advanced degrees before 1949, perhaps 2,000 to 3,000 were on the mainland of China in 1950.[8]

In May 1950 the roster of Chinese natural scientists totalled 862 names, of which 174, or 20 per cent., were outside the country. Some 225 of these natural scientists were reported to be engaged principally in research before the Communists came to power.[9] A number of these men fled from China with the Communist take-over, but the majority remained.[10] Almost the entire roster of the 190 physical and natural scientists who at present are members of the Department Committees of the Chinese Academy of Sciences is made up of the men who were leaders in science and rising research scientists before 1949. About 150 of them are known to have received training abroad, eighty of them in the United States and most of the remainder in Europe and Japan. These men, many of them former members of the Academia Sinica under the Republic, are Chinese equivalents to Soviet Academicians.

Before 1949 most of China's basic research was carried on in twenty-one research institutes under two national academies: The Academia Sinica (established in 1928) with thirteen institutes and the National Academy of Peking (established in 1929) with eight institutes. Altogether seventeen of these institutes were concerned with mathematics, physical and life sciences. In addition, the National Geological Survey of China (established in 1916) had eight research laboratories with thirty senior scientists and about 200 technical specialists. Various government ministries had others. Thus the military establishment operated the

---

[7] These are crude projections from figures on college graduates presented in *Chung-kuo Chiao-yü Nien-chien* (*Chinese Yearbook of Education*) (Shanghai: 1948). Anderson Shih, Director of Union Research Institute, Hong Kong, in " The Comparative Status of Science and Education between Communist China and USSR " (paper read at the Third International Sovietological Conference, September 18–24, 1960, Lake Kawaguchi, Japan), p. 11, estimates that some 20,000 scientists and technicians were scattered over China in 1949.

[8] Leo A. Orleans, *Professional Manpower and Education in Communist China* (Washington: National Science Foundation, 1961), p. 77.

[9] Kuo Mo-jo, " General Report on 1950 Work and Main Points of 1951 Programme of the Chinese Academy of Sciences," *Hsin Hua Yueh-pao*, May 1951, in CB 153, pp. 4–11; *K'o-hsueh T'ung-pao*, No. 19, 1959, p. 613.

[10] Anderson Shih, *loc. cit.*, p. 2. Shih reports that over 90 per cent. of China's professors and scientists had been approached and urged to remain at their posts before the Communists established their government.

Air Force Research Bureau, the Central Ordnance Research Institute, and the Army Medical Research Institute. Under the Ministry of Health there was a National Institute of Medical Research with fifteen departments. The Ministry of Economics operated the Huanghai Industrial Research Institute and the National Industrial Research Bureau with seventeen departments. The Ministry of Agriculture had a research bureau with twelve departments. The Ministry of Education supported a variety of university research departments, the National Institute of Compilation and Translation, scientific equipment production plants and a number of provincial science institutes. Finally, a number of industrial plants carried on some engineering research.[11]

During the early period of Communist control, the country's scientific resources were under-utilised, or diverted to other purposes. " The most advanced form of all-out technological assistance " from the Soviet Union admittedly provided the specialised skills needed for " the overwhelming majority of the important industrial and technical facilities developed during the First Five-Year Plan." While the educational system was recast and expanded to emphasise science, technology and engineering, and to produce hastily trained technical staffs for the new industrial plants and modern facilities introduced by the Russians, the existing research institutes, industrial laboratories and government research organisations merely underwent reshuffling, rehabilitation and minor expansion.[12]

From the Communist viewpoint there was, in fact, little need for change in the function and organisation of science as it existed in 1949. On some points there were strong similarities in the outlook and policies of Nationalists and Communists. Both looked on science as a tool with which to develop China's resources and national strength:

> To be able to shoulder the heavy responsibility of reviving our nation and completing our revolution, we must have at all costs a clear idea of the content and meaning of science; we must propagate the spirit of science and we must utilise the methods of science; so that one man will be as efficient as ten, and in one day ten days' work will be done.[13]

This passage from a wartime directive by Chiang Kai-shek finds

11 Joseph Needham and Dorothy Needham, *Science Outpost: Papers of The Sino-British Science Co-operation Office, 1942–46* (London: 1948). Chart opposite p. 32 and *passim*; *The China Yearbook, 1931*, Shanghai, pp. 454 *et seq.*; *China Handbook, 1937–45*, New York, pp. 350 *et seq.*; *China Handbook, 1950*, New York, pp. 657 *et seq.*

12 Nieh Jung-chen, " China's Programme in Science and Technology," *Jen-min Jih-pao*, September 27, 1959, in CB 608, pp. 1–11.

13 Chiang Kai-shek, " The Way and Spirit of Science," in Needham, *op. cit.*, p. 79. Also see Chow Tse-tsung, *The May Fourth Movement* (Cambridge: Harvard University, 1960), pp. 344–345.

echoes in Communist statements and the provisions of the Common Programme promulgated by the Communist authorities in September 1949: " Efforts shall be made to develop the natural sciences in order to serve industrial, agricultural and national defence construction." Both the Nationalists and the Communists were equally interested in applied science and technology. The Communists at first merely sought to improve on existing research priorities and organisational patterns. They seemed to have been less concerned about science during this period than the politics of scientists and the " rehabilitation of ideology."

Nor was the imposition of central governmental control a major problem in the transition from one government to the next. Most of China's science was already under government agencies and direction. This was true of the national academies established in the first years of Nationalist rule. Subsequently, wartime mobilisation of national resources and the development of government research agencies, both industrial and academic, enlarged the government's place in science. Thus one authority replaced another when the Communists took over the country. Only a few university research programmes and industrial scientific laboratories and programmes remained to be brought under governmental management.

The Communist leaders were intent, however, on establishing firm control over existing institutions. On coming to power, the Chinese Communists took over and reorganised research centres, took active steps to mobilise scientists in support of the régime and developed a mass information programme for the popularisation of science.

Immediately following the establishment of the new régime in October 1949, Ch'en Po-ta, deputy chief of the Communist Party Propaganda Department and vice-president of the Marx-Lenin Institute, made a quick trip to the Soviet Union to consult with S. I. Vavilov, the President of the Soviet Academy of Sciences. In discussing the problems facing China in the field of science, Ch'en in particular explored the role and organisation of the Soviet Academy of Sciences, the Russian system for planning scientific research and the connection between science and technology.[14] Following Ch'en's return to China, the State Administrative Council at its second meeting on October 25 ordered the establishment, on November 1, 1949, of a Chinese Academy of Sciences directly under the jurisdiction of the Central People's Government,[15] " to direct and promote the development of science in China."

14 I. N. Kiselov, *loc. cit.*, p. 2.
15 *China Digest*, VII, No. 4, November 16, 1949, p. 23.

Kuo Mo-jo, a literary and cultural figure who was to become a notable spokesman for the new régime, upon his appointment as President of the new Academy, promptly went to the Soviet Union in November for further information and discussion about scientific organisation. Following his trip, Vavilov's book, *Thirty Years of Soviet Science*, was translated into Chinese to serve as a guide, along with Stalin's *Marxism and Problems of Linguistics*, for the organisation of the natural sciences in China.[16]

The Communist Party, of course, already had made preparations to bring scientists within its network of mass organisations. Plans for this were laid at a meeting convened in Peking during July 1949 where it projected an All-China Conference of Scientific Workers.[17] This conference, with about 470 participants meeting in Peking on August 18-24, 1950, formally established two key organisations. One was an All-China Federation of Natural Science Societies with " the aim of rallying all the scientific societies and organising all the scientific workers so as to carry out scientific research work for the improvement of production technique, and thus to promote New Democratic economic and cultural construction." [18] The other was the All-China Association for the Dissemination of Scientific and Technical Knowledge designed to assist the government popularise science.[19]

In terms of research, the Academy of Science was the significant body during this period. Until 1956 it was the agency of the government charged with official responsibility for national co-ordination and administration of research and, through its institutes, the main agency for research activities.[20] Its initial tasks were to (1) reorganise and consolidate the research institutes of the country; (2) provide for a continuation of research activities and plans, relating them to requirements in industry, education and national construction; (3) compile a national

---

16 Ch'ien San-ch'iang, "Modern Science in China," *Kuang-ming Jih-pao*, July 21, 1953, in CB 257, p. 5.

17 Coching Chu, "Science in New China," *Culture and Education in New China* (Peking: Foreign Languages Press, n.d.), p. 69.

18 *Jen-min Shou-ts'e 1953* (Tientsin: *Ta Kung Pao*), in CB 257, p. 8.

19 *Ibid.* p. 29. The purposes of this organisation are thus described: " The activities of the Association are directed toward the workers, peasants and soldiers, and its aims are: (1) to enable the labouring people to master a scientific knowledge of production so as to give full play to their powers in national economic construction; (2) to explain all natural phenomena from the materialistic viewpoint so as to get rid of superstitious notions; (3) to extol our accomplishments in scientific technique and the inventions resulting from the creative efforts of the labouring people so as to promote the people's patriotic spirit; and (4) to popularise medical and health knowledge so as to safeguard the people's state of health."

20 T'ao Meng-ho, "China's New Academia Sinica," *China Monthly Review*, November 1957, in CB 153, p. 21.

roster of scientists and work out assignments for them on a planned basis; (4) develop plans to increase China's scientific manpower in co-operation with the universities through training programmes, foreign education, and recruitment of Chinese scientists abroad; and (5) educate research workers in Marxist-Leninism.[21]

From 1949 to 1953, the Academy rehabilitated and reconstructed scientific activities more or less along pre-existing lines. With the formulation of the First Five-Year Plan (1953–1957), the Academy was reorganised with Russian assistance, slowly enlarged and expected to play a key role in the allocation of scientific resources.[22] However, very little was achieved. In short, as the Communist authorities in China have stated, " the scientific and technological work carried out during this period was rather scattered, and less research work of a creative nature was carried out." [23] The new Communist leadership in China, in effect, at first left science to the scientists. The scientists, however, were given little time for science, for they were mobilised for the Korean War effort and put through programmes of political indoctrination.

EXPANSION OF SCIENTIFIC FACILITIES

Once the decision to expand scientific work was made, the Chinese Communist authorities acted forcefully. Funds budgeted for science within the allocations to culture, education and health rose from about $15 million in 1955 to just short of $100 million in 1956. Since then the budget for science has represented about one per cent. of the total national budget. In 1960 this amounted to about $440 million, calculated on the basis of non-official exchange rates. While most of the increase seems to have been in support of industrial research and technological development, the budget of the Academy of Sciences was increased almost three-fold between 1953 and 1957, rising to almost $37 million. In 1956 and 1957 the Chinese Communists report that they spent over $9 million in British sterling to purchase scientific literature from non-Communist countries. The rapid rise in expenditures for science is clear from the following table:

---

[21] Kuo Mo-jo, " General Report on 1950 Work and 1951 Programme of the Chinese Academy of Sciences," *Hsin Hua Yueh-pao*, May 1951, in CB 153, pp. 4–11.

[22] Russian advisers, about a dozen in number, introduced an additional organisational level in the Academy by grouping the research institutes within four, later five, departments. The Academy adopted Soviet administrative practices, probably including accounting and reporting procedures and systems of internal communications. It followed Russian advice in the consolidation and redistribution of research projects, and, in principle, accepted the Russian reward and status system of Academicians.

[23] Nieh Jung-chen, *loc. cit.*, p. 4.

TABLE I

Budgeted Expenditures for Science
Units: thousand dollars
(thousand yuan)

YEAR	Total Science-Budget (a)	National Budget (b) (per cent.)	Academy of Science	Science Budget (per cent.)	Research in Educational Institutions(c)	Science Budget (per cent.)	Imports of Scientific Literature from non-Communist countries(d)
1950	408 (1,000)	0·015	1,224(c) (3,000)				
1951	3,212 (7,870)	0·07	—	—	—	—	—
1952	4,628 (11,340)	0·07	—	—	—	—	—
1953	13,000 (31,900)	0·15	13,000(c) (31,900)	100·0	—	—	—
1954	13,836 (33,890)	0·14			—		
1955	15,410 (38,000)	0·14	—	—	300(c) (740)	·019	—
1956	99,590 (244,000)	0·8	27,800(d) (66,740)	27·0	2,440(c) (6,000)	·024	5,040 (11,800)
1957	119,600 (293,000)(f)	1·0	36,735(c) (90,000)	27·5	4,166(d) (10,000)	·04	4,200 (11,500)
1958	156,734(f) (384,000)	0·9	—	—	—	—	—
1959	334,700 (820,000)	1·57	—	—	—	—	—
1960	441,224(g) (1,081,000)	1·54	—	—	—	—	—

2·45 Yuan=$1·00 (h)

Notes

(a) Helen and Yi-Chan Yin, *Economic Statistics of Mainland China (1949–57)* (Cambridge; Harvard Center for East Asian Studies, 1960), p. 92.
(b) Sources: State Statistical Bureau, *Ten Great Years: Statistics of the Economic and Cultural Achievements of the People's Republic of China* (Peking: Foreign Languages Press, 1960), p. 23; Tseng Shan, " Report on Examination of the Final State Accounts and the Draft 1960 State Budget," NCNA, April 10, 1960, in *Survey of the China Mainland Press* (hereafter SCMP) (Hong Kong: U.S. Consulate-General), 2240, pp. 3–6.
(c) Approximate figures calculated from indices given by Kuo Mo-jo, *Jen-min Jih-pao*, July 6, 1957, in CB 467, pp. 8, 9.
(d) Kuo Mo-jo, *ibid*.
(e) NCNA, June 4, 1957.
(f) Li Hsien-nien, budget speech, *Jen-min Jih-pao*, Feb. 12, 1958, p. 3.
(g) *Fianay SSSR*, Moscow, No. 9, September, 1960, p. 92.
(h) These conversions are based on unofficial exchange rates with non-*bloc* countries, but it may be noted that in October 1960, 1 yuan equalled 1 rouble in Chinese transactions within the Sino-Soviet *bloc* and 4 roubles equalled U.S. $1.00 at the official rate of exchange. Using this rate, the dollar figure for the 1960 budget for science, is reduced from $441,224,000 to $270,250,000, but its percentage of the national budget is unaffected.

A large proportion of the increase in the science budget has gone into buildings, especially at Peking and such new centres as Sian and Lanchow. In some cases, these buildings were criticised as extravagant and the costs of construction were far above official building standards.[24] The development of new research centres in the past two years may have absorbed much of the recent increase in budget allocations. Near Peking at Chung kuan-ts'un a new national centre for education and science is being built to accommodate, when completed, a hundred thousand students and scientists. However, the competition for materials and equipment in short supply, probably also for qualified people, apparently has prevented scientific bodies from expanding as rapidly as planned. For a number of years, more funds were budgeted for science than were spent.[25] Yet the number of centres and the amount of suitable space for scientific research have been vastly improved. Comparable improvements have also been made in other respects.

Although still dependent upon Soviet and Eastern European sources for many complex instruments, China has rapidly increased her production of scientific apparatus both for teaching and research purposes. Most institutes also seem to have some shop facilities for building research equipment. Within the Academy of Sciences special responsibility for instrument development is lodged with the Institute of Optical and Precision Instruments at Ch'ang-ch'un. Under the First Ministry of Machine Building, the Shanghai Scientific and Technical Instrument Research Institute and its attached General Instruments Factory is a major producer of scientific and technical equipment. In addition, there are a number of other industrial plants making scientific instruments, such as the Nanking Scientific Instrument Plant, the T'ung-chi Instrument Plant in Canton, the Pu Fah Scientific Apparatus Plant and the Ta Hua Electric Instrument Plant in Shanghai and the State Electronic Tube Plant in Peking.[26] In 1958 the State Scientific and Technological Commission decided to establish regional scientific supply centres in Tientsin, Peking, Shenyang, Shanghai, Canton and Wuhan.[27] This tremendous effort to develop production of scientific and industrial equipment may be partly due to a desire to save foreign exchange in view of the high cost of foreign equipment.[28]

The need for scientific literature has been met by major acquisitions of Soviet and Western journals and books. In 1958, the Chinese

24 Li Hsien-nien to the National People's Congress (hereafter NPC), NCNA, July 8, 1955.
25 Kuo Mo-jo to the NPC, NCNA, June 18, 1956, in CB 400, pp. 1–5.
26 *China Reconstructs*, March 1956, p. 19; *Kuang-ming Jih-pao*, January 31, 1958, p. 1;
    Far Eastern Economic Review, Hong Kong, July 6, 1956; J. Tuzo Wilson, *One Chinese Moon*, (Toronto, New York, London: 1959), p. 78 *passim*.
27 NCNA, January 26, 1958.
28 Li Fu-ch'un to the NPC, May 23, 1957.

Academy of Sciences received from its Soviet counterpart 46,132 titles in exchange for 29,831. The Soviet All-Union Institute of Scientific and Technical Information (VINITTI) sent China thirteen series of its *Reference Journal*, forty-eight series of its *Express Information*, the *Bulletin of Technical Economic Information*, reviews, pamphlets, etc. In 1958 the Institute also sent 400,000 bibliographical cards on materials which it was processing.[29] A strenuous effort to secure Western scientific books and periodicals, both back and current publications, led to purchases in pounds sterling of over $5 million in 1956 and $4 million in 1957—sums claimed to be larger than spent for the same purpose by the Soviet Union, as well as Japan and India, during these years.[30] Major responsibility for acquisitions falls on the Institute of Scientific and Technological Information, which apparently was separated from the Academy in 1959 and made a separate agency under the Scientific and Technological Commission. It now publishes eighty-nine periodicals and has arranged exchange of scientific information with most countries in the world.

Although there still is "a scarcity of materials from foreign countries" in some fields,[31] the general library facilities have been reported to be fairly adequate.[32] The Library of the Academy of Sciences, which in 1957 had 2·5 million volumes in its various branches and institutes, has been expanded and stocked with much current literature from abroad, including the United States. It now claims to have over six million titles and exchange arrangements with 1,290 institutes in fifty-six countries.[33]

For the past few years the Chinese have also had access to the research facilities of other Communist countries, notably at the nuclear research centre at Dubna, near Moscow, where as early as 1957 eleven Chinese scientists were working.[34] Benefits in research facilities, as well as scientific personnel, also accrue to the Chinese from the joint research projects which they have undertaken with the Soviet Union. In addition to earlier contracts, a master agreement providing for such co-operation for a five-year period, 1958–62, was signed on December 11, 1957.[35] One major project, the survey of the Heilungkiang river basin, in which 300 Chinese scientific workers and 130 Soviet scientists from the Russian

29 I. N. Kiselov, *loc. cit.*, pp. 6, 7.
30 Kuo Mo-jo to the NPC, *Jen-min Jih-pao*, July 6, 1957, in CB 467, p. 9.
31 *Scientia Sinica*, VIII, No. 10, 1959, p. 1158.
32 Kuo Mo-jo to NPC, *Jen-min Jih-pao*, July 6, 1957, in CB 467, p. 9; Wilson, *op. cit.*, *passim*.
33 Chang-tu Hu *et al.*, *China: Its People, Its Society, Its Culture* (New Haven: 1960), p. 450; *Scientia Sinica*, Vol. VIII, No. 11, in *Science News Letter*, Washington, D.C., December 10, 1960, p. 387.
34 *K'o-hsueh*, XXXIII, No. 2, 1957.
35 *K'o-hsueh T'ung-pao*, No. 6, 1958, p. 165.

Academy of Sciences took part, was completed in early 1960 after three years of work.[36]

Since 1957 the Chinese have acquired some very modern and advanced research equipment and facilities. The Russians provided the Institute of Atomic Energy at Peking with a nuclear research reactor, put into operation on September 27, 1958, a cyclotron and another type of accelerator.[37] The Chinese themselves have built a high tension multiplier and several small accelerators. They are now building electronic digital computers, automatic swing curve computers, radio telescopes and other delicate and complex equipment.[38]

Most scientific research is concentrated in institutes. In general, the institutes of the Academy of Sciences concentrate on most of the work in basic science and on more difficult and fundamental problems. Their resources too, however, are primarily committed to investigating applied rather than theoretical problems. The major emphasis now is on the research institutes connected with industry and communications, reported in 1958 to be 415 in number with 14,700 research and technical personnel.[39] The growth of research facilities is summarised in the table overleaf. Statistics for research centres outside of the Academy are scanty up to 1958 and after this date are not included here because, with the Great Leap Forward, they lack definition which permits comparison with the institutes of the Academy of Sciences.

In terms of scientific resources, mainland China now has the institutional basis for advanced scientific research in several fields. Rapid progress is being made in extending and raising general scientific and technological levels of research in industry, agriculture and health, but advanced scientific achievement on a broad scale appears to be impeded by one major deficiency: the supply of highly trained scientists. This is illustrated in the Academy of Sciences which has more research centres than the Soviet Academy of Sciences, but far fewer research scientists. In 1959 the Chinese Academy had 105 research institutes to Russia's eighty-seven, but only 7,000 members on its research staff compared to Russia's 14,000.[40]

---

[36] *Kuang-ming Jih-pao*, December 1, 1959, p. 1, in JPRS: 3132 (April 1, 1960), pp. 12, 13.

[37] For a review of the Chinese capabilities in the nuclear field, see A. Doak Barnett, "The Inclusion of Communist China in an Arms-Control Programme," *Daedalus* (Proceedings of the American Academy of Arts and Sciences, Vol. 88, No. 4), Fall 1960, pp. 831–845.

[38] NCNA, September 15, 1959, and September 28, 1959; *Druzhba, Peking*, November 12, 1958, p. 28 and February 4 1959, p. 9.

[39] State Statistical Bureau, *Ten Great Years: Statistics of the Economic and Cultural Achievements of the People's Republic of China* (Peking: Foreign Languages Press, 1960), p. 203.

[40] Figures on the Soviet Academy as reported in the *New York Times*, July 23, 1959.

TABLE II

Growth of Scientific Research Institutes and Personnel
(1949—1959)

| | ACADEMY OF SCIENCES | | | | | | | OTHER | |
| | Research Institute | Research Staff | | | | Total Research Staff | Total Employees | Research Departments and Institutes | Research Staff |
YEAR		Senior	Associate	Assistant and Technical	Student				
1949	14(a)	224(b)	—	—	—	660(c)	—	110(a)	—
1950	17(d)	—	—	—	—	—	—	—	—
1951	e)	—	—	—	30(c)	—	—	—	—
1952(f)	25(g)		317	661		1,292	5,239	—	—
1953(h)	25		347		1,378	1,725	—	20(i)	1,000(i)
1954(j)	41		350	—	—	—	—	58	
1955(k)	47	428	421		1,634	2,483	—	60	3,940
1956(l)	66	—	—	—	320(m)	4,475	—	105	10,307
1957(n)	68	746	725	4,005	340(m)	5,506	17,336	(o)	—
1958	90	—	—	—	1,600(p)	—	—	—	—
1959	105(q)	(800)	(800)	—	1,900(p)	7,000(q)	40,000(q)	—	—

Notes

(a) Kuo Mo-jo reported on June 17, 1950, that the Academy had fourteen institutes, one observatory, and one industrial research unit. He said that there also were ninety-three natural science institutions, seventeen scientific institutes and twenty-nine factories making scientific appliances in China.—*Culture and Education in China*, (Peking: Foreign Languages Press, n.d.), p. 8.

(b) *K'o-hsueh T'ung-pao*, No. 19, October 11, 1959, p. 613. Chu K'o-chen put the figure of research institutes in China in 1949 at 270.—*Nauka I Zhizn'*, Moscow, XXVI, No. 9, September 1959, in JPRS 3283 (May 19, 1960), p. 2.

(c) Coching Chu, "Scientific Research and University Education," *Ta Kung Pao*, October 29, 1950, in CB 153, pp. 32–36.

(d) Ch'ien San-ch'iang, "Modern Science in China," *Kuang-ming Jih-pao*, July 21, 1953, in CB 257, pp. 1–5. This includes the Tsu-chin-shan Observatory.

(e) Li Ssu-kuang, "Science Serves the People," *People's China*, August 16, 1951 (in CB 153, pp. 12–20). Three of the bodies listed were not institutes. Li said that before 1949 there were about 190 research centres and programmes in China: thirty-two in engineering and technology, 112 in agriculture, seventeen in geology and eleven in medicine and pharmacology.

(f) *Peking Review*, No. 5, April 1, 1958, p. 12; *Jen-min Shou-ts'e*, 1958, p. 597, for all except research institutes.

(g) Ch'ien San-ch'iang, *loc. cit.* He includes the Tsu-chin-shan Observatory, and states there were twenty-eight institutes in 1952, but his list shows only twenty-five.

(h) Anderson Shih, *op. cit.*, p. 16; Kuo Mo-jo, "Report Concerning the Basic Conditions of the Chinese Academy of Sciences and Its Future Work," *Jen-min Jih-pao*, March 26, 1954 in CB 359 pp. 15–22. In addition to twenty-five research institutes Kuo lists four independent research rooms, four preparatory offices for research institutes, one observatory, one scientific instrument collection and one custodial committee for bacteriological specimens.

(i) Ch'ien San-ch'iang, *loc. cit.*

(j) Kuo Mo-jo, in Report to National People's Congress, NCNA, Peking, July 21, 1955, CB 351, p. 21; NCNA, Peking, April 29, 1955, SCMP No. 1038 p. 17.

(k) Anderson Shih, *op. cit.*, p. 16; *Drushba*, Peking, March 27, 1956, p. 2. Also *K'o-hsueh T'ung-pao*, 1955, No. 11, and SCMP 1061, p. 27.

(l) Po I-po to the National People's Congress, NCNA, Peking, July 1, 1957, on figures for 1956, except for students.

(m) *Ragvitiye Ekonomiki Stran Narodny Demokratii*, (Moscow: 1958), p. 223.

(n) *Jen-min Jih-pao*, January 3, 1958; *Peking Review*, No. 5, April 1, 1958, p. 12, for 1957 figures with two exceptions.

(o) The State Statistical Bureau is said to have reported " over 500 scientific research institutes with more than 20,000 research workers," in 1957. Peking Radio Broadcast, April 13, 1959.

(p) These are enrolment figures for students at the Academy's universities.

(q) *K'o-hsueh T'ung-pao*, 1959, No. 19, pp. 613, 614.

SHORTAGE OF SCIENTISTS

The men and institutions inherited from the previous era provided a base on which the Chinese Communists could build during the past ten years, but these were not adequate for the ambitious programmes being launched. To meet the shortage of first-rate scientists, the Communists have taken three measures to expand their number: inducing Chinese scientists abroad to return; sending students to the Soviet Union and Eastern Europe for advanced training; and developing a programme of graduate training in China.

Although over 1,500 students who were studying abroad returned to the China mainland by the end of 1952,[41] the Chinese estimated in 1958 that about 10,000 Chinese scientists and students still remained in the United States, England, France and Japan. Persuading these people to return, they saw as " one of the most important methods " of meeting their immediate needs for trained manpower.[42] A few hundred returned between 1952 and 1958, principally from the United States; very few have done so since 1958. However, among those who returned prior to 1958 were one or two hundred men who constitute a significant portion of the total number of capable scientists available to the régime.

As a second step, the Chinese Communists sent students abroad for advanced training. Thus far these students have proved to be Communist China's main source of young scientists with post-graduate training. By May 1957, 7,075 Chinese students—a good deal fewer than the 10,000 called for in the First Five-Year Plan—had been sent to fourteen countries for study. Of these, 1,331 went for post-graduate training.[43] Most of the students went to the Soviet Union, 6,572 by the end of 1958.[44] Of those studying in Russia, 300 completed their training and returned to China in 1956; 351 in 1957; 600 were scheduled to return in 1958; and about 1,200 in 1959—making a total of 2,400. In 1960 another 1,300 students returned from Russia and other Socialist countries after completing from two to five years of study.[45]

41 *China Handbook, 1953–54*, (Taipei: 1953), p. 409.

42 Tseng Wen-ching, *The Socialist Industrialisation of China*, 1959, in JPRS: 3800 (August 31, 1960), p. 113.

43 *Druzhba*, Peking, May 30, 1957.

44 *Hua Ch'iao Jih-pao*, New York, February 17, 1959.

45 NCNA, July 18, 1957; NCNA, February 14, 1959, June 27, 1959, and July 16, 1960; *Druzhba*, November 5, 1957, p. 21.

The 3,700 students who have returned to China after their study abroad include those who had done post-graduate work. How many is uncertain. Less than 20 per cent. of the students sent abroad during the First Five-Year Plan were post-graduate students; about 40 per cent. (139) of the students returning from the Soviet Union in 1957 were reported to have been in post-graduate studies. Perhaps altogether 1,200 to 1,500 have received advanced degrees, most of these in engineering and fields of applied science, but very few—possibly only a couple of hundred—in the basic physical and natural sciences.[46] Almost all have been assigned upon their return to the Academy of Sciences, to scientific and technological institutes of the various ministries and bureaux, and to universities as teachers.[47]

Additionally, several hundred Chinese scientists, advanced students and technicians with research potentialities had their qualifications up-graded by going to the Soviet Union for periods of study and training in research. Beginning in 1953, several hundred Chinese scientists have visited the Soviet Union for varying periods to observe Russian research and for short-term research experience and training. Part of this pro-gramme was specifically designed to strengthen the Academy of Sciences. According to a Russian report, " From 1956 on, the institutes of the Academy of Sciences USSR began to enrol, at the request of the Academy of Sciences of the Chinese People's Republic, Chinese aspirants and operators [*i.e.*, students seeking degrees and those receiving formal research experience]; for instance, during 1958, 300 Chinese specialists received training in practice and instruction in the system of the Academy of Sciences USSR." [48]

China's need for scientists will finally have to be met through her own educational and training programmes. The leaders of the Academy of Sciences certainly recognise this. The President of the Academy, Kuo Mo-jo, in a speech to the National People's Congress in 1955 noting that the country's progress had been made possible by Soviet scientists and specialists, argued that China could not continue to depend on the Soviet Union for scientists and needed " a strong army of scientists " of its own. He warned that without this, it was hard to imagine how the plans for building Socialism and Communism could succeed.[49] Nieh Jung-chen, the chairman of the Scientific and Technological Commission, put the matter succinctly in 1958 when he said : " It is obvious that if we cannot conduct our research independently and creatively, if we cannot fight

[46] Science is not listed among the subjects of specialisation of the 1,300 students who returned to China in 1960.

[47] Tseng Wen-ching, *op. cit.*, p. 118.

[48] I. N. Kiselov. *loc. cit.*, p. 6.

[49] NCNA, July 21, 1955, in CB 351, pp. 20–24.

for our own rejuvenation, it will be eternally impossible for us to catch up with the advanced scientific level of the world." [50] The Twelve-Year Science Plan called for the training of 10,500 graduate students by the end of 1967, but there are those who are now urging that the figure at least be doubled.[51]

In fact, very little has been accomplished. The Academy of Sciences undertook to develop a graduate training programme in 1955, but the poor and uneven preparation of the students in advanced fields of science presented problems which could only be solved at earlier stages in education. Moreover, many of the best students were sent to the Soviet Union. In order to prepare a select group of undergraduates for advanced work and to develop a sound programme of graduate study and research training, the Academy recently has established two educational institutions of its own in co-operation with the Ministry of Higher Education. One is the University of Science and Technology at Peking which opened in the fall of 1958 with an enrolment of 1,600 students. The other was organised by the institutes of the Shanghai Branch of the Academy in 1959 with an initial enrolment of 300 students.[52]

Some post-graduate work has been attempted in senior universities and technical colleges. By the end of 1956, 4,841 students had been accepted for elementary graduate training, mostly for two-year periods and primarily in preparation for teaching.[53] The Ministry of Higher Education announced in July 1956 that educational institutions would admit 1,015 for more intensive graduate training, covering a four-year course. Rigorous graduate standards were finally introduced in September 1957, when the Ministry of Higher Education announced post-graduate openings: 161 at universities; sixty-five at institutes of technology; sixty-four at colleges of agriculture and forestry; five at the English Department of the Peking Foreign Languages School, and fifty-three others.[54]

The shortage of senior scientists is likely to persist for a long time, well beyond 1967. Among graduate students, a relatively small proportion appear to be concentrated in the basic sciences, partly because the need for engineers and technicians to meet the goals of the five-year plans has higher priority and also because only a limited number of first-rate scientists can be spared for education, full- or part-time, from the research projects pressed upon them. Despite demands of party

---

[50] Nieh Jung-chen, " The Road of Development of Our Country's Scientific and Technical Work," *Hung Ch'i* (Red Flag), No. 9, October 1, 1958, in Union Research Service (URS), Vol. 13 No. 19, pp. 278–279.
[51] Tseng Wen-ching, *op. cit.*, p. 113.
[52] NCNA, September 20, 1958; *Druzhba*, October 15, 1958, p. 29; NCNA, Peking, June 18, 1959.
[53] *Narodnyy Kitay*, Peking, No. 16 (August 16, 1957), p. 20.
[54] *Kuang-ming Jih-pao*, August 9, 1957, in SCMP 1626, p. 2; *Ibid.* September 13, 1957.

enthusiasts and the urgent requirements of state planners, only a few students can be trained at one time, as the President of the Academy of Sciences pointed out in 1955 to the National People's Congress: "The idea of mass production cannot be entertained." He also emphasised that the process of training could not be speeded up: "Generally speaking, a university graduate is required to take from five to ten years of post-graduate research work without a break in order to become a more advanced scientist." His hope was that during the Second or Third Five-Year Plan, the small number of those being trained in the Academy would be able to make their contribution to national construction.[55] In the sciences, as distinct from engineering, it is not likely that by 1960 more than a couple of hundred students had completed their training in China itself for the equivalent of a doctoral degree.

The shortage of research personnel for the new facilities which were being built and for work in priority fields was so severe that Kuo Mo-jo, on returning from a trip to the Soviet Union in early 1958, proposed that: (1) some scientists in allied fields be diverted to work in areas where shortages of scientists were most acute; (2) the Russian system of using students for research should be adopted; and (3) that able secondary school students should be recruited and given intensive short-term training to prepare them for work in the research projects of the Academy.[56] Thus the shortage is not only at the upper levels, but also extends throughout the entire research establishment.

The most critical shortage, however, appears to be in the higher ranks. How many scientists are there in China with the ability and training to conduct advanced research? Precise information for answering this question is not available. Any estimate may need radical revision. In mathematics, there are less than 400 scientists engaged in research.[57] In the natural sciences, there probably are not over 1,200 scientists with advanced degrees, or their equivalent, actively engaged, full- or part-time, in research.[58] Of these, half or more are connected with the Academy of Sciences. Most of the remainder are associated with industrial research institutes and the science departments of the

---

55 Kuo Mo-jo to the NPC, July 21, 1955, in CB 351, pp. 20–24.

56 *K'o-hsueh T'ung-pao*, No. 7, 1958, p. 198.

57 According to *K'o-hsueh T'ung-pao*, No. 18, 1959, p. 1, 342 mathematicians published 983 papers between 1950 and 1958.

58 This figure, subject to radical revision. is arrived at as follows: 862 names on the 1950 roster of natural scientists, less 174 abroad, equals 688; 200 completed training or were up-graded through further training in the Soviet Union by 1960; 150 completed training or were further trained to post-graduate levels in China; probably less than 100 returned to China after 1949 from the United States, Europe and Japan with post-graduate degrees at the doctoral level in the natural sciences: gross total, 1,338. From this should be subtracted losses through death, those inactivated for political unreliability, retirement and ill-health, and those involved in other activities, such as politics, administration, etc.

better universities. The most rapidly expanding group appears to be in engineering, probably making up a significant proportion of the 1,200 to 1,500 who have completed their post-graduate training in the USSR and returned to China.

The government is trying to encourage university professors to supervise and conduct research and in 1957 set aside $4 million for this purpose. In the case of some of the research institutes of the Academy, faculty members from the neighbouring universities seem to provide, on a part-time basis, all of the scientific guidance available to the research staff, whose regular members may be made up entirely of young college graduates.[59]

Some, perhaps a good deal, of advanced research in some fields has been made possible only because of the assistance of Soviet scientists who have been sent to China to initiate and organise research programmes. Over a hundred Soviet experts were at work in Peking alone by November 1957.[60] For example, in physics a Soviet scientist, who served as a consultant between 1956 and 1958, initiated a series of studies in Kirin; another served as a consultant and participant in research in the Department of Physics of Metallic State at Peking University; and many Russian physicists came to China for brief periods as lecturers and consultants.[61] In chemistry, the Russians in 1956 sent N. P. Luzhnaya to work for half a year in the six chemical institutes of the Academy of Sciences and others were sent to direct research studies as part of the Soviet Union's contribution to the thirty projects of the Twelve-Year Science Plan involving inorganic chemistry.[62] But these are temporary expedients.

THE CONTROL OF SCIENCE

In view of the small number of scientists and the large scale of the government's development programme, the use of Chinese scientists became a matter of critical importance to the régime. Where should the direction and control of China's scientific resources be lodged?

As has been indicated, the leaders of Communist China until 1956 left to China's scientists the responsibility for governing their own professional activities. In 1954 and 1955, following the termination of the Korean War, the Academy of Sciences lost its cabinet rank under

[59] See "Chemistry Department of Northwest University and Sian Chemistry Research Institute Join Efforts in Scientific Research," *Kuang-ming Jih-pao*, December 23, 1959, in Union Research Service (hereafter URS), Vol. 19, No. 12, pp. 174–176.

[60] *Vestnik Akademii Nauk SSSR*, Moscow, 1959, No. 9, p. 50.

[61] *Fisika Metallov i Metallovedeniye*, Vol. VIII, 1959, No. 6, pp. 820–828, in JPRS: 2425 (March 31, 1960), pp. 1–13.

[62] *Zhurnal Neoorganicheskoy Khimi*, Vol. III, 1958, No. 2, pp. 542–545, in JPRS: 2568 (April 27, 1960), pp. 1–9.

the Constitution adopted in September 1954, but received endorsement as " the supreme academic organ of the state charged with the important mission of directing and promoting scientific work throughout the country." [63] The Academy was reorganised and divided into four departments. In June 1955 at a national meeting the Academy was given prestige and national character through the appointment of 233 members to its four new departments. Its institutes were strengthened; its control over scientific personnel increased; and it was empowered to encourage science through a system of national science awards, by improving the material and social status of scientists, and by developing co-ordinated direction over scientific research throughout the country.

At the inaugural meeting, Vice-Premier Ch'en Yi, a member of the Party's Politburo, asked the scientists " to use their own labour and wisdom " to meet the needs of the state and the requirements of science. This idea had been endorsed earlier by the Party paper, *Jen-min Jih-pao*. It asked for recognition that " scientific workers have their own mission, which is to conduct research." [64] Later at the Eighth Party Congress in September 1956, Yü Kuang-yuan, the head of the Science Division of the Propaganda Department of the Central Committee of the Party, stated that—

> In leading scientific work, the Party should rely on scientists to the fullest extent. Modern sciences are finely divided into various fields. Only the specialists know the fine points of a certain field of science. When we have scientific problems, we must learn humbly from specialists. [65]

In keeping with this approach, responsibility for formulating the Twelve-Year Science Plan was placed largely upon Chinese and Soviet scientists. It thus represented " The crystallisation of the collective wisdom of scientists." [66]

At the Eighth Congress of the Communist Party, however, there also was a restatement of the purpose of scientific inquiry. The Party adopted the Second Five-Year Plan, which called for the development by the end of 1962 of a " self-contained industrial network." In this scheme, heavy industry was made the first priority as the foundation of economic development and national defence. This required more and better industrial technology. Therefore, the Party concluded that it " should actively and selectively develop research in science," in order to meet the needs of national construction. [67]

The Communist Party operated on " the principle of subservience of scientific research to the requirements of the state." This meant the

[63] *Jen-min Jih-pao*, June 3, 1955.
[64] *Ibid*., February 27, 1955.
[65] Peking Radio, September 26, 1956.
[66] Kuo Mo-jo to the NPC, NCNA, June 18, 1956, in CB 400, p. 3.
[67] Yü Kuang-yuan to the Party Congress, Peking Radio, September 26, 1956.

pursuit of scientific research and scientific activities had to be according
to plan and not along the lines of the personal research interests of
individual scientists. Plans determined the character and quantity of
work required of scientists and science to meet staged goals for national
development. The principle of " subservience " required central direction
and control to ensure fulfilment of the plans.[68]

When the Academy of Sciences convened its second national conference, May 23–30, 1957, Party policies had begun to take effect and the
role of the Academy had changed. In connection with the preparation
of the Twelve-Year Science Plan, the State Planning Commission
appointed on March 14, 1956, a Scientific Planning Committee, chaired
by Ch'en Yi. In May 1957, before the second national conference of the
Academy of Sciences, it was transformed into a standing commission of
the State Council, and its membership increased from thirty-five to 106.[69]
The Commission replaced the Academy of Sciences as the " national
organ for policy making " in scientific matters. It was charged with
responsibility for organising scientific institutions and undertakings,
collating and co-ordinating plans for scientific research in each area,
integrating plans and activities in science with national plans and programmes, supervising the execution of all plans, controlling the use of
research funds, establishing working standards and pay scales for
scientists, developing training programmes, organising international
exchanges and communications among scientists and promoting the
recruitment of Chinese scientists abroad.

This was not surprising. The Academy had a poor record in serving
claimants for scientific assistance. As the state's programmes began to
develop, the demands for scientists became urgent and competitive in
many sectors of the state; heavy industry, light industry, higher education,
health, agriculture, defence, and the research institutes of the Academy
of Sciences itself. In 1955 the head of the Academy admitted that the
Academy, which was charged with providing for national needs, had
given no study to " the needs of national construction," prepared no plans
for the development of science, made no rational distribution of research
institutes to meet the requirements of new production bases, and
developed no effective national science roster with a system of assigning
scientists to priority jobs.[70]

Moreover, scientists were not administrators and many complained
constantly about the administrative tasks laid on them. But there was
also a deeper problem. Among the scientists there was strong feeling

---

68 This subject has been dealt with in great and reiterative volume. Examples are:
Chou En-lai to the NPC, June 26, 1957; Kuo Mo-jo to the NPC, July 5, 1957.
69 *Communist China, 1957*, Union Research Institute, Hong Kong, 1958, p. 119.
70 NCNA, Peking, June 2, 1955, SCMP 1066, pp. 6–8; NCNA, Peking, July 21, 1955,
in CB 351, pp. 20–24.

that the Academy and China's scientists should devote themselves to research on basic theoretical problems, seek to develop new branches of science, improve standards of research and raise the level of science education rather than to give their time to problems of industrialisation and elementary science training where their skills were under-utilised.

Realising that scientific and technical knowledge was essential for the achievement of their plans, the government, however, was eager to find ways of releasing " the activity and creative efforts of scientists in a more effective way." It hoped that with policies of liberality and greater freedom, scientists and intellectuals would respond with a greater effort in support of the régime's programmes. Instead, latent differences between scientists and the Communist Party broke into a " bitter struggle " in 1957 when the Party in its " Hundred Flowers " campaign found itself involved in deep and sharp controversy with intellectuals all over China.[71] The question of control over science received sharp and explicit answer and definition.

Had the Communist Party not had a prepared and dogmatic position on the matter, the debate might have gone along lines in other countries where thoughtful people are disturbed and perplexed by the relationship which should prevail between science and government. Essentially, the issue concerned the nature of scientific activity. Was science a self-sustaining and independent area of human inquiry with its own disciplines, subject-matter and intrinsic purposes? Did the natural sciences have a " class " character? If not, did the " class " character of the scientists affect scientific work? While the scientists argued over the emphasis to be given to theoretical as opposed to applied research, to the pursuit of new knowledge and understanding for their own sake *versus* subordination of science to planned programmes for technological achievement, the Party was interested in the locus of decision-making and authority.

There could be no doubt of the position of the Communist leaders in this contest. They attacked the scientists for arguing that " laymen cannot lead experts." The statement of a Vice-Premier that " a bitter struggle exists between us and the bourgeois scientists who maintain that Communists are laymen," defined part of the problem.[72] When scientists advocated academic leadership on the grounds that scientists and not politicians were qualified to guide scientific work, the Party charged them with political motives and opposition to the principle of " letting politics

---

[71] For general accounts of this controversy, see Theodore H. E. Chen, *Thought Reform of the Chinese Intellectuals* (Hong Kong Un., 1960); Roderick MacFarquhar, *The Hundred Flowers Campaign and the Chinese Intellectuals*, (New York: Praeger, 1960).

[72] *Hung Ch'i*, No. 9, October 1, 1958.

be in command." Communist leaders interpreted the criticisms of scientists as an attempt " to oust the Party from the field of science." The head of the state's Scientific and Technological Commission later pointed out that " Should we allow science to take the course directed by bourgeois experts, the scientific work of our country would completely drift away from its political mission in Socialist construction." Hence there must be " absolute Party leadership over science and technology " as the " basic guarantee for full manifestation of the superiority of Socialism, and for speedy development of scientific techniques in our country." [73]

As the outcome of this " struggle," China's political planners and policy-makers took firmer control in the direction and administration of science policy and operations. The Scientific Planning Commission was replaced by an even more powerful body under the State Council with jurisdiction over both scientific and technological activities. This is the Scientific and Technological Commission established on November 23, 1958, through a merger of the Scientific Planning Commission and the State Technological Commission. A group of senior and reliable Communist Party members, under the chairmanship of Marshal Nieh Jung-chen, a Vice Premier and member of the Central Committee of the Party, now control science. While the character of this body manifests the importance the régime attaches to science and to the co-ordination of science with technological and industrial development, none of the members of the commission are leading scientists.[74]

The functions of this Commission with respect to science are similar to those of the Scientific Planning Commission, but its jurisdiction is wider. It supervises not only research activities but also the associations of scientists and the organisations disseminating scientific information. The two national bodies active in these fields since 1950, the All-China Federation of Natural Science Societies and the All-China Association for the Dissemination of Scientific and Technical Knowledge, were combined on September 23, 1958, to form the People's Republic of China Association for Science and Technology, which was subsequently placed under the control of the Commission.[75] In December 1959 the Scientific and Technological Commission undertook to extend its direct control through local commissions, over scientific research in all parts of China,

[73] Nieh Jung-chen to the First National Congress of the Scientific and Technical Association of the People's Republic of China, *Hung Ch'i*, No. 9, October 1, 1958, in URS, Vol. 13, pp. 278–297.

[74] The members of the Scientific and Technological Commission include: Nieh Jung-chen (chairman); five vice-chairmen: Han Kuang, Liu Hsi-yao, Chang Yu-hsuan, Fan Ch'ang-chiang, and Wu Heng; and, in addition, An Tung, Chao Shou-kung, Chü Kang-chien, Sui Yun-sheng, and Wang Shun-t'ung. Scientific personalities such as Kuo Mo-jo and Li Ssu-kuang, who were on the Scientific Planning Committee, are not included on the Commission.

[75] For the Resolution setting up the " Science Association," see *Hua Hsueh T'ung-pao*, 1958, No. 12, pp. 673, 674.

TABLE III

Organisation of Science in Communist China

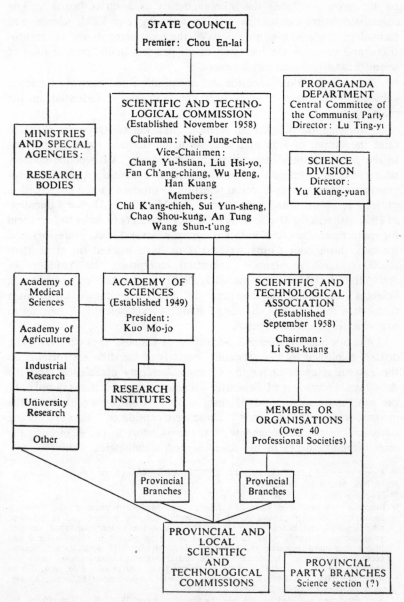

as well. These commissions " under the leadership of the Party committees," organise and co-ordinate the activities of the branches and institutes
of the Academy of Sciences, industries and higher educational institutions
on the principle "that the whole country is a chess board." The
commission's responsibilities include mapping out local science and
technological plans, assigning parts of the local plans to various institutions, and ensuring the inclusion of all projects in the overall plan of
scientific and technical development.[76]

The national framework for the organisation and control of science
subsequent to these changes and developments is indicated in the
chart opposite:

" Storming the heights of science," like the country-wide drive to
raise the output of iron and steel through backyard furnaces, has led
to the diffusion and decentralisation of research. All over the country
universities and technical schools expanded or developed research programmes—mostly with direct application to production and construction
projects in industry and agriculture. The Ministry of Higher Education
in 1957 assigned 6,700 assistants to faculty members in order to free them
for more research.[77] Under this programme over 23,000 professors and
teachers throughout China were said to have worked on more than
20,000 research problems.[78] Industrial enterprises, the Academy of
Agriculture (established on March 1, 1957) and the Academy of Medical
Sciences (established on December 11, 1955) were caught up in mass
research with " peasant scientists " and " worker scientists " helping to
over-achieve research targets.[79]

Dramatic results emerged, according to Chinese spokesmen: " The
articles published by the academic journals of the different societies in
the natural sciences under the Chinese Academy of Sciences and the
All-China Federation of Scientific Societies contained, for example, 47
per cent. more words in 1958 than in 1957. Compared with 1952, the
increase was twenty-one times." These were considered " most convincing
statistics " of the achievements of the mass effort to break through the
scientific bottle-necks in the scientific and technological fields.[80]

---

[76] *Kuang-ming Jih-pao*, December 19, 1959, in URS, Vol. 19, p. 173.

[77] NCNA, March 15, 1957.

[78] *Pei-ching Jih-pao*, October 7, 1957, p. 4.

[79] Research was developed under the Academy of Medical Sciences at the Research
Institute of Hematology and Blood Transfusion, with six sections, and at the same
time hospital and health organisations throughout the country launched research
programmes. Scientific work in agriculture had been centred in three national and
fifteen provincial research institutes, but suddenly in 1958 agricultural research,
according to reports, was metamorphosed and throughout China research teams and
institutes were at work: 157 at the provincial level, 190 in *chuan* or *ch'ü*, 771 in
hsien or county and 7,690 in communes. *Jen-min Jih-pao*, April 12, 1960; *Kuang-
ming Jih-pao*, December 25, 1960.

[80] Nieh Jung-chen reported by *Jen-min Jih-pao*, September 27, 1959, in CB 608, p. 10.

The overall range and distribution of the research activities in 1958 as reported by the State Statistical Bureau at Peking, is indicated in the following table:

TABLE IV

Scientific Research Institutes and Personnel (1958)*

	Number of Institutes	Personnel (*thousands*)	
		Total	Of which: research & technical personnel
Total	848	118·6	32·5
Of which:			
Basic science	170	28·3	5·9
Industry and communication	415	59·2	14·7
Agriculture, forestry, animal husbandry and fishery	134	10·8	1·2
Medical science and public health	101	12·1	2·2

NOTE: Data covers the institutes of natural sciences and technology under the various ministries of the Central People's Government, provinces, municipalities directly under the central authority, autonomous regions, seven municipalities and the Chinese Academy of Sciences. Institutes of philosophy, social sciences, literature and the arts are not included.

Source: State Statistical Bureau, *Ten Great Years: Statistics of the Economic and Cultural Achievements of the People's Republic of* China, (Peking: Foreign Language Press, 1960), p. 203.

This fury of effort " to achieve greater, faster, better and more economical results " was in compliance with " the guide-line of walking on two legs " enunciated by the Party's Central Committee and Mao Tse-tung. It calls for more work " both at the Central Government and local levels simultaneously on a big, intermediate and small scale." [81] Under a policy of uniting scientific research, education and production, local scientific bodies are being developed to form a " national scientific research network." From Chinghai in the west to Kirin in the north-east the development and organisation of science has been added to the responsibilities of provincial and local governments. Each province appears to be organising a scientific work committee under the sponsorship of the Scientific and Technological Commission to establish

[81] *Jen-min Jih-pao*, October 11, 1959, in CB 608, p. 13.

branches of the Academy of Sciences and of the Association for Science and Technology. At lower levels the directives call for " scientific research and science popularisation organs." [82]

These local, mass organised activities may be a useful means for reorienting social attitudes and quickening the diffusion of technical skills in the population, but they have little bearing on China's capacity for advanced scientific achievement in the present decade. The central government recognises this and is not allocating its research funds for these mass research activities, which are charged to local and provincial budgets. The central government reserves its funds for research in nationally controlled scientific, industrial and educational institutions. Scientific achievement depends, then, more on the universities and academies, particularly the Academy of Sciences. Although the latter's share in the national budget for science and research was only 27 per cent. in 1957, it remains the major centre of theoretical and academic research.

THE ACADEMY OF SCIENCES

The Academy of Sciences serves a unique function in a country short of scientists and without highly developed technological and research facilities. It is an institutional device, first inaugurated in China by the Nationalists when they came into power, enabling a technically and scientifically under-developed country to carry on scientific work at an advanced level. First-rate minds trained in the best scientific institutions abroad are brought together in a few centres where scarce and costly facilities are concentrated. Thus at minimum cost and within a technologically and scientifically retarded environment, China is able to carry on some work which is abreast of world scientific progress. Moreover, these science centres serve as reservoirs of scientific talent and knowledge to be drawn upon by other groups and enterprises in the country needing specialised assistance and guidance. They also provide the resources for the advanced training of new generations of scientists.

Almost all of the leading scientists of China are associated with the Academy of Sciences. First of all, most of the research scientists appear to be on the staffs of the Academy's institutes. Secondly, eminent scientists outside of the Academy are appointed to serve together with senior scientists in the Academy as members of the national scientific committees attached to each of the five departments into which the work of the Academy has been divided. Finally, most, if not all, of the research

[82] See, for example, Report of Yuan Jen-yuan to the Chinghai Provincial People's Congress, *Chinghai Jih-pao*, Sining July 4, 1958, in JPRS: 5847 (November 7, 1960), p. 46; Wang Huan-ju to the Kirin People's Congress, *Kirin Jih-pao*, Ch'ang-ch'un, May 27, 1960, in JPRS: 4135 (October 24, 1960), p. 14.

institutes of the Academy have scientific committees, usually with a dozen or more members, composed of scientific specialists in the appropriate field to help plan and guide substantive work.

On June 3, 1955, the State Council appointed 233 of China's leading scientists as members of the Academic Departments of the Academy.[83] On May 31, 1957, twenty-one additional appointments were announced at the closing session of the second national meeting of the Department Committees.[84] The Department Committees were to meet simultaneously once a year to discuss the work of their departments and of the Academy, but thus far have been convened in full sessions only twice—in June 1955 and in May 1957. A third meeting concerned only with the natural sciences was held at Shanghai with 131 members in attendance.[85]

Originally meant to be " the supreme organ of the Academy of Sciences," the Department Committees have not been empowered with authority and progressively have lost importance. Once acclaimed as the equivalent of Academicians in the Soviet Union, and promised such recognition and status in 1955, no titles and responsibilities have been conferred upon them as yet.[86] Although many of the scientists believe that direction of the Academy should be in professional hands, the government clearly is not prepared to turn control of the Academy over to men who are not altogether in accord with its views and policies.

At the level of the research institutes, however, the views of scientists appear to be taken into account in carrying out priority projects and programmes. Although not in a position to direct over-all policies of the Academy, the members of the scientific committees of the institutes provide expert guidance on the character and direction of research. Through these committees, the best of the younger and older scientists, probably well over a thousand altogether, are drawn into the work of the Academy at its technical levels. In addition, some of the institutes are able to mobilise wider counsel and support through national conferences of scientists in their fields. In April 1958, for example, the Institute of Chemistry at Chung-kuan-ts'un, the new research and educational centre four miles from Peking, called a conference attended by 120 chemists from institutes, industries and universities.[87]

The direction and control of work in the Academy of Sciences is exercised by the Academy Council and its Standing Executive Committee. This body is responsible to the State Council, apparently through

---

83 The members are listed in SCMP 1062, pp. 37 *et seq.*
84 The list of names appears in CB 460, p. 17.
85 NCNA, May 12, 1960, in SCMP 2262, pp. 29–31.
86 Kuo Mo-jo's speech to the Department Committees of the Academy, *Jen-min Jih-pao*, June 12, 1955, in CB 359, p. 11; *Jen-min Jih-pao*, June 3, 1955, in SCMP 1064, pp. 14, 15.
87 NCNA, April 9, 1958.

TABLE V

Organisation of the Academy of Sciences

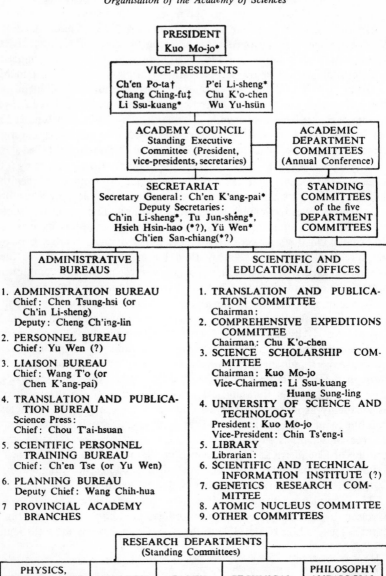

PRESIDENT
Kuo Mo-jo*

VICE-PRESIDENTS
Ch'en Po-ta†   P'ei Li-sheng*
Chang Ching-fu‡   Chu K'o-chen
Li Ssu-kuang*   Wu Yu-hsün

ACADEMY COUNCIL
Standing Executive
Committee (President,
vice-presidents, secretaries)

ACADEMIC
DEPARTMENT
COMMITTEES
(Annual Conference)

SECRETARIAT
Secretary General: Ch'en K'ang-pai*
Deputy Secretaries:
Ch'in Li-sheng*, Tu Jun-sheng*,
Hsieh Hsin-hao (*?), Yü Wen*
Ch'ien San-chiang(*?)

STANDING
COMMITTEES
of the five
DEPARTMENT
COMMITTEES

ADMINISTRATIVE
BUREAUS

1. ADMINISTRATION BUREAU
   Chief: Chen Tsung-hsi (or
   Ch'in Li-sheng)
   Deputy: Cheng Ch'ing-lin

2. PERSONNEL BUREAU
   Chief: Yu Wen (?)

3. LIAISON BUREAU
   Chief: Wang T'o (or
   Chen K'ang-pai)

4. TRANSLATION AND PUBLICA-
   TION BUREAU
   Science Press:
   Chief: Chou T'ai-hsuan

5. SCIENTIFIC PERSONNEL
   TRAINING BUREAU
   Chief: Ch'en Tse (or Yu Wen)

6. PLANNING BUREAU
   Deputy Chief: Wang Chih-hua

7 PROVINCIAL ACADEMY
   BRANCHES

SCIENTIFIC AND
EDUCATIONAL OFFICES

1. TRANSLATION AND PUBLICA-
   TION COMMITTEE
   Chairman:
2. COMPREHENSIVE EXPEDITIONS
   COMMITTEE
   Chairman: Chu K'o-chen
3. SCIENCE SCHOLARSHIP COM-
   MITTEE
   Chairman: Kuo Mo-jo
   Vice-Chairmen: Li Ssu-kuang
                  Huang Sung-ling
4. UNIVERSITY OF SCIENCE AND
   TECHNOLOGY
   President: Kuo Mo-jo
   Vice-President: Chin Ts'eng-i
5. LIBRARY
   Librarian:
6. SCIENTIFIC AND TECHNICAL
   INFORMATION INSTITUTE (?)
7. GENETICS RESEARCH COM-
   MITTEE
8. ATOMIC NUCLEUS COMMITTEE
9. OTHER COMMITTEES

RESEARCH DEPARTMENTS
(Standing Committees)

| PHYSICS, MATHEMATICS AND CHEMISTRY | BIOLOGY | EARTH SCIENCES | TECHNICAL SCIENCES | PHILOSOPHY AND SOCIAL SCIENCES |

the Scientific and Technological Commission. Thus far no constitution of the Academy has been published although a committee for drafting a constitution, headed by Chu K'o-chen, was appointed in 1957.[88] Nonetheless, it is possible from scattered references to piece together a rough picture of the administration and organisation of the Academy.

Policy and organisational matters are in the hands of a small group of " reliable " scientists and Communist Party representatives in the Academy Council.[89] Under the Council and a Secretariat, located at the Academy's headquarters next to the National Library in Peking, the work of the Academy is divided between administrative and scientific activities. The administrative offices and services seem to be staffed in large part by Party members, few of whom have any scientific background, although the Party has sought to train some of its cadres for scientific administration.[90]

Scientific activities are now organised under five, formerly four, departments: (1) Physics, Chemistry and Mathematics; (2) Biology; (3) Earth Sciences (*i.e.*, geology, geophysics and meteorology); (4) Technical Sciences; and (5) Philosophy and Social Sciences. Each department has a director, deputy director, departmental committee, standing committee and secretary or secretariat to supervise the work of the institutes and research projects within its jurisdiction.[91] The standing committee of each department, composed of the director, deputy director, and " several members elected by the department concerned," is supposed to meet once a month " to handle routine matters of the department."

The organisation of the Academy is indicated in the chart on p. 125.

The scientific work of the Academy is carried on in its institutes and by its research teams. These now number over a hundred and they have been rapidly increased in number.

Each institute has its own character, depending upon its size, location, type of research, leadership, national importance assigned to its activities, and other factors. They vary greatly in size. Some with big laboratories, major research facilities, or large comprehensive projects, such as the Institute of Nuclear Physics, the Institute of Geology, or the Institute of Geography, have hundreds of employees. Smaller and newer institutes may have less than a dozen members on their professional research staff.

---

88 *Jen-min Jih-pao*, May 31, 1957.
89 While no list of the members of the Academy Council has been found, its Standing Committee probably includes the President, Vice President and Secretaries of the Academy.
90 This was discussed by Yü Kuang-yuan at the Eighth Party Congress, Peking Radio, October 9, 1956.
91 See Appendix for " Regulations on the Organisation of the Departments of the Chinese Academy of Sciences."

Each is under a director, all of whom seem to have scientific qualifications, usually one or more deputy directors, and a Scientific Committee. The larger institutes appear to be organised along the lines indicated in the following chart:

TABLE VI

Organisational Structure of Research Institutes

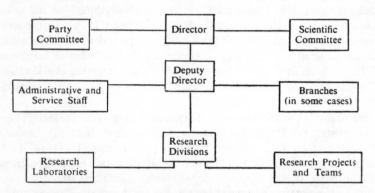

Work taking place in the research institutes of specific academies and ministries of the government has been dealt with by others.

Within the institutional arrangements for directing and conducting scientific activity, however, there are many factors which have an important bearing on China's capacity for scientific achievement. Some of these are the product of doctrines and decisions by China's rulers; others inhere in the history and tradition of the Chinese people. The large picture is complex and difficult to evaluate; but a few features of the situation seem to be clear enough to justify summary comment.

In Sum: Two Steps Forward: One Step Backward

First, like much of the world, China possesses a retarded scientific culture. Modern science is a foreign import, Western in origin, which is only beginning to take root in what the Communists describe as a " backward " society. Hence, China's modern scientists, in a sense, are still cultural aliens and, in the case of the older Western-trained scientists, political aliens, within their own society. They face the problem of adapting a foreign yet trans-national scientific culture, with its precise experimental and speculative methods, to the Chinese situation. In a scientifically unsophisticated environment they are bearers of ideas and working habits which China's political leaders, hedged by Marxist dogmatic certainties, do not appear to comprehend and trust. Yet they have a tremendous advantage. The ambition to industrialise China's economy and to modernise her society has led China's leaders to open the way to systematic scientific activity and to mobilise the entire population of a tradition-bound country to accept and utilise scientific and technical concepts and innovations.

Secondly, China's national ambition has resulted in major emphasis upon the applied sciences, engineering and technology in support of national development programmes. Clearly the Chinese are devising strenuous means for increasing the speed of technical change and are attempting consciously and drastically to foreshorten transitional stages through which other nations have passed on the way to industrialisation.[92] Scientific research, as in the Soviet Union, is strongly linked to production. Research institutes are called upon to "set up experimental factories so that the results of their research can be readily applied to production."[93] But they are not bound entirely to Soviet and other models, and are willing to experiment and take some risks without regard to cost. China's science overlord, Nieh Jung-chen, stated the official attitude: "We can afford to be a little bolder in scientific attempts than in economic construction, because even if we fail, our economic loss will not be very big, but if we succeed, the result will be significant. Besides, initial failures in scientific experiments often provide conditions for eventual success."[94] The Chinese may well obtain some striking successes by their rate of innovation and application of scientific methods in transforming an underdeveloped economy and society.

Thirdly, research in basic science, nonetheless, is not altogether neglected, but even here the Communist leaders exhibit strong pragmatic motives. They support research because "the choice of technical policy and formulation of production plans often have to depend on the result of research" and because research "will open up new avenues for the development of production."[95] In the Academy of Sciences, as President Kuo Mo-jo has suggested, a few scientists of the highest calibre are or should be engaged in taking "scientific theories to a higher level."[96] Some contributions can be expected from these talented minds in their own fields of specialisation. By and large, neither the direction of the main body of research, the amount of time given to theoretical problems, nor the quantity and character of research facilities suggest that China will soon be a major contributor to theoretical knowledge over a broad

---

[92] Nieh Jung-chen, *Jen-min Jih-pao*, Sept. 27, 1959, in GB 608, p. 9; *Hung Ch'i*, No. 9, October 1, 1958, in URS, Vol. 13, No. 19, pp. 283, 286. Many Chinese Communist statements and writings seem to have an underlying feeling or fear that time is running out and speed is important.

[93] *Hung Ch'i*, No. 9, October 1, 1958, in URS, Vol. 13, No. 19, p. 295.

[94] *Ibid*. pp. 284, 285.

[95] *Ibid*. p. 287.

[96] *Jen-min Jih-pao*, May 24, 1957, in CB 460.

range of scientific inquiry. Meanwhile, the Chinese Communist Government and China's scientists are searching the scientific literature of the world for ideas which can be applied in China, and which will serve to enrich their own research.

Fourthly, the scale of support given to scientific research in Communist China is still very modest by international standards.[97] Even after 1957, when over 1 per cent. of the central government budget, exclusive presumably of military research and development, was allocated to science, the outlay totalled no more than $400 to $500 million. With limited personnel and facilities, more money probably cannot be used profitably. Even before 1957 the Academy of Sciences did not spend its entire allocation.[98] Comparisons are difficult. Nonetheless, since the Chinese Communists have set Russia up for emulation as the world's leader in science and have modelled their own Academy of Sciences on the Soviet Academy of Sciences, it may be useful to compare the two Academies as the focal agencies of scientific activity in these countries.

By 1959 the Chinese Academy of Sciences claimed to have about 7,000 scientific workers. It is estimated that of these 800 were senior researchers with doctorate-level training; 800 were associate researchers with the equivalent of a master's or bachelor's degree in science and with research experience; 5,400 were research assistants, advanced trainees and technicians with higher or technical school training in science; and 1,900 were selected science students, most of whom were working for bachelor's, and a few for advanced degrees in the special training institutes of the Academy. Including administrative and service personnel, 40,000 people were employed by the Academy.

Ten years earlier, in 1949, the Soviet Academy of Sciences had 6,053 scientific workers divided into the following categories: 918 senior researchers; 2,455 associate researchers; 2,680 research assistants; 1,734 students working for bachelors' and advanced degrees; and a total of 20,000 employees, including administrative and service staff.[99]

The striking difference is in the ratio of trained scientists to junior personnel and technicians in the two Academies. The Russians had more than twice as many in the senior and associate category (3,373) as had the Chinese (1,600). On the other hand, in China a large number of technicians, junior personnel and service staff had been assigned to the Academy, giving it twice as many employees as the Russian Academy ten years before. The broader, nation-wide picture likewise illustrates

97 The reported science budget of the Soviet Union for 1961 is $4.44 billion (4 billion new roubles at the official rate of exchange of $1.11 to the rouble), or 5 per cent. of the total budget—reported in the *New York Times*, December 21, 1960.
98 Kuo Mo-jo to the NPC, June 18, 1956, Peking, June 18, 1956, in CB 400, pp. 1–5.
99 Conway Zirkle and Howard A. Meyerhoff, *Soviet Science* (Washington: American Association for the Advancement of Science, 1952), p. 73.

the distance China has to travel. Ignoring the question of quality, Russia was reported in 1955 to have about 3,000 organisations for scientific research with 100,000 research personnel [100]; whereas in China in 1957 there were 580 research institutes with 28,000 research and technical personnel.[101] By 1959 the Soviet Union was reported to have 310,000 scientists of whom 10,500 had the degree of Doctor of Science and 94,000 the degree of Candidate of Science.[102]

China thus is far behind the Soviet Union in its over-all scientific resources. To catch up with the Soviet Union even in a few sectors of science and technology in the next seven years and thus reach advanced world levels in these fields will require an extraordinary performance.

Fifthly, co-operation with the Soviet Union in science has steadily increased during the past ten years and shows no signs of diminishing. China's needs for scientific assistance account for this in large part. China is far from self-sufficient in scientific resources; years, probably decades, of development will be needed before she reaches the point of producing the scientists she requires. Communist China's dependence upon the Soviet Union during the past decade may have been also motivated by other considerations. The record suggests that Peking felt China's senior scientists were ideologically unprepared and politically unreliable to qualify as architects of a new organisation and plan for science in China. Thus they turned to the Soviet Union for " socialist " scientists to revamp scientific research and organisation instead of to their own specialists whose backgrounds were both non-Communist and Western in orientation. In any case, the magnitude of Soviet assistance and guidance appears to have given Chinese scientific endeavours the imprint of Soviet science with its strengths and weaknesses.

Sixthly, a remarkable feature of scientific organisation in Communist China is the development of large and top-heavy administrative super-structures. This, as has been noted, is capped by the State Scientific and Technological Commission, and is also evident in the administration of the Academy of Sciences and provincial systems for science develop-ment and control. At the national level some of the organisational and developmental tasks undertaken by the Party and State Council clearly required strong political direction and authority. This the scientists were not in a position to provide. Moreover, after 1957 the resources provided to science were sufficient in volume to require allocation by the top rank of state planners. In addition, there was an extension of the Party administrative system throughout scientific establishments, adding additional bureaucratic channels. The launching of mass science

[100] Kuo Mo-jo to the NPC, NCNA, July 21, 1955, in CB 351, pp. 21, 22.
[101] *Ten Great Years, op. cit.,* p. 189.
[102] Reported in the *New York Times,* December 26, 1960.

and technological programmes required a further proliferation of administrative and organisational bodies running from Peking to the communes. Whether the tremendous pressure to produce " results " has led to the over-organisation of science, is hard to judge. On its face, this would appear to be possible.

Seventhly, a related problem is that of communication between scientists and top political leaders. In contrast to the Soviet Union where a large number of scientists are members of the ruling élite and are even within the inner circle of political power, Chinese senior scientists as a group appear to have little or no direct and intimate association with Mao Tse-tung and senior Party officials. This anomalous situation might be ascribed to several factors: the Party's distrust of most Western-trained, bourgeois scientists; the absence of any scientists among the senior members of the Party; a feeling of uneasiness on the part of politicians and generals in associating with highly trained specialists; a possible " intellectual lag " on the part of China's first-generation Communist leaders to grasp the full implications of science and scientific modes of thought; and a reluctance to admit newcomers and those untested by political and military trials to the inner circle of power. A situation in which scientists have relatively little influence may have serious consequences by leading the régime both to over- and under-estimate the implications of scientific and technological developments.

This situation may change as new generations of scientists appear, although reports on the Chinese policy of rigidly segregating Chinese students studying in the Soviet Union from participation in normal student and public activities may be an indication that the Chinese are not entirely at ease about the effect of influences emanating from other quarters within the *bloc.* In any event, the Chinese Communists seek to correct the situation by giving preference to students with Party and worker-peasant backgrounds for training in the sciences, and by recruiting into the Party those science students who have requisite political and ideological qualifications. In 1957 over 62 per cent. of the research students in the Academy were either members of the Communist Party or of the Communist Youth League.[103] Political tests are also applied in selecting students for admission to the new University of Science and Technology in Peking.

Eighthly, the presence and supervisory intervention of the Communist Party is evident throughout the entire range of scientific organisations. The Central Committee of the Party exercises controlling influence through the Science Division, headed by Yü Kuang-yuan, of its Propaganda Department under Lu Ting-yi. As Party supervisors have grown in sophistication, these Party administrators and units are probably not

[103] Kuo Mo-jo to the NPC, *Jen-min Jih-pao,* in CB 467, p. 12.

as obstructive as they once were and may, in fact, facilitate research and concentrated work by clearing the way for the fulfilment of planned targets.

Ninthly, as in most countries, the social sciences are neglected. There is an understandable reluctance on the part of governments and societies to expose their political and social systems and beliefs to objective and scientific research and analysis. In a country controlled by men with firm and explicit ideological predispositions and under an authoritarian or totalitarian system, reluctance tends to crystallise into bristling opposition. " Social sciences have a clearly defined class character " and, therefore, have only one major task to perform, the creative application of the " real science " of Marxism-Leninism to human history and social phenomena.[104] This, of course, is the incessant function of the Party. Consequently, social science research in an academic sense has become unimportant and been restricted to supporting the propaganda activities of the régime, or to working in a few applied fields, such as developing educational methods, working on linguistic problems, or improving the efficiency of industrial and labour practices. Despite the fact that the President of the Academy of Sciences is the Director of its First Institute of History, the social sciences receive little support from the Academy. Moreover, many of China's natural and physical scientists do not accept Marxist social science as scientific and some have urged that the social sciences be removed from the Academy and separately organised.[105] Clearly social scientists in China cannot be expected to make more than the most meagre contributions in theory and application to their disciplines.

Finally, while we are too remote from the scene of science in China to identify and evaluate all of its main organisational features, there is no doubt that science has been shaped to support the developmental programmes of the régime and, in particular, the building of modern heavy industries. In developing science, the priorities in 1960 are placed in three clear categories. The first and " primary task " is research " relating to the development of the national economy." Research on " pioneering science and technology," in which China is " very weak," is placed in the second category as an area in which " energetic efforts " are required. The lowest priority is assigned to " research on fundamental theories." [106] There is no doubt that science and technology are harnessed in Communist China to the goal of national economic development and power.

[104] *Ibid.*
[105] *Ibid.*, p. 13; *Jen-min Jih-pao*, May 27, 1957, in CB 460, p. 10.
[106] " Ch'ang Chin-fu Maps Scientific Tasks," NCNA, June 6, 1960, in CB 622, p. 33.

The Literary World of Mao Tse-tung *

By HOWARD L. BOORMAN

" Who says we have not had any creative workers? Here's one
right here! " (Laughter).
Mao Tse-tung, *Oppose Party Formalism* (February 8, 1942).

POETRY and politics are rare companions in the competitive world of
practical affairs today. In Moscow, Nikita Khrushchev, with peasant
shrewdness, is addicted to Russian proverbs to enliven his rhetoric; but
there are few indications that he is sympathetic with the creative writer
and none that he himself will rank with Pushkin in the annals of his
nation's literature. In Washington, the appearance of Robert Frost at
John F. Kennedy's inauguration in January 1961 was an event at once
exceptional and gratifying to admirers of Frost's artistic integrity; the
elderly poet's advice to the young president of the United States to stress
the Irish and underplay the Harvard in his background may yet have
enduring significance. Only in Peking, however, do we find a world
leader who combines distinctive political abilities and literary talents.
Indeed the juxtaposition of strategic and artistic instincts in Mao Tse-tung
is so unusual in the post-Churchillian world that the case merits more
than passing note.

The outsider surveying the literary world of Mao Tse-tung confronts
several possible avenues of approach. Contemporary Chinese literature
may be studied, first, as the subject of literary criticism; second, as
the source of data regarding the society which has produced it; or, third,
as the product of particular political and social conditions. The first
approach is predominantly aesthetic; it views literature as a verbal art
form, studies the artistic devices peculiar to creative writing, stresses
appreciation of the unique qualities which inhere in a work of literature
to give it distinctive beauty, emotional power, moral verity, or new
awareness of the potentialities of life. The second approach attempts
to delineate and describe a society through the mirror of its literature.
The third approach aims—not at literary, aesthetic, or social criticism—
but rather at the establishment of a sense of historical perspective.

Clearly Chinese Communist literary policies cannot be made intelligible without reference to what the Chinese authors themselves have

* I acknowledge with gratitude the assistance provided by Mr. Yong-sang Ng of the
research project on Men and Politics in Modern China, Columbia University.

actually been writing or without reference to aesthetic considerations. Such appraisal, however, is outside the scope of this article. Nor do I attempt the use of contemporary Chinese literature as social documentation, if only because the existence of nation-wide controls over literature has sharply limited traffic on this avenue. Chinese writing today appears to have become a literature unlikely, except by omission or oversight, to reveal much about the real problems of real people living in the People's Republic of China.

Rather this article attempts to survey the evolving political influences which have shaped Chinese imaginative writing in the past two decades. During the 1930s and 1940s, despite the Nationalist censorship so sharply condemned by the literary left, a genuine literature of social protest— a literature which served as a sort of national conscience—did emerge and exist in China. Since the Communist victory in 1949–50, the authorities at Peking have erected a new control system designed to inhibit the production of imaginative writing as that term is conventionally used in the West. Aware of the function of literature as an instrument of social stimulus, the Communist leaders now emphasise the production of what appear to the bourgeois mind to be essentially propaganda and educational materials cast in the forms traditionally employed by literature: fiction, drama and verse. At the same time, the attitudes which Communist China displays toward its writers and artists, and the views which it holds of the proper position of art and literature in the life of the society afford important insights into China's deeper aspirations. Peking's theories regarding the social role of literature do delineate the values held by the ruling group, the leadership of the Chinese Communist Party, and the style of life which its policies are shaping. The following pages outline some basic assumptions and aims of Chinese Communist literary policies as expounded by Mao Tse-tung, and describe some salient features of the bureaucratic structure through which creative writing is now controlled in the People's Republic.

I

The political control of literature in Communist China rests ultimately upon the theoretical foundations of Marxism-Leninism. Though precise definition of the relationship between European Socialism before Lenin and Chinese Communism after Mao Tse-tung is elusive, some important strands do link the remote worlds of nineteenth-century Europe and twentieth-century China. These strands are both theoretical and practical. Of major importance is the instinct inherent in Marxism that its doctrine offers a new instrument for systematic analysis and radical reshaping of history and human society, the crusading faith based upon a set of imperatives both philosophical and political. Chinese Communism owes its theoretical faith in dialectical and historical materialism to Karl Marx. But it owes a more practical and penetrating debt to Vladimir Lenin. Lenin it was who developed a specific analysis of " imperialism," a framework for supporting the concept that non-Western nationalism would be a useful ally of the Western proletariat in the general revolutionary struggle against capitalism. At the same time, Leninist doctrine laid emphasis upon conscious action as a critical factor in stimulating social change. And Lenin laid stress, finally, upon the need for organisation as a key to action, on the vital necessity of developing a disciplined political party with absolute authority to lead the revolution and build the new society.[1]

More immediately, Chinese Communist literary policies have been affected by Russian experiments and experiences in fashioning " Socialist realism " as the main doctrinal guide in shaping literature and art in the U.S.S.R.[2] The most succinct definition of Socialist realism in its classic form was given in a statute passed by the First All-Union Congress of Soviet Writers in August 1934:

> Socialist realism is the basic method of Soviet literature and literary criticism. It demands of the artist the truthful, historically concrete representation of reality in its revolutionary development. Moreover, the truthfulness and historical concreteness of the artistic representation of reality must be linked with the task of ideological transformation and education of workers in the spirit of Socialism.

This innocent formula embraces, on the one hand, a link between Communist " Socialist realism " and the earlier critical realism of nineteenth-century Europe and, on the other, an element which the Soviets described as new and distinctive in literary theory.[3] The link lies in the

---

[1] For concise and lucid appraisal, see Alfred G. Meyer, *Marxism: the Unity of Theory and Practice* (Cambridge: Harvard Un. Press, 1954) and *Leninism* (Cambridge: Harvard Un. Press, 1957). See also Edmund Wilson, " Marxism and Literature," in *The Triple Thinkers* (London: John Lehmann, 1952), pp. 188–202. Originally published in 1938, this remains a perceptive essay by a distinguished literary critic who has also read Marx thoughtfully.

[2] Of the large literature available on the subject, see especially the recent books by Avrahm Yarmolinsky, *Literature under Communism: the Literary Policy of the Communist Party of the Soviet Union from the end of World War II to the Death of Stalin* (Bloomington: Indiana Un. Press, Russian and East European Series, Vol. 20, 1960), and Harold Swayze, *Political Control of Literature in the USSR, 1946–1959* (Cambridge: Harvard Un. Press, 1962). A classic account written from inside the movement is Leon Trotsky, *Literature and Revolution* (New York: Russell & Russell, 1957). Originally published in 1924, this volume remains a brilliant short analysis, charged with Trotsky's usual polemical gusto, of the problems confronting Russian authors during the early period after the Bolshevik revolution.

[3] See the revealing examination of Soviet literary doctrine offered by an unknown writer. Abram Tertz (pseudonym), *On Socialist Realism* (New York: Pantheon Books, 1960), pp. 24–25, with an introduction by Czeslaw Milosz. Milosz himself has discussed the relationship between political responsibility and artistic creativity in *The Captive Mind* (New York: Vintage Books, 1955), a brilliant volume confirming the fact that it is simpler to write about the intellectual under Communism than to be one.

truthfulness of the representation, a quality shown by earlier writers in the stream of modern realism: Balzac, Maupassant, Tolstoy and Chekhov, for example. The distinctive element lies in the alleged ability of Socialist realism to portray the future in the present, to grasp reality " in its revolutionary development," and to instruct readers in accordance with that development " in the spirit of Socialism." Viewing literature as the artistic crystallisation of the political aspirations of the Communist Party, Socialist realism is concerned not only with portraying " life as it really is " but also with depicting " life as it ought to be." On the basis of this theory, official Soviet criticism during the Stalinist era erected three fundamental standards for estimating the merit of a work of literature: first, the truthfulness, or " Party-mindedness," of its portrayal of reality; second, the work's pedagogical potential; and, third, its intelligibility to the " broad masses " of the people.[4]

In China, the impact of Marxism-Leninism helped to create the type of intellectual and emotional environment necessary for the existence of a Chinese Communist movement and for the emergence of Mao Tse-tung as its leader. Essentially, Mao's historic role stems from the fact that he has been a man of sufficient stature and imagination to adopt Marxism-Leninism and to apply its mystique and its radical faith in a technologically primitive peasant land which no European or Russian Communist leader ever truly comprehended viscerally, however much he may have attempted intellectually. In the same fashion, Mao was able to absorb the general elements of the Soviet pattern of political control over modern Russian literature and to apply them to the specific stream of modern Chinese literature as it had developed during the 1920s and 1930s. Peking's official doctrine has conventionally stressed the point that Mao's success has lain in his integration of the " universal truth " of Marxism-Leninism with the concrete " practice of China's revolution." The same claim may be made for the evolution of Chinese Communist literary policy under Mao's direction.

The development of a unified literary line in the Chinese Communist Party first took place during the Sino-Japanese war, as Mao consolidated his control over the central Party apparatus. After the Japanese action in north China in July 1937, Mao and the Chinese Communist leadership evolved a strategic programme at once simple and comprehensive: total conquest of national power. In pursuit of this goal, the Chinese Communists fashioned a working programme which affected increasingly broad areas of the countryside of north, east and central China. This programme included, for example, mobilisation of peasant discontent wherever possible; manipulation of the latent forces of Chinese patriotism; and the projection of Mao's " New Democracy " as the most

[4] See Swayze, *op. cit.*, p. 17.

progressive political programme in China. Utilising these and other devices, Mao's commanders, commissars, and cadres gradually wove a network of " liberated areas " in the face of the Japanese invasion. Since the Chinese Communist movement was in armed opposition to the Nationalist Government, its doctrine and practice were of necessity overwhelmingly oriented toward problems of power. Yet Yenan's doctrine was often discreetly muted to encompass the political logic of the united front, and practice was consciously patriotic to embrace the logistical and intelligence requirements of guerrilla warfare in the rural areas.

One mark of the growing political shrewdness of the Chinese Communist leadership was the fact that it came to emphasise the " cultural front " as of equal importance with military operations. Mao himself argued that literature was as critical a factor as guerrilla warfare in the total revolutionary programme in China. In retrospect, this emphasis provides a notable measure of the calibre of the two major antagonists of the period. Mao consistently recognised the important social role of literature as an instrument of criticism and reform during an interlude of political disintegration. Chiang Kai-shek just as consistently viewed the war against the Communists solely in military, never in intellectual, terms.

Though Mao's view of the social role of literature was doubtless influenced by earlier Marxist or Soviet analysis, his grasp of the problem was nevertheless consciously native.[5] Mao himself was a man of the May Fourth generation, and his diagnosis inevitably began with examination of the seminal outburst which had been the May Fourth movement of 1919.[6] In his major statement, *On New Democracy* (January 1940), Mao placed the May Fourth movement as the principal line of demarcation running through China's " democratic revolutionary movement " and dividing the old from the new.

> The May Fourth movement was an anti-imperialist as well as an anti-feudal movement. Its outstanding historical significance lies in a feature which was absent in the revolution of 1911, namely, a thorough and uncompromising opposition to imperialism and a thorough and uncompromising opposition to feudalism.[7]

Bringing orthodox class analysis to the phenomenon, Mao argued that before 1919 China's new cultural movement, her " cultural revolution,"

---

[5] A convenient summary of Mao's views is given in *Mao Tse-tung on Art and Literature* (Peking: Foreign Languages Press, 1960), translated from the Chinese text published by the People's Literature Publishing House in December 1958. Arranged chronologically, most of the contents are taken from the *Selected Works of Mao Tse-tung*, with some additions of more recent materials.

[6] The most extended study of the movement, based on wide research in contemporary sources, is Tse-tsung Chow, *The May Fourth Movement: Intellectual Revolution in Modern China* (Cambridge: Harvard Un. Press, 1960).

[7] See Mao Tse-tung, *Selected Works* (New York: International Publishers, 1955), Vol. III (1939–41), pp. 145–146. The following quotations are taken from this translation of *On New Democracy*, p. 145 *et seq.* The Chinese text is found in *Mao Tse-tung hsuan-chi* (Peking: Jen-min Ch'u-pan-she, 1952), Vol. II, pp. 655–704.

had been led by the bourgeoisie and directed against the "old culture of the feudal class." The May Fourth movement opened the way for a distinctly new historical period, the era of the "new-democratic culture," defined as the "anti-imperialist, anti-feudal culture of the broad masses of the people under the leadership of the proletariat."

Since the dawn of Chinese history, according to Mao, "there had never been such a great and thorough-going cultural revolution." As the "ideological reflection" of the political and economic revolution, the cultural revolution from the May Fourth movement to the time of Mao's speech (January 1940) was divided into four periods: (1) 1919–21; (2) 1921–27; (3) 1927–37, and (4) 1937–40. The first period, from the May Fourth outburst to the founding of the Chinese Communist Party, was an interlude during which the cultural revolution was confined to the intelligentsia and had only limited contact with the workers and peasants. The second period, from 1921 to 1927, was the era of the temporary Communist-Kuomintang alliance and of the Northern Expedition. In class terms, this was defined as a united front of the proletariat, the peasants, the urban petty bourgeoisie, and the (national) bourgeoisie. The decade from 1927 to 1937 was a "new revolutionary period" comprising "on the one hand a period of counter-revolutionary campaigns of 'encirclement and annihilation,' and on the other a period of the deepening of the revolutionary movement." And the fourth period was, of course, the then current period of the "war of resistance" against Japan.

The core of the "new democratic culture" section of *On New Democracy* summarised what was to become the conventional Communist analysis both of the May Fourth movement and Lu Hsün, the most articulate and influential critic of the post-1919 Chinese society:

> Its influence is so great and its power so tremendous that it is practically invincible wherever it goes. The vast scope of its mobilisation is unparalleled in any other period of Chinese history. And Lu Hsün was the greatest and the most militant standard-bearer of this new cultural force. He was the supreme commander in China's cultural revolution; he was not only a great man of letters, but also a great thinker and a great revolutionary. Lu Hsün had the most unyielding backbone and was totally free from any trace of obsequiousness and sycophancy; such strength of character is the greatest treasure among the colonial and semi-colonial peoples.[8]

Writing only about three years after Lu Hsün's death in October 1936, Mao lauded an already near-legendary "Lu Hsün, the Communist," as the "giant of China's cultural revolution," conveniently ignoring the fact that the real Lu Hsün had never joined the Party. Despite increasing contact with the underground Communist apparatus in Shanghai during

[8] *Ibid.* p. 144.

the period of the repressive Kuomintang actions of the early 1930s, he remained an intransigent individualist. Though Lu Hsün became China's most prominent symbol of left-wing intellectual opposition to the Kuomintang, he never succumbed to the lure of institutionalisation in the Marxist-Leninist faith.[9]

The sweep of Mao's vision may explain, if not excuse, his imprecision. Nearly a decade before Communism gained power at Peking, he was attempting during the winter of 1939–40 at his remote Shensi base to describe the system of " New Democracy " which, even then, he planned to bring to fruition in China. " National in form, new-democratic in content ": such was Mao's prescription for the cultural sector of his general revolutionary formula. Culture should be " national, scientific, and mass." It should be national in the sense that it should oppose " imperialist oppression " and uphold the " dignity and independence of the Chinese nation "; scientific in the sense that it should oppose all " feudal and superstitious ideas " and stand for the " unity of theory and practice." And it should be " mass " in the sense that it should be " in the service of the toiling masses of workers and peasants who constitute more than 90 per cent. of the nation's population, and it should gradually become their culture."

In essence, Hu Shih's earlier " literary revolution " and the entire May Fourth movement had incorporated a bold attack upon the classical language in favour of a simpler medium which could be understood not only by trained scholars but also by all Chinese with a minimum standard of literacy. So too did Mao Tse-tung in his *On New Democracy* (January 1940) call for linguistic and literary reform as an integral part of the Communist programme of cultural reorientation. Yet Mao's proposals were more drastic than those of the explorers and experimenters of the 1917–27 decade. Mao argued not only that a written form of the everyday spoken language of China should properly be used for general communication but also that the intellectuals should consciously learn the language of the common people. The Chinese written language, he stated, " must be reformed in certain ways, and our spoken language must be brought close to that of the people; we must know that the people are the inexhaustibly rich source of our revolutionary culture."

Two years later, in May 1942, Mao framed a more specific definition of the new policies through which the Communists planned to control the course of literary development in China. This definition was offered at the Yenan Forum on art and literature, a landmark in the history

⁹ See Harriet C. Mills, " Lu Hsün and the Communist Party," *The China Quarterly*, No. 4, October–December 1960, pp. 17–27.

of Chinese Communist cultural policy, where Mao made two significant speeches.[10]

The first, on May 2, was designed to raise issues for discussion. Observing that since the outbreak of the Sino-Japanese war in July 1937 more and more " revolutionary artists and writers " had come to Yenan and other Communist base areas, Mao referred to the necessity of merging the talents of these individuals with " the people." The purpose of the meeting, he stated, was " to fit art and literature properly into the whole revolutionary machine as one of its component parts, to make them a powerful weapon for uniting and educating the people and for attacking and annihilating the enemy. . . ." To achieve this objective Mao presented several problems requiring solution: the standpoint, the attitude, and the audience of the writers.

The proper standpoint (*li-ch'ang*), Mao stipulated, should be " that of the proletariat and the broad masses of the people." The correct standpoint in turn determined the appropriate attitude (*t'ai-tu*): whether to " praise " or " expose." Both were necessary, Mao stated, in accordance with whether the writer was dealing with (a) the enemy, (b) the allies in the united front, or (c) " our own people, namely, the masses and their vanguard " (*i.e.*, the Communist Party). With respect to audience (*kung-tso tui-hsiang*), he stated that literary works produced in the Shensi-Kansu-Ninghsia border region and other anti-Japanese bases should be designed for a specific audience: workers, peasants, soldiers and revolutionary cadres. If " writers from the intelligentsia " were to produce works which would be welcomed by the common people, they must first " transform and remould their thoughts and feelings." If such writers were to become Communist revolutionary writers, they must have a serious knowledge of Marxism-Leninism. True, the essential task of the writer is to create literary works. But " Marxism-Leninism is the science that all revolutionaries should study, and artists and writers cannot be exceptions."

Three weeks later, Mao summed up the forum's deliberations. In a concluding talk on May 23, 1942, he drew a firm line across the page of modern Chinese creative writing and promulgated what has since become, with some later variations, the " correct " analysis of the literary and aesthetic principles designed to guide the " progressive " writers and artists of China.

With characteristic pragmatism, Mao began: " In discussing any problem we should start from actual facts and not from definitions." After summarising the " present situation " as viewed from Yenan in the

---

[10] See Mao Tse-tung, *Selected Works* (New York: International Publishers, 1956), Vol. IV (1941–45), pp. 63–93. The Chinese text is found in *Mao Tse-tung Hsuan-chi* (Peking: Jen-min Ch'u-pan-she, 1953), Vol. III, pp. 849–880.

spring of 1942, Mao turned to " our problems." These, he stated, were basically two: " for whom " to work, and " how to serve." Quoting Lenin's famous 1905 statement, *Party Organisation and Party Literature*, Mao echoed this classic definition of the ideological basis of proletarian literature. Mao concurred that literature must be shaped by a clear " Party spirit " and must be designed for the masses, specifically for the workers, peasants and soldiers. As to the problem of " how," Mao stipulated that " popularisation " was a more pressing task than " elevation," that is, that literature should be brought down to the level of the common people to explain Communist programmes in simple, concrete language. Writing should be consciously native: in substance drawing upon China's rich storehouse of " revolutionary tales " and folk literature capable of being interpreted in an appropriate political light; in style drawing upon the pithy language of the common people. Writing should turn its back upon bourgeois themes or subjective inspiration, and should be based upon immersion in the everyday life of the common people of China.

Mao then turned to the broader issue of the relationship between literature and politics. In the world today, he stated, " all culture, all art and literature belong to definite classes and follow definite political lines. There is in reality no such thing as art for art's sake, art which stands above classes or art which runs parallel to or remains independent of politics." Literature, in short, exists primarily for politics (interpreted as meaning " class politics and mass politics "), not for amusement or entertainment. Thus Communist literary activity occupies a definite and assigned place in the Party's total revolutionary work and must serve the particular political purposes defined by the Party. Commenting finally on literary criticism as a principal method of " struggle," Mao distinguished two basic criteria: political and artistic. At the time Mao spoke (May 1942), the foremost problem confronting both China and the Chinese Communist Party was " resistance to Japan." According to the political criterion, therefore, all literary works were " good " which encouraged national unity and resistance to Japan. At the same time, Mao recognised that, to be politically effective, literary works also had to be artistically effective. " What we demand is unity of politics and art, of content and form, and of revolutionary political content and the highest possible degree of effectiveness in artistic form. Works of art, however politically progressive, are powerless if they lack artistic quality."

In a general way, the literary standards prescribed by the leader of the Communist Party of China in 1942 were similar to those created by the doctrinal demands of Socialist realism in the U.S.S.R. Literature must, first of all, be truthful in its depiction of real life as seen through the glass of *partiinost*, the " Party-minded spirit " which views all situations in relation to the " correct " Communist Party line at any given point in time. It must, secondly, incorporate a pedagogical element to give it maximum effectiveness in inculcating appropriate ethical and political values as required by the Communist revolution. And it must, thirdly, be intelligible to the common people. To be socially effective as a device for instruction and edification, a work of literature must be successful in creating an impact that is extensive as well as intensive.

Mao's Yenan talks on literature were neither original nor unopposed. In large part, they represented his summation of theories which had been widely discussed in leftist literary circles in China since the 1930s. His call for linguistic and literary reforms echoed programmes advocated earlier by leaders of the League of Left Wing Writers. His stress on the necessity for popularisation was as much pragmatic as political, a reflection of the fact that *pai-hua* literature, as it had developed during the 1920s and 1930s, was tending to become almost as incomprehensible to the average Chinese reader as classical *wen-yen*. Nor did Mao's ideas go unchallenged; a small but influential group of left-wing writers and literary critics continued in fact to oppose his dictates through the 1940s and even the early 1950s.

Because of his personal position as unchallenged leader of the Chinese Communist movement, Mao's 1942 statements did nevertheless have widespread practical importance, both in the Communist-controlled areas and outside. Within the " border regions " the Communists increasingly attempted to link imaginative writing with the political demands of nationalism, agrarian reform and the united front. Genuinely interesting talents, displayed by new authors working completely in the new native " revolutionary " pattern stipulated by Mao, did emerge. Chao Shu-li, for example, Shensi peasant born and bred, demonstrated an authentic command of rural idiom; a considerable virtuosity in linking humour, satire and pathos; and notable effectiveness in creating peasant literature with a political message for peasants.[11] In the Nationalist areas, the major established authors of twentieth-century China, increasingly dissatisfied with the intellectual turbidity and artistic aridity of the Kuomintang leadership, gradually moved towards the political left. Yenan's resolute anti-Japanese stand, its lack of venality, its Spartan way of life and its nascent " New Democracy " constituted potent appeals which Chungking could hardly match.

II

All was not simple and sweet. In the Communist areas, both in Shensi and elsewhere, the unavoidable frictions created in attempting to wed

---

[11] See Cyril Birch, " Fiction of the Yenan Period," *The China Quarterly*, No. 4, October–December 1960, pp. 1–11, followed by Birch's translation of the short story " Mai-chi " (" The Sale of a Hen "), pp. 12–16.

literary creativity and political orthodoxy were apparent during the 1940s, as similar tensions had earlier been manifest at Shanghai during the 1930s. Yet the broad fact remained that Chinese Communism, well before it won national control, had gained substantial support from many thoughtful and patriotic Chinese writers. The assassination in July 1946 at Kunming of Wen I-to, prominent poet, scholar and spokesman of the liberal Chinese intellectuals who opposed the National Government, aroused national attention and widespread criticism of the Kuomintang. By the late 1940s, almost all the serious writers of China had indicated their tacit agreement with Mao Tse-tung's political programme; after 1949, every top-ranking author remained on the mainland.[12] Such a beginning appeared auspicious. The literary front could lay claim to a substantial body of writing produced despite frustrating conditions of military conflict, political suppression and censorship, and economic insecurity during the three decades following the May Fourth movement. With optimism tinged by fatalism, the literati looked forward to reaping the benefits which Mao's consistent attention to " cultural work " appeared to promise.

The situation of the writers since has been largely a tale of ingenuous affection deceived. In practical terms, the establishment of the Central People's Government marked the close of the literary period sparked a generation earlier by Ch'en Tu-hsiu, Hu Shih, *New Youth* and the Chinese Renaissance. The post-1949 era has been marked by total emphasis upon the creation of a " people's literature " on a truly national basis. This emphasis has been accompanied by the establishment of a new control mechanism capable of applying rigorous standards to all writers on the mainland, Communist and non-Communist alike. The hypothesis that politics has a profound impact upon literature has ripened into the axiom that politics is the essence of literature. Understanding of the relation between the two may thus best be assisted by an assessment of Peking's general policy intentions.

In the political sphere, Peking's primary objectives have been, first, consolidation of total power and construction of an effective apparatus of political control and, second, forced development of maximum national power. The driving ram-jet engine behind this programme of social engineering is the distinctive organisation-cum-ideology which is the Communist Party of China. Leninist by tradition and by necessity, the Communist Party now dominates all aspects of life on the mainland, acting in part as the innovating agent in imposing change, in part as

---

[12] Of the top-ranking literary figures, only Lao She, who was in the United States at the time, was absent when the new government was established in October 1949. He returned to China slightly later, toward the end of 1949, and has remained in Peking. See Cyril Birch, " Lao She: The Humourist in his Humour," *The China Quarterly*, No. 8, October–December 1961, pp. 45–62.

the reflector of evolving forces and aspirations in contemporary Chinese society. The new totalitarian marriage of apparatus and doctrine, coupled with a technological control system which never existed before in China, thus gives the Chinese Communist élite a degree and a type of power which is in important respects completely new.

As the nature of the society is now being shaped to correspond with the priorities of the Communist political system, so too has the position of literature in the society changed drastically. Now, as formerly in the Communist-controlled areas in the countryside, the Party seeks expository works which preach a simple, social moral attuned to its immediate purposes. But now the mobilisation of fiction as the handmaiden of politics has been carried through on a national scale. In pursuit of its ambitious goals, Peking confronts the problem of purposeful stimulation of over 650 million Chinese dwelling within the borders of the People's Republic. To that end, Peking must strive to eliminate illiteracy to make literature comprehensible to the common people [13]; while simultaneously it must use literature to reach those who can read in order to secure maximum public support for its programme of planned national modernisation. The political structure of Communist China is in important respects similar to a military organisation which operates through command, not consent. Within this command context, literature is a sort of independent regiment staffed by technicians skilled in the use of prose, poetry and drama for the mobilisation of mass support for centrally determined political objectives.

An outstanding characteristic of modern single-party dictatorship is its reliance upon bureaucratic organisation to render its controls effective on a broad scale. As in other realms of Chinese life, it has been necessary to create a large bureaucratic apparatus to translate the Communist Party's literary precepts into actual practice. The political control of literature in the People's Republic of China has been little studied to date, and the following account is confined to description of the apparatus affecting the production of literary works. It does not attempt to analyse the precise techniques of control or to assess the manner in which changes in the political climate within China have affected the style and operation of the system.

The primary instrument of political control in Communist China is the central apparatus of the Communist Party itself. Thus the Party's central organisation, specifically the department of propaganda of the Central Committee, acts as the general source of ideological orthodoxy and the central arbiter of its transmutation into " literature." Director

---

[13] See Father Paul L.-M. Serruys, *Survey of the Chinese Language Reform and the Anti-illiteracy Movement in Communist China* (Berkeley: University of California, Center for Chinese Studies, Studies in Chinese Communist Terminology, No. 8, February 1962).

of the propaganda department of the party is Lu Ting-yi, long a high-ranking figure in the central hierarchy, an alternate member of the Political Bureau since September 1956 and a member of the Secretariat of the Central Committee since September 1962. Of the seven deputy directors of the department, the most prominent is Chou Yang, an alternate member of the Central Committee and the key figure in articulating the Party line in the field of literature. The propaganda department of the Central Committee also includes a literature and arts division, headed by Sung Yang, of whom little is known.

The Communist Party rules mainland China through an apparatus composed of what are ostensibly governmental organisations and institutions, but it has ensured from the outset that all such organs function only under its own political supervision. In the national government structure at Peking, the principal channel of direction and control is the Ministry of Culture. Since its establishment in 1949, this ministry has been headed by the novelist Mao Tun. Creatively inactive in recent years, Mao Tun has been the ranking government official in the field of literature and the arts though he himself is not a Communist Party member. He has eight vice-ministers, of who Ch'ien Chun-jui, now an alternate member of the Central Committee, is probably the most influential Communist. The Ministry of Culture has broad administrative authority in the cultural field, including literature, and is the top level in a nation-wide pyramid of subordinate bureaus which direct cultural affairs at the provincial and local levels. Neither Mao Tun nor the Ministry of Culture, however, plays any major role in policy formulation.

The Chinese Academy of Sciences, also a part of the governmental machinery at Peking, may be mentioned because of its position as the principal centre of advanced research in the People's Republic. President of the Academy since 1949 has been Kuo Mo-jo, one of the most versatile of living Chinese intellectuals and a significant force on the cultural scene since the 1920s. Prolific as poet, playwright, novelist, short story writer, essayist and critic, Kuo formally joined the Communist Party in 1959. Under its department of philosophy and social sciences, the Academy has an Institute of Literary Studies, where senior scholars pursue advanced research on China's classical literature, as well as other organs which have more indirect connection with literature and literary history: the research institutes on linguistics and philology, minority nationality languages and archaeology.

Outside the Party and government structure, the key apparatus facilitating Party direction of literature is the All-China Federation of Literary and Art Circles. The Federation, established in the summer of 1949 slightly before the establishment of the Central People's Government, is one of the largest and most influential of the " people's organisations " which Peking has created to channel political controls throughout the country.[14] Reorganised at its second congress in 1953, the Federation held its third national congress of writers and artists at Peking in July–August 1960. That meeting elected a national committee of 224 persons, from among whom were elected the chairman and fifteen vice-chairmen of the Federation. Kuo Mo-jo was re-elected chairman, with Mao Tun and Chou Yang as the top vice-chairmen. Other vice-chairmen elected in 1960 included Pa Chin, Lao She, Hsu Kuang-p'ing (widow of Lu Hsün), T'ien Han, Ou-yang Yu-ch'ien (died 1962) and Hsia Yen, as well as Mei Lan-fang (died 1961) and other senior figures in the arts. Well-known literary figures who became members of the national committee in 1960 but were not elected to vice-chairmanships included Chang T'ien-yi, Ch'eng Fang-wu, Hsieh Ping-hsin (previously a vice-chairman), Hsiung Fo-hsi, Liu Pai-yu and Yü P'ing-po.

The All-China Federation of Literary and Art Circles is essentially a holding company responsible for co-ordinating the activities of nine national organisations representing major branches of the arts: literature, drama, painting, music, dance, folklore, vocal music, films and photography. The literary subdivision of the Federation is the Chinese Writers' Union. Like its Russian counterpart, the Union of Soviet Writers, this organisation is intended to be the principal professional body in contemporary Chinese literary life,[15] responsible to and supervised by the Central Committee of the Party. The Writers' Union is designed to provide a forum for the interchange of ideas, an organisation through which professional writers may aid and stimulate each other, and a direct channel through which the Communist Party, aided by the Party fraction in the Union, can transmit its mandates and elucidate its view of the tasks confronting contemporary Chinese literature. Mao Tun, in addition to his post as Minister of Culture in the government, has also served as chairman of the Chinese Writers' Union since 1949. The Union now has four vice-chairmen: Chou Yang, Pa Chin, Shao Ch'uan-lin and Lao She. As a national association, the Writers' Union also supervises branches in the provinces and autonomous regions, and at the sub-provincial level as well. In organisation and operations, these branches are similar to the national Union, though their apparatus is naturally simpler.

Information about the activities and interrelationships of the various parts of the bureaucracy which controls the complex range of activities involved in the production of literary works in Communist China is

---

[14] See *The People's New Literature* (Peking: Cultural Press, 1950), for English translations of four reports given at the first Congress of the All-China Federation of Literary and Art Circles in July 1949. Reports are by Chou En-lai, Kuo Mo-jo, Mao Tun and Chou Yang, and the pamphlet has a foreword by Emi Siao.

[15] For an appraisal of the Soviet Writers' Union, see Swayze, *op. cit.*, Chap. 6, " Bureaucratic Controls and Literary Production," pp. 224–258.

scanty.[16]   As a general rule, policy decisions of the central apparatus of the Party, speeches by top Party officials, leading editorials in the major newspapers and theoretical journals published in Peking—all these have the force of military orders.   In specific cases, the top Party echelons may issue instructions through the propaganda department of the Central Committee.   And, not least important, Peking's ranking literary bureaucrats, both vice-chairmen of the Chinese Writers' Union, are also ranking Communists.   Chou Yang has been close to Mao Tse-tung since the 1930s; Shao Ch'uan-lin, while less prominent, is now secretary of the Communist Party fraction in the Writers' Union.   The Party thus exercises continuing political surveillance through the editorial offices of the leading literary journals and publishing houses.

The two leading literary magazines in China today are *Jen-min Wen-hsueh* (*People's Literature*: PL) the organ of the Chinese Writers' Union, and *Wen-yi Pao* (*Journal of Literature and the Arts*) the organ of the All-China Federation of Literary and Art Circles.[17]   Both are monthlies; and it is hardly surprising to record the fact that, in both influence and circulation, they dominate the literary scene throughout the country.   *People's Literature*, normally running about 80 pages, prints current short novels and some poems; *Wen-yi Pao*, with about 40–50 pages, specialises in shorter literary pieces and literary criticism.   Though the precise techniques of Party control are often cloudy, it is clear that few are exempt from pressures.   Feng Hsueh-feng, for example, at the time of his downfall, was both a vice-chairman of the Writers' Union and editor-in-chief of the People's Literature Publishing House.   This company, one of the specialised houses established by the Communists to publish literary works for the general reader, occupies a key place in the preparation and distribution of approved books.   Here, as elsewhere in the publishing realm, editors, cultural cadres, and authors are doubtless plagued continually by the tensions created by the potentially conflicting demands for ideological reliability and artistic potency.

The organisation of writing on a national basis may be viewed, at one level, as an aspect of the programme of coercive persuasion and indoctrination which has been so prominent a part of the Communist

---

[16] Some guidance is provided by Franklin W. Houn, *To Change a Nation: Propaganda and Indoctrination in Communist China* (New York: The Free Press of Glencoe, 1961).   See especially Chap. 3, "The Printed Word and the Dogma," pp. 91–154.

[17] A useful index guide to the contents of *Jen-min Wen-hsueh* is given in Takashi Aiura, "Jimmin bungaku sodai shosetsu, sambun, ho-koku ichiranhyo," *Journal* of Osaka University of Foreign Studies, 1961, No. 9, pp. 93–145.   Prepared in the Chinese literature seminar, this guide lists 947 items included in *Jen-min Wen-hsueh* during the period from October 1949 to November 1959, arranged by year and month with summary of contents.

Samples of three short novels, translated from PL (issues of October through December 1961), are given in *China News Analysis* (Hong Kong), No. 414, March 30, 1962.

control system in China.[18] This programme, played in a distinctively Chinese key and aimed at a higher degree of saturation than superficially similar programmes in other totalitarian political systems, has been a major element in Peking's mobilisation effort. At another level, the Chinese Communists have gone beyond the general thought reform programme to launch specific attacks against writers accused of being lax in political reliability or lethargic in production of the approved brands of fiction. The primary instrument employed in these campaigns has been public criticism by the Communist Party. The major purpose has been to compel the writers thus stigmatised to recognise and accept the strict guidance of the Party in literary, no less than in political, matters.

This series of campaigns aimed at reaffirming the primacy and purity of Party leadership has encompassed both non-Communist and Communist writers, including some veteran Party members. The roots of these attacks may be found in the period during the Sino-Japanese war when the Communists, confronted with expanding Party membership and with extended geographical lines of control, embarked upon a thorough-going programme of tightening intra-Party discipline along strict Leninist lines.[19] Both at Yenan during the early 1940s and in the Communist-controlled areas of the North-east after 1945, the Party authorities dealt abruptly and harshly with Communist writers who ventured overt criticism of Mao's official policies.

Since their victory on the mainland, Communist attacks on writers and literary scholars have intermittently been intensified.[20] One major campaign, launched in the autumn of 1954, focused upon Yü P'ing-po, leading non-Communist scholar of classical Chinese literature, for alleged ideological errors in assessment of the famous eighteenth-century novel, *Hung Lou Meng* (*The Dream of the Red Chamber*). The essence

[18] The most informed brief introduction to this controversial subject is Harriet C. Mills, "Thought Reform: Ideological Remoulding in China," *The Atlantic*, special issue on China, December 1959, pp. 71–77. More extended first-hand accounts and academic studies include the following: Theodore H. E. Chen, *Thought Reform of the Chinese Intellectuals* (Hong Kong: Hong Kong Un. Press, 1960); Robert Ford, *Wind between the Worlds* (New York: David McKay, 1957); Robert Jay Lifton, *Thought Reform and the Psychology of Totalism: a Study of "Brainwashing" in China* (New York: Norton, 1961); Allyn and Adele Rickett, *Prisoners of Liberation* (New York: Cameron Associates, 1957); and Edgar H. Schein *et al.*, *Coercive Persuasion: A Socio-Psychological Analysis of the "Brainwashing" of American Civilian Prisoners by the Chinese Communists* (New York: Norton, 1961).

[19] See Boyd Compton, *Mao's China: Party Reform Documents, 1942–44* (Seattle: University of Washington Press, 1952). Compton provides a solid introduction, followed by translation of twenty-two documents used in "study" and discussion groups in the Communist areas during the *cheng-feng* campaign. A slightly revised group of documents is given in *Cheng-feng Wen-hsien* (Peking: Hsin-hua Shu-tien, May 1950).

[20] In addition to the summary provided by Franklin W. Houn, *op. cit.*, pp. 130–40, see also Shau-wing Chan, "Literature in Communist China," *Problems of Communism*, VII, No. 1 (January–February 1958), pp. 44–51, and Cyril Birch, "The Dragon and the Pen," *Soviet Survey*, special China issue, No. 14 (April–June 1958), pp. 22–26.

of Peking's criticisms of Yü, a prominent authority on the novel, was that he had failed to emphasise that the novel portrayed the class struggle and exposed, through its characters, the evils of China's feudal society. Having vilified Yü for his failure to employ Marxist categories of analysis, the Communists went on to denounce him as a " bourgeois idealist " tainted with the poisonous doctrines of Hu Shih, attacks which were as virulent as they were manifestly absurd, since Yü P'ing-po had often differed with Hu Shih's opinions concerning early Chinese fiction and drama. Feng Hsueh-feng, then a vice-chairman of the Chinese Writers' Union and editor of the influential *Wen-yi-Pao,* lost his editorship for having taken Yü's part in the controversy. Yü P'ing-po in the end emerged from the sustained attack, made the necessary concessions to Marxist interpretation, and applied himself with remarkable resilience to his *Hung Lou Meng* studies.[21]

Less fortunate was Hu Feng, himself a leading independent Marxist literary critic who had been a disciple of Lu Hsün in Shanghai in the 1930s. After the establishment of the new régime at Peking in 1949, Hu Feng became increasingly critical of the attempts of his old antagonist, Chou Yang, and of Chou's fellow bureaucrats in the central apparatus to dominate all literary activity in China. This smouldering resentment erupted in a general statement, " Views on Literary Questions" which Hu Feng boldly submitted to the Central Committee of the Party in July 1954. In reply to this overt criticism of the sterility of literature under its rigid rule Peking launched a massive counter-attack. The Communist authorities declared Hu Feng of " bourgeois reactionary " thinking and in July 1955 arrested both Hu and other members of his " clique " on charges of " counter-revolutionary " activities.

Though the charge that he disagreed with Peking's current literary policies was valid, there was no evidence proving that Hu Feng's ideas were anti-Marxist in principle or that he actually intended to subvert or sabotage political authority. Peking's manipulation of the case demonstrated that the political aspects of the controversy overshadowed the literary. Peking's programme of political mobilisation during 1955 required that heterodox views be exposed and eradicated. A revolutionary by conviction, Hu Feng found himself unable to sustain his stand in favour of freedom of expression for the creative writer during a period when the demands of political utilitarianism outweighed those of artistic integrity.

An interlude of liberalisation in ideological controls came during the " hundred flowers " campaign launched in mid-1956 with the explicit aim of giving intellectuals and " cultural workers " a greater sense of

---

[21] I am indebted to Professor David Hawkes of Oxford University for background information on Yü P'ing-po.

participation in the tasks of " Socialist construction " and of leavening the literary scene with fresh forms of expression. The apparent relaxation in Communist policy heralded by Lu Ting-yi's speech of May 1956 [22] did in fact bring forth a short-lived spasm of literary realism. One short story, " Young Newcomer to the Organization Department," published in the September 1956 issue of *People's Literature*, provides a perceptive account of the growing disillusion experienced by an enthusiastic Communist Party worker in the face of bureaucracy, lethargy, and indifference.

Yet the attempt to win over and mobilise the intellectuals was too brief to sustain significant new literary production, and the interlude of criticism was followed in 1957 by a new rectification campaign in the Party and a general nation-wide drive against " rightist elements " antithetical to Peking's policies. The most dramatic case affecting the literary world during this period was that of Ting Ling, prominent Chinese Communist authoress and Stalin Prize winner, who was attacked for leading an " anti-Party conspiracy " within the Communist ranks. Chou Yang himself led the attack on Ting Ling and her associates.

Amidst the tangle of polemical verbiage contributed by Chou Yang and other pillars of orthodoxy,[23] many questions regarding these major cases of non-conformity remain obscure. It is clear, however, that the Communist authorities at Peking still affirm the validity of the general literary principles enunciated by Lenin in 1905 and articulated in China by Mao Tse-tung in 1942.[24] They still decree, first, that literature must be subordinate to politics; second, that the Communist Party must direct the course of contemporary Chinese literature; and third, that the essential purpose of literature is to educate workers, peasants, and soldiers in the policies determined by the Party leadership. The continued relevance of Mao's literary precepts was again stressed in May 1962, on the twentieth anniversary of the talks at the Yenan Forum on art and literature, when Peking's policy line stressed the ultimate political responsibilities of the creative writer. " China's literature and art must bring into full play its militancy and inspire the whole people to strive for the nation's prosperity and make efforts to establish a new socialist life," the official *People's Daily* stated.

[22] Lu Ting-yi, *Let a Hundred Flowers Blossom, a Hundred Schools of Thought Contend* (Peking: Foreign Languages Press, 1958). The speech was given in Peking on May 26, 1956, and published originally in the *People's Daily* of June 13, 1956.

[23] One sample may suffice to indicate the style of the discourse. Chou Yang, in denouncing the errant behaviour of Ting Ling and Ch'en Ch'i-hsia, summarised the official line: " Instead of remoulding themselves in the spirit of collectivism, they want to remould the Party and the revolution according to their individualist outlook." See Chou Yang, *A Great Debate on the Literary Front* (Peking: Foreign Languages Press, 1958), p. 13.

[24] See Lin Mo-han, *Raise Higher the Banner of Mao Tse-tung's Thought on Art and Literature* (Peking: Foreign Languages Press, 1961).

By intent and by necessity, Chairman Mao remains the Male Muse of the Arts in Peking's current mythology. In the real world, however, it is clear that neither the Central Committee of the Party, the Chinese Writers' Union nor the Party officials in the principal editorial offices at Peking and Shanghai are omnipotent. The process of influencing and controlling literary production depends also upon author and reader.

At one level, the task begins at the desk of the individual author, where the subtle process of personal censorship inherent in the Chinese Communist political system is first activated and finally resolved. Supported by stipend and encouraged by royalties, the creative writer nevertheless occupies a precarious position, constantly measuring his margin of freedom between the wall of schematism and the brink of non-conformity. At still another level, the enormous and newly literate reading public plays an essential role as ultimate consumer. Though the choice of Chinese literary works to be approved and published, and of non-Chinese works to be translated, is determined in large part by the Party's prescriptions as to what he should read, the reader himself is still not defenceless. Reader reaction (reception or resistance) is not an integral part of the control process, but it is still influential in China as in the Soviet Union. The authorities at Peking thus temper their proletarian predilections with a measure of pragmatism in publishing policy. The major traditional works of Chinese fiction are available, as indeed is a wide range of Chinese translations of Western books. Shakespeare, Dickens, and Hardy; Mark Twain and Jack London; Zola, Maupassant, Balzac, and Victor Hugo; Goethe and Heine: all are part of the literary fare still available in Chinese translation in the People's Republic of China today.[25]

III

Available they may be, but Western works form only a minor pattern in the literary world of Mao Tse-tung's China, dedicated as that nation is to the downfall of bourgeois society. The dominant motif is still the distinctive blend of nationalism and radicalism which has come to mark Chinese Communism today. Within this larger political context, the meshing of doctrine and discipline is as notable in literature as in any other major field of activity in China. Indeed the very speed and sureness with which the authorities at Peking have moved in imposing political controls over literature (much faster than the Communists in Moscow did during a comparable period after 1917) suggest that Mao Tse-tung and his associates have been working in harmony with some

[25] See the special article on translations into Chinese from Western languages in *The Times Literary Supplement*, September 21, 1962, p. 741.

longer historical trends. On any realistic estimate, neither Marx, Lenin, Stalin, nor Mao Tse-tung may be held solely responsible for the pattern of intellectual and social revolution in contemporary China. The new formulae are supported by elements in the Chinese political tradition. They are also buttressed by the Russian impact on China during the three decades before Communism engulfed that country, and by the particular demands, frequently turbulent and usually strident, of modern Chinese nationalism and anti-imperialism.

Mao Tse-tung's brand of totalitarianism has certain roots in the massive tradition of bureaucratic government, variously labelled authoritarian or despotic, found in dynastic China. The paternalistic Confucian system, dependent as it was on status and hierarchy, on obligation and obedience, was based in part upon autocratic assumptions and administered by a sophisticated bureaucracy well attuned to the practical requirements of wielding power. For centuries prior to the metamorphosis of mainland China into a major power in the international Communist system, the Chinese political heritage consistently placed greater emphasis upon group ethics and group responsibility than on individual autonomy.

Peking's present programme of intellectual and literary reorientation has also been aided by the impact of Russian ideas among the Chinese intelligentsia after 1917.[26] While the Western powers were still dominant on the China coast during the 1920s and 1930s, the influence of Russian literature was both strong and subtle. The works of the nineteenth-century titans—Pushkin, Gogol, Turgenev, Dostoyevsky, Tolstoy, and Chekhov—were all found in China's bookshops. Gorky was also popular, and considerable attention was paid to Soviet authors of the early post-revolutionary authors despite the Kuomintang censorship during the 1930s.[27] The attraction of modern Russian fiction arose partly because it depicted problems and tensions which paralleled those with which sensitive Chinese were naturally concerned. Thus the inflow of Russian ideas, particularly the themes of social idealism, patriotism and humanitarianism, fed the mole of intellectual revolution in its burrowing under the bustling international concessions in Shanghai and the other treaty ports.

Another manifest segment of Russian influence was, of course, sharply focused and highly political. After the 1917 revolution, the

---

[26] See Benjamin Schwartz, " The Intelligentsia in Communist China," *Daedalus* issue on " The Russian Intelligentsia," Summer 1960, pp. 604–621.

[27] A list of translations of foreign works into Chinese up to March 1929 is given in Chang Ching-lu (ed.), *Chung-kuo Hsien-tai Ch'u-pan Shih-liao* (Peking: Chung-hua Shu-chu, 1954), Vol. I, pp. 271–323. Russian authors and their works are given on pp. 277–287. Another list in the same work gives the names of Soviet authors available in Chinese translation up to May 1930, *ibid.* Vol. II, p. 280 *et seq.* Almost all important writers of the Soviet period are represented.

Soviets brought to China a shrewdly conceived, partially true, and reasonably palatable diagnosis of Chinese national frustration. Foreign " imperialism " and domestic " feudalism," the Leninist argument ran, were the twin evils blocking progress toward independence and modernisation. The blending of Russian and Chinese revolutionary styles has also been aided by two particular elements inherent in the mystique of Marxism-Leninism: a probing insight into mass psychology in countries attempting the process of rapid transition from traditional to industrial society and, second, a deep passion for material improvement and modernisation.[28] All these elements helped Communism in China before 1949 to take advantage of the growing mood of protest; they have unquestionably helped Communism in power since 1949 to enforce discipline, regimentation and centralisation of decision.

Yet the intellectual component in Marxism which allegedly provides " scientific " description and analysis of reality is only the warp of the ideological pattern in contemporary China. The pattern also embraces an indigenous emotional woof, dyed in the vat of modern Chinese nationalism. The projectile force of nationalism, which Peking has now seized and directed into anti-American channels, is in part a newer version of the deep Chinese antagonism toward Western intrusion manifest during the nineteenth century. The traditional hostility of the official-gentry class toward foreigners was sharpened and broadened during the early twentieth century as a result of the impact in China of the Russian revolution and the ideas of Lenin. Both the Chinese Communist Party and the post-1924 Kuomintang were strongly, often violently, anti-imperialist. Harnessing the deep-seated Chinese distrust of the West and of its ambiguous intentions toward China, Mao Tse-tung has now organised modern Chinese nationalism for his specific political purposes. Peking's " anti-imperialist nationalism " lays primary stress upon the demands of national solidarity over competing demands for individual rights. Though giving little place to what the West would define as democratic participation, Peking's appeal to Chinese nationalistic aspirations has tapped significant sources of popular energy in that country.

Viewed against this backdrop of historical and cultural motifs, the peregrinations of the Party line toward contemporary Chinese literature gain additional significance. Peking's political emphasis today is on the sustained expansion of national power. In pursuit of his objective, the Chinese Communists have made a massive effort to instil a sense of unity into the Chinese nation and a sense of purpose into contemporary Chinese life. The long-term success of their endeavour is problematic.

---

[28] See Adam B. Ulam, *The Unfinished Revolution: an Essay on the Sources of Influence of Marxism and Communism* (New York: Random House, 1960).

But the immediate accomplishments, as well as the obvious shortcomings, must be recognised. For some in China, the Communists have transformed uncertainty into conviction. For many others, the Communists have restored a sense of confidence in China as a vigorous nation capable of decisive action (not least, of expelling the Westerners and extirpating the Western enclaves) and have inculcated a renewed sense of self-respect for China as a distinctive cultural entity with a proud past and a manifest destiny.

Perhaps the major requirement in assessing tradition and transition in the literary world of Mao Tse-tung is, therefore, a sense of perspective.[29] In the non-Communist tradition, literature is conventionally held to be an individual expression of experience, real or imagined; and the normal relation between writer and product is assumed to comprise integrity, spontaneity and sincerity. For the writer working on a large scale, the purpose of creation is the communication of a complex vision, inherently personal and frequently moral, of man and of life. Secure in his individualist bias, the non-Communist critic is thus likely to conclude that the authorities at Peking, through their collectivist preconceptions and prejudices, have doomed the Chinese literary field to stunted growth for an indefinite period.

Actually, however, the links between literature and society are inevitably intricate.[30] Contemporary Chinese literature may be of dubious value as a guide to present social reality in China. But it still has substantial significance in clarifying the values of the society which has shaped and produced it. In earlier centuries, the traditional historian of China had a definite didactic function: he was consciously constructing a corpus of precedents to guide future generations of scholar-officials in the theory and practice of public administration as it should be conducted in accordance with Confucian ethical standards.[31] Today the writer in Communist China is, in a perverse way, similarly charged with a didactic mission: he is attempting to channel all the energies of his nation into the construction of the " New China."

29 See T'ien-yi Li, " Continuity and Change in Modern Chinese Literature," *The Annals* of the American Academy of Political and Social Science, Vol. 321, January 1959, pp. 90–99.

30 Irving Howe, *Politics and the Novel* (New York: Horizon Press, 1957) is a provocative study of some aspects of this subject. The volume has chapters on Stendhal, Dostoyevsky, Conrad, Turgenev and Henry James; a section on American novelists (" The Politics of Isolation ") commenting on Hawthorne (*The Blithedale Romance*), Henry Adams (*Democracy*) and Henry James (*The Bostonians*); and an appraisal of several distinctively twentieth-century writers: Malraux, Silone, Koestler and Orwell. Leo Lowenthal, *Literature and the Image of Man: Sociological Studies of the European Drama and Novel, 1600–1900* (Boston: Beacon Press, 1957), is a thoughtful study of the changing image of man in relation to society as revealed in some of the major literary works of the Western world during the past three centuries.

31 See E. Balazs, " L'histoire comme guide de la pratique bureaucratique," in W. G. Beasley and E. G. Pulleyblank (eds.), *Historians of China and Japan* (London: Oxford Un. Press, 1961), pp. 78–94.

IV

The vision of social change, while itself a major feat in a tradition-bound civilisation, is certainly not new in modern China. But the implementation of change on a national basis under determined and dedicated direction is new. Chairman Mao has added implementation to imagination, and the political results of the addition process are certain to outlast him.

In the literary realm, however, the situation still shelters deviant conduct. While all professional writers in the People's Republic must follow the demands of the " mass line in literature " in writing for " the people," one prominent non-conformist amateur stands aloof from Peking's doctrinal demands. Contemporary China's best-selling and most-translated author is—in his poetry at least—a conspicuous exception to the rules articulated in Peking.

Snow Scene (1945)

The grandeur that is the northern country—
    an expanse of the good earth ice-bound,
    snow-covered for thousands of miles around.
Surveying the Great Wall, to its north and south,
    nothing but whiteness meets the eye.
The torrents of the mighty Huang Ho
    into insignificance pale.
Silver snakes dance atop the mountains,
    waxen elephants roam the plains,
    as if to wrest heaven's domain.
Let us wait for the sky to clear
    when, clothed in radiant colours,
    the land becomes more magnificently dear.
For such an enchanting empire, little wonder
    countless heroes matched wits with one another.
Alas! The ambitious emperors of Ch'in and Han
    could scarcely boast of literary lore.
E'en the founders of the great houses T'ang and Sung
    became nought before the sages of yore.
As to the redoubtable Genghis Khan,
    pampered child of fortune he was,
    excelled only on the field of battle.
Gone are they all.
For leaders truly worthy of homage,
    must yet be sought among men of our own age.[32]

---

[32] Mr. Yong-sang Ng has prepared this translation. Peking's official English version appears in *Mao Tse-tung: Nineteen Poems* (Peking: Foreign Languages Press, 1958), p. 22, and is also quoted on page 65 below.

Written in the *tz'u* form, the poem marks a definite return to the past in both conception and style. Its presentation is in the orthodox Chinese statesman-scholar tradition, opening with a reference to the beauties of nature and then turning to a political theme. Blending sharp imagery and vivid metaphor, manifesting a strong sense of history and of change on the part of the author, the poem stands as an unusually effective example of traditionalism, formal excellence, and romantic heroism.

The culprit?

Mao Tse-tung himself is the outstanding exception to the canons of proletarian and utilitarian literature which he has brought to his country and his people.[33]

---

[33] Aware of this stubborn fact, Mao has suggested that it is inadvisable to encourage young people to write verse in the classical style " because these forms would cramp their thought and are also difficult to master." See his January 1957 letter to Tsang K'o-chia, then editor of the magazine *Poetry*, included in *Mao Tse-tung on Art and Literature, op. cit.*, pp. 135–136. See also Ping-ti Ho, " Two Major Poems by Mao Tse-tung : a Commentary, with Translations," *Queen's Quarterly* (Kingston, Ontario, Canada), LXV, 2, Summer 1958, pp. 251–262. Robert Payne has a chapter on " The Poetry of Mao Tse-tung " in his revised biography, *Portrait of a Revolutionary: Mao Tse-tung* (New York: Abelard-Schuman, 1961), pp. 230–248.

Multiplicity in Uniformity:
Poetry and the Great Leap Forward

By S. H. CHEN

THE Great Leap Forward has not only been measured by the claimed increases of grain and steel production by so many million tons. Peking boasts too that the Leap produced, in 1958 alone, millions and millions of poems and songs. These products, both in themselves as art and in their way and manner of accomplishment, should reveal a picture of how the mental life, or, more precisely, how the mental as well as physical energy, of the nation is being vigorously mobilised, organised and directed. For, as much of the steel was, regardless of its quality, produced in " backyard furnaces," so are myriads of these poems and songs, regardless of their aesthetics, made by farm teams in the fields, workers in the factories, and labourers building roads or bridges. The people are goaded and urged, instructed and inspired by tireless party cadres who exhort all social and racial groups that, among other purposes, there has to be a new epoch of poetry production to celebrate the new era in Chinese history.

There is enough evidence to show that the phenomenal, *quantitative* success is real. And the immediate effect of this success may be readily observed as therapeutic. It is as if the gasping, agonising interjections of " ai-ya! a-yo! " of men, and of women too, under the back-crushing weight of iron or earth, were transformed into facilely rhythmic and, more important, " ideologically correct " words, which they are told to recite or sing pridefully as their own invention. Whatsoever rest periods (one would hesitate to say " leisure ") they may get, they are not allowed to remember their fatigue, but are called on to enjoy the uplifting pastime of poetry-contests, which, they are told, would make a Tu Fu or Li Po out of them, or better. For those great poets Tu and Li were unfortunately born in the wrong age of " feudalism," and much of their writing must be regarded as " incorrect " or " retarded." But, today, under the leadership of Chairman Mao and the Communist Party, the people's poetry can never be " incorrect." One example out of myriads, from a song reportedly by peasants in Shensi Province, goes like this:

Each year our farm production grows,
Grains and cotton pile up mountain high, Hurrah!
Eat the grains, but don't forget the sower,
The Communist Party's our dear Ma and Pa.

Let this not be too easily dismissed as a puerile jingle. Think of it rather as the first words which the anonymous baby of the Revolution is taught proudly to sing and imitate. Innocent, docile, yet capable of lusty outcry, such a baby is to be regarded as the ideal model for the millions of the toiling masses in their elementary literary education. All who sing in its voice are praised, for it is also adored as the symbol of the awaited happy future. But for the present, these voices serve splendidly an immediate purpose, and strike a resounding note that dominates all proclamations of literary value, true or false. The poet-critic Hsiao San commented on the above-quoted poem in the *People's Daily* of February 11, 1958, in an article entitled " The Best Poetry," a panegyrical piece which was echoed, moreover, by practically all other professional poets and writers, often in even more ecstatic eulogies:

> "This is the first year of our Second Five-Year Plan, also the first of the fifteen years in which our steel and other important industrial productions will catch up with those of England. . . . At this time, all over our whole country how innumerable are the beautiful songs being sung, and how innumerable are the magnificent poems [like this] being composed! These are the best poetry."

If the question of criteria for " magnificent " " best poetry " like this must raise any sensitive brow, the reports on the salutary social effect of the do-it-yourself mass production of songs and poems by all the people merit some credence. One on village life in Shansi Province, in the *Wen-Hui Pao*, April 15, 1958, referring to poetry and song production during the Great Leap, epitomised the effect well enough:

> "It has tempered the labourers' spiritual life. . . . Popular today in the country is this observation: ' In the past, people worked with knitted brows and sour faces; today they work with glad brows and smiling faces. Where in the past there were idle visits, quarrels and gossips, today there are songs, dances and studies of culture.' "

Songs and dances had been used earlier as a powerful means for organisation, indoctrination and mobilisation of the masses even when the Communists were preparing to seize power before 1949. But never until the past two years had there been such a hyper-intensification of the efforts to sow seeds of poetry and stir up every bit of even the humblest soil, tapping the oldest roots of folk art to bring forth poetry from the masses, but *for* the ambitious state programme on its gigantic and perilous road of national construction. The establishment of the Communes during the past two years, the virtually atavistic return to ancient communal life, and the emotional and physical strains thus caused by the Great Leap, seem to be reasons obvious enough for the possibility, as well as the need, of this stupendous mass poetry movement.

And on the theoretical level, the overwhelming phenomena of "success," even if only quantitative, as some Peking or Shanghai critics in their sober moments amid the deafening general claque dare admit, has encouraged a unique revisionist outcry in the otherwise severely anti-revisionist atmosphere of China as regards Marxian doctrines. "Is Marx's Principle of Unbalance between Art Production and Material Production Applicable to Socialist Literature?"[1] is a rhetorical question put as the title of an article in the *Wen-Yi Pao* (No. 2, 1959), and firmly answered no. After citing cases of the colossal literary Great Leap along with the economic, its author, Chou Lai-hsiang, concludes that this "Marxian theory of unbalance . . . is outdated." For "new conditions have appeared" in China today; the contradiction which Marx saw between the three factors, "productive forces," "social relations" and "consciousness," caused by the modern division of labour, which segregated and "imprisoned" the artist, is believed to have vanished, and the author declares that "the harmonious compatibility between art production and material production will be the eternal law." How valid this new theory is, or indeed how long it will be allowed to stand as Party policy changes, it is hard and perhaps entirely futile to estimate.

The works and ideas expressed by a writer may any time be torn to pieces once he is described as a "rightist" or something similar—witness the degradation of the Stalin Prize-winning novels of Miss Ting Ling along with the personal attacks on her.[2] But for the moment Mr. Chou Lai-hsiang's daring article is sufficient indication of the intoxicated frenzy aroused by the production of multimillion poems among the masses, which drove at least one critic to overreach himself in even challenging a part of the Marxism canon.[3]

Nor should we too readily dismiss the expression of extreme enthusiasm among all the writers and poets, some long since well-established like Kuo Mo-jo, Mao Tun, Feng Chih and others, as mere lip-service under duress. The production of countless songs and poems by the proletarian hosts in such a short time cannot but be impressive to them. Accustomed to finer craftsmanship as they may have been, they cannot

---

[1] This apparently refers to Marx's ideas in *Critique of Political Economy*, though citations in Mr. Chou's article are from a Chinese version: *Marxism and Literature*.

[2] See a sample tirade in *Wen-hsueh P'ing-lun*, No. 1, 1959, pp. 67–83.

[3] Polemics, though not violent, have already been set off by this article. In *Wen-yi Pao*, No. 4, 1959, Chang Huai-chin is raising objections which in no way, however, reflect on the enthusiasm for the Great Leap in poetry production.

but now admire the sheer plenitude of the products. The Shensi peasant poem we have just quoted may in itself as a single piece be indeed trivial and ludicrous, just as a drop of salt water is trivial and even distasteful. But in China today it is not just drops, but raging, roaring, gigantic ocean-waves made out of them that are confronting, converging on and converting the old world of letters for the time being. And conceivably, in so far as literature affects as well as reflects life, society and culture, there will be consequences which at present we can only try to gauge.

Let us first try to see how these waves, the " high tides of creation " among the masses, *ch'uang-tso kao-ch'ao*, as all the journals are reporting, have been actually raised, and then also examine the character of the works in a few more directions and details. Their impressiveness being primarily in their overwhelming quantity, we resort to some statistics. When one first read of the " million poem movement " in many journals, it seemed simply to be common hyperbole. And, incidentally, hyperboles have so overloaded Chinese prose literature during the Great Leap that perhaps only an admirer of the Elizabethan euphuistic style can enjoy them. But then one sees that the production of " million poems " are reported by units, like quotas, from the small community, county or town to the provincial level. And a million or millions of poems are expected not only from each province of greater population and higher literacy, but from such remote frontier ones as Inner Mongolia and Yunnan. The fulfilment of these quotas can be calculated on the basis of more or less precise figures which are available. The *Wen-hsueh P'ing-lun*, a most sophisticated journal, edited by well-known pre-Communist authors and Peking University professors, published a sample of partial statistics on the literary products of the workers in 1958, as compared with the year before, in its February 1959 issue.

Among workers in Shanghai, the number of participants in literary creation jumped from 889 in 1957 to over 200,000 in 1958, having produced in the one year more than five million works. Those in a much smaller town, T'ang Shan in Hopei Province, produced over two million. " In Tien Tzin and T'ang Shan, many ' thousand-poem small groups (*hsiao-tzu*) ' and ' ten thousand-poem workshops (*ch'ê chien*) ' have appeared." The productivity of a small town in Luan County of Hopei Province is perhaps regarded as fair average for both town and country, and is much more closely scanned. Though the figure of the population is not given, the times of individual participation in literary activities in 1958 are recorded as 1,428,428. Then more specifically we are told that 6,038 workers participated in poetry-and-song movements, and produced a total of 83,133 poems and songs throughout the year.

The production therefore averages over twelve poems and songs *per capita.*

Even if one is not so carried away as to apply, as far as arithmetic goes, the average to the 600,000,000 of the Chinese population to obtain a production figure of over six billion poems a year, the quantitative success of the Multimillion-Poem Movement would still remain true to its claim. But confirmation of the enormity of sheer numbers should not leave unanswered another question: Considering the high percentage of illiteracy, 60 per cent. according to a recent estimate despite intensive anti-illiteracy efforts in recent years, how can so many peasants and labourers write at all, not to speak of composing poems and songs? The fact is that these poems and songs were not written, but are said to have been "produced" or "created" by the masses. And they are produced by the method of suggestion, often mass suggestion, in the name of "collaboration," and "inducement" on the part of the cadres and other cultural workers.

The task of the cadres and their helpers nominally, however, is only to "collect," to put down in writing for those who cannot write, as well as to copy down the small percentage that are written and published. They are published, though seldom in printing, but in large characters on bulletin boards and walls all over prominent places in towns and villages. The task of the "collectors" bears an exquisite classical name, *ts'ai feng,* "collection of airs of the states," a term that has in ancient tradition glorified the most treasured *Classic of Poetry,* or *Shih-Ching,*[4] of over two thousand years ago, largely gathered under the Chou dynasty from folk songs as direct voices of the people. Eulogies, extolling the revival of this beautiful tradition under the present government and party, are of course plentiful. There is indeed the distinction that the ancient songs in sharp image and clear tone criticised the state governments and princelings and with deeply moving pathos sang of the people's suffering under inhuman enforcements of labour and conscription, whereas the present songs and poems only express tearful gratitude to Chairman Mao and the Party, preach devotion to the government, and are hilariously joyful about the hardest labour imaginable. The justification however is simple: under Communism all is changed for the positive.

True, a proposition has been made that today's creation by the people be "faithfully recorded and scientifically preserved."[5] And the question of "faithful transcription" versus "retouch" has been raised.[6] But the great Kuo Mo-jo himself, perhaps still the most influential

---

[4] English translation by Arthur Waley, entitled *The Book of Songs* (London: Allen and Unwin, 1937).
[5] *Wen-yi Pao,* No. 2, 1959, p. 10.   [6] *Min-chien Wen-hsueh,* April, 1958.

literary pundit in Peking today, gave his blessing to the " golden touch."
" We all know," he proclaimed in an interview, " that a poem can be
touched from stone into gold! " How many of the " collected " items
did, or needed to, undergo the golden touch cannot be determined. But
the general uniformity of millions of the " hallelujahs " can already be
decided in the process of their production. One report of exemplary
success in remote Yunnan Province is revealing (*Wen-yi Pao*, No. 2,
1959). The cadres as a " literary brigade " penetrate deeply into the
mountainous country, not by themselves, but through a hierarchy of a
local party organisation down to the village cells. Native grade school
teachers are called on to co-operate. It is a frontier district where both
Chinese and minority aborigines reside, and the rate of literacy is very
low. When the village crowds gather, the intention to " collect airs " is
explained, and one can imagine that the benevolence of Chairman Mao
and the Communist Party is extolled as the principal theme of the oratory.
Glorification of national achievements in reconstruction comes next,
then homage to " labour heroes," " model workers " and their selfless
dedication, and the praise of achievements in the locality. The crowds
are induced into a festive mood. The declared purpose of the gathering
is to collect from them songs and tunes which they have long since
known. But the themes for creating new songs, as we can see, have
been effectively suggested.

New words, however crudely put together, are glamorised as befitting
the new ideology. And they fill the familiar old tunes as substitute for
the " unreconstructed " old words of native folk airs. This, thanks to
the great latitude of rhyming patterns in the Chinese language and its
immense richness in homophones, can be done in moments of effective
mass suggestion almost as easily as if by reflex action. If the sentiment
expressed in these new " airs " thus " collected " for permanent record
may be illusory and transient, the psychological appeal in the process
of the " collection " is at least real at the time. The more illiterate people
are, after such a long, glorious Chinese literary tradition, the greater
usually is their respect and envious admiration for learning and for
literary ventures. They cannot but feel grateful and elated, when they
find suddenly in their midst college graduates and venerable school *shien-
sheng* (masters) who not only sing unashamedly their rustic tunes, seeking
avidly for the words, but cajole them to produce more new ones on
simple but exalted high-sounding themes, and dignify their improvisa-
tions as the best composition. Of course the heavy demand for the
production of iron or grain is at no time let up. The farmers and
workers worry about the next day's work, and even some local party
leaders are dubious about the song-and-poem festivals. But, as the

Yunnan report says, the people soon find the poem-collectors are busy by their side as they work. In a mining village, "When they pump the bellows, we (the collectors) pump the bellows. When they break the ores, we break the ores." Thus they sing and improvise with the collectors' help, and perhaps also get suggestions, being corrected as well as recorded in the process. One song thus produced is given as an example of the new song-makers' joy, gratitude and pride:

> Chairman Mao's good leadership, so good,
> College graduates come here to "pick up our tune." [7]
> Yellow mud on our legs, but as man to man,
> I sing a tune to greet our "next of kin." [8]

No wonder the small literary brigade could report that in "about ten days over a thousand items were collected," in this distant corner of Yunnan Province. "Every village, every hamlet, all the fields and all the hilltops are filled with songs. While the people are singing old songs, they invent so many new ones at the same time that you can collect and collect, but they never end." Thus millions and millions of such songs and poems were produced and collected during one year of the Great Leap, with more and more to come.

An indication of how the quantitative immensity may at this time be changing even the concept of the quality of poetry can be noted in the current numerical phrases when the poems are counted. Instead of by "pieces," which would be *shou*, the old "classifier" which every student of Chinese knows, poems are sometimes spoken of in terms of *lou* or *ch'ê*, "basketfuls" or "carloads." This seems to denote, though perhaps inadvertently, the feeling that these poems are just so much goods or cargo, extracted as well from everyone's mental and emotional force as from the physical, in collectivised, quick production. The traditional concept of a poem as a long and painstakingly wrought gem is by implication bourgeois and passé.

It is not easy to show what these poems are like in translation. For the majority of them chime with sonorous, if totally unsubtle, rhymes, and flow with lilting rhythm, or are declaimed staccato, in the traditional patterns of five or seven syllables to each line, with free variations, however, as befitting everyday speech and local slang. Translations are bound to miss all the elements but the central idea; and the idea, when translated, amounts to no more than the few pious themes we have noted. In discussing the poems we must nevertheless choose a

---

[7] This is *kua tiao-tzu*, a local slang, possibly gaining new glamour on account of the new movement. It literally means "hoist the tune," indicating, we suspect, its being hung up high for public notice, as well as picked for preservation.

[8] Here, *ch'in jen*, refers to the "graduates," *i.e.*, the visiting cadres. Kinship terms occupy a prominent position in the diction of the new folk poetry. See discussion to follow.

few samples. It is important to bear in mind, however, that it is not each single sample as it stands that counts, but the tremendous, overwhelming aggregations of them that make the impact today on Chinese mental and social life. We have compared the individual pieces with drops of salt-water, which, when gathered into surging waves, make a striking spectacle. We might as well note here that " multiplicity in uniformity " may, under certain conditions, be accredited as an aesthetic quality to natural and human phenomena. George Santayana recognised it, for instance, in the starry firmament and in democracy. This quality may be denied of the " Million-Poem " movement for the lack of lustre and individuality of its ingredients, but its magnitude of uniform aggregations may instead impress the observer with its collective dynamism and awesome singleness of purpose.

Whatever the aesthetic judgment may be, it is immediately discernible that the " creation " of poetry by the Chinese masses, besides the practical therapeutic effect we have mentioned, attempts also to achieve what any new literature usually does, as soon as it becomes a social influence, except that this influence on Chinese society is at once inflated with political inspiration and also effectively controlled. We are speaking of the results which this new literature has shown in producing efficacious myths through large, definitive public images which fuse concepts and emotions together, and are capable of direct mass appeal. The creative force, however manipulated, is the folk mentality, which is at the same time the object of the appeal and the source from which the materials for this myth-making are derived. This song, perhaps the most popularly quoted, is an example of the image which the new masses have created of themselves:

> *In Heaven there is no Jade Emperor,*[9]
> *Nor is there a Dragon King in the sea.*
> *I am the Jade Emperor,*
> *I am the Dragon King.*
> *Hoy, you Three Sacred Mountains and Five Holy Peaks,*
> *Make way!*
> *Here I come.*[10]

But the Chinese masses today are *les enfants terribles* only to the old gods, in heaven or under the sea. Their songs are exhorting them at the same time to see themselves as the most docile citizens on earth, the devout worshippers of one idea, of one ruling power, and of one man. The " Mountain Climb Song " of Inner Mongolia has many versions which, in endless couplets of staccato monotone, characterising the hypnotic effect on the uphill climber, goes like this:

[9] Being the Chinese folk concept of Godhead in heaven.
[10] Included in *Hung-ch'i ke-yao*, ed. by Kuo Mo-jo and Chou Yang, 1958.

> We worship no god, nor temples build,
> Chairman Mao's love is greater manifold.
> Gods we destroy, and temples tear down,
> Better than gods we worship the One Man.
> Mountains may shake, earth may quake, and we are not afraid,
> But we dare not forget what the Chairman said.

It has proved a happy accident indeed that Mao Tse-tung's name
can so easily produce sonorous rhymes in association with objects which
signify good omen or meaning to the folk imagination, and which are
therefore familiar in the repertoire of old folk songs: The sun's glorious
red *hung*, the warm spring wind *fêng*, the dew that makes all plants
green *ching*, and the lamplight *teng*, the radiant star *hsing*, and so on
ad infinitum. And Mao becomes all these in the mass production of
impromptu poems, among fervent millions in poetry contests over the
whole country. Another word that has by repeated use and fusion with
folk songs quickly gained a magical ring is " Party," *Tang*. It no longer
stands for the mere concept of a political structure, or the rather faceless
body of an organisation; it becomes incarnate, as it were, in the images
sometimes of the great sun, *t'ai yang*, sometimes of the beloved mother,
ch'in niang, sometimes of the flower that spreads its fragrance, *hsiang*.
These sound effects of the originals cannot possibly of course be reproduced in translation. And here is not the occasion to discuss versification.
But we have indicated the most popular rhyme endings and the power-
fully suggestive connotations that are associated with the word Party,
and thus metaphorise the *Tang* into a shining image with myriads of
songs singing its glory. Actually most of the popular rhyme endings
associated in this instance are in the " level tone " of the Chinese
language, and the *Tang* comes in their midst with a down and up
crescendo of a pealing, rising tone. But even this, on occasions, is not
without some effect of a distinctive, if awesome, ring.

In creating images of the toiling masses themselves, ancient legendary
heroes and heroines who have long inhabited the folk imagination have
been brought to life. The tiger-killer Wu Sung, the lady-warriors Hua
Mu-lan and Mu Kuei-ying, the fabulous teen-age fighter Lo Cheng and
many other characters from the story books are conjured to appear in
shining armour among the working crews as labour heroes. But perhaps
one of the most prominent figures is the more ancient Yü Kung, or Mr.
Foolish, who succeeded in moving a whole mountain with crude picks
and shovels, with the unshakeable faith that if he could not accomplish
the feat himself, the continuous efforts of his sons and grandsons for a
thousand generations would do so. " Moving mountains," with the
pride and faith of Mr. Foolish, has indeed become perhaps the most

exalted trope in the language of the Chinese masses today, and may occasionally produce a quaint piece of folk poetry like this:

> *Two full baskets I carry on a pole,*
> *How their weight makes the pole bend;*
> *But my dear wife, you come and see,*
> *I'm carrying a mountain at each end.*

It is a long-established and exceedingly popular practice of Chinese folk poetry to begin with one or two lines of piquant statements of natural or domestic objects, which, apparently unrelated to the main theme of the poem, would set its temper and tone by associations of rhyme, and create an atmospheric effect with emotive connotations. This device has given old Chinese folk songs their peculiar charm of naturalness and spontaneity. The natural or domestic objects are evoked from immediate environments and associated directly with intimate personal feelings, to effect in their unpredictable, unpremeditated way, an authenticity of poetic emotion. The plums fall, and a girl thinks of marriage; the reed leaves are covered with white dew and one longs for a friend; the spinning wheel creaks, and a wife dreams of her soldier husband on the frontier. Now in the millions of new folk poems where the same device is employed, thousands of flowers, plants, natural elements and domestic implements of all districts and provinces, too, are on display to aid the poetry production. And in reading them one feels a welcome relief from monotony by sensing the richly varied flavours of folk soil from all parts of China today. To this extent the works carry the mark of genuine products of each native locality, in the open air and on the spot, despite the centrally controlled hard-driven machine.

But even with this device, each new poem as a whole still has a totally different quality as compared with the old. The old Chinese folk poetry so devised owes much of its great moving power to the vital interaction whereby familiar, conspicuous natural objects are juxtaposed with intimately felt, individualised emotions, and thus the objects are made unique symbols of private emotion, and private emotion in turn gains a universal dimension as an individual experience. But in the new airs of folk " creation," where the natural objects are present, they are without the benefit of emotive individualisation, but are often made mere ornaments of public pronouncements and generalised ideas, without any quality of experience. About the same public event, the election of local representatives, Yunnan produced the camellia to embellish a verse, Fukien the red peach, and Manchuria, as expected, the soya bean.[11]   Here is one example:

> Golden beans, silver beans,
> Cast them, but cast with care,
> Elect a good man, to do a good job,
> Cast the beans in this earthen ware.

Naive, trivial and insignificant this in itself may be. But it is not so insignificant when realised as a sample product of a feverishly earnest nation-wide movement to turn up the deepest roots of folk tradition under the Communist sun, and to draw out and convert the last reserve of individual feeling into a collectivised consciousness.

Another instance of such conversion that is evident in the " Million-Poem " movement is the new usage imposed on old kinship terms. Kinship terms are as abundant in the Chinese language as the varieties of flowers and plants in the far-flung Chinese provinces. The kinship terms are used to denote the Chinese meticulous sense and high regard for clearly defined human relationship.   Some terms were almost sacred to the individual, such as father, mother and ancestor.   These, if they had been extended at all in their applications, would be to the royal monarch or to heaven and earth in appropriate moments of political or religious sentiment in bygone days.   And thanks to the downfall of the monarchy we might say that these terms even gained a more strictly observed individual dignity.   No Chinese in the recent past, unless forced by sadistic lynchers or maniacs, would have for his life called anyone else a parent.   And the term *ch'in jen,* " next of kin," besides its normal application to the closest blood relations, was reserved for a special, strictly private occasion, as the most intimate term of endearment between lovers.   Perhaps no other part of the new poems and songs therefore offends so poignantly the sensibility of a Chinese poetry reader outside mainland China today, making him feel so acutely a creeping of the flesh, as the constant invocation of Chairman Mao, the Party and the cadres as pa, ma, and *ch'in jen,* " next of kin."   This may be the result not simply of political duress, but of a vigorous campaign for the rejection of all old values held for and by the individual.   The individual should feel himself to be nil, and his most cherished kinship terms are surrendered, along with his precious self, to the state into which he is supposed to have been newly born.   These terms, too, like himself must be made to serve, to express infantile devotion with infantile senti-mentality.   And of course these most familiar emotive expressions can

---

[11] See *Chung-Kuo Ke-yao Tzu-liao*, Second Series, II, " *Sung Ke* " or " Songs of Praise " Section.   Ed. by Ch'u Ch'iu-po Literary Society, Chinese Department, University of Peking.

with some suggestion become most handy to fill up the vacuity of the vocabulary of the illiterate when they are induced to believe that they are in the exalted state to produce poetry. Whatever the reasons for the practice, one's instinctive reaction to this grotesque transference of the meaning of words begins at least with a strong distaste.

But in this presentation we have tried not to allow taste, that variable though better educated neighbour, to prejudice or to interfere with our interpretation of an important phenomenon in the life of a half billion of humanity. What has or has not been accomplished is much more momentous than good or bad taste. What the phenomenon means, in the short view, is an attempt carried out with some measure of success to convert and control the mental as well as the physical energy of hundreds of millions of individuals so as to form a collective conscious-ness dedicated in collective labour to serve a gigantic state in the making. And in the longer view, perhaps the vision of thoroughly remodelling not only a colossal human community, but every man and his soul in it as well, is not held without some genuine conviction among certain most active zealots in their intoxicated moments of enthusiasm for the mass poetry movement. Even for the sake of poetry itself, some of them may be sincerely entertaining the hope of a rosy future, when the general level of poetic education of the whole population is sufficiently raised.

Kuo Mo-jo, like an optimistic prophet, wrote a short piece of exhortation,[12] entitled " Hail, New ' Airs of the States ' Today, New ' Elegies of Chu ' Tomorrow! " But the prophecy may also portend an inauspicious omen, or foreshadow a stubborn " contradiction," as the current parlance may prefer to call it. The " Elegies " sprang up in the 4th century B.C., about five hundred years after the " Airs of the States," when, in Marxian terms, the old social order (that of a " slave society " according to Mr. Kuo's own sociological view) entirely col-lapsed, and Chü Yuan, the first individual poet in Chinese history, solitary and passionately defiant, arose in tragic magnificence. If there was any folk tradition behind his works, he sublimated it so as to distil and focus all human passions into an individualised expression of one living, feeling, suffering human being singing of himself in a uniquely personal form.

We all know that Marxism does not believe in history repeating itself, but strongly advocates giving history a helping hand. Nor is anyone suggesting that Mr. Kuo in drawing the analogy wants by any means to imply the present system has to collapse in order that the new advent of the individual genius of Chü Yuan may be possible. All we can point out is that for such a future of Chinese poetry as Mr. Kuo

12 *Chung-Kuo Ch'ing-nien Pao*, April 16, 1958.

visualises the "helping hand," now very busy indeed in all respects, is not really helping at all. The busy hand, for that matter, is actually pointing in an opposite direction. It has indeed succeeded in drawing immense power to raise stupendous tidal waves of mass creation. But at what expense of pulverising and obliterating the last remnants of man's individuality we have already seen. The spectacle of "multiplicity in uniformity" as one impressive aspect of the high tide we have also noted. But a high tide, unlike the stars in the firmament, does not stay constant. And, unless something else is done, the tide, as it rolls away, may leave only worthless alkalis on a barren shore, having drained away what fertility the land may already have had.

At least for the present, there is much evidence that the tide is swallowing up, or at least stunting, any individual talent that may exist. Many writers of proven poetic gifts are absorbed in writing panegyrics to extol the movement, or joining the cadres in the literary brigades. Others, amid the deafening claque, are exhausting themselves to produce sedulous imitations to echo the roaring tide, or one might say, add mere drops to the surging waves. Tien Chien, for instance, the famed "drummer of the times," whose militant songs aided the Communist Party to power, has since then become the furthest advanced in accepting "collectivism" for poetic creation. And "collectivism" means complete submersion of the poet's self, soul and flesh, into the collective body of the masses. In a preface to a collection of his poems, entitled "My Vow," [13] he writes: "I sometimes also call myself a poet. But it is merely a borrowed term. It is a title borrowed from the collective body." To belong with the collective body is regarded as more important for a poet than even to write poetry. Tien Chien preaches the moral with a fable. Though the logic is forced and the metaphor somewhat mixed, it is still revealing. A boatman from the sea is beckoning to thousands of young poets, and says:

"The great sea . . . is made of innumerable streams. The streams are dug by the People, forming beautiful designs with their labour. And I know the sea, for my sweat and blood are the sea water. The water of the sea is my sweat and blood. If you want to write about this sea, come and live in my boat. If you just stay here, even though you do not write any poetry in all your life, that still will be all right."

But even under the menace of entire submersion of the poet's self, of total assimilation of the individual man into the collective body, one still hears a lone voice or two, striking a very different note. Muffled as they may be by the roaring waves from a distant shore, listen closely and

[13] In *Hai Yen Sung* (Peking: 1958).

you hear the authentic cadence and ring which pulsate whenever poetry
bespeaks man's own mind:

> Have more trust in man,
> Trust that " man " [14] is more trustworthy than your " Interference "
> Trust that " man's " " conscience " need not be forced into unity.
> Trust that " man " needs no urging whip, nor white lines of the race
>   course,
> But needs only a torch to beckon his heart and spirit to advance.
>
> .   .   .   .   .   .
>
> Have more trust in man,
> Trust that every ordinary heart
> Is prone to come near truth as rivers toward the sea.
>
> .   .   .   .   .   .
>
> Trust that to release man's " innate knowledge," and " true instinct,"
> Means far, far more than to release atomic energy,
> Trust that our achievement is not only in having delivered the atom,
> The deliverence of the human heart, that alone is the tallest banner
>   of our day.

These are stanzas from a very long poem, " Have More Trust In
Man," by Chang Ming-chüan, published in Peking in May, 1957. The
voice, ironically, would not have become audible to us today amidst the
loud droning and din of the million songs, had it not been so extensively
quoted in a severe piece of criticism of it, as testimony against Chang
Ming-chüan by another poet, in a recent volume entitled *Communist
Style*.[15] The volume is devoted chiefly to high praises of the million
poems and songs from the collective body as model " Communist style,"
but carried an attack on Chang with the above quotations in a separate
essay as evidence to indict him as " rightist," throwing " anti-party hand-
grenades," and being " anti-thought-reform," " obliterating Party-
leadership " and sounding " bugle calls to individualism." One reads
with some relief, however, that after all these bombastic blasts, Chang
was merely advised to " change his heart and wash his face and become
a new man." Whether or how he will change, or whether as one defiant
individual he still has to meet with some worse fate, it is hard to guess.
But as the waves of " collectivism " rise to their peak, his appeal for
" trust in man " may be only one contradicting voice that has been
accidentally brought to our attention. In industrial and rural production, the Chinese Communists may have succeeded in telescoping many
decades of history into a few short years. And this has been done by
continually invoking the law of contradiction. The present million-poem
movement, when all is said and done, at least still indicates a realisation
of poetry as one of China's most valuable national assets. But if Mr.

[14] All quotation marks are as in the original.
[15] Tien Chia, *Lun Kung-ch'an Chu-yi Feng-ke* (Peking: 1958).

Kuo Mo-jo's prophecy of "Airs of the States Today, and Elegies of Chu Tomorrow" [16] contains any truth, and if the telescoping of five hundred years of poetic advancement from communal folk production to individual genius is to be at all possible, the contradiction there must not only be more carefully heeded, but much more wisely solved, than in the production of material goods. And since upon international cultural exchange and progress rests the only hope of a viable civilised human future, this, may it be realised in Peking, is as much a concern of the whole world as of China.

---

[16] Several poets during the past few years showed promising talent in long narrative poetry, which we lack space to discuss here. In any case, the impact of the multitudes of folk poems seems to be the most engrossing phenomenon today.

From Friendship to Comradeship: The Change in Personal Relations in Communist China

By EZRA F. VOGEL

IN the first fifteen years of Communist rule on the Chinese mainland, personal relationships have undergone an important transformation, a transformation which testifies to the success of the régime in penetrating and influencing the private lives of its citizens. From the view of the individual, the change in personal relationships arises principally from the uncertainty as to whether private conversation will remain private or whether it will in some way be brought to the attention of the authorities. When one no longer confides in a friend for fear that he might pass on the information, either intentionally or unintentionally, an element of trust is lost. When a person no longer invites a friend to his home for fear the friend might see something that he would later be called upon to describe, the nature of the relationship is altered. When a person begins to watch carefully and think about what he might be revealing to his friend and wonders under what circumstances this information might be brought to the attention of the authorities, friendship as a relation of confidence and personal commitment is weakened.

To say that friendship as an ultimate value has been weakened is not to say that friendliness has gone. Indeed, a new morality which stresses friendliness and helpfulness between all citizens has become widely accepted. The new morality does not distinguish between people on the basis of personal preferences. Like the Protestant ethic in which all are equal under God, comradeship is a universalistic morality in which all citizens are in important respects equal under the state, and gradations on the basis of status or degree of closeness cannot legitimately interfere with this equality. This article is concerned with exploring the decline of friendliness and the rise of comradeship.

THE RISKS OF FRIENDSHIP

The success of the régime in preventing friendships from interfering with what it defines as national goals and purposes has been achieved in large part because of people's fears. The fear arises because people are continually supplying information which causes friends to suffer.

The opportunities for supplying information are legion and cannot be avoided entirely. Information may be supplied in private interviews, in small group discussions, or in large assemblies. It may be supplied formally or casually, wittingly or unwittingly.

Refusal to supply information about a friend is rare because it would cause the authorities to take a more serious view of the problem. When an individual refuses to testify against a friend, the case is no longer regarded by the régime as that of an idiosyncratic individual, but as a group of two and possibly more conspiring to resist the régime, and the risks become greater. For most citizens the question is not whether to supply information, but how and how much to supply to minimise the consequences for one's self and one's friend.

Although friendships have been broken as a result of information supplied, the profound effect on friendship in Communist China is not so much a direct result of cases of broken friendship as the indirect result, the growth of the feeling that it is not worth the risk to confide to a friend information which could potentially be damaging. In fact, supplying information about a friend does not necessarily lead to a break in friendship since both recognise the pressures to co-operate. Indeed, even under pressure, most people make serious attempts to minimise the rupture in personal relationships. If the opportunity is available, a friend will first consult the accused to find what information has already been supplied and then, in slightly different terms, supply the same information without giving forth any new "materials." Even if the opportunity for consultation is not available, the friend may try to guess what information might be known already to minimise the possibility of contradictory stories or new material which might increase the suspicions. Or he might supply testimony which, though critical of the accused, subtly presents the friend's good side or suggests mitigating factors. For example, this could take the following form: " Since he has done such goods things as ————, I was shocked at his being so base as to ————." If he suspects he will be called upon to denounce a friend in a small meeting, he may first ask the friend for suggestions about what to say. At a minimum he would apologise to his friend afterwards. But even if friendships do not break with criticisms they are often strained. There is a fine line between supplying the bare minimum of information and a little more than the minimum, and many friendships have turned on this fine line.

Although betrayal of friends is possible at any time, the greatest opportunities arise during rectification campaigns. At the time of these campaigns, lines between the loyal and the deviants are drawn more sharply, and the loyal must prove their loyalty by criticising their deviant friends. More meetings are held for expression of opinions about neighbours and fellow workers, and more histories of friends, and especially suspect friends, must be written. More wall posters must be hung to denounce those who have committed errors, and large assemblies called to publicise the more serious cases. Friendships are under the most serious strain during these campaigns, and the prevailing mood is that it is unwise to trust anyone.

Of course, campaigns are opportunities for those who bear old grudges to express them by finding evidence that one's object of hate made precisely the kind of mistakes that the campaign is designed to correct. Indeed, people with old grudges continuously watch their rivals and save up instances of potentially culpable behaviour for just such campaigns. One obviously tries to avoid letting such a rival obtain any information which he might later use for criticism.

In addition to the danger of rivals, two kinds of persons are considered especially likely to betray a friend: the activist-opportunist and the suspect. An activist who is anxious to join the Young Communist League or the League member anxious to join the Communist Party in order to advance his own career has to prove that he is very loyal to the régime. One of the best ways to prove it is by showing that friendships do not stand in the way of his loyalty to the régime, that when necessary he will report on a friend. Of course, there is considerable variation among activists as to how energetically they report on friends, but there are always some who even seek opportunities for reporting. Many eager young people feel that their chances of rising within the régime are improved if they can furnish exciting bits of information which cast doubts upon some of their fellows. Most superiors whose job it is to receive such information apparently prefer to feel safer and have more reports (even if some are not later substantiated) rather than run the risk of not getting information which is important. Hence, they are anxious to give sufficient encouragements and rewards so that activists will continue to bring in their " little reports."

The suspect is dangerous partly because he is in a somewhat desperate situation, and he is anxious to do something that might eliminate or at least minimise his difficulties. Reporting on friends is one obvious way to extricate one's self, and the continued pressures for supplying information are hard to resist. The suspect may first be called upon to supply very unimportant and seemingly irrelevant details, and this is then used as a wedge for acquiring more information.

The suspect is dangerous not only because he is more motivated to accuse others, but because he is called upon to give much more detailed information about all aspects of his life. The mere fact of being an acquaintance of a suspect is sufficient to implicate the other person. Indeed, the régime relies very heavily on such objective factors as who had contact with whom, who is related to whom, who lives near or works with whom. Even if not guilty by association, a person is at least a suspect by association.

Direct betrayal is certainly not the only danger of friendship, and perhaps not even the most important. The risks of friendship arise in large part from the masses of information which are continually gathered in autobiographies, school essays, small group discussions, and even in casual conversation. The many channels of gathering information make it possible that the most innocent sounding statement might eventually be used or distorted by the régime to discredit a friend. Several times during their school years, students are expected to write autobiographies which begin from the age of eight. All cadres, all people of importance, and all people who are under serious suspicions must also write autobiographies. Some people are called on to write annual reports about their activities. Checks are sometimes made to see that a person mentioned by another will in his own report mention the other. Furthermore, the discussions in small groups in the school, neighbourhood, or place of work may be used as information, and this information reflects not only on the person giving the information but on all other persons whom he mentions.

In school, children are called upon incidentally to tell about things at home. Although the primary purpose of these school discussions may not be to gather information about doubtful families, a teacher would be expected to pass on any reports that do create serious doubts about certain families.

Not only contacts, but even incidental details may create risks if reported. For example, any information about dress or house furnishings or eating habits, no matter how innocuous it may seem to the reporter, might be taken to mean that a person is not truly a member of the peasant or proletariat class.

The risks of friendship are thus almost omnipresent. They vary from serious accusations which might send one to labour reform or death down to the petty annoyances of neighbourhood jealousies being discussed in small group meetings which at most would lead to verbal criticism. The impact of these risks is not limited to friendships broken as a result of betrayal. The total impact is much more profound. It includes the reluctance to let any other person know something which might have adverse effects if known by the authorities. The possibilities of the other person casually mentioning or recalling it in a group meeting before thinking of the significance or of deliberately supplying critical information are so great that it is thought safer not to expose a friend to such information. But it is the very withholding of information from friends which changes the nature of friendship.

THE ROUTINISATION OF RISKS

In the period since 1949 not only has the régime had to develop and modify its techniques for governing, but also the people have had to learn how to live under Communist rule. In the early period, after a period of rumours and worries of the wildest sort, the people seemed to settle down to learning seriously what was expected of them. Not only did they have to study ideology, find out what they were expected to perform at work, and how they were to be organised, but they had to learn to live with the risks of friendship.

The risks of friendship became most apparent in the early campaigns; rural land reform, thought reform of the intellectuals, and 3-anti and 5-anti against cadres and businessmen. These campaigns involved self-criticism, criticism of others and struggle against those accused of thoughts and behaviour not in keeping with the purposes of the régime. Most people were apparently completely unprepared psychologically for being denounced by their friends, and the impact on those criticised in these early campaigns was sometimes devastating. People in Shanghai, for example, compared the 3-anti and the 5-anti campaigns to the 1929 Wall Street crash, and the feeling at the time was that one must be careful in walking along the street to watch for the bodies falling from tall buildings.

The risks have probably not become any less severe. The campaigns of 1955, 1957 and 1959 also involved large numbers of people, and the struggle sessions were also very intense. Although probably in no campaign were as many people killed as in the land reform and counter-revolutionary campaign, labour reform and labour re-education have continued on a sizeable scale. In addition to these major campaigns, group discussion, self-criticism and criticism continue between campaigns. While the risks of friendship have probably not lessened to any considerable extent, people have become more accustomed to it and have grown to treat it as a routine which does not upset their own personal equilibrium. They have become less concerned about whether a friend can be trusted and more willing to take for granted the need to be cautious. They have become less anxious about conversations with friends and more willing simply to exclude certain things from the discussion to avoid the tensions and strains in their personal relationship.

By virtue of having seen how the régime operates for a number of years, people have become much more skilful in distinguishing between what is risky and what is not. They know how to watch for clues that campaigns are in the offing, and they detect hints about kinds of behaviour likely to be criticised. They have become more sophisticated in supplying evidence. They know how to state their arguments in ways that sound sincere without presenting new information which would be damaging to themselves or their friends. They are less earnest in trying to state what they really believe and more willing to say what they think they are expected to say. Indeed, so clear have the procedures and practices become that people criticised by the régime often are considered not unfortunate but foolish, foolish for having taken stands which would almost inevitably lead to trouble. But there is still a measure of uncertainty, of surprises, and many people, because of their background or their class position, or their situation within a neighbourhood or work group, cannot escape risks no matter how well they understand them. And although people are more resigned to criticism, the experience of being criticised, denounced and isolated can still be very devastating.

REDUCING THE RISKS

Although people are generally cautious in their conversations and their associations, they cannot avoid saying everything which involves risks, and the desire for intimacy leads people to take some small risks with people with whom they feel relatively safe. Great care is taken, therefore, in distinguishing the various degrees of risk in seeing various people and in talking about certain topics.

Obviously people avoid others who have more suspicious backgrounds. Children of landlords not only have difficulty finding partners when they reach the marriageable age, but they have difficulty in finding friends at all. People who have been criticised in a campaign and gone through a period of labour reform or re-education may, if they prove themselves, be allowed to return to their former work and salary, and some are even allowed to return to positions as high as they had before. But even if they return, it is hard for them to have close relationships with anyone except other people who have been similarly criticised. They are avoided not so much because they are generally despised for their errors. They are avoided because of the risks involved in associating with them.

People also avoid activist-informers, but here the danger is not of being seen with such a person but of saying something that might be used as " material " with unfortunate results. One must, of course, be polite to the activist-informer and avoid saying or doing anything that might antagonise him. But one also tightens up in his presence. When the Youth Leaguer comes around, people are respectful but aloof, and idle chatter usually ceases until he goes away, and people hurry to return to their work or to some place else. Sometimes it is not readily apparent which member of a group it is who is serving as informer. But over a period of time, judging by the criticisms that the superiors make and the opportunities for various colleagues to have acquired the knowledge on which the criticisms are based, one can generally determine who is serving as informer. Although people cannot physically avoid contact with activists in their own group, they can be much more on their guard.

People also avoid contacts with strangers, since one can never be sure what their standing with the régime might be. Even a relative in another city who was formerly in good standing with the régime might have fallen into disfavour without one's knowing about it. If he is now in difficulty, exchanging letters with him will cause a lot of "trouble" and many people feel that the risks involved aren't worth it; it is not the content of the letter but the mere fact of sending the letter which causes the trouble.

Similarly it is rare even for fellow professionals living in different communities to have much contact. Within a single urban area, one can keep well-informed on the current political standing of one's colleagues and thus have contact with the acceptable ones without running too much risk. With fellow professionals in other communities there is always a much greater risk, and hence people are reluctant to associate with fellow professionals from different communities.

People are similarly cautious in associating with people who have newly arrived from the outside, and even greater risks are involved in having too much contact with foreigners. Even members of the Party who are authorised to have such contacts with outsiders may be cautious since even they would be suspect if they had too much contact, just as before 1949 some cadres who had originally been sent to work as undercover agents in Kuomintang organisations were later suspect since they might have taken over some of the Kuomintang's attitudes during their association with it.

Adults are also cautious with children, not because of fear of being associated with certain children and not (except in very rare cases) because they are afraid that children will be called upon to betray them. It is because children often lack precautions in talking to others. Whereas most adults can be counted on to be cautious in giving out information which could conceivably reflect on their family or friends, children are often lacking in discretion, and they might unwittingly blurt out revealing information.

Rarely is anyone so foolish as to complain to a friend about the régime. Even if one were to complain about the food or clothing, this might be taken as a reflection of one's bourgeoisie background or—if not from a bourgeoisie background—of bourgeoisie influences in one's background or at least bourgeoisie tendencies in thought or behaviour. It is rare to invite others to one's home, especially if one has some articles of furniture or food that might be considered as bourgeois.

This does not mean that one cannot express opinions to one's friends, but one must always be careful to say things which if quoted will not be interpreted badly. One cannot say, " Oh, the food is bad this year," but one could if pressed defend a statement like, " It is a great pleasure to serve our great country, and what does it amount to if one has a few little inconveniences like having a little less rice." While the ability to express opinions in ways which do not reflect doubts about one's love for the régime is an art which is now highly cultivated, the expressions of subtle criticisms have not fully replaced the expression of frank criticism. Even two people with long-term loyalties and mutual fondness ordinarily do not express verbally their doubts, their troubles, their tribulations. It is not worth the risk, and there is commonly an implicit comrade's agreement that they will not say anything that would create in the other a conflict about whether or not he should reveal something. Indeed, there are modes of mutual understanding and fondness which do not require confiding one's innermost thoughts; and many people prefer not to strain the relationship by saying something that the other might be under pressure to reveal. It is not simply prudence and self-protection, but considerateness to the other and to their relationship.

The Limits of Influence and Help

Not only has friendship as a relationship of confidence greatly declined, but another kind of friendship has declined for very different reasons. This is the kind of relationship where one gave economic assistance or used his influence in an organisation to help a friend.

The reasons for this change are not hard to find. The régime has carried on a concerted attack on nepotism and the use of personal influence. In addition to enforcing severe sanctions against violators, the régime has placed the critical decisions about placement in schools or jobs in the hands of committees rather than single individuals. Very commonly outsiders do not even know who it is who makes the decisions. Entrance to schools or firms is decided by entrance examinations in combination with other criteria by a committee who do not even say why people are rejected or admitted. Because these decisions are made by committees and not by individuals, because the personnel on these committees is subject to frequent changes, and because their decisions are subject to review by other parts of the régime, it is very unlikely that one individual can be a personal benefactor. Of course, one person may recommend another and this may have some effect on the final decision, but the decision would be made by a larger committee and the person applying for the job would have to have the necessary qualifications as judged by other criteria. Even Communist Party members are subject to the same discipline of committee decisions and hence lack the power to offer help to people on the basis of particular considerations. It is true that Party members must be loyal and not just competent, but the loyalty is to the Party, not the Party secretary.

Not only do individuals ordinarily not have the influence to provide others with opportunities for schooling or employment, but few individuals any longer have the resources of private wealth to offer sizeable economic assistance to others. The régime has not had to rely on a concerted attack on "feudalistic" relations between people from the same locality, from the same school, or the same clan to weaken these friendship bonds between the benefactor and the recipient. They have been weakened by the inability of individuals to command the resources by which they can effectively serve as benefactors.

The New Ethic: Comradeship

In place of friendship as a relationship of mutual trust and privacy or as a "feudalistic" relationship between benefactor and recipient, the concept of comradeship has become gradually diffused throughout the population. Originally the term comrade was used among the members of the loyal band of Communists to signify a faithful and trusted follower in the context of a wider society in which many people were not comrades. It implied a fundamental equality, and even today in Party meetings, Party members are regarded as fundamentally equal, even though in their work units they would have superior-subordinate relationships to carry out their activities.

With the takeover of the mainland and the enunciation of the New Democracy in 1949, the term "comrade" was gradually extended in practice to include the population at large. At first it was used for officials, and then perhaps gingerly and almost playfully (as with any group learning new terms) it was gradually used by people in talking to each other until it became fairly widespread. It was not used, however, among close friends. It was used to describe the relationship of one person to another in their role as fellow citizens. As one's activities and responsibilities as a citizen of the state came to play an important part in one's life, so did the relationship between citizens become a critical mode of interpersonal relations. It became the dominant basis for all interpersonal relations and was supported by propaganda and by the very small group discussions that played such a key role in the weakening of friendship.

The essence of the term comrade lies not only in the loyalty to Communism (counter-revolutionaries, landlords and other "enemies of the people" would not be addressed as comrades) but in the universal nature of comradeship. In a very fundamental sense, every citizen is a fellow comrade, and there is no longer such a sharp line even between friends and comrades. Part of the ethic underlying the concept of comrade is that there is an important way in which everyone in the society is related to every other person. Hence it is perfectly natural for people to address others whom they never met before. The other side of the concept is that one should not have special relationships with certain people which would interfere with the obligations to anyone else. A special relationship between two people is not considered sacred and not even praiseworthy; this would not be a comradely relationship and it would be considered suspect and illegitimate.

An important element in "comradeship" is the accent on "helping" other people. "Helping" is at times a euphemism for getting another person to fall in line and do what is expected of him, whether by logical arguments, forceful persuasion, or repeated reminders. This kind of "helping" is something that one should do for a comrade, for anyone else in the society. But "helping" also means spending time to be of assistance to a person in need. A student who is having trouble with his lessons should be helped by someone who can give the assistance. An old person on the street should be given assistance by someone located coveniently nearby. A newcomer to a group should be helped by someone already on hand to become acquainted with the new place, to find all the facilities that he will need.

There is a positive value placed on being of assistance to others, on spending time and energy to make things easier for them. Indeed, some refugees from mainland China find it difficult to adjust in Hong Kong to the fact that no longer are people really looking after them and caring for them.

Although activists are likely to be the best informers, they are also likely to be the best comrades. Activists are expected to and do in fact spend considerable time assisting their colleagues and neighbours. They assist new arrivals, they make suggestions for how to do things, they try to arrange help for the needy. Comrades are concerned for their fellow citizens, and this concern includes both seeing that they stay in line and that they be given assistance when they need it within the limits of the possibilities of the time and place.

Comradeship is also strongly egalitarian in its underlying ethic. Because of their work position, some people have considerably more authority and power than others. But as fellow citizens, as comrades, they are in many fundamental respects regarded as equals. A person who is a Party member or who has more education or a higher status in his personal relations with others is supposed to behave as an equal. Of course, this does not entirely work out in practice, but the underlying ethic is clear, and a case where it was not practised would be considered an abuse.

VARIATIONS ON A THEME

The pattern of caution and reserve in personal relationships paradoxically is probably the greatest among Party members, whom the régime considers very reliable, and the intellectuals, whom the régime considers very unreliable. What is common to these two groups is that they are subjected to more study meetings, self-criticism, and criticism. The Party members are subjected to intense control because of their power and responsibility. Because of their power, the régime demands of them a much higher level of loyalty and discipline than it demands of ordinary citizens, and it exercises constant vigilance lest impure elements or impure thoughts affect the ranks of the Party. The intellectuals are subjected to intense control because of their unreliability, their lack of discipline, and because the régime recognises their potential for influence, especially influence on the minds of youth.

Party members who are least in danger of being rightists, *i.e.*, those with the purest backgrounds and thoughts, may have a feeling of security and camaraderie unknown anywhere else in the society. The Party, being the one organisation where frequent meetings and organisational strength are not suspect, gives its members a group spirit in place of more intimate friendship.

Factory workers and peasants are less subject to pressures, not only because they have a " good " class background but because the demands of keeping up production place some limits on the frequency and length of meetings. Since educational institutions can tolerate more political meetings without clearly and visibly affecting the results, they are more prone to such intrusions.

Peasants are subject to less intrusion than are factory workers partly because the rural organisation, even under the commune, is not as tight and highly controlled and structured as factory organisation. Partly peasants are less controlled because the distance from political power centres is farther and because the proportion of Party members, Youth Leaguers, etc., is less. Peasants may be just as reticent to express criticism to authorities, but the concern about private conversation being brought to the attention of authorities is certainly not as great as in other groups, and the extent to which opinions could deviate before being reported is undoubtedly much greater. This is not to say that peasants have not been affected by the same pressures; the régime's exploitation of local community cleavages, the sending in of outsiders into rural areas, and the informing activities of Youth Leaguers and local Party members have affected friendship patterns even in remote rural areas.

CLOSER COMRADES

Although comrades are theoretically equal and close companions, in practice some are more close than others. While they would be reluctant to admit it, people who grew up under certain economic conditions and have been assigned a certain family status do tend to feel more comfortable with comrades who have been assigned the same status. When a comrade goes to the city or is assigned with other comrades to go to a rural area, he is likely to associate with comrades from his same area who can speak the same dialect and share the same local tastes in food and opera and join in discussion of local news or mutual friends. A comrade may feel tense in talking to a comrade who has power over him and become somewhat stiff and formal when talking to a comrade under him, but will relax with a comrade of about his own level. Though more intimate with comrades in his own small group, a person may feel freer with an acquaintance in another group because there is less danger that their conversation will have to be reported and discussed in a meeting. Young people of the same sex do not sense the slight embarrassment and reserve that can characterise relations between men and women. A better-educated person may feel somewhat cautious with a less-educated comrade because he cannot display his inward feeling of superiority, and the less educated may try to suppress the embarrassment he feels in trying to behave like an equal when he in fact feels inferior. Comrades of the same educational level do not have this problem.

So prominent are political considerations that subtle shadings in political attitudes often separate closer comrades from other comrades. Often these political shadings are not discussed openly, but they are sensed and understood. A comrade who was criticised in a campaign several years ago feels closer to another comrade who was criticised in the same campaign. An activist is more likely to feel comfortable with another activist; a League member can talk more easily to another League member. And, even within the Communist Party, a mildly enthusiastic Party member is more likely to feel closer to another who is mildly enthusiastic, a former rightist is likely to feel closer to another former rightist.

There are many ways to express this closeness. Comrades can talk together, go to movies, or go on walks together. While they are not in the position to do big things for each other like offer major financial assistance or find jobs, there are many little favours they can do for each other. They can share their tight rations, they can help each other with their washing or sewing. They can share their books or their clothes. They can assist each other with their lessons or their work. A comrade who has some special political information might in the context of some casual conversation simply say that it is not wise to do such and such, thereby indirectly warning of some impending political campaign. They would ordinarily avoid any kind of political discussion that might conceivably be embarrassing if later discussed with authorities, but they can make subtle criticisms in ways that would later be defensible. Within the confines of not discussing items which might be politically embarrassing later, there can be considerable loyalty between comrades, and the easy-going affability, kindness and considerateness which characterise friendship in other parts of the world are also found among comrades in Communist China.

Within certain confines, the régime has gradually grown to accept the existence of closer comradeship. The programme of having everyone discuss almost everything about himself and his friends which characterised China in the early period after takeover, has generally given way to a sharpening of the line between what the régime needs to know and what it doesn't need to know. As long as these relationships do not seem threatening to the régime and are kept within bounds, comrades are given freedom to be closer to some comrades than others. While comrades may associate fairly freely on an individual basis, they rarely assemble in a large group except under official auspices. Large groups are inevitably anathema since their potential for damage caused by unified opposition is much greater. Hence, any sizeable group must have its activities very carefully authorised, and its activities must be reported in great detail by very reliable comrades. Because their friendships are potentially more dangerous, men are watched more carefully than women, and old women are perhaps given more leeway in their friendships than any other group in the population.

The practice of not interfering with non-threatening relationships inevitably involves a distinction between the politically reliable and the politically unreliable. Comrades with very clean records of continued activism and support for the régime are given considerable leeway in forming close relationships. But the régime is much more suspicious of budding friendships when one of the pair has some " problems in his background." More frequent observations and reports are required of associates of suspects. Even without any special reason, suspects may be called upon to report on their activities and engage in criticisms of themselves and their comrades. Special meetings may be called, and if these friendships appear too close, they may suffer all the more and even be assigned to different (and often lower) positions in places where they could not possibly have contact with each other. Hence, those who have suspicious backgrounds must be much more cautious in forming relationships and more reserved even in seeing the same person too many times lest it lead to further suspicions. They are in fact, as the régime wishes them to be, relatively isolated.

While some comrades are in fact closer to other comrades, there is a limit as to how close they can become. The limit is dictated partly by fear, but it is supported by the ethic of comradeship which demands that friendships do not interfere with one's role as a citizen, that an individual's commitment with another individual not interfere with his commitment to the collectivity.

As a moral ethic, comradeship is very similar to the moral ethic governing work relationships in the West. One is expected to be friendly but not to form such deep friendships that they interfere with doing the work. In work relationships one can be considerate, kind and relaxed without developing a special private relationship and commitment to the other person. One can discuss some limited personal matters, but it is inappropriate to talk too much about one's personal tastes. If two people are continually together, whispering, going everywhere together, it is regarded as lack of consideration for the rest of the group.

What is unique about Communist China is not the presence of a universalistic ethic governing personal relations, but the absence of a private ethic to supplement the public ethic and support the commitment of the individual to his friend. In most Western countries, close personal relationships may exist outside of a work context giving personal support to the individual for the tensions which exist in his more formal work requirements. In Communist China, the universalistic ethic penetrates much more deeply into personal lives so that it is difficult to gain personal support from the tensions generated in the more formal relationships. This is not as severe a problem as one might imagine. For the citizen who is bitterly attacked by comrades, the combination of criticism and avoidance by friends can be devastating. But most Chinese people do not seem to require as high a level of personal support as people in many other societies. Their needs for dependent gratification are not so great, and the support of friends and especially of family members, even if expressed only by attitude rather than by potentially dangerous conversation, appears to be sufficient. But the individual is also tightly integrated into his small group, whether it be at work or in the neighbourhood, and to the extent that he cannot stand completely independent of social pressures and requires some support, he is dependent on his small group which is closely integrated with the régime, and this support is conditional on his showing the proper political attitudes, a situation which gives the régime considerable leverage in getting the individual's co-operation. The general small group support for being a good comrade is not the same as the relatively unconditional support which a friend offers his friend, but it has become an important psychological substitute. A person relies on his comrades not only for expediency but to satisfy his desires for personal companionship.

The growth of the new universalistic ethic has been important to the régime not only because it reduces the threats to political control. It is important because a modernising society undergoing rapid social change and reorganisation requires a basis of personal relations which makes it possible for people of different social backgrounds, from different geographical areas, with different personal tastes to have relationships with each other. This can only be supplied by a universalistic ethic. But the all-pervasiveness of the universalistic ethic, its penetration into private lives can only be understood in terms of the régime's desires for the power to be able to influence people even in small matters of their daily lives. Because people rise into membership in the Young Communist League and the Communist Party partly because they have proved their willingness to place the goals of the Party above the goals of friendship, it has assured that the leaders, even more than the average people, will be comrades first and friends second.

Foreign Relations

Diplomacy and Revolution:
The Dialectics of a Dispute

By RICHARD LOWENTHAL

THE policy declaration and the appeal to the peoples of the world adopted last December by the Moscow conference of eighty-one Communist parties mark the end of one phase in the dispute between the leaderships of the ruling parties of China and the Soviet Union—the phase in which the followers of Mao for the first time openly challenged the standing of the Soviet Communists as the fountain-head of ideological orthodoxy for the world movement. But the "ideological dispute" which began in April was neither a sudden nor a self-contained development: it grew out of acute differences between the two Communist Great Powers over concrete diplomatic issues, and it took its course in constant interaction with the changes in Soviet diplomatic tactics. Hence the total impact of that phase on Soviet foreign policy on one side, and on the ideology, organisation and strategy of international Communism on the other, cannot be evaluated from an interpretation of the Moscow documents alone, but only from a study of the process as a whole, as it developed during the past year on both planes.[1]

To say that the 1960 Chinese challenge to Soviet ideological authority grew out of pragmatic disagreements over foreign policy is not to take the view that the varieties of Communist ideology are a mere cloak for

---

[1] I have not attempted here to deal with the impact of the dispute on Chinese foreign policy, as distinct from Chinese ideology. Owing to the absence of diplomatic relations with the main enemy, the scope for Chinese diplomacy outside the *bloc* is somewhat limited. As experts on the subject have suggested in past issues of this review, the chief effect of the dispute in this field seems to have been to make the Chinese leaders try to mend some of their national quarrels with neutral Asian states, notably Burma, Nepal and Indonesia, and to reduce the temperature of their conflict with India: apparently they realised at some point that the multiplication of these quarrels made them needlessly vulnerable to Soviet criticism of their general views on war and peaceful co-existence—views that had, after all, been formulated primarily with an eye to relations with the "imperialist" West, and above all with the United States. On the main issue, the repetition of the proposal for an atom-free zone in the Pacific on August 1 may have been intended to stake out a Chinese negotiating position in case of Soviet-American agreement on a permanent ban on nuclear tests —a price to be exacted for agreement to be kept out of the nuclear club.

conflicts of national interest. The profound differences in the history of the Soviet and Chinese Communist parties, both in the strategy by which they conquered power and in the methods they used afterwards for transforming society, have clearly produced a different ideological climate, different forms of inner-party life and a different " style of work "; and the fact that Mao Tse-tung could only win control of the Chinese party and lead it to victory by repeatedly defying Stalin's advice has contributed to the formation of a Chinese Communist leadership which is highly conscious of those differences.

This is not the place either to discuss the origin and nature of the distinctive ideological climate of Chinese Communism in detail, or to trace its various manifestations from Mao's first " rectification " movement of 1941 to the methods adopted after his victory for the " re-education " of hostile classes, or from the reaction to Soviet " de-stalinisation " and the subsequent crisis in the Soviet *bloc* to the " Hundred Flowers " campaign and to the creation of the communes. Suffice it to say that while some of these manifestations of Chinese originality took an apparently " liberal " and others an apparently " extremist " form, their common characteristic is a historically conditioned tendency to believe that almost anything is possible to a revolutionary party armed with the right consciousness—an exaltation of faith and will over all " objective conditions " of the productive forces and all given class structures which exceeds that shown by the Bolshevik model, and is even more remote from the original Marxian doctrine than the latter.

A party leadership conditioned by this ideological climate will obviously perceive both the internal problems and the national interests of the state it governs in a peculiar way; to that extent, the ideological difference constitutes a kind of permanent potential for rivalry between the two Communist Great Powers. Yet it does not by itself explain the timing and content of any particular dispute between them. For given the manifestly overriding importance of their common interests, the potential rivalry can only become actual when concrete policy disagreements arise which cannot be settled by the ordinary means of intra-*bloc* diplomacy, and which the weaker and dependent ally regards as sufficiently vital to take recourse to the public use of the ideological weapon. This was done by China in muted hints during the 1958 disagreements, and much more openly in 1960.

THE CHINESE VIEW

In both cases, Chinese misgivings seem to have been based on a sense of insufficient Soviet diplomatic and military support in their long-standing conflict with the United States, and to have been acutely aggravated by Mr. Khrushchev's efforts to achieve a Soviet-American *détente*

—by his repeated bids for a " summit conference " without Communist
China, and by his visit to the U.S. in September 1959. The Chinese
leaders apparently feared, probably not without reason, that such a
détente would further diminish Soviet interest in taking serious risks on
their behalf, and increase Soviet interest in preventing them from taking
any such risks themselves. Above all, Soviet willingness to make disarmament one of the main items on any summit agenda, combined with
the agreed temporary ban on nuclear test explosions and the continued
negotiations for a permanent ban, must have given rise to Chinese anxiety
lest the Russians might be willing on certain conditions to enter a commitment to close the " nuclear club." The mere fact of negotiation on
that subject apparently precluded them from receiving Soviet aid in
developing nuclear weapons of their own, and thus helped to delay their
becoming a world power of the first rank; an actual Soviet commitment
would have faced them with the choice of either accepting permanent
inferiority in this field, or—if they went ahead successfully in developing
and testing the weapon themselves—of defying an agreement of the
world's leading powers in isolation.

Whatever the Chinese may have said in their private representations
to Moscow, they did not think it advisable to spell out these fears in
public. But during the winter of 1959–60—roughly from Khrushchev's
visit to Peking, on his return from his talks with Eisenhower, at the
beginning of October to the Moscow conference of the Warsaw Pact
states in early February—they openly attacked the assumptions on which
the effort to achieve a Soviet-American *détente* was officially based.[2]
The core of their argument was that the policy of American " imperialism " and of Eisenhower, its " chieftain," could not change in
substance even if it was temporarily disguised by peace-loving phrases;
hence nothing could be gained by seeking an understanding with the U.S.
in an atmosphere of *détente*, only by isolating this " main enemy " and
putting maximum pressure on him. A period of quite visible, concrete
disagreement on policy towards the Eisenhower administration thus
preceded the Chinese Communists' generalised, ideological attack on
Soviet authority.

The most striking characteristic of that period is the apparent uncon-
cern with which the Soviet leaders pursued their preparations for a
" summit conference," despite the increasingly outspoken Chinese protests. The impression that Mao Tse-tung had refused to approve the
concept of a *détente* based on " mutual concessions " as advanced by
Khrushchev was confirmed when the latter, addressing the Supreme Soviet

---

[2] For a full study of the development of the Chinese arguments during that phase, see
A. M. Halpern, " Communist China and Peaceful Coexistence," *The China Quarterly*,
No. 3, p. 16.

on his return to Moscow, coupled his advocacy of that concept with blunt warnings against the " Trotskyite adventurism " of a policy of " neither peace nor war," [3] and when the theoretical organ of the Chinese Communists developed an analysis of American foreign policy directly opposed to Khrushchev's optimism in the following months.[4] Nevertheless, Khrushchev announced to the Supreme Soviet in January 1960 a substantial reduction of Soviet conventional forces and military expenditures as his advance contribution to the ten-power disarmament negotiations, and also indicated willingness to help overcome the deadlock in the negotiations on an inspection system for a permanent ban on nuclear test explosions—a most sensitive issue from the Chinese point of view.

Within a week, the standing committee of the Chinese National People's Congress, in a resolution formally approving the Soviet disarmament proposals, solemnly announced to the world that China would not be bound by any agreements to which she was not a party; but when this stand, together with warnings against illusions about a change in the character of American policy, was repeated at the conference of Warsaw Treaty ministers in early February by the—possibly uninvited— Chinese observer, his speech was not published in any European member state of the Soviet *bloc*, and the declaration adopted by the conference showed virtually no concessions to his point of view.[5] To cap it all, Khrushchev spent most of the remainder of February, including the tenth anniversary of the Sino-Soviet alliance, in India and Indonesia, two countries with which China was involved in acute conflicts of national interest, and showed throughout the journey an almost ostentatious detachment from Chinese claims and actions.

All during the winter, the Chinese thus experienced the inherent weakness in the position of a dependent ally who urges the stronger partner to pay more heed to his interests, but is unable to switch sides if the latter turns a deaf ear: none of their objections, raised first in secret and then with increasing publicity, were able to deflect Khrushchev from his course. There remained to them one weapon—to interfere directly not with the Soviet policy of *détente*, but with the *détente* itself—by urging on Communist and revolutionary nationalist movements in the non-Communist world a bolder forward policy than was compatible with the plans of Soviet diplomacy. But this meant that the Chinese Communists must set themselves up as rivals to their Russian comrades in

---

[3] Moscow Radio, October 31, 1959.

[4] *e.g.* Yü Chao-li, "The Chinese People's Great Victory in the Fight against Imperialism," *Peking Review*, September 22, 1959, from *Red Flag*, No. 18, 1959; *idem*, "Excellent Situation for the Struggle for Peace," *Peking Review*, January 5, 1960, from *Red Flag*, No. 1, 1960; editorial, *People's Daily*, January 21, 1960.

[5] See the text of both the declaration and K'ang Sheng's speech in *The China Quarterly*, No. 2, pp. 75–89.

advising these movements—in other words, that they must generalise the dispute and raise the question of ideological authority.

During the later part of the winter 1959–60, a number of cases became known where Chinese representatives had opposed Soviet delegates in closed sessions of the directing organs of such international front organisations as the World Peace Council, the Afro-Asian Solidarity Committee, the World Federation of Trade Unions, etc. The central issue in these clashes was whether the "peace campaign" was the priority task to which all other forms of revolutionary struggle must be subordinated, as the Russians maintained, or whether it was only one among many forms of the struggle against imperialism, which must in no circumstances be isolated and "set in opposition" to more militant forms of revolutionary action, as the Chinese argued. It was as a platform for these discussions in the international movement that the Chinese Communists published in April their ideological statements on the teachings of Lenin —documents which, despite all later elaborations and modifications, have remained basic for that phase of the dispute.[6]

THE QUESTION OF WAR

It has been implied in subsequent Soviet polemics, against "dogmatists and sectarians," and innumerable times spelt out in Western comment, that the central thesis of those Chinese statements was the continued validity of Lenin's belief in the inevitability of world war. That is not so. Every one of the Chinese documents in question quoted with approval the sentence in the 1957 Moscow declaration (based in turn on the resolution of the Twentieth Congress of the CPSU) that, owing to the growth of the forces of peace, " it is now realistically possible to prevent war." What none of them approved, however, is the formula of the Twenty-first Congress on the emerging possibility " even before the full victory of Socialism in the world, while capitalism continues to exist in part of the world, to banish world war from the life of human society." The difference is that, in the Chinese view, the latter phrase implies the disappearance of any serious *danger* of world war while capitalism still exists; the Chinese Communists felt that this presupposed a change in the nature of imperialism—and that they had to deny such a possibility in order to contest the Khrushchevian hope of converting the ruling circles of the U.S. to a genuine acceptance of " peaceful coexistence " from realistic motives.

---

6 Yü Chao-li, " On Imperialism as a Source of War in Modern Times," and " On the Way for all Peoples to struggle for Peace," NCNA, March 30, 1960, from *Red Flag*, No. 7, 1960; Editorial " Long Live Leninism," *Peking Review*, April 26, 1960, from *Red Flag*, No. 8, 1960; Editorial, *People's Daily*, April 22, 1960; Lu Ting-yi, " Get United under Lenin's Revolutionary Banner," speech at Lenin commemoration meeting in Peking, April 22, 1960 (NCNA same date).

The picture drawn by the Chinese was that of an unchanged, though weakened, imperialism which would resort to war whenever it could to defend its sphere of exploitation, but might be prevented from doing so in any particular case by the " forces of peace." In practice, they agreed with the Soviets in regarding an all-out attack on the Soviet *bloc* as unlikely, but argued that inter-imperialist war was still possible, and insisted that colonial wars against national liberation movements were virtually inevitable: the latter could only be " stopped " by vigorous support for the revolutionary movements. But the Communists would fail to give support if they were " afraid " of another world war, if they " begged the imperialists for peace," or if they tolerated or even spread illusions about the warlike nature of imperialism, instead of mobilising the masses everywhere for an all-out struggle against it.

This analysis implied three charges of " muddle-headed concessions to revisionism " against Khrushchev's policy : exaggeration of the dangers of nuclear war, which might paralyse the will to resist imperialism or at any rate lead to excessive caution; illusions about the growth of a " realistic " tendency towards peaceful coexistence among such " chieftains of imperialism " as Eisenhower, which might lead to a relaxation of vigilance among the Communist governments and movements; and as a result, excessive reliance on diplomatic negotiation as a means to avert war, causing a desire to restrain revolutionary movements and " just wars " of liberation, instead of welcoming them as the best means to weaken the imperialists and stop *their* wars. Accordingly, the Chinese ideologists argued that it was all right for a Communist to seek a meeting with Eisenhower, but wrong to say that he believed in the latter's peaceful intentions; all right to propose " general and complete disarmament," but wrong to tell his own followers that there was a real chance of obtaining it; all right to propagate peaceful coexistence, but wrong to advise the Algerian nationalists to try and negotiate a cease-fire with President de Gaulle. They accepted peace *propaganda* as a means of revolutionary struggle against imperialism, but not peace *diplomacy* of a kind which might even temporarily mitigate the forms of that struggle.

THE SOVIET REPLY

The Russians, aware that there could be no serious negotiation without an atmosphere of *détente* and at least the pretence of believing in the peaceful intentions of the other side, recognised that this was an attack on their whole coexistence diplomacy; but they had to answer it on the ideological plane. Through the mouth of Otto Kuusinen, a member of the secretariat of the CC CPSU who had begun work in the Comintern in Lenin's time, they insisted [7] that Lenin had differentiated between militarist diehards and possible partners for peaceful coexistence in the imperialist camp, and had foreseen that changes in military technique might one day make war impossible. They argued that the growing strength of the " Socialist camp " and the destructive potential of nuclear weapons and long-range rockets had in fact provided a realistic basis for a diplomacy based on similar differentiation at the present time, and claimed as telling proof of their thesis the success of Khrushchev's personal diplomacy in general, and of his " historic visit " to the U.S. in particular, in largely dispersing the climate of the Cold War and restoring businesslike relations between the two different social systems. Yet only a few weeks later Khrushchev himself, even while maintaining this position in theory, reversed himself in practice to the extent of wrecking the summit conference on the ground that negotiation with Eisenhower had become impossible after his assumption of responsibility for the U 2 incident.

Western discussion of the causes of this *volte-face* has necessarily remained inconclusive in the absence of direct evidence of the motives of the Russian rulers and the course of their deliberations in the critical period. But a coherent analysis of the Sino-Soviet dispute is impossible without at least venturing a hypothesis. I have elsewhere stated my reasons for rejecting the theory that a decisive weakening of Khrushchev's position by some combination of " neo-Stalinist " or " pro-Chinese " elements in the Soviet leadership took place at that time [8]; indeed, I know of no convincing evidence for the assumption that such a grouping exists at all. On the other hand, Khrushchev's Baku speech of April 25 showed his anxieties, following a number of authorised American policy statements, lest the summit meeting might fail to yield the Western concessions on Berlin which he expected, and his desire to increase the pressure in that direction; and his initial reaction to the U 2 incident is consistent with the assumption that he regarded it not as a reason for evading the summit conference, but as an occasion for making the pressure more effective by driving a wedge between Eisenhower and his " diehard militarist " advisers. [9]

By marking the complete failure of this crude attempt at differentiation, the President's assumption of personal responsibility for the spy-flights, whatever its other merits or demerits, must have been a double blow to Khrushchev: it deprived him of the last hope of obtaining substantial concessions at the summit, and it put him clearly in the wrong

---

[7] Speech at Lenin commemoration meeting in Moscow, April 22, 1960: *Pravda*, April 23.

[8] " The Nature of Khrushchev's Power," *Problems of Communism*, July/August 1960.

[9] See Khrushchev's speeches to the Supreme Soviet on May 5 and 7, and at the reception of the Czechoslovak Embassy in Moscow on May 9.

on one important part of his public argument with his Chinese allies. A failure to reach his summit objectives thus became certain at the very moment at which, from the viewpoint of his prestige in the " Socialist camp " and the Communist world movement, he could least afford such a failure: hence it seems natural that, with the full support of his colleagues, he decided rather to wreck the conference in advance unless he could still force a last-minute differentiation by obtaining a public apology from Eisenhower.

Within a few days, Khrushchev demonstrated by his refusal to go ahead with an East German peace treaty pending a possible summit conference with Eisenhower's successor that he had not abandoned the " general line " of his diplomacy but only intended to change the time schedule. But the Chinese Communists not only were not content with that, but felt that now they had been proved right by events, they were in a strong position to force a broad change of policy by pressing home their ideological attack.

PEKING PRESSES ITS ATTACK

The attempt was made officially and in fact publicly at the beginning of June at the Peking session of the General Council of the WFTU by the Chinese Vice-President of that body, Liu Chang-sheng, and there is reason to suppose that even more comprehensive and outspoken criticisms of Soviet policy were circulated non-publicly at the same time, at least to selected leaders of the Communist world movement. Liu's speech [10] went beyond the April documents in demanding a " clarification " of the Communist attitude towards war, denouncing " indiscriminate " opposition to war and calling for active support for " just wars " of liberation; in sharply opposing the formulation of the Soviet Twenty-first Congress about " eliminating war forever while imperialism still exists " as " entirely wrong " and leading to " evil consequences of a serious nature which, in fact, we already see at present," though he too admitted the possibility of preventing a new world war; and in condemning any belief that proposals for general and complete disarmament could be accepted, and that the funds formerly earmarked for war purposes could be used for the welfare of the masses and for assisting underdeveloped countries while imperialism still existed as " downright whitewashing and embellishing imperialism " and thus " helping imperialism headed by the U.S. to dupe the people."

Yet the Chinese had misjudged their chances of forcing a change of the Soviet line. At the WFTU session, they found themselves vigorously counter-attacked by both the Russian and the major European movements, and finally isolated with only the Indonesian trade unions on their

[10] NCNA, June 8, 1960.

side. Moreover, this seems to have been the point at which the Soviet leaders decided to give battle in defence of their ideological authority, and first of all to whip into line those European satellite parties which had in the past shown signs of sympathy for Chinese intransigence. They took the initiative in calling a conference of all ruling Communist parties to meet on the occasion of the Rumanian party congress later that month; and in the meantime the Soviet press began to publish warnings against the dangers of " dogmatism " and " sectarianism " in the international movement,[11] while the Italian delegates returning from Peking published the fact that the Chinese had been isolated and defeated in a major international discussion on the problems of the struggle for peace and disarmament.[12]

Now that the issue of authority was out in the open, the field of the dispute kept broadening. Already in April, the speaker at the Peking celebration of Lenin's birthday, Lu Ting-Yi, had claimed for Mao's creation of the communes the succession to Lenin's concept of " uninterrupted revolution," and had attacked people who in Socialist construction " rely only on technique and not on the masses " and deny the need for further revolutionary struggle in the transition to the higher stage of Communism.[13] Now *Pravda* quoted Engels and Lenin for their criticism of the Blanquist wish to " skip all the intermediate stages on the road to Communism " in the illusion that " if power were in their hands, communism could be introduced the day after tomorrow." [14] Yet the original Sino-Soviet disagreement about the communes had been ended in the winter of 1958–59 with the withdrawal of the Chinese claim that this institution constituted a short cut to the Communist stage, and an understanding that the Chinese would go on developing and the Soviets and their European satellites rejecting that institution without further debate. The revival of the issue now only made sense as part of the attempt by each side to throw doubt on the other's ideological orthodoxy.

THE BUCHAREST CONFERENCE

On the eve of the Bucharest conference, a *Pravda* editorial stated bluntly that " among Socialist countries, there cannot be two opinions on the question of peace or war. Socialists believe that in present conditions there is no necessity for war, that disarmament is not only needed but possible, and that peaceful coexistence between nations is a vital necessity." [15] Coupled with a quote from Khrushchev's December speech to

[11] Articles on the fortieth anniversary of Lenin's " Leftwing Communism, an Infantile Disorder," by D. Shevlyagin in *Sovyetskaya Rossiya*, June 10, and by " N. Matkovsky " in *Pravda*, June 12, 1960; *Pravda* editorial " Full Support " on the Soviet disarmament proposals, June 13, 1960.
[12] Foa in *Avanti*, June 15; Novella in *Unita*, June 19, 1960.
[13] NCNA, April 22, 1960.   [14] N. Matkovsky on June 12.   [15] June 20, 1960.

the Hungarian party congress about the need for all Communist governments to " synchronise their watches," and his warning that " if the
leaders of any one of the Socialist countries would set themselves up to
be above the rest, that can only play into the hands of our enemies," this
indicated the Soviet leaders' intention to force a clear decision that would
be binding on all ruling parties.

But at Bucharest, this intention was at least partly foiled by the
Chinese. Khrushchev's public attack [16] on people who quote the words
of Lenin without looking at the realities of the present world, and whom
Lenin would set right in no uncertain manner if he came back today,
was plain enough for all the satellite leaders to understand that the time
for manoeuvring between the two colossi was over, and for all but the
Albanians to rally round. His account of how Soviet strength and Soviet
skill had again and again foiled the war plans of the " imperialists," from
Suez in 1956 to the Turkish-Syrian crisis of 1957 and the U.S. landing in
the Lebanon after the Iraqi revolution of 1958, if historically dubious, was
propagandistically effective as a demonstration of the meaning of his
" peace policy " for a Communist audience. But the Chinese delegate
P'eng Chen was clearly instructed neither to submit nor to carry the
ideological debate to a conclusion at this point: he evaded a decision by
a skilful withdrawal to prepared positions.

In public, P'eng Chen appeared as the advocate of Communist unity
at almost any price, to be achieved on the basis of the 1957 Moscow
declaration to which all but the Yugoslavs had agreed.[17] This committed
the Chinese once more to recognition of the possibility of preventing or
" checking " imperialist wars—a possibility that, P'eng claimed, could
only be fulfilled by the united strength of the " Socialist camp " and the
determined mobilisation of mass action against the imperialists. But it
was also intended to commit the Russians once again to the 1957 thesis
that the aggressive circles of the U.S. were the main enemy of peace and
all popular aspirations, and that " revisionism " was the main danger
within the ranks of the Communist movement. Having said that much,
the Chinese representative spoke no word about *détente*, disarmament or
the " elimination of war from the life of mankind " before the disappearance of capitalism.

Behind the scenes, he seems to have argued that the 1957 conference
of ruling Communist parties had been called chiefly to settle problems of
Communist power and " Socialist construction "; the questions now in
dispute, being concerned with world-wide revolutionary strategy, could
only be decided by a conference representing the whole Communist
movement. Khrushchev might well complain about Chinese " factional "

---

[16] Speech at the Bucharest Congress on June 21, 1960, as carried by TASS.
[17] Text in NCNA, June 22, 1960.

methods of carrying the quarrel into the ranks of other parties; in the end he had to agree to put up the dispute officially for worldwide inner-party discussion in preparation for a November conference in Moscow, and to content himself with a brief interim communiqué which, while stressing the primary importance of the " peace campaign," did not go beyond the 1957 declaration on any controversial point.

This fell far short of what the Soviet leaders had expected. The decisive showdown was not only postponed for several months, but it would take place before an audience of revolutionary parties many of whose members were less closely tied to Soviet control than the East European satellites, and might well regard the Chinese slogans of unconditional revolutionary solidarity as more attractive than the Soviet readiness to subordinate their struggle to the needs of co-existence diplomacy whenever that seemed expedient. Thus an Algerian Communist might prefer Chinese offers of aid for the F.L.N. to the repeated Russian advice favouring negotiation with de Gaulle; an Iraqi Communist might recall that neither Soviet support for Kassem's régime nor his own party's Soviet-ordered retreat from its earlier offensive policy had obtained for it a legal, let alone a dominating, position under that régime; an Indonesian Communist might resent the manner in which Khrushchev had ignored his party during his official visit, and the general Soviet wooing of the " bourgeois nationalist " régime of Soekarno that limited the democratic rights of the Communists as well as of other parties and favoured a neutralist *bloc* with the " renegade " Tito. And would not the Communists of Latin America be sensitive to the Chinese argument that as Yankee imperialism was the main enemy, any attempts to relax Soviet-American tension were bound to weaken Soviet support for them as well as for China?

Yet without the co-operation of these movements, Khrushchev's co-existence diplomacy could not be carried through: he needed their discipline, and the Chinese had launched their ideological attack on his authority precisely in order to undermine that. Now they had created a situation in which the objects of the struggle, the Communist movements *in partibus infidelium*, were to act to some extent as its arbiters. True, the Russians had still the advantage of the prestige and resources of a world Power as well as of older organisational ties: all the foreign Communists knew that the Soviets *could* help them more—financially, diplomatically, and ultimately militarily—than the Chinese, yet they were less certain that the Soviets *would* always help them to the limits of their ability. Hence Khrushchev seems to have felt that in preparation for the November meeting, not only the circulation of new Soviet documents and the dispatch of new emissaries to the wavering parties were needed, but

above all new proofs of the spirit of revolutionary internationalism ani-
mating his foreign policy.

SOVIET FOREIGN POLICY HARDENS

The fact that he had already decided to postpone his new summit
approach until after the U.S. presidential elections made it easier for him
to furnish that proof: for he could now afford to increase rather than
relax tension for a time without serious damage to his future diplomatic
chances, and perhaps even in the hope to improve them by creating a dark
backdrop for the next display of his sunny smile—provided only that he
did not allow matters to get really out of hand. The weeks after Bucharest
thus offered the strange spectacle of the Soviet leaders conducting themselves on the world stage in the very style which Peking's ideological
theses had seemed to demand, while at the same time launching a
vigorous campaign against those theses throughout the Communist world
movement !

The Bucharest communiqué had not yet been published when Russia
demonstratively walked out of the ten-power disarmament talks at
Geneva, just before the Western counter-proposals for which she had
been calling so insistently were officially submitted. There followed
within a few days the shooting down of an American plane over the
Arctic, the first Soviet note on the Congo accusing all the Western powers
of backing Belgian military intervention as part of a plot to restore
colonial rule, and as a climax Khrushchev's personal threat to use intercontinental rockets against the U.S. if the latter should attack Cuba.
Yet during the same period, Khrushchev used his visit to Austria to insist again and again on the horrors of nuclear world war and on the need
to avoid even local wars because of the risk that they might spread; and
even in his most reckless gestures he took care not to do anything irrevocable. The Geneva test negotiations were *not* broken off; the Cuban
rocket threat was soon " explained " as symbolic, while in the Congo the
Russians refrained from backing their policy with force; and a proposal
for taking the disarmament negotiations out of the U.N. and for calling
instead for a disarmament conference of " all governments " including
China, which the Chinese managed to get adopted by a Stockholm session
of the World Peace Council in July, was promptly dropped down the
memory hole by Moscow in favour of Khrushchev's suggestion that all
heads of government of the member states should personally attend the
next U.N. assembly session in order to discuss the Soviet plan for general
and complete disarmament.

The same contradiction between the desire to keep the lines of negotiation open and the need to pose constantly as an uninhibited revolutionary agitator also dominated Khrushchev's subsequent behaviour at the

U.N. assembly itself. He did not back the neutrals' initiative for a new summit meeting but left the onus of killing it to the West. He depreciated the importance of his own proposals for " general and complete disarmament," for the sake of which so many heads of government had come, by devoting far more energy to his attack on " colonialism " in general and on the U.N. secretariat in particular, and by choosing a language and style of behaviour more apt to inspire revolutionary movements outside than to influence delegates inside the assembly hall. He followed his attack on the secretariat by proposals for a reform of the latter and of the Security Council which appealed to the natural desire of the new African and Asian member states for stronger representation in the leading organs of the U.N., but then suggested that any such changes in the Charter should be postponed until the delegates of the Chinese People's Republic had been seated. These inconsistencies are incomprehensible unless the fact is borne in mind that during all that time Khrushchev was engaged in an effort to prove his revolutionary zeal and international solidarity in preparation for the Moscow conference.

Meanwhile the line for the ideological campaign itself had been laid down by a meeting of the central committee of the CPSU in mid-July, which had approved the conduct of its delegation at Bucharest, led by Khrushchev, oddly enough after a report by secretariat member F. R. Kozlov who had not been there. As developed during late July and August in the Soviet press and the statements of pro-Soviet leaders of foreign Communist parties, the campaign showed some significant changes of emphasis.[18] It was more uncompromising than ever on the need to avoid the horrors of nuclear war, and the rejection of all attempts to belittle them or to regard any kind of international war as desirable. It insisted that good Marxist-Leninist revolutionaries were entitled and indeed obliged to adopt on this matter conclusions different from Lenin, both because of the new techniques of destruction and because of the change in the relation of world forces to the disadvantage of imperialism. It vigorously defended the possibility not only of stopping each particular war, but of altogether " eliminating war from the life of society " with the further growth of the strength of the " Socialist camp," even while capitalism still existed on part of the globe, as the Twenty-first Congress had laid down; and it claimed that the Soviet programme of general and complete disarmament was a realistic policy goal that could be achieved, even though this might require time, " mutual concessions " and compromises. Any opposition to this general line of peaceful coexistence

---

[18] F. Konstantinov and Kh. Momdzhan, " Dialectics and the Present," *Kommunist* No. 10, 1960; *Pravda* editorial, July 20; speech by M. A. Suslov, *Pravda*, July 30; Y. Frantsev, *Pravda*, August 7; B. Ponomarev, *Pravda*, August 12; Togliatti speech to Italian CC, *Pravda*, July 28; T. Zhivkov in August issue of *World Marxist Review*.

was to be eliminated from the Communist movement as " Trotskyite adventurism."

MOSCOW AND PEKING SHIFT THEIR GROUND

But the new campaign no longer laid stress on Khrushchev's differentiation between " realistic statesmen " and " diehard militarists " in the enemy camp, and no longer mentioned " relaxation of international tension " as a condition of coexistence diplomacy. Instead, the goals of peace and disarmament were now put forward, in language first used by the Chinese critics, as having to be " imposed " on the imperialists by the strength of the " Socialist camp " and the relentless struggle of the masses. Peaceful coexistence was now described as " the highest form of the class struggle," and justified as leading not to an even temporary weakening, but to an intensification of revolutionary movements everywhere, including civil wars and colonial revolts whenever the imperialists attempted to hold back the rising tide by force. It was only international wars, wars between states, that should be avoided by the policy of peaceful coexistence; and it was explicitly admitted that imperialist intervention against revolutionary movements might lead to " just wars of liberation," and that in that case the duty of the Socialist camp was to support the latter—though not necessarily with troops—and to seek to end the intervention. In short, it was now claimed that there was no contradiction at all between the diplomacy of coexistence and the policy of unconditional revolutionary solidarity : both had become compatible in an age where, owing to the growing strength of the " Socialist camp," the " dictatorship of the proletariat had become an international force " as once predicted by Lenin.

This interpretation of Soviet policy evidently placed its authors in a very strong position to meet the Chinese ideological challenge; yet as the Chinese had intended, and as Khrushchev's simultaneous actions illustrated, it was bound greatly to reduce the credibility and effectiveness of the coexistence campaign in non-Communist eyes. The Soviets could hope to succeed in restoring their international ideological authority to the exact extent to which they were prepared temporarily to weaken the political impact of their diplomacy. It was an expression of that dilemma that when the chief ideological spokesman of Yugoslav Communism, Vice-President Edvard Kardelj, published a pamphlet in defence of coexistence and against the Chinese cult of revolutionary war,[19] *Pravda* immediately turned against him and accused him of all the revisionist sins of which the Chinese had accused the Soviets [20]—not only because he had been so tactless as to name the Chinese as his target,

[19] " Socialism and War," first published in *Borba*, August 12–20, 1960.
[20] A. Arzumanyan and V. Koryonov. *Pravda*, September 2, 1960.

which the Soviets had never done, but because he had taken a consistent position with which they could not afford to identify themselves. For Kardelj had argued that real peaceful coexistence between states with different social systems required that these systems should not become the basis of permanent " ideological *blocs* " in foreign policy; and this concept was, of course, as incompatible with Soviet practice as with the new definition of coexistence as " the highest form of the class struggle."

During the same period, the Chinese Communists were also shifting their ground. They stopped belittling the horrors of nuclear war and claiming that only cowards could fear them,[21] and repeatedly protested their willingness to fight for peaceful coexistence and the prevention or stopping of wars. But they kept rubbing in the formula of the Moscow declaration of 1957 about the role of the aggressive U.S. circles as the centre of world reaction and the need for vigilance against its war plans camouflaged by peace talk, which they felt had been borne out by Khrushchev's experience with Eisenhower; and they pictured peaceful coexistence and disarmament as goals which could be " imposed " on the enemy only " to some extent " and for limited periods, without the slightest assurance of permanence or completion before the final, worldwide victory of the Communist cause.[22] In other words, they remained adamant in their rejection of the thesis of the Twenty-first Congress about " eliminating war from the life of mankind " before that final victory.

THE QUESTION OF ROADS TO POWER

Parallel with that, the Chinese concentrated on extolling the importance of revolutionary violence, including revolutionary war. While the Russians now *admitted* that peaceful coexistence did not *exclude* colonial uprisings and civil wars, and that imperialist intervention in these cases *might lead* to " just wars of liberation," the Chinese stressed revolutionary violence as the normal and classical road for the advance of the Communist cause, and support for just wars as the *criterion* of true internationalism. In fact, they abandoned the safe ground of the 1957 Moscow declaration (on which they were otherwise relying in that phase) to the extent of attacking its thesis, taken over from the Twentieth Congress of the CPSU, that the Communist seizure of power might take place in some countries without violent upheaval and civil war, as a peaceful revolution carried out with the help of the legal parliamentary

---

21 The last Chinese statement on those lines seems to have been the article on the tenth anniversary of the outbreak of the Korean War by Gen. Li Chih-min, *People's Daily*, June 25, 1960.

22 *People's Daily* editorial commenting on Bucharest communiqué, June 29 ; Liao Ch'engchih's speech to Bureau of World Peace Council in Stockholm, July 10 ; Ch'en Yi's speech in Peking, NCNA, July 15 ; Li Fu-ch'un's speech to the Vietnamese party congress, NCNA, September 6.

institutions. Ignoring the examples given by the Russians at the time—such as the annexation of Esthonia and the Czechoslovak coup of February 1948—the Chinese now insisted that the bourgeoisie would never and nowhere abandon power without resorting to violence, and that it was " muddle-headed " at best to confuse the peaceful construction of Socialism *after* the seizure of power with the necessarily violent conquest of power itself.[23]   To this, the Soviets replied with renewed charges of " Blanquism." [24]

Of all the differences raised in the 1960 dispute, this argument on the violent and non-violent roads to power was probably the least serious and most purely demagogic one. The Soviets had started talking about the " parliamentary road " in order to ease the tactical position of the Communist parties in the West, and it was the latter who made propagandist use of the formula; at any rate, it contains nothing to which the Chinese could object from the point of view of their interests. But in the weeks before the crucial Moscow meeting, the Chinese effort was chiefly directed at those Communist parties in underdeveloped countries for which the Chinese experience had long been regarded as a natural model —parties which had developed alternately in co-operation or violent conflict with nationalist dictators, but which had certainly no prospect of gaining power by " parliamentary " means. By dragging in the slogan of the " peaceful road " which nobody had thought of applying to those parties, the Chinese were trying to suggest to them that the real motive for the Soviet counsels of restraint occasionally tendered to them (and which were in fact due to the diplomatic expediency of " keeping in " with the nationalist dictators concerned) was a general renunciation of revolution for the sake of " peace "—that the Soviets were passing from the Leninist policy of coexistence between states to the " revisionist " position of peace between classes!

The Soviets replied to this twist by a similar piece of demagogy—accusing the Chinese of a sectarian refusal to work with broad nationalist movements against imperialism unless these movements subscribed in advance to Communist principles and leadership.[25]   As a general charge, this was as untrue as the Chinese attack on the alleged " revisionism " of Moscow's " peaceful road "; the close contacts maintained by Peking with the Algerian and many African nationalists proved that daily. But Peking's conflicts with the Indian and Indonesian governments, due in fact not to doctrinaire prejudice but to Chinese chauvinism, and its

---

[23] In public, this came out most clearly in the last weeks before the Moscow Conference, notably in comments on the publication of the fourth volume of the works of Mao, *e.g. People's Daily*, October 6, and above all *Red Flag* editorial, November 2. But it is clear from Soviet reaction that the point must have been raised internally before.
[24] A. Belyakov and F. Burlatsky in *Kommunist* No. 13, 1960.
[25] Y. Zhukov in *Pravda*, August 26.

support for leftish malcontents in several Asian Communist parties against Moscow's wooing of nationalist dictators gave to the charge a semblance of substance.

Soviet-Chinese relations seem to have reached their low point in August and early September. It was during that period that an unusually large number of Soviet technicians left China, while many Chinese students returned from Russia: that the organ of the Soviet-Chinese Friendship Society disappeared from the streets of Moscow; and that the expected Chinese scholars failed to turn up at the Orientalists' Congress there. It was then, too, that a number of Soviet provincial papers printed an article explaining that in contemporary conditions, not even a huge country like China could build Socialism in isolation and without the aid and backing of the Soviet Union,[26] while Peking's theoretical voice published a statement of the need for China to rely chiefly on her own resources for the fulfilment of her plans.[27] We do not know the inside story behind those visible symptoms—whether Moscow really tried to apply economic pressure and failed, or whether Peking made a gratuitous demonstration of her capacity for " going it alone." Chinese criticism, at any rate, had not been silenced by October 1st, when the Russians used the eleventh birthday of the CPR to make again a show of friendship; on the contrary, some of Peking's most polemical utterances came in the last weeks before the Moscow conference,[28] whereas the Soviet ideological campaign had rather abated since the middle of September. But by then the Soviets could afford to stop arguing in public, for the Chinese had been largely, though not completely, isolated in the international movement: early in September, even the North Vietnamese party fell in line with the Soviet position.[29]

The mere duration of the Moscow conference—almost three weeks of argument behind closed doors—showed that agreement on a new common statement of principles was anything but easy. This time, the Chinese had sent the strongest possible team short of exposing Mao himself to the risk of defeat—a delegation led by Liu Shao-ch'i and the Party secretary Teng Hsiao-p'ing; and reports that he fought for every clause and comma, and finally yielded to the majority view on some crucial points only under the threat of an open ideological breach do not seem implausible. Halfway through the debates, the anniversary of the 1957 declaration was commented on by editorials in Moscow and Peking which

---

[26] S. Titarenko in *Sovyetskaya Latviya, Bakunsky Rabochy et al.*, August 16, 1960.

[27] Li Fu-ch'un in *Red Flag*, No. 16, 1960.

[28] *Cf.* the articles quoted in note 22 above; also Marshal Lo Jui-ch'ing's article for the (North) *Korean People's Forces Journal* on the tenth anniversary of Chinese intervention in Korea, NCNA, October 25, 1960.

[29] See P. J. Honey's analysis of the North Vietnamese Party Congress in *The China Quarterly*, No. 4, p. 66.

still showed a marked difference of emphasis [30] on the primacy of revolutionary struggle in the *People's Daily*, on the " general line " of peaceful coexistence in *Pravda*; while at the same time a Chinese delegate to a session of the Afro-Asian Solidarity Committee threw off all restraint and claimed publicly that there could be no peaceful coexistence in those countries before the liquidation of colonialism, as the oppressed peoples would never accept " coexistence between the rider and the horse." [31] But it seems established that as the Moscow conclave wore on, the Chinese were only able to retain the support of a few Asian parties that were traditionally dependent on them or largely recruited from the Chinese minorities, of some rather weak Latin American parties, and of the faithful Albanians long tied to them by common enmity against the Yugoslav " revisionists."

The Moscow Statement

The long document on the strategy of international Communism that was agreed in the end thus marks a clear Soviet victory on almost all the points that had still been in dispute in the preceding three months. But the Soviet position as defended since the July session of the central committee of the CPSU already contained substantial concessions to the original Chinese criticism of Soviet policy.

The 1960 Moscow declaration starts from the Soviet analysis that Lenin's views are partly outdated because the present epoch is no longer primarily that of imperialism, but of the growing preponderance of the " Socialist world system " over the forces of imperialism. On this basis, it accepts not only the possibility of ending war forever with the worldwide victory of Socialism, but of " freeing mankind from the nightmare of another world war even now "—of " banishing world war from the life of society even while capitalism still exists in part of the world." The thesis of the Twenty-first Congress of the CPSU which the Chinese had fought to the last has thus been reluctantly accepted by them, and so has the full description of the horrors of nuclear war. The declaration also proclaims the possibility not of preventing all local wars, but of " effectively fighting the local wars unleashed by the imperialists " and extinguishing them, and stresses the unanimity of all Communists in their support for " peaceful coexistence " and negotiation as the only alternative to destructive war. Finally, it recognises the " historic " importance which a fulfilment of the Soviet programme for general and complete disarmament would have, and states that its achievement, though difficult, may be accomplished in stages if the masses and the governments of the " Socialist camp " resolutely fight for it.

[30] *People's Daily*, November 21 ; *Pravda*, November 23.
[31] NCNA, November 21.

At the same time, " peaceful coexistence " is described as " a form of the class struggle " (not, as in some Soviet documents, as " the highest form," because in the Chinese party doctrine that rank remains reserved for revolutionary war). The hope of preserving peace is squarely based on the strength of the " Socialist camp," the revolutionary movements and their sympathisers; it is admitted that the latter may be found also in " certain strata of the bourgeoisie of the advanced countries " who realise the new relation of forces and the catastrophic consequences of a world war, but this appears as a marginal factor. Gone are Khrushchev's " realistic statesmen " and his successful goodwill visits; the emphasis is on the fact that the aggressive, warlike nature of imperialism has not changed, and that " American imperialism " as such—not only, as stated in 1957, " the aggressive imperialist *circles* of the United States "—has become the " main centre of world reaction, the international gendarme, the enemy of the peoples of the whole world." While condemning " the American doctrine of the Cold War," the document thus defines coexistence in rigid Cold War terms.

The declaration allots to the " peace campaign " pride of place as likely to unite the broadest possible fronts under Communist leadership, and rejects the " slander " that the Communists need war for extending their sway or believe in " exporting revolution." But it also calls for the most determined international support, both by the mass movement and by " the power of the Socialist world system," of revolutionary movements anywhere against " the imperialist export of counter-revolution." The statement that " the Socialist states . . . have become an international force exerting a powerful influence on world developments. Hence real possibilities have appeared to settle the major problems of our age in a new manner, in the interest of peace, democracy and Socialism . . . " assumes a special meaning in this context: for the first time since Stalin's victory over Trotsky, active support for international revolution is proclaimed as an obligation of the Soviet Government and all other Communist governments. But the crucial question of whether that obligation includes the risk of war, of whether " peaceful coexistence " or " revolutionary solidarity " is to receive priority in case of conflict, is not settled explicitly—for the possibility of conflict between the two principles is not admitted.

On the question of violent or peaceful roads to power; the view of the Russians and of the 1957 declaration that both may be used according to circumstances is clearly upheld. Equally " broadminded " are the declaration's new directives for the policy of the Communists in underdeveloped countries towards their " national bourgeoisie "— *i.e.*, toward the nationalist, neutralist and non-Communist, though in fact hardly ever bourgeois régimes that have emerged from the struggle for

national independence. The Communists are advised to aim at " national
democratic " régimes, defined by their willingness to support the Soviet
bloc against the " imperialists," to create the preconditions of progressive
internal development by land reform, and to grant full freedom for the
activity of the Communist Party and of Communist-controlled " mass
organisations." They are told that those sections of the " national
bourgeoisie " which oppose land reform and suppress the Communists,
having taken a reactionary turn at home, will sooner or later also side
with imperialism abroad. But again, the crucial question of a nationalist
dictatorship that is willing to take Soviet aid and to vote anti-Western
in the U.N., but gaols its own Communists, is shirked; nor is there any
clear indication of who is to interpret the ambiguous directives in case
of conflict.

IDEOLOGICAL AUTHORITY

Thus matters come back to the ultimate issue of ideological authority
—of the right to interpret ambiguous principles in a changing situation.
Here, the Soviets score a clear but very limited victory : they emerge as
the most successful, but not as the only orthodox interpreters of the
true doctrine. The Soviet Union is hailed as the only country that,
having completed " Socialist construction," is engaged in building the
" higher stage " of Communism; the Chinese communes are not even
mentioned, and the Soviet argument that Communist abundance is not
possible short of the highest level of technical productivity, including
automation, is hammered home. The CPSU is unanimously declared
to be " the universally recognised vanguard of the world Communist
movement," and its superior experience in conquering power and transforming society is stated to have fundamental lessons for all parties; the
decisions of its Twentieth Congress in particular are said to have opened
a new era for the whole international movement. But that new era now
turns out to be an era of polycentric autonomy—just as the bolder spirits
thought at the time.

For under the new declaration, the spiritual authority of the CPSU
is not incarnated in the shape which all doctrinaire authority, and
certainly all authority in the Bolshevik tradition, requires by its nature—
the shape of hierarchical discipline. It is not only that the declaration
repeats the ancient pious formula about the independence and equality
of all Communist parties; it is that it fails to establish a visible, single
centre for their dependence. It provides for irregular conferences, whether
world-wide or regional, for mutual co-ordination, and for bipartite consultations betwen any two parties in case of differences. This may be
intended to rule out the circulation of Chinese attacks on CPSU policy
to third parties before they have raised the matter in Moscow directly;

but it does not, on the face of it, prevent them from broadening the discussion again the next time they fail to get satisfaction in their direct contact with the " vanguard of the world movement." Clearly, the primacy of that vanguard is no longer that of an infallible Pope: the rule of *Moscow locuta, causa finita* is valid no more. For the first time in its forty years of history, international Communism is entering a " conciliary " period.

One phase of open ideological controversy between Moscow and Peking has thus ended. The Chinese have withdrawn their open challenge to the Marxist-Leninist orthodoxy of the Soviet Communists, but not before they had extracted from it as much advantage for their foreign policy as they could hope to gain without risking an open breach. The underlying differences of interest and viewpoint remain, though their public expression will now be muted for some time. But the phase that has now closed has not only had a considerable immediate impact on Soviet foreign policy; it is bound to produce lasting changes in the constellation of factors shaping that policy, in Soviet-Chinese relations, and in relations within the Communist world movement.

A measure of the immediate effect is the uncertainty of direction shown by Soviet diplomacy from the wrecking of the summit conference in May to the end of 1960. Having set out to induce the U.S., by a mixture of pressure and courtship, to abandon some exposed positions and allies for the sake of a temporary understanding with their chief antagonist, the Kremlin did not indeed abandon that objective, but wavered visibly between it and the Chinese objective of isolating the U.S. as the one irreconcilable enemy. The oscillations were too fast, the conciliatory gestures too half-hearted, and the brinkmanship too risky to be explained merely as the conscious use of zig-zag tactics to " soften up " the opponent; even if the Soviets intended all the time to reserve the next serious offer of relaxation for the next American President, a cool calculation of diplomatic expediency would hardly have led them to commit themselves in the meantime to the point to which they have gone over, say, Laos or Cuba. By depriving them of the power automatically to subordinate all revolutionary movements everywhere to Soviet diplomatic needs, the Chinese forced Stalin's successors to compete for authority over those movements by playing up to them to some extent; and this meant that, while failing to impose on the Kremlin a policy made in Peking, the Chinese forced it to deviate from its own concepts to a significant extent.

Nor have they lost this power of interference as a result of the Moscow conference. True, they have failed to establish a power of veto over Soviet diplomacy in general and Soviet-American contacts in particular, as would have been the case if the Chinese theses of an unconditional priority of revolution over peace and of the hopelessness of any serious disarmament agreement with the "imperialists" had been adopted. There is nothing in the Moscow declaration that would make it *impossible* for the Soviets still to agree with the Western powers on a permanent ban on nuclear test explosions with proper guarantees of inspection, hence on an attempt to close the "atomic club." But there is much in it that will enable the Chinese to make it more difficult, and generally to raise suspicion against any direct Russo-American talks, and nothing that specifically endorses Mr. Khrushchev's methods of personal diplomacy, from his pursuit of summit meetings to his proposals for "reforming" the United Nations. In fact, if the text of the declaration is viewed in the context of the events leading up to it, it suggests that the Soviet Communist Party was only able to win on the controversial questions of principle by silently disavowing some of the more spectacular actions of its leader, and that the latter has emerged from the fight with his personal prestige noticeably impaired.

The declaration's approval of the "general line" of peaceful co-existence and of the aim to eliminate world war in our time permits the Soviets to go on pursuing their strategy of using both negotiation and violence short of world war as means to gain their ends; but it is not enough to assure them of tactical freedom to decide, in the light of their own interests alone, when and how far to use one or the other. To regain that freedom of manoeuvre, the Soviets would have either needed a plain and brutal statement that local revolutions may in certain circum-stances have to be subordinated to the interest of preserving world peace and thus protecting the achievements of "Socialist construction" against a nuclear holocaust; or they would have required an equally plain recognition of their right to act as the only legitimate interpreters of revolutionary doctrine for the world movement, and to enforce the strategic and tactical consequences of their interpretation by means of centralised discipline. But either way of ensuring Soviet primacy, so natural in the Stalinist age when the Soviet Union alone was "the fatherland of all toilers," proved impossible in the post-Stalinist age of "the Socialist World System" proclaimed by Khrushchev himself.

On one side the doctrine that "the dictatorship of the proletariat has become an international factor," first announced in Russia by M. A. Suslov and now substantially incorporated in the declaration, amounts to a partial repeal of Stalin's "Socialism in a single country": it does not, of course, deny what was achieved under the latter slogan, but it restores, in the new world situation, the idea of a duty of the Communist powers to aid the progress of world revolution for which Trotsky fought. Even if this principle of solidarity is not formulated as an absolute and unlimited obligation, it is enough to expose Soviet diplomacy to constant pressure to take bolder risks—pressure of the kind which the Chinese mobilised effectively during the past year, and are free to use again.

POLYCENTRIC COMMUNISM

On the other hand, the declaration's recognition of the Soviet Communist Party as the " vanguard " of the world movement falls far short of establishing a permanent and unchallengeable doctrinaire authority, let alone a single centre endowed with disciplinary powers. It even falls far short of the position conceded to the Soviet Union and the Soviet Communist Party at the time of the 1957 Moscow declaration—on Mao Tse-tung's initiative. Then, the Soviet Union was consistently described as being " at the head of the Socialist camp," and Mao publicly went out of his way to speak of the need for a single leader both among Communist states and parties, and to insist that only the Russians could fill both roles.

Now, the Chinese talk quite openly and naturally about the special responsibilities of " the two great Socialist powers," the Soviet Union and China; and in the declaration itself, the vanguard role of the Soviet party is balanced in part by the recognition of the " enormous influence " exerted by the Chinese revolution on the peoples of Asia, Africa and Latin America by its encouraging example to all movements of national liberation. In 1957, the failure to found a new formal international organisation only increased the influence of the large international liaison machinery developed within the secretariat of the central committee of the CPSU, compared with which all bilateral and regional contacts were bound to be of subordinate importance. Now, the failure formally to establish a single centre legitimates the *de facto* existence of two centres in Moscow and Peking, both with world-wide links and without any agreed division of labour, which will continue to cooperate on the basis of the declaration but also to give different advice on the questions it has left open and to compete for influence. And if Moscow is still the stronger power and the older authority, Peking is closer in its type of revolutionary experience and the emotional roots of its anti-colonialist ardour to those parts of the world where the chances of Communist revolution are most promising.

In a long-range view, the relative victory of the Soviets in the 1960 phase of the dispute thus appears less important than the fact that this phase has marked a new stage in their abdication of their former position of exclusive leadership. The reports that the Soviets themselves expressed during the Moscow conference a wish that they should no longer be described as being " at the head of the Socialist camp " may well be true : finding themselves unable any longer to exert effective control over the whole world movement, they may have preferred not to be held responsible for all its actions by their enemies. In a *bloc* containing two great powers, in an international movement based on two great revolutions, such a development was indeed to be expected as soon as important differences appeared between them. But while the two protagonists remain as determined to continue to co-operate as they are unable to settle their disagreements, the result is not a two-headed movement with neatly separated geographic spheres of control, but a truly polycentric one: many Communist parties outside the Soviet *bloc* may in future be able to gain increased tactical independence, based on their freedom of taking aid and advice from both Moscow and Peking, simultaneously or alternately—with all the risks that implies for the future unity of its doctrine and strategy.

The victory of Communism in China, and the subsequent growth of Communist China into a great power, thus appears in retrospect as the beginning of the end of the single-centred Communist movement that Lenin created, and the single-centred Soviet *bloc* that Stalin built. The process took a decisive step forward in 1956, when the Twentieth Congress of the CPSU recognised the existence of a " Socialist world system " and of different roads to power, and when the destruction of the Stalin cult inflicted an irreparable blow on the type of Soviet authority that had depended on the infallibility of the " father of nations." Mao's victory had killed the uniqueness of the Soviet Union; Khrushchev's speech buried the myth built around that uniqueness.

It was at that moment that the spectre of " polycentric Communism " first appeared. But when destalinisation was quickly followed by the crisis of Russia's East European empire, the façade of single-centred unity was restored in the following year with the help of China's prestige and Mao's authority. Now that China herself has brought back the spectre she helped to exorcise three years ago, the process is no longer reversible. This time, polycentric Communism has come to stay.

China and the Bomb—
Chinese Nuclear Strategy*

By MORTON H. HALPERIN

THE detonation of a nuclear device by the People's Republic of China on October 16, 1964, made it unmistakably clear that China attached a very high priority to becoming a militarily effective nuclear power as soon as possible. Although the effect on Chinese economic development has probably been relatively limited thus far, the Chinese are devoting substantial resources to their nuclear programme and may be expected to have militarily effective systems within this decade. The Chinese appear to be considerably further along in the development of nuclear weapons and delivery systems than had been previously anticipated.

Analysis by the American Atomic Energy Commission has indicated that the Chinese employed uranium and not, as had been expected, plutonium in the first test device. This indicates that the Chinese almost certainly have an operating gaseous diffusion plant for the production of weapons-grade uranium 235. The French gaseous diffusion plant, which is just about to produce its first fissional material, is estimated to cost approximately one billion dollars. This contrasts with the cost of a nuclear reactor which for an industrialised country is in the order of $50 million for a reactor capable of producing about one weapon per year. The Chinese costs may be expected to be two or three times greater. The Chinese appear to have not only the diffusion plant but two reactors producing weapons-grade plutonium. Given the combined resources of the diffusion plant and the two reactors (whose efficiency can be significantly upgraded by the use of some weapons-grade uranium), the Chinese may well be able to produce in considerable excess of the one to two bombs per year previously estimated and are very likely

* This article draws on material prepared for the Council on Foreign Relations Project, " The United States and China in World Affairs." I am grateful to Robert Blum, Director of the China Project, for support of my research and for permission to use the material. I am also grateful to the Center for International Affairs and the East Asian Research Center, Harvard University for support of my research. Many of the points made here are discussed in greater detail and documentation in my forthcoming book *China and the Bomb*, to be published by Praeger.

in a position to be able to detonate one or more additional devices in
the very near future. The exact extent of the rate at which they will be
able to stockpile fissional material is impossible to estimate in the
absence of more precise data on the size of the diffusion plant. With
the available enriched uranium, the Chinese are undoubtedly devoting
significant attention to developing fusion weapons and may be able
to detonate a fusion device (hydrogen bomb) in the very near future.
The emphasis given to the manufacture of a diffusion plant much earlier
in the development of nuclear weapons than done by any other state
suggests that the Chinese attach very high priority to the development
of fusion weapons, presumably for use in a counter-population as
opposed to a tactical military role.

The Chinese are undoubtedly aware of the importance of developing
adequate delivery systems and appear, according to a number of recent
reports, to be attaching very high priority to the development of medium-
range ballistic missiles. The Chinese may well be able to test a short-
range surface to surface missile in the very near future and can now
be expected to have a medium-range missile capability sometime before
the end of the decade and perhaps within three years. For the
immediate future the Chinese should be able to convert the small
number of TU-4 planes which they have to hold fission devices with an
explosive power of approximately twenty kilotons. Such planes would
be vulnerable both to destruction on the ground and to destruction by air
defence systems but would at least pose some threat to nearby Asian
cities.

In addition to the cost in economic resources, which can be expected
to grow steadily once the Chinese begin relatively large-scale production
of fissionable material and delivery systems, the Chinese commitment
in terms of scientific and technical manpower appears to be very heavy.
There is little public information available about the structure of the
Chinese nuclear missile programmes but some things can be inferred.
The nuclear programme appears to be under the control of Wang Kan-
chang, who was trained in the West, and the missile programme under
the direction of Chien Hsueh-shen, who has worked on American rocket
programmes and who returned to China in 1955. The nuclear programme
is undoubtedly staffed by scientists trained at the Joint Research Institute
in Dubna in the Soviet Union, at which some 950 Chinese scientists
have trained.

This major commitment makes clear that China attaches a very high
priority to becoming a militarily effective nuclear power. Peking has
indicated not only in the statement issued by NCNA at the time of the
detonation, but also previously, what motivations lay behind China's
effort to enter the nuclear club. The Chinese desire for a national nuclear

capability stems fundamentally from the aspiration to make China a great power, the pressure to admit China to the United Nations and otherwise to acknowledge China's great power status. More specifically these motivations may be summarised as follows: (1) the desire for a more credible deterrent against an American attack; (2) the desire for increased influence within the Communist world; (3) the desire for additional means of supporting wars of national liberation, and (4) the desire for additional means for establishing Chinese hegemony in Asia.

DETERRING AN AMERICAN ATTACK

The statement issued by NCNA announced the Chinese detonation and went on to state:

> This is a major achievement of the Chinese people in their struggle to increase their national defence capability and oppose the United States imperialist policy of nuclear blackmail and nuclear threats.
>
> To defend oneself is the inalienable right of every sovereign state. And to safeguard world peace is the common task of all peace-loving countries.
>
> China cannot remain idle and do nothing in the face of the ever-increasing nuclear threat posed by the United States. China is forced to conduct nuclear tests and develop nuclear weapons. . . .
>
> The development of nuclear weapons by China is for defence and for protecting the Chinese people from the danger of the United States' launching a nuclear war.[1]

The Chinese have consistently made the argument that the more Socialist countries that have nuclear weapons the more successful is deterrence likely to be—an argument analogous to that advanced by certain groups in Britain and France.[2]

The theme of the need for more than one Socialist country to have nuclear weapons in order to deter the United States was expressed in a *People's Daily* editorial on August 9, 1962. The editorial noted that China has consistently opposed nuclear tests and favoured the banning of nuclear weapons, but it continued:

> We hold, however, that when imperialism is stubbornly hindering and opposing agreement on the suspension of nuclear tests and the prohibition of nuclear weapons and is using such weapons to threaten the people of the world, the Socialist countries, to ensure the security of the Socialist camp and defend world peace, naturally must possess nuclear weapons, and moreover, nuclear weapons of better quality than those of U.S. imperialism.
>
> The Socialist countries love peace; nuclear weapons in their hands and nuclear tests conducted by them are entirely different in nature from

[1] NCNA Statement, text in *New York Times*, October 17, 1964, p. 10.
[2] The Chinese have sometimes argued that any increase in the number of countries possessing nuclear weapons was desirable. See, for example, Ch'en Yi's interview with Reuter's manager, Walton Cole, October 5, 1961.

nuclear weapons in the hands of the imperialist bloc and nuclear tests conducted by that bloc. The possession of nuclear weapons and the carrying out of nuclear tests by the Socialist countries can only be a telling blow against the imperialist policy of the nuclear arms drive and nuclear blackmail and therefore helps to prevent war; it will help force imperialism to accept some kind of agreement on the discontinuance of nuclear testing and the prohibition of nuclear weapons and so will help the cause of world peace.[3]

The Chinese position on the value of a number of Socialist national nuclear forces, while recognising the danger of the spread of nuclear weapons, particularly to Germany, was discussed in detail in the Chinese statement of August 15:

In fighting imperialism and aggression and defending its security, every Socialist country has to rely in the first place on its own defence capability, and then—and only then—on assistance from fraternal countries and the people of the world. For the Soviet statement to describe all the Socialist countries as depending on the nuclear weapons of the Soviet Union for their survival is to strike an out-and-out great-power chauvinistic note and to fly in the face of the facts.

The Chinese Government has always fully appreciated the importance of the Soviet Union's possession of nuclear weapons. However, such possession must in no way be made a justification for preventing other Socialist countries from increasing their own defence capabilities. . . . If the Soviet Government is earnest about abiding by the Moscow Statement and really wants to fight the imperialist policies of aggression and war and to defend world peace, there is no reason why it should try so hard to obstruct other Socialist countries from increasing their defence capabilities.[4]

The Chinese argument presented here is simply that the more Socialist countries that have nuclear weapons the better because it increases the general strength of the Socialist camp and because it increases deterrence by making more credible in the eyes of the United States the likelihood of a nuclear response. This is a position that would suggest not that nuclear weapons are necessary for China because of any breakdown in the Sino-Soviet alliance, but merely because they add to the overall strength and credibility of bloc deterrence. However, the Chinese have gone beyond this to argue not only that the Russians have tried to use their nuclear dominance to control the Socialist camp, but also that the Russians have not put nuclear weapons at the disposal of the other Socialist countries during crises or cast a protective umbrella over wars of national liberation when they should. In addition, the Chinese have suggested that since the aim

[3] *Jen-min Jih-pao* (*People's Daily*), August 9, 1962, abridged translation in *Peking Review*, No. 33, 1962.

[4] " Statement by the Spokesman of the Chinese Government—A Comment on the Soviet Government Statement of August 3," August 15, 1963, translated in *Peking Review*, No. 33, 1963.

of the test-ban agreement is apparently a détente with the West, in the future the Russians are even less likely to be willing to use their nuclear strength to promote the aims of other Socialist countries and to protect them against American nuclear threats. In the absence of Soviet support, the Chinese are likely to seek to deter the United States by making nuclear retaliatory threats directed at Asian countries. In order to accomplish this, they appear to be developing an intermediate-range missile force which could be targeted on Asian cities. The Chinese could expect such a capability to serve as a powerful deterrent against an American attack on China as the result of the expansion of a Sino-American conflict on the Chinese periphery.

INFLUENCE WITHIN THE COMMUNIST BLOC

In their detonation statement the Chinese leaders made only passing reference to their dispute with the Soviet Union and the need for China to develop nuclear capability in order to combat Soviet influence in the international Communist movement. They remarked simply that the test ban " tried to consolidate the nuclear monopoly held by the three nuclear powers and tie up the hands and feet of all peace-loving countries. . . ."

Long before the Chinese were prepared to discuss conflicts within the Communist bloc over nuclear strategy, they discussed this issue in the guise of considering the contradictions arising within NATO over nuclear strategy. For example, in February of 1963 a Chinese commentator in an article entitled " Imperialist Contradictions Around the Question of Great Nuclear-Power Status " declared:

> A country which has fine delivery vehicles (long-range missiles and guided missiles) and a large quantity of nuclear bombs of great variety is a super state, and only a super state is qualified to lead the world and to control and direct those countries which do not have nuclear weapons or have only a small number of nuclear weapons without fine delivery vehicles.[5]

This article went on to explain how the United States desired to control Europe, the United Kingdom desired to control France and France desired to control West Germany. It concluded:

> Today, the United States is attempting to assert its leadership and impose the second-class nation status on the imperialist countries of Western Europe. That is why this sharp contradiction has developed to such an unprecedented degree. . . .
> All these are indications that France will not give up its own independent nuclear force and deprive itself of the great nuclear-power

5 Ouyang Hsing, " Imperialist Contradictions Around the Question of Great Nuclear-Power Status," *Chinese Youth*, Nos. 3–4, February 10, 1963. Translation in *Selections from China Mainland Magazines* (SCMM) (Hong Kong: U.S. Consulate-General) No. 355, p. 18.

status, to the point of handing over the military security and political future of its own and those of the Common Market as a whole to U.S. control.[6]

Through the early months of 1963 the Chinese press, radio and NCNA released a series of articles highlighting the growing stresses and strains in the NATO Alliance over the question of national nuclear forces. The broadcasts expressed sympathy for the French position and described the multilateral force as a crude attempt by the United States to continue its control over the countries of the NATO Alliance by being the only power to control nuclear weapons. While prior to the heating up of the controversy at the time of the test-ban negotiations in June the Chinese never drew the relevant analogies for their own situation, it was clear that this was the implication of their remarks.[7]

This allusion to the situation in Europe, and in particular the French opposition to American nuclear policy, continued after the signing of the test ban. For example, NCNA reported on July 24, 1963, that French newspapers and news agencies had all expressed their strong opposition to the U.S. intention to bar France from developing its independent nuclear force and to weaken France's resistance to American efforts to control its allies by means of nuclear superiority. According to NCNA the French papers maintained that the United States tried to use the possibility of an agreement on the test ban to attain its aims but they pointed out that France had made it clear that it would never be bound by the test-ban agreement.[8] Thus the Chinese have sought by analogy to make their case for the need for a Chinese nuclear capability by stressing the French need for such a force and the American attempt to dominate its alliance by being the sole Western nuclear power.[9]

The Chinese have made it clear that their presentation of the discussion about contradictions within the NATO Alliance applies equally to Sino-Soviet differences. There have been veiled suggestions in the Sino-Soviet polemics that the Chinese have resisted Soviet proposals

[6] *Ibid.*

[7] Among the large number of programmes and despatches that might be cited, see, for example, Peking Home Service broadcast, January 8, 1963 (printed in BBC *Summary of World Broadasts* (*SWB*), FE/1145/A1/2); and NCNA despatch from London of January 10, 1963 (printed in *SWB*, FE/1147/A1/1); and a Peking Home Service broadcast, February 21, 1963 (printed in *SWB*, FE/1183/A1/2). See also Yang Chunfong, " A Nuclear Force Without a Name," *Peking Review*, No. 24, 1963.

[8] NCNA despatch broadcast, July 24, 1963, and on the Peking Home Service (printed in *SWB*, FE/1310/A1/1).

[9] However, the Chinese have also been influenced by the great difficulties that the French have encountered in developing their own national nuclear force. In a sense the quoting of the French experience highlights the difficulties in resisting these pressures as well as the analogous existence of the pressures in the Western camp. For an analysis of the French nuclear programme, see Ciro Elliott Zoppo, " France as a Nuclear Power," in R. N. Rosecrance (ed.), *The Dispersion of Nuclear Weapons: Strategy and Politics* (New York: Columbia University Press, forthcoming).

for co-operation in the nuclear military field which presumably would involve the stationing of Soviet nuclear forces on Chinese territory under Soviet control. For example, the Chinese have charged that " in 1958 the leadership of CPSU put forward unreasonable demands designed to bring China under Soviet military control. These unreasonable demands were rightly and firmly rejected by the Chinese Government." [10] The Chinese statement goes on to declare that soon after this the Russians tore up the alleged agreement to provide China with information on new technology. Details of the Sino-Soviet disagreement on this point have not yet been made clear in the Sino-Soviet polemics but they at least suggest, in light of the great attention given by the Chinese to the French-U.S. situation, that some sort of analogous debate has taken place.

The Chinese have accused the Russians of desiring not only to control all the nuclear weapons within the Communist camp but also as a consequence to have a monopoly of the right to speak on questions of nuclear weapons and nuclear policy for the Socialist camp.[11]

The Peking régime has clearly concluded that in order to have equal influence with the Soviet Union within the Socialist camp, China will have to develop an indigenous nuclear capability. It has concluded from Soviet pressure to prevent the Chinese development of such a capability, as well as the corresponding efforts by the United States to halt diffusion within the capitalist camp, that in fact nuclear weapons are an important source of intra-alliance power. Peking's influence within the international Communist movement may be expected to rise because of China's nuclear detonation and the fall of Khrushchev. The Asian parties are likely to be even more firmly drawn into the Chinese camp and more Communist Parties may move into a neutral position seeking to end the rift.

SUPPORTING WARS OF NATIONAL LIBERATION

Closely related to the Chinese desire for nuclear weapons to increase their influence within the Communist camp is their feeling that the nuclear power of the Soviet Union has not been used adequately in the support of wars of national liberation. This theme emerges quite clearly in the Chinese detonation statement:

> The Chinese people firmly support the struggles for liberation waged by all oppressed nations and the people of the world. We are convinced

---

10 " The Origin and Development of the Differences Between the Leadership of the CPSU and Ourselves, Comment on the Open Letter of the Central Committee of the CPSU," *People's Daily*, September 6, 1963. Translation in pamphlet (Peking: Foreign Languages Press, 1963), p. 26.

11 " Statement by the Spokesman of the Chinese Government—a Comment on the Soviet Government's Statement of August 3," August 15, 1963, translated in *Peking Review*, No. 33, 1963.

that, by relying on their own struggles and also through mutual aid, the peoples of the world will certainly win victory.

The mastering of the nuclear weapons by China is a great encouragement to the revolutionary peoples of the world in their struggles and a great contribution to the cause of defending world peace. . . .

The Chinese do not believe that nuclear weapons can be used directly in wars of national liberation. In fact, they argue to the contrary that neither the imperialist countries nor those engaged in a war of liberation can use nuclear weapons. The way in which the war is fought, including the intermingling of forces of both sides, makes the use of such weapons inappropriate.[12] In fact this is the area in which the Chinese believe that it is the loyalty of men that is important and not the particular weapons system. Nevertheless, the Chinese believe that the Russians are unwilling to support wars of national liberation and hence the Chinese must assume this role and can assume it more effectively if they are a nuclear power.

The Chinese accuse the Russians of believing that " a single spark from a war of national liberation or from a revolutionary people's war will lead to a world conflagration destroying the whole of mankind." [13] On the contrary the Chinese argue that Communist régimes can only be established with the use of violence and that the Russians are in fact greatly overestimating the danger that any war of national liberation or Soviet intervention in a local war will lead to general nuclear war. They argue that the pressures against such a war are very great and that the Russians are being cowardly in retreating in the face of Western pressure.

Chinese Hegemony in Asia

A fourth Chinese motive for acquiring nuclear weapons, but one about which the Chinese are most reluctant to talk, is the feeling that it would increase the Chinese ability to establish their hegemony in Asia. As Chinese actions in the aftermath of their nuclear detonation suggest, Peking is unlikely to try to resort to explicit forms of nuclear blackmail or nuclear threats to expand the area of Chinese influence in the Far East. Rather, the Chinese will try by their nuclear detonation and their developing nuclear capability to remind the countries of Asia of the presence on their borders of a major military power with whom they

---

[12] " Two Different Lines on the Question of War and Peace, Comment on the Open Letter of the Central Committee of the CPSU," *People's Daily*, November 19, 1963. Translation in pamphlet (Peking: Foreign Languages Press, 1963), p. 27.

[13] " A Proposal Concerning the General Line of the International Communist Movement. The Letter of the Central Committee of the Communist Party of China in Reply to the Letter of the Central Committee of the Communist Party of the Soviet Union of March 30, 1963," June 14, 1963. Translation in pamphlet (Peking: Foreign Languages Press, 1963), pp. 31–32.

will have to come to terms. The Chinese recognise that being the only Asian nuclear power substantially increases their prestige among Asian elites and will strengthen the argument of those, such as Prince Sihanouk of Cambodia and General Ne Win of Burma who feel that small countries in Asia must make their peace with Peking.

The Chinese are unlikely to see their development of nuclear weapons as opening up wholly new possibilities for expanding Chinese influence in Asia, rather, it will simply reinforce Chinese conventional military power and Chinese ability to support wars of national liberation in enabling the Peking régime to make an implicit threat of military action against her neighbours while relying on political moves to bring these countries into the Chinese orbit. There would seem to be no situation in which the actual employment of nuclear weapons would be contemplated by the Chinese or would, in fact, be useful in expanding Chinese influence.

THE DANGERS TO CHINA OF A NUCLEAR DETONATION

In its detonation statement, Peking made it quite clear that it was sensitive to and would try to deal with the two problems created by a Chinese detonation and the attempt by China to become a nuclear power. The first of these problems involves the widespread opposition in the world to further testing of nuclear weapons; the second stems from the fear that the United States (or perhaps even the Soviet Union) might use the excuse of a Chinese detonation to launch an attack against China perhaps restricted to Chinese nuclear facilities.

In dealing with the first problem, the Chinese statement fell back on essentially the same position as the Chinese had adopted at the time of the signing of the test-ban treaty. The statement declared:

> The Chinese Government has consistently advocated the complete prohibition and thorough destruction of nuclear weapons. Should this have been realised, China need not have developed the nuclear weapon. But this position of ours has met the stubborn resistance of the United States imperialists.
>
> The Chinese Government pointed out long ago that the treaty on the partial halting of nuclear tests signed by the United States, Britain and the Soviet Union in Moscow in July, 1963, was a big fraud to fool the people of the world. . . .
>
> The Chinese Government hereby formally proposes to the governments of the world that a summit conference of all the countries of the world be convened to discuss the question of the complete prohibition and thorough destruction of nuclear weapons, and that, as a first step, the summit conference should reach an agreement to the effect that the nuclear powers and those countries which will soon become nuclear powers undertake not to use nuclear weapons, neither to use them against non-nuclear countries and nuclear-free zones, nor against each other.

If those countries in possession of huge quantities of nuclear weapons are not even willing to undertake not to use them, how can those countries not yet in possession of them be expected to believe in their sincerity for peace and not to adopt possible and necessary defensive measures?

The Chinese Government will, as always, exert every effort to promote the realisation of the noble aim of the complete prohibition and thorough destruction of nuclear weapons through international consultations. . . .

We are convinced that nuclear weapons, which are after all created by man, certainly will be eliminated by man.

Peking has sought to justify its refusal to sign the test-ban treaty on the grounds that the treaty is simply an effort by the current nuclear powers to maintain their nuclear domination. The Chinese have argued that they would be prepared to forgo the testing of nuclear weapons provided there was agreement on the complete prohibition and destruction of nuclear weapons. The assertion of this position by the Chinese is in contrast to the general line that they have taken with the Russians that it is wrong to stress the desirability or the possibility of disarmament and that disarmament is in fact impossible until imperialism and capitalism are abolished. Nevertheless the Chinese recognition of the widespread support for the nuclear test-ban treaty led them, both after the signing of the test-ban agreement and after their detonation of a nuclear device, to issue a call for total nuclear disarmament and to propose a summit conference of all the nations of the world to discuss nuclear disarmament.[14] During his trip through Africa in the summer of 1964, Chou En-lai was repeatedly to explain the Chinese opposition to the test-ban treaty and did so on the basis of these Chinese statements.[15] The Chinese probably anticipate similar attacks at the Afro-Asian Conference next year and may be expected again to emphasise their desire for total nuclear disarmament.

The Chinese appear to have been relatively successful in reducing the immediate adverse impact of their first nuclear test. While only Cambodia (and less officially Indonesia) issued statements welcoming the test and viewing it as a step toward world peace, very few countries were willing to condemn the test. Despite their opposition to the Chinese effort to become a nuclear power, most Afro-Asian countries

---

[14] The Chinese statements following the signing of the test-ban treaty are remarkably similar to those which they issued following their own detonation. It was clear that when they issued these statements in the summer of 1963 they were doing so partly to lay the groundwork for their justification for their own nuclear test a year later. The Chinese statements following the test ban have been reprinted in the pamphlet *People of the World, Unite, For the Complete, Thorough, Total and Resolute Prohibition and Destruction of Nuclear Weapons!* (Peking: Foreign Languages Press, 1963).

[15] See, for example, Robert A. Scalapino, " Sino-Soviet Competition in Africa," *Foreign Affairs,* July 1964, p. 643.

simply expressed their regret and stressed the importance of bringing China into the United Nations and into disarmament talks. While it does not appear likely that China will be voted into the U.N. at the 1964 session, it now appears at least possible and probably likely that the situation will change in 1965, at least in part because of the Chinese nuclear test. The failure of Indian Prime Minister Lal Bahadur Shastri to get any support for the Indian proposal, made at the recent Cairo Conference, to send a delegation to Peking to urge China not to test, underlines the caution with which most countries are going to treat the emergence of a nuclear China.

With the exception of countries allied to the United States, only India and Japan issued condemnations of the test in the immediate aftermath of the detonation. Both countries decried the test as a threat to world peace and one which would require them to re-examine their own military programmes, although in both cases the governments reaffirmed their own decisions not to become nuclear powers. The most immediate adverse effect of the Chinese detonation was in Japan where even the left wing of the Japanese Socialist Party has condemned the test. In fact a visiting delegation of the Socialist Party in Peking was forced to speak out against the test at a public banquet when the Chinese made favourable references to their effort to become a nuclear power. The Japanese Communist Party can be expected to be further isolated by its support of the Chinese nuclear testing and the Socialist Party can be expected to move further from the policy of rapprochement with China.

A theme which runs through both the Chinese efforts to counteract the adverse reaction to their position on nuclear testing as well as their desire to avoid provoking an American attack on China is their discussion of the question of not using nuclear weapons first. The NCNA statement at the time of detonation not only chided the United States for refusing to indicate that it would never use nuclear weapons first but also made such a commitment for the People's Republic of China: " The Chinese Government hereby solemnly declares that China will never at any time and under any circumstances be the first to use nuclear weapons."

Peking appears to be aware that its testing of a nuclear device, its attempt to become a nuclear power, raises the possibility that the United States (or perhaps the Soviet Union) will decide to destroy the Chinese capability to produce nuclear weapons before China has an effective deterrent against such a move. In order to deter such a possibility, the Chinese can be expected to be even more cautious in taking military action around their periphery than they have been in the past, at least until they have a nuclear delivery capability. At the same time, they will probably continue to stress in their official statements not only that they will not use nuclear weapons first but also that they understand the grave consequences which would result from a nuclear war, that they will, therefore, not be aggressive in threatening the use of nuclear weapons, and that they will strive to prevent nuclear war. All these themes were touched on in the Chinese statement:

> On the question of nuclear weapons, China will commit neither the error of adventurism nor the error of capitulationism. The Chinese people can be trusted. . . . We sincerely hope that a nuclear war would never occur. We are convinced that, so long as all peace-loving countries and people of the world make common efforts and persist in the struggle, a nuclear war can be prevented.

Particularly since the Sino-Soviet dispute has become more public and more intense, the Chinese have gone out of their way to try to counteract the Soviet attempt to portray them as nuclear warmongers who are neither aware of nor fear the destructive consequences of nuclear war. Peking recognises that to try to capitalise on the belief that the Chinese leaders were irrational and reckless would be simply to increase the strength of those in the West who are arguing for a pre-emptive move to destroy the Chinese capability. The Chinese have therefore been stating since 1961 that they understand fully the consequences of nuclear war and will do everything they can to avoid it. At the same time the Chinese argue that to overemphasise the danger of nuclear war, to continually harp on the theme of the need to avoid nuclear war, can only serve to demoralise those striving to overthrow imperialist régimes and the countries and nations which do not possess nuclear deterrent power. In their most candid statement discussing this dilemma, the Chinese declared:

> We hold that in order to mobilise the masses of the people against nuclear war and nuclear weapons it is necessary to inform them of the enormous destructiveness of these weapons. It would be patently wrong to under-estimate this destructiveness. However, U.S. imperialism is doing its utmost to disseminate dread of nuclear weapons in pursuit of its policy of nuclear blackmail. In these circumstances, while Communists should point out the destructiveness of nuclear weapons, they should counter U.S. imperialist propaganda of nuclear terror by stressing the possibility of outlawing them and preventing nuclear war; they should try and transmute the people's desire for peace into righteous indignation at the imperialist policy of nuclear threats and lead the people to struggle against the U.S. imperialist policies of aggression and war. In no circumstances must Communists act as a voluntary propagandist for the U.S. imperialist policy of nuclear blackmail. We hold that the U.S. imperialist policy of nuclear blackmail must be thoroughly exposed and that all peace-loving countries and people must be mobilised on the most extensive scale to wage an unrelenting fight against every move made by the U.S. imperialists in their plans for aggression and war. We are deeply convinced that, by relying on the united struggle of all forces defending

peace, it is possible to frustrate the U.S. imperialist policy of nuclear blackmail. This is the correct and effective policy for achieving a ban on nuclear weapons and preventing a nuclear war.[16]

For the short run the Chinese probably expect to get relatively modest gains in terms of their striving for great power status and in their competition with the Soviet Union within the international Communist movement and with the "intermediate zone" by their detonation of a nuclear device. They are also aware of the short-run costs. In the long run they undoubtedly see a nuclear capability as giving them an ability to deter an American attack and thus to assure the permanence of the Communist régime and, at the same time, laying the groundwork for a more vigorous attempt to expand Chinese influence throughout the world.

[16] "The Differences between Comrade Togliatti and Us," *People's Daily*, December 31, 1962. Translation in pamphlet (Peking: Foreign Languages Press, 1963), pp. 15–16.

Chou En-lai on Safari

By W. A. C. ADIE

CHOU EN-LAI'S recent "western expedition" to Africa [1] and the Mediterranean was Peking's greatest diplomatic effort to date outside the Communist world. Coming at a time when China had openly split from Russia and yet remained at odds with America, India, and most other countries, it marked a turning point in Peking's foreign policy and perhaps in the entire post-war structure of international relations.

When Chou En-lai intervened in the Eastern European crisis of 1956, a Chinese presence was asserted in Europe for the first time since the Mongol Yuan dynasty; it heralded Peking's assertion of ideological independence from Moscow. His latest safari renewed links with Africa and the Mediterranean forged and then broken by the Chinese Ming dynasty; it marks Peking's determination to assert its ideological supremacy over Moscow. The present situation has apparently inspired some of China's leaders to project the vision of a schismatic international and "third force"—drawn up from the nations of Africa, Asia, Latin America and even Europe (France in particular)—against the "double hegemony" of the nuclear giants who, the Chinese and de Gaulle complain, divided the world between themselves at Yalta. [2]

---

[1] Chou had planned to visit those African countries that recognised China. The disturbances in East Africa in mid-January, however, forced him to modify his plans. In the end he visited ten countries. China had already exchanged diplomatic recognition with eight of these—the United Arab Republic (May 1956), Algeria (December 1958), Morocco (November 1958), Ghana (July 1960), Mali (October 1960), Guinea (October 1959), Sudan (February 1959), and Somalia (December 1960). Chou made a special visit to Tunisia to establish diplomatic relations. But because of the revolution in Zanzibar in January (China had recognised the overthrown government in December 1963) and the mutinies in Tanganyika (recognised December 1961), Uganda (October 1962) and Kenya (whose independence celebrations had been attended by the Chinese Foreign Minister in December 1963) Chou had to cross these countries off his visiting list. However, he did manage a face-saving visit to Ethiopia.

On his seven-week tour Chou was accompanied by Marshal Ch'en Yi, the Foreign Minister, and an impressive entourage of more than fifty. It included K'ung Yuan, Deputy Director of the State Council's Office in Charge of Foreign Affairs; Huang Chen, Vice-Minister of Foreign Affairs (now Ambassador to France); Wang Yü-t'ien, Director of the West Asian and African Department of the Foreign Ministry; Kung P'eng, Director of the Information Department of the Foreign Ministry; and Liu Hsi-wen, Director of the Asian and African Department of the Ministry of Foreign Trade.

[2] "All the World's Forces Opposing U.S. Imperialism, Unite!", *People's Daily*, January 21, 1964; *Peking Review*, No. 4, 1964. In his talks with a delegation of French Deputies, Mao said, " France, Germany, Italy, Britain—if she can cease to be

Although much of Chou's activity in Africa can be explained in diplomatic terms, a strong psychological impulse towards a more revolutionary approach also appears to exist within the Chinese Communist Party. The Party leadership claims to be waging a "class struggle" in defence of Maoism (true revolutionary Marxism-Leninism) against Khrushchev's "good friends"[3] within its ranks and against the allied forces of "reaction" inside China and imperialism and revisionism in the world at large. There are indications that the Party leadership believes that these two struggles are near a "turning point."[4] Certain unfavourable developments within China and the Communist world and other favourable internal and international conditions seem to have combined to impose a policy of "daring to act, daring to win" in order to roll back the wheel of counter-revolution. Their train of thought seems to be that if the danger of what is represented as a "reactionary comeback" is to be nipped in the bud, China must find allies abroad to form the "broadest possible United Front" for a "struggle" against the "corrupting revisionist influence" of Russia and the "imperialist oppression of the United States." And according to current Chinese doctrine Africa is one of the main centres of struggle—one of the "storm centres of revolution."

Chou En-lai wound up his tour with a rousing speech in Mogadishu on February 3, on the excellent revolutionary prospects in Africa. Whatever others in China and Africa might have read into his remarks, on the surface he was talking about the prospects for revolutions of national-liberation, rather than any social revolution which could be labelled a "Communist take-over."[5] At a press conference the

America's agent—Japan and ourselves (China)—that is the third force." *L'Humanité*, February 21, 1964. Lack of space precludes discussion of this new " United Front " of China and France adumbrated by Mao and de Gaulle, an essential feature of which can already be seen to be the same sort of rivalry for influence in Africa, Latin America and Asia that had already marked the Sino-Soviet relationship; its ultimate purpose is to " transform " the other partner, by first gaining control of the " intermediate zone." On French policy see the article by J. Vernant in *Politique Etrangere*, No. 6, 1963.

[3] *People's Daily–Red Flag* editorial, March 31, 1964. *Peking Review*, No. 14, 1964.

[4] On " turning points " see *The Selected Military Writings of Mao Tse-tung*, IV (Peking: Foreign Languages Publishing House, 1963), p. 344. The passage from " The present situation and our tasks " deals with the " turning point from growth to extinction " for Chiang, after the People's Liberation Army had " turned back the wheel of counter-revolution." The poems by Mao published this January, especially the last written in January 1963, indicate that a new turning point is at hand, like when Mao crossed the Yangtse in spite of " well-meaning " advice, no doubt from the Russians. See poems and article by Kuo Mo-jo in *Red Flag*, No. 1, 1964: " Heaven and earth revolve; time presses . . . wipe out all harmful creatures until no enemy remains."

[5] The time has come when the term " Communist " has more emotive content than precise significance. The Chinese tend to use the term " Marxist-Leninists " to denote those revolutionaries of whom they approve, but such terms as " populists," or " national-socialists " would be more accurate. The veteran Comintern agent M. N. Roy has pointed out that " Communism " in Asia is essentially the nationalism and

same day he denied (and later events seem to support this) that the Zanzibar revolution, which began on January 12, was the work of " the Communists." " Is it not crediting us with others' merits to say that such incidents were caused by us?", Chou asked.

He went on to say that the United States Government:

> pursues a colonial policy of interference and adopts an arrogant attitude in an attempt to control other countries . . . [but] . . . not only the peoples cannot be held down, but even those in power in various countries sometimes find it unbearable. . . . Consequently the whole thing will burst, and this is the sorrow of U.S. imperialism.[6]

Analysts of Chinese Communist behaviour are used to seeing cases of the common psychological phenomenon by which if China is suffering economic difficulties, for example, a lot of propaganda will appear about an economic crisis in the United States. Chou is undoubtedly stating the sober truth about certain unpopular régimes, but his wish to think that the " whole thing will burst " is perhaps strengthened by a feeling that relations between those in power in China and the masses are not good enough either. As the *People's Daily* put it, " sometimes barriers exist between the leadership and the masses." [7] The intensity of the present campaign to maintain discipline, revolutionary *élan* and " class struggle," which in its new form exalts the Army for learning and creatively developing the thought of Mao Tse-tung, must indicate to experienced observers that something unusual is brewing. A shortish article entitled " The whole country must learn from the Liberation Army," published in the *People's Daily* on February 1, mentioned Mao's name twenty-five times. Since then the paper has been full of pictures of soldiers—one shows the model warrior Kuo Hsing-fu studying Mao's works, with the caption " The Source of Strength." On the international news page there are pictures of guerillas in Africa, Vietnam, etc., whose " source of strength " is also Mao.[8]

Some Chinese and Chinese-inspired statements seem to imply that *all* African governments and frontiers will eventually have to be swept away in the course of armed struggle. This provoked Suslov's charge that " After all, it is absurd to say that the working people of Algeria, Ghana, Mali and certain other countries are faced with the task of

---

racism of the educated middle class, which plays up the misery of the masses with the ambition of achieving dictatorial power. See *Radical Humanist*, January 13 and 20, 1952. This is equally true of Africa and Latin America.

6 *Peking Review*, No. 7, 1964.

7 *People's Daily*, February 7, 1964.

8 Describing Captain Kuo's methods of Socialist education, Peking Radio said on February 17 that vigorous bayonet practice was necessary to promote class hatred and show how to " eliminate our class enemy."

starting armed revolt." [9] Suslov was, of course, over-simplifying the issue; but this was the setting in which Chou had to play his diplomatic part, and woo the independent African rulers.

In Africa, Chou En-lai was embarrassed by the need, as Patrick Seale put it in the *Observer*, to wear the diplomat's topper and the guerilla's beret at the same time (his Foreign Minister, Ch'en Yi, actually wore the beret, though with a somewhat French air). His difficulties were most probably compounded by a lack of clarity and consensus among China's leaders about what China's policy towards Africa should in fact be. There is reason to believe that " socialism in one country " does have its powerful advocates in China, even though the official call to press on with revolution in the world is often heard. China faces much the same conflict between its diplomatic and revolutionary policies as Russia did in the inter-war years. It would not be surprising if some of Chou's activities in Africa were more concerned with preserving a United Front at home than with the Africa question itself. In any case, the Maoist epistemology and method of work require that China's policy towards Africa remain ambiguous and flexible. At present Peking's indeterminate " minimum programme " seems to call for a denial of Africa's resources to the West; there are hints of a " maximum programme " which would include liberation and unification of Africa by a sort of " Southern Expedition," similar to the joint Communist-Nationalist Northern Expedition to unite China in 1927,[10] and increased Chinese participation in the exploitation of Africa's mineral and agricultural resources.

THE RECONNAISSANCE

One thing, however, was certain: China needed to know much more about Africa and train more personnel before any policy could be successful. Chou was most probably telling the truth when he said that he was in Africa to " understand and learn more," and sincere in regretting that he had not been able to visit Africa sooner. A fore-warning of such reconnaissance missions as Chou's was given last October when Chou Yang called for a drive to learn more about the world

[9] Suslov's Report to the plenary meeting of the Soviet Central Committee, delivered on February 14, 1964, released April 3, 1964. *Soviet Booklets*, II, No. 3 (London: 1964).
[10] The Kenyan Minister of Home Affairs, Mr. Oginga Odinga, expressed this idea all too clearly during his visit to Peking in May 1964. He called for a general war, " I repeat, war," against the present South African régime and said, " Comrades, the war in Africa needs your help " This passage was censored by NCNA. The Chinese have recently disbursed large sums in the hope of securing a foothold in such places as Basutoland, which offer opportunities for operations against South Africa. At a Peking rally in April, Mao Tse-tung hailed the armed rising in Pondoland and predicted the outbreak of violent revolution in South Africa with great vehemence (NCNA, April 1964).

" to meet the needs of revolution." According to Mao, to learn about something is to change it, not to change one's own mind. Knowledge is knowledge of struggle. This is all very well, but it does not settle for China's leaders the issue of how they are to "change reality" in Africa—that is, what "contradictions" are they going to exploit.[11]

Until the first fact-finding mission by Liu Ch'ang-sheng's delegation to the Afro-Asian People's Solidarity Council Meeting at Conakry in June 1961, the Chinese seemed to use Africa mainly as a canvas on which to paint heroic pictures of "struggles," in order to refute the revisionists. While Liu was touring Africa a secret document on foreign policy was circulated to high ranking military officers. Africa was presented as heading in the same direction as China, but a long way behind. It held out little prospect of Africa getting beyond the stage of nationalist revolution for some years to come:

> Some places in Africa are like China at the time of the Boxer rebellion, some are at the stage of the 1911 Revolution, some at the period of the May Fourth [1919] movement. They are far from the 1949 era of [Communist control in] China. What matters now in Africa is anti-imperialism and anti-colonialism; anti-feudalism is not yet important. It is time not for social revolution but for national revolution, time for a broad United Front. In Africa there are many rightists, not many leftists in power; the rightists must lose their prestige and position; then others will come forward and carry out the national revolution. We must explain the revolution from the Taipings onwards . . . they must act for themselves, foreign assistance being secondary . . . if there were one or two among the independent countries which would effect a real nationalist revolution their influence would be great and a revolutionary wave would roll up the African continent.[12]

It is not quite clear to what extent a "real nationalist revolution" involves the beginning of a social revolution, but since 1961 the Chinese Communist Party's line seems to have become more optimistic (or rather impatient) on this score. The fact is, however, that the whole policy of developing contacts with the western countries beyond the seas "in the interests of the revolution" is ambivalent. If it leads to the collapse of existing African governments, it will appear to have always been world-wide subversion and conversion disguised as national diplomacy. But if it leads to a *détente* between China and the West,

---

11 Mao observed in *On Practice* (Peking: Foreign Languages Press, 1958), p. 8: "If you want to acquire knowledge you must take part in the practice of changing reality. If you want to know the taste of a pear, you must change the pear by eating it as food." This is reminiscent of Plekhanov's remark that Lenin " desires unity the way a man desires unity with a piece of bread."

12 *Bulletin of Activities*, No. 17, 1961. Several other articles in the *Bulletin* show China's particular interest in the Congo, and its resources: compare with the articles on Africa in *Peking Review*, No. 27, July 5, 1960, No. 2, January 10, 1964, and No. 16, April 5, 1964. I have discussed China's plans for the Congo in my article on " China and Africa Today " *Race*, April 1964.

its object will appear to have always been to establish normal diplomatic and trade relations for China under cover of Messianic slogans about world revolution. The root cause of this ambivalence is the old problem of whether China is to be identified with a single nation-state or a universal " way of life," which the present generation of leaders have not yet entirely solved.

DIPLOMATIC METHOD

From the point of view of gaining influence and not just learning in the normal sense, Chou was not in a strong position in Africa. The countries of Africa, unlike some of those in Asia, are beyond China's long shadow. Generally speaking, they are not caught in situations which would enable the Chinese to gain influence by exploiting the balance of power. The great powers would rather let Africa be independent than start a second " scramble for Africa." The African states can play China off against the United States, the Soviet Union, Britain and France. But China cannot make it worthwhile for any African state to sever its links with these countries and throw its lot in with China.[13]

In his diplomat's topper, Chou had to talk about peaceful co-existence and woo the same national bourgeois politicians that Peking criticises the Russians for favouring (such as Nasser). Throughout his trip diplomacy was stretched to the limit. De Gaulle had yet to recognise Peking, so he for one had not to be offended—especially as other countries were expected to follow his lead. To build " the United Front from above " Chou had to reassure his hosts about China's position on the nuclear test-ban treaty and the Sino-Indian border dispute —none of them supported China's policy. He had to try to win friends and pave the way for further Chinese trade missions and embassies by playing on two themes—the need for another Bandung Conference, which by implication would mark a " turning point " in the " struggle " against colonialism and neo-colonialism, and the pseudo-racialist notion that " we Afro-Asians " should get together and exclude all outside influences. There was no point in China trying to press the Africans with China's views against Yugoslavia, Russia or the United States, with which many African countries have good relations.

In the guerilla's beret, Chou was expected to prepare " the United Front from below " (as the eventual basis of China's leadership of the

[13] At present China's willingness to spend money and provide means of transport, guerilla training, propaganda media, etc., even to the most reactionary elements, has the effect of making it easier for opportunists to exploit the new cold war than the old. It forces the Russians or others to go in where otherwise they might have held back (Somalia, for instance). Then they are in, not China; but confusion increases.

" third force ") by appealing to the discontented sub-elites of Africa and by personifying the second wave of revolution, not co-existence and non-alignment. But it would have been diplomatically suicidal for Chou to have openly voiced the line that China had taken up in the dispute with Russia:

> Violent revolution is a universal law of proletarian revolution. To realise the transition to socialism, the proletariat must closely rely on the peasants, establish a broad united front based on the worker-peasant alliance and insist on proletarian leadership of the revolution.[14]

Peking had the good sense not to pull the red carpet from under Chou by publicising this line in Africa while he was there (they waited until the day after he returned home). This dilemma found expression, for those able to interpret the Maoist doubletalk, in restatements of the Chinese interpretations of terms such as " peace," " non-alignment," and the "Bandung spirit" as synonyms for struggle (especially armed struggle) against "imperialism, colonialism, and neo-colonialism." [15] In Egypt, for example, Chou spoke about "world peace" (to be achieved by struggle), and about the world being divided between "Imperialist" and "Afro-Asian' states (including China) more than about peaceful co-existence and non-alignment.

In seeking the "common ground" on which to build his broad United Front, Chou was prepared to speak at length and say as little as possible. He said that China's policy towards Africa was guided by the principles that:

1. It supports the African peoples in the fight against imperialism and old and new colonialism and for winning and safeguarding of national independence;
2. It supports the governments of African countries in their pursuance of a policy of peace, neutrality and non-alignment.
3. It supports the African peoples in their desire to realise solidarity and unity in the form of their choice;
4. It supports the African countries in their efforts to settle their differences through peaceful consultations;
5. It maintains that the sovereignty of the African countries must be respected by all other countries and that all encroachment and interference from whatever quarter should be opposed.

Unable to secure support on specific issues, Chou fell back on a series of verbal formulas acceptable to African leaders and Maoists

---

[14] *People's Daily–Red Flag* joint editorial, March 31, 1964.
[15] On the problems raised by the vague and different meanings attached to political terms see my article on "The Study of Chinese Politics" in *Political Studies*, February 1964. Such problems deserve greater attention, if later accusations of bad faith between China and the nations it deals with are to be avoided.

alike, which each side could interpret in its own way. In its editorial reviewing Chou's tour the *People's Daily* indicated the points he had been trying to work into the communiqués:

> In the communiqués issued after their talks, Premier Chou En-lai and the leaders of the African Countries agreed: In order to prevent world war, it is necessary to wage an unremitting struggle against the imperialist policies of aggression and war; the contemporary national liberation movement is an important force in defence of world peace; imperialism and old and new colonialism must be completely liquidated in Africa; Asian-African solidarity must be strengthened with the utmost effort and, in the opinion of many countries, active preparations should be made for a second Asian-African conference; disputes among Asian-African countries should be settled through peaceful negotiations on the basis of Asian-African solidarity; national economies should be developed by mainly relying on one's own strength supplemented by foreign assistance.[16]

To this extent his trip must be considered quite a success. His sometimes evasive public utterances, however, seemed stereotyped and jargon-ridden, contrasting sharply with the more thoughtful and original remarks of some of the African leaders. Politeness and genuine admiration for a great country and people also led to African praise for the Chinese rulers and some of their methods. Some of Chou's hosts have rarely had such an important guest as the Premier of China. As an individual he seems to have made a very good impression, perhaps because he did not at all fit the image of the "Chinese war maniacs" projected by Soviet propaganda.

Many readers will remember the good impression Chou made in India and at Bandung in 1955. It took some time for the mutual disillusion of India and China to turn their first excessively naïve hopes of brotherhood and "peaceful co-existence" into the present bitter hostility.[17] Most African leaders are in a better position to avoid woolly-minded hypocrisy and self-deception in dealing with China, and their realism will perhaps spare them the need for an agonising reappraisal later. Although Africa is not on China's doorstep as India is, if Peking does get an unreal picture of the situation in Africa it can cause a great deal of trouble for independent African governments by encouraging guerilla warfare, in the belief that this is really in the interests of "the masses," and they objectively want revolution.[18]

---

[16] *People's Daily*, February 6, 1964.
[17] On the euphoria of the "Hindi-Chini Bhai-bhai" period see V. B. Karnik (Ed.), *China Invades India* (Bombay: Allied publishers, 1963), p. 157ff.
[18] The Chinese contend that their minority view really represents the will of the majority, "including those whose consciousness has not yet been aroused." See *People's Daily–Red Flag* joint editorial, No. VII, February 2, 1964. This idea of retrospective justification by a future majority was denounced by Lenin in a polemic against Plekhanov and Trotsky (see Suslov, *loc. cit.*, p. 72). Such logic can only be refuted by "life itself."

THE UNITED ARAB REPUBLIC
DECEMBER 14–21

Chou En-lai's tour of Africa began at Cairo airport on December 14 with full diplomatic pomp and the flattery of a twenty-one gun salute, usually reserved for heads of state. This could not hide the fact that President Nasser was still in Tunisia conferring with President Bourguiba, most probably about what line they should take towards Chou En-lai.

Chou En-lai cannot have expected that it would be easy to win President Nasser over to the Chinese point of view. President Nasser has a much more sophisticated attitude towards Maoist double-talk than he had at Bandung. The good impression made by Chou En-lai at that time was soon dissipated by the practical development of Sino-Egyptian relations. Since the events in Iraq in 1959 Nasser has regarded the Chinese with some reserve. But he has been too successful an exponent of positive neutralism to be ignored. He has received more American and Soviet aid than any other African leader. He survived Suez and has the local Communist Party under lock and key. He has won considerable independence and his prestige is high among the non-aligned countries. Perhaps this is why Chou En-lai chose to spend a week in Egypt, the longest stay of his African tour.

As China could do nothing that would make it worthwhile for President Nasser to change his position, Chou En-lai was faced with a situation that called for his talents as a Grand Master of United Front Work. All he could hope to do was to project the image of a reasonable and peace-loving China, make the most of a few specific points of agreement in the discussions, and get some mutually acceptable (although differently interpreted) formulas written into the final communiqué. Even in this Chou faced great difficulties. President Nasser evidently preferred to keep political discussions to a polite minimum, giving his guest time to see and realise the significance of Egypt's historic monuments and the Aswan Dam, in which the Russians have invested £117 million.

Chou lost no time in enunciating the theme that China and Africa shared a history and a future of " struggle " (this was to recur throughout his tour, with reference to the ever-flowing Yangtse and an appropriate African river, where available). While seeking the basis for a United Front in other issues, Chou evidently could not abandon China's stand on the nuclear test-ban treaty or the border dispute with India. These were precisely the issues on which China needed to explain her position and gain support. (But of the countries Chou visited none supported China on these two issues.) Chou said that the three powers that drew up the test-ban treaty monopolise nuclear weapons;

China wanted a total ban on such weapons. To scotch Soviet allegations of Chinese callousness, he declared that " a large scale nuclear war would be a great disaster for all mankind." On the Colombo proposals (of which Egypt was one of the six sponsors) he took the line that China accepts them in principle as the basis for direct negotiations, and that China and India should meet to settle the border question peacefully without preconditions.

The United Front approach was especially noticeable in Chou's efforts to get support for a second Bandung Conference at the same time as Yugoslavia, India, Ceylon and Egypt were trying to organise a second Belgrade conference. Chou declared, perhaps to India's relief, that China was an aligned country and could not attend, but he raised no objection to a second Belgrade conference. He thought that if the Afro-Asian states sought common ground while retaining their differences and settled their problems without intervention by imperialism, then the second Bandung conference would be as successful as the first. But Chou got little reward for all his efforts. In the final communiqué President Nasser would only declare his willingness to " preserve " the " spirit " of Bandung.

The form of words that found their way into almost all communiqués (listed above) were given their first airing in Cairo on December 21. Slightly more specific was China's declaration of support for the people of Palestine, Yemen and Oman, and the recognition by Egypt of China's right to Formosa and a place in the United Nations.

In Egypt Chou stated, perhaps for home consumption, that " China . . . has a special destiny . . . to support countries which have not yet won victory or are about to win it." But neither President Nasser or Chou's later hosts acknowledged this self-imposed mission.

ALGERIA
DECEMBER 21–27

It was no coincidence that on the eve of Chou En-lai's arrival President Ben Bella's official newspaper, *Le Peuple,* carried a full-page interview in which Mr. Khrushchev explained that peaceful co-existence and the struggle for liberation were compatible. This was clearly aimed at undermining one of Chou's main theses—the thesis that the Algerian armed revolution was a " brilliant example " of the " correct way " for oppressed nations to win their independence. Chou's thesis may well have flattered the Algerians. Nevertheless, it became increasingly clear that having struggled to win their independence the Algerians were only interested in associating themselves with China in so far as it would enhance, not detract from, Algeria's independence and

influence. Ben Bella later said in an interview with *Jeune Afrique* that
Algeria would have to balance its policy so that the Sino-Soviet dispute
in no way affected Algeria's independence.

Chou responded with tact to Ben Bella's sensitivities. He publicly
approved of Ben Bella's highly pragmatic blend of socialism and the
way he dealt with the French. He stressed that China had no monopoly
of revolutionary truths. He even went so far as to praise the first
Belgrade conference, and added that the Bandung and Belgrade
conferences were pursuing " the same aim of consolidating peaceful
co-existence." He seemed to get on well with Ben Bella and was
allowed to address a meeting of F.L.N. cadres, which no other foreign
statesman has been invited to do.

Chou tried to develop some enthusiastic co-operation by playing on
Ben Bella's dream of liberating southern Africa. He offered China's
help in opening up roads across the Sahara. On Chou's arrival NCNA
reports lauded Algeria as one of the most important centres of African
revolutionaries in exile and mentioned the considerable support Algeria
gave these people. Some Algerian officials, however, are having
second thoughts about the wisdom of harbouring revolutionaries
ostensibly devoted to the liberation of Africa. In this connection
Ben Bella's expulsion of Jacques Vergès after the latter's visit to Peking
in 1963 may be significant. Vergès had served Ben Bella as special
adviser on African affairs and edited *Révolution Africaine* in Algiers.
His views on returning from Peking may have been too Maoist for
Ben Bella's liking. Vergès now edits the pro-Chinese *Révolution*
in Paris.[19]

Perhaps some Chinese share the feeling of some Algerians that
Algeria's closer involvement in the " struggles " of southern Africa
would create conditions for purging Algeria's bourgeois elements and
carrying the revolution a step further. Be this as it may, Ben Bella

[19] It has published material critical of the Algerian Government and its tone suggests
that most existing African régimes need to be overthrown by a second revolution like
that in Zanzibar, whose Foreign Minister " Babu " is on the magazine's editorial
board. " In no former colony is any lasting solution conceivable without completely
overturning social and economic structures "—Vergès in Vol. 1, No. 9, on " The
People's Victory in Zanzibar." Though it claims to incorporate the original
Algerian-inspired *Révolution Africaine*, Algerians say that all ties have been severed
since Vergès insisted on basing his line on Chinese and Cuban experience, rather
than on Ben Bella's ideas.

While Chou was in Algeria he had a long interview with Colonel Boumedienne,
Chief of the Army, and the Army paper *El Djeish* published a long article on the
Chinese method of " Land Reform " (controlled social revolution in an agrarian
society). On March 7 changes in the military structure of the country were
announced, which had the effect of removing control of the Army from Col.
Boumedienne and putting it directly under the President (*France Observateur*, March
12, 1964). Subsequently, Ben Bella has indicated that Soviet aid will enable him
to maintain control.

seems determined not to play the part of an African Chiang Kai-shek. In the final communiqué both sides agreed that "effective support" was needed to destroy "apartheid régimes" and "colonialism seeking a comeback," but no concrete suggestions were made. No tribute was paid to Ben Bella's efforts in this direction, although Chou En-lai later praised those of President Nkrumah.

The communiqué was hardly a diplomatic triumph for Chou En-lai. First of all Ben Bella and he could not readily agree on how "socialist" Algeria was at present. Algeria claims to be carrying out "socialist reconstruction"; Mr. Khrushchev goes so far as to say that Ben Bella is transforming Algeria "on the basis of Socialism"; after a lengthy wrangle the Chinese would only agree to the formula that Algeria had "decided to take the Socialist road." On the test question of a Bandung or a Belgrade conference, Ben Bella, a great admirer of President Tito, was only willing to "develop the spirit of Bandung." In fact what the communiqué concealed was more interesting than what it said. There was no mention of "turning points" in Afro-Asian history, no thanks for aid, no support for China's entry into the United Nations, or rights to Formosa.

Only four months later Ben Bella was receiving the full red carpet treatment in Moscow, before being made a Hero of the Soviet Union.

MOROCCO
DECEMBER 21–30

Trading interests keep Sino-Moroccan relations on an even keel where political interests alone could not. Last year Morocco's imports from China—mainly green tea—totalled $6·9 million. This was almost balanced by China's purchase of $6·3 million worth of Berliet lorries, phosphate fertilisers and cobalt, a strategic material. In fact Morocco trades with both China and Cuba despite American pressure. During Chou's visit ideology was played down—King Hassan spoke amiably of the fondness of Moroccan collectors for Chinese "crockery" (*sic*); both sides were really interested in stepping up trade.

China's support for the Moroccan opposition to the King had considerably strained diplomatic relations. For this reason and the fact that the border dispute with Algeria had led to an enstrangement between the King and Presidents Ben Bella and Nasser, the King wanted Chou En-lai's stamp of approval for his rule. Chou responded to Hassan's dignified reception like a courtier of France or of old Cathay, lavishing more fine words on the King than on any other of his hosts in Africa. In the joint communiqué:

Premier Chou En-lai praised the successes achieved by His Majesty's Government and the Moroccan people in their efforts to consolidate national independence and develop the national economy and for the evacuation of foreign military bases, as well as their support to the African peoples in their struggle for independence.

The last compliment was not paid to Ben Bella. Even so King Hassan did not respond with talk of " turning points " or support for a Bandung conference. Chou had to be satisfied with the fact that Morocco supported the restoration of China's rightful place in the United Nations.

On December 30, Chou broke his African tour as he had planned and spent several days in Albania, China's naval base in the Mediterranean. The ultra-revolutionary tone of Chou's utterances there and of the joint Sino-Albanian communiqué were in stark contrast to his reasonable African image. The gist of it all was that the victory of the world revolution, even in the industrial countries, is just round the corner, thanks to the upsurge of the " national liberation struggle " of Africa, Latin America and Asia.

TUNISIA
JANUARY 9–10

The invitation that Chou En-lai received from President Bourguiba on December 28, to visit Tunisia and establish diplomatic relations, was one of his few tangible diplomatic gains. Although Tunisia supported China's admission to the United Nations, neither side had previously expressed any interest in strengthening diplomatic relations. Under President Bourguiba, Tunisia has avoided hysterical attitudes towards the West, carried out moderate socialist reforms, and received more American aid per person than any other country in Africa. But when China set out to establish her diplomatic presence in Africa, President Bourguiba was quite prepared to exchange recognition.

President Bourguiba left Chou En-lai in no doubt that China's attitudes towards the United Nations, the use of force in the settlement of border disputes, and the test-ban treaty " have not failed to arouse doubt and concern among us." [20] According to President Bourguiba his talks with Chou En-lai were conducted " with the frankness of friendship ":

I told him what shocked us in his manner, style and conceptions. I said " You come to Africa as the enemy of the capitalist states, of the West, of the neutralists and the non-aligned, of India, of Tito, of Khrushchev, of everybody. You have not chosen an easy policy.

[20] President Bourguiba's speech at a reception in honour of Chou En-lai, B.B.C.'s *Summary of World Broadcasts*/ME/1450.

I'll say that. Don't expect to score much in Africa. Others won't tell you straight; I will—you won't get far in this continent." [21]

In the communiqué both sides expressed their satisfaction with "the sincerity and friendliness" which characterised the talks. It seemed, however, that President Bourguiba had put Chou En-lai on a very sticky wicket. Even though France had recently withdrawn from the base at Bizerta, President Bourguiba was apparently too astute to be drawn into an endorsement of that all-purpose word "struggle," and so both sides expressed "support for the African peoples that are continuing their efforts for decolonisation." This was followed by three paragraphs on the importance of peace. Tunisia had been represented at the first Bandung Conference, but Chou was unable to persuade Bourguiba to support a second. But the last sentence of the communiqué made all this worthwhile for China—it was the agreement to exchange diplomatic recognition.

GHANA
JANUARY 11–16

Premier Chou En-lai received a much more enthusiastic reception in Ghana than in North Africa. Compliments were exchanged and ideological sympathy displayed. Accra Radio said that Chou represented a group of dedicated social builders, people who had transformed a semi-dependent, semi-feudal China into a socialist society which commanded the respect of the whole world. The Ghana *Daily Graphic* greeted Chou as an "old friend, friend not only of Ghana but of the oppressed millions of the world." The communiqué, however, suggested that these sentiments, genuine though they might be, were a veneer which covered up some diplomatic knots.

At the farewell banquet President Nkrumah indicated that Chinese methods should be copied by Africa not only for the liberation of the continent but also in reconstruction:

> We have learned with interest the methods by which the people of China have mobilised their resources for the reconstruction of their country and the improvement of their living conditions . . . the example of China's determination, organisation, discipline and unity cannot be lost on Africa at this time.

In the final communiqué Chou "admired the role of Ghana and its leader in the vanguard of the national liberation movement in Africa, in promoting African solidarity and in defending world peace." (Only the unlikely combination of King Hassan of Morocco and President Nkrumah were flattered in this way.) Both parties agreed that there

[21] *Jewish Observer and Middle East Review*, April 3, 1964.

could not be lasting peace in the world without a resolute struggle against imperialism and colonialism, and said that everything should be done to get the United Nations' forces out of the Congo (after which African countries should be on their guard against neo-colonialist intrigues there).

President Nkrumah was the only one of Chou's hosts who considered an " Afro-Asian-Latin American anti-imperialist conference " desirable; and the first to voice active support for a second Bandung conference. Chou reiterated China's support for increased Afro-Asian representation in the United Nations' organisations, and reaffirmed that this question should not be linked in any way with the question of the restoration of China's rights at the United Nations, which Ghana supports. It was interesting that Ghana " objected " (not a strong diplomatic word) to any attempt to create " two Chinas." This suggested that Ghana does not insist on China's right to Formosa and might accept the idea of " one China and one Formosa."

President Nkrumah and Premier Chou En-lai clearly did not see eye to eye on several issues. According to the communiqué their " exchanges of opinions " revealed a " community " (not an " identity " or " complete identity ") of views. They definitely disagree over the nuclear test-ban treaty. Although the course of the Sino-Indian border dispute since the Colombo proposals were put forward (with Ghana as a sponsor) was discussed at length, President Nkrumah showed no willingness to change his view in China's favour.

No thanks were offered for Chinese aid as Ghana has yet seen little of the £8 million that was offered by China in 1961. On the other hand, there were no Chinese lectures on the need for self-reliance—there is a lot of foreign capital in Ghana, especially in the Volta river project.

Even President Nkrumah's Marxist sympathies have not drawn them closer together. Chou politely ignored his remark that Ghana was determined to build and sustain a Socialist society. The Chinese are just as unhappy as the Russians about " African roads to socialism," which allegedly " hamper socialist ideology and strengthen the position of bourgeois ideology." The Chinese are not consoled by Nkrumah's attempt to translate Marxism to meet the needs of Africa, just as Mao did to meet the needs of China. In his recent book *Consciencism* [22] he denied that the class struggle or revolution was needed for the transition to socialism in Africa. He believed that socialism can evolve from the traditional communalism of African society. According to the Chinese view the African version of Socialism should be worked out

[22] K. Nkrumah, *Consciencism* (London: Heinemann, 1964).

in the course of armed " struggles " such as that waged by Pierre Mulele in the Congo, just as Mao adapted Marxism-Leninism to Chinese conditions in the course of twenty years of continuous warfare.

MALI
JANUARY 16–21

Mali welcomed the Chinese envoys with exceptional enthusiasm; in his speech of welcome Modibo Keita set the tone of the visit by stressing the reasonable cost of Chinese assistance, the ease with which Chinese technicians adapted themselves to Malian life and the competence with which they worked without interfering in Mali's affairs. Special numbers of *L'Essor,* the organ of the Union Soudanaise-R.D.A., hailed the five principles of China's policy towards Africa and China's method of self-reliance; China gives us assistance, the paper said, to " strengthen our economic struggle which is another form of the struggle against imperialism." This same struggle is also helped by £28 million of Soviet and Eastern European aid and the benefits of being an associate member of the Common Market.

However, political struggle was not forgotten. NCNA reported that Mao's Fourth Volume and other works were being eagerly bought at the Chinese Economic Exhibition in Bamako, but Modibo Keita used the words " our country never shrinks from any solution for the achievement of African unity if there are *objective* conditions for its realisation " (emphasis added). Although the French once denigrated Modibo Keita as an " unrepentant Communist," he stated in a speech in December 1962 that " we are not Marxist-Leninists, Mali is searching for her own road to Socialism." [23]

If the final communiqué contains several points favourable to the Chinese which were not endorsed by other African leaders, the reason probably lies more in Modibo Keita's appreciation and expectation of Chinese economic aid than in his ideological views. The two parties, the communiqué said, exchanged views extensively on the experiences they had had in national construction and the prospects for economic development of the African and Asian countries. They held that to consolidate national independence the young countries must first and foremost count on their own forces (Chou cautioned that China's aid was " very limited "), they must rely on their own people and fully tap their own natural resources. Although it described the world scene as dominated by the national liberation struggle, the communiqué did not mention China's right to Formosa (which has

---

[23] *Horoya,* December 26, 1962. The version in Keita's own paper *L'Essor,* December 22, 1962, omits this passage.

also been giving effective aid to African countries). Unlike Sékou Touré, Keita included in his communiqué the eight points which Chou had been trying to get accepted as the principles governing Chinese aid.[24] Before getting down to such economic matters the two parties supported "the African, Asian, and Latin American peoples in their sacred struggle" (especially in South Africa) and endorsed "the idea of a second conference of the independent countries of Asia and Africa"— a weaker formula than Nkrumah's.

In exchange for Mali's enthusiasm, Chou accorded her the accolade of being "resolved to embark on the road to Socialism," like Algeria. This may mean, if anything, that Mali is considered to be a more amenable subject for "United Front" tactics than Ghana or Guinea. The Mali army was at the time engaged in operations against Touareg rebels, which would be facilitated by the trans-Saharan road Chou offered to build from Algeria.

GUINEA
JANUARY 21–26

The political case history of President Sékou Touré will undoubtedly give the Chinese plenty to think about as they work out their policy (or, like many governments, conflicting policies) towards Africa. He has been aptly described as:

> A determined and dynamic Pan-African, whose speeches and writings reveal a coherent and radical philosophy both eloquent and imaginative . . . perhaps the single most influential and significant figure on the continent for the younger, more radical African leaders. They see in his career the symbol of an African nationalism that challenged a colonial government [France] head-on and yet survived without capitulating to the dominion of the Eastern bloc.[25]

China managed to raise its political stock in Guinea by timely economic aid. When food was scarce in Guinea in 1959, after France had granted Guinea independence and cut Guinea from its economic grace, China stepped in with 15,000 tons of grain. Then in 1960 when Sékou Touré visited China he was offered an interest free loan of £9 million. China's support for Guinea was all the more acceptable after Russian diplomats were expelled from Guinea at the end of 1961 for intriguing against Sékou Touré. But in turn China's influence was counterbalanced by

---

[24] The eight points included mutual benefit and respect for sovereignty (no strings), interest free loans, help for self-reliance, selection of projects which require less investment while yielding quicker results, the use of best quality equipment at international market prices, and the assurance that Chinese experts would enjoy the same living standards as the experts of the country they were sent to help. All these points reflect China's experience of Soviet aid.

[25] Ronald Segal, *African Profiles* (Harmondsworth: Penguin, 1963), p. 314.

better relations (and more aid) from the United States. In October 1962, Sékou Touré had talks with President Kennedy, whom he later described as "very aware of African problems."

Clearly, however, Sékou Touré does feel that he has much in common with the Chinese. Welcoming Chou En-lai he said that despite differences between Guinea and China there were fundamental points in common:

> If it is true that revolution can neither be imported nor exported, it is just as true that revolution born in similar historical conditions, based on the same principles, directed towards similar goals necessarily partake of the same nature . . .

and he expressed considerable admiration for the Chinese Communist Party. But the key passage of the speech was that:

> Outside the classical dogmas and theories of Socialism a new truth peculiar to the peoples which have been subject to foreign domination is being confirmed, particularly in Africa . . . This presupposes absolute equality and freedom . . . guaranteed by a regime of "national democracy" transcending the inevitable differences that exist in our society . . .

The Guinean people, he said, had decided on a "non-capitalist road of development" (the approved Russian formula for African Socialism). Just as he had done in Ghana, Chou En-lai thought it best to ignore such references.

After what the French and Russians had done in Guinea Chou evidently thought that it was a perfect spot for a whole-hearted denunciation of imperialism, colonialism and neo-colonialism. Neo-colonialism was singled out for special treatment. It had become, he said, "the most dangerous, the most ferocious enemy of the national liberation movement . . . it corrupted the revolutionary will of the patriotic forces." Even this did not rouse Sékou Touré to go beyond the usual anti-imperialist generalities.

Chou's talks with Sékou Touré, according to the joint communiqué, yielded "an extensive identity of views . . . on the questions discussed" (but which questions were not discussed?). Chou reiterated his point that aid was always mutual and not unilateral. Guinea's stand was "an extremely great support for the Chinese people."

In turn Guinea supported China's "just struggle" for "complete unification" of its territory and the restoration of its rights in the United Nations. Moreover, Guinea was one of the two countries that came out in support of a second Bandung conference and was not represented at the preparatory meeting for a second Belgrade conference. But on the question of the Sino-Indian border dispute, Guinea refused to commit itself.

THE SUDAN
JANUARY 27–30

In most African countries Chou En-lai's claims of traditional friendship and " struggle " alongside China rested on the most tenuous evidence, if any. But in the Sudan much was made of the fact that the Sudanese people had " finally punished " General Gordon, who had fought against the Taiping rebels on behalf of the Chinese Imperial Government.

With cotton exports to China running at £8·8 million in 1962 (the last year for which complete figures are available) the Sudanese Government had no wish to offend China, although it has resented China's support for the exiled Sudanese Communist A. M. Kheir. There was not much public enthusiasm about Chou En-lia's visit, although the official reception was friendly.

Chou could claim little success in the Sudan. According to the communiqué he had " exchanged views and opinions " with President Abboud but there was little in the way of an identity of views. There was the usual declaration of support for those struggling against imperialism and reference to peaceful co-existence. President Abboud reaffirmed his support for China's entry into the United Nations and came out quite strongly in favour of another Bandung conference. But within two months Sudan, too, was represented on the preparatory meeting in Colombo for a second Belgrade conference.

ETHIOPIA
JANUARY 30–FEBRUARY 1

Chou En-lai's embarrassment at having to cancel his visit to Kenya, Tanganyika and Uganda was somewhat eased when he managed to get an impromptu invitation from Emperor Haile Selassie, a pillar of independence and respectability, and host to the Organisation of African Unity. The Emperor, however, was unenthusiastic. Apparently he had agreed to the visit because he felt it was difficult for him to ignore the representative of 700 million people, and it would give him a chance to put Ethiopia's case against Somalia's territorial claims to Chou before he arrived in Mogadishu.

The Ethiopian public were quite unaware of Chou En-lai's presence. The Emperor received his guests at Asmara, well away from the capital, Addis Ababa. Frank exchanges were not confined to private discussions. At a banquet in Chou's honour the Emperor criticised China's stand on the Sino-Indian border dispute, the test-ban treaty and the United Nations, before ending on the imperial note of " We ask that you give full weight to the words We have spoken." In reply Chou patiently repeated the ambiguous and provisional formulas of the United Front:

> Our two countries differ in systems, and the policies we pursue are not completely the same, but since we are getting together our aim is to seek common grounds and to try to eliminate or reserve our differences *for the time being.* (Emphasis added.)

In the communiqué both parties could agree on the formula that:

> the Addis Ababa conference was a turning point in the history of . . . African unity, just as the Bandung conference was a turning point in the history of the liberation of Afro-Asian countries and the development of Afro-Asian solidarity . . . the time [is] ripe for convening a second Afro-Asian conference.

Nevertheless, Ethiopia, like the other countries Chou visited (with the exceptions of Guinea and Mali) was represented in Colombo on March 23 at the preparatory meeting for a second Belgrade conference. The Emperor did support China's entry into the United Nations and " agreed to the normalisation of relations between the two Governments in the near future."

The reports that Chou later said baldly in Mogadishu that Ethiopia was controlled by foreigners fit in neither with the official reports of what he said, nor with his character. At this stage he had nothing to gain by offending the Emperor, but he did perhaps need to justify his visit to Ethiopia to some of the more revolutionary elements in Africa and at home. That is what he seemed to be doing when he said:

> The U.S. Government applied pressure to Ethiopia . . . But contrary to their expectations . . . China issued a friendly joint communiqué with Ethiopia . . . To oppose control from the outside is also part of the national revolutionary movement.

SOMALIA
FEBRUARY 1–4

China's policy towards Somalia raised real diplomatic problems for Chou En-lai. In 1962 Somalia's relations with Kenya and Ethiopia began to deteriorate as Somalia pressed for a Greater Somalia. In August 1963, when no one else would support Somalia, China stepped in and offered aid totalling £8 million. This pleased the Somalis but aroused the suspicions of the Ethiopians and Kenyans. This was not forgotten even though within a few months Russia had offered Somalia more than two and a half times as much aid. Not surprisingly, Chou En-lai was quick to point out that China's attitude towards disputes among African countries is that of non-involvement, and that China appeals to the countries concerned to settle their dispute peacefully.

There was not much popular excitement over the visit. Radio Mogadishu said that China's liberation struggle was a lesson for Africans who had not yet achieved complete political and economic freedom. The *Corriere della Somalia* was more interested in China's economic, especially agricultural, aid. Although Premier Shermarke stressed that Communism was "against the principles of the Somali people," the joint communiqué mentioned a "complete identity of views . . . on the maintenance of peace and stability in Asia and Africa." It was also announced that China would help Somalia to build roads and perhaps aerodromes and increase other aid. Russia promptly announced she would build seventeen factories for Somalia. As usual in the Black Africa part of his visit, Chou managed to get Somalia's support not only for China's admission to the United Nations, but also for another Bandung conference. This did not stop Somalia later attending the preparatory meeting for another Belgrade conference.

CONCLUSION

It is too early to say whether or not the Organisation of African Unity will be capable of dealing with attempts by the Chinese and others to divert and exploit the "holy war" to liberate South Africa and unify the continent; China's own experience of the Comintern's fatal efforts to exploit the 1927 Northern Expedition may serve as a useful guide. As Tang Tsou points out in his book on *America's Failure in China*, the Peking leadership will only face up to reality after they have tried repeatedly to change it, and failed.[26] If Africa and the other countries concerned stand fast, determined to go their own way, Mao's new conception of a "third force" consisting of China, Japan and Western Europe as well as the countries of Asia, Africa, and Latin America could develop towards the adoption of a normal and realistic view of the outside world by Peking, *pari passu* with the normalisation of her relations with other independent nation states.

[26] Tang Tsou, *America's Failure in China* (Chicago: Chicago Univ., 1963), p. 218.

China in the Postwar World*

By A. M. HALPERN

HISTORY is not going to find it easy to render a full judgment on the Second World War. The impact of the technological developments which that war stimulated is still working itself out. These developments alone have set to the politicians of various countries a series of problems which demanded action and which required a more complex, sustained intellectual effort than was needed in earlier times. The more advanced and more powerful the country, the more the problems arising from technological development, especially in weaponry, placed themselves in the centre of attention. For a full decade after the end of the war, it was generally thought that the bipolar distribution of power was a lasting phenomenon. The second postwar decade produced some evidence that this might not be so, but even now no one can be quite sure what qualifications or exceptions to bipolarity are significant today or will be in the future. The decolonisation process, attended by the emergence of many new, for the most part modernising, states and paralleled by the restructuring of European politics, clearly is one of the major phenomena of the period. Here, too, the future is obscure. Throughout the period, there has been a pervasive uncertainty as to what cultural and social values the world's peoples would subscribe to and what political leadership they would follow.

The recent foreign policy of any state can be studied as a series of adjustments to the various uncertainties of the postwar world. The historian of the future will have the leisure to describe that world in its manifold aspects and to decide which of these were in the long view basic and which were not. The meaning of events will appear less uncertain in retrospect than at the time of occurrence. The political actors of the time, however, have had to commit themselves in terms of the priorities they could see. The nature of the postwar world was not something given in the observable facts, which had to appear in identical form to everyone. Any one actor had no choice but to see that world in terms of his own values and ambitions, his resources, the decisions that he had to make, and his sense of history. It was not, perhaps, a particularly advantageous period for an only partially equipped state to establish itself as a great world power.

* The material in this article is to be incorporated in a book-length study of Communist China's foreign policy which the author is preparing for the Project on the United States and China in World Affairs at the Council on Foreign Relations.

INITIAL OUTLOOK

There is more reason in the case of the Chinese Communists than in most cases to treat the set of attitudes existing at the time they took power as a baseline. The notion of a baseline is unavoidably artificial. The Chinese outlook of 1949 was no virgin birth, freshly sprung from the brow of Mao Tse-tung. It derived from an accumulation of political and military experiences over the span of a generation, especially from the climactic actions of the four years between V-J day and October 1, 1949. But Mao and his companions have left no doubt that they regarded the end of the war and their own ascension to power as events which created a new constellation of world relationships.

Accordingly there was a felt need on the part of the Chinese Communist Party (CCP) leadership to make some explicit statements of their major assumptions about the world situation and of their broad strategic principles. It can be noted parenthetically that Communists, and the Chinese Communists perhaps more than others, in any case are verbalisers by custom. The politics of transformation seems to require not merely that one should think before acting but that one should theorise before, during, and after action. This political style, having fewer reference points in accepted tradition, demands a higher degree of self-consciousness and permits fewer premises to remain tacit than do other styles.

The need to be explicit exists especially when the world situation appears ambiguous or when a major change in the world situation is believed to have taken place. Between V-J day and October 1, 1949, one or both of these conditions obtained. During this period the Chinese Communist Party issued only a few, brief public statements which specifically analysed China's position in the world. They are nevertheless useful in establishing a baseline because of the circumstances under which they were produced. Furthermore, they represented the convictions of the small group which shared leadership for years before the conquest of power and has since then continued to exercise it. There have been some deaths and some purges. But taken as a whole the leading group has shown an ability, for which there are few precedents, to make the transition from an aspiring counter-elite to the central group of rulers and managers of a nation in the course of building. As far as the evidence goes, it tends to show that the nuclear group in the Chinese Communist leadership makes itself responsible collectively not only for all obviously major decisions but for discussing and passing on many matters which in other countries are handled by staff work at lower levels. Whatever has remained constant and whatever has changed of their initial estimate of the world situation therefore has had operational consequences.

Of the various possible ways of describing the postwar world, the Chinese Communist leadership has chosen consistently to emphasise above all political relations. They were, and fundamentally still are, wedded to a view of the world as the arena of a conflict between two ideologies, two forms of society, two international alliance systems. Any other factors or trends, if noted at all, were and are regarded as subsidiary. The world-view in which conflict is not a temporary malfunction, but an inherent structural feature, requires recognition of a permanent enemy and does not permit mental reservations in one's basic attitude towards him. For the Chinese Communists, the external enemy was and remains imperialism.[1] Their initial outlook contained a strong sense of mission in respect to this enemy, a mission which by definition transcended mere nationalism. Even the Common Programme,[2] which was a least-common-denominator kind of document designed to be palatable to non-Communists, specified that the Chinese People's Republic (C.P.R.) " shall accord the right of asylum to foreign nationals who seek refuge in China because they are oppressed by their own governments. . . ." The original and persisting concept was of foreign policy not just as a shield, but as a spear, and of China as a whole-hearted volunteer in the anti-imperialist ranks.[3] In this way China was to enter into the mainstream of world history.

Further, an integral part of the initial CCP outlook was faith in the future, a conviction of being in the service of destiny. Some well-known Maoist slogans—among them " Imperialism and All Reactionaries are Paper Tigers "; " Despise the Enemy Strategically, Respect Him Tactically "; and " Man Will Conquer Weapons, Weapons Will Not Conquer Man "—predate the assumption of power in 1949. These slogans and the so-called " revolutionary optimism " they express have never been absent from the consciousness of the CCP leaders. In 1958 and after, following a period when emphasis on them was not appropriate to the foreign policy the C.P.R. was carrying out, they were revived in a context very different from that of 1949. All have been employed in anti-Khrushchevian polemics in the past few years.

---

[1] It becomes necessary, to avoid awkward circumlocutions, to use terms like " imperialism " which are part of the Communist vocabulary. Using these terms does not require accepting the theoretical framework in which they were generated or the judgments the Communists attach to them. " Imperialism " can be defined in a purely enumerative sense, as applying to those powers to whom the Chinese apply it at any given point of time. The identities of these powers are usually well enough known.

[2] Passed by the Chinese People's Political Consultative Conference on September 9, 1949.

[3] It is, of course, true that the diffusion of industrialisation and the post-war bipolarity of military power helped to reduce the number of apparently possible patterns of cultural and political development. Nevertheless, the unanimity with which for many years the western world accepted the idea that two and only two value systems, two and only two forms of society were available to choose between, was surprising. The idea surely was not consistent with the liberal intellectual tradition.

By citing these slogans and by referring to the sense of mission and the world view whose point of departure is political conflict, I do not in any sense mean to imply that the Chinese Communist mentality is wholly lacking in a sense of reality. I do mean to argue that they place a higher value on morale and a lower value on physical capabilities than some other elites do. They have insisted on the importance of courage in many contexts. The CCP customarily describes unsuccessful deviationists in its past history as having " lost confidence in the revolution." In the recent past, when they described Khrushchev and his circle as " outwardly tough as bulls, but inwardly cowardly as mice," the condemnation was meant to apply simultaneously in the psychological, moral, and political senses. For Mao and his circle, losing one's nerve is both a sin and a shame. Further, there is no reason to underrate the real-world effectiveness of the CCP outlook. Because of it, the CCP leaders undertook tasks which previous Chinese leaders had not accomplished. Of these we need only note the unification and political organisation of the country.

Again, prejudices do not automatically produce policy. To suppose that the world outlook of the CCP leaders would lead them, as it were by instinct, to pursue nothing but an aggressive course under all circumstances would be to regard them as amateur or romantic revolutionaries, which they are not. They are men of action, not of impulse. Their experience of struggling for power laid down grooves in which their later behaviour ran; it did not put blinders on them. Their habit has been never to underestimate the possibilities of a situation, but to make a careful survey of their resources and of how they can best be applied. They are accustomed to economising on means and to utilising temporary alliances. A succinct statement of their methods of operation in the early '40s [4] is worth pondering. It describes the struggle against the Kuomintang as having been guided by the principles of " justifiability, expediency and restraint." These are respectively: to fight only in self-defence, but never to fail to strike back; to arrange forces so as to be sure of victory; and to make truces before the adversary can launch a new attack. The Chinese Communists have not invariably observed these principles in their dealings with the outside world, and history does not always oblige by arranging things to fit anyone's maxims. Still, in reviewing recent events, it would be hard to find a neater statement of what the Chinese thought they were doing on India's North East Frontier in 1962.

4 In Hu Chiao-mu, *Thirty Years of the Communist Party of China*, 4th ed. (Peking: 1959), p. 66.

FOREIGN RELATIONS: EARLY PHASE

On the eve of taking power, the CCP had made a firm decision on its basic problem in foreign relations—to break China's ties with the imperialist powers and to align it with the Soviet bloc. In his well-known article " On People's Democratic Dictatorship " [5] Mao stated his position in the bluntest possible terms. He would lean to one side, he would be provocative, he would do business only with countries who met his conditions regarding mutual respect. He would look for no assistance from the British and American Governments, but would expect " genuine and friendly assistance " only from the Soviet bloc. In practice this meant not just the reduction of the influence of the major imperialist powers, but the removal of their physical presence. It was made impossible for British and French businesses and educational enterprises to continue to operate, and Western diplomatic installations were caused to withdraw under spectacular conditions. Relations with some of the smaller European countries were restored in fairly short order, but the Chinese chose to make an example of the British and a few others by " negotiating " the details of recognition and diplomatic relations. The C.P.R. accepted a British chargé d'affaires but not an ambassador.

It has been argued that Mao's anti-imperialist policy was inevitable. Between 1945 and 1949, the United States had shown no signs of being prepared to tolerate Communist rule in China, but only of looking for alternatives to it. U.S., and to a lesser degree British and French, presence could then only become an obstacle to the full attainment of national independence and sovereignty in a China under Communist rule. The recognised need for foreign assistance could be satisfied only from the other direction. Mao's article just cited indicates, however, that non-Communist Chinese could and did think of alternatives and were reluctant to foreclose the future in quite so drastic a way, but would have preferred an independent, nationalist posture.

On the level of expediency, there were other considerations besides the potent ones mentioned above. Mao was determined to establish the legitimacy of the new government on the basis of its having a Communist character. Although—perhaps one might better say because—the CCP did not intend to construct a one-party state in form, it was essential to construct one in substance. Areas where the authority of the CCP was to be unconditional were best marked off at the outset. Foreign policy as a whole was one of these. To permit the imperialists to remain physically might have provided a basis for doubt as to where authority lay and for questions as to the wisdom of official policy. Only some years later, when the party's authority was consolidated, would it be possible to resume

---

[5] Written to commemorate the 28th anniversary of the CCP, July 1, 1949.

limited dealings with the British, the French, the Japanese, the Germans and others. The CCP also thought it necessary to destroy what remained of imperialist prestige. During the first few years of the Communist régime, there was a sustained propaganda effort to denigrate the historical role of imperialist powers in China and to engrave on the popular mind an image of imperialism, especially of the United States, as an enemy whose ferocity was uninhibited. The propaganda effort relied heavily on recounting atrocities, both historical and current, as well as on a quasi-scholarly argument that represented imperialist hostility as a case of predestination.

The anti-imperialist policy could not be convincing, even to the CCP, if it did not rest on an estimate of the relevant balances of power. Chinese Communist public discussions of this subject contain an element of propaganda which must be discounted, but which is very difficult to measure. Any conclusions about the real calculations of the Chinese are necessarily tentative. Still, the contention that imperialism is by nature aggressive has been so regularly made by the Chinese that one must take it as a well-rooted and permanent belief. But it is a general rather than a specific calculation. Any single Chinese statement that the United States plans to commit aggression cannot be directly taken as a sign that they regard the likelihood of war as high at the moment. The whole body of such statements can, however, be taken as meaning that they seriously plan for the contingency of war in the future.

In recent years, they have emphasised that the determining factors are not subjective but a matter of natural law. Imperialism, it is said, cannot change its nature; it must create wars. The official CCP estimate in the immediate postwar years was that while the United States was actively planning to attack the Soviet Union, it would be prevented from doing so by the political resistance of the world's peoples.[6] This estimate, at the time it was made, had the purpose of reassuring CCP cadres in regard to the prospects of the Chinese revolution. The concept of a world balance between military capability in the physical sense and countervailing political resources survived into the period after the takeover of power. In later years there were several important revisions of the Chinese estimate of the balance of power. During the first two years of the régime, however, the Chinese accepted the Zhdanov line. They gave verbal support to anti-imperialist dissident and insurrectionary movements, especially in Asia, though it appears that in most cases they could give little more. China's significant contribution to the strength of the Viet Minh lay in the Communist conquest of the mainland, but the operational consequences of this event did not become fully apparent

---

[6] " Some Points in Appraisal of the Recent International Situation " (April 1946), in *Selected Works of Mao Tse-tung*, IV (Peking: Foreign Languages Press, 1961).

until some time passed. The Trade Union Conference of Asian and Australasian Countries, to which Liu Shao-ch'i made an important opening address in Peking on November 16, 1949, did not develop into an effective channel. In early 1950 a number of important leaders of the Japan Communist Party took refuge in China after being purged from public life. For the first two years, however, Chinese assistance to Asian revolutionary movements was ideological and political rather than material.

To describe imperialism as inherently aggressive carries some implication that imperialism has the initiative and that Communism requires a defensive strategy—or more properly a counter-attacking strategy. Over the years, with the major exception of 1957–62, it appears that this has been the Chinese view. The view accords with their domestic military experience, which they have projected onto the international level. In recent writings, they make much use of the term " tit-for-tat struggle," which derives from their anti-Kuomintang strategy. The term itself implies that the first moves will come from the enemy, but that use of the initiative, far from being an advantage, is in the end self-defeating. By the same token the Chinese Communists have consistently regarded the local balance of power as unfavourable. On this level they have seen their problem as that of countering encirclement. The United States has had greater freedom to deploy its forces in Asia than the C.P.R. has had. As the United States has made use of this freedom, the Chinese have analysed capabilities as signifying intentions and have felt themselves confirmed in the belief that the nature of imperialism cannot change.

The structure of imperialism, however, can change, and so can the structure of Communism. In the early years of the C.P.R.'s existence, and pretty much through 1957, the Chinese held to the concept that the conflict between two international alliance systems, both having great internal solidarity, determined the shape of international relations. From the beginning they believed that the United States was the essential imperialist centre. For the first few years, one of their favourite phrases described the United States as stepping into the shoes of Nazi Germany and Fascist Japan. This phrase soon lost its timeliness. The Chinese continued to speak of two camps, while noting as of more or less theoretical interest that the former metropolitan countries must resent that their postwar weakness permitted the United States to replace them in their former colonies. If one can apply some current Chinese phraseology to prior times, the " basic contradiction " in the world was between the Socialist and the imperialist camps. From 1957 to 1962, the Chinese argued that the Socialist camp must preserve its solidarity and pursue a common pattern of action, when it quite obviously was doing no such thing. In the same period, they began to detect more substantial signs than before of frictions within the western world. These derived both from economic competition and from discrepant military ambitions, the classical sources of inter-imperialist conflict according to Marxist-Leninist theory. It was not until late 1962 that the Chinese openly departed from the view of the two-world conflict as the controlling pattern. Until then, even while evaluating the changes that were going on, they clung to formulas comparing the strength of the " East Wind " and the " West Wind," originally enunciated in 1957. In mid-1963,[7] they specified that there were four " fundamental contradictions in the contemporary world "—between the two camps, between classes in the capitalist countries, between " oppressed nations " and imperialism, and among imperialist countries. Of these the third was said to be at present the most important.

This digression has taken us a long way from Mao's determination in 1949 to align China with the Soviet bloc. His estimate of the situation at that time was the original simple one, allowing only two options. Again, it has been argued that the choice was in any case inevitable because of the very important tangible advantages involved. The Sino-Soviet Treaty of February 1950 and the agreements signed concurrently or soon after contained important provisions relating to the C.P.R.'s military security and future economic development. Once the decision to follow an anti-imperialist policy had been made, there was no other source of support available. Soviet economic co-operation over the following several years was not prodigal in monetary terms, but it was directed exactly at making up for the C.P.R.'s major deficiencies in techniques and personnel.

Expediency alone does not completely account for the C.P.R.'s alignment with the Soviet Union. There was also the calculation, ideologically conditioned, that this move was essential to the attainment of the objectives that Mao regarded as constituting China's mission, and the calculation that it was in accord with the world power balance of the time and of the future. Further, the pre-existing foreign contacts of the CCP, going back many years, were with the international Communist movement, in which the Party had well-understood organisational connections. Over the next several years, up to about the 20th Congress of the CPSU in early 1956, the Sino-Soviet relationship was a congenial one. During these years the C.P.R. gave at least verbal support to all aspects of Soviet foreign policy, and with few or no qualifications. The relationship changed during these years, but the degree of co-ordination of action remained high.

---

[7] In *A Proposal Concerning the General Line of the International Communist Movement*, June 14, 1963, *Peking Review*, No. 25.

It appears more accurate to say that in 1950 the tangible benefits to the C.P.R. followed from the desire to unite with the Soviet bloc rather than being the origin of this desire. Non-Communists in China had reservations about the necessity and the wisdom of the exclusive alliance, since they did not subscribe to the CCP's analysis of the world power balance. In 1950, the CCP itself accepted monolithism knowingly and gladly. There was, however, one important reservation. The status of the C.P.R. in the Soviet bloc was never that of a mere Soviet satellite. The Chinese could work with Stalin, but they were well aware that he had advised them badly on several earlier occasions.[8] Within the Communist movement, the Chinese claimed, and were accorded for a time, a special role as the classic model for revolutions in colonial and semi-colonial countries.[9] Mao also could co-operate with Stalin without sacrificing the principle of national independence. Independence has two sides, autonomy and security. From the Chinese standpoint, imperialism is a threat primarily to the latter, monolithic Communism primarily to the former.

THE KOREAN WAR

Up to the outbreak of the Korean war, the major concerns of Chinese foreign policy were to establish their anti-imperialist posture, arrange their alignment with the Soviet Union, define their role in the international Communist movement, and complete the establishment of C.P.R. sovereignty within the legal boundaries of China as they saw them. Their unfinished business was primarily in Formosa and Tibet, where the omens were good in both cases. These concerns as a whole were not the first priority tasks of their complete programme. The major claim on their attention was domestic affairs, the job of " national regeneration." The initiation of hostilities in Korea in 1950 can be rather confidently taken as a Russian move, if only because it made sense in terms of Russia's resources and situation (especially in regard to the peace treaty with Japan) and did not make sense in Chinese terms. For the Chinese, however, the course of events imposed the need for serious decisions in the foreign area. These decisions were of such scope that they defined some basic aspects of China's world position, and in this sense the war was a most important formative experience.

---

[8] This has finally been stated flatly. The article " On the Question of Stalin," *People's Daily* and *Red Flag*, September 13, 1963, specifies that, " In the late twenties, the thirties and the early and middle forties, . . . Comrades Mao Tse-tung and Liu Shao-chi resisted the influence of Stalin's mistakes." This " revelation " merely confirms what informed readers had understood much earlier from, for example, Hu Chiao-mu's 1951 pamphlet, cited above.

[9] The uses made by the Chinese of this claim over a longer period have been treated in a past number of this journal. See A. M. Halpern, " The Foreign Policy Uses of the Chinese Revolutionary Model," *The China Quarterly*, No. 7.

It is as yet impossible to determine how much Sino-Soviet co-ordination there was before the outbreak of hostilities. It seems likely that Mao would not have been able to veto the move, even if he had had the chance and had wanted to use it. It also seems likely that he fully expected the operation to be a quick, complete success. The decision to intervene was thus not foreseen from the very beginning, but made in the light of events as they developed over a period of time.

In trying to identify the critical considerations, the question again arises whether there were any options. Public statements on behalf of the United States and the United Nations had offered guarantees of the security of China's borders. Either the Chinese did not trust them, or (as I think more likely) they could not reconcile themselves to the situation that would result from accepting them. What was at stake was first, that freedom for any imperialist power to deploy its forces in the whole of Korea would compromise China's security, and, secondly, China's status as a power. In the latter regard, successful intervention would establish the C.P.R.'s claim that no Asian problems could be settled without its participation, while acceptance of an unpalatable result would compromise the claim. The demand for great power status was implicit in the term " national regeneration " by which Mao summarised his domestic objectives. The Korean situation supplied a test which gave content to the demand.

Thus the C.P.R. made a decision for war under conditions which Maoist military doctrine would have defined as unfavourable and somewhat to the disadvantage of domestic objectives. After the first encounter, the geography did not permit mobility. Chinese forces operating on alien territory could not take full advantage of their accustomed methods of logistics and intelligence. Nevertheless the C.P.R., by the behaviour of its representatives who were invited to appear at the United Nations in November-December 1950, passed up the chance to apply the principle of restraint by accepting a relatively advantageous truce and at the same time misused one of their best chances of being seated in the United Nations. Instead they committed themselves to what turned into a succession of positional battles and paid an enormous price in casualties. Monolithism could hardly have asked for more.

The two years of relative military inactivity from June 1951 to July 1953 also had their points of danger. The armistice negotiations, in which the Chinese gained some of their points but lost their major demand for a general settlement of Asian problems, were a test of nerves. The experience, however, was important in confirming the Chinese Communist (also the Stalinist) view of negotiation as one of the methods of tit-for-tat struggle. In the first half of 1952, the public health situation in North Korea posed a real threat to the Chinese position there. They coped with the difficulty in part through the world-wide propaganda campaign in which the United States was charged with using germ warfare, a campaign which depended on the closest co-ordination of Chinese and Soviet facilities. For that matter, the whole strategy of the Korean war period was based on co-ordination with Stalin, as is shown by the speed with which the first moves towards concluding the armistice were made after his death. It was not merely a matter of the Chinese pulling the Russian chestnuts out of the fire, but rather, as the pregnant phrase recently used by the Chinese puts it, of the C.P.R. being willing to stand " in the front line of defence of the Socialist camp so that the Soviet Union might stay on the second line." [10]

If the results are judged in terms of the major Chinese stakes—security and great-power status—the C.P.R. had reason to be satisfied. It made other important gains in prestige throughout the world, especially in Asia, as well as in military equipment. It gained a standing in North Korea which after 1958 ripened into close alliance and mutual support. It became the channel of communications for the Soviet bloc with North Vietnam and obtained a significant voice in North Vietnamese affairs. Soon after the armistice, the leading role allotted to Chou En-lai at the 1954 Geneva Conference exemplified the rise in China's international position. The Soviet Union would not again make a move in Asia without taking the C.P.R. into account.

The costs were considerable. Apart from casualties and the cost of purchasing Soviet equipment, the C.P.R. was no longer able to move effectively against Formosa and the Nationalist Government. The C.P.R. was excluded from taking part in the peace treaty with Japan, which then established relations with the Nationalists. Their chance to be seated in the United Nations was put off for an indefinite time, and recognition by several countries was similarly postponed. Thus they helped isolate themselves and reduced their own scope for diplomatic manoeuvre, though not to an intolerable degree. By the time of the armistice, situations in Southeast Asia, which they might have been able to exploit had they not been tied down in Korea, no longer offered openings. As a result of the Korean war and the war in Vietnam, the United States took on commitments in Asia which it had not definitely planned to assume in 1949–50, and the local balance of power was thereby shifted unfavourably to the C.P.R.

There is no sure ground for making an estimate of the lessons of Korea as the Chinese saw them. In later years, especially from 1958 on, they have used the Korean war as something of a clincher in arguing the case for the importance of armed struggle as against Khrushchev's

10 See " Two Different Lines on the Question of War and Peace," *People's Daily* and *Red Flag*, November 19, 1963.

policy of accommodation in dealing with the West. But the real lessons of the war probably had to do with their military planning. They have since shown as little enthusiasm as anyone else for a repetition of the experience. Apparently they have decided that military conflicts in which their interests are engaged against those of the United States must be kept very small and preferably conducted by proxy. As a direct result of the war, they reorganised their armed forces and began a programme of modernisation. Differences of opinion developed about the missions of the armed forces and their relation to other agencies of the Government. Ultimately their military relationship to the Soviet Union came to be an issue.

In the broadest terms, it appears that for several years the Chinese accepted that they would not have a strategic war capability but would have a tactical capability and be tied into a Soviet-managed system for strategic purposes. Soviet military thinking was changing, however, and a discrepancy developed over the question of nuclear sharing. The year 1958 appears to have been crucial. The Chinese now openly hint at a Soviet proposal which would have extended Soviet control over the Chinese armed forces. The Chinese preferred to keep their independence, especially when they found that they could not count on the support they would have liked in such operations as their 1958 action against the offshore islands. Although they probably remain in the Soviet system for purposes of strategic defence, they cannot depend on Soviet support in the more likely contingency of limited war, and they have not been able to obtain the material needed to keep up the efficiency of their forces in being. The maintenance of an independent posture, specifically an independent nuclear capability, has come to occupy the centre of their military thinking. This is not to say that they look forward to attaining in the foreseeable future a capability for conducting strategic war. They apparently have two uses for a nuclear capability of minor proportions. One is for defence. The other is to gain greater freedom of manoeuvre in conventional operations.

Neither the Korean nor later experiences diminished the value the Chinese place on morale. They still regard it as the factor which ultimately decides the outcome of wars. Their tactics are still a combination of military with political and psychological techniques. They remain more completely Stalinist in this respect than in any other.

FOREIGN RELATIONS: CONCILIATORY PHASE

From about the time of the 1951 cease-fire in Korea, signs appeared of a general shift in world Communist strategy. The underlying theory was revealed later, in the documents of the 19th Congress of the CPSU (1952), but the pattern of action had already emerged before the

Congress took place. The key concept in foreign policy was " peaceful co-existence." In terms of operations, this meant broadening the base of the peace movement to provide for co-operation with a range of non-Communist pacifists whom the Communists had up to then criticised on ideological grounds and accused of being " objectively " tools of the bourgeoisie. Throughout this period, which can be regarded as lasting to about the end of 1957, the Communist intention was to use the peace movement as a weapon against imperialism. In the short term the movement was to help prevent wars. In the long term it was to weaken the ability of imperialist governments to follow policies which the Communist countries regarded as threats. The Chinese view on this point has not changed. From about 1958 on, their differences from the Soviet Union grew sharper, culminating in 1963 in the C.P.R.'s denunciation of the partial nuclear test ban treaty.

During the period 1951–57, the controlling calculation on the Communist side was that a serious imbalance of strategic military power had come into being. If there ever was a time when the Soviet Union was in great physical danger, this was it. The indicated policy was to avoid war, reduce tension, and limit by political means the ability of the United States to deploy its forces—in short, a strategy of denial. Stalin himself, however, apparently retained ambivalent feelings about this policy. It was not until after his death that war situations in Asia were liquidated. On the Chinese side, the need for reducing tensions was further supported by the demands of the First Five-Year Plan, which seemed to require a " stable international environment."

Under these circumstances the Chinese developed the method called " people's diplomacy." Basically this is a tactic of discovering points of agreement between the C.P.R. and non-governmental political groups —either parties or movements—in other countries, and promoting mutual support. There is a certain inherent contradiction in the tactic. On the one hand it is intended to influence incumbent governments to adopt policies more favourable to China than they would do spontaneously. On the other hand it tends to intensify divisions between incumbent governments and their oppositions, and sometimes the result is to stiffen the attitude of the government towards China. The tactic has had a mixed history. With the great reduction of tension in Asia brought about by the 1954 Geneva Agreement, it became feasible for the C.P.R. to transcend people's diplomacy and to deal with some Asian countries on the government-to-government level. The basis of these dealings was that the C.P.R. could co-operate with countries with whom it had no conflicts of interest, which in Chinese theory of the time might mean all Asian countries. This approach produced the Five Principles of Peaceful Co-existence and the co-operative posture of the C.P.R. at the 1955

Bandung Conference. The transition is illustrated by the efforts of the Chinese to create institutional channels of communication. In 1952 they created the Peace Liaison Committee for the Asian and Pacific Region, a typical instrument of people's diplomacy by its composition. The organisation lapsed into inactivity especially after the post-Bandung creation of the Afro-Asian People's Solidarity Organisation, in which both governments and non-governmental organisations are represented.

The major weakness of people's diplomacy as such is that it did not effectively promote Chinese access to all Asian countries. In the case of Thailand it led to what has been called the " honeymoon phase " of Sino-Thai relations in 1955–57, but with the accession to power of Marshal Sarit the relationship was shown to be shallow. The first aim of the C.P.R. was to expand its own influence in Asia and to limit or reduce the American presence in the area. They achieved enough during the period to establish China as a factor in Asia which a number of countries felt could be dealt with productively. But it became apparent by the end of 1957 that the American presence was not reduced but increased. The C.P.R. in later years did not abandon people's diplomacy. From 1957 to 1963 it occupied less of their attention than other methods. Since 1963 there has been a considerable revival of the method and a good deal of energy devoted to the institutionalisation of Third World communications. But many things happened in the meantime.

Another noteworthy development of 1952 was emphasis on trade. The Chinese trade offensive began with the Moscow Economic Conference of that year. The theoretical guideline was the concept, elaborated in the documents of the 19th Congress of the CPSU, of two parallel world markets. There was thus from the outset a political element involved, in that there was some hope of using trade to compete with imperialism for influence in the so-called " intermediate zone." Trade with Asian countries also helped promote people's diplomacy, by drawing business groups into the orbit of communication, and was compatible with state-to-state diplomacy as well. The peak Chinese effort to use economic techniques, including economic warfare, came in 1956–58. Especially in the last year of this period, the Chinese pushed the export of textiles to Southeast Asia at uneconomic prices, to compete with Japan and India. In particular, they made a real effort to capture the markets of Malaya and Singapore.[11] On the whole the export drive was a failure, since China did not have the capacity to sustain it. In subsequent years, one could occasionally see signs of nostalgia for the

---

[11] Further details and discussion of C.P.R. economic strategy for this period are to be found in A. Doak Barnett, *Communist Economic Strategy: The Rise of Mainland China* (Washington: National Planning Association, 1959) and A. Boone, " The Foreign Trade of China," *The China Quarterly*, No. 11, July-September, 1962.

concept of parallel world markets, but rather as something that ought to be than as something that is. The C.P.R.'s trade now seems, on the whole, to be regulated by pragmatic economic considerations.

Economic assistance by the C.P.R. to non-Communist countries was initiated in practice only toward the end of the period, with the $22 million grant to Cambodia in 1956. Its original rationale was stated in the resolutions of the Bandung Conference. Its scope has been increased rather steadily in later years, though always within modest limits as compared with the programmes of major aid-giving countries. Formal loans and grants to Cambodia, Nepal, Ceylon, Indonesia and Burma, extended for the most part in the period following 1957, now total over $250 million. Loans and grants to African countries now total approximately $150 million. These began, if one includes reported assistance to the Algerian Provisional Government, in 1959. The majority of credits to governments were extended from 1960 on. Besides Algeria, Ghana, Guinea, Mali, Somali, and Kenya have been recipients. In the Middle East, following a cash grant to the United Arab Republic in 1956, Chinese loans were made to Yemen and later to Syria. The total of aid committed was about $410 million by 1962 and is now over $500 million, but the amount actually disbursed is much less—for Africa, about 25 per cent. of the amount committed.[12]

China's aid has been comparatively efficient in operation and has been administered with considerable political and psychological sensitivity. In general, the C.P.R.'s practice in this field has been consistent with its rather simple doctrine that the function of aid is to reduce the recipient country's dependence on others. Recently a new ideological emphasis has been supplied, which derives from the Chinese contention in anti-Soviet polemics that self-reliance (following the Chinese example) is essential to true national independence.[13]

The 1951–57 period of Chinese Communist foreign policy was rich in ideas and flexible in action. During the period it appeared that the C.P.R. was scoring a series of successes and rapidly growing in influence. Yet in striking a balance of gains and losses for the period as a whole, one arrives at a rather simple result. The C.P.R. achieved sufficient weight in Asia, which was at that time its primary area of interest, to become a great power in the area. This is true at least in the sense that all Asian countries in one way or another came face to face with the C.P.R. and

---

[12] Chinese economic aid to bloc countries began in 1953 with a $200 million grant to North Korea. By the end of 1961, commitments exceeded $1,500 million, of which almost two-thirds was drawn on.

[13] A comprehensive, though obviously propagandistic, statement of the C.P.R.'s doctrine on foreign aid is given by Ai Ching-chu, " China's Economic and Technical Aid to Other Countries," *Peking Review*, No. 34, August 21, 1964.

found that it was an element in their environment which could not be ignored. Though the patterns of amity and hostility have shifted, awareness of the C.P.R. has not declined subsequently.

The C.P.R.'s prestige and influence in the Soviet bloc also grew during the period. In early 1955 Molotov declared that the Socialist camp now had two heads, the Soviet Union and the C.P.R. This meant, I believe (though it cannot be fully proved), that the Soviet Union conceded Asia to be a sphere of Chinese influence, where they themselves would not be particularly active. By the beginning of 1960 it was clear that no pattern of co-operation existed any longer. The seeds of conflict within the bloc were already sown at the 20th Congress of the CPSU in 1956. During the following year there appeared to be a significant rise in the C.P.R.'s prestige and leverage in the Communist areas of Europe. This also did not last—not that the C.P.R. has now no leverage at all or even necessarily less impact in European Communist circles, but obviously its ways of affecting developments are not at all those that it appeared to have when Chou En-lai was invited in 1956–57 to intervene in Moscow's dealings with Poland and Hungary.

The limits of Chinese success during the period have already been indicated. They apparently seemed important enough to some CCP leaders to sustain a sharp change of line in late 1957. There remains a hypothetical question: If the C.P.R. had continued the 1951–57 line of foreign policy, would its position today be stronger or weaker?

1957 PERSPECTIVE

I propose here to deal with the very important developments in Chinese Communist foreign policy after 1957 only in broad terms, confining the discussion to major premises and scanting the description of events. The period in question contains two important changes of phase, which can be dated more or less as taking place in November 1957 and July 1963. The conspicuous events to which the changes can be tied are the Moscow meeting of ruling Communist Parties in 1957 and the signing of the tripartite partial nuclear test-ban treaty in 1963. Just as the notion of a 1949 baseline is artificial, the idea of taking a sort of cross-sectional reading of Chinese strategic perspectives at precisely these points is artificial but nonetheless a useful device.

It is known, at any rate, that Mao Tse-tung went to the 1957 Moscow meeting convinced that the world Communist line needed overhauling. The Chinese had been disturbed by the theses advanced at the 20th Congress of the CPSU and even more disturbed by the events in Hungary at the end of 1956. In China itself, the experimental thaw of the Hundred Flowers period in 1957 had traumatic repercussions and led to a sharp swing to the left in the CCP's domestic line. In August and October, Russian successes in launching an intercontinental missile and orbiting an artificial satellite indicated that nuclear parity was at hand. The time was ripe also in that in July 1957 Khrushchev had consolidated his power by winning a fight against the anti-Party group. If there was to be a divergence of preferences regarding world Communist strategy, it would be better to face it at the earliest suitable moment, and there was no one left who was better situated than the CCP to do it.

From what little has been revealed of Mao's address to the Moscow meeting, it appears that he argued that in the previous decade Communist successes had occurred when Communists had boldly met imperialist initiatives (the tit-for-tat struggle) and losses had occurred when Communists had yielded ground. In short, the conciliatory approach of 1951–57 might have been justified during a period of weakness, when the situation required a strategy of consolidating past revolutionary gains, but it was now outdated.

Mao's first major premise was that a decisive shift had occurred in the world balance of power. This was expressed in the catchword: "The East Wind prevails over the West Wind." There appear to have been real differences in the military estimates of the C.P.R. and the Soviet Union. These differences became greater as time passed, especially as regards sharing of nuclear weapons. By the middle of 1959 at the latest the Russians made it clear that they would not actively help the C.P.R. obtain an independent nuclear capability.[14] The Chinese did not abandon the East Wind-West Wind slogan until 1962, by which time it was obvious that the supposed imbalance of military power in favour of the Soviet Union did not exist.

A corollary to this first premise was that a worldwide confrontation with imperialism was now possible, and that important results could be achieved quickly. It appears that the Chinese were particularly sanguine regarding the Middle East and thought of it as an area where a vital blow could be struck at Western interests. In this and in other situations Khrushchev's policy was to avoid a head-on clash, to work towards a reduction of Soviet-U.S. antagonism in the over-all sense, though by no means to appear soft in specific situations or to overlook propaganda opportunities. In Chinese eyes his methods were mere sabre-rattling, not to be mistaken for real struggle, of which one of the best examples was their own performance in the Korean war. By October 1959, it was clear that Khrushchev preferred accommodation

---

[14] The " revelations " made by the Chinese, especially in " The Origin and Development of the Differences between the Leadership of the CPSU and Ourselves," *People's Daily* and *Red Flag*, September 6, 1963, do not altogether clarify what agreements were actually made at what times.

with the United States to confrontation. Thereafter the Chinese could put obstacles in his way but could not stop him.

The second major premise was that the Socialist camp should be unified in ideology and organisation and that the CPSU should carry out the responsibilities of being its sole head. The origin of the problem is to be found in Stalin's death. Not long after that the new leadership in the Soviet Union arrived at a calculated decision that Stalin's centralised, dictatorial methods of control should be modified before they produced resistance or rebellion, both in the domestic sphere and in the international movement. In the autumn of 1953, the catchword " proletarian internationalism " began to enjoy a certain vogue in Asian Communist writings, as it still does. The Chinese gained something in status and freedom and seem on the whole to have enjoyed both, though they themselves were delicate enough so that they never used the phrase " Socialist camp under two leaders." When Mao demanded at the 1957 Moscow meeting that the CPSU should have exclusive title to the role of vanguard of the Socialist camp, he was not necessarily proposing to renounce any of the CCP's right to its own opinion, but rather to turn the united efforts of the camp against imperialism.[15] By October 1959, however, the prospects for the kind of monolithism Mao had in mind had become very dim. Soon after that the C.P.R. adopted positions, for example on the important matter of disarmament, which were not just different from but opposed to those of the Soviet Union.

The third major premise was that actions of the C.P.R. would be supported by the Soviet Union and the whole Socialist camp. Thus China could use the favourable state of the world power balance to overcome the unfavourable state of the local power balance. The test came soon. In the operations against Quemoy in 1958, Soviet co-operation was available more in the preparatory phase than in the phase of action, and at the critical points it did not meet the specifications the Chinese would have liked to set. A year later, the Soviet position on the C.P.R.'s conflict with India amounted in Chinese eyes not just to non-support but to betrayal.

The fourth premise was that the Third World could be handled by pressure rather than by conciliation. The Chinese at this point assigned

---

[15] A recent explanation of the Chinese stand reads: " It was only logical that the CPSU should carry forward the revolutionary tradition of Lenin and Stalin, shoulder greater responsibility in supporting other fraternal Parties and countries and stand in the van of the international Communist movement. . . . We hold that the existence of the position of head does not contradict the principle of equality among fraternal Parties. It does not mean that the CPSU has any right to control other Parties; what it means is that the CPSU carries greater responsibility and duties on its shoulders." See " The Leaders of the CPSU are the Greatest Splitters of Our Time," *People's Daily* and *Red Flag*, February 4, 1964.

to the Third World a lower priority than they had previously done. They felt free to express disapproval, if not contempt, for those leaders of non-aligned countries who represent what the Chinese call the " national bourgeoisie." In this area, too, the C.P.R. reappraised its position about the end of 1959, and some changes in approach then followed. Settlements of previously undetermined border problems were a conspicuous example. There was not, however, a return to the categorical kind of treatment of Asian and African countries as uniformly having " no conflicts of interest " with the C.P.R. Instead the C.P.R. developed a differentiated approach depending on a variety of factors.

It appears in retrospect that the 1957 perspective was viable for barely two years. The Chinese, though they must at the time have been more painfully aware of its weaknesses than any outside observer could possibly be, did not abandon it. There is a suggestive parallel with C.P.R. domestic policy, whose general temper and vicissitudes ran a similar course to foreign policy. In the latter case, the Chinese clung to most of their verbal postures and fought for their views in a series of intra-mural controversies with the Soviet Union. The bitterness has deepened with each engagement, and the number of third parties involved has steadily grown. For the time being, the fight remains a family fight, and the prospects of rapprochement are poor but not absolutely nil.

Throughout the period another trend has been observable. In 1957 the horizons of the Chinese had widened, so that they thought of their arena of action as the whole world. The Sino-Soviet dispute itself required them to act more and more as an autonomous factor on a world scale. At the same time, Africa (to a much smaller degree also Latin America) emerged as an area where the Chinese could engage themselves. The years 1961 and 1962 were in many ways the low point in the C.P.R.'s international effectiveness. Measured in terms of 1957 objectives, C.P.R. foreign policy was a shambles. By the middle of 1963 the Chinese developed a new strategic outlook.

The 1957–63 period does not lend itself easily to summation. It was overshadowed by the development through several stages of the Sino-Soviet conflict. The pattern of C.P.R. actions through the period was not what would result from the steady application of a consistent grand design. What characterised it was rather a series of false starts and shifts of approach. Also, it was on the whole reactive. Many of the goads to action were developments elsewhere, not under the control of the C.P.R., rather than the putting into practice of C.P.R. plans.

A good deal of the area of Sino-Soviet disagreement on world Communist strategy can be indicated simply by noting that the Soviet

Union's views differed from the C.P.R.'s on every one of the Chinese
premises discussed above. The difference with regard to how to handle
the United States was a key issue. A number of related issues soon came
into the open. The Chinese made it clear that they had no desire to
negotiate with the United States, especially not with the purpose of
stabilising a *status quo* in Asia which did not suit them, and that in any
case they would not permit the Soviets to negotiate for them. The
question of disarmament was directly involved. Soviet economic sanctions applied in the summer of 1960 affected the Chinese economy
generally and their atomic development programme particularly, but the
loss of Soviet technical assistance did not hold the Chinese back from
proceeding with efforts which culminated in the atomic detonation of
October 16, 1964. In the area of Third World strategy, the difference
in Chinese and Soviet strategic concepts led into competition for
influence. By the time of the Afro-Asian Solidarity Conference at Moshi
in February 1963, the Chinese were openly exploiting racial appeals
in order to exclude the Soviet Union from participation.

The dispute with the Russians went through several phases. The 1960
Moscow conference, it is now admitted, settled nothing permanently. It
made the Chinese aware of the danger of being isolated and spurred
them into efforts to increase their base of support within the world
movement—efforts which have succeeded beyond what seemed reasonably expectable at the time. No more advantageous occasion for
reaching a *modus vivendi* arose later. Khrushchev personally vitiated
what chance might have existed at the 22nd CPSU Congress in October
1961 by his unexpected attack on Albania. In the spring of 1962,
concurrent with the meeting of the National People's Congress in
Peking, there were signs that another attempt was being made. It
was the last chance. At meetings of European Communist Parties
following the Cuban incident, the Chinese drew the line openly, and by
June 1963 they made it clear that they were willing to accept a split in
the Communist movement.[16] Further, by dwelling on territorial questions,

---

16 This challenge was successful. The Chinese position has since become stronger, since
   conditions have become less favourable for a Soviet initiative toward " excommuni-
   cating " the CCP. The CCP's awareness of the tactical situation is well expressed
   in its Central Committee's letter of July 28, 1964, to the Central Committee of the
   CPSU, in reference to Khrushchev's proposal for a meeting of 26 Communist Parties
   to take place in December 1964. " You are falling into a trap of your own making
   and will end by losing your skin. . . . We firmly believe that the day your so-called
   meeting takes place will be the day you step into your grave. . . . Once again we
   sincerely advise you to rein in on the brink of the precipice. . . . But if you refuse
   to listen and are determined to take the road to doom, well, suit yourselves! Then
   we will only be able to say:
   " *Flowers fall off, do what one may;*
   Swallows return, no strangers they."
                                        " With fraternal greetings."

the C.P.R. underlined that its disagreements with the Soviet Union extend to state as well as Party relations.

In its Asian relations, the C.P.R.'s central objective was still to weaken U.S. influence and strengthen its own. This objective supplies a thread of connection between a number of developments, each of which has some important individual characteristics. The most important, and to the C.P.R. the most promising, situation of direct conflict of interests took place, in the end, in Laos and Vietnam. Here the C.P.R. role has been to push developments as far as they can safely go, without itself being directly involved. In the same connection, it has made significant gains in its relations with Cambodia. Conflict with India received conspicuous expression in the NEFA border battle of 1962. Its roots, however, go much deeper, to India's relations with the United States and the Soviet Union, India's role in Afro-Asian affairs and as a non-aligned country, and a growing divergence between Indian and Chinese world views and strategies.

As a by-product of Sino-Indian conflict, the C.P.R. settled a number of outstanding border questions with other Asian countries and was also able to reorganise its relations with Pakistan. Also somewhat related was the growth of Sino-Indonesian co-operation on matters of mutual interest. The outcome so far, however, has been mutual accommodation in a form dictated as much by the interests of others as by Chinese ambitions. In its relations with Japan, after a number of abortive moves, the C.P.R. in late 1962 reached a practical solution by abandoning some untenable demands and agreeing to proceed, at least for the present, within the limits allowed by Japanese politics.

1963 PERSPECTIVE

The 1963 perspective grew out of C.P.R. reactions to earlier trends. It is a distinctive adaptation to developments within the bloc, including some which resulted from its own endeavours, and to the increasingly pluralistic pattern of international relations. Its major premises appear to be four.

First is the premise of self-reliance. During 1962 the last prospect of economic support from the Soviet Union on terms acceptable to the C.P.R. apparently vanished. Decisions were made to base economic recovery and future development on China's own resources, so that no outside power could affect the C.P.R. economy as the Russians had by withdrawing their technicians in 1960. The principle has been given an ideological phrasing and has been recommended both to other Communist countries and the emerging nations generally.

Second is the premise of independence from the Soviet Union in foreign policy and opposition to the Soviet " general line of peaceful co-existence." Of the many issues in the Sino-Soviet dispute, the one the C.P.R. seems to regard as central is the applicability of co-existence in dealing with the United States. In this matter the C.P.R. charges that the Russians, for nationalistic reasons, have misapplied the principle and are subject to being accused of practising "class collaboration." In its fight against Khrushchev's "modern revisionism" the CCP has been able to make this point an important test issue and a means of making others declare themselves. In order to present an effective opposition, the CCP needed allies within the bloc. Starting with Albania, it has been able to attract to its side a number of Communist Parties, especially Asian, not all of whom are its puppets, and fractions of many other Parties throughout the world. The process began (omitting Albania) in 1961, not long after the 1960 Moscow Conference of 81 Communist and Workers' Parties. The most valuable test issues were Cuba and the test ban treaty. Only when several of its moves had produced enough results to ensure that the CCP would not be isolated in the world movement or in the bloc did the Chinese take the decisive step. July 1963 is a significant benchmark because it was only then that the CCP had the backing it needed to challenge Khrushchev to expel them from the world movement under conditions where it was clear that they were not bluffing. Fundamental organisational questions are now at issue within the world movement as a result of Khrushchev's reluctance to pick up the gauntlet.

Third is the premise that the anti-imperialist struggle continues. More and more, however, the C.P.R. defines the struggle as anti-American. A part of its diplomatic pattern of action is to create or exploit differences of interest between the United States and the European countries or Japan as a means of isolating the United States. A special category, designated the "second intermediate zone," has been established. The CCP has some hope that in the longer run the imperialist world will conform to Lenin's prediction and contribute to its own destruction. The immediate struggle against "U.S. imperialism" proceeds not by direct confrontation but indirectly—that is to say on the territory of third parties—whether the means employed are political, economic or military.

Fourth is the premise that for the present the decisive area of struggle is the Third World. The Chinese have revived a number of their practices of 1954–57, but under changed circumstances. They are now active in Africa as well as Asia and have their eyes on Latin America. In these areas they compete for influence not only with the imperialists but with the Soviet Union and with some non-aligned countries. Tactical methods range from state-level negotiations to a fight for control of revolutionary groups. In Asia the pattern is barely distinguishable from traditional power politics. Perhaps the major difference is that there is a renewed burst of energy going into the creation of third-world institutions and that the whole effort is conceived as an interim, though relatively long-term, one which ultimately will be superseded by the emergence of revolutionary situations in Europe.

The C.P.R.'s strategic concepts at this time rest on a belated, partial recognition that the whole world situation is no longer bipolar but pluralistic.[17] In view of the past, one must ask for how long the present perspective will be viable. It seems to conform to China's actual capacities rather better than the 1957 perspective did to her capacities at that time. The C.P.R. can be expected to achieve some gains in respect to its smaller-scale short-term goals. Its longer-range goals, as always, are drawn in terms of the maximum potentialities it sees in the present situation. These goals are less likely to be attained. When the time comes for the next major revision of Chinese strategy, it is likely to take a direction that is not included in their present perspective.

The statements made by the Chinese on the occasion of their 15th National Day show little or no disposition to look backward over the course of their foreign relations. In tone and content they supply a strong hint that the Chinese feel themselves to be standing on the threshold of a new major period in history. On October 16 they achieved their first independent nuclear explosion, which had been long expected, but which showed somewhat greater technical advancement than the outside world had foreseen. Two days earlier Khrushchev had been ousted from his positions of Party and state leadership. Both events open up avenues of development for the C.P.R. and add to the number of alternatives open to it, but neither affects the basic Chinese perspective.

Chinese statements at the time of the nuclear detonation and before do not indicate an unrealistic view of what a small nuclear capability means to them. Militarily, it adds to their security and gives them more freedom of manoeuvre, but it does not by itself yet overturn the local balance of power or eliminate the sense of being encircled. Its effects on their prestige are as yet incalculable and the substantive consequences of an increase in prestige can only be guessed at. Presumably the impact will be partly negative as well as positive. Up to now, the matters that have been immediately affected are UN representation and the C.P.R.'s place in disarmament negotiations.

The Chinese evidently hoped that Khrushchev could be overthrown as far back as two years ago. Their handling of relations with the Soviet Union and the world Communist movement can hardly be understood on any other assumption. Also, it is very probable that Khrushchev's handling of China was an important factor leading to his fall.

[17] One might pause here long enough to speculate what the course of events might have been if the CCP had anticipated this state of affairs in 1949, or, more to the point, in 1957. By the latter date a trend toward pluralism was already envisaged by several middle powers, *i.e.*, countries like Britain, France and Japan.

It has generally been recognised that there was an element of personal antagonism between Mao and Khrushchev in the Sino-Soviet dispute. It will now be possible to measure a little more accurately how important this element was. But one should not expect that Mao will now be catapulted into "leadership" of the world Communist movement. He has himself indicated that "leadership" is something of an illusion,[18] and it has become even more of one in the past year as several Communist Parties have shown their independence. Soviet policies, furthermore, were not Khrushchev's individual creation, no matter how much of a personal impress he gave them. Even if decorum and dialogue are resumed, there will still be differences of interest in relation to the United States, the Third World, and nuclear proliferation. The Chinese paid a high price to consolidate their independence. It is not likely that they will now give any of it up cheaply, especially if they have really grasped the meaning of pluralism in world affairs.

Explanatory Formulas

Those who study China naturally try to summarise as simply as possible the essential characteristics of Chinese behaviour. One of the student's functions is, after all, to make his subject predictable. There is a natural tendency, then, toward the production of formulas which attempt to reduce behaviour to simple patterns. Some such formulas are inevitably too simple.

It is sometimes asked whether Chinese policy is based on ideology or on national interest. Neither concept is altogether clear, and the two are not mutually exclusive. Communist ideology is not pure philosophy but also political analysis and strategy. To deny its motive power it seems to be necessary to argue, as De Gaulle does, that it is a great illusion and that there is in reality no such thing as a Communist foreign policy; that ideological disagreement between Marxists means that Marxism is irrelevant to foreign relations. The decline of Communist monolithism has led some observers to emphasise that it was never 100 per cent. complete, and that it was an error to have overlooked the seeds of controversy when they were first planted. But if Communism under Stalin was not perfectly monolithic, there was in his time an international alliance system that was as nearly so as any known to history. National interest is not in itself a clear guide to action in an ambiguous world. While it is accepted in this paper that a drive towards great power status has been a constant motive of the C.P.R., it is a motive that has not always pulled in an opposite direction from ideology. It has been argued here that in a number of situations the Chinese have had

---

[18] See especially "The Leaders of the CPSU are the Greatest Splitters of Our Time," *People's Daily* and *Red Flag*, February 4, 1964.

options and that their choices have reflected both their great power ambitions and their sense of a world revolutionary mission.

A variant of the national interest interpretation is the " Middle Kingdom " thesis. When stated so as to assert that the real policy of the C.P.R. is to restore traditional Chinese suzerainty in a defined portion of Asia and nothing more, this thesis seems clearly not to correspond to the record. If it were true, it would imply that Chinese Communist foreign policy is not oriented towards the international system that now exists, but towards one that expired over a century ago; and it would make the CCP the first Chinese dynasty that ever expressed the belief that the fate of the world hung on the fortunes of the outer barbarians.

The national interest thesis raises another question of considerable difficulty—the relation of foreign to domestic policy. The truism that these two aspects of national policy affect each other is well enough demonstrated as a general proposition so that it must apply to China as well. The question is in what ways and how much. The Chinese Communist policy maker appears to have little need to take account of public opinion, though there is some fugitive evidence that at times he feels its pressure. Some instances have been noted earlier of cases where domestic priorities have affected foreign policy, *e.g.*, during the period of the First Five-Year Plan or in relation to present patterns of foreign trade. Also, especially prominently during the period of the Great Leap Forward, there has evidently been a close consonance of overall temper in the CCP approach to domestic and international problems. Anti-revisionism has been a domestic as well as a foreign campaign. We have also noted above that the CCP tends consistently to try to generalise, on the level of international strategy and tactics, its domestic revolutionary experience. But there is little to support the idea that the primary use of foreign policy to the C.P.R. is to promote domestic programmes.

There has been some discussion of the degree of rationality of Chinese foreign policy. To say that the Chinese behave in this area with consistent and perfect rationality seems to me tantamount to saying they are not human, not responsive to the calls of honour, ambition or self-esteem. In a sense some of their basic objectives are inherently non-rational, as are other people's. No one can possibly be sure that Communism will defeat imperialism, or vice versa, or even that a proposition framed in these terms has enough real-world content to be a useful guide to action. Yet it appears that the CCP to some extent evaluates its actions in terms of a judgment of how they will contribute to the complete liquidation of imperialism. A more workable query would deal with the relative importance of information and *a priori* judgment in Chinese Communist policy making. We have noted above that the CCP shows some tendency to estimate situations in terms of potential development as much as or more than in terms of present actuality and that it often adopts a course aimed at realising maximum gains, though it does not necessarily always expect to attain the maximum.

Similarly, the Chinese are said to be cautious. It is certainly true that they are not the opposite of cautious, which would be reckless. But as a description of their overall bent, " caution " seems a poor word. A truly cautious man is not only prudent in his procedures but tends to direct himself to the safer rather than the maximum options. Chinese caution also depends on what is at stake and how seriously it is believed to be threatened. When the stakes are high and the threat is imminent, the Chinese are capable of putting everything at risk.

Throughout this paper C.P.R. policies and actions have been described as if they were based on unanimity of the leadership. It should at least be noted in passing that this is certainly not the case in the planning phase and that the shifts and changes that have taken place are hardly to be understood except if one supposes that there is more than one tendency at work. As for a general formula which would enable us to assemble the recorded facts in coherent fashion, the one stated at the beginning of this paper seems to me to have some virtues. It treats the C.P.R. as working towards great power status in the rapidly changing postwar environment by methods chosen in the light of the CCP's values and ambitions plus China's resources, and with a variety of adaptations to the CCP's perception of the state of the world. The most dubious term in this formula is " postwar." One may be uncertain when the period ended, but " postwar " does not seem the right word to use for the world as is exists today.

Index